FRENCH XX
BIBLIOGRAPHY

A BIBLIOGRAPHY FOR THE STUDY OF
FRENCH LITERATURE AND CULTURE SINCE 1885

VOLUME XV, NO. 2, ISSUE NO.

72

COMPILED AND EDITED BY
ALISA BELANGER

D1593670

YOUNGSTOWN STATE
UNIVERSITY

NOV 0 4 2021

W.F. MAAG LIBRARY
SERIALS DEPARTMENT

SUP

Selinsgrove
SUSQUEHANNA UNIVERSITY PRESS

© 2021 by Rosemont Publishing & Printing Corp.

All rights reserved. Authorization to photocopy items for internal or personal use, or the internal or personal use of specific clients, is granted by the copyright owner, provided that a base fee of $10.00, plus eight cents per page, per copy is paid directly to the Copyright Clearance Center, 222 Rosewood Drive, Danvers, Massachusetts 01923. [978-1-57591-218-9/21 $10.00 + 8¢ pp, pc.]

Associated University Presses
10 Schalks Crossing Road
Suite501-330
Plainsboro, NJ 08536

The paper used in this publication meets the requirements
of the American National Standard for Permanence of Paper
for Printed Library Materials Z39.48-1984.

ISBN 978-1-57591-218-9 (issue no.72)
International Standard Serial Number 0085-0888
Library of Congress Catalog Card Number 77-648803

Printed in the United States of America

Z
2173
.F7
no. 72

CONTENTS

PAGE

Table of Abbreviations v

PART ONE: General Subjects 23993

    Anthologies and Collections 23993

    Bibliography 23995

    Bibliophilism and Publication 23996

    Comic and Graphic Novels 23998

    Crime Fiction 24002

    Francophone Literature 24003

    Gender and Sexuality 24009

    Literary History: France 24013

    Literary Themes and Topics 24017

    Literary Theory and Aesthetics 24021

    Memoirs and Autobiography 24026

    Miscellaneous 24027

    Novel and Short Story 24030

    Philosophy, Psychology, and Religion 24032

    Poetry 24036

    Surrealism 24038

    Theater 24039

    Translation and Plurilingualism 24041

PART TWO: Author-Subjects (arranged alphabetically by name of author,
theater actor, or theater director) 24043

iii

PART THREE: Cinema 24269

   Section I. Cinema in General 24269

   Section II. Individual Directors, Cinema Authors, Cinema Theorists, and
   Actors (arranged alphabetically) 24274

TABLE OF ABBREVIATIONS

BAnQ	Bibliothèque et Archives nationales du Québec
BnF	Bibliothèque nationale de France
Cor	Cornell University
LoC	Library of Congress
Naz	Nazareth College
PrQ	Proquest Search Engines
RIT	Rochester Institute of Technology
UaB	SUNY University at Buffalo
Syr	Syracuse University
UofR	University of Rochester
Web	World Wide Web

PART ONE

General Subjects

ANTHOLOGIES AND COLLECTIONS

RR1.   • Arditi, Metin, & Alain Bouldouyre: *Dictionnaire Amoureux de l'Esprit Français*. Paris: Plon. 669p. [BAnQ] (Apollinaire, Arnaud, Camus, Péguy, Ringuet)

RR2.   • Bégaudeau, François, & Hubert Artus: *Gilets Jaunes: Pour un Nouvel Horizon Social*. Vauvert: Au Diable Vauvert. 236p. [BAnQ] (Ernaux)

RR3.   • Boase-Beier, Jean, & Marian Vooght: *Poetry of the Holocaust: An Anthology*. Todmorden: Arc Publications. 243p. [Cor] (Cayrol, Desnos)

RR4.   • Cannone, Belinda, & Christian Doumet: *Dictionnaire des Mots Parfaits*. Vincennes: Thierry Marchaisse. 209p. [BnF] (Bénabou)

RR5.   • Chédeville, Élise: *A Cent à l'Heure: 13 Nouvelles sur la Vitesse*. Paris: Flammarion. 109p. [WC] (Delerm)

RR6.   • Cito, Myriam, Nathan Maggetti, & Elisa Ruckstuhl: *La Prose: Anthologie Suisse (Quelques Textes Finalistes du Pija 2019)*. Charmey: Éditions de l'Hèbe. 219p. [WC]

RR7.   • Contarini, Silvia, Claire Joubert, & Jean-Marc Moura: *Penser la Différence Culturelle du Colonial au Mondial: Une Anthologie Transculturelle*. [Sesto San Giovanni]: Mimésis. 473p. [WC]

RR8.   • Dalle, Maxime, Yves Delafoy, & Archibald Ney: *"Raskar Kapac": L'Anthologie*. Grézillac: Éditions du Rocher. 471p. [BnF] (Matzneff)

RR9.   • Dotoli, Giovanni, Mario Selvaggio, Alain Rey, & Emma V. Puggioni: *Le Vampire dans la Poésie Française: XIX-XXe Siècles: Anthologie*. Paris: L'Harmattan. 477p. [Cor]

RR10.   • Foucault, Michel, Georges Dumézil, Émile Benveniste, Claude Lévi-Strauss, Roland Barthes, Jean F. Joliot-Curie, Guillaume Roubaud-Quashie, Lukas Tsiptsios, & Jean Ristat: *Les Lettres Françaises: Cinquante Ans d'Aventures Culturelles: Anthologie Depuis 1942*. Paris: Hermann. 1025p. [BnF] (Paulhan, Vilar)

RR11.   • Fournier, Jean-Louis, & Alain Bouldouyre: *Dictionnaire Amoureux du Nord*. Paris: Plon. 531p. [BAnQ]

RR12.   • Fragos, Emily: *Poems of Paris*. New York: Alfred A. Knopf. 256p. [WC] (Prévert)

RR13.   • Frank, Edwin: *The Red Thread: Twenty Years of Nyrb Classics: A Selection*. New York: New York Review Books. 261p. [WC] (Bespaloff)

RR14.   • García, Tizón E.: *Herido Leve: Treinta Años de Memoria Lectora*. Madrid: Páginas de Espuma. 651p. [LoC] (Bove, Schwob)

RR15.   • Goust, Dominique: *L'Art du Pastiche: Anthologie Buissonnière de la Littérature Française: De Rutebeuf à Anouilh*. Paris: Omnibus. 543p. [BnF] (Laurent)

RR16.   • Grenier, Nicolas, & Patrick Clastres: *Jeu, Set et Match!: Une Anthologie Littéraire du Tennis*. Le Crest: Les Éditions du Volcan. 208p. [BnF] (Alphonse Daudet)

RR17.   ● Guentchev, Lubomir, & Alain Vuillemin: *Anthologie de Poètes Français et Allemands*. Cordes-sur-Ciel: Rafael de Surtis. 191p. [BnF]

RR18.   ● Henry, Jean-Marie, & Zaü: *La Cour Couleurs: Anthologie de Poèmes Contre le Racisme*. [Voisins-le-Bretonneux]: Rue du Monde. Nouvelle edition revue et corrigée. 67p. [BnF] (Velter)

RR19.   ● Lacelle, Andrée, & Pelletier F. Baril: *Poèmes de la Résistance*. Sudbury, ON: Éditions Prise de parole. 103p. [WC] (Hédi Bouraoui)

RR20.   ● *La France: Anthologie 2019: Recueil [de Textes Primés Lors du Concours Littéraire 2019*. Bort-les-Orgues: Association la Méridienne du monde rural. 89p. [BnF]

RR21.   ● Lapointe, Jeanne, Marie-Anne Beaudet, Mylène Bédard, Claudia Raby, & Juliette Bernatchez: *Rebelle et Volontaire: Anthologie 1937-1995*. Montréal: Leméac. 252p. [BAnQ] (Roy)

RR22.   ● Lavalou, Armelle: *Paris, Une Anthologie Littéraire: De François Villon à Michel Houellebecq*. Paris: Parigramme. 1087p. [BnF]

RR23.   ● Lebech, Mette: *European Sources of Human Dignity: A Commented Anthology*. Oxford: Peter Lang. 345p. [WC]

RR24.   ● Levisalles, Nathalie: *Méditerranée, Amère Frontière: Récits*. Arles: Actes Sud. 141p. [Cor] (Slimani)

RR25.   ● Michel, Louise, & Eric Fournier: *À Mes Frères: Anthologie de Textes Poétiques et Politiques*. Montreuil: Libertalia. 165p. [BAnQ]

RR26.   ● Morgenrath, Christa, Eva Wernecke, José E. Agualusa, Ellen Banda-Aaku, Ken Bugul, Aya Cissoko, Youssouf A. Elalamy, Tendai Huchu, Sonwabiso Ngcowa, Okwiri Oduor, Nii A. Parkes, Chika Unigwe, Jutta Himmelreich, Gudrun Honke, Michael Kegler, & Manfred Loimeier: *Imagine Africa 2060: Geschichten Zur Zukunft Eines Kontinents*. Wuppertal: Peter Hammer. 191p. [WC]

RR27.   ● Olivri, Thomas: *Total Geek-Art: Une Anthologie Artistique de la Pop Culture*. Paris: Huginn & Muninn. 414p. [WC]

RR28.   ● Pichler, Michalis: *Publishing Manifestos: An International Anthology from Artists and Writers*. Cambridge, MA: MIT Press. 339p. [Cor] (Debord)

RR29.   ● Pinguet, Jérémie: *Aimer, Rimer: 150 Poèmes Pour Réinventer l'Amour*. Paris: l'Harmattan. 288p. [BnF] (Maulpoix)

RR30.   ● Riester, Franck: *Notre-Dame: Une Anthologie de Textes d'Écrivains: Le Patrimoine Littéraire Défend le Patrimoine Architectural*. Paris: Points. 93p. [WC]

RR31.   ● Rouquet, Guy: *Le Livre de L'autre: 30 Écrivains Racontent le Rôle de l'Autre dans la Naissance de leur Oeuvre*. Bègles: Le Castor Astral. 187p. [WC] (Camus, Goffette, Khoury-Ghata, Lemaire)

RR32.   ● Saint-Pol-Roux, Max Jacob, Victor Segalen, Gwenn Darras, & Yvan Guillemot: *Anthologie de la Poésie en Bretagne au XXe Siècle*. Rennes: Calligrammes-Bernard Guillemot. 340p. [WC]

RR33.   ● Séité, Yannick, & Sylvie Patron: *Textuel: Une Anthologie, 1976-2016*. Paris: Hermann. 313p. [BnF] (Kristeva)

RR34.   ● Stableford, Brian M.: *Tales of Enchantment and Disenchantment: A History of Faerie with an Exemplary Anthology of Tales*. Encino, CA: Black Coat Press. 668p. [WC] (Lorrain, Mendès)

RR35.   ● *Un Temps aux Écrivains: Anthologie Littéraire Trimestrielle*. Villeurbanne: MaBoZa. 249p. [WC]

RR36.   ● Zouari, Fawzia, & Youma Fall: *Voix d'Écrivaines Francophones: Anthologie*. Orléans: Regain de lecture. 189p. [WC]

RR37.   Murat, Michel: "Décontextualisation et Recontextualisation: Le Travail des Anthologies Poétiques." *Littérature*, *194*, 2, 50. [Syr] (Hocquard)

RR38.   Ruprecht, Alvina: "Christiane P. Makward & Judith G. Miller, Eds. and Trans. Plays by French and Francophone Women: A Critical Anthology." *Theatre Research in Canada*, *21*, 2. [Naz]

RR39.   Spanu, Michael: "Michaël Abecassis & Marcelline Block, an Anthology of French and Francophone Singers from A to Z." *Volume!*, *15-2*, 1, 169. [WC]

BIBLIOGRAPHY

RR40.   ● Bennani, Fatiha, & 'Abd -R. Ṭankul: *85 Ans de Littérature Marocaine de Langue Française (1932-2017)*. Paris: L'Harmattan. 115p. [UofR]

RR41.   ● DiMercurio, Catherine C.: *Contemporary Authors: Volume 417. A Bio-Bibliographical Guide to Current Writers in Fiction, General Nonfiction, Poetry, Journalism, Drama, Motion Pictures, Television, and Other Fields*. Farmington Hills, MI: Gale. 449p. [WC]

RR42.   ● DiMercurio, Catherine C.: *Contemporary Authors: Volume 418. A Bio-Bibliographical Guide to Current Writers in Fiction, General Nonfiction, Poetry, Journalism, Drama, Motion Pictures, Television, and Other Fields*. Farmington Hills, MI: Gale. 450p. [WC]

RR43.   ● DiMercurio, Catherine C.: *Contemporary Authors: Volume 419. A Bio-Bibliographical Guide to Current Writers in Fiction, General Nonfiction, Poetry, Journalism, Drama, Motion Pictures, Television, and Other Fields*. Farmington Hills, MI: Gale. 450p. [WC]

RR44.   ● DiMercurio, Catherine C.: *Contemporary Authors: Volume 420. A Bio-Bibliographical Guide to Current Writers in Fiction, General Nonfiction, Poetry, Journalism, Drama, Motion Pictures, Television, and Other Fields*. Farmington Hills, MI: Gale. 450p. [WC]

RR45.   ● DiMercurio, Catherine C.: *Contemporary Authors: Volume 421. A Bio-Bibliographical Guide to Current Writers in Fiction, General Nonfiction, Poetry, Journalism, Drama, Motion Pictures, Television, and Other Fields*. Farmington Hills, MI: Gale. 450p. [WC]

RR46.   ● Dimerman, Julien, Peggy Errebei, & Sylvie Levêque: *Bibliographie de la Littérature Française, XVIe-XXIe Siècle: Année 2018. Revue d'Histoire Littéraire de la France*, *119*, hors série. Paris: Classiques Garnier. 767p. [WC]

RR47.   ● Dumont, Paula: *Entre Femmes: 250 Oeuvres Lesbiennes Résumées et Commentées: Tome 2*. Paris: L'Harmattan. 260p. [Cor]

RR48.   ● Núñez, Maria L., Brigitte Praplan, & Damien Tornincasa: *Famille, Familles!: Une Bibliographie en Faveur de la Diversité*. Lausanne: Institut Suisse Jeunesse et Médias. 112p. [WC]

RR49.   González García, Ana Margarita: "Le Livre des Apparitions." *Anales de Filología Francesa*, *27*, 593-4. [RIT] (Cardinal)

RR50.   "Les Livres." *Les Lettres Romanes*, 73, 291-297. [UaB] (Serge)

RR51.   Lodge, Sally, & Shannon Maughan: "Spring 2019 Children's Announcements: Publishers M-Q." *Publishers Weekly*, *266*, 5, 43. [PrQ]

23995

RR52.   Michaud, Stéphane: "Éléments de Bibliographie." *Revue de Littérature Comparée*, *371*, 3, 363. [Naz] (Bensoussan)

RR53.   "Nota Bene." *World Literature Today*, *93*, 1, 77. [RIT] (Reza)

RR54.   Price, Richard, & Sally Price: "Bookshelf 2018." *Nieuwe West - Indische Gids*, *93*, 1, 73-98. [RIT] (Franketienne)

RR55.   Yamashiro, Aiko: "Annual Bibliography of Works about Life Writing, 2017-2018." *Biography*, *42*, 1, 175-292. [PrQ] (Cardinal, Sarraute)

BIBLIOPHILISM AND PUBLICATION

RR56.   ● Absalyamova, Elina, Nuijs L. Van, & Valérie Stiénon: *Figures du Critique-Écrivain: Xixe-XXie Siècles*. Rennes: Presses Universitaires de Rennes. 329p. [Cor] (Kristeva, Blanchot, Péguy, Perec)

RR57.   ● Baltazar, Julius, & Marc-Édouard Gautier: *Julius Baltazar: Un Rimbaud Déguisé en Cosmonaute*. [Angers]: Ville d'Angers. 302p. [WC] (Guillevic)

RR58.   ● Beresniak, Ariel, Chatenet A. Du, Nathalie Moine, Yitshok Niborski, Natalia Krynicka, & Anne Goscinny: *Imprimé chez Beresniak: Le XXe Siècle Entre les Lignes*. Paris: Bibliothèque Medem. 164p. [Cor] (Goscinny)

RR59.   ● Bergounioux, Pierre, & Jacques Barral: *Le Corps de la Lettre*. Saint-Clément-de-Rivière: Fata Morgana. 54p. [WC]

RR60.   ● Bosco, Henri, & Alain Tassel: *Lettres à Quelques Amis Écrivains*. Paris: Classiques Garnier. 135p. [Cor] (Marcel)

RR61.   ● Breuil, Eddie: *Méthodes et Pratiques de l'Édition Critique des Textes et Documents Modernes*. Paris: Classiques Garnier. 921p. [Cor]

RR62.   ● Brogniez, Laurence, Clément Dessy, & Clara Sadoun-Édouard: *L'Artiste en Revues: Arts et Discours en Mode Périodique: [Colloque, Université Libre de Bruxelles, 28-30 Octobre 2013]*. Rennes: Presses Universitaires de Rennes. 498p. [WC] (Copeau)

RR63.   ● Demanze, Laurent: *Un Nouvel Âge de l'Enquête: Portraits de l'Écrivain Contemporain en Enquêteur*. [Paris]: Corti. 291p. [Cor] (Carrère, Daoud, Modiano)

RR64.   ● Deville, Patrick: *L'Étrange Fraternité des Lecteurs Solitaires*. Paris: Seuil. 54p. [BAnQ]

RR65.   ● Gaudet, Gérald, & Pierre Vadeboncoeur: *Écrire, Aimer, Penser: Entretiens sur l'Essai et la Création Littéraires*. Montréal: Nota Bene. 266p. [BAnQ] (Suzanne Jacob, Vadeboncoeur)

RR66.   ● Gorius, Alain, & Thieri Foulc: *Page(s: Bibliophilie Contemporaine & Livres d'Artistes: 2019, 22e Édition*. Paris: Association Page(s. 125p. [WC] (Bernard Noël)

RR67.   ● Goy, Héloïse, & Tatiana Lenté: *Bibliothérapie: 500 Livres Qui Réenchantent la Vie*. Vanves: Hachette. 295p. [BnF]

RR68.   ● Jey, Martine, & Laetitia Perret: *L'Idée de Littérature dans l'Enseignement*. Paris: Classiques Garnier. 362p. [LoC] (Péguy)

RR69.   ● Lavoie, Brian F.: *Maple Leaves: Discovering Canada Through the Published Record*. Dublin, OH: OCLC Research. 34p. [WC]

RR70. ● Le Bras, L.: *Les Manuscrits de l'Extrême*. Paris: Bibliothèque nationale de France. 199p. [LoC] (Guyotat)

RR71. ● Matisse, Pierre, Joan Miró, & Élisa Sclaunick: *Ouvrir le Feu: Correspondance Croisée, 1933-1983, Augmentée de Lettres d'André Breton, Jacques Dupin et Pierre Loeb*. [Strasbourg]: L'Atelier Contemporain-François-Marie Deyrolle. 763p. [Cor]

RR72. ● Minella, Anne-Marie, & Jean-Yves Bosseur: *Dialogues Contemporains: Les Collaborations de Jean-Yves Bosseur*. Château-Gontier: Aedam Musicae. 285p. [WC] (Dorion)

RR73. ● Moulin, Joanny, Phương N. Nguyễn, & Yannick Gouchan: *La Vérité d'une Vie: Études Sur la Véridiction en Biographie*. Paris: Honoré Champion. 407p. [LoC] (Dotremont)

RR74. ● Obrist, Hans U.: *Les Entretiens Infinis: Conversations, 2014-2018*. Paris: Fondation Cartier pour l'Art Contemporain. 298p. [BnF] (Varda)

RR75. ● Price, Leah: *What We Talk About When We Talk About Books: The History and Future of Reading*. New York: Basic Books. 214p. [UofR]

RR76. ● Quignard, Marie-Françoise: *L'Enfer de la Bibliothèque: Eros Au Secret*. [Paris]: Bibliothèque nationale de France. 319p. [WC]

RR77. ● Talon-Hugon, Carole: *L'Art Sous Contrôle: Nouvel Agenda Sociétal et Censures Militantes*. Paris: Presses Universitaires de France – Humensis. 137p. [BAnQ] (Lepage)

RR78. ● Villaumé, Cécile: *Des Écrivains Imaginés*. Paris: Le Dilettante. 218p. [Cor] (Bloy)

RR79. Aron, Paul: "La Reconversion des Écrivains Catholiques Après-Guerre en Belgique Francophone: Le Cas de l'Hebdomadaire Vrai." *Contextes*, 23. [PrQ] (Gevers)

RR80. Basch, Sophie: "La Postérité Littéraire et Artistique de la Victoire de Samothrace: Petite Anthologie." *Revue d'Histoire Littéraire de la France*, 119, 3, 615-628. [RIT]

RR81. Bridenne, Florence: "Les 10 Ans du Prix Littéraire de la Porte Dorée au Salon Littexil." *Hommes & Migrations*, 1327, 4, 145. [UaB] (Lopes)

RR82. Gavalda, Élisabeth: "De Prospero à Ses Cahiers. L'Aventure d'une Revue." *La Revue des Revues*, 61, 1, 44. [UofR] (Vinaver)

RR83. Glynn, Dominic, Sébastien Lemerle, & Erika Fülöp: "Digital Authorship and Social Media: French Digital Authors' Attitudes Towards Facebook." *French Cultural Studies*, 30, 2, 121-137. [UofR] (Bon)

RR84. Ouvry-Vial, Brigitte: "La Conception Éditoriale du Lecteur en France des Années 1950 à la Fin des Années 1970: En Particulier dans les 'Discours d'Escorte' de Jean Cayrol, Jean Paulhan et Gaëtan Picon." *Mémoires du Livre*, 10, 2. [WC]

RR85. Radwan, Jérôme: "Quelques Repères Significatifs Pour Ne Pas Oublier l'Action du Bouquiniste Bruxellois de 'La Borgne Agasse,' Jean-Pierre Canon (25 Décembre 1941 - 12 Janvier 2018)." *Textyles*, 54, 197-199. [Cor] (Guillaumin)

RR86. Vieira, Willian: "In the Name of Real Names: Literary Game, Self-Censorship and Literary Ontology." *Alea: Estudos Neolatinos*, 21, 2, 219-237. [Cor] (Angot)

COMIC AND GRAPHIC NOVEL

RR87. ● Badir, Sémir, Maria G. Dondero, & François Provenzano: *Les Discours Syncrétiques: Poésie Visuelle, Bande Dessinée, Graffitis*. Liège: Presses Universitaires de Liège. 149p. [LoC]

RR88. ● Barry, Alpha O.: *L'Information Dessinée en Afrique Francophone: Postures Critiques et Transmission de Savoirs*. Pessac: Presses Universitaires de Bordeaux. 375p. [Cor]

RR89. ● Bazin, Gaby: *Lettrages et Phylactères: L'Écrit dans la Bande Dessinée*. [Gap]: Atelier Perrousseaux. 215p. [WC]

RR90. ● Béghain, Véronique, & Isabelle Licari-Guillaume: *Les Traducteurs de Bande Dessinée =: Translators of Comics*. Bordeaux: Presses Universitaires de Bordeaux. 151p. [WC]

RR91. ● Berthou, Benoît, & Jacques Dürrenmatt: *Style(s) de (la) Bande Dessinée*. Paris: Classiques Garnier. 428p. [WC]

RR92. ● *Bd!: Collection de Monsieur M. Dit Nanette, et à Divers: Vente, Paris, 25 Mai 2019*. Paris: Coutau-Bégarie & Associés. 96p. [BnF]

RR93. ● Boum: *Rues de Montréal: Histoires Urbaines en Bande Dessinée*. Montréal: Planches: FBDM. 141p. [BAnQ]

RR94. ● Bourgoin, Marie, & Matthieu Rémy: *Fanzinorama: Une Histoire de la Bande Dessinée Underground*. Paris: Hoëbeke. 189p. [WC]

RR95. ● Caboche, Elsa, & Désirée Lorenz: *La Bande Dessinée à la Croisée des Médias: [Actes des Journées d'étude, Maison des Sciences de l'Homme et de la Société, Université de Poitiers, 9-10 Octobre 2014]*. Tours: Presses Universitaires François-Rabelais. 201p. [BnF]

RR96. ● Chalvin, Antoine, Jean-Léon Muller, Katre Talviste, & Marie Vrinat-Nikolov: *Histoire de la Traduction Littéraire en Europe Médiane: des Origines à 1989*. Rennes: Presses Universitaires de Rennes. 433p. [Cor]

RR97. ● Chauvaud, Frédéric, & Denis Mellier: *Les Êtres Contrefaits: Corps Difformes et Corps Grotesques dans la Bande Dessinée*. Rennes: Presses Universitaires de Rennes. 367p. [WC]

RR98. ● Delisle, Philippe: *La Bd au Crible de l'Histoire: Hergé, Maurras, les Jésuites et Quelques Autres*. Paris: Karthala. 195p. [BAnQ]

RR99. ● Delorme, Isabelle: *"Ma Vie N'est Pas Croustillante": Exposition de Planches de Bande Dessinée Mémorielle, 28 Janvier-29 Mars 2019: Travaux Réalisés dans le Cadre des Ateliers Artistiques de Sciences Po en 2018*. Paris: Bibliothèque de Sciences Po. 112p. [WC]

RR100. ● Delorme, Isabelle: *Quand La Bande Dessinée Fait Mémoire du XXe Siècle: Les Récits Mémoriels Historiques en Bande Dessinée*. Dijon: Les Presses du Réel. 501p. [LoC] (Satrapi)

RR101. ● Deprêtre, Evelyne, & German A. Duarte: *Transmédialité, Bande Dessinée & Adaptation*. Clermont-Ferrand: Presses Universitaires Blaise Pascal. 305p. [BAnQ]

RR102. ● Duhoo, Jean-Yves: *Un Beau Bébé: Cahier Spécial Bd de l'Édition Charente Libre du 24 Janvier 2019*. Angoulême: Charente Libre. 64p. [WC]

RR103. ● Eisner, William E., Anne Capuron, & Arthur Clare: *Les Clés de la Bande Dessinée: Intégrale*. Paris: Delcourt. 540p. [BnF]

RR104. ● Federici, Sandra: *L'Entrance des Auteurs Africains dans le Champ de la Bande Dessinée Européenne de Langue Française (1978-2016)*. Paris: L'Harmattan. 353p. [Cor]

RR105. ● Fripiat, Bernard, & Laurent Petitguillaume: *L'Orthographe en Bd*. [Paris]: Larousse DL. 255p. [BAnQ]

RR106. ● Fumeux, Christophe, François Dougier, & Pauline Testut: *Bande Dessinée, Illustrations: Dessins Originaux, Planches, Illustrations, Albums Rares, Albums Dédicacés: Vente, Paris, Hôtel Drouot, Samedi 7 Décembre 2019*. Paris: Coutau-Bégarie & Associés. 96p. [WC]

RR107. ● Glaude, Benoît: *La Bande Dialoguée: Une Histoire des Dialogues de Bande Dessinée (1830-1960)*. Tours: Presses Universitaires François-Rabelais. 391p. [Cor]

RR108. ● Gonick, Larry: *La Biologie en Bd*. [Paris]: Larousse. 313p. [BAnQ]

RR109. ● *La Bande Dessinée, Une Invention Genevoise?: Les Trésors de la Bibliothèque: Rodolphe Töpffer, 16.11.2019 - 18.01.2020: Programme*. Genève: Bibliothèque de Genève. 37p. [WC]

RR110. ● *La Revue Dessinée: L'Information en Bande Dessinée*. Lyon: La Revue Dessinée. 226p. [WC]

RR111. ● Le Breton, R.: *Écrire Une Bande Dessinée: Scénario et Art Séquentiel*. Avignon: Scénario 2.0. 144p. [BnF]

RR112. ● Lesage, Sylvain: *L'Effet Livre: Métamorphoses de la Bande Dessinée*. Tours: Presses Universitaires François Rabelais. 431p. [WC]

RR113. ● *Les Grands Maîtres de la Bd Mondiale*. [Paris]: Beaux Arts Éditions. 239p. [BAnQ] (Hergé)

RR114. ● Lungheretti, Pierre, & Laurence Cassegrain: *La Bande Dessinée, Nouvelle Frontière Artistique et Culturelle: 54 Propositions pour une Politique Nationale Renouvelée: Rapport au Ministre de la Culture*. Paris: La Documentation Française. 162p. [BnF]

RR115. ● Mars, L. L.: *Bande Dessinée & Grand Public*. Paris: Adverse. 15p. [BnF]

RR116. ● Meesters, Gert, Frédéric Paques, & David Vrydaghs: *Les Métamorphoses de Spirou: Le Dynamisme d'une Série de Bande Dessinée*. Liège: Presses Universitaires de Liège. 199p. [LoC]

RR117. ● Miniac, Jean-François: *Bd, Une Histoire Française et . . . Belge !: Pratt, Uderzeo, Hergé, Franquin, Moebius, Zep*. Paris: Oracom. 130p. [WC]

RR118. ● Nabizadeh, Golnar: *Representation and Memory in Graphic Novels*. New York, NY: Routledge. 198p. [Cor] (Satrapi)

RR119. ● Peeters, Benoît: *La Bande Dessinée Entre la Presse et le Livre. Fragments d'une Histoire*. Paris: BNF Editions. 1 vol. [WC]

RR120. ● *Rock & Bd Réunion*. Saint-Joseph (Réunion): Contrebande. 87p. [BnF]

RR121. ● Rommens, Aarnoud, & Benoît Crucifix: *Abstraction and Comics: Volume 1*. Liège: Presses Universitaires de Liège. 447p. [WC]

RR122. ● Rommens, Aarnoud, & Benoît Crucifix: *Abstraction and Comics: Volume 2*. Liège: Presses Universitaires de Liège. 441p. [RIT]

RR123. ● *Secrets de la Bande Dessinée*. Paris: BNF-Centre national de la littérature pour la jeunesse. *La Revue des livres pour enfants*, Hors-série, 5. 160p. [WC] (Sfar)

William F. Maag Library
Youngstown State University

RR124. ● Simon, Raphaëlle, & Laurent Bidot: *L'Histoire des Saints en Bande Dessinée*. Grenoble: Glénat. 96p. [BnF]

RR125. ● Sous, Jean-Louis: *Mises en Abîme: Psychanalyse, Bd*. Paris: Saint Honoré. 128p. [WC]

RR126. ● Sun, Zi, & Pete Katz: *L'Art de la Guerre: En Bande Dessinée*. Paris: Éditions Contre-dires. 128p. [BnF]

RR127. ● Terrades, Olivier: *Bande Dessinée in Extenso: D'Autres Intermédialités au Prisme de la Culture Visuelle*. Paris: Le Manuscrit. 416p. [BnF]

RR128. ● Vangindertael, Zoé: "Le Musée et la Bande Dessinée: Enjeux d'une Relation Symbiotique." *Marges*, 29, automne-hiver, 16-29. [WC]

RR129. ● Yuio: *Dessiner, Illustrer: Mode d'Emploi en Bd*. Paris: Eyrolles. 127p. [BnF]

RR130. ● Zep, & Valott: *Quelques Héros de la Bande Dessinée*. Lausanne: [Galerie du Marché]. 40p. [WC]

RR131. Aggarwal, Kusum: "Cassiau-Haurie (Christophe), Histoire de la Bande Dessinée au Cameroun. Préface de Raphaël Thierry. Paris: L'Harmattan, 2016, 234 p. – ISBN 987-2-343-08333-9." *Études Littéraires Africaines*, 48, 233. [LoC]

RR132. Arnould, Paul: "Sylvain Lesage, Publier la Bande Dessinée. Les Éditeurs Franco-Belges et l'Album, 1950-1990: Villeurbanne, Presses de l'ENSSIB, Coll. Papiers, 2018, 424 Pages." *Questions de Communication*, 36, 2, 328. [Cor]

RR133. "Bande Dessinée dans les Cases Africaines." *Jeune Afrique*, 59, 3027, 74-77. [Syr]

RR134. "Bande Dessinée Kadhafi et Sarkozy Sont dans un Bateau." *Jeune Afrique*, 59, 3032, 64-67. [Syr]

RR135. "Bande Dessinée Les Damnés de la Ville." *Jeune Afrique*, 59, 3048, 76-79. [Syr]

RR136. "Bande Dessinée Les Statues Meurent Aussi." *Jeune Afrique*, 59, 3034, 76-79. [Syr]

RR137. Blanchard, Marianne, etal.: "Co-construction et Expérimentation d'une Bande Dessinée Numérique pour la Classe: Les Grandiloquents, Épisode sur la Gravitation." *Tréma*, 51. [WC]

RR138. Blanchard, Marianne, & Hélène Raux: "La Bande Dessinée, Un Objet Didactique Mal Identifié." *Tréma*, 51. [WC]

RR139. Blin-Rolland, Armelle: "'Tu Te Décolonises': Comics Re-Framings of the Breton Liberation Front (FLB)." *Studies in Comics*, 10, 1, 73-91. [PrQ]

RR140. Bumatay, Michelle: "African Bande Dessinée Festivals and Competitions: Participation, Patronage, and Performance." *Research in African Literatures*, 50, 2, 35-48. [RIT]

RR141. Calargé, Carla: "Une Ville de Marges: Quand la Bd Donne à Voir Beyrouth." *Nouvelles Études Francophones*, 34, 1, 30-44. [UaB]

RR142. Calargé, Carla, & Alexandra Gueydan-Turek: "Introduction: De la Case à la Gouttière. La Bande Dessinée d'Expression Française et ses Marges." *Nouvelles Études Francophones*, 34, 1, 6-10. [UaB]

RR143. Caraco, Benjamin: "Enseigner la Bande Dessinée: Le Cas de l'Atelier d'Illustration de l'École des Arts Décoratifs de Strasbourg." *Sociétés & Représentations*, 47, 1, 237. [Cor]

RR144.   Chopelin, Paul: "La Révolution Française en Bande Dessinée. Actualité de l'Édition." *Annales Historiques de la Révolution Française, 398*, 4, 147. [UofR]

RR145.   Delorme, Isabelle: "L'Échappée Belle du Roman Graphique dans l'Édition Française." *Sociétés & Représentations, 48*, 2, 195. [Cor]

RR146.   Forsdick, Charles: "*Bande Dessinée* and the Penal Imaginary: Graphic Constructions of the Carceral Archipelago." *European Comic Art, 12*, 2, 1-16. [Naz]

RR147.   Gerbier, Laurent: "La Bande Dessinée du Réel et la Poésie de la Non-Fiction." *Quinzaines*, 1210, 4-6. [Syr]

RR148.   Gerbier, Laurent: "Les Études de Bande Dessinée et l'Édition Universitaire." *Quinzaines*, 1210, 10-11. [Syr]

RR149.   Giaufret, Anna: "La Bande Dessinée Québécoise A-t-Elle Peur des Anglicismes?" *Circula*, 9, 106-122. [WC]

RR150.   Gilbert, Marc-Antoine: "L'Imaginaire de l'Identité dans *L'Ascension du Haut Mal* de David B." *Nouvelles Études Francophones, 34*, 1, 86-96. [UaB]

RR151.   Gueydan-Turek, Alexandra: "Le Renouveau de la Bande Dessinée Maghrébine Contemporaine: Vers une Éthique Relationnelle." *Nouvelles Études Francophones, 34*, 1, 45-59. [Syr]

RR152.   Guillaud, Étienne, & Juliette Mengneau: "Un Détour par la Bande Dessinée: Retour sur des Expériences d'Apprentissage de la Sociologie en Licence." *Socio-Logos*, 14. [PrQ]

RR153.   Han, Sangjung: "La Bande Dessinée Française et Mai 68." *Société d'Études Franco-Coreennes*, 88, 245-259. [WC]

RR154.   Hervey, Yoann, Fabien Meynier, Céline Saturnino, & Sophie Pierre: "De la Bande Dessinée au Cinéma: Puissances et Fragilités des Corps chez Alejandro Jodorowsky." *Entrelacs*, 16. [BAnQ]

RR155.   Hureau, Maxime: "La Bande Dessinée Comme Forme Académique: Réflexions sur le Déploiement de Nick Sousanis." *Belphégor, 17*, 1. [Syr]

RR156.   Husson, Laurent: "Pascal Robert, La Bande Dessinée, Une Intelligence Subversivevilleurbane, Presses de l'ENSSIB, Coll. papiers, 2018, 311 Pages." *Questions de Communication, 36*, 2, 331. [Cor]

RR157.   King, Andrea, & Kristiana Karathanassis: "Language and Loss in Michel Rabagliati's *Paul à Québec* and Sarah Leavitt's *Tangles*." *Canadian Literature, 238*, 84, 100, 182-183. [RIT]

RR158.   Kohn, Jessica: "La Bande Dessinée, 'Une Menace pour la Culture'?, Jean Gaugeard, Les Lettres Françaises, 1966." *Parlement[s], Revue d'Histoire Politique, 29*, 1, 123. [Cor]

RR159.   Laurel, Maria H., María-Pilar Tresaco, & Ana-Isabel Moniz: "Imagination et Bande Dessinée: Vingt Mille Lieues sous les Mers." *Carnets*, deuxième série, 15. [Cor]

RR160.   Leduc, Véro: "Est-ce Vraiment une Bande Dessinée?" *Canadian Journal of Disability Studies, 8*, 1, 58-97. [Cor]

RR161.   Lesage, Sylvain: "Écrire l'Histoire en Images: Les Historiens et la Tentation de la Bande Dessinée." *Le Mouvement Social, 269*, 1, 47-65. [UofR]

RR162.   Lesage, Sylvain: "Paniques Morales et Bande Dessinée. Loi N° 49-956 sur les Publications Destinées à la Jeunesse." *Parlement[s], Revue d'Histoire Politique, 29*, 1, 225. [Cor]

RR163.   Lesage, Sylvain: "Quand La Bande Dessinée Fait Mémoire du XXe Siècle. Les Récits Mémoriels Historiques en Bande Dessinée by Isabelle Delorme (Review)." *Le Mouvement Social*, *269*, 1, 258. [UaB]

RR164.   Lesage, Sylvain: "Une Bande Dessinée Adulte? Usages et Mésusages de la Légitimation." *Belphégor*, *17*, 1. [Syr]

RR165.   Moine, Florian: "Construire la Légitimité Culturelle du Neuvième Art: Le Musée de la Bande Dessinée d'Angoulême." *Belphégor*, *17*, 1. [Syr]

RR166.   Peeters, Benoit: "Rodolphe Topffer: Inventeur et Theoricien de la Bande Dessinee." *Kultura*, 165, 259-262. [UaB]

RR167.   Pellitteri, Marco: "Le Son dans la Bande Dessinée – Réprésentation et Imagination de la Dimension Auditive." *Todas As Letras Revista de Língua e Literatura*, *21*, 1. [Syr]

RR168.   Portal, Claire: "'S'il Vous Plaît . . . Dessine-Moi (. . .)' La Géodiversité dans la Bande Dessinée, Quelques Repères de la Case au Récit." *Géomorphologie: Relief, Processus, Environnement*, *25*, 4, 253-268. [Cor]

RR169.   Robert, Pascal: "Le Stéréotype dans la Bande Dessinée Franco-Belge: Jeux et Plasticité Narrative." *Hermès, La Revue*, *83*, 1, 111. [UofR]

RR170.   Robinson, Nova: "Jerry Cans and Shrapnel Collections: Using Graphic Memoirs to Teach about the Lebanese Civil War." *Arab Studies Journal*, *27*, 2, 114-45. [RIT]

RR171.   Sanchez, A.-C.: "Mode et Bande Dessinée, Si Loin, Si Proches." *Oeil*, 726. [UofR]

RR172.   Schechner, Stephanie: "Wendy Michallat. French Cartoon Art in the 1960s and 1970s: Pilote Hebdomadaire and the Teenager Bande Dessinée. Leuven Up, 2018." *Studies in 20th & 21st Century Literature*, *43*, 2. [Naz]

RR173.   Screech, Matthew: "French Cartoon Art in the 1960s and 1970s: 'Pilote Hebdomadaire' and the Teenager 'Bande Dessinée' by Wendy Michallat." *French Studies*, *73*, 3, 496. [UaB]

RR174.   Simioni, Elena: "Se Débrouiller à Dakar: Langue(s) et Culture(s) Urbaines dans la Bande Dessinée Goorgoorlou de T. T. Fons." *Il Tolomeo*, 1. [WC]

CRIME FICTION

RR175.   ● Daeninckx, Didier, & Patrick Boucheron: *Le Roman Noir de l'Histoire*. Lagrasse [France]: Verdier. 810p. [UofR]

RR176.   ● Delbos, Françoise: *Polar? Vous Avez Dit Polars?: Polar, Psychanalyse et Discours Capitaliste*. Paris: La Petite Librairie. 88p. [BnF]

RR177.   ● Fuligni, Bruno: *La Police des Écrivains*. Paris: CNRS. 260p. [WC]

RR178.   ● Libens, Christian: *Une Petite Histoire du Roman Policier Belge de Langue Française*. Neufchâteau: Weyrich. 97p. [LoC]

RR179.   ● Marc, Bernard: *Mémoires du Crime: Le Légiste Témoigne: De la Belle Epoque aux Années Folles (1910-1925)*. Paris: MA éditions – ESKA. 288p. [WC]

RR180.   ● McDermid, Val: *Scènes de Crime: [200 Ans d'Histoires et de Sciences Criminelles]*. Paris: Les Arènes. 421p. [BnF]

RR181. ● Ménard, Noëlle: *Le Polar S'Écrit à l'Ouest: Une Enquête Très Académique*. [Nantes]: Coiffard. 133p. [WC]

RR182. ● Reed, Sarah M. A.: *Translating Cultural Identity: French Translations of Australian Crime Fiction*. Oxford: Peter Lang. 244p. [LoC]

RR183. ● Salado, Régis, & Carin Trevisan: *Ecrits, Images et Pensées de Prison: Expériences de l'Incarcération*. Paris: Hermann. 331p. [WC] (Calet)

RR184. "Afrique-France Alexandre Djouhri: Sa Vie Est un Roman Noir." *Jeune Afrique*, *59*, 3048, 40-42. [UofR]

RR185. "La Sélection Polar, Essai, Bd et Jeunesse." *Historia*, 870, 78-87. [BAnQ]

RR186. Moulin, A. M.: "Un Genre Nouveau, Le Polar Éthique?" *Medecine Sciences: M/S*, *35*, 1, 78-79. [WC]

RR187. Ostojic, Zvezdana: "Legacies of the Rue Morgue: Science, Space, and Crime Fiction in France." *MLN*, *134*, 4, 841-4. [RIT] (Butor, Leroux)

RR188. Platini, Vincent, Jean-Bernard Pouy, & Marin Ledun: "Roman Noir: Écrire une 'Autre Histoire'?" *Agone*, *63-64*, 1, 99. [Cor]

RR189. Sarr, M. M., & E. Bertho: "Méditerranéennes les Migrations entre Enquête et Polar." *Multitudes*, *76*, 3, 202-206. [Cor]

FRANCOPHONE LITERATURE

RR190. ● Amuri, Mpala-Lutebele M.: *Oralité, Traditions et Modernité en Afrique au XXIe Siècle*. Paris: L'Harmattan. 576p. [WC] (Condé, Hampâté Bâ, Kourouma)

RR191. ● Battiston, Régine, & Daniel Annen: *Les Littératures Suisses entre Faits et Fiction*. Strasbourg: Presses Universitaires de Strasbourg. 254p. [WC]

RR192. ● Bédia, Jean-Fernand, & Koléa Zigui: *Lumières Postcoloniales: Pour Un Nouvel Esprit Critique Littéraire en Afrique Francophone*. Paris: L'Harmattan. 367p. [Cor] (Beti, Aimé Césaire, Dadié, Kourouma)

RR193. ● Bertho, Elara: *Sorcières, Tyrans, Héros: Mémoires Postcoloniales de Résistants Africains*. Paris: Honoré Champion. 518p. [WC]

RR194. ● Boutaghou, Maya, & Anne Donadey: *Représentations de la Guerre d'Indépendance Algérienne*. Paris: Classiques Garnier. 249p. [WC] (Bey, Venaille, Marker)

RR195. ● Carrier, Roch: *Leçons Apprises et Parfois Oubliées*. Montréal: Libre Expression. 309p. [BAnQ] (Aquin)

RR196. ● Chassaing, Irène: *Dysnostie: Le Récit du Retour au Pays Natal dans la Littérature Canadienne Francophone Contemporaine*. [Québec]: Les Presses de l'Université Laval. 267p. [Syr] (Hébert, Huston, Laferrière, Maillet)

RR197. ● Clément, Daniel: *Les Récits de Notre Terre: [volume 3]*. [Québec]: Presses de l'Université Laval. 156p. [Cor]

RR198. ● Clément, Daniel: *Les Récits de Notre Terre: Les Naskapis*. [Québec]: Presses de l'Université Laval. 172p. [Cor]

RR199. ● Corinus, Véronique, Mireille Hilsum, & Mélikah Abdelmoumen: *Nouvel État des Lieux des Littératures Francophones: Cadres Conceptuels et*

Création Contemporaine. Lyon: Presses Universitaires de Lyon. 237p. [UofR] (Kwahulé)

RR200. • Cornille, Jean-Louis: *Lémures: Hantologie de la Littérature Malgache en Français*. Caen: Passage(s). 110p. [UofR] (Rabemananjara)

RR201. • Corsin, Julie: *Approche de la Culture et Littérature Féminines Francophones sur le Continent Américain aux XXe et XXIe Siècles*. Paris: Indigo - Côté Femmes. 199p. [Cor] (Baron Supervielle)

RR202. • Crainic, Corina, & François Paré: *Martinique, Guadeloupe, Amériques: Des Marrons, du Gouffre et de la Relation*. Laval: Presses de l'Université Laval. 140p. [Syr] (Glissant, Simone Schwarz-Bart)

RR203. • De Luca, Y.: *Intertextualité dans le Roman Québécois: Les Charmes du Mythe*. Trento: Tangram Edizioni Scientifiche. 187p. [LoC]

RR204. • Dia, Fadel: *Un Homme de son Temps: Hommage au Professeur Assane Seck*. Paris: L'Harmattan-Sénégal. 144p. [LoC] (Cheikh Anta Diop)

RR205. • Diagne, Ibrahima, & Hans-Jürgen Lüsebrink: *L'Intertextualité dans les Littératures Sénégalaises: Réseaux, Réécritures, Palimpsestes*. Paris: L'Harmattan. 289p. [UofR] (Birago Diop, Senghor)

RR206. • Diakité, Boubakary: *Écritures et Désécriture dans les Romans Africains*. Paris: L'Harmattan. 224p. [UofR] (Deleuze, Kourouma)

RR207. • Diard, Dominique: *Polyphonies Diverselles du Tout-Monde: Tout-Monde ou "Multivers" à l'Oeuvre dans la Fiction Caribéenne Contemporaine*. Caen: Passage(s). 174p. [UofR] (Chamoiseau, Glissant)

RR208. • Diop, Mamadou, & Mamadou K. Ba: *Mythe et Littératures Africaines: La Mise en Texte de l'Imaginaire*. Paris: l'Harmattan. 247p. [UofR] (Ben Jelloun, Hampâté Bâ, Kourouma, Tadjo)

RR209. • Eba'a, Germain, & Jean-Marcel Essiene: *Immigration et Francographie: Bilan, Enjeux et Perspectives*. Saint-Denis: Connaissances et Savoirs. 211p. [Cor] (Chedid, Cheng, Laferrière, Maalouf)

RR210. • Forter, Greg: *Critique and Utopia in Postcolonial Historical Fiction: Atlantic and Other Worlds*. Oxford: Oxford UP. 227p. [UofR] (Chamoiseau)

RR211. • Gendre, Annick: *Polyphonies Littéraires Francophones Transcontinentales: Frontières, Fronts Tierces?* Paris: L'Harmattan. 208p. [UofR] (Bianciotti)

RR212. • Guéna, Pauline, & Guillaume Binet: *L'Amérique des Écrivains: Road Trip*. Paris: 10/18. 206p. [BnF]

RR213. • Halden, Charles: *Nouvelles Études de Littérature Canadienne Française*. Ann Arbor, MI: F.R. de Rudeval. 377p. [WC] (Conan, Nelligan)

RR214. • Hél-Bongo, Olga: *Roman Francophone et Essai: Mudimbe, Chamoiseau, Khatibi*. Paris: Honoré Champion. 301p. [Cor]

RR215. • Ippolito, Christophe: *Vers des Identités Culturelles Postfrancophones: Pour des Littératures en Langue Française Libérées des Errements de la Francophonie*. Caen: Passage(s). 278p. [UofR]

RR216. • Izzo, Justin: *Experiments with Empire: Anthropology and Fiction in the French Atlantic*. Durham: Duke UP. 282p. [UofR] (Chamoiseau, Hampâté Bâ, Leiris, Rouch)

RR217. • Jia, Jie, & Pierre Dimech: *Pieds-noirs: Français à Part Entière ou Entièrement à Part?; Accueil et Reconstruction Identitaire des Français d'Algérie de 1962 à Nos Jours*. La Chaussée d'Ivry: Atelier Fol'fer. 272p. [WC]

RR218.	● Jouve, Edmond, & Rodolphe Alexandre: *Quelle Francophonie en Guyane?* Paris: L'Harmattan. 261p. [UofR]

RR219.	● Kana, Nguetse P., & Mangoua R. Fotsing: *Littératures Francophones et Géographie.* Dschang: Presses Universitaires de Dschang. 208p. [WC] (Bekri, Daoud, Kourouma, Maximin, Monénembo)

RR220.	● Kassab-Charfi, Samia, & Adel Khedher: *Un Siècle de Littérature en Tunisie: 1900-2017.* Paris: Honoré Champion. 548p. [WC]

RR221.	● Kizzi, Akila: *Marie-Louise Taos Amrouche: Passions et Déchirements Identitaires.* Paris: Fauves. 487p. [WC]

RR222.	● Kramer, Pascale, Daniel Roulet, Carl Spitteler, Etienne Barilier, & Camille Luscher: *Helvétique Équilibre: Dialogues avec le "Point de Vue Suisse" du Prix Nobel de Littérature 1919.* Chêne-Bourg, Genève: Zoé. 125p. [BnF] (Rolland)

RR223.	● Lançon, Daniel, & Ridha Boulaâbi: *Voix d'Orient: Mélanges Offerts à Daniel Lançon.* Paris: Geuthner. 260p. [Cor] (Lanson, Le Bris)

RR224.	● Laurichesse, Jean-Yves, & Sylvie Vignes: *États des Lieux dans les Récits Français et Francophones des Années 1980 à Nos Jours.* Paris: Classiques Garnier. 358p. [BnF] (Alexakis, Bon, Ernaux, Glissant, Réda)

RR225.	● Leupin, Alexandre, & Dominique Aurélia: *La Louisiane et les Antilles, une Nouvelle Région du Monde.* Pointe-à-Pitre: Presses Universitaires des Antilles. 217p. [BnF] (Glissant)

RR226.	● Llorens, Natasha M.: *Waiting for Omar Gatlato: A Survey of Contemporary Art from Algeria and Its Diaspora.* Berlin: Sternberg Press. 261p. [Cor] (Allouache, Fanon)

RR227.	● Lucrèce, André: *Antilles: Les Paroles, les Visages et les Masques.* Paris: L'Harmattan. 246p. [LoC] (Alexis, Glissant, Saint-John Perse, Zobel)

RR228.	● Lüsebrink, Hans-Jürgen, & Sarga Moussa: *Dialogues Interculturels à l'Époque Coloniale et Postcoloniale: Représentations Littéraires et Culturelles, Orient, Maghreb et Afrique Occidentale (de 1830 à Nos Jours).* Paris: Kimé. 406p. [Cor] (Beti, Bouvier, Chraïbi, Sebbar)

RR229.	● Mabanckou, Alain, & Abdourahman A. Waberi: *Dictionnaire Enjoué des Cultures Africaines.* Paris: Fayard. 335p. [BAnQ]

RR230.	● Macfarlane, Heather: *Divided Highways: Road Narrative and Nationhood in Canada.* Ottawa: University of Ottawa Press. 165p. [Syr] (Archambault, Poulin)

RR231.	● Marcotte, Sophie: *Regards sur les Archives d'Écrivains Francophones au Canada.* [Ottawa]: Les Presses de l'Université d'Ottawa. 332p. [Naz] (Aquin, Guèvremont, Roy)

RR232.	● Marcu, Ioana: *La Problématique de l'"Entre(-)deux" dans les Littératures des "Intranger.e.s."* Paris: L'Harmattan. 342p. [Cor] (Charef)

RR233.	● M'Baye, Babacar, & Besi B. Muhonja: *Gender and Sexuality in Senegalese Societies: Critical Perspectives and Methods.* London: Lexington Books. 319p. [WC] (Bâ)

RR234.	● Mbembe, Achille, & Felwine Sarr: *Politique des Temps: Imaginer les Devenirs Africains.* Dakar, Sénégal: Jimsaan. 398p. [WC] (Dib)

RR235.	● Mongo-Mboussa, Boniface: *Désir d'Afrique.* Paris: Gallimard. 379p. [BnF] (Kourouma)

RR236.	● Montigny, Éric, & François Cardinal: *La Révolution Z: Comment les Jeunes Transformeront le Québec.* Montréal: Les Éditions La Presse. 235p. [BAnQ] (Godbout)

RR237. ● Moura, Jean-Marc: *Littératures Francophones et Théorie Postcoloniale.* Paris: PUF. 3e edition. 230p. [UofR]

RR238. ● Ngo, Nlend N. L.: *Dynamique de Transculturation du Christianisme: L'Expérience du Missionnaire Protestant Jean-René Brutsch au Cameroun (1946-1960).* Paris: Karthala. 375p. [Cor]

RR239. ● Ouasmi, Lahcen, & Fatiha Bennani: *Hommages: Fatema Mernissi, Assia Djebar, May Ziade, Mohammed Khair-Eddine.* Casablanca: Faculté des Lettres et des Sciences Humaines de Casablanca Ben M'sik. 178p. [WC]

RR240. ● Poliquin, Laurent: *Les Foudres du Silence: L'Estomac Fragile de la Littérature Francophone au Canada.* Paris: L'Harmattan. 286p. [UofR] (Roy, Thibodeau)

RR241. ● Quaghebeur, Marc: *Écritures de Femmes en Belgique Francophone après 1945.* Bruxelles: P.I.E. Peter Lang. 410p. [LoC] (Nys-Mazure)

RR242. ● Ransom, Amy J., & Dominick Grace: *Canadian Science Fiction, Fantasy, and Horror: Bridging the Solitudes.* Cham: Springer International. 380p. [WC]

RR243. ● Redouane, Najib, & Yvette Szmidt: *Kamal Benkirane: Voix Marocaine au Canada.* Paris: L'Harmattan. 298p. [UofR]

RR244. ● Roche, Anne: *Algérie: Écritures de l'Autre.* Paris: Kimé. 274p. [LoC] (Djaout, Yacine)

RR245. ● Sabry, Randa: *Voyager d'Égypte vers l'Europe et Inversement: Parcours Croisés (1830-1950).* Paris: Classiques Garnier. 498p. [Cor] (Lorrain)

RR246. ● Tolliver, Cedric R.: *Of Vagabonds and Fellow Travelers: African Diaspora Literary Culture and the Cultural Cold War.* Ann Arbor: University of Michigan Press. 232p. [Cor] (Alexis)

RR247. ● Toudoire-Surlapierre, Frédérique, & Ethmane Sall: *Les Rébellions Francophones.* Paris: Orizons. 278p. [Cor] (Chamoiseau, Boubacar Boris Diop, Kourouma, Labou Tansi)

RR248. ● Touré, El H. S. N., & Hamidou Kane: *Pilotage des Politiques Publiques au Sénégal de 1960 à 2012.* Dakar: L'Harmattan-Sénégal. Préface de Cheikh Hamidou Kane. 431p. [LoC]

RR249. ● Vandyck, Agnes O.: *African Visionaries.* Legon-Accra, Ghana: Sub-Saharan Publishers. 316p. [WC] (Bâ)

RR250. ● Warner, Tobias: *The Tongue-Tied Imagination: Decolonizing Literary Modernity in Senegal.* New York: Fordham UP. 342p. [Syr] (Bâ, Boubacar Boris Diop, Sembène)

RR251. Ahondoukpè, Mireille: "L'Annonce Faite à Marie: De l'Héritage Africain à une Lecture Postcoloniale." *Tydskrif Vir Letterkunde,* 56, 2, 76-82. [Naz] (Amrouche, Glissant, Saint-John Perse)

RR252. Azeb, Sophia: "Crossing the Saharan Boundary: Lotus and the Legibility of Africanness." *Research in African Literatures,* 50, 3, 91-115. [RIT] (Haddad, Senghor)

RR253. Barnes, Leslie, Ashok Collins, & Gemma King: "Introduction: Truth and Representation in French and Francophone Studies." *Australian Journal of French Studies,* 56, 2, 117-124. [Naz] (Darrieussecq)

RR254. Beránková, Eva Voldřichová: "Les Notions d'Américanisation et d'Américanité: Naissance, Évolution et Applications Littéraires dans le Québec Contemporain." *Écho des Études Romanes*, *15*, 1, 117. [PrQ] (Carrier, Poulin)

RR255. Bonn, Charles: "Un Siècle de Littérature en Tunisie, 1900-2017." *Revue de Littérature Comparée*, 372, 486-9. [PrQ] (Nina Bouraoui, Meddeb)

RR256. Bonner, Christopher: "Alioune Diop and the Cultural Politics of Negritude: Reading the First Congress of Black Writers and Artists, 1956." *Research in African Literatures*, *50*, 2, 1-18. [RIT] (Alexis, Rabemananjara)

RR257. Bryce, Jane: "African Futurism: Speculative Fictions and 'Rewriting the Great Book'." *Research in African Literatures*, *50*, 1, 1-19. [RIT] (Labou Tansi, Tadjo)

RR258. Burnett, Joshua Yu: "'Isn't Realist Fiction Enough?': On African Speculative Fiction." *Mosaic*, *52*, 3, 119-35. [PrQ] (Bâ)

RR259. Calvo Martín, Beatriz: "Écrire Au-Delà de la Fin des Temps? Les Littératures au Canada et au Québec." *Anales de Filología Francesa*, 27, 581-3. [PrQ] (Michel Marc Bouchard, Brossard, Dupré, Poulin)

RR260. Chamoiseau, Patrick, & Reeck Matt: "Weaving a Creole Patrimony." *World Literature Today*, *93*, 1, 54-58. [Naz]

RR261. Chochotte, Marvin: "Making Peasants *Chèf*: The *Tonton Makout*, Militia and the Moral Politics of Terror in the Haitian Countryside during the Dictatorship of François Duvalier, 1957–1971." *Comparative Studies in Society and History*, *61*, 4, 925-53. [PrQ] (Alexis)

RR262. Danticat, Edwidge: "All Geography is within Me." *World Literature Today*, *93*, 1, 58. [RIT] (Alexis)

RR263. Dulude, Sébastien, et al: "Les Herbes Rouges." *Lettres Québécoises*, 174, 4-22. [Web] (Beausoleil)

RR264. Ferrer, Carolina: "Les Littératures Franco-Canadiennes dans un Monde Globalisé: Une Analyse Métacritique." *Journal of Canadian Studies*, *53*, 3, 623-658. [UofR]

RR265. Frelier, Jocelyn A.: "Osons la Fraternité! Les Écrivains aux Côtés des Migrants. Sous la Direction de Patrick Chamoiseau et Michel Le Bris." *French Studies*, *73*, 2, 334. [UofR]

RR266. George, Olakunle, & Taiwo A. Osinubi: "African Literature and Social Change: Tribe Nation, Race / Author's Response." *Journal of the African Literature Association*, *13*, 3, 338-334. [UaB] (Bâ)

RR267. Githire, Njeri: "Hunger and Irony in the French Caribbean: Literature, Theory, and Public Life." *Nieuwe West - Indische Gids*, *93*, 1, 156-7. [RIT] (Pineau, Simone Schwarz-Bart)

RR268. Glynn, Dominic, Sébastien Lemerle, & Claire Ducournau: "Une Visibilité à Négocier: 'Monde Noir' et 'Continents Noirs,' Deux Collections Françaises de Littérature Africaine." *French Cultural Studies*, *30*, 2, 138-152. [UofR] (Mabanckou)

RR269. Grenier, Benoît: "Sur les Traces de la Mémoire Seigneuriale au Québec: Identité et Transmission au Sein des Familles d'Ascendance Seigneuriale." *Revue d'Histoire de L'Amérique Française*, *72*, 3, 4-40. [RIT] (Roy, Saint-Denys Garneau)

RR270. Jaji, Tsitsi, Martin Munro, & David Murphy: "Introduction: The Performance of Pan-Africanism." *Research in African Literatures*, *50*, 2, VII-XI. [PrQ] (Alexis)

RR271.   Kemedjio, Cilas: "In Praise of My Mentors and Mentees: Mentoring as an Institution of African Literature." *Journal of the African Literature Association*, *13*, 1, 5-14. [UaB] (Beti)

RR272.   Kirouac Massicotte, Isabelle, Élise Lepage, & Mathieu Simard: "La Région dans la Littérature du Québec: État des Lieux et Nouvelles Perspectives." *Voix et Images*, *45*, 1, 7-13. [Web] (Bessette)

RR273.   Li, Xiaofan Amy: "East Asian Francophone Writers and Racialized Aesthetics? Gao Xingjian and Aki Shimazaki." *Esprit Créateur*, *59*, 2, 134-49. [PrQ]

RR274.   Mahmoud, Alaaeldin: "Beyond the Colonial/Orientalist Encounter: 'European' Cultural Contributions to Arab Modernity." *Hungarian Cultural Studies*, 12, 46-64. [RIT] (Henein)

RR275.   Mara, Kathryn: "Unmasking the African Dictator: Essays on Post-colonial African Literature." *Research in African Literatures*, *50*, 1, 215-6. [RIT] (Kourouma)

RR276.   Mistreanu, Diana: "Echoes of Contemporary Indian Francophone Literature: A Cognitive Readong of Shumona Sinha's *Fenêtre sur l'Abîme* (2008)." *Politeja*, 59, 177-94. [PrQ] (Makine)

RR277.   Montes Nogales, & Vicente Enrique: "La Tradición Maliense en Recas: Las Funciones Sociales de un *Griot Bambara*." *Estudios de Asia y Africa, 54*, 3, 431-56. [RIT] (Hampâté Bâ)

RR278.   Moura, Jean-Marc: "Migrations Littéraires Transatlantiques Contemporaines. Des Littératures de Langue Française et de Leurs Relations à l'Amérique du Nord." *Contemporary French and Francophone Studies*, *23*, 1, 7-22. [Naz] (Glissant)

RR279.   Murdoch, H. A.: "Memorial Tribute: J. Michael Dash." *Research in African Literatures*, *50*, 3, 166-8. [RIT] (Alexis)

RR280.   Murray-Román, Jeannine: "Connecting Histories: Francophone Caribbean Writers Interrogating their Past." *Nieuwe West - Indische Gids*, *93*, 1, 140-1. [RIT] (Pineau)

RR281.   Orock, Rogers: "Rumours in War: Boko Haram and the Politics of Suspicion in French-Cameroon Relations." *The Journal of Modern African Studies*, *57*, 4, 563-87. [RIT] (Beti)

RR282.   Pucherova, Dobrota: "What is African Woman? Transgressive Sexuality in 21st-Century African Anglophone Lesbian Fiction as a Redefinition of African Feminism." *Research in African Literatures*, *50*, 2, 105-22. [PrQ] (Bâ)

RR283.   Romain, Pascale: "Face à l'Indigénisme: Analyse Comparative des Œuvres de Pétion Savain et de Jean-René Jérôme et Jacques Gabriel." *Journal of Haitian Studies*, *25*, 1, 127-151. [UaB] (Alexis)

RR284.   Saint-Martin, Lori: "Sister-Brother Incest, Androgyny, and Death: *Les Souffleurs* by Cécile Ladjali and *Ce Qu'Il en Reste* by Julie Hivon." *Esprit Créateur*, *59*, 3, 19-33. [RIT]

RR285.   Sajed, Alina: "Re-remembering Third Worldism: An Affirmative Critique of National Liberation in Algeria." *Middle East Critique*, *28*, 3, 243-260. [Syr] (Amrouche)

RR286.   Sarse, V.: "The Signification of the Forbidden Word 'Nègre' in African Literatures Written in French." *Svet Literatury*, 59, 64-73. [Cor] (Oyono, Sassine)

RR287.   Stern, Kristen: "Disidentifying African Authors at a French Literary Festival: Mabanckou and Miano at Étonnants Voyageurs." *Research in African Literatures*, *50*, 2, 49-67. [RIT] (Le Bris)

RR288.   Tartakowsky, Ewa: "Notes de Lecture: Algérie, les Écrivains dans la Décennie Noire." *Hommes & Libertés*, 186, 61-2. [PrQ] (Boudjedra, Djebar, Dib, Khadra)

RR289.   Tcheutou, Arnaud: "L'Hymne National du Cameroun: Un Chant Patriotique sans Ancrage Géo-Identitaire." *Journal of the African Literature Association*, *13*, 1, 64-79. [Syr] (Kane, Ngandu Nkashama)

RR290.   Zabus, Chantal: "Transing the Algerian Nation-State: Textual Transgender and Intersex from Pre-Independence to the Black Decade." *Acta Neophilologica*, *52*, 1-2, 69-96. [RIT] (Djaout)

GENDER AND SEXUALITY

RR291.   ● Adler, Laure, & Camille Viéville: *The Trouble with Women Artists: Reframing the History of Art*. Paris: Flammarion. 158p. [UaB] (Cahun, Calle)

RR292.   ● Alfaro, Amieiro M., Stephane Sawas, & Cano A. B. Soto: *Xenographies Féminines dans l'Europe d'Aujourd'hui*. Bruxelles: Presses Interuniversitaires. 194p. [WC] (Beyala, Gallaire)

RR293.   ● Alfonsi, Isabelle: *Pour une Esthétique de l'Émancipation: Construire les Lignées d'un Art Queer*. Paris: B42. [UaB] (Cahun)

RR294.   ● Allison, Maggie, Elliot Evans, & Carrie Tarr: *Plaisirs de Femmes: Women, Pleasure and Transgression in French Literature and Culture*. New York: Peter Lang. 255p. [WC] (Chawaf, Catherine Millet, N'Diaye, Vivien, Varda)

RR295.   ● Altınay, Ayşe G.: *Women Mobilizing Memory*. New York: Columbia UP. 525p. [Syr] (N'Diaye)

RR296.   ● Aquino, Eloisa: *The Life and Times of Butch Dykes: Portraits of Artists, Leaders, and Dreamers Who Changed the World*. Portland, OR: Microcosm. 222p. [WC] (Cahun)

RR297.   ● Arias, Maldonado M.: *(Fe)male Gaze: El Contrato Sexual en el Siglo XXI*. Barcelona: Anagrama. 104p. [LoC] (Catherine Millet)

RR298.   ● Atack, Margaret: *Making Waves: French Feminisms and Their Legacies 1975-2015*. Liverpool: Liverpool UP. 279p. [WC] (Ernaux, Huston)

RR299.   ● Auzoux, Amélie, & Camille Koskas: *Erotisme et Frontières dans la Littérature Française du XXe Siècle*. Paris: Classiques Garnier. 406p. [UofR] (Ernaux, Jouve, Larbaud, Morand, Pieyre de Mandiargues)

RR300.   ● Badiou, Alain, & Barbara Cassin: *Homme, Femme, Philosophie*. Paris: Fayard. 228p. [Cor]

RR301.   ● Beauvoir, Simone, Marguerite Duras, Marguerite Yourcenar, Annie Ernaux, & Guillaume Gallienne: *Ça Peut Pas Faire de Mal: Les Femmes Écrivains: Simone de Beauvoir, Marguerite Duras, Marguerite Yourcenar, Annie Ernaux*. [Paris]: Gallimard. 239p. [BAnQ]

RR302.   ● Bizais-Lillig, Marie, & Sandra Schaal: *Éducations Sentimentales en Contextes Orientaux*. Strasbourg: Presses Universitaires de Strasbourg. 411p. [BnF] (Djebar)

RR303.   ● Boëtsch, Gilles, & Tiffany Roux: *Sexualités, Identités & Corps*

Colonisés: XVe Siècle-XXIe Siècle. Paris: Centre National de la Recherche Scientifique. 667p. [Cor] (Slimani)

RR304. ● Bourdeau, Loïc: *Horrible Mothers: Representations Across Francophone North America*. Lincoln: University of Nebraska Press. 213p. [Syr] (Arcan, Huston)

RR305. ● Busby, Margaret: *New Daughters of Africa*. Oxford: Myriad. 805p. [UaB] (Boni, N'Diaye)

RR306. ● Carquain, Sophie, & Pauline Duhamel: *J'aimerais Te Parler d'Elles: 50 Femmes Audacieuses*. Paris: Albin Michel Jeunesse. 93p. [BAnQ] (Varda)

RR307. ● Civale, Cristina: *El Arte en Tetas: Mujeres Artistas Que Cambiaron la Historia del Arte*. [Argentina]: Milena Caserola. 201p. [WC] (Calle)

RR308. ● Coffey-Glover, Laura: *Men in Women's Worlds: Constructions of Masculinity in Women's Magazines*. London: Palgrave Macmillan. 256p. [WC]

RR309. ● Coly, Ayo A.: *Postcolonial Hauntologies. African Women's Discourses of the Female Body*. Lincoln: University of Nebraska Press. 264p. [UofR] (Bessora)

RR310. ● Currey, Mason: *Daily Rituals: Women at Work: 143 Artists on How They Paint, Write, Perform, Direct, Choreograph, Design, Sculpt, Compose, Dance, Etc*. New York: Alfred A. Knopf. 394p. [UaB] (Bernhardt, Duras, Sagan, Varda)

RR311. ● Demers, Patricia: *Women's Writing in Canada*. Toronto: University of Toronto Press. 342p. [Cor] (Roy)

RR312. ● Di Spurio, L.: *Du Côté des Jeunes Filles: Discours, (Contre-) Modèles et Histoires de l'Adolescence Féminine (Belgique, 1919-1965)*. Bruxelles: Éditions de l'Université de Bruxelles. 296p. [Cor]

RR313. ● Durá, Marga, & Coco Escribano. *Mujeres Poderosas: Que Te Inspirian Para Plantarle Cara a la Vida*. Barcelona: Grijalbo. 207p. [WC] (Beauvoir)

RR314. ● Gagnet, Michaëlle: *L'Amour Interdit: Sexe et Tabous au Maghreb*. Paris: L'Archipel. 205p. [BAnQ] (Slimani)

RR315. ● Jahn, Andrea: *In the Cut: Der Männliche Körper in der Feministischen Kunst= The Male Body in Feminist Art*. Bielefeld: Kerber. 303p. [WC] (Calle)

RR316. ● Lucey, Michael: *Someone: The Pragmatics of Misfit Sexualities, from Colette to Hervé Guibert*. Chicago: The University of Chicago Press. 310p. [UofR] (Duras, Genet, Guibert, Leduc)

RR317. ● Lugan, Anne-Marie, & Mona Chollet: *Femmes-Femmes sur Papier Glacé: La Presse "Féminine," Fonction Idéologique*. Paris: La Découverte. 303p. [BAnQ] (Maspero)

RR318. ● Maurel-Indart, Hélène: *Femmes Artistes et Écrivaines dans l'Ombre des Grands Hommes*. Paris: Classiques Garnier. 283p. [Cor] (Pozzi, Valéry, Yourcenar)

RR319. ● McIlvanney, Siobhán, & Cheallaigh G. Ni: *Women and the City in French Literature and Culture: Reconfiguring the Feminine in the Urban Environment*. Cardiff: University of Wales Press. 302p. [UofR]

RR320. ● Meyer-Plantureux, Chantal: *Antisémitisme et Homophobie: Clichés en Scène et à l'Écran: XIXe-XXe Siècles.* Paris: CNRS. 398p. [Cor] (Bernhardt, Brasillach, Cohen, Guitry, Némirovsky, Rebatet)

RR321. ● Mohssine, Assia, & Rédouane Abouddahab: *Genres Littéraires et "Gender" dans les Amériques.* Clermont-Ferrand: Presses Universitaires Blaise Pascal. 377p. [WC] (Arcan)

RR322. ● Morrill, Rebecca, Karen Wright, & Louisa Elderton: *Great Women Artists.* London: Phaidon. 463p. [Syr] (Cahun, Calle)

RR323. ● Mouillaud-Fraisse, G.: *Féminisme et Philosophie.* [Paris]: Gallimard. 366p. [Cor] (Beauvoir)

RR324. ● Prin-Conti, Wendy: *Femmes Poètes de la Belle Époque: Heurs et Malheurs d'un Héritage.* Paris: Honoré Champion. 230p. [UofR] (Delarue-Mardrus, Krysinska, Noailles, Vivien)

RR325. ● Proulx, François: *Victims of the Book: Reading and Masculinity in Fin-de-Siècle France.* Toronto: University of Toronto Press. 390p. [Syr] (Barrès, Bourget, Vallès)

RR326. ● Robson, Kathryn: *I Suffer, Therefore I Am: Engaging with Empathy in Contemporary French Women's Writing.* Cambridge: Legenda. 140p. [BnF] (Angot, Darrieussecq, Nothomb)

RR327. ● Steiner, Liza: *Sade Aujourd'hui: Anatomie de la Pornocratie.* Paris: Classiques Garnier. 480p. [Cor] (Catherine Millet)

RR328. ● Still, Edward J.: *Representing Algerian Women: Kateb, Dib, Feraoun, Mammeri, Djebar.* Berlin: De Gruyter. 222p. [Syr] (Yacine)

RR329. ● Thérenty, Marie-Ève: *Femmes de Presse, Femmes de Lettres: De Delphine de Girardin à Florence Aubenas.* Paris: CNRS. 399p. [Cor] (Duras)

RR330. ● Viala, Alain: *La Galanterie: Une Mythologie Française.* Paris: Seuil. 391p. [WC] (Beauvoir)

RR331. Bras, Pierre: "Le Collectif 490 Des Hors-La-Loi du Maroc Reçoit le Prix Simone-de-Beauvoir pour la Liberté des Femmes 2020." *L'Homme et la Société,* 209, 9-12. [RIT] (Slimani)

RR332. Cairnie, Julie: "Truth and Reconciliation in Postcolonial Hockey Masculinities." *Canadian Literature,* 237, 103,119,183. [PrQ] (Carrier)

RR333. Campbell, Cary: "National Allegory as Feminist Critical Discourse: Boni, Tadjo, and Ivoirité." *Research in African Literatures,* 50, 1, 36-52. [PrQ]

RR334. Coste, Marion: "Les Mauvaises Mères dans *Femme Nue, Femme Noire* de Calixthe Beyala et *Contours du Jour Qui Vient* de Léonora Miano." *Études Littéraires Africaines,* 47, 67. [LoC]

RR335. Eloit, Ilana: "American Lesbians are Not French Women: Heterosexual French Feminism and the Americanisation of Lesbianism in the 1970s." *Feminist Theory,* 20, 4, 381-404. [Naz] (Wittig)

RR336. Fox, Meghan C.: "Alison Bechdel's Fun Home: Queer Futurity and the Metamodernist Memoir." *Modern Fiction Studies,* 65, 3, 511-37. [RIT] (Colette)

RR337. Gaden, Élodie: *Écrire la "Femme Nouvelle" en Egypte Francophone: 1898-1961.* Paris: Classiques Garnier. 434p. [UofR]

RR338. Glenn, Susan A.: "Writing the Feminist Past." *Jewish Social Studies,* 24, 2, 17-32. [PrQ] (Bernhardt)

RR339.　　Gurel, Perin: "Transnational Feminism, Islam, and the Other Woman: How to Teach." *Radical Teacher*, *113*, 71, 74,122. [PrQ] (Satrapi)

RR340.　　Hétu, Dominique: "Writing Herself into Being: Quebec Women's Autobiographical Writings from Marie de L'incarnation to Nelly Arcan by Patricia Smart." *Ariel*, *50*, 1, 177-180. [Naz] (Blais, Théoret)

RR341.　　Hoskin, Rhea A.: "Femmephobia: The Role of Anti-Femininity and Gender Policing in LGBTQ+ People's Experiences of Discrimination." *Sex Roles*, *81*, 11-12, 686-703. [RIT]

RR342.　　Kenny, Oliver: "Eroticism, Pornography, Love: The Discursive Politics of Reactionary French Scholarship on Sexual Imagery." *Studies in Arts and Humanities Journal*, *5*, 2, 30-50. [RIT] (Hocquard, Catherine Millet)

RR343.　　Leguen, Brigitte: "Autofiction Versus Writing the Self in Contemporary French Women Writers." *Feminismo-s*, 34, 121-41. [PrQ] (Calle, Desautels, Ernaux, Leduc)

RR344.　　Lévesque, Andrée: "Writing of the Self in New Brunswick and Quebec." *Acadiensis*, *48*, 1, 132-142. [UaB] (Arcan)

RR345.　　Ncube, Gibson: "Self-Imposed Exile, Marginality, and Homosexuality in the Novels of Abdellah Taïa, Rachid O., and Eyet-Chékib Djaziri." *Journal of Homosexuality*, *10*, 1080, 1-17. [WC]

RR346.　　Ojong, Vivian B.: "The Social Dynamics of Feminism in the Context of African Migration." *Gender and Behaviour*, *17*, 3, 13920-13931. [UaB] (Bâ)

RR347.　　O'Neil-Henry, Anne: "Middlebrow Matters: Women's Reading and the Literary Canon in France since the Belle Époque." *French Forum*, *44*, 3, 465-8. [PrQ] (Colette, Sagan, Tinayre)

RR348.　　Overell, Rosemary: "More than a Hashtag: Excitement, Anguish and the Semblant of #MeToo." *Theory & Event*, *22*, 4, 792-819. [RIT] (Catherine Millet)

RR349.　　Provitola, Blase A.: "In Visibilities: The Groupe du 6 Novembre and the Production of Liberal Lesbian Identity in Contemporary France." *Modern & Contemporary France*, *27*, 2, 223-241. [Naz]

RR350.　　Pucherova, Dobrota: "What is African Woman? Transgressive Sexuality in 21st-Century African Anglophone Lesbian Fiction as a Redefinition of African Feminism." *Research in African Literatures*, *50*, 2, 105-22. [RIT] (Beyala)

RR351.　　Riva, Silvia: "'Awa' et Autres Revues Féminines en Afrique Francophone: Par-Delà les Lieux Communs." *Storia delle Donne*, 15, 11-30. [PrQ] (Zobel)

RR352.　　Rivera, Serena: "Women in Twentieth-Century Africa." *Journal of International Women's Studies*, *20*, 2, 432-5. [RIT] (Liking)

RR353.　　Segarra, Marta: "For a Genealogy of French Lesbian Literature." *Feminismo-s*, 34, 79-96. [PrQ] (Cahun, Monnier, Vivien)

RR354.　　Stamper, Christine N., & Mollie V. Blackburn: "'I Will Not Be a 17 Year Old Virgin': Female Virginity and Sexual Scripting in Graphic Narratives for Teenagers." *Journal of Graphic Novels and Comics*, *10*, 1, 47-66. [UaB] (Maroh)

RR355.　　Swanson, Elizabeth: "Rape, Representation, and the Endurance of Hegemonic Masculinity." *Violence Against Women*, *25*, 13, 1613-30. [PrQ] (Dongala)

RR356.   Szczur, Przemyslaw: "Contre l'Homophobie Religieuse. Les Relations entre l'Homosexualité Masculine et la Religion chez Quelques Écrivains Belges Francophones." *Synergies Pologne*, *16*, 89, 99,147. [PrQ] (Eekhoud)

LITERARY HISTORY: FRANCE

RR357.   ● Adler, Aurélie, Marie-Françoise Lemonnier-Delpy, & Herta L. Ott: *Figurations Épiques et Contre-Épiques de la Grande Guerre*. Rennes: Presses Universitaires de Rennes. 309p. [UofR] (Echenoz, Mac Orlan, Martin du Gard, Rolland)

RR358.   ● Al-Matary, Sarah: *La Haine des Clercs: L'Anti-intellectualisme en France*. Paris: Seuil. 392p. [Cor] (Houellebecq, Zola)

RR359.   ● Amadieu, Jean-Baptiste: *Le Censeur Critique Littéraire: Les Jugements de l'Index, du Romantisme au Naturalisme*. Paris: Hermann. 632p. [Cor] (Zola)

RR360.   ● Apap, Anabel: *Écrire par Devoir de Mémoire: La Tragédie du Rwanda Vue par le Collectif "Écrire par Devoir de Mémoire."* Caen: Passage(s). 168p. [WC] (Boubacar Boris Diop, Lamko, Monénembo, Tadjo)

RR361.   ● Arbus, Pierre: *1914-1918 Grande Guerre ou Contre-Révolution?: Ce Que Disent les Imaginaires*. Paris: Téraèdre. 274p. [Cor] (Guilloux, Gance)

RR362.   ● Bernanos, Georges, & François Angelier: *Monsieur Ouine*. Talence: l'Arbre Vengeur. 413p. [Naz]

RR363.   ● Bernanos, Georges, Ramiro Maeztu, & Francisco J. Martínez: *Escritos Inéditos en Torno a la Guerra Civil Española*. Granada: Nuevo Inicio. 145p. [WC]

RR364.   ● Bertrand, Stéphane, & Sylvie Freyermuth: *Le Nationalisme en Littérature: Des Idées au Style (1870-1920)*. Bruxelles: Peter Lang. *Convergences*, 95. 261p. [WC] (Barrès, Maurras, Psichari)

RR365.   ● Blin, Louis: *La Découverte de l'Arabie par les Français: Anthologie de Textes sur Djeddah, 1697-1939*. Paris: Geuthner. 786p. [WC]

RR366.   ● Bonazzi, Mathilde: *Mythologies d'un Style: Les Éditions de Minuit*. Genève: La Baconnière. 213p. [Cor] (Chevillard, Wittig)

RR367.   ● Bragança, Manuel: *Hitler's French Literary Afterlives, 1945-2017*. Cham: Palgrave Macmillan. 130p. [Syr] (Dard, Genet, Schmitt)

RR368.   ● Camps, Christian, & Alem N. Sagnes: *Les Camps de Réfugiés Espagnols en France: 1939-1945*. Cazouls-leš-Beźiers: Éditions du Mont. 340p. [WC] (Semprun)

RR369.   ● César, Marc, & Laure Godineau: *La Commune de 1871: Une Relecture*. [Grâne (Drôme)]: Créaphis. 591p. [Cor] (Vallès)

RR370.   ● Chare, Nicholas, & Dominic Williams: *The Auschwitz Sonderkommando: Testimonies, Histories, Representations*. Cham: Palgrave Macmillan. 278p. [Syr] (Lanzmann)

RR371.   ● Charpentier, Pierre-Frédéric: *Les Intellectuels Français et la Guerre d'Espagne: Une Guerre Civile par Procuration (1936-1939)*. Paris: Le Félin. 696p. [Cor] (Bernanos, Brasillach, Claudel, Jacques Maritain, Malraux, Simon)

RR372.   ● Chessex, Jacques, & Isabelle Falconnier: *Dire la Gloire et la*

Menace: Articles Parus dans l'Hebdo du 01.03.2000 au 30.08.2001. Vevey: L'Aire. 150p. [WC]

RR373. ● Comfort, Kathy: *Refiguring les Années Noires: Literary Representations of the Nazi Occupation.* Lanham: Lexington Books. 207p. [UofR] (Cayrol, Céline, Delbo, Duras)

RR374. ● Corbin, Christophe: *Revisiting the French Resistance in Cinema, Literature, Bande Dessinée, and Television (1942-2012).* Lanham: Lexington Books. 235p. [Syr]

RR375. ● Curtis, Lara R.: *Writing Resistance and the Question of Gender: Charlotte Delbo, Noor Inayat Khan, and Germaine Tillion.* Cham: Palgrave Macmillan. 159p. [Syr]

RR376. ● Demenet, Philippe & Christiane Taubira: *Ils Ont Rêvé l'Europe: [Erasme, Voltaire, Montesquieu, Jean-Jacques Rousseau, Goethe, Victor Hugo, Romain Rolland, Stefan Zweig, Heinrich Mann, André Gide, Albert Camus, Georges Bernanos, Louise Weiss, Vaclav Havel, Emmanuel Levinas, Jorge Semprun, Simone Veil].* Montrouge: Bayard. 205p. [BnF]

RR377. ● Demm, Eberhard: *Censorship and Propaganda in World War I: A Comprehensive History.* London: Bloomsbury Academic. 329p. [WC] (Barbusse)

RR378. ● Dubosson, Fabien: *Dés-admirer Barrès: Le Prince de la Jeunesse et ses Contre-Lecteurs (1890-1950).* Paris: Classiques Garnier. 806p. [UofR] (Aragon)

RR379. ● Durozoi, Gérard: *Histoires Insolites du Patrimoine Littéraire.* [Vanves, France]: Hazan. 271p. [LoC] (Luca)

RR380. ● El Gammal, J., & Jérôme Pozzi: *Le Grand Est 1870-2019: Forces et Cultures Politiques.* Nancy: Presses Universitaires de Nancy. 336p. [BnF] (Marin)

RR381. ● Gouttefangeas, Maud: *Au Théâtre des Pensées: Péguy, Valéry, Artaud, Michaux.* Dijon: Éditions Universitaires de Dijon. 260p. [Cor] (Péguy)

RR382. ● Grenouillet, Corinne, & Anthony Mangeon: *Mémoires de l'Événement. Constructions Littéraires des Faits Historiques (XIXe-XXIe Siècle).* Strasbourg: PU Strasbourg. 380p. [UofR] (Marc Bloch, Certeau)

RR383. ● Hello, Yves: *La Résistance à la République en Vendée: De Dreyfus à Pétain, 1894-1944.* La Crèche: La Geste. 434p. [WC] (Maurras, Zola)

RR384. ● Heymann, Catherine, & Tobar E. Mächler: *Réceptions Réciproques de la Littérature Française en Colombie et de la Littérature Colombienne en France.* Binges: Orbis Tertius. 188p. [LoC]

RR385. ● Jouanneau, Daniel: *Dictionnaire Amoureux de la Diplomatie.* Paris: Plon. 903p. [Cor] (Saint-John Perse)

RR386. ● Keuer, Philippe, & Philippe Wilmouth: *Vivre La Drôle de Guerre en Moselle et à la Frontière: Septembre 1939-Mai 1940.* Metz: Paraiges Histoire. 207p. [BnF] (Dorgelès)

RR387. ● Laget, Thierry: *À L'Ombre des Jeunes Filles en Fleurs et le Prix Goncourt 1919.* Paris: Honoré Champion. 355p. [Cor] (Aragon, Rachilde, Rivière)

RR388. ● Lamonde, Yvan: *Brève Histoire des Idées au Québec, 1763-1965.* Montréal: Boréal. 253p. [BAnQ] (Vadeboncoeur)

RR389. ● Marot, Patrick: *L'Inscription Littéraire des Savoirs.* Paris: Classiques Garnier. 401p. [Cor] (Segalen)

RR390. ● Menusier, Antoine: *Le Livre des Indésirés: Une Histoire des Arabes en France.* Paris: Les Éditions du Cerf. 364p. [Cor] (Begag)

RR391. • Moret, Jean-Marc, & Domingo Gasparro: *De Lautréamont à Francis Bacon: Les Films de Cocteau Comme Lien Intertextuel*. Paris: Honoré Champion. 452p. [Cor] (Salmon, Soupault)

RR392. • Morlat, Patrice: *La République des Frères: Le Grand Orient de France de 1870 à 1940: Penser la Cité Idéale*. Paris: Perrin. 843p. [Cor] (Jaurès)

RR393. • Moussa, Sarga, & Daniel Lançon: *L'Esclavage Oriental et Africain: Au Regard des Littératures, des Arts et de l'Histoire (XVIIIe-XXe Siècles)*. Paris: Presses Sorbonne Nouvelle. 297p. [LoC] (Kessel)

RR394. • Nadim, Roxana: *Le Roman de Barcelone: Un Mythe Littéraire Interculturel au XXe Siècle*. Paris: Classiques Garnier. 446p. [BnF] (Simon)

RR395. • Ndiaye, Macodou, & Florence Alexis: *Les Noirs en France du 18ème Siècle à Nos Jours*. Paris: Paari Éditeur. 345p. [WC] (Fanon, Loti, U Tamsi)

RR396. • Pagès, Alain: *L'Affaire Dreyfus: Vérités et Légendes*. Paris: Perrin. 283p. [Cor] (Péguy)

RR397. • Provini, Sandra: *Renaissance Imaginaire: La Réception de la Renaissance dans la Culture Contemporaine*. Paris: Classiques Garnier. 1 vol. [BnF] (Céline, Oulipo)

RR398. • Rastier, François: *Exterminations et Littérature: Les Témoignages Inconcevables*. Paris: PUF. 411p. [Cor] (Littell, Semprun)

RR399. • *Revue d'Histoire Littéraire de la France, Vol.4 (2019)*. Paris: Classiques Garnier. 256p. [WC]

RR400. • Saenen, Frédéric: *Scripta Manent. Critiques Littéraires*. Bruxelles: Samsa. 200p. [WC] (Drieu La Rochelle, Louys)

RR401. • Serre-Floersheim, Dominique: *La Rhétorique de la Haine: La Fabrique de l'Antisémitisme par les Mots et les Images*. Paris: Honoré Champion. 282p. [Cor]

RR402. • Sobanet, Andrew, & Lawrence D. Kritzman: *Revisioning French Culture*. Liverpool: Liverpool UP. 372p. [UofR] (Kofman)

RR403. • Stroev, Alexandre: *Les Intellectuels Russes à la Conquête de l'Opinion Publique Française: Une Histoire Alternative de la Littérature Russe en France de Cantemir à Gorki*. Paris: Presses Sorbonne Nouvelle. 367p. [LoC] (Bataille)

RR404. • Toker, Leona: *Gulag Literature and the Literature of Nazi Camps: An Intercontexual Reading*. Bloomington, IN: Indiana UP. 281p. [Syr] (Semprun, Wiesel)

RR405. • Vaché, Jacques, Arthur Cravan, & Julien Torma: *Lettres de Guerre*. Saint-Didier: Escalier. 101p. [Cor] (Aragon)

RR406. • Vernier, Jean-Marie: *L'Héritage Européen: Essai sur la Culture Intellectuelle de l'Europe*. Paris: L'Homme Nouveau. 336p. [LoC] (Gilson, Rougemont)

RR407. Atack, Margaret: "Abjection, Derision and Power: Writing in the Voice of the Victim in Three French Post-War Texts." *Law, Culture and the Humanities*, October. [Naz] (Cohen, Gary, Kristeva)

RR408. Baghiu, Ştefan: "The Functions of Socialist Realism: Translation of Genre Fiction in Communist Romania." *Primerjalna Knjizevnost*, 42, 1, 119-32. [PrQ] (Barbusse)

RR409. Brito, Manuel: "La Vanguardia Como Nexo Primordial Entre los

Poetas del Lenguaje Norteamericanos y Algunas Editoriales Francesas (1975-2018): Revista de Estudios Franceses." *Çédille*, 16, 227-55. [RIT] (Hocquard)

RR410.   Broch, Ludivine: "Colonial Subjects and Citizens in the French Internal Resistance, 1940-1944." *French Politics, Culture & Society*, 37, 1, 6-31. [RIT] (Tillion)

RR411.   Delbrel, Yann: "L'Écriture contre les Excès de l'Épuration." *Revue Droit Littérature*, 1, 285-297. [Web] (Béraud)

RR412.   Dreyfus-Armand, Genevi: "La Presse de l'Exil Républicain Espagnol en France (1939-1975): Antifranquisme et Identités Collectives: Revista de Estudios Franceses." *Çédille*, 16, 117-29. [PrQ] (Cassou)

RR413.   Gleyse, Jacques: "Le Mai 68 de l'Éducation Physique: Du Trotskisme à la Critique du Sport et à l'Éducation Corporelle." *Staps*, 126, 4, 65. [Cor] (Maspero)

RR414.   Hitchcott, Nicki: "The (Un)Believable Truth about Rwanda." *Australian Journal of French Studies*, 56, 2, 199-215. [RIT] (Boubacar Boris Diop, Monénembo)

RR415.   Hughes, Joe: "Scenes of Post-War French Thought." *Angelaki*, 24, 6, 22-40. [UaB] (Lacoue-Labarthe)

RR416.   Jeanpierre, Laurent: "'Intellectuals' Melancholia: The End of the French Intellectual (London/New York, Verso, 2018): European Journal of Sociology." *Archives Européennes de Sociologie*, 60, 3, 504-9. [PrQ]

RR417.   Juengel, Scott J.: "Stars without a World." *Modernism/Modernity*, 26, 3, 521-42. [PrQ] (Man)

RR418.   Magalí Andrea Devés: "La Revista Rumbo: Un Eslabón en la Unidad de los Intelectuales 'Por la Defensa de la Cultura' (Buenos Aires, 1935)." *Orbis Tertius*, 24, 30. [PrQ] (Barbusse)

RR419.   Malakhov, Vladimir: "Why Tajiks are (Not) Like Arabs: Central Asian Migration into Russia Against the Background of Maghreb Migration into France." *Nationalities Papers*, 47, 2, 310-24. [PrQ] (Belghoul)

RR420.   Miller, J. H.: "Poetics Today?" *University of Toronto Quarterly*, 88, 2, 101. [PrQ] (Man)

RR421.   Moulin, Joanny: "The Ghosts of World War II: The Year in France." *Biography*, 42, 1, 49-54. [PrQ] (Alain, Nimier)

RR422.   Quaghebeur, Marc: "Transgressions et Histoire." *Synergies Pologne*, 16, 11-30. [RIT] (Lemonnier, Mertens)

RR423.   Rieff, David: ". . . And If There Was Also a Duty to Forget, How Would We Think about History Then?" *International Review of the Red Cross, 101*, 910, 59-67. [PrQ] (Todorov)

RR424.   Schey, Taylor: "Romanticism and the Poetics of Political Despair." *ELH*, 86, 4, 967-96. [PrQ] (Man)

RR425.   Shaheen, Aaron: "Spiritualizing Prostheses: Anna Coleman Ladd's Portrait Masks for Mutilated Soldiers of World War I." *Modernism/Modernity*, 26, 3, 639-62. [PrQ] (Aragon)

RR426.   Stammers, Tom: "La Mondialisation de la Révolution Française (vers 1930-1960): Origines et Éclipse d'un Paradigme Historiographique." *Annales: Histoire, Sciences Sociales*, 74, 2, 297-335. [RIT] (Halévy, Édith Thomas)

RR427.   Starr, Deborah A.: "Book Reviews: On the Mediterranean and the Nile: The Jews of Egypt. Bloomington: Indiana UP, 2018. 226 pp." *Association for Jewish Studies. AJS Review*, 43, 2, 492-4. [RIT] (Jabès)

RR428.   Stayer, Jayme: "Poetry and Theology in the Modernist Period by Anthony Domestico (Review)." *Modernism/ Modernity*, 26, 1, 233-5. [RIT]

RR429.   Teyssier, Arnaud: "Crise Française, Crise de l'État: Quand l'État N'Arbitre Plus la Guerre Civile: Les Non-Dits et Vrais Enjeux d'une Crise." *Le Débat*, 206, 142. [RIT] (Halévy)

RR430.   Zwick, Hé: "Dehors [Outside]." *Migration Letters*, 16, 1, 123-4. [PrQ] (Bernanos)

LITERARY THEMES AND TOPICS

RR431.   ● Abbasian, Pooya: *De l'Amour: [Exposition, Palais de la Découverte (Paris) du 8 Octobre 2019 au 30 Août 2020]*. Arles: Actes Sud. 76p. [BAnQ] (Bauchau)

RR432.   ● Aguiar, Marian, Charlotte Mathieson, & Lynne Pearce: *Mobilities, Literature, Culture*. Cham: Palgrave Macmillan. 322p. [WC] (Leblanc)

RR433.   ● Ahmad, Dohra, & Edwidge Danticat: *The Penguin Book of Migration Literature: Departures, Arrivals, Generations, Returns*. [New York]: Penguin Books. 281p. [Cor] (Charef, Satrapi)

RR434.   ● Angelis, Zoe, & Blake Gutt: *Stains: Communication and Contamination in French and Francophone Literature and Culture = Les Taches*. Berlin: Wien Peter Lang. 254p. [WC] (Bataille, Cadiot, Duras)

RR435.   ● Bauer, Dominique, & Michael J. Kelly: *The Imagery of Interior Spaces*. [Goleta, California]: Punctum Books. 241p. [WC] (Goncourt)

RR436.   ● Benert, Britta: *Langue(s) et Littérature de Jeunesse*. Wien: LIT. 301p. [WC]

RR437.   ● Bharat, Meenakshi: *Representing the Exotic and the Familiar: Politics and Perception in Literature*. Philadelphia: John Benjamins. 363p. [WC] (Segalen)

RR438.   ● Boissieras, Fabienne, & Régine Jomand-Baudry: *L'Énigme de la Mémoire: Études Pluridisciplinaires*. Paris: CNRS. 379p. [BAnQ] (Artaud, Leiris, Vialatte)

RR439.   ● Bowker, M. H.: *Misinterest: Essays, Pensées, and Dreams*. [Santa Barbara]: Dead Letter Office. 161p. [WC] (Renard)

RR440.   ● Boyer-Weinmann, Martine, & Denis Reynaud: *Vestiaire de la Littérature: Cent Petites Confections*. Ceyzérieu, [France]: Champ Vallon. 374p. [Cor] (Barthes)

RR441.   ● Braudel, Fernand, Paul Valéry, & Jacques Barozzi: *Le Goût de la Méditerranée*. [Paris]: Mercure de France. 107p. [BnF]

RR442.   ● Bridet, Guillaume: *Décentrer le Cosmopolitisme: Enjeux Politiques et Sociaux dans la Littérature*. Dijon: Éditions Universitaires de Dijon. 198p. [Cor] (Eberhardt, Israti)

RR443.   ● Broich, Jacqueline M., Wolfram Nitsch, & Daniel Ritter: *Terrains Vagues: Les Friches Urbaines dans la Littérature, la Photographie et le Cinéma Français*. Clermont-Ferrand: Presses Universitaires Blaise Pascal. 224p. [WC] (Serres, Rivette)

RR444. ● Butel, Yannick: *Arts et Perspectives Révolutionnaires*. Aix-en-Provence: Presses Universitaires de Provence. 134p. [WC]

RR445. ● Caccamo, Emmanuelle: *De la Ville Intelligente à la Ville Intelligible*. Québec, PQ: Presses de l'Université du Québec. 190p. [WC] (Le Clézio)

RR446. ● Cadieu, Morgane: *Marcher au Hasard: Clinamen et Création dans la Prose du XXe Siècle*. Paris: Classiques Garnier. 214p. [UofR] (Calle, Perec)

RR447. ● Campbell, Carolyn, & Joe Cornish: *City of Immortals: Père-Lachaise Cemetery, Paris*. [Novato, CA]: Goff Books. 199p. [WC] (Bernhardt)

RR448. ● Castorio, Jean-Noël: *Rome Réinventée: L'Antiquité dans l'Imaginaire Occidental, de Titien à Fellini*. Paris: La Librairie Vuibert. 437p. [LoC] (Yourcenar)

RR449. ● Caws, Mary Ann: *Creative Gatherings: Meeting Places of Modernism*. London: Reaktion Books. 352p. [Syr] (Apollinaire)

RR450. ● Chauveau, Sophie: *Sonia Delaunay: La Vie Magnifique*. Paris: Tallandier. 411p. [WC] (Apollinaire)

RR451. ● Christ, Birte, & Ève Morisi: *Death Sentences: Literature and State Killing*. [Cambridge]: Legenda. 246p. [Cor] (Camus)

RR452. ● Couser, G. T., & Susannah B. Mintz: *Disability Experiences: Memoirs, Autobiographies, and Other Personal Narratives*. Farmington Hills, MI: Macmillan Reference USA. 2 volumes. 913p. [UofR] (Alphonse Daudet)

RR453. ● Crinquand, Sylvie, & Véronique Liard: *Les Confidences ou l'Intime Partagé*. Dijon: Éditions Universitaires de Dijon. 186p. [LoC]

RR454. ● Cruickshank, Ruth: *Leftovers: Eating, Drinking and Re-Thinking with Case Studies from Post-War French Fiction*. Liverpool: Liverpool UP. 230p. [UofR] (Dariesseussecq)

RR455. ● Danaï, Oyaga O.-B.: *Le Mythe: Unité et Transversalité d'un Genre*. Paris: L'Harmattan. 272p. [LoC] (Kwahulé)

RR456. ● Defraeye, Julien, & Élise Lepage: *Approches Écopoétiques des Littératures Française et Québécoise de l'Extrême Contemporain*. [Québec]: Université Laval. 159p. [WC]

RR457. ● Dihal, Kanta: *Perspectives on Evil: From Banality to Genocide*. Boston: Brill. 290p. [LoC] (Littell)

RR458. ● Domestici-Met, Marie-José, & Alexis Nuselovici: *Mobilités Contemporaines: De l'Exil à l'Expatriation*. Aix-en-Provence Cedex: Presses Universitaires d'Aix-Marseille. 150p. [Cor] (Morand)

RR459. ● Donnelly, Anne: *Condamné à Mer: Rêveries Marines autour des Origines*. Bordeaux: Zeraq. 87p. [BnF] (Ferré)

RR460. ● Dupuy, Lionel: *L'Imaginaire Géographique: Essai de Géographie Littéraire*. Pau: PUPPA. 193p. [WC] (Gracq)

RR461. ● Gally, Michèle, & María P. Suárez: *Figuras de Perceval: Del Conte du Graal Al Siglo XXI = Figures de Perceval: Du Conte du Graal au XXIe Siècle / María-Pilar Suárez & Michèle Gally (dirs.)*. Madrid: Servicio de Publicaciones de la Universidad Autónoma de Madrid. 356p. [WC] (Quignard)

RR462. ● Gally, Michèle: *Le Bonheur: Dictionnaire Historique et Critique*. Paris: CNRS. 602p. [Cor] (Éluard, Le Clézio, Prévert)

RR463. ● George, Marion: *Von Der Magie der Literarischen Reihe: Der Atridenmythos bei Giraudoux, Sartre, Yourcenar und Anouilh*. Berlin: Trafo. 489p. [BnF] (Giraudoux)

RR464. ● Gillespie, Margaret, Paglianti N. Novello, & Michel Collet: *Méta-morphoses: Corps, Arts Visuels, Littérature: La Traversée des Genres: [Journée d'Études, Université de Franche-Comté, Mai 2016]*. Binges: Éditions Orbis Tertius. 235p. [BnF] (Apollinaire)

RR465. ● Grivel, Charles: *Le Corps Défait: Études en Noir de la Littérature Fin-de-Siècle: Zola, Huysmans, Lorrain, Rachilde, Goncourt, Villiers de L'Isle-Adam, Gourmont et Quelques Autres*. [Lille]: Les Âmes d'Atala. 154p. [WC] (Rachilde)

RR466. ● Guilbert, Cécile: *Ecrits Stupéfiants: Drogues et Littérature de Homère à Will Self*. Paris: Robert Laffont. 1401p. [WC]

RR467. ● Guillaume, Isabelle: *Imaginaires de la Chasse de 1870 à 1914*. Paris: Honoré Champion. 449p. [Cor] (Renoir)

RR468. ● Keller-Privat, Isabelle, & Karin Schwerdtner: *La Lettre Trace du Voyage à l'Époque Moderne et Contemporaine*. [Nanterre]: Presses Universitaires de Paris-Nanterre. 253p. [Cor] (Bonnefoy)

RR469. ● La Soudière, M.: *Arpenter le Paysage: Poètes, Géographes et Montagnards*. Paris: Anamosa. 320p. [BAnQ] (Gracq, Trassard)

RR470. ● Le Clézio, J. M. G., & Jun Xu: *Quinze Causeries en Chine: Aven-ture Poétique et Échanges Littéraires*. [Paris]: Gallimard. 206p. [Cor]

RR471. ● Lestringant, Frank: *Bribes d'Îles: La Littérature en Archipel de Benedetto Bordone à Nicolas Bouvier*. Paris: Classiques Garnier. 254p. [WC] (Bou-vier, Michaux, Prévert)

RR472. ● Leupin, Alexandre: *L'Hérésie Poétique: Du Moyen Âge à la Modernité*. Paris: Hermann. 446p. [LoC] (Catherine Millet)

RR473. ● Medina, Arjona E.: *Agapè: De l'Amour dans le Patrimoine Litté-raire*. Paris: L'Harmattan. 288p. [LoC] (Le Clézio, Catherine Millet)

RR474. ● Metse, Euterpe: *Ruins in the Literary and Cultural Imagination*. Cham: Palgrave Macmillan. 306p. [WC] (Lanzmann)

RR475. ● Navarro, Justo: *Petit Paris*. Barcelona: Editorial Anagrama. 236p. [UofR] (Malet)

RR476. ● N'Gaïde, Abderrahmane, Yoro K. Fall, Cheikh Guèye, Malick Diagne, & Moustapha Sène: *Esquisse d'une Topologie Historique: Une Rue N'est Pas Une Simple "Machine à Marcher" . . . : (Hommage au Pr. Yoro Khary Fall, 1949-2016)*. Dakar: L'Harmattan-Sénégal. 150p. [LoC] (Cheikh Anta Diop)

RR477. ● Nicholson, Matthew: *Re-situating Utopia*. Leiden: Brill. 113p. [LoC] (Marin)

RR478. ● Noacco, Cristina, & Sophie Duhem: *L'Homme Sauvage dans les Lettres et les Arts*. Rennes: Presses Universitaires de Rennes. 529p. [WC] (Le Clézio, Simon)

RR479. ● Pahud, Stéphanie, & Frédéric Beigbeder: *Chairissons-Nous!: Nos Corps Nous Parlent*. Lausanne: Favre. 217p. [BnF] (Beigbeder)

RR480. ● Parlea, Vanezia: *Îles Réelles, Îles Fictionnelles*. Clermont-Ferrand: Presses Universitaires Blaise Pascal. 263p. [WC] (Devi, Gracq)

RR481. ● Peyrani, Béatrice, & Ann Bandle: *Ils Ont Changé Le Monde sur le Léman: Voltaire, Rousseau, De Staël, Byron, Chateaubriand, Stendhal, Dumas, Flau-bert, Hugo, Rolland*. Genève: Slatkine. 295p. [WC]

RR482. ● Pierrat, Emmanuel: *Faut-il Rendre des Œuvres d'Art à l'Afrique?* Paris: Gallimard. 282p. [LoC] (Apollinaire)

RR483.　● Rabaté, Jean-Michel: *Rire au Soleil: Des Affects en Littérature*. Paris: Campagne Première. 211p. [Cor] (Blanchot)

RR484.　● Rausing, Sigrid: *Europe: Strangers in the Land*. London: Granta. 264p. [RIT]

RR485.　● Shattuck, Roger: *La Época de los Banquetes: Historia de la Bohemia y las Vanguardias en el París de la "Belle Époque."* Madrid: Antonio Machado Libros. 412p. [WC] (Apollinaire)

RR486.　● Stone, Jonathan: *Decadence and Modernism in European and Russian Literature and Culture: Aesthetics and Anxiety in the 1890s*. Cham: Palgrave Macmillan. 219p. [Syr] (Rodenbach)

RR487.　● Sylvos, Françoise: *Utopies et Dystopies Coloniales: [Actes du Colloque, Saint-Denis de La Réunion, 8-9 Décembre 2014]*. Sainte-Clotilde (Réunion): Éditions K'A. 29p. [WC] (Le Clézio)

RR488.　● Thiesse, Anne-Marie: *La Fabrique de l'Écrivain National: Entre Littérature et Politique*. [Paris]: Gallimard. 440p. [Cor]

RR489.　● Tillier, Bertrand: *L'Artiste dans la Cité: 1871-1918*. Ceyzerieu: Champ Vallon. 271p. [WC]

RR490.　● Vöing, Nerea: *Arbeit und Melancholie: Kulturgeschichte und Narrative in der Gegenwartsliteratur*. Bielefeld: Transcript Transcript. 400p. [Cor] (Beigbeder)

RR491.　● Weyembergh, Maurice: *Littérature et Terreur: La Description du Phénomène Terroriste dans le Roman*. Paris: L'Harmattan. 283p. [WC] (Khadra)

RR492.　● Wolf, Nelly: *Le Peuple à l'Écrit: De Flaubert à Virginie Despentes*. Saint-Denis: Presses Universitaires de Vincennes. 201p. [Cor] (Bon, Ernaux, Guitry, Poulaille)

RR493.　Belot, F.: "The Struggle for Life: 'L'Assassinat Scientifique' in Daudet, Barrès, and Bourget." *Dix-neuf*, *23*, 1, 58-69. [UaB]

RR494.　Boudreau, Annette: "L'Identité Assignée: Du Lieu et Ses Manifestations Discursives." *Minorités Linguistiques et Société/ Linguistic Minorities and Society*, 12, 51-66. [Web] (Beauchemin)

RR495.　Bronsther, Jacob: "Torture and Respect." *The Journal of Criminal Law and Criminology*, *109*, 3, 423-490. (Améry) [UofR]

RR496.　Desorbay, Bernadette: "Pour Une Relation Compossible du Même et de l'Autre l'Exotisme, de Segalen à Glissant et Chamoiseau." *Intercâmbio*, 12, 46-67. [PrQ]

RR497.　Djanikian, Ani: "La Symbolique du Miroir dans le Théâtre Mythologique Français: Subversion du Mythe." *Revue de Littérature Comparée*, *369*, 48, 60, 124, 126. [PrQ] (Anouilh, Giraudoux)

RR498.　Gyssels, Kathleen: "'Chemin de Dames': Le Tirailleur Sénégalais de Léon-Gontran Damas à David Diop." *French Studies in Southern Africa*, *2019*, 49, 122-139. [Cor]

RR499.　Henry-Tierney, P.: "Marie Claire's Transgressive Trio: Erotic Alterity in Christine Angot, Claire Castillon, and Tatiana de Rosnay." *Esprit Createur*, *59*, 3, 73-85. [UaB]

RR500.　Jeanneret, Yves: "L'Urbanité, C'est Là et Ça Va Donner: Le Motif de la Donnée dans les Représentations de la Ville." *Questions de Communication*, *36*, 2, 25. [Cor] (Marin)

RR501.　Jordan, S.: "Overstepping the Boundaries: Sexual Awakening, Trauma, and Writing in Annie Ernaux's *Mémoire de Fille* and Christine Angot's *Une Semaine de Vacances.*" *Esprit Createur*, *59*, 3, 5-18. [UaB]

RR502.   Mensch, James: "Trust and Violence." *Studia Phaenomenologica*, 19, 59-73. [Syr] (Améry)

RR503.   Rosellini, M.: "A 'Curious' Literature: The Editorial Production of Erotic Libertinism." *Dix-Septième Siècle*, *283*, 2, 311-328. (Apollinaire)

RR504.   Wicky, Érika: "Psyché et Narcisse, Portraits et Miroirs." *Esprit Créateur*, *59*, 1, 142-53. [PrQ] (Bernhardt)

RR505.   Ziethen, Antje: "Convergences Urbaines: La Ville dans les Littératures Africaines de l'Atlantique Noir." *Journal of the African Literature Association*, *13*, 2, 188-200. [UaB] (Dongala, Lopes)

LITERARY THEORY AND AESTHETICS

RR506.   ● Arasteh-Roodsary, Sona L., etal.: *Dynamik der Form: Literarische Modellierungen Zwischen Formgebung und Formverlust.* Heidelberg: Universitätsverlag Winter. 266p. [Syr] (Echenoz)

RR507.   ● Bähler, Ursula, Peter Fröhlicher, & Reto Zöllner: *A Quoi Bon la Littérature? Réponses à Travers les Siècles, de Rabelais à Bonnefoy.* Paris: Classiques Garnier. 365p. [Cor] (Breton, Reverdy, Simon)

RR508.   ● Beaudet, Marie-Andrée, Micheline Cambron, Lucie Robert, Paul Aron, Luc Bonenfant, Sandria P. Bouliane, Pierre Rajotte, Adrien Rannaud, Rivières M.-J. Des, Lucie Robert, Chantal Savoie, Esther Trépanier, Alain Vaillant, & Alain Viala: *La Littérature Comme Objet Social II: Mélanges Offerts à Denis Saint-Jacques.* Montréal: Nota Bene. 251p. [BAnQ] (Miron)

RR509.   ● Bénac-Giroux, Karine: *Poétique et Politique de l'Altérité: Colonialisme, Esclavagisme, Exotisme (XVIIIe-XXIe Siècles).* Paris: Classiques Garnier. 602p. [BnF] (Claudel, Fanon, Genet)

RR510.   ● Benoît, Eric: *Effets de Lecture: Pour une Énergétique de la Réception.* Pessac: Presses Universitaires de Bordeaux. 354p. [BnF] (Péguy)

RR511.   ● Bernadet, Arnaud: *La Phrase Continuée: Variations Sur un Trope Théorique.* Paris: Classiques Garnier. 408p. [LoC] (Saint-John Perse)

RR512.   ● Bertrand, Romain: *Le Détail du Monde: L'Art Perdu de la Description de la Nature.* Paris: Seuil. 277p. [BAnQ] (Ponge)

RR513.   ● Biglari, Amir, & Nathalie Watteyne: *Scènes d'Énonciation de la Poésie Lyrique Moderne: Approches Critiques, Repères Historiques, Perspectives Culturelles.* Paris: Classiques Garnier. 359p. [Cor] (Dupré, Guillevic)

RR514.   ● Boisson, Bénédicte, & Noémie Courtès: *Saluts, Rappels et Fins de Spectacle (XIXe-XXIe Siècles).* Paris: Classiques Garnier. 353p. [BnF] (Novarina)

RR515.   ● Bonnier, Xavier, & Ariane Ferry: *Le Retour du Comparant: La Métaphore à l'Épreuve du Temps Littéraire.* Paris: Classiques Garnier. 502p. [Cor] (Cadiot, Chamoiseau)

RR516.   ● Bouju, Emmanuel, Yolaine Parisot, & Charline Pluvinet: *Pouvoir de la Littérature: De l'Energeia à l'Empowerment.* Rennes: Presses Universitaires de Rennes. 360p. [BnF] (Barthes, Marin, U Tamsi)

RR517. ● Bouygues, Élodie, & France Marchal-Ninosque: *Genèse des Seuils*. Besançon: Presses Universitaires de Franche-Comté. 252p. [Cor] (Barthes, Rochefort)

RR518. ● Burns, Lorna: *Postcolonialism After World Literature: Relation, Equality, Dissent*. New York: Bloomsbury Academic. 255p. [Syr] (Daoud)

RR519. ● Carle, Zoé: *Poétique du Slogan Révolutionnaire*. Paris: Presses Sorbonne Nouvelle. 323p. [Cor] (Luca)

RR520. ● Diepeveen, Leonard: *Modernist Fraud: Hoax, Parody, Deception*. Oxford: Oxford UP. 205p. [UaB]

RR521. ● Dodane, Claire, & Jacqueline Estran: *Genre et Tradition(s): Regards sur l'Autre et sur Soi au XXe Siècle*. Paris: L'Harmattan. 280p. [LoC] (Deleuze, Foucault, Triolet)

RR522. ● Eide, Marian: *Terrible Beauty: The Violent Aesthetic and Twentieth-Century Literature*. Charlottesville: University of Virginia Press. 304p. [UaB] (Wiesel)

RR523. ● Faizand, de M. F.: *Face à l'Impressionnisme: Réception d'un Mouvement, 1900-1950*. Mont-Saint-Aignan: Presses Universitaires de Rouen. 284p. [BnF] (Mauclair, Malraux)

RR524. ● Fernandes, Carla, & Ilana Heineberg: *Histoires de la Littérature et Fragments de Littératures Oubliées: Mondes Américains en Interaction*. Binges: Orbis Tertius. 312p. [LoC] (Apollinaire)

RR525. ● Forrest, Jennifer: *Decadent Aesthetics and the Acrobat in French Fin de Siècle*. Andover: Routledge. 216p. [Cor] (Goncourt, Laforgue, Mendès, Mirbeau)

RR526. ● Fumaroli, Marc, Paul-Victor Desarbres, & Maxence Caron: *Partis Pris: Littérature, Esthétique, Politique*. Paris: Robert Laffont. 1041p. [BAnQ] (Butor, Girard, Guitry, Paulhan, Sollers, Vauthier, Vitrac)

RR527. ● Gandhi, Leela: *Postcolonial Theory: A Critical Introduction*. New York: Columbia UP. 275p. [Naz] (Memmi)

RR528. ● Germoni, Karine, & Claire Stolz: *Aux Marges des Discours Rapportés: Formes Louches et Atypiques en Synchronie et en Diachronie*. Louvain-la-Neuve: L'Harmattan. 464p. [BnF] (Simon)

RR529. ● Glover, Douglas H.: *The Erotics of Restraint: Essays on Literary Form*. Windsor, ON: Biblioasis. 201p. [WC] (Camus)

RR530. ● Gomez-Géraud, Marie-Christine, & Jean-René Valette: *La Question du Langage*. Paris: Honoré Champion. 577p. [WC]

RR531. ● Grau, Donatien, & Jean-Luc Moulène: *Titres: Une Histoire de l'Art et de la Littérature Modernes*. [Paris]: Klincksieck. 253p. [WC] (Apollinaire, Jarry, Tzara)

RR532. ● Hillaire, Norbert: *La Réparation dans l'Art*. [Lyon]: Nouvelles Éditions Scala. 348p. [BnF] (Ponge)

RR533. ● Hollister, Lucas: *Beyond Return: Genre and Cultural Politics in Contemporary French Fiction*. Liverpool: Liverpool UP. 290p. [UofR]

RR534. ● Janowska-Augustyn, Joanna, Jean-Pierre Dubost, & Sarah J. Sasson: *Penser et (D)écrire l'Illustration: Le Rapport à l'Image dans la Littérature des XVIIIe et XIXe Siècles*. Clermont-Ferrand: Presses Universitaires Blaise-Pascal. 445p. [WC] (Mallarmé)

RR535. ● Jollin-Bertocchi, Sophie, & Serge Linarès: *Changer de Style:*

Écritures Évolutives aux XXe Et XXIe Siècles. Boston: Brill-Rodopi. 272p. [Syr] (Barthes, Chaillou, Char, Duras, Ernaux, Le Clézio, Régnier, Simon)

RR536. • Joqueviel-Bourjea, Marie: *Nu(e): Une Revue, des Voix, la Poésie; Une Esth/éthique de la Rencontre.* Paris: Hermann. 290p. [BnF] (Valéry)

RR537. • Joubert, Jean-Marc, & François Ploton-Nicollet: *Pouvoir, Rhétorique et Justice.* Paris: Classiques Garnier. 393p. [WC] (François Mauriac)

RR538. • Jouve, Vincent: *Pouvoirs de la Fiction: Pourquoi Aime-t-on les Histoires?* Malakoff: Armand Colin. 191p. [Cor] (Zola)

RR539. • Khatibi, Abdelkebir, & P. B. Yalim: *Plural Maghreb: Writings on Postcolonialism.* Oxford: Bloomsbury Academic. 197p. [UofR]

RR540. • Leger, Marc J.: *The Idea of the Avant Garde and What It Means Today 2.* Bristol: Intellect. 350p. [Cor] (Carax)

RR541. • Liljesthröm, Valeria, & Yasmina Sévigny-Côté: *Ecritures Francophones: Ironie, Humour et Critique Sociale.* Paris: Hermann. 174p. [Syr] (Beyala, Chamoiseau, Glissant, Kane, Labou Tansi, Mabanckou, Stétié)

RR542. • Lorandini, Francesca: *Au-delà du Formalisme: La Critique des Écrivains Pendant la Seconde Moitié du XXe Siècle (France-Italie).* Paris: Classiques Garnier. 385p. [UofR] (Tournier)

RR543. • Lund, Christian: *Looking Writing Reading Looking.* [Humlebæk, Denmark]: Louisiana Museum of Modern Art. 171p. [WC] (Roubaud)

RR544. • Lusson, Pierre, Georges Perec, Jacques Roubaud, & Peter Consenstein: *A Short Treatise Inviting the Reader to Discover the Subtle Art of Go.* Cambridge, MA: Wakefield Press. 201p. [LoC] (Roubaud)

RR545. • Määttä, Simo, Mélanie Buchart, & Aslak Djupsjö: *Sources du Savoir, Sources de l'Information, Sources de l'Énonciation.* Helsinki: Société Néophilologique. 139p. [WC]

RR546. • Malela, Buata B., Gérald Désert, & Hans Färnlöf: *Les Marges dans les Capitales Littéraires, Artistiques et Politiques.* Paris: Les Éditions du Cerf. 214p. [Cor] (Confiant)

RR547. • Marein, Marie-Françoise, Bérengère Moricheau-Airaud, Christine Copy, & David Diop: *Les Illusions de l'Autonymie: La Parole Rapportée de l'Autre dans la Littérature.* Paris: Hermann. 389p. [Cor] (Cixous, Mirbeau)

RR548. • Martin, Serge: *L'Impératif de la Voix, de Paul Éluard à Jacques Ancet.* Paris: Classiques Garnier. 323p. [Cor] (Mabanckou)

RR549. • Mokwe, Edouard: *Les Pensées Littéraires d'Aimé Césaire et d'Edouard Glissant Aujourd'hui, Pour un Vivre-Ensemble Harmonieux.* Muenchen: LINCOM. 98p. [WC]

RR550. • Moss, Ceci: *Expanded Internet Art: Twenty-first Century Artistic Practice and the Informational Milieu.* New York: Bloomsbury Academic. 160p. [WC] (Lyotard)

RR551. • Nayrolles, Jean: *Du Sacrificiel dans l'Art.* Paris: Kimé. 294p. [Cor] (Jaurès)

RR552. • Née, Patrick: *Naissance de la Critique Littéraire et de la Critique d'Art dans l'Essai.* Paris: Classiques Garnier. 429p. [Cor] (Apollinaire, Mallarmé)

RR553. • Ouachene, Nadia: *L'Oralité, de la Production à l'Interprétation.* Paris: L'Harmattan. 297p. [Cor] (Le Clézio)

RR554.　● Pizzi, Katia: *Italian Futurism and the Machine*. Manchester, MI: Manchester UP. 304p. [Naz] (Marinetti)

RR555.　● Plossu, Bernard, & Bernard Noël: *Lire, Écrire*. Crisnée, Belgique: Yellow Now. 93p. [LoC]

RR556.　● *Pourquoi l'Art?: Chimériques Esthétiques*. Kfar-Saba: Société d'Études Benjamin Fondane. 158p. [WC]

RR557.　● Rancourt, Jacques, & Christian Noorbergen: *La Vie au Sol: Haïkus et Photographies: [Livre-Catalogue Publié à l'Occasion d'une Exposition à la Bibliothèque Gaston Miron de l'Université Paris 3, du 14 Novembre au 13 Décembre 2019]*. Paris: Transignum. 49p. [WC] (Miron)

RR558.　● Rondepierre, Éric: *Double Feinte: Territoire des Fictions Secondes*. Paris: Tinbad. 182p. [LoC] (Genet, Nougé)

RR559.　● Said, Edward W., Moustafa Bayoumi, & Andrew Rubin: *The Selected Works of Edward Said, 1966-2006*. New York: Vintage Books. 602p. [BAnQ]

RR560.　● Saint-Amand, Denis: *Le Style Potache*. Geneve: La Baconnière. 189p. [WC] (Chevillard)

RR561.　● Sorlin, Sandrine: *Stylistic Manipulation of the Reader in Contemporary Fiction*. London: Bloomsbury Academic. 264p. [WC]

RR562.　● Thérien, Claude, & Suzanne Foisy: *Temporalités Esthétiques et Artistiques*. Rennes: Presses Universitaires de Rennes. 190p. [WC]

RR563.　● Toorn, Nicolaas: *Le Jeu de l'Ambiguité et du Mot: Ambiguïté Intentionnelle et Jeu de Mots chez Apollinaire, Prévert, Tournier et Beckett*. Leiden: Brill. 198p. [WC]

RR564.　● Vallury, Rajeshwari S.: *Theory, Aesthetics, and Politics in the Francophone World: Filiations Past and Future*. Lanham: Lexington Books. 165p. [Syr] (Barthes, Genet)

RR565.　● Vandenberghe, Pascal: *Cannibale Lecteur: Chroniques Littéraires et Perles de Culture*. Lausanne: Favre. 347p. [BnF] (Werth)

RR566.　Alan, Morris: "Book Review: Poétique et Usages de la Liste Littéraire: Le Clézio, Modiano, Perec." *Modern Language Review, 114*, 2, 382-383. [Naz]

RR567.　Alvarez-Prendes, Emma: "Le Triple Fonctionnement de l'Adverbe Honnêtement en Français Contemporain: Propriétés et Liens avec les Marqueurs d'Attitude Énonciative." *Journal of French Language Studies, 29*, 1, 93-111. [PrQ] (Aymé)

RR568.　Barnard-Naudé, Jaco: "'I Have Forgotten My Umbrella': On the Abdications of Style in Law and Rhetoric." *African Yearbook of Rhetoric, 9*, 1, 1-13. [Cor] (Lacoue-Labarthe)

RR569.　Bermudez, V.: "Dynamics of Poetic Interpretation: Emotion and Cognitive Aesthetics in Literary Reading." *Signa, 28*, 139-171. [Syr] (Gaspar)

RR570.　Brezault, Eloise: "Scoring Race: Jazz, Fiction, and Francophone Africa." *Research in African Literatures, 50*, 2, 262-3. [RIT] (Beti)

RR571.　Carreto, Carlos F. Clamote: "Déterritorialiser la Littérature: Herméneutique et Mondialisation." *Synergies Portugal, 7*, 93-112. [RIT] (Rouaud)

RR572.　Cuesta Abad, José Manuel: "Pasiones de la Filología." *Rilce, 35*, 1, 43-63. [RIT] (Man)

RR573.　Danblon, Emmanuelle: "Qui a Peur de la Rhétorique?" *Studii de Lingvistica, 9*, 75-84. [RIT]

RR574. Fontanille, Jacques, & Alessandro Zinna: "Le Dialogue entre la Sémiotique Structurale et les Sciences. Hommage à Algirdas Julien Greimas." *Langages*, *213*, 1, 5. [UofR]

RR575. Harvey, Robert: "'Du Bon Usage des 'Espaces Autres'." *Literatura: Teoría, Historia, Crítica*, *21*, 1, 279-295. [Naz] (Antelme)

RR576. Hétu, Dominique: "De la Temporalité et des Mythes dans les Espaces Littéraires." *Canadian Literature*, *238*, 126,127,183. [PrQ] (Tremblay)

RR577. Hussain, Amina: "Theorising Post-Truth: A Postmodern Phenomenon." *Journal of Comparative Literature and Aesthetics*, *42*, 1, 150-62. [RIT] (Man)

RR578. Insausti, Gabriel: "100 Years of Futurism." *Rilce*, *35*, 2, 712-5. [RIT] (Marinetti)

RR579. Joslin, Isaac: "Aesthetics and Intertexts of Resistance and Liberation in the African Diaspora: Hip-Hop and Créolité." *Journal of Comparative Literature and Aesthetics*, *42*, 2, 72-84. [RIT] (Confiant)

RR580. Lahiri, Madhumita: "The Pose of the Author: Colonial Africa and the Operations of Genre." *Social Dynamics*, *45*, 1, 53-74. [Syr] (Barthes)

RR581. Lim, Pierre-Mong: "What is a World? On Postcolonial Literature as World Literature." *Revue de Littérature Comparée*, 372, 489-92. [PrQ] (Nina Bouraoui)

RR582. Lucey, Michael: "Real-Time Literary Texts." *College English*, *82*, 1, 41-54. [RIT]

RR583. Martin, Marie, Élisabeth Nardout-Lafarge, Jan Baetens, & Nadja Cohen: "L'Écriture et la Projection: Un Nouveau Genre dans la Littérature Française Contemporaine?" *Études Françaises*, *55*, 2, 115-133. [UofR] (Alféri)

RR584. Ndlovu-Gatsheni, Sabelo: "Discourses of Decolonization/ Decoloniality." *Papers on Language and Literature*, *55*, 3, 201, 226, 300. [PrQ] (Cixous)

RR585. Ousselin, Edward: "Poétique et Usages de la Liste Littéraire: Le Clézio, Modiano, Perec. Par Gaspard Turin." *French Studies*, *73*, 1, 146. [UofR] [UaB]

RR586. Philippe, Pascal Haensler: "Stealing Styles." *Orbis Litterarum*, *74*, 3, 173-90. [PrQ] (Cixous)

RR587. Renaud, Lise: "The Concept of Paratext in Thinking About the Configuration of Digital Practices." *Communication & Langages*, *202*, 4, 83. [Cor] (Genette)

RR588. Sanson, Hervé: "Une Esthétique du Bazar." *Expressions Maghrébines*, *18*, 1, 175-196. [UaB] (Deguy, Zumthor)

RR589. Skenderovic, Damir, & Christina Spti: "From Orientalism to Islamophobia: Reflections, Confirmations, and Reservations." *ReOrient*, *4*, 2, 130-43. [PrQ] (Daoud)

RR590. Stepanov, Brigitte: "Post/Past Violence: The Aftermath of Revolutions and Literature as Reconciliation." *Contemporary French and Francophone Studies*, *23*, 3, 307-315. [Naz] (Bey)

RR591. Tchokothe, Ré: "Archiving Collective Memories and (Dis)Owning." *Afrika Focus*, *32*, 1, 171-81. [RIT] (Hampâté Bâ)

RR592. Uzel, Jean-Philippe: "Appropriation Artistique Versus Appropriation Culturelle." *Esse*, *97*, 10-9. [RIT] (Mnouchkine)

RR593. Vachhani, Sheena J.: "Rethinking the Politics of Writing Differently through Écriture Féminine." *Management Learning*, 50, 1, 11-23. [PrQ] (Cixous, Irigaray)

RR594. Van Cranenburgh, A., K. van Dalen-Oskam, & J. van Zundert: "Vector

Space Explorations of Literary Language." *Language Resources and Evaluation*, *53*, 4, 625-650. [UaB]

RR595.   Wenger, Jonathan: "La Naissance de l'Écrivain." *Revue Historique Neuchâteloise: Musée Neuchâtelois: Revue d'Histoire Régionale Fondée en 1864*, 1-2, 47. [WC] (Rougemont)

RR596.   Williany, Vania: "The Comparable Nuance of Complicity and Resistance in the Development of Postcolonial Theories." *K@ta*, *21*, 2, 84-92. [RIT] (Césaire)

RR597.   Xiangrong, Chen, & Raymond Rocher: "La Littérature Française Contemporaine A-t-Elle Sa Place dans le Manuel 'Le Français'?" *Synergies Chine*, *14*, 145, 158, 251. [RIT] (Pennac)

MEMOIRS AND AUTOBIOGRAPHY

RR598.   ● Altounian, Janine: *L'Effacement des Lieux: Autobiographie d'une Analysante, Héritière de Survivants et Traductrice de Freud*. Paris: PUF. 274p. [BAnQ] (Laplanche)

RR599.   ● Baillargeon, Mercédès: *Le Personnel Est Politique: Médias, Esthétique, et Politique de l'Autofiction chez Christine Angot, Chloé Delaume, et Nelly Arcan*. West Lafayette, IN: Purdue UP. 206p. [Syr]

RR600.   ● Delerm, Philippe: *L'Extase du Selfie: Et Autres Gestes Qui Nous Disent*. Paris: Éditions de Noyelles. 107p. [WC]

RR601.   ● Fouet-Fauvernier, Jeanne: *Écritures de la Survie en Milieu Carcéral: Autobiographies de Prisonniers Marocains des Années de Plomb*. Paris: L'Harmattan. 294p. [LoC] (Serhane)

RR602.   ● Grell-Borgomano, Isabelle, Jean-Michel Devésa, & Théo Ananissoh: *L'Écriture du Je dans la Langue de l'Exil*. Louvain-la-Neuve: EME Éditions. 359p. [WC] (Arrabal, Cixous, Goldschmidt, Kristof, Lê)

RR603.   ● Hiemer, Elisa-Maria: *Autobiographisches Schreiben als Ästhetisches Problem: Jüdische Vielfalt in der Polnischen und Deutschen Gegenwartsliteratur*. Wiesbaden: Harrassowitz. 212p. [Cor] (Bachelard)

RR604.   ● Puccini, Géraldine: *L'Intime de l'Antiquité à Nos Jours*. Pessac: Presses Universitaires de Bordeaux. 1 vol. [WC] (El Maleh)

RR605.   ● Resina, Joan R.: *Inscribed Identities: Life Writing as Self-Realization*. New York: Routledge. 221p. [UofR] (Kristeva, Semprun)

RR606.   ● Vandyck, Agnes O., & Molly Nyagura: *African Visionaries*. Legon-Accra: Sub-Saharan Publishers. 316p. [LoC] (Tadjo)

RR607.   Ball, Andrew J.: "Listening by Echo: Voice, Eidetic Image, and the Retrospective Self." *Journal of Comparative Literature and Aesthetics*, *42*, 2, 60-71. [PrQ]

RR608.   Bernard, Isabelle: "Histoire et Paysages dans Quelques Écritures de Terrain Contemporaines: Jean-Christophe Bailly, François Bon, Patrick Deville et Marie Richeux." *Arcadia*, *54*, 2, 231. [RIT]

RR609.   Boisclair, Isabelle: "L'Agentivité Sex/tex/tuelle de la Travailleuse du Sexe à Travers le Prisme de l'Écriture au Je." *Recherches Feministes*, *32*, 1, 35, 47, 260, 266, 270, 275. [PrQ] (Sarrazin, Théoret)

RR610.   Dennis, Laura: "La Vie des Autres: Sophie Calle et Annie Ernaux,

Artistes Hors-la-Loi by Ania Wroblewski (Review)." *Women in French Studies*, 27, 230-231. [UaB]

RR611. Ferreira-Meyers, Karen: "Récit de Vie, Récit de Soi – Cendrars, Djian, Houellebecq, Rachid O., Abdallah Taïa et Alii. Christophe Ippolito (dir.)." *French Studies in Southern Africa*, 49, 247-249. [Cor]

RR612. Hajj, Sleiman El: "Archiving the Political, Narrating the Personal: The Year in Lebanon." *Biography*, 42, 1, 84-91. [RIT]

RR613. Kwak, Youna: "How to Read Barthes: Autobiography's Intimacy Effect." *French Forum*, 44, 3, 405-21. [PrQ] (Sollers)

RR614. Lipscomb, Antonella: "Vers Une Nouvelle Autobiographie: Subversions et Transformations du Genre dans les Autobiographies Contemporaines Françaises." *Anales de Filología Francesa*, 27, 179-98. [PrQ] (Bosquet, Leduc)

RR615. Peñalver Vicea, Maribel: "Pulsions Meurtrières du Moi." *Anales de Filología Francesa*, 27, 257-76. [RIT] (Detambel, Nobécourt)

RR616. Rodgers, Catherine: "Utilisations Contrastées du Discours Autofictionnel: D'Après *Une Histoire Vraie* de Delphine de Vigan et *Place Colette* de Nathalie Rheims." *Esprit Créateur*, 59, 3, 34-46. [PrQ] (Doubrovsky)

RR617. Rosario, Nandan, & Sunaina Arya: "A Philosophy of Autobiogrpahy: Body & Text." *Journal of Comparative Literature and Aesthetics*, 42, 1, 194-9. [RIT] (Satrapi)

RR618. Said, Brahim Ahmed: "Pour Une Réception de l''Ambiguïté Générique' du Roman Autobiographique." *Anales de Filología Francesa*, 27, 53-73. [RIT]

RR619. Soto Cano, Ana Belén: "Dans l'Eau Je Suis chez Moi: Esquisse Autofictionnelle de l'Autre Francophonie." *Anales de Filología Francesa*, 27, 347-64. [RIT]

RR620. Vieira, Willian: "Em Nome do Nome Real: Jogo Literário, Autocensura e Defesa da Autoficção." *Alea: Estudos Neolatinos*, 21, 2, 219-237. [Naz] (Angot)

RR621. Wallart, Kerry-Jane: "Women's Life Writing and the Practice of Reading: She Reads to Write Herself." *Études Anglaises*, 72, 1, 116-8. [PrQ] (Sarraute)

RR622. Zeh, Miriam: "Elsewhere in Elsewhen—Autofiction as Utopia." *Utopian Studies*, 30, 1, 127-135. (Doubrovsky)

MISCELLANEOUS

RR623. ● Audétat, Michel, Bruno Pellegrino, & Alice Rivaz: *Prix Alice Rivaz: Bruno Pellegrino: Là-Bas Est Un Mois d'Automne: Lausanne, Cercle Littéraire, 29 Novembre 2018*. Lausanne: Association Alice Rivaz. 25p. [WC]

RR624. ● Ballestra-Puech, Sylvie: *Lectures de Lucrèce*. Genève: Droz. 465p. [BnF] (Réda)

RR625. ● Bauer, Franck, Chantal Liaroutzos, & Christian Nicolas: *Le Désir Demeuré Désir: Mélanges autour de Franck Bauer*. Caen: Presses Universitaires de Caen. 396p. [Cor] (Péret, Simon)

RR626. ● Bock-Côté, Mathieu: *L'Empire du Politiquement Correct: Essai sur la Respectabilité Politico-Médiatique*. Paris: Les Éditions du Cerf. 299p. [Cor] (Finkielkraut)

RR627. ● Broch, Julien: *Médecins et Politique (XVIe-XXe Siècles): Études d'Histoire des Idées Politiques et Sociales.* Bordeaux: LEH. 335p. [WC] (Céline, Léon Daudet)

RR628. • Comoy, Fusaro E., & Hélène Gaillard: *Street Art, Récit et Poésie: Réflexions sur les Pratiques Artistiques Urbaines à l'Occasion de la Rétrospective Ernest Pignon-Ernest à Nice en 2017.* Dijon: Éditions Universitaires de Dijon. 114p. [WC]

RR629. • Coulon, Marc-Antoine, & Fressange I. La: *Paris: Fashion Flair.* Paris: Flammarion. 280p. [WC]

RR630. • Cronin, Susie, Sofia Hewson, & Fathaigh C. Ó.: *#noussommes: Collectivity and the Digital in French Thought and Culture.* New York: Peter Lang. 162p. [LoC] (Meschonnic)

RR631. • Di Felice, P., & Pierre Stiwer: *European Month of Photography: Emop: 7e Mois Européen de la Photographie: Printemps 2019, Luxembourg.* Luxembourg: Café-Crème. 108p. [WC] (Calle)

RR632. • Dossin, Catherine: *France and the Visual Arts Since 1945: Remapping European Postwar and Contemporary Art.* London: Bloomsbury Visual Arts. 287p. [Syr] (Calle, Varda)

RR633. • English, Darby, & Charlotte Barat: *Among Others. Blackness at Moma.* New York: Museum of Modern Art. 488p. [Syr] (Sembène, Palcy)

RR634. • Fargue, Léon-Paul, Maurice Denis, & Laurent Freitas: *Paris Nabi: Bonnard, Denis, Vuillard et les Autres.* [Saint Clément de Rivière]: Fata Morgana. 64p. [BnF] (Fargue)

RR635. • Gourmont, Remy, & Christian Buat: *Dialogues des Amateurs sur les Choses du Temps: Suivi de Nouveaux Dialogues des Amateurs.* Paris: Classiques Garnier. 632p. [WC] (Bernhardt)

RR636. • Hilali, Bacar D.: *Des Autofictions Arabes.* Lyon: Presses Universitaires de Lyon. 482p. [Cor] (Doubrovsky)

RR637. • Jambou, Louis: *La Musique entre France et Espagne: XVIe-XXe Siècles.* Paris: L'Harmattan. 434p. [BnF]

RR638. • Jannelle, Fabien: *Mémoire des Textes: Les Textes de Références sur l'Art et la Culture.* Nantes: M Médias: [La Scène]. 98p. [BnF] (Copeau)

RR639. • Jünger, Ernst, Banine, Armand Petitjean, Henri Plard, François Poncet, Henri Thomas, & Julien Hervier: *Essais.* [Paris]: Le Livre de Poche. 1152p. [BnF] (Henri Thomas)

RR640. • Lambert, Jérémy: *Archives: Le Futur du Passé.* Woluwe-Saint-Pierre: Association Charles Plisnier. 192p. [WC] (Plisnier)

RR641. • Liébert, Adeline: *L'Ici et le Lointain: Déplacements avec François Cheng, Hector Bianciotti, Claudio Magris et Gérard Macé.* Paris: Classiques Garnier. 543p. [Cor]

RR642. • Marec, Yannick, & Jacques Poisat: *Hôpitaux et Médecine en Guerre: De la Création du Service de Santé Militaire aux Conflits Contemporains.* Mont-Saint-Aignan: Presses Universitaires de Rouen et du Havre. 387p. [WC] (Duhamel)

RR643. • Naepels, Michel: *Dans la Détresse. Une Anthropologie de la Vulnérabilité.* Paris: EHESS Editions. 136p. [LoC] (Simon)

RR644. • Nettleton, Claire: *The Artist as Animal in Nineteenth-Century French Literature.* Cham: Palgrave Macmillan. 241p. [Syr] (Laforgue)

RR645. ● Ottinger, Didier: *Francis Bacon au Scalpel des Lettres Françaises*. Paris: Centre Pompidou. 165p. [LoC] (Deleuze, Littell)

RR646. ● Oudghiri, Rémy, & Ana Nuño: *Pequeño Elogio de la Fuga del Mundo: De Petrarca a Pascal Quignard*. Madrid: Alfabeto. 159p. [WC] (Quignard)

RR647. ● Perry, Nicole, & Marc-Oliver Schuster: *Vergessene Stimmen, Nationale Mythen: Literarische Beziehungen Zwischen Österreich und Kanada = Forgotten Voices, National Myths: Literary Relations between Austria and Canada*. [Innsbruck]: Innsbruck UP. 191p. [BnF] (Monique Bosco)

RR648. ● Rollot, Jean: *Bordeaux, Port d'Amérique, Port d'Amours*. Bordeaux: Le Festin. 113p. [BnF] (Guérin)

RR649. ● Samlak, Noureddine, & Khireddine Mourad: *Marrakech, Une Ville d'Hier et d'Aujourd'hui*. Marrakech: Etablissement Afaq. 380p. [WC] (Ollier)

RR650. ● Staub, Lyutsiya: *Revisiting Renoir, Manet and Degas: Impressionist Figure Paintings in Contemporary Anglophone Art Fiction*. Tübingen: Narr Francke Attempto. 229p. [WC]

RR651. ● Taladoire, Eric: *Essai Bibliographique sur l'Archéologie Francophone de la Mésoamérique =: Bibliographical Essay Upon the French-Speaking Contributions to Mesoamerican Archaeology = Ensayo Bibliográfico sobre la Arqueología Francófona de Mesoamerica*. Summertown, Oxford: Archaeopress. 231p. [WC]

RR652. ● Titeca, Kristof: *Rebel Lives: Photographs from Within the Lord's Resistance Army*. Veurne: Hannibal. 287p. [WC] (Littell)

RR653. ● Viatte, Germain, François Cheng, Supervielle S. Baron, Martine Sagaert, & René Ceccatty: *Geneviève Asse*. Paris: Galerie Antoine Laurentin. 78p. [WC] (Baron Supervielle)

RR654. ● Vincent-Arnaud, Nathalie, & Frédéric Sounac: *L'Accordeur de Piano dans la Littérature et au Cinéma*. Dijon: Éditions Universitaires de Dijon. 106p. [LoC]

RR655. Ángeles, Sirvent Ramos: "Estado Actual de la Investigación en Literatura Francesa y Género. Perspectiva desde España y Francia. A Modo de Introducción." *Feminismo-s*, 34, 13-42. [PrQ] (Baron Supervielle, Desautels, Mokeddem, Dominique Rolin, Thériault, Turcotte)

RR656. Benedicty-Kokken, Alessandra: "Direct Democracy: Collective Power, the Swarm, and the Literatures of the Americas." *Nieuwe West - Indische Gids*, *93*, 3, 343-4. [RIT] (Chauvet)

RR657. Conord, Fabien: "Les Dernières Indépendances des Colonies Françaises: Les Comores et Djibouti (1962-1980)." *Studia Politica; Romanian Political Science Review*, *19*, 1, 9, 33, 145, 149. [RIT] (Perret)

RR658. Duffy, Jean H.: "Jean Dubuffet's Beautiful People." *Word & Image*, *35*, 2, 191-209. [UofR] (Limbour)

RR659. Hamdi, Tahrir: "The Arab Intellectual and the Present Moment." *Arab Studies Quarterly*, *41*, 1, 59-77. [RIT] (Althusser)

RR660. Querido, Pedro: "Non-Embodied Old Voices? Problematizing Old Age, Embodiment, and Scepticism in Radio Art." *Modern Language Review*, *114*, 3, 423. [RIT] (Pinget)

RR661. Reddick, Yvonne: "Tchibamba, Stanley and Conrad: Postcolonial Intertextuality in Central African Fiction." *Tydskrif Vir Letterkunde*, *56*, 2, 54-66. [Naz] (Mudimbe)

RR662.   Samiei, Mohammad: "Weapons of Mass Destruction in Context; Investigating the Links between Militarization and Godlessness of Modern Politics." *Journal of World Sociopolitical Studies*, *3*, 3, 551-78. [PrQ] (Claude Mauriac)

RR663.   Taylor, Jack: "Language, Race, and Identity in Adichie's Americanah and Bulowayo's We Need New Names." *Research in African Literatures*, *50*, 2, 68-85. [PrQ] (Bâ)

NOVEL AND SHORT STORY

RR664.   ● Abada, Medjo J. C.: *Épistémogéographies: Les Fabriques de l'Espace et du Savoir dans la Fiction*. Paris: L'Harmattan. 222p. [UofR] (Beti, Chedid, Giono, Kourouma, Labou Tansi)

RR665.   ● Afana, Nga V. M.: *Tourisme et Littérature: L'Étape du Cameroun dans le Roman d'Escale Français*. Saint-Denis: Connaissances et Savoirs. 154p. [BnF] (Leiris)

RR666.   ● Alphant, Marianne, Harry Blake, Rachid Boudjedra, & Philippe Forest: *Le Nouveau Roman*. Paris: Artpress. 144p. [BnF] (Duras, Ollier, Pingent, Sarraute)

RR667.   ● Armstrong, Joshua: *Maps and Territories: Global Positioning in the Contemporary French Novel*. Liverpool: Liverpool UP. 238p. [Syr] (Darrieussecq, Houellebecq, Salvayre, Toussaint)

RR668.   ● Audet, René, & Nicolas Xanthos: *Ce Que le Personnage Contemporain Dit à la Critique*. Paris: Presses Sorbonne Nouvelle. 209p. [Cor] (N'Diaye)

RR669.   ● Bedrane, Sabrinelle, Claire Colin, & Christine Lorre-Johnston: *Le Format Court: Récits d'Aujourd'hui*. Paris: Classiques Garnier. 440p. [Cor] (Sebbar)

RR670.   ● Biaggini, Olivier, & Philippe Guérin: *Entre les Choses et les Mots: Usages et Prestiges des Listes (Espace Roman, XVIe-XXIe Siècles)*. Paris: Presses Sorbonne Nouvelle. 373p. [WC]

RR671.   ● Bray, Bernard, & Odile Richard-Pauchet: *Roman par Lettres: Usages Poétiques de la Première Personne dans la Littérature Française*. Paris: Classiques Garnier. 524p. [Cor] (Schwob)

RR672.   ● Bray, Patrick M.: *Price of Literature: The French Novel's Theoretical Turn*. Northwestern UP. [Evanston, IL]: Northwestern University Press. 168p. [Syr] (Proust)

RR673.   ● Carretta, Simona, Bernard Franco, & Lanter J. Sarfati: *La Pensée sur l'Art dans le Roman des XXe et XXIe Siècles*. Paris: Classiques Garnier. 358p. [WC] (Chazal, Mirbeau, Quignard, Simon)

RR674.   ● Chaabene, Rached: *L'Histoire au Péril de la Fiction dans la Nouvelle "Historique."* Paris: L'Harmattan. 216p. [UofR] (Dib)

RR675.   ● Diallo, Falémé Djibril, & Bégong-Bodoli Betina: *Le Romancier Négro-Africain Francophone et la Question des Indépendances Africaines: 1970-2000*. Dakar: Harmattan-Sénégal. 357p. [WC] (Fall, Kourouma, Labou Tansi, Mudimbe)

RR676.   ● Dion, Robert, & Andrée Mercier: *La Construction du Contemporain: Discours et Pratiques du Narratif au Québec et en France depuis 1980*. [Montréal]: Les Presses de l'Université de Montréal. 409p. [Syr]

RR677. ● Dufour, Philippe, Bernard Gendrel, & Guy Larroux: *Le Roman de Mœurs: Un Genre Roturier à l'Âge Démocratique*. Paris: Classiques Garnier. 372p. [UofR] (Céard, Verne)

RR678. ● Faggion, Lucien, Christophe Regina, & Alexandra Roger: *L'Humiliation: Droit, Récits et Représentations (XIIe-XXIe Siècles)*. Paris: Classiques Garnier. 603p. [Cor] (Romains)

RR679. ● Frackowiak, Jean-François: *La Tentation Symbolique du Roman Français au Tournant du XXIe Siècle: Henry Bauchau, Sylvie Germain, Philippe Le Guillou*. Paris: Champion. 435p. [UofR] (Germain)

RR680. ● Gauvin, Lise: *Le Roman Comme Atelier: La Scène de l'Écriture dans les Romans Francophones Contemporains*. Paris: Karthala. 194p. [Cor] (Chamoiseau)

RR681. ● Hamilton, Njelle W.: *Phonographic Memories: Popular Music and the Contemporary Caribbean Novel*. New Brunswick, NJ: Rutgers UP. 236p. [Syr]

RR682. ● Haussmann, Diana: *Zelebrieren, Vergessen, Erneuern: Das Spannungsfeld der Afrikanität bei Fatou Diome, Léonora Miano und Alain Mabanckou*. Berlin: Frank & Timme. 440p. [WC]

RR683. ● Hodgson, Andrew: *The Post-War Experimental Novel: British and French Fiction, 1945-75*. New York: Bloomsbury Academic. 208p. [Syr] (Queneau)

RR684. ● Holland, Rachel: *Contemporary Fiction and Science from Amis to Mcewan: The Third Culture Novel*. Lancaster: Palgrave Macmillan. 211p. [Syr] (Houellebecq)

RR685. ● Jaquier, Claire: *Par-delà le Régionalisme: Roman Contemporain et Partage des Lieux*. Neuchâtel: Livreo-Alphil. 137p. [BnF] (Roud)

RR686. ● Lani-Bayle, Martine, & Gaston Pineau: *Mettre l'Expérience en Mots: Les Savoirs Narratifs*. Lyon: Chronique Sociale. 247p. [WC] (Morin)

RR687. ● Morrison, Anthea: *New Crossings: Caribbean Migration Narratives*. Jamaica: University of West Indies Press. 201p. [LoC] (Condé)

RR688. ● Ogawin, Kokou A.: *Le Milieu Naturel Africain dans les Romans Français du XXe Siècle*. Paris: L'Harmattan. 377p. [UofR]

RR689. ● Rabaté, Dominique: *Petite Physique du Roman: (des Années 1930 à Aujourd'hui)*. Paris: Corti. 298p. [UofR] (Duras, Echenoz, Gracq, Manchette, Modiano)

RR690. ● Repinecz, Jonathon: *Subversive Traditions: Reinventing the West African Epic*. East Lansing: Michigan State UP. 283p. [Syr] (Boubacar Boris Diop, Fall, Hampâté Bâ, Ouologuem)

RR691. ● Ricardou, Jean, & Erica Freiberg: *Révolutions Minuscules: Pour une Théorie du Nouveau Roman et Autres Écrits: 1971*. [Bruxelles]: Les Impressions Nouvelles. 431p. [WC] (Pleynet)

RR692. ● Sennhauser, Anne: *Devenirs du Romanesque: Les Écritures Aventureuses de Jean Echenoz, Jean Rolin et Patrick Deville*. Paris: Honoré Champion. 398p. [UofR] (Echenoz)

RR693. ● Stampfli, Anaïs: *La Coprésence de Langues dans le Roman Antillais Contemporain*. New York: Peter Lang. 1 vol. [LoC] (Maximin, Simone Schwarz-Bart)

RR694. ● Vargas, Llosa M., Albert Bensoussan, Rubén Gallo, & Daniel Lefort: *L'Atelier du Roman: Conversation à Princeton avec Rubén Gallo*. Paris: Gallimard. 296p. [BAnQ] (Bensoussan)

RR695. ● Zigoli, Antonin: *La Nouvelle Africaine Francophone*. Saint-Denis: Publibook. 182p. [WC] (Ben Jelloun, U Tamsi)

RR696. Arráez, José Luis: "Analyse du Processus d'Animalisation et de Réification de la Femme Accusée de 'Collaboration Horizontale' à Travers la Fiction Romanesque: Revista de Estudios Franceses." *Çédille*, 15, 55-81. [RIT] (Germain)

RR697. Bernard, Isabelle: "Le Secret de Famille dans Non-Dits et Mentir Vrai de Gisèle Fournier." *Arcadia*, *54*, 1, 47. [PrQ] (N'Diaye)

RR698. Bizek-Tatara, Renata: "De la Transgression à la Norme. Le Fantastique Belge." *Synergies Pologne*, 16, 101, 111, 147. [PrQ] (Gevers, Hellens, Lilar, Mallet-Joris, Ray)

RR699. Eslin, Jean-Claude: "Novel and the History of the 20th Century/ Le Roman et l'Histoire du XXe Siècle." *Svet Literatury*, *XXIX*, 59, 84-9. [RIT] (Martin du Gard)

RR700. Hartmann, Lori: "Allegories of Justice: Crime and Punishment in Three African Novels." *Africa Today*, *66*, 2, 109-131. [Naz] (Sembène)

RR701. Heise, Ursula K.: "Science Fiction and the Time Scales of the Anthropocene." *ELH*, *86*, 2, 275-304. [RIT] (Greimas)

RR702. Knox, Katelyn: "Postcolonial Paris: Fictions of Intimacy in the City of Light by Laila Amine (Review)." *Studies in the Novel*, *51*, 3, 458-60. [PrQ]

RR703. Murat, Michel: "1927: Fin du Roman?" *Littérature*, *193*, 1, 76. [UofR] (Berl)

RR704. Quayson, Ato: "Modern African Literary History: Nation-and-Narration, Orality, and Diaspora." *Journal of the African Literature Association*, *13*, 1, 131-152. [Syr] (Beyala, Daoud, Tadjo)

RR705. Soare, Oana: "Le Nouveau Roman dans la Roumanie des Années 1967-1968." *Philologica Jassyensia*, *15*, 2, 135-48. [RIT] (Butor, Claude Mauriac)

RR706. Tatsumi, Takayuki: "The Future of Cyberpunk Criticism: Introduction to Transpacific Cyberpunk." *Arts*, *8*, 1. [RIT] (Todorov)

PHILOSOPHY, PSYCHOLOGY, AND RELIGION

RR707. ● Axelrod, Mark: *Notions of Otherness: Literary Essays from Abraham Cahan to Dacia Maraini*. New York: Anthem Press. 87p. [Syr] (Wittig)

RR708. ● Barbier, Jean: *L'Alternance Féconde: Une Philosophie de la Contemplation et de la Création*. Paris: Les Éditions du Cerf. 285p. [LoC] (Gilson, Simone Weil)

RR709. ● Barontini, Riccardo, & Julien Lamy: *L'Histoire du Concept d'Imagination en France: De 1918 à Nos Jours*. Paris: Classiques Garnier. 352p. [WC] (Frénaud)

RR710. ● Bennett, Jill, & Mary Zournazi: *Thinking in the World: A Reader*. London: Bloomsbury Academic. 350p. [Syr] (Serres)

RR711. ● Bismuth, Léa, & Mathilde Girard: *La Besogne des Images: Art, Littérature, Philosophie*. Trézélan: Filigranes. 233p. [LoC] (Bataille)

RR712. ● Blackburn, Simon, Tony Allan, R. G. Grant, Diana Loxley, Kirsty Seymour-Ure, Marcus Weeks, Iain Zaczek, & Will Buckingham: *Philoso-*

phers: Their Lives and Works. New York: DK Publishing. 360p. [BAnQ] (Kristeva, Simone Weil)

RR713. ● Bonord, Aude: *François d'Assise, un Poète dans la Cité: Variations Franciscaines en France (XIXe-XXe Siècles)*. Paris: Classiques Garnier. 243p. [LoC] (Green, Rouaud)

RR714. ● Braunstein, Jean-François: *L'Épistémologie Historique: Histoire et Méthodes*. Paris: Ed. de la Sorbonne. 270p. [WC] (Cavaillès)

RR715. ● Breu, Clarissa: *Biblical Exegesis Without Authorial Intention?: Interdisciplinary Approaches to Authorship and Meaning*. Boston: Brill. 241p. [WC] (Man)

RR716. ● Brunier-Coulin, Claude, and Jean-François Petit. *Le Statut Actuel De La Métaphysique*. Paris : Orizons. 420p. [LoC] (Certeau)

RR717. ● Caron, Maxence: *Fastes: De la Littérature Après la Fin du Temps; Suivi de, Manifeste du Maxencéisme*. Paris: Les Belles Lettres. 632p. [LoC] (Beckett, Sollers)

RR718. ● Casteel, Sarah P.: *Caribbean Jewish Crossings: Literary History and Creative Practice*. Charlottesville: University of Virginia Press. 352p. [Syr] (André Schwarz-Bart)

RR719. ● Chretien, J. L.: *Spacious Joy: An Essay in Phenomenology and Literature*. New York: Rowman & Littlefield International. 198p. [Cor] (Claudel, Michaux)

RR720. ● Cohen-Levinas, Danielle, & Perrine Simon-Nahum: *Survivre. Résister, Se Transformer, S'Ouvrir: Nouveaux Colloques des Intellectuels Juifs 2019*. Paris: Hermann. 296p. [Cor] (Wiesel)

RR721. ● David, Pascal, & Jean-Noël Dumont: *La Philosophe Comme Expérience Spirituelle: Attention et Consentement*. Valence: Peuple Libre. 147p. [LoC] (Blondel, Henry, Simone Weil)

RR722. ● De Sutter, L.: *Qu'est-ce Que La Pop'Philosophie?* Paris: Presses Universitaires de France. 111p. [LoC] (Deleuze)

RR723. ● Descamps, Olivier, & Rafael Domingo: *Great Christian Jurists in French History*. Cambridge: Cambridge UP. 485p. [Cor] (Jacques Maritain)

RR724. ● Dopatka, Ulrich: *Phänomenologie der Absoluten Subjektivität: Eine Untersuchung zur Präreflexiven Bewusstseinsstruktur im Ausgang von Edmund Husserl, Jean-Paul Sartre, Michel Henry und Jean-Luc Marion*. Paderborn: Wilhelm Fink. 435p. [WC]

RR725. ● Fabre, Michel, & Loïc Clavier: *Le Religieux sans la Religion: Vivre et Éduquer sans Absolu?: 1850-1950*. Mont-Saint-Aignan: Presses universitaires de Rouen et du Havre. 244p. [BnF] (Durkheim)

RR726. ● Fournier, Martine, & Romina Rinaldi: *Corps et Esprit: Les Influences Réciproques*. Auxerre: Sciences Humaines. 82p. [WC] (Serres)

RR727. ● Ghosh, Ranjan: *Philosophy and Poetry: Continental Perspectives*. New York: Columbia UP. 336p. [Syr] (Bataille, Blanchot)

RR728. ● Goh, Irving: *L'Existence Prépositionnelle*. Paris: Galilée. 109p. [Cor] (Irigaray)

RR729. ● Gouarné, Isabelle: *Les Sciences Sociales Face à Vichy: Le Colloque "Travail et Techniques" de 1941*. Paris: Classiques Garnier. 334p. [Cor] (Marc Bloch, Mauss)

RR730. ● Hanink, James G.: *In Search of Harmony: Metaphysics and Politics*. Washington, DC: Catholic University of America Press. 368p. [WC] (Raïssa Maritain)

RR731. ● Hemmens, Alastair: *The Critique of Work in Modern French Thought: From Charles Fourier to Guy Debord*. Cham: Palgrave Macmillan. 226p. [Syr] (Breton)

RR732. ● Ibáñez, Tomás: *Contra La Dominación: En Compañía de Castoriadis, Foucault, Rorty y Serres*. Barcelona: Gedisa. 318p. [LoC]

RR733. ● Jellab, Aziz: *Une Fraternité à Construire: Essai sur le Vivre Ensemble dans la Société Française Contemporaine*. Boulogne-Billancourt [France]: Berger-Levrault. 424p. [Cor] (Durkheim, Péguy)

RR734. ● Kahang'a, Rukonkish D., & Claude Ozankom: *Philosophie et Tradition Sapientielle Africaine: Hommage au Professeur Dominique Kahang'a Rukonkish*. Paris: L'Harmattan. 245p. [LoC]

RR735. ● Katz, Steven T.: *Holocaust Studies: Critical Reflections*. New York: Routledge. 353p. [Cor] (Wiesel)

RR736. ● Knasas, John F. X.: *Thomistic Existentialism et Cosmological Reasoning*. Washington, DC: The Catholic University of America Press. 327p. [WC] (Gilson)

RR737. ● Kojève, Alexandre, & Robert B. Williamson: *The Concept, Time, and Discourse*. South Bend, IN: St. Augustine's Press. 259p. [WC]

RR738. ● Le Guellec-Minel, A.: *La Mémoire Face à l'Histoire: Traces, Effacement, Réinscriptions*. Rennes: Presses Universitaires de Rennes. 375p. [Cor] (Hamelin)

RR739. ● Lienhard, Marc: *Rire avec Dieu: L'Humour chez les Chrétiens, les Juifs et les Musulmans*. Genève: Labor et Fides. 307p. [BAnQ]

RR740. ● Linfield, Susie: *The Lions' Den: Zionism and the Left from Hannah Arendt to Noam Chomsky*. New Haven: Yale UP. 389p. [Syr] (Memmi)

RR741. ● Majer, Krzysztof, Justyna Fruzińska, Józef Kwaterko, & Norman Ravvin: *Kanade, di Goldene Medine?: Perspectives on Canadian-Jewish Literature and Culture = Perspectives sur la Littérature et la Culture Juives Canadiennes*. Boston: Brill. 362p. [WC] (Kattan, Thériault)

RR742. ● Marciano, Raphy: *Juifs et Chrétiens, les Promesses d'un Dialogue*. Paris: Les Éditions du Cerf. 323p. [LoC] (Wiesel)

RR743. ● McQuillan, Martin: *Critical Practice: Philosophy and Creativity*. New York: Bloomsbury Academic. 240p. [Syr] (Cixous)

RR744. ● Mezei, Balázs M.: *Philosophies of Christianity: At the Crossroads of Contemporary Problems*. Cham: Springer. 288p. [WC] (Gilson)

RR745. ● Milon, Alain: *Leçon d'Économie Générale: L'Expérience-limite chez Bataille-Blanchot-Klossowski*. [Paris]: Presses Universitaires de Paris Nanterre. 338p. [WC]

RR746. ● Morana, Cyril, Éric Oudin, & André Comte-Sponville: *Petite Philosophie de l'Art: De Platon à Deleuze*. Paris: Eyrolles. 184p. [BnF]

RR747. ● Moriarty, Michael, & Jeremy Jennings: *The Cambridge History of French Thought*. Cambridge: Cambridge UP. 570p. [Syr] (Foucault)

RR748. ● Moscovici, Claudia, & Joseph Polak: *Holocaust Memories: A Survey of Holocaust Memoirs, Histories, Novels, and Films*. Lanham, MD: Hamilton Book. 231p. [Cor] (Wiesel)

RR749. ● Ong-Van-Cung, Kim S.: *Les Formes Historiques du Cogito: XVIIe-XXe Siècles*. Paris: Classiques Garnier. 381p. [Cor] (Foucault)

RR750. ● Perry, Catherine, & Safoi Babana-Hampton: *Femmes d'Islam dans la Littérature, le Cinéma et l'Art Contemporains*. Paris: L'Harmattan. 259p. [UofR] (Djebar, Fall, Serreau)

RR751. ● Petit, Jean-François: *La Crise Moderniste Revisitée: Actes du Colloque des 12 et 13 Février 2019 (Institut Catholique de Paris)*. Paris: Karthala. 270p. [BnF] (Blondel)

RR752. ● Potter, Martin, Małgorzata Grzegorzewska, & Jean Ward: *In Wonder, Love and Praise: Approaches to Poetry, Theology and Philosophy*. Berlin: Peter Lang. 221p. [LoC] (Blanchot)

RR753. ● Raghuramaraju, A.: *Calibrating Western Philosophy for India: Rousseau, Derrida, Deleuze, Guattari, Bergson and Vaddera Chandidas*. New York: Routledge. 102p. [Syr]

RR754. ● Rasimi, Olivier, & André Comte-Sponville: *La Vierge à l'Enfant: Les Hautes Figures de l'Amour*. Paris: Citadelles & Mazenod. 201p. [WC]

RR755. ● Remiche, Benoît, Isabelle Graesslé, Eli Bar-Navi, Isabelle Benoit, Anne-Marie Impe, Maroussia Mikolajczak, & Régis Debray: *Dieu(x), Modes d'Emploi*. Bruxelles: Tempora. 319p. [WC]

RR756. ● Rosenblum, Rachel: *Mourir d'Écrire?: Shoah, Traumas Extrêmes et Psychanalyse des Survivants*. Paris: PUF. 188p. [LoC] (Carrère, Kofman, Perec)

RR757. ● Rudrum, David, Ridvan Askin, & Frida Beckman: *New Directions in Philosophy and Literature*. Edinburgh: Edinburgh UP. 486p. [WC] (Cixous)

RR758. ● Samrout, Ghada: *À Bord du Mot: Études Littéraires*. Paris: L'Harmattan. 257p. [Cor] (Stétié)

RR759. ● Sedjari, Ali: *Le Vivre Ensemble entre le Droit et les Valeurs*. Tanger: Virgule. 447p. [WC] (Khatibi)

RR760. ● Sim, Stuart: *Post-truth, Scepticism & Power*. Cham: Palgrave Macmillan. 175p. [Syr] (Lyotard)

RR761. ● Sousa, Luís A., & Ana Falcato: *Phenomenological Approaches to Intersubjectivity and Values*. Newcastle upon Tyne: Cambridge Scholars. 324p. [WC] (Marcel)

RR762. ● Stetter, Jack, & Charles Ramond: *Spinoza in Twenty-First-Century American and French Philosophy: Metaphysics, Philosophy of Mind, Moral and Political Philosophy*. New Delhi: Sydney Bloomsbury Academic. 396p. [UofR]

RR763. ● Usher, Phillip J.: *Exterranean. Extraction in the Humanist Anthropocene*. Bronx: Fordham UP.240p. [Syr] (Serres)

RR764. ● Van Loon, J.: *The Thinking Woman*. New Brunswick, NJ: Rutgers University Press. 248p. [Syr] (Kristeva)

RR765. ● Vries, Hent: *Miracles et Métaphysique*. Paris: PUF. 403p. [WC] (Gilson)

RR766. ● Winock, Michel: *Les Figures de Proue de la Gauche Depuis 1789*. Paris: Perrin. 436p. [Cor] (Beauvoir)

RR767. ● Zarka, Yves C., & Avishag Zafrani: *La Pheńomeńologie et la Vie*. Paris: Les Éditions du Cerf. 592p. [BAnQ] (Henry)

RR768. Andrews, Molly: "The Narrative Architecture of Political Forgiveness." *Political Psychology*, *40*, 3, 433-447. [UofR] (Améry)

RR769.   Anidjar, Gil: "On the Political History of Destruction." *Reorient*, *4*, 2, 144-165. [Naz] (Améry)

RR770.   Bergoffen, Debra: "From the Shame of Auschwitz to an Ethics of Vulnerability and a Politics of Revolt." *The Journal of Speculative Philosophy*, *33*, 3, 527-536. (Améry)

RR771.   Crosson, J. B.: "Inventive Traditions: Authority and Power in African Diasporic Religions." *Religious Studies Review*, *45*, 4, 451-459. [UofR] (Mudimbe)

RR772.   Decout, Maxime: "Ce Que la Judéité Fait à la Pensée de la Littérature." *Esprit Créateur*, *59*, 2, 42-55. [PrQ] (Jean-Richard Bloch, Cohen, André Schwarz-Bart)

RR773.   Desjardins, D. D.: "Philosophy of the Sublime as Theory and Experience." *Philosophy and Literature*, *43*, 1, 71-88. [RIT] (Zola)

RR774.   Du Champs, C., & R. Burnet: "Barabbas: Conséquences Littéraires de l'Histoire de la Réception d'un Personnage Biblique." *Revue Théologique De Louvain*, *50*, 1, 21-38. [Cor] (Ghelderode)

RR775.   Dunca, Petru: "Dimensions of Sacrifice in Rite – Hermeneutical Perspectives." *Hermeneia*, 22, 101-12. [PrQ] (Caillois)

RR776.   Fauré, Clémentine: "Huguenots ou Barbares ... Ces Adversaires Sont les Mêmes: Charles Maurras, André Gide, et l'Esthétique Comme Résistance à la Race." *Esprit Créateur*, *59*, 2, 150-64. [RIT]

RR777.   Mba, Chika C.: "African Philosophy in the Age of Neoliberal Capitalism." *History Compass*, 17, 3. [UaB] (Mudimbe)

POETRY

RR778.   • Aceves, Raúl, & Laura Solórzano: *En Esta Luz del Poema*. Guadalajara, Jalisco: Al Gravitar Rotando. 70p. [LoC] (Saint-Denys Garneau)

RR779.   • Artaud, Antonin, Antonio Bertoli, & David Giannoni: *Révolte Contre la Poésie*. Bruxelles: Maelström. 1 vol. [WC]

RR780.   • Artous-Bouvet, Guillaume: *Inventio: Poésie et Autorité*. Paris: Hermann. 212p. [LoC] (Pinson)

RR781.   • Barda, Jeff: *Experimentation and the Lyric in Contemporary French Poetry*. Cham: Palgrave Macmillan. 327p. [Syr] (Alféri, Cadiot, Hocquard, Roche)

RR782.   • Casado, Miguel: *Un Discurso Republicano: Ensayos Sobre Poesía*. Madrid: Libros de la Resistencia. 256p. [WC] (Bernard Noël, Ponge)

RR783.   • Collot, Michel: *Le Chant du Monde dans la Poésie Française Contemporaine*. Paris: Corti. 355p. [Cor] (Cheng, Deguy, Emaz, Jaccottet, Bernard Noël, Pinson, Velter)

RR784.   • Cortázar, Julio, Sylvie Protin, & Jacques Jouet: *Produit du Hasard: Hypertexte et Poésie Combinatoire*. Lyon: Presses Universitaires de Lyon. 189p. [BnF]

RR785.   • Creswell, Robyn: *City of Beginnings: Poetic Modernism in Beirut*. Princeton, NJ: Princeton UP. 259p. [Syr] (Saint-John Perse)

RR786.   • Debord, Guy, & Bras L. Le: *Poésie, Etc*. Paris: L'Échappée. 589p. [BnF]

RR787.   • Dethurens, Pascal: *L'Émerveillement: De la Présence dans la*

Poésie et l'Art Modernes. [Strasbourg]: L'Atelier contemporain. 246p. [LoC] (Bonnefoy)

RR788. ● Duffett, Michael, & Mark Pirie: *The Presence of Love: Poems Selected and New*. Wellington: HeadworX. 84p. [WC] (Bonnefoy)

RR789. ● *Earth and Mind: Dreaming, Writing, Being: Nine Contemporary French Poets - Yves Bonnefoy, Jacqueline Risset, Salah Stétié, Vénus Khoury-Ghata, Tahar Ben Jelloun, André Velter, Marie-Claire Bancquart, Jean-Claude Pinson, Jacques Dupin*. 2019, Vol. 1. Beaverton: Ringgold. [PrQ]

RR790. ● Ehlers, Sarah: *Left of Poetry: Depression America and the Formation of Modern Poetics*. Chapel Hill, NC: University of North Carolina Press. 291p. [Naz] (Roumain)

RR791. ● Epstein, Jean, Nicole Brenez, & Sarah Keller: *La Poésie d'Aujourd'hui: La Lyrosophie et Autres Écrits*. Paris: Independencia. 511p. [BnF] (Giraudoux, Paulhan)

RR792. ● Gayraud, Irène: *Chants Orphiques Européens: Valéry, Rilke, Trakl, Apollinaire, Campana et Goll*. Paris: Classiques Garnier. 786p. [Cor]

RR793. ● Grafe, Adrian, & Nicolas Wanlin: *Trouver une Langue: Poésie et Poétique = Finding a Language: Poetry and Poetics*. Arras: Artois Presses Université. 264p. [WC] (Mallarmé)

RR794. ● Hoagland, Tony: *The Underground Poetry Metro Transportation System for Souls: Essays on the Cultural Life of Poetry*. Ann Arbor, MI: The University of Michigan Press. 152p. [Cor] (Apollinaire)

RR795. ● Hubner-Bayle, Corinne, Éric Dayre, & Guillaume Artous-Bouvet: *Le Réel de la Poésie*. Paris: Kimé. 246p. [Cor] (Dupin, Jaccottet, Rimbaud, Saint-John Perse)

RR796. ● Labarthe, Patrick, Johannes Bartuschat, Martina Albertini, Sara Ferilli, & Numa Vittoz: *La Tradition Européenne du Sonnet*. Genève: Slatkine. 286p. [Cor] (Bonnefoy)

RR797. ● Lloze, Évelyne, Samia Kassab-Charfi, & Idoli Castro: *Périples et Escales: Écrire le Voyage en Poésie*. Paris: Hermann. 345p. [LoC] (Esteban, Gaspar, Labou Tansi, Sacré)

RR798. ● Malela, Buata B.: *Aimé Césaire et la Relecture de la Colonialité du Pouvoir: Avec Sartre, Fanon, Glissant, Kourouma, Badian, Schwarz-Bart, Dadié et Ouologuem*. Paris: Anibwe. 317p. [WC]

RR799. ● McMahon, Fiona, Giuseppe Sangirardi, Brigitte Denker-Bercoff, & Cécile Iglesias-Slicaru: *Penser le Genre en Poésie Contemporaine*. Paris: Classiques Garnier. 341p. [LoC] (Maulpoix)

RR800. ● Nardone, Jean-Luc: *Poésie Paysage: Mélanges Offerts à Jean Nimis*. Toulouse: Université de Toulouse II-Jean Jaurès. 155p. [WC]

RR801. ● Rajkumar, Joanna: *Lignes Sans Réponses: Trois Expériences Poétiques des Limites du Langage*. Paris: Classiques Garnier. 730p. [UofR] (Michaux)

RR802. ● Réda, Jacques: *Quel Avenir Pour la Cavalerie?: Une Histoire Naturelle du Vers Français*. [Paris]: Buchet Chastel. 211p. [Cor] (Apollinaire)

RR803. ● Ringlet, Gabriel: *Le Regard Éclairé. Tome 1*. Châtelineau: Le Taillis Pré. 137p. [WC] (Daumal)

RR804. ● Rodriguez, Antonio, Isabelle Falconnier, & M. de Francesco: *Le Poème et le Territoire: Promenades Littéraires en Suisse Romande: Dans les Pas de Jorge Luis Borges, Lord Byron, Blaise Cendrars, Victor Hugo, Philippe Jacottet,*

Adam Mickiewicz, Rainer Maria Rilke, Alexandre Voisard. Lausanne: Noir sur Blanc. 223p. [BAnQ] (Chessex, Jaccottet, Jouve, Roud)

RR805. ● Royer, Jean: *L'Autre Parole: Poèmes Didactiques.* Montréal: Noroît. 179p. [BAnQ] (Goffette)

RR806. ● Torrent, Céline: *Le Poétique Instinct à Travers la Danse. De Mallarmé à Aujourd'hui.* Paris: L'Harmattan. 600p. [LoC] (Char, Maulpoix, Quignard, Valéry)

RR807. ● Vashkevich, Nadezda: *L'Heureux Phœnix: Pourquoi Écrit-on des Sonnets Aujourd'hui?: Étude sur le Sonnet Actuel en France et en Russie (1940-2013).* Paris: L'Harmattan. 220p. [Cor] (Aragon, Bonnefoy, Desnos)

RR808. ● Vinclair, Pierre: *Prise de Vers: À Quoi Sert La Poésie?* Sainte-Colombe-sur-Gand: La Rumeur Libre Éditions. 159p. [WC] (Mallarmé)

RR809. ● Vulpe, Nicola: *Insult to the Brain: An Altogether Unreliable Account of My Conversations with Poets, Mostly About Dying, but Also About Other Matters Both Great and Trivial.* Buffalo: Guernica. 130p. [WC] (Verhaeren)

RR810. Azérad, Hugues: "Lire en Relation: Édouard Glissant et Aimé Césaire à la Démesure Baroque de Lautréamont." *Dalhousie French Studies*, 113, 111-122. [UofR]

RR811. Baños Gallego, Pedro: "À la Recherche des Traits Fondamentaux du Poème en Prose: Revista de Estudios Franceses." *Çédille*, 15, 83-107. [RIT] (Brossard, Krysinska)

RR812. Baños Gallego, Pedro: "Les Frontières du Poème en Prose: Pour une Délimitation Générique: Revista de Estudios Franceses." *Çédille*, 16, 173-204. (Krysinska, Saint-Pol Roux)

RR813. Feshchenko, Vladimir: "Graphic Translation of Experimental Verse as a Strategy of Poetic Text's Transcreation." *Studia Metrica et Poetica*, 6. [WC] (Apollinaire)

RR814. Labrusse, Sébastien: "'L'Antériorité de l'Être sur la Parole.' Réflexions sur la Question des Limites du Langage." *Le Philosophoire*, 52, 2, 35. [PrQ] (Bonnefoy)

RR815. Métayer, Guillaume: "Poesia e Melancolia. A Invenção da Vontade de Potência?" *Cadernos Nietzsche*, 40, 2, 9-32. [Cor] (France)

RR816. Moltedo, Ennio: "Five Poems." *World Literature Today*, 93, 1, 33. [PrQ] (Atlan)

RR817. Suhr-Sytsma, Nathan: "Theories of African Poetry." *New Literary History*, 50, 4, 581-607. [RIT] (Damas, Birago Diop, U Tamsi)

SURREALISM

See also 1784, 1803, 3722, 4190, 4854, 4860.

RR818. ● Dempsey, Amy: *Surrealism.* London: Thames and Hudson. 175p. [Syr]

RR819. ● Gobyn, Ronny, & Sam Stourdé: *Variétés: Avant-garde, Surréalisme et Photographie: 1928-1930.* Arles: Actes Sud. 367p. [WC]

RR820. ● Janover, Louis, & Maxime Morel: *Front Noir, 1963-1967: Surréalisme et Socialisme de Conseils.* Paris: Non-lieu. 232p. [Cor]

RR821. ● Kries, Mateo, & Tanja Cunz: *Objects of Desire: Surrealism and Design 1924-Today*. Weil am Rhein: Vitra Design Museum. 368p. [Syr]

RR822. ● Laxton, Susan: *Surrealism at Play*. Durham, NC: Duke UP, 363p. [Syr]

RR823. ● Ottinger, Didier, Salvador Dalí, René Magritte, & Marie Sarré: *The Surrealist Movement from Dalí to Magritte: Crisis and Rebirth in 1929*. Budapest: Madgyar Nemzeti Galéria. 243p. [WC]

RR824. ● Richardson, Michael: *The International Encyclopedia of Surrealism: Volume 3*. Sydney: Bloomsbury Visual Arts. 540p. [UaB] (Breton)

RR825. Bohn, Willard: "Revisiting the Surrealist Image." *Romance Quarterly*, *66*, 2, 91-106. [Naz] (Breton, Reverdy)

RR826. Bridet, G.: "1925: Fin de l'Ère Chrétienne, An I du Surréalisme?" *Littérature*, *193*, 1, 45-59. [UaB]

RR827. Greenshields, Will: "Lacan Contra the Surrealists." *Nottingham French Studies*, *58*, 1, 64-81. [UaB] (Breton)

RR828. Hopkins, David: "The Surrealist Toy, Or the Adventures of the Bilboquet." *The Sculpture Journal*, *28*, 2, 175-92. [PrQ] (Caillois)

RR829. Spiller, Neil: "Feverish Delirium: Surrealism, Deconstruction and Numinous Presences." *Architectural Design*, *89*, 4, 86-93. [Naz] (Jarry)

RR830. Strange, Kristen: "Conference Review: 'Surrealisms: The Inaugural Conference of the International Society for the Study of Surrealism' Bucknell University Humanities Center, Lewisburg, Pennsylvania (November 1-3, 2018)." *Journal of Surrealism and the Americas*, *10*, 1, 106. [PrQ]

RR831. Suther, Jensen: "Allegories of the Future: Towards a Critical Theory of Surrealism." *CR: The New Centennial Review*, *19*, 2, 231. [PrQ]

RR832. Turk, Boštjan M.: "Les Apories du Surréalisme." *Acta Neophilologica*, *52*, 1-2, 183-198. [WC]

RR833. Vidal, P. "Dalí-Magritte: Le Face-à-Face de Deux Titans du Surreálisme." *Oeil*, 729. [UofR]

THEATER

RR834. ● Allegret, Yan: *Comme le Vent Épouse les Formes de la Plaine: Journal d'Avignon 2018: Récits*. Fontenay-sous-Bois: Quartett. 101p. [BnF] (Bobin)

RR835. ● Bégoc, Janig, & Sylvain Diaz: *Le Texte au Risque de la Performance: La Performance au Risque du Texte*. Strasbourg: Université de Strasbourg. 132p. [WC] (Marc Bloch, Mouawad)

RR836. ● Bobin, Christian, Franco G. Brambilla, Tino Aime, & Emanuele Borsotti: *Cuore di Neve*. Torino: Elledici. 39p. [WC]

RR837. ● Boisson, Bénédicte, & Noémie Courtes: *Saluts, Rappels et Fins de Spectacle (XIXe-XXIe Siècles)*. Paris: Classiques Garnier. 353p. [BnF]

RR838. ● Bouchet, Pauline: *Les Voix du Théâtre Québécois Contemporain: De l'Auteur au Personnage et Vice-Versa*. Bruxelles: Peter Lang, 201p. [WC] (Chaurette, Mouawad, Tremblay)

RR839. ● Brun, Catherine, Jeanyves Guérin, & Marie-Madeleine Mervant-Roux: *Genèses des Études Théâtrales en France: XIXe-XXe Siècles*. Rennes: Presses Universitaires de Rennes. 427p. [Cor] (Marcel)

RR840.　● Buch, Marina-Rafaela: *Le Théâtre Nippon dans le Théâtre Français du XXe Siècle: D'un Regard Kaléidoscopique à une Réception Productive*. Gottingen: Vandenhoeck & Ruprecht. 333p. [WC] (Genet)

RR841.　● Butel, Yannick: *La Critique, Un Art de la Rencontre: L'Origine du (i.e. d'un) Geste II: [Actes du Colloque International, Aix-En-Provence, Marseille, 2-4 Novembre 2016]*. Aix-en-Provence: Presses Universitaires de Provence. 229p. [Cor] (Vitez)

RR842.　● Cazaux, Chantal: *L'Opéra de Paris: 350 Ans*. Paris: L'Avant-Scène Opéra, Éditions Premières Loges. 163p. [WC]

RR843.　● Chaouche, Sabine: *The Stage and Its Creative Process*. Paris: Classiques Garnier. 341p. [WC] (Vitez)

RR844.　● Didier, Alain, & Prosper Mérimée: *Théâtre: Doctrine, Production, Critique*. Paris: L'Harmattan. 207p. [WC] (Ghéon)

RR845.　● Donaty-Prost, Brigitte, & Jean Rohou: *Les Classiques sur la Scène des Années 1880-1960: Célébrer, Explorer, Éduquer*. Pézenas: Domens. 317p. [WC] (Antoine, Copeau, Vilar)

RR846.　● Fall, Marouba: *Théâtre et Tradition en Afrique Noire Francophone: Exemple du Théâtre Sénégalais de Langue Française: Essai*. Dakar: L'Harmattan-Sénégal. 307p. [Cor] (Birago Diop, Liking, Senghor)

RR847.　● Grisel, Daniel: *Jo Tréhard. Maître d'Oeuvre d'un Théâtre Populaire, Caen de 1945 à 1972*. Cabourg: Cahiers du Temps. 256p. [WC] (Ferré)

RR848.　● Lécroart, Pascal: *Formes et Dispositions du Texte Théâtral du Symbolisme à Aujourd'hui: Enjeux Littéraires, Politiques, Scéniques*. Besançon: Presses Universitaires de Franche-Comté. 356p. [WC] (Giono, Jarry, Koltès, Mouawad, Vauthier)

RR849.　● Mortier, Daniel, Chantal Foucrier, Jean-Pierre Morel, Anne-Rachel Hermetet, & Ariane Ferry: *Frontières du Théâtre: Mélanges Offerts à Daniel Mortier*. Paris: Classiques Garnier. 376p. [BnF] (Chaurette)

RR850.　● Parisse, Lydie: *Les Voies Négatives de l'Écriture: Dans le Théâtre Moderne et Contemporain*. Paris: Lettres Modernes Minard. 283p. [Cor] (Beckett, Maeterlinck, Novarina, Tardieu)

RR851.　● Sergoï, Timotéo: *Traverser Le Monde Avec un Sac de Plumes: Trente-cinq Ans de Théâtre Hors des Théâtres*. Esneux: Murmure des Soirs. 162p. [WC] (Cros)

RR852.　● Shtutin, Leo: *Spatiality and Subjecthood in Mallarmé, Apollinaire, Maeterlinck, and Jarry: Between Page and Stage*. Oxford: Oxford UP. 226p. [UofR] (Jarry)

RR853.　Beaufils, Éliane: "Théâtralisations Radiophoniques de Poèmes." *Germanica*, 64, 1, 183. [Cor] (Meschonnic)

RR854.　Caune, Jean: "L'Incommunication, Moteur de la Dynamique Théâtrale." *Hermès*, 84, 2, 151. [Cor] (Reza)

RR855.　Denyer, Heather J.: "Transcending Reality in African Theatre." *PAJ: A Journal of Performance and Art*, 41, 3, 98–102. [PrQ] (Kwahulé)

RR856.　Foster, Kendrick: "Give Thy Thoughts a Tongue: Theater and Conflict Resolution." *Harvard International Review*, 40, 2, 24-7. [PrQ] (Lamko)

RR857.　Heppelmann, Eva: "Book Reviews: Staging Creolization: Women's Theater and Performance from the French Caribbean." *Theatre Survey*, 60, 2, 307-9. [RIT] (Ina Césaire)

RR858.   Losco-Lena, M.: "Quand la Photographie de Scene Masque l'Innovation Scenique." *Revue d'Histoire du Théâtre*, *3*, 283, 97-110. (Antoine)

RR859.   Manuel, Pedro: "Complicating the Implication: Animism and Spectrality in Performances Without Humans." *Performance Research*, *24*, 6, 16-21. [UaB] (Marleau)

RR860.   Opondo, Sam O., & Michael J. Shapiro: "Subalterns 'Speak': Migrant Bodies, and the Performativity of the Arts." *Globalizations*, *16*, 4, 575-591. [RIT] (Sembène)

RR861.   Schreier, Lise: "'Le Plus Parisien de Tous Les Nègres': Victor Cochinat et l'Expérience de la Couleur." *Esprit Créateur*, *59*, 2, 88-102. [RIT] (Coppée)

RR862.   Spedalieri, Francesca: "Women, Collective Creation, and Devised Performance: The Rise of Women Theatre Artists in the Twentieth and Twenty-First Centuries." *Theatre History Studies*, 38, 246-9. [PrQ] (Mnouchkine)

TRANSLATION AND PLURILINGUALISM

RR863.   ● Edwards, Natalie: *Multilingual Life Writing by French and Francophone Women: Translingual Selves*. London: Routledge. 176p. [Syr] (Pineau, Salvayre)

RR864.   ● Gouyon, Matignon L.: *Dictionnaire Inuit: Dialecte du Nunavik*. Paris: L'Harmattan. 256p. [LoC]

RR865.   ● Kadiu, Silvia: *Reflexive Translation Studies: Reflexive Translation Studies*. London: UCL Press. 181p. [WC] (Meschonnic)

RR866.   ● Kershaw, Angela: *Translating War: Literature and Memory in France and Britain from the 1940s to the 1960s*. Cham: Palgrave Macmillan. 293p. [UofR]

RR867.   ● Lehmkuhl, Ursula, & Lutz Schowalter: *Translating Diversity: Concepts, Practices, and Politics*. Münster: Waxmann. 237p. [WC] (Poulin, Tremblay)

RR868.   ● Lombez, Christine: *Traduire, Collaborer, Résister: Traducteurs et Traductrices sous l'Occupation*. Tours: Presses Universitaires François Rabelais. 420p. [WC] (Albert-Birot, Man)

RR869.   ● Murugaiyan, Appasamy: *Langues de l'Inde en Diasporas: Maintiens et Transmissions = Ndian Languages in Diaspora: Retention and Transmission: Colloque International: 29-31 Octobre 2015, Mémorial Acte, Point-à-Pitre, Guadeloupe: Actes du Colloque*. Paris: SCITEP. 444p. [BnF] (Devi)

RR870.   ● Nathanaël: *Hatred of Translation*. New York: Nightboat Books. 203p. [WC]

RR871.   ● Poulin, Jacques: *La Traduction Est une Histoire d'Amour; Suivi de, L'Anglais N'est Pas Une Langue Magique*. Montréal: Leméac. 268p. [WC]

RR872.   ● Rosmarin, Léonard A.: *Becoming a Francophile: A Half-Century Love Affair*. Oakville, ON: Mosaic Press. 241p. [WC] (Atlan, Pinget, Wiesel)

RR873.   ● Williamson, Sophie: *Translation*. London: Whitechapel Gallery. 238p. [Syr]

RR874.   Caws, Mary Ann: "Essays in Experiment." *College Literature*, *46*, 1, 254-6. [PrQ] (Bonnefoy)

RR875.   Edwards, Natalie: "Translingual Life Writing: Vassilis Alexakis, Hélène Cixous, Lydie Salvayre." *Esprit Créateur*, *59*, 4, 124-136. [UaB]

RR876.   Glover, Kaiama L.: "'Blackness' in French: On Translation, Haiti, and the Matter of Race." *Esprit Créateur*, *59*, 2, 25-41. [PrQ] (Depestre, Mars)

RR877.   Glynn, Dominic, Sébastien Lemerle, & Subha Xavier: "The Global Afterlife: Sino-French Literature and the Politics of Translation." *French Cultural Studies*, *30*, 2, 153-165. [UofR] (Cheng)

RR878.   Iloh, Ngozi O.: "Translating Yvonne Mété-Nguemeu's Femmes de Centrafrique: Âmes Vaillantes au Cœur Brisé from a Feminist Perspective." *Revista Ártemis*, *27*, 1, 115-31. [PrQ] (Liking)

RR879.   Lindqvist, Yvonne: "Translation Bibliomigrancy: The Case of Contemporary French Caribbean Literature in Sweden." *Meta*, *64*, 3, 600. [PrQ] (Chamoiseau)

RR880.   Lombez, Christine: "La Réception de la Poésie Espagnole Traduite en France sous l'Occupation (1940-1944): Le Cas de F. García Lorca et de ses Traducteurs." *Revue de Littérature Comparée*, *372*, 423, 435, 498, 500. [RIT] (Roblès)

RR881.   Masson, Jean-Yves: "La Traduction Entre Critique et Création." *Revue de Littérature Comparée*, *369*, 85, 97, 125, 127. [PrQ]

RR882.   McKeane, John: "Universalism and the (Un)Translatable." *Translation Studies*, *12*, 1, 64-77. [PrQ] (Badiou)

RR883.   Meadwell, Kenneth: "Poesis and Translation." *Canadian Literature*, *238*, 157, 158, 183. [RIT] (Nelligan)

RR884.   Robertshaw, Matthew: "Kreyòl Anba Duvalier, 1957–1986: A Circuitous Solution to the Creole Problem?" *Nieuwe West - Indische Gids*, *93*, 3, 231-57. [RIT] (Depestre)

RR885.   Sasaki, Yu: "Content with Failure? Cultural Consolidation and the Absence of Nationalist Mobilization in the Case of the Occitans in France." *Social Science History*, *43*, 2, 213-41. [RIT] (Mistral)

RR886.   Steriu, Luminiţa, & Monica Vlad: "De Quelques Marqueurs de Reformulation dans l'Écriture des Mémoires de Master en Roumain Langue Maternelle et en Français Langue Étrangère." *Studii de Lingvistica*, *9*, 2, 247-67. [PrQ] (Bekri)

RR887.   Tavares, Otávio Guimarães, Juliana Steil, & Jamille Pinheiro Dias: "Literature and Translation." *Ilha do Desterro*, *72*, 2, 11-6. [RIT] (Du Bouchet)

RR888.   Tissot, Damien: "In Between Borders: Space, Gender, and Translation." *Philosophy & Rhetoric*, *52*, 3, 265-279. [Naz]

RR889.   Tremblay, Christian: "Langues et Politiques, Des Destins Imbriqués Mais Distincts (II)." *Philologica Jassyensia*, *15*, 1, 269-84. [RIT]

RR890.   Xavier, S.: "The Global Afterlife: Sino-French Literature and the Politics of Translation." *French Cultural Studies*, *30*, 2, 153-165. [RIT]

PART TWO

Author-Subjects

ABOUET, Marguerite.
See also 51, 140.
RR891.   Leslie, Goufo Z.: "Parcours Figuratif de la Femme dans la Bande Dessinée Aya de Yopougon de Marguerite Abouet et Clément Oubrerie." *Alternative Francophone*, 10, 156-168. [Syr]
RR892.   Miranda, Déborah Alves, & Josilene Pinheiro Mariz: "Liberdade Sexual Feminina em Aya de Yopougon: Uma Leitura a Partir de Três Personagens." *Antares: Letras e Humanidades*, *11*, 22, 72-92. [Web]

ACCAD, Évelyne.
See also 452.
RR893.   ● Accad, Évelyne, Roula Zoubiane, & Pirouz Eftékhari: *Un Amour Tissé dans la Tourmente: Récit à Trois Voix*. Paris: L'Harmattan. 372p. [BnF]

ADAM, Paul.
RR894.   Alluin, Bernard: "Notes Sur le Lion d'Arras de Paul Adam." *Nord'*, *73*, 1, 97. [Cor]
RR895.   Domain, Magali: "La Grande Guerre de Paul Adam." *Nord'*, *73*, 1, 83. [Cor]

ADAMOV, Arthur.
RR896.   ● Adamov, Arthur, & Max Chaleil: *L'Arbitre aux Mains Vides: Écrits de Jeunesse*. Paris: Éditions de Paris. 211p. [BnF]
RR897.   ● Ortlieb, Gilles, Laurent Terzieff, Pierre Minet, & Jacqueline Adamov-Autrusseau: *Un Dénuement: Arthur Adamov*. Paris: Fario. 67p. [WC]
RR898.   Bakary, Kone: "L'Écriture Dramatique d'Arthur Adamov, une Esthétique de l'Absurde." *Revue Malienne de Langues et de Littératures*, 4, 122-131. [Web]

ADIAFFI, Jean-Marie.
RR899.   Diawara, Youssouf: "Silence, On Développe (Jean-Marie Adiaffi Adé) et la Question de l'Interdiscursivité." *International Journal of Humanities and Cultural Studies*, *5*, 4, 19-28. [Web]
RR900.   Kanga, Konan Arsène: "Le 'Silence Triomphant' du Héros comme Stratégie Narrative dans *Les Naufragés de l'Intelligence* de Jean-Marie Adé Adiaffi." *Littérature, Langues et Linguistique*, 2, 6. [Web]

ALAIN [Emile Auguste Chartier].
See also 421.
RR901.   Lempereur, Alain: "Négociation Responsable: La Grande Joie de Persévérer dans Son Être avec Autrui." *Question (s) de Management*, 4, 57-66. [Web]

ALAIN-FOURNIER.
See also 3754, 4030.

RR902. ● Laffrat, Jean-Louis, & Alain Fournier: *Le Petit Jean-Louis: Un Gamin de Cussangy.* Paris: Soga. 269p. [BnF]

RR903. Boddy, Trevor: "High Arctic, High Design." *The Canadian Architect*, *64*, 6, 28-34. [RIT]

RR904. Lewis-Stempel, John: "In the Limelight." *Country Life*, Jul 10, 98-9. [PrQ]

ALBERT-BIROT, Pierre.
See also 868.

RR905. ● Aurouet, Carole, & Marianne Simon-Oikawa: *Pierre Albert-Birot (1876-1967): Un Pyrogène des Avant-Gardes.* Rennes: Presses Universitaires de Rennes. 250p. [Cor]

RR906. Baillaud, Bernard: "Carole Aurouet et Marianne Simon-Oikawa (dir.), Pierre Albert-Birot (1876-1967). Un Pyrogène des Avant-Gardes, Presses Universitaires de Rennes, Coll. 'Interférences', 2019, 252 p." *La Revue des Revues*, *62*, 2, 126. [UofR]

ALBIACH, Anne-Marie.
RR907. ● Albiach, Anne-Marie, Marie-Louise Chapelle, & Claude Royet-Journoud: *La Mezzanine: Le Dernier Récit de Catarina Quia.* [Paris]: Seuil. 270p. [BAnQ]

ALEXAKIS, Vassilis.
See also 224, 875.

RR908. Dehner-Armand, Rebecca: "Two Stories by Vassilis Alexakis." *Delos*, *34*, 2, 209-222. [UaB]

RR909. Morello, André-Alain: "Vassilis Alexakis-Entre Nomadisme Linguistique et Géographie de la Dépossession." 317-326. In 224.

ALEXIS, Jacques-Stephen.
See also 227, 246, 256, 261, 270, 279, 283, 432.

RR910. Boadas, Aura Marina: "Poétiques du Réalisme Merveilleux chez Jacques Stephen Alexis et Miguel Bonnefoy." *Il Tolomeo*. *21*, 1. [WC]

RR911. Del, Rossi S.: "L'Humanisme Panaméricain de Jacques Stephen Alexis." *Il Tolomeo*. *21*, 1.. [WC]

RR912. Kwaterko, Józef: "Omniscience et Polyphonie: Esthétique de l'Engagement dans l'Espace d'un Cillement de Jacques Stephen Alexis." *Il Tolomeo*, *21*, 1. [WC]

RR913. Newman, Scott: "From Marvellous Realism to World Literature: Rethinking the Human with Jacques Stephen Alexis." *Francosphères*, *8*, 1, 1-21. [Cor]

RR914. Schallum, Pierre: "Vodou, Mystique et Égypte Antique dans les Arbres Musiciens: Jacques Stéphen Alexis et la Question de l'Un." *Il Tolomeo*, *21*, 1. [WC]

ALFÉRI, Pierre.
See also 583, 781.

RR915. ● Alféri, Pierre: *La Sirène de Satan: Précédé de et la Rue.* Lacelle: Hourra. 44p. [BnF]

RR916. • Zukofsky, Louis, Pierre Alféri, & David Lespiau: *Un Objectif: & Deux Autres Essais*. Genève: Héros-limite. 55p. [WC]

ALLAIN, Marcel.
See also 4698.
RR917. • Bocquet, Olivier, Julie Rocheleau, Marcel Allain, & Pierre Souvestre: *The Wrath of Fantômas*. London: Titan Comics. 1 vol. [LoC]
RR918. • Schmitz, Gordon L.: *Fantômas und das Geheimnis des Phantoms der Oper*. Framersheim: Brighton. 212p. [WC]

ALLAIS, Alphonse.
RR919. • Allais, Alphonse, & Stéphane Trapier: *En Ribouldinguant!* Talence: Arbre Vengeur. 192p. [BAnQ]

ALTHUSSER, Louis.
See also 659.
RR920. • Althusser, Louis, & G. M. Goshgarian: *History and Imperialism: Writings, 1963-1986*. Cambridge: Polity Press. 191p. [WC]
RR921. • Althusser, Louis, G. M. Goshgarian, & Alcira N. Bixio: *Las Vacas Negras: Entrevista Imaginaria (el Malestar del XXXII Congreso): ¡Lo Que No Está Bien, Camaradas!* Madrid: Akal. 302p. [WC]
RR922. • Althusser, Louis, Yves Vargas, & G M. Goshgarian: *Lessons on Rousseau*. London: Verso. 144p. [Cor]
RR923. • Backer, David I.: *The Gold and the Dross: Althusser for Educators*. Leiden: Brill. 80p. [Cor]
RR924. • Cheloni, Roberto: *L'Apparizione di Figure Eminenti: L'Altro Volto del Transgenerazionale: Kafka, Joyce, Althusser*. Roma: Armando. 176p. [WC]
RR925. • Seppmann, Werner: *Dasœ Elend der Philosophie: Über Louis Althusser*. Kassel: Mangroven. 379p. [WC]
RR926. • Sirmasac, Hakan: *Philosophische Distinktionen und Wissenschaftliche Analytik Nach Louis Althusser: Prozesse - Strukturen - Theorien*. Baden-Baden: Nomos. 268p. [WC]
RR927. Alant, Jaco: "Louis Althusser en Jacques Derrida. Raakpunte Van Sin en die Sintuiglike in Twee Tydgenootlike Tekste." *Litnet Akademies*, *16*, 3, 50-74. [WC]
RR928. Alvares, de F. J. G.: "Étienne Balibar e Louis Althusser." *Pensata*, *8*, 1. [WC]
RR929. Armstrong, Nancy: "What Use Is Althusser?" *Cultural Critique*, 103, 13-18. [UaB]
RR930. Bargu, Banu, & Robyn Marasco: "The Political Encounter with Louis Althusser." *Rethinking Marxism*, *31*, 3, 239-241. [Naz]
RR931. Berdet, M.: "The Concept of 'Phantasmagorical Interpellation': A Theoretical Proposal Inspired by Walter Benjamin and Louis Althusser." *Isegoria*, 61, 505-524. [Cor]
RR932. Cockshott, Paul: "Althusser's Theory of Ideology: Reversion to Idealist Mystery." *Critique*, *47*, 4, 551-583. [UaB]
RR933. Cotten, Jean-Pierre: "La Correspondance Althusser-Sève: Amitié, Compagnonnage Politique et Divergences Théoriques." *La Pensée*, *397*, 1, 59. [Syr]

RR934.   Douet, Yohann: "Althusser, Poulantzas et le Problème de l'Autonomie de la Politique." *L'Homme & La Société*, *209*, 1, 157. [Naz]

RR935.   Fuchs, C.: "Revisiting the Althusser/e. P. Thompson-Controversy: Towards a Marxist Theory of Communication." *Communication and the Public*, *4*, 1, 3-20. [Cor]

RR936.   Galano, Jean-Michel: "Althusser: Éléments de Rétrospection." *La Pensée*, *397*, 1, 72. [UofR]

RR937.   Giraldo, Zuluaga C., & Arboleda G. M. López: "El Amor Como Afectación y Afecto en La Vida de Louis Althusser: Una Montaña Muchas Veces Pintada." *Ces Psicología*, *12*, 1, 112-121. [Naz]

RR938.   Gordillo, Ignacio: "The Idea of Event in Althusser and Badiou Philosophy's: A Way to Rethink the Political Subjectivities." *Oxímora. Revista Internacional de Ética y Política*, 15, 33-50. [WC]

RR939.   Harris, Neal: "How to Be a Marxist in Philosophy by Louis Althusser Edited and Translated by G. M. Goshgarian." *Studies in Social and Political Thought*, 28. [WC]

RR940.   Ichikawa, Elisa Y., & Eline G. O. Zioli: "A Escola e as Identidades dos Alunos do Campo: Um Estudo a Partir de Bourdieu e Althusser." *Cadernos Ebape. br*, *17*, 1, 25-36. [Syr]

RR941.   Jan, Matija: "Drugi Teoreticizem Lousia Althusserja =: The Second Theoreticism of Louis Althusser." *Phainomena*, *28*, 108-109, 329-353. [WC]

RR942.   Lopez, Arboleda G. M., & C. G. Zuluaga: "Love as Effect and Affection in the Life of Louis Althusser: A Mountain Painted Many Times." *Revista Ces Psicologia*, *12*, 1, 112-121. [Naz]

RR943.   Marasco, R.: "Althusser's Gramscian Debt: On Reading Out Loud." *Rethinking Marxism*, *31*, 3, 340-362. [Naz]

RR944.   Pavón-Cuéllar, David: "Lacan and Althusser on Psychology: the Political Ethos of Serving Ideals and Justifying Ideology." *Psychotherapy and Politics International*, *17*, 2. [Cor]

RR945.   Pippa, Stephano: "Void for a Subject: Althusser's Machiavelli and the Concept of 'Political Interpellation'." *Rethinking Marxism*, *31*, 3, 363-379. [RIT]

AMÉRY, Jean.
See also 495, 502, 768, 769, 770.

RR946.   ● Ataria, Yochai, Amit Kravitz, & Eli Pitcovski: *Jean Améry: Beyond the Mind's Limits*. Cham: Palgrave Macmillan. 345p. [Syr]

RR947.   Brandl, L.: "Über Die Rampe: Jean Améry in Wien. Eine Revision." *Literatur und Kritik*, 533-534, 5-10. [Syr]

RR948.   Fernández, López J. A.: "'Der Schmerz War, der er War." Tortura y Teorización del Dolor en Jean Améry." *Isegoría*, 60, 285. [Naz]

RR949.   Fuchs, A.: "Geschichte - Wahrheit - Versöhnung: Zur Aktualität Jean Amérys." *Zeitschrift fur Evangelische Ethik*, *63*, 3, 168-179. [UaB]

RR950.   Lelle, Nikolas: "Arbeit, (Un)freiheit, Tod Erwiderungen von Jean Améry, Primo Levi Und Tibor Wohl auf die Kz-Devise 'Arbeit Macht Frei'." *Zeitschrift Für Geschichtswissenschaft*, *67*, 6, 538-551. [Syr]

RR951.   Traverso, Enzo: "Jean Améry. Entre la Razón Crítica y la Desesperanza." *Acta Poética*, *40*, 2, 41-60. [RIT]

AMROUCHE, Jean.
See also 251, 285.

ANGOT, Christine.
See also 86, 326, 499, 501, 620, 2777.

RR952.   Baroud, Rana: "#mots-dièse et Écritures de Soi: Essai sur un Activisme Contemporain." *Relief, 13,* 1, 125-135. [Syr]

RR953.   Hauksson-Tresch, Nathalie: "De l'Utilité des Théories Linguistiques et Littéraires lors d'un Procès d'Écrivain: L'Exemple du Procès Intenté à la Romancière Française Christine Angot." *Bergen Language and Linguistics Studies, 10,* 1, 11. [WC]

RR954.   Mihelakis, Eftihia, Vincent Lavoie, & Ania Wroblewski: "Marie Darrieussecq et Christine Angot, Récidivistes du Réel." *Captures, 4,* 1, mai. [WC]

RR955.   Ngamaleu, Jovensel: "Écriture du Moi et Violation de la Vie Privée d'Autrui ou la Judiciarisation de l'Autofiction: Les Petits de Christine Angot et Belle et Bête de Marcela Iacub." *Anales de Filología Francesa, 27,* 1, 199-216. [Naz]

RR956.   Pelletier, Laurence: "*Un Tournant de la Vie* de Christine Angot." *Spirale, 267,* hiver, 57-58. [WC]

RR957.   Soualah, Keltoum: "'Inceste Scriptural': Adversités Vécues et Normes Subverties dans l'Inceste de Christine Angot." *Cahiers Erta,* 18, 105-123. [WC]

ANOUILH, Jean.
See also 497.

RR958.   ● Kucharuk, Sylwia: *Jean Anouilh: En Quête de la Métathéâtralité.* Lublin: Wydawnictwo Uniwersytetu Marii Curie-Skłodowskiej. 236p. [WC]

RR959.   Coker, L. S.: "Happy as the Lark: Broadway Presents Joan of Arc." *Revue Française d'Études Américaines. 161,* 4, 72. [Syr]

RR960.   Gonçalves, Rodrigo Tadeu: "A Tradutora e o Diálogo Intermidiático em Antigonick de Anne Carson." *Classica, Revista Brasileira de Estudos Clássicos, 32,* 1, 79-91. [WC]

RR961.   Koulouris, Theodore: "*Antigone* and its Context: Looking at Antigone. Pp. x + 247. London and New York: Bloomsbury Academic, 2018. Cased, £85, US$114. ISBN: 978-1-350-01711-5." *The Classical Review,* 69, 2, 380-3. [PrQ]

RR962.   Mazari, Negar: "Approche 'Innovante' du Mythe d'Orphée: Étude de la Transition du Monde Antique au XXème Siècle par l'Eurydice de Jean Anouilh d'Après la Mythanalyse de Gilbert Durand." *Recherches en Langue et Littérature Françaises, 12,* 22, 69-86. [WC]

RR963.   Vozdova, M.: "Character of Old Duchess in the Theatrical Universe of Jean Anouilh." *Etudes Romanes de Brno, 40,* 2, 123-141. [UofR]

RR964.   Vozdová, Marie, & Jiřina Matousková. "Towards a Bergsonian Reading of Le Bal des Voleurs by Jean Anouilh." *Romanica Olomucensia, 30,* 2, 333-345. [WC]

ANTELME, Robert.
See 575.

ANTOINE, André.
See also 845, 858.

RR965.　● Tait, Peta. *Antoine; Stanislavski; Saint-Denis*. New York: Metheun Drama. 25p. [WC]

APOLLINAIRE, Guillaume.

See also 1, 449, 450, 464, 482, 485, 503, 524, 531, 552, 563, 792, 794, 802, 813, 852.

RR966.　● Apollinaire, Guillaume, & Marion Baudriller: *Alcools: Poésie*. [Paris]: Larousse. 239p. [WC]

RR967.　● Bernard, Julie: *Mon Coffret à Poèmes: À Suspendre, Exposer et Partager: 15 Poèmes-Affiches d'Apollinaire, Desnos, Topor et de Poètes d'Aujourd'hui*. [Voisins-le-Bretonneux]: Rue du Monde. 1 coffret. [WC]

RR968.　● Blanc, Lydia P.: *Apollinaire, "Alcools": Parcours, Modernité Poétique?* Paris: Ellipses. 108p. [BnF]

RR969.　● Delbreil, Daniel: *Dictionnaire Apollinaire [A-L]*. Paris: Honoré Champion. 614p. [Cor]

RR970.　● Delbreil, Daniel: *Dictionnaire Apollinaire [M-Z]*. Paris: Honoré Champion. 614-1234p. [Cor]

RR971.　● Fernandez-Miranda, Elena: *Les Fantasmes d'Apollinaire*. Paris: L'Harmattan. 361p. [Cor]

RR972.　● *Guillaume Apollinaire: Mars 2019*. Paris: Librairie Jean-Claude Vrain. 1 vol. [Cor]

RR973.　● Huguet, Alexandra: "Alcools, de Guillaume Apollinaire." *NRP*, 34, 1. [WC]

RR974.　● Kornhauser, Jakub, & Wacław Rapak: *Apollinaire - "L'Esprit Nouveau" - Les Avant-Gardes*. Kraków: Jagiellonian UP. 296p. [WC]

RR975.　● Morhange-Bégué, Claude, & Pierre Lartigue: *Alcools (1913), Guillaume Apollinaire: 1re Générale & Techno: Nouveau Bac*. Paris: Hatier. 128p. [WC]

RR976.　● Tammen, Johann P.: *Wind und Windporzellan: Nachdichtungen von Guillaume Apollinaire Bis Valentino Zeichen*. Göttingen: Wallstein. 231p. [Cor]

RR977.　● Zinenberg, Dominique: *Pour Saluer Apollinaire*. Saint-Chéron: Unicité. 93p. [BnF]

RR978.　Alliot, Julien: "Guillaume Apollinaire et les Femmes?: Que Sait le Poète?" *La Revue Lacanienne*, 20, 1, 201. [Cor]

RR979.　"Apollinaire: De Quoi Moudre Entretiens avec Claude Debon et Victor Martin-Schmets." *Quinzaines*, 1207, 4-6. [UaB]

RR980.　Bories, Anne-Sophie: "Sex, Wine and Statelessness: Apollinaire's Verse Without Borders in 'Vendémiaire'." *Modern Languages Open*, 1, 14. [WC]

RR981.　Campa, Laurence: "Apollinaire et ses Amis. Le Louvre en ses Ambivalences." *Revue d'Histoire Littéraire de la France*, 119, 3, 579-588. [RIT]

RR982.　"Dans La Peau d'Apollinaire: [Dossier]." *Français dans le Monde: Revue de l'Enseignement du Français hors de France*, 421, janvier-février, 52-61. [WC]

RR983.　Delbreil, Daniel: "Book Review: Lettres Reçues par Guillaume Apollinaire. 'Bibliothèque des Correspondances'." *Revue d'Histoire Littéraire de la France*, 119, 4, 1000-1005. [RIT]

RR984.　Dereuse, P.: "Rimbaud, Apollinaire, Dotremont de l'Écrit à l'Image." 88-97. In 2197.

RR985.   Fiorentino, Francesco, & Luca Bevilacqua: "Déconstruction des Modèles et Ironie Littéraire: Quelques Remarques sur l'Effet de Distanciation dans la Poésie d'Apollinaire." *Revue Italienne d'Études Françaises*, 9. [Syr]

RR986.   Foss, Colin: "Shtutin, Leo. Spatiality and Subjecthood in Mallarmé, Apollinaire, Maeterlinck, & Jarry: Between Page and Stage." *French Review*, 93, 2, 267. [RIT]

RR987.   Gayraud, I.: "Apollinaire et l'Orphisme Pictural: Entre Critique d'Art et Création." *RLC - Revue de Littérature Comparée*, 369, 1, 61-73. [Naz]

RR988.   Lévesque, Isabelle: "Guillaume Apollinaire, Les Obus Miaulaient." *Quinzaines*, 1207, 8-9. [UaB]

RR989.   Lévesque, Isabelle: "Guillaume Apollinaire, Tout Terriblement." *Quinzaines*, 1207, 7. [UaB]

RR990.   Matore, Daniel: "Pound's Transmissions: Typography, Phonography, and Notation." *Modernism/Modernity*, 26, 2, 351-73. [PrQ]

RR991.   Michelson, A.: "Painting, Instantaneism, Cinema, America, Ballet, Illumination, Apollinaire*." *October*, 169, 65-74. [Naz]

RR992.   Petrova, Anastassia D.: "Guillaume Apollinaire, Innovator: L'Enchanteur Pourrissant (The Enchanter Rotting) as the Literature Progress Embodiment." *Astra Salvensis*, 7, 13, 447-462. [WC]

RR993.   Soudani, Hind: "Quelle Sémiotique pour la Poésie Artistique de Guillaume Apollinaire?" *Études de Linguistique Appliquée*, 196, 4, 345. [UofR]

RR994.   Udasmoro, Wening: "Women and Pleasure in Guillaume Apollinaire's Calligram Collection *Poèmes à Lou*." *K@ta*, 20, 2, 60-67. [UaB]

AQUIN, Hubert.
See also 195, 231.

RR995.   Bélanger, David, Rosalie Lavoie, & Aurélie Lanctôt: "Vignettes: David Bélanger sur Hubert Aquin, Janette Bertrand et Michèle Lalonde." *Liberté*, 325, 76. [UaB]

RR996.   Harvey, François: "Hubert Aquin Fade Out: Excentration, Falsification et Disparition dans les Derniers Écrits Aquiniens." *Études Françaises*, 55, 2, 137. (UofR)

ARAGON, Louis.
See also 378, 387, 405, 425, 807.

RR997.   ● Aragon, Louis, & François Eychart: *Les Annales de la Société des Amis de Louis Aragon et Elsa Triolet*. Paris: Delga. *Les Annales de la Société des Amis de Louis Aragon et Elsa Triolet*, 20. 465p. [WC]

RR998.   ● Aragon, Louis, & Marie-Thérèse Eychart: *La Grande Gaîté: Suivi de Tout Ne Finit Pas par des Chansons*. Paris: Gallimard. 142p. [WC]

RR999.   ● Beaulieu, D. A., Louis Aragon, & Charles H. Ford: *On Syntax*. Malmö, Sweden: Timglaset. 13p. [UaB]

RR1000.   ● Ledroit, André: *Le Grand Débat du Siècle: À la Manière de Nos Plus Grands Poètes Jean de la Fontaine, Victor Hugo, Jacques Prévert, Louis Aragon: Nouvelles*. Saint-Denis: Édilivre. 25. [BnF]

RR1001.   ● Noël, Bernard: *Aragon*. Bordeaux: Éditions des Vanneaux. 61p. [BnF]

RR1002. ● Piégay, Nathalie, Josette Pintueles, & Fernand Salzmann: *Dictionnaire Aragon*. Paris: Honoré Champion. 2 vols. 1035p. [Cor]

RR1003. ● Vasseur, Bernard: *Aragon Stalinien?: Mythe et Réalité*. Auxerre: HDiffusion. 102p. [WC]

RR1004. ● Vigier, Luc: *Cahiers Aragon, Vol. 2*. Meurcourt: Éditions les Cahiers. 240p. [WC]

RR1005. Bougnoux, Daniel: "Le Droit Romain N'Est Plus. Note sur un Conte Écrit par Aragon en 1944." *Histoire de la Justice*, 29, 1, 397. [WC]

RR1006. Muzzi, Nino: "Louis Aragon: L'Amore Come Assoluto." *Poesia*, 345, 2-19. [WC]

RR1007. Perrot, Mathieu: "'Les Charmants Contours de la Danseuse'. A Portrait of Humour in Traité du Style by Louis Aragon." *Romanica Olomucensia*, 30, 2, 315-332. [WC]

RR1008. Vigier, Luc: "Louis Aragon 'J.R. 75 / Le Cadeau à Jean'." *Quinzaines*, 1212, 3-4. [Syr]

ARCAN, Nelly.
See also 304, 321, 340, 344, 599.

RR1009. Bouhadid, Nadia: "Identité Queer: Absence et Négation de Soi dans Folle de Nelly Arcan." *Anales de Filología Francesa*, 27, 1, 35-52. [Syr]

RR1010. Courville, Vanessa: "Nelly Arcan. Trajectoires Fulgurantes by Isabelle Boisclair et al. (Review)." *University of Toronto Quarterly*, 88, 3, 415-418. [RIT]

RR1011. Galis, Polly: "Hyper-conformity as Counter-Narrative in Nelly Arcan's *À Ciel Ouvert*." *Esprit Créateur*, 59, 3, 86-98. [UofR]

RR1012. Michel, Amélie: "La Violence Énonciative dans Putain de Nelly Arcan: Entre Intériorisation et Renversement des Rapports de Pouvoir Liés à la Sexualité." *Études Littéraires*, 48, 3, 133. [UaB]

RR1013. Savignac, Rosemarie: "Fantômes et Impostures dans La Fureur de Ce Que Je Pense de Marie Brassard d'Après des Textes de Nelly Arcan." *Canadian Literature*, 239, 31-49. [Naz]

ARCHAMBAULT, Gilles.
See also 230.

RR1014. ● Archambault, Gilles: *Tu Écouteras Ta Mémoire: Cent Très Brefs Récits*. Montréal: Boréal. 136p. [BAnQ]

RR1015. ● Péan, Stanley, & Gilles Archambault: *De Préférence La Nuit*. Montréal: Boréal. 263p. [BAnQ]

ARLAND, Marcel.
RR1016. ● Calmont, Jeanne: *La Collection Marcel Arland: Dans l'Amitié des Peintres: Vente à Paris 28 Mars 2018 14 H*. Paris: Sotheby's France. 139p. [WC]

ARNAUD, Noël.
RR1017. ● Damaggio, Jean-Paul: *Noël Arnaud, par ses Complices*. Angeville: La Brochure. 154p. [BnF]

ARON, Raymond.
See also 1.

RR1018. ● Adair-Toteff, Christopher: *Raymond Aron's Philosophy of Political Responsibility: Freedom, Democracy and National Identity.* Edinburgh: Edinburgh UP. 186p. [UofR]

RR1019. ● Aron, Raymond, Dominique Schnapper, & Fabrice Gardel: *L'Abécédaire de Raymond Aron.* Paris: Éditions de l'Observatoire – Humensis. 233p. [Cor]

RR1020. ● Nelson, Scott B.: *Tragedy and History: The German Influence on Raymond Aron's Political Thought.* New York: Peter Lang. 307p. [WC]

RR1021. ● San, Mauro C.: *Raymond Aron e Gli Stati Uniti: Anni di Guerra, Sguardi di Pace (1945-1972): Successo o Fallimento dell'Egemonia Americana?* Milano: FrancoAngeli. 164p. [LoC]

RR1022. ● Stewart, Iain: *Raymond Aron and Liberal Thought in the Twentieth Century.* Cambridge: Cambridge UP. 327p. [Syr]

RR1023. Agassi, Joseph: "Raymond Aron's Contributions." *Philosophy of the Social Sciences,* December 25. [RIT]

RR1024. Davis, Reed M.: "L'Abécédaire de Raymond Aron, Textes Choisis par Dominique Schnapper et Fabrice Gardel: Paris: L'Observatoire, 2018, 240 pp. 19 Euros. ISBN:979-1032905739." *Society, 56,* 6, 642-644. [UofR]

RR1025. Drochon, Hugo: "Raymond Aron's 'Machiavellian' Liberalism." *Journal of the History of Ideas, 80,* 4, 621-642. [Naz]

RR1026. Haine, Jean-Yves: "Raymond Aron's Remarkable Relevance for Our Decaying World." *European Review of International Studies, 6,* 1, 47-58. [UaB]

ARP, Jean.

RR1027. ● Arp, Jean: *Hans and Jean Arp - Twenty Sketchbooks.* Gottingen: Steidl. 1 vol. [WC]

RR1028. ● Jedrzejczyk, Malgorzata, & Katarzyna Sloboda: *Composing the Space: Sculptures in the Avant-Garde.* Köln: Walther König. 230p. [WC]

RR1029. ● Kornhoff, Oliver: *Arp: Purzelblätter: Bestandskatalog der Papierarbeiten im Arp Museum Bahnhof Rolandseck.* Remagen: Landes-Stiftung Arp Museum Bahnhof Rolandseck. 303p. [WC]

RR1030. ● Martinoli, Simona, & Roland Scotti: *Public Arp: Jean Arp: Arte e Architettura in Dialogo.* Bellinzona: Casagrande. 175p. [WC]

ARRABAL, Fernando.
See also 602.

RR1031. ● Aranzueque-Arrieta, Frédéric: *Arrabal, une Oeuvre-Vie Panique: Essai Panique.* Bordeaux: Moires. 509p. [Cor]

RR1032. ● Arrabal, Fernando: *¡Pintapollos Trotskistas! Y Otros Artículos.* Madrid: Reino de Cordelia. 237p. [LoC]

RR1033. ● Arrabal, Fernando, & J. San Martin: *Sarah & Victor.* Paris: Au Crayon Qui Tue. 4 Cahiers. [BnF]

RR1034. Arrabal, Fernando: "Héros et Héroïnes Passés et Présents des Échecs." *Ligeia, 32,* 169-172, 84. [PrQ]

RR1035. Branco, António: "O Processo de Criação de Fando e Lis, de Fernando Arrabal: Uma Memória Cartográfica." *Urdimento, 3,* 36, 357-375. [WC]

RR1036. Ruiz del Olmo, F. J., & Jésus Del Río: "Entre La Tragedia Griega y las Películas de Carretera: Iré Como un Caballo Loco (1973) de Fernando Arrabal." *Alpha, 47,* 135-147. [Naz]

RR1037.   Sprinceana, I.: "The Shape of Resistance: Objects as Fetishes in El Cementerio de Automóviles (1957) by Fernando Arrabal and Ederra (1982) by Ignacio Amestoy." *Anales de la Literatura Espanola Contemporanea*, 44, 2, 439-460. [UaB]

ARTAUD, Antonin.
See also 381, 438, 779.
RR1038.   ● Acca, Fabio: *Fare Artaud: Il Teatro della Crudeltà in Italia (1935-1970)*. Spoleto: Editoria et Spettacolo. 408p. [WC]
RR1039.   ● Artaud, Antonin: *Khabar Eni Kathar Esti: Le Manuscrit de Rodez*. Rodez: Archives Départementales de l'Aveyron. 68p. [BnF]
RR1040.   ● Artaud, Antonin: *La Danza del Peyote*. Aprilia: Ortica. 207p. [WC]
RR1041.   ● Artaud, Antonin: *La Vitre d'Amour: Suivi de la Montagne des Signes: Et Autres Textes*. Paris: Caractères. 75p. [BnF]
RR1042.   ● Artaud, Antonin: *Les Nouvelles Révélations de l'Être*. [Saint-Clément-de-Rivière]: Fata Morgana. 38p. [UaB]
RR1043.   ● Artaud, Antonin, Balthus, & Raoul Albé: *Balthus*. Madrid: Casimiro. 85p. [WC]
RR1044.   ● Artaud, Antonin, & Rodolfo Cortizo: *El Treatro de la Crueldad: Ciencia, Poesía y Metafísica*. Madrid: La Pajarita de Papel. 124p. [WC]
RR1045.   ● Artaud, Antonin, & Alex Giuzio: *Il Teatro e la Crudeltà*. Roma: E/O. 149p. [WC]
RR1046.   ● Artaud, Antonin, & Olivier Penot-Lacassagne: *Les Nouvelles Révélations de l'Être: Suivi de Lettres et Sorts*. [Paris]: Prairial. 117p. [BnF]
RR1047.   ● Artaud, Antonin, Giuseppe Rocca, & Giuliano Zincone: *Il Teatro e il Suo Doppio, e il Teatro di Séraphin*. Roma: Audino. 151p. [WC]
RR1048.   ● Artaud, Antonin, Paule Thévenin, Jacques Derrida, & Simon Werle: *Antonin Artaud: Zeichnungen und Portraits*. München: Schirmer/Mosel. 253p. [WC]
RR1049.   ● Broyart, Benoît, & Laurent Richard: *Nanaqui: Une Vie d'Antonin Artaud*. Grenoble: Glénat. 123p. [WC]
RR1050.   ● Duménil, Lorraine: *Artaud et le Cinéma*. Paris: Nouvelles Éditions Place. 121p. [WC]
RR1051.   ● Macherez, Felix: *Au Pays des Rêves Noirs: Antonin Artaud au Mexique*. Sainte-Marguerite-sur-Mer: Équateurs. 204p. [BnF]
RR1052.   ● Mèredieu, Florence: *Bacon, Artaud, Vinci: Une Blessure Magnifique*. Paris: Blusson. 165p. [Cor]
RR1053.   ● Palazzeschi, Yves: *Antonin Artaud, d'une Révélation à l'Autre: 1923-1937*. S.l.: Yves Palazzeschi. 93p. [BnF]
RR1054.   ● Perriera, Giuditta, & Pia Valentinis: *Il Suono del Candore: L'Abisso di Cristallo di Antonin Artaud*. Palermo: RueBallu. 76p. [WC]
RR1055.   ● Sircar, Ronojoy: *Remember, Repeat, Inhabit. A Study of Antonin Artaud, Krzysztof Kieslowski and Nikhil Chopra*. London: Bloomsbury Academic. 200p. [WC]
RR1056.   ● Thévenin, Paule, & Jacques Derrida: *Antonin Artaud: Drawings and Portraits*. Cambridge, MA: The MIT Press. 255p. [WC]
RR1057.   Corral, Fulla A.: "Antonin Artaud sur la Scène Espagnole (1969-2016)." *Anales de Filología Francesa*, 27, 1, 419-448. [Syr]

RR1058.   Crombez, Thomas: "De Intrede van Antonin Artaud in België." *Documenta*, *25*, 2, 159-180. [WC]
RR1059.   Lamberechts, Luc: "Gene A. Plunka (red.), Antonin Artaud and the Modern Theater." *Documenta*, *13*, 3, 188-190. [WC]
RR1060.   López, Paola A.: "El Heroísmo de Antonin Artaud." *Praxis Filosófica*, 49, 151-170. [Naz]
RR1061.   Pennisi, G.: "The 'Fluid Mask' of Antonin Artaud: Effects of Corporeal Hyperreflexivity on Schizophrenic Subjects." *Mediterranean Journal of Clinical Psychology*, 7, 1. [WC]
RR1062.   Slote, Sam: "Namelessness from Artaud to Beckett." *Samuel Beckett Today/ Aujourd'hui*, *31*, 1, 130-146. [RIT]
RR1063.   Templeton, Michael: "Ambivalent Texts, the Borderline, and the Sense of Nonsense in Lewis Carroll's 'Jabberwocky'." *International Journal of English Studies*, *19*, 2, 1-18. [PrQ]

ATLAN, Liliane.
See 816, 872.

AUDIBERTI, Jacques.
See 1083.

AUDOUX, Marguerite.
RR1064.   Audoux, Marguerite: *Valserine, and Other Stories: English and French Versions*. [N.p.]: Forgotten Books. Édition originale, 1912. 299p. [WC]

AUGIÉRAS, François.
RR1065.   ● Augieras, François, & Dirk Höfer: *Eine Reise auf den Berg Athos*. Berlin Matthes & Seitz: Berlin. 280p. [WC]
RR1066.   Osman, Ladan: "Alien Citizen Field Notes." *World Literature Today*, *93*, 2, 42-3. [PrQ]

AYMÉ, Marcel.
See also 567.
RR1067.   ● Akérib, Agnès: *Marcel Aymé, Pourfendeur du Délit d'Opinion: Adaptation Libre de sa Correspondance*. Paris: Triartis. 62p. [BnF]
RR1068.   ● Aymé, Marcel, & May Angeli: *L'Éléphant: Un Conte du Chat Perché*. Paris: Les Éditions des Éléphants. 44p. [BnF]
RR1069.   ● *Cahier Marcel Aymé*. Villers-Robert: Société des Amis de Marcel Aymé. *Cahier Marcel Aymé*, 37. 148p. [WC]

BÂ, Mariama.
See also 233, 249, 250, 258, 266, 282, 346, 663.
RR1070.   ● Bâ, Mariama, & Pérez S. Martín: *Mi Carta Más Larga*. Barcelona: Wanafrica. 137p. [WC]
RR1071.   ● Ndiaye, Bassirou, & Lamarana P. Diallo: *La Souffrance: Une Clef de Lecture pour l'Oeuvre Romanesque de Mariama Bâ*. Dakar: Harmattan-Sénégal. 193p. [UofR]
RR1072.   Dieng, Mamadou: "Les Femmes, la Communication et le Pouvoir Traditionnel dans l'Oeuvre de Mariama Bâ." *French Review*, *92*, 4, 40-53. [RIT]

RR1073.   Faye, Diome: "Economic Violence, Sexual Exploitation and Psychological Trauma: A Comparative Study of the Predicament of Women in Gloria Naylor's The Women of Brewster Place and Mariama Ba's So Long a Letter." *Journal of Advances in Education and Philosophy, 3*, 9, 335-341. [WC]

BACHELARD, Gaston.
See also 603.

RR1074.   ● Alison, Aurosa, & Jean-Jacques Wunenburger: *Épistémologie et Esthétique de l'Espace chez Gaston Bachelard*. [Milan]: Mimésis. 312p. [BnF]

RR1075.   ● Hiéronimus, Gilles, & Julien Lamy: *Imaginaire et Praxis: Autour de Gaston Bachelard*. Paris: Classiques Garnier. 190p. [WC]

RR1076.   ● Wavelet, Jean-Michel: *Gaston Bachelard, l'Inattendu: Les Chemins d'une Volonté*. Paris: L'Harmattan. 267p. [LoC]

RR1077.   Abreu, Bernardes S. T.: "Representações Poéticas do Sertão na Perspectiva do Filósofo-Professor Gaston Bachelard." *Revista Profissão Docente, 19*, 42 1-20. [Syr]

RR1078.   Almeida, Tiago S.: "Erguendo Barreiras Contra o Irracionalismo: História das Ciências e Diagnóstico da Atualidade em Gaston Bachelard." *Tempo, 25*, 3, 715-736. [Naz]

RR1079.   Araújo, Alberto F.: "O Cântico do Silêncio em La Flamme d'une Chandelle de Gaston Bachelard." *Síntese: Revista de Filosofia, 46*, 144, 93. [UaB]

RR1080.   Basso, Elisabetta, Emmanuel Delille, Gaston Bachelard, & Ludwig Binswanger: "Correspondance Gaston Bachelard-Ludwig Binswanger (1948-1955): Transcrite, Traduite et Éditée par Elisabetta Basso et Emmanuel Delille." *Revue Germanique Internationale*, 30, 183-208. [Cor]

RR1081.   Corsellas, Maximiliano S.: "El Conocimiento Simbólico y el Mito del Fuego en las Culturas Antiguas. Aportes desde la Imaginación Creadora de Gastón Bachelard." *Tábano*, 15, 48-59. [WC]

RR1082.   Da Rocha, G. K.: "Hountondji and Bachelard: Pluralism as a Methodological and Phenomenological Concept in Approaching the Cultural Knowledge of Africa." *Filosofia Theoretica, 8*, 2, 97-110. [WC]

RR1083.   Gao, Yanping: "Between Matter and Hand: On Gaston Bachelard's Theory of Material Imagination." *Journal of Comparative Literature and Aesthetics, 42*, 1, 73-81. [PrQ]

RR1084.   Kumar, A.: "The Designer's Philosopher Gaston Bachelard and The Poetics of Space." *Economic and Political Weekly, 54*, 47, 77-78. [UofR]

RR1085.   Souto, Caio: "Objeto em Perspectiva e Sujeito em Devir na Epistemologia Histórica de Gaston Bachelard." *Intelligere*, 8, 13. [WC]

BADIOU, Alain.
See also 300, 882, 938, 1118, 2132, 3322, 3412, 4729.

RR1086.   ● Badiou, Alain: *Trump*. Cambridge: Polity. 68p. [UaB]

RR1087.   ● Badiou, Alain, & Véronique Pineau: *Le Séminaire*. [Paris]: Fayard. 351p. [WC]

RR1088.   ● Druon, Serge: *Alain Badiou et la Guerre des Infinis: Une Lecture Critique de L'Immanence des Vérités: Essai*. Saint-Denis: Édilivre. 239p. [BnF]

RR1089.   ● Henry, Chris: *The Ethics of Political Resistance: Althusser, Badiou, Deleuze*. Edinburgh: Edinburgh UP. 236p. [Syr]

RR1090. • Völker, Jan: *Badiou and the German Tradition of Philosophy*. Sydney: Bloomsbury Academic. 220p. [WC]

RR1091. • Wald, Lasowski A., Pierre Soulages, & Alain Badiou: *Dialogue avec Alain Badiou sur l'Art et sur Pierre Soulages*. Paris: Cercle d'Art. 108p. [WC]

RR1092. Badiou, Alain: "Lessons from the 'Yellow Vests' Movement." *African Yearbook of Rhetoric*, 9, 1, 14-19. [Cor]

RR1093. Badiou, Alain, & Duane Rousselle: "Love Must Be Reinvented." *Theory & Event*, 22, 1, 6-17. [PrQ] (Char)

RR1094. Barakat, Zeina M.: "Happiness, Alain Badiou, Bloomsbury, 2019 (ISBN 978-1-4742-7553-8), viii + 128 pp., Pb £12.99." *Reviews in Religion & Theology*, 26, 4, 572-577. [UofR]

RR1095. Baruchello, Giorgio: "Alain Badiou and Marcel Gauchet, What Is to Be Done? A Dialogue on Communism, Capitalism, and the Future of Democracy (Malden, MA: Polity Press, 2016)." *Nordicum-mediterraneum*, 13, 1. [Syr]

RR1096. Bencin, Rok: "Rethinking Representation in Ontology and Aesthetics Via Badiou and Rancière." *Theory, Culture & Society*, 36, 5, 95-112. [UaB]

RR1097. Bustamante, Óscar P.: "Das Dilemma der Liebe und die Poetik der Aufrichtigkeit. Heinrich Heine und Alain Badiou." *Auc Interpretationes*, 8, 1, 66-79. [WC]

RR1098. Carvalho, Wanderley M., & Neto O. França: "Singular e Universal em Alain Badiou e a Hipótese da Cientificidade da Psicanálise." *Psicologia Usp*, 30. [RIT]

RR1099. Denkova, Lidia: "Alain Badiou – Philosophical Tango with the Elusive Theatre." *Sledva: Journal for University Culture*, 39, 14-15. [LoC]

RR1100. Eckstrand, Nathan: "Does Fidelity to Revolutionary Truths Undo Itself?" *Radical Philosophy Review*, 22, 1, 59-84. [WC]

RR1101. Filloy, Constanza: "La Introducción del Vacío en la Filosofía de Alain Badiou: Sobre la Transformación de la Cuestión de lo Uno y lo Múltiple." *Revista de Filosofía Diánoia*, 64, 83, 153. [UaB]

RR1102. Giannakakis, Vangelis: "Adorno, Badiou and the Politics of Breaking Out." *Theory & Event*, 22, 1, 18-43. [PrQ]

RR1103. Gordienko, Andrey: "The Cause of the People: Sartre's Encounter with Lacan in Badiou's Theory of the Subject." *Paragraph*, 42, 2, 188-204. [Naz]

RR1104. Griffith, James: "A Cartesian Rereading of Badiou's Political Subjectivity." *Philosophy Today*, 63, 1, 93-100. [RIT]

RR1105. Hong, Kisook: "The Concept of Truth and Subject in Alain Badiou - Beyond Lacan." *Phenomenology and Contemporary Philosoph*, 80, 33-55. [WC]

RR1106. Idziak, Urszula, & Bartosz P. Bednarczyk: "The Noble Family As 'Singular Multiplicity'? Redefining the Smoczynski–Zarycki's Totemic Definition of Nobility Through the Lenses of Alain Badiou's Mathematical Ontology." *Acta Universitatis Sapientiae, Social Analysis*, 9, 1, 53-69. [Naz]

RR1107. Jansen, Stef: "Anthropological (In)fidelities to Alain Badiou." *Anthropological Theory*, 19, 2, 238-258. [RIT]

RR1108. Kobialka, Michal: "'In Praise of Theatre' by Alain Badiou (Review)." *Cultural Critique*, 102, 1, 211-221. [UaB]

RR1109. Kulik, Karyna: "Alain Badiou's Concept of Ethics." *Cherkasy University Bulletin: Philosophy*, 1, 88-92. [WC]

RR1110.   Luzar, Robert: "The Multiplicity of (Un-)Thought: Badiou, Deleuze, Event." *Comparative and Continental Philosophy*, *11*, 3, 251-264. [Cor]

RR1111.   Madarasz, Norman R.: "Bioética das Verdades e a Exceção Imanente: Sobre Política, Matemática e Ética no Sistema Filosófico de Alain Badiou." *Veritas (Porto Alegre)*, *64*, 3, 35598. [Syr]

RR1112.   McGill, Kenneth: "Ontology, Belief and the Politics of Sanction: An Application of Badiou's Theory of the Event." *Anthropological Theory*, *19*, 2, 259-78. [PrQ]

RR1113.   Paccoud, Antoine: "Badiou, Haussmann and Saint-Simon: Opening Spaces for the State and Planning between 'Post-Politics' and Urban Insurgencies." *Planning Theory*, *18*, 3, 339-358. [UofR]

RR1114.   Pocius, K.: "The Subject and the Real: Ethical Implications of A. Badiou's Philosophy." *Problemos*, 96, 71-82. [UaB]

RR1115.   Portela, Luciana: "Dina Dreyfus, Alain Badiou e os Programas de Filosofia da Rádio-Televisão Escolar Francesa nos Anos 1960. Entrevista com Alain Badiou." *Anuário Antropológico*, 1, 331-346. [Cor]

RR1116.   Varela, Pequeño M.: "Los Fundamentos Onto-Lógicos de la Metafísica de Alain Badiou: La Relación Entre Ser y Ser-Ahí." *Logos*, 52, 139-159. [Naz]

RR1117.   Vlieghe, Joris, & Piotr Zamojski: "Out of Love for Some-Thing: An Ontological Exploration of the Roots of Teaching with Arendt, Badiou and Scheler." *Journal of Philosophy of Education*, *53*, 3, 518-30. [PrQ]

RR1118.   Yi, Sohyon: "A Study on the Religious Imagination in Yi Chung-Jun's Come Low Unto Us - Focusing on Alain Badiou and Eric L. Santner's Philosophical View." *Comparative Korean Studies*, *27*, 3, 193-223. [LoC]

BANCQUART, Marie-Claire.
RR1119.   ● Bancquart, Marie-Claire: *Toute Minute Est Première*. [Bègles]: Le Castor Astral. 207p. [WC]

RR1120.   ● Bancquart, Marie-Claire, & Claude Ber: *Toute Minute Est Première: Suivi de Tout Derniers Poèmes: Anthologie Personnelle*. Bègles: Le Castor Astral. 207p. [WC]

RR1121.   ● Bancquart, Marie-Claire, de B. A. Préta, & Marie-Claire Bancquart: *Terre Énergumène: Précédé de dans Le Feuilletage de la Terre et de Verticale du Secret*. Paris: Gallimard. 398p. [WC]

RR1122.   Bonhomme, Béatrice: "Marie-Claire Bancquart (1932-2019): L'Ouverture de l'Être au Monde vers un Infini Poétique." *Hermès*, *84*, 2, 229. [UofR]

BARBUSSE, Henri.
See also 377, 408, 418.
RR1123.   Bălă, Laurenţiu: "Le Poilu en Traduction Roumaine. Étude de Cas: Le Feu d'Henri Barbusse." *Linguistica*, *58*, 1, 77-87. [Naz]

BARILIER, Étienne.
RR1124.   ● Barilier, Etienne: *Alfred Métraux: Ou la Terre Sans Mal*. Lausanne: Presses Polytechniques et Universitaires Romandes. *Le Savoir Suisse*, 142. 167p. [WC]

BARON SUPERVIELLE, Silvia.
See 201, 653, 655.

BARRAULT, Jean-Louis.

RR1125. • Londré, Felicia H.: *Barrault; Mnouchkine; Stein.* New York: Metheun Drama. 242p. [WC]

RR1126. Bovet, Jeanne, Marie-Madeleine Mervant-Roux, & Pascal Lécroart: "'Langage Insolite' ou 'Langage Naturel'? Jean-Louis Barrault et Antoine Vitez Face au Verset Claudélien." *Revue Sciences/ Lettres*, 6. [WC]

BARRÈS, Maurice.

See also 325, 364, 378, 493.

RR1127. • Desclaux, Jessica: *L'Orient des Écrivains et des Savants à l'Épreuve de la Grande Guerre: Autour d''Une Enquête aux Pays de Levant' de Maurice Barrès.* Grenoble: UGA. 181p. [Cor]

RR1128. Desclaux, Jessica: "Le Musée du Louvre dans la Cartographie Artistique et Idéologique de Maurice Barrès." *Revue d'Histoire Littéraire de la France, 119*, 3, 533-552. [RIT]

RR1129. Leymarie, M.: "Sur l'Antisémitisme de Maurice Barrès (1): De l'Enfance à la Veille de l'Affaire Dreyfus." *Archives Juives, 52*, 1, 125-143. [Cor]

RR1130. Paigneau, David: "Du Moi Comme Apophatisme: Maurice Barrès, Emil Cioran, Philippe Muray." *Anales de Filología Francesa, 27*, 1, 217-242. [Naz]

RR1131. Shervashidse, Vera V.: "Paul Claudel's Cosmism and Maurice Barres's Egotism." *Studia Litterarum, 4*, 2, 144-161. [Cor]

BARTHES, Roland.

See also 10, 440, 516, 517, 535, 564, 580, 613.

RR1132. • Baldwin, Thomas: *Roland Barthes: The Proust Variations.* Liverpool: Liverpool UP. 189p. [Cor]

RR1133. • Barthes, Roland: *Les Cours et les Séminaires de Roland Barthes: La Préparation du Roman: Cours au Collège de France (1978-1979 et 1979-1980).* Paris: Points. 741p. [WC]

RR1134. • Bishop, Ryan, Sunil Manghani, Victor Burgin, Christine Berthin, & Sean Cubitt: *Seeing Degree Zero: Barthes/Burgin and Political Aesthetics.* Edinburgh: Edinburgh UP. 440p. [Syr]

RR1135. • Carluccio, Daniele: *Roland Barthes Lecteur.* Paris: Hermann. 340p. [UofR]

RR1136. • Diaz, José-Luis, & Mathilde Labbé: *Les XIXe Siècles de Roland Barthes.* Bruxelles: Les Impressions Nouvelles. 272p. [Cor]

RR1137. • Ffrench, Patrick: *Roland Barthes and FLM. Myth, Eroticism and Poetics.* London: Bloomsbury Academic. 320p. [WC]

RR1138. • Guittard, Jacqueline, Émeric Nicolas, & Mark Antaki: *Barthes Face à la Norme: Droit, Pouvoir, Autorité et Langage(s).* Paris: Mare et Martin. 340p. [LoC]

RR1139. • Irala-Hortal, Pilar: *El Síndrome de Barthes: La Construcción Retórica de la Imagen Fotográfica.* Madrid: Fragua. 189p. [WC]

RR1140. • Meng, Qingya: *L'Échec du Voyage en Chine (1974), de Sollers, Kristeva, Pleynet et Barthes.* Paris: Complicités. 187p. [WC]

RR1141. • Messager, Mathieu: *Roland Barthes.* Paris: Que Sais-Je?.127p. [Cor]

RR1142. Alves, Ana M.: "L'Empreinte de Roland Barthes sur l'Univers Frontalier Hustonien." *Quêtes Littéraires*, 9. [WC]

RR1143. Araujo, Rodrigo C.: "Poligrafias de Barthes." *Revista Mosaicum, 30*, 30, 15-32. [WC]

RR1144. "Badmington, Neil. The Afterlives of Roland Barthes." *Forum for Modern Language Studies*, *55*, 1, 117. [UaB]

RR1145. Bastos, Almir S., & Junior E. G. Melgar: "A Relevância Filosófica do Conceito de Neutro de Roland Barthes." *Relacult. 5*, 1. [WC]

RR1146. Beaudin, Pearson N.: "Merleau-Ponty and Barthes on Image Consciousness: Probing the (Im)Possibility of Meaning." *Dianoia: the Undergraduate Philosophy Journal of Boston College*, *6*, 1, 8-18. [WC]

RR1147. Benhaïm, André: "Barthes on the Beach." *The Yearbook of Comparative Literature*, 62, 162-173. [UofR]

RR1148. Brandini, Laura T.: "Autoridade e Alteridade na China de Roland Barthes." *Revista Letras Raras*, *8*, 4. [WC]

RR1149. Brazil, Kevin: "W. G. Sebald's Revisions of Roland Barthes." *Textual Practice*, *33*, 4, 567-584. [UaB]

RR1150. Broclain, Elsa, Benoît Haug, Pénélope Patrix, & Cécile Raulet: "Claude Coste et Sylvie Douche (éds.), Barthes et la Musique: Rennes, PUR, 2018." *Transposition*, 8. [WC]

RR1151. Coste, Claude: "Roland Barthes: Création, Émotion, Jouissance." *French Studies*, *73*, 2, 318-319. [UofR]

RR1152. Coste, Claude: "Roland Barthes: Le Regard du Caméléon." *Faux Titre*, 434, 244-263. [UaB]

RR1153. De Paula, J. R.: "Exercícios de Aproximação: A Experiência Literária a Partir de Roland Barthes e Maria Gabriela Llansol." *Revista Letras Raras*, *8*, 4. [WC]

RR1154. De Pourcq, M. J. G. M.: "Travel, Classicism and Writing in Barthes's 'En Grèce'." *Barthes Studies*, 5, 23-52. [WC]

RR1155. Di Sevo, R. D.: "A Era Das Cartas: O Diário da Procura de Compagnon por Barthes." *Palimpsesto*, 18, 30. [WC]

RR1156. Díaz, Valentín: "Roland Barthes, Vita Nova. Santiago de Chile, Marginalia, 2018, 72 Páginas." *Orbis Tertius*, 24, 30. [Naz]

RR1157. Duarte, Miguel M.: "Photography and Writing, or the Intimacy of the Image: A Dialogic Encounter between Barthes's Camera Lucida and Blanchot's Philosophy of Otherness." *Photographies*, *12*, 3, 283-301. [Syr]

RR1158. Echazarreta, Carmen: "Reseña Del Libro La Cámara Lúcida. De Roland Barthes." *Communication Papers*, 8, 17. [WC]

RR1159. Emery, Jacob: "Introduction: Thinking with Roland Barthes's Mythologies: Fifty Years After 1968 and Four Hundred Years Before." *The Yearbook of Comparative Literature*, 62, 1-20. [UofR]

RR1160. Facioni, S.: "La Parola Scissa. Certeau E Barthes Interpreti Di Ignazio Di Loyola." *Bollettino Filosofico*, 34, 170-178. [WC]

RR1161. Ferraz, Bruna F.: "Roland Barthes e Italo Calvino: Leitores do Japão." *Revista Letras Raras*, *8*, 4. [WC]

RR1162. Ferraz, Paulo P.: "As Metalinguagens de Roland Barthes." *Remate de Males*, *39*, 2, 849-866. [WC]

RR1163. García, Hubard G.: "Quizás . . . Barthes y Derrida." *Acta Poética*, *40*, 1, 63-85. [WC]

RR1164.   Garcia-Catalan, S., T. Sorolla-Romero, & M. Martin-Nunez: "Reclaiming Detail: Barthesian Subtleties and Catalysis in Tv Fiction." *Palabra Clave*, *22*, 3, 711-739. [Naz]

RR1165.   Haustein, K.: "How to Be Alone with Others: Plessner, Adorno, and Barthes on Tact." *Modern Language Review*, *114*, 1, 1-21. [RIT]

RR1166.   Kim, Hui-Teak: "A Study on the Formation and Development of the Concept of Translinguistics: Focusing on the Discussions of Saussure, Benveniste and Barthes." *Semiotic Inquiry*, 61, 37-68. [LoC]

RR1167.   Koike, H.: "The Noeme of Photography: The Paradigmatic Shift in the Photographic Theory of Roland Barthes." *Kunstiteaduslikke Uurimusi*, *28*, 3-4, 7-22. [PrQ]

RR1168.   Lasowski, Aliocha W.: "De Gide à Barthes, Carnets en Musique: La Petite Ritournelle du Journal." *Revue des Sciences Humaines*, 335, 149-162. [Syr]

RR1169.   Lèal, Alfredo: "El Fracaso de la Fotografía: Una Respuesta Intermedial al Programa Fenomenológico de Camera Lucida de Roland Barthes." *Fotocinema. Revista Científica de Cine y Fotografía*, 2, 19, 189. [Cor]

RR1170.   Lee, Kyungmin, & Taegu Lee: "Analysis of Gender Expression from 'Your Name' by Using Barthes's Semiotics." *The Journal of Image and Cultural Contents*, 16, 231-248. [WC]

RR1171.   Lopes, Luiz: "Roland Barthes Caminhando Contra os Absolutos." *Revista Letras Raras*, *8*, 4. [WC]

RR1172.   Marquez, I.: "'Roland Barthes and You Are Now Friends': Facebook and the Friendship Myth." *Signa*, 28, 937-957. [Syr]

RR1173.   Márquez, Israel: "'Roland Barthes y Tú Ahora Sois Amigos': Facebook y el Mito de la Amistad." *Signa*, 28, 937. [Syr]

RR1174.   Matei, Alex: "Roland Barthes et le Minimalisme Affectif Comme Signe d'Actualité." *Dacoromania Litteraria*, 5, 33-44. [WC]

RR1175.   Moudileno, Lydie: "Barthes's Black Soldier: the Making of a Mythological Celebrity." *The Yearbook of Comparative Literature*, 62, 57-72. [Naz]

RR1176.   Nugraha, D. N. S., & W Dyahrini: "Semiotic Analysis of Roland Barthes in Suluk Wujil by Sunan Bonang." *Journal of Advanced Research in Dynamical and Control Systems*, *11*, 3, 304-308. [WC]

RR1177.   Oliveira, Priscila, Ribeiro B. Costa, & Bylaardt C. Ottoni: "Uma Ferida no Coração do Amor: A Escrita no Diário de Luto de Roland Barthes." *Revista Letras Raras*, *8*, 4. [WC]

RR1178.   Pagan, N. O.: "Barthes the Phenomenologist and the Being of Literature." *Mosaic*, *52*, 1, 17-32. [UaB]

RR1179.   Phillips, Matt: "*Album: Unpublished Correspondence and Texts* by Roland Barthes (Review)." *French Studies*, *73*, 1, 142-143. [UofR]

RR1180.   Rabaté, Jean-Michel: "Barthes's Mythological 'Photogeny'." *The Yearbook of Comparative Literature*, 62, 104-119. [Naz]

RR1181.   Regis, J.: "The Notation in the Work of Barthes. Uses, Meanings and Variations." *Estudios de Teoria Literaria*, *8*, 16, 227-238. [WC]

RR1182.   Reisdoerfer, Hiago M.: "Fait Divers: As Contribuições De Roland Barthes Para O Jornalismo." *Temática*, *15*, 3. [WC]

RR1183.   Robinson, John T.: "Argument for Method: An Application of Barthes' Language Codes in Poetry." *Crossroads*, *26*, 3, 60-76. [Cor]

24059

RR1184.   Ronel, Yoav: "'Exiled from All Gregarity': Profane Love, Poetics and Political Imagination in Barthes and Agamben." *Theory Now. Journal of Literature, Critique, and Thought*, 2, 1. [WC]

RR1185.   Sari, Ika R., Muhammad Luthfie, & Koesworo Setiawan: "The Meaning of Journalist Independence in the Post Film (Roland Barthes' Semiotics Analysis)." *Jurnal Komunikatio*, 5, 1. [WC]

RR1186.   Sarvenaz, Safavi, & G. Ü. Agah: "Bringing Back the Image into its Frame: Barthes' Soldier and the Contextual Frame of Human Perception and Interpretation of Signs." *Semiotica*, 229, 87-100. [PrQ]

RR1187.   Sirvent, Ramos A.: "Los Diarios de Roland Barthes." *Anales de Filología Francesa*, 27, 1, 331-346. [Syr]

RR1188.   Swami, S.: "Barthes Tells the Story Wrong." *Poetry*, 214, 4. [Naz]

RR1189.   Szymon, Wróbel: "Roland Barthes Reads the Map and the Territory by Michel Houellebecq." *Philosophy Study*, 9, 12. [LoC]

RR1190.   Tan, Ian: "Thomas Gould, Silence in Modern Literature and Philosophy: Beckett, Barthes, Nancy, Stevens." *The Wallace Stevens Journal*, 43, 2, 277-278. [Naz]

RR1191.   Teixeira, Derick D. S.: "Walter Benjamin e Roland Barthes Às Margens da Escritura." *Cadernos Benjaminianos*, 14, 1, 87. [WC]

RR1192.   Tenev, Darin: "Language Models and the Study of Literature (Bulgarian Guillaumist School Versus Roland Barthes and the Saussurean Legacy)." *History of Humanities*, 4, 2, 389-400. [UaB]

RR1193.   Varga, Z. Z.: "Description Degree Zero and the Un-Reality Effect: Roland Barthes on Description." *Primerjalna Knjizevnost*, 42, 2, 91-104. [Naz]

RR1194.   Vizzardelli, S.: "Erotismo Della Morte o Ciclo di Isteresi. La Perversione Tra Barthes e Deleuze." *Aut Aut.* 382, 91-105. [Syr]

RR1195.   Wahnon, S.: "On Interpretation in Barthes: Towards a Plural Hermeneutics." *Rilce*, 1, 17-42. [Naz]

RR1196.   Wampole, Christy: "Poujade's Infowars: On Barthes's Anti-Anti-Intellectualism." *The Yearbook of Comparative Literature*, 62, 73-103. [Naz]

RR1197.   Wardiani, Sri R.: "Muslimah's Clothing Brand, Identity, and Myths in Barthes Semiotic Study." *El Harakah (Terakreditasi)*, 21, 1, 83. [RIT]

RR1198.   Weller, Shane: "Active Philology: Barthes and Nietzsche." *French Studies*, 73, 2, 217-233. [UaB]

RR1199.   Wermer-Colan, Alex: "Roland Barthes After 1968: Critical Theory in the Reactionary Era of New Media." *The Yearbook of Comparative Literature*, 62, 133-156. [Naz]

RR1200.   Wilson, H. R.: "The Theatricality of Grief: Suspending Movement, Mourning and Meaning with Roland Barthes." *Performance Research*, 24, 4, 103-109. [Cor]

RR1201.   Wismanto, Agus: "Strukturalisme Mistik: Tahayul/ Mitos/ Dongeng de Saussure (1857-1913) & Roland Barthes (1915-1980)." *Sasindo*, 6, 1. [WC]

RR1202.   Yustiana, Melia, & Ahmad Junaedi: "Representasi Feminisme Dalam Film Marlina Si Pembunuh Dalam Empat Babak (Analisis Semiotika Roland Barthes)." *Koneksi*, 3, 1, 118. [WC]

BATAILLE, Georges.
See also 403, 434, 711, 727, 745, 2913.

RR1203.   ● Lippi, Silvia: *Trasgressioni: Bataille, Lacan.* Napoli: Orthotes. 234p. [WC]

RR1204.   ● Marczuk, Monika, & Nicola Apicella: *Cahiers Bataille: Dictionnaire Critique de Georges Bataille.* Meurcourt: Editions les Cahiers. 303p. [BnF]

RR1205.   ● Romano, Onofrio: *Georges Bataille: Depensare la Crescita.* Milano: Jaca Book. 80p. [WC]

RR1206.   André, Tobias: "Georges Bataille: Tant de Traces du Temps à Lascaux." *Annales Littéraires de l'Université de Besançon,* 995, 131-138. [LoC]

RR1207.   Austin, Guy: "The Stink of the Sacred: A Bataillean Reading of Gainsbourg's Film Je T'aime Moi Non Plus." *French Cultural Studies, 30,* 1, 34-43. [RIT]

RR1208.   Benedetti, Francesco: "Jacqueline Risset, Georges Bataille." *Rivista di Letterature Moderne e Comparate, 72,* 4, 437-438. [Syr]

RR1209.   Chaouat, Bruno: "De Immundo: Georges Bataille's Gnostic Existentialism." *Yale French Studies,* 135, 249. [PrQ]

RR1210.   Chen, Meng-Shi: "The Quest for Ecstatic Sovereignty: Georges Bataille's Obsession with the Lingchi Photos." *Culture and Dialogue, 7,* 2, 213-236. [LoC]

RR1211.   Louette, Jean-François: "'Jean Lombre' ou les Amis Déconcertés Georges Ambrosino et Georges Bataille, L'Expérience à l'Épreuve. Correspondance et Inédits (1943-1960)." *Critique, 75,* 864, 451-459. [UaB]

RR1212.   Luna, V. S.: "Politics of Creation. the Persistence of Surrealism in the Readings of Walter Benjamin, Maurice Blanchot, & Georges Bataille." *Literatura: Teoria, Historia, Critica, 21,* 1, 197-223. [Naz]

RR1213.   Mohamed, Ahmed: "La Contagion Psychique de La Haine Familiale dans les Fictions de Georges Bataille: Une Exploration Psychanalytique." *Le Divan Familial, 42,* 1, 85. [Cor]

RR1214.   Moraes, Marcelo J.: "Sobre a Mesa de Mármore do Café, uma Iguaria Canibal: Perspectivas do Olho, Entre Walter Benjamin e Georges Bataille." *Ars (São Paulo), 17,* 36, 57-78. [Syr]

RR1215.   Morais, Vasques P.: "O Erotismo Como Experiência Infinita, em Georges Bataille." *Sapere Aude, 10,* 19, 398-406. [WC]

RR1216.   Mosquera, Varas A. C.: "Ezquerra, J. Y Fortanet, J.(eds.), La Luz de un Gran Frío. Ensayos Sobre Georges Bataille, Madrid, Ediciones Casus-Belli, 2017. 245 pp." *Anales del Seminario de Historia de la Filosofía, 36,* 1, 271-275. [Naz]

RR1217.   Pytko, Mateusz: "'I Did Myself as a Dog'. Leo Lipski's Piotruś in the Light (and Darkness) of the Henri Bergson's and Georges Bataille's Theories of Laughter." *Tekstualia, 4,* 59, 95-116. [LoC]

RR1218.   Ribeiro, Rodrigues Tadeu: "Por um Antropomorfismo Dilacerado: Georges Bataille e a Arte Contemporânea." *Analógos, 19,* 1. [WC]

RR1219.   Rose, Mitch: "The Diversity We Are Given: Community Economies and the Promise of Bataille." *Antipode, 51,* 1, 316-333. [UaB]

RR1220.   Santiago, Tainá M. S., & Natanael D. Azevedo: "O Discurso Sobre Reprodução entre Filosofias E Pinturas: De Georges Bataille a Francisco Brennand." *Revista Philia | Filosofia, Literatura & Arte, 1,* 1, 202-219. [WC]

RR1221.   Taylor, Leila: "The Amorous Annihilation of Will: An Examination of Georges Bataille's Death & Sensuality through Bryan Fuller's Hannibal." *Horror Studies, X,* 1, 45-59. [PrQ]

RR1222.   Tremblais, M.: "El Concepto de Heterología a Través de la Presencia de lo Abyecto en Histoire de l'Œil u Madame Edwarda de Georges Bataille." *Cedille*, 16, 427-449. [Syr]

RR1223.   Weeks, Harry: "'The Weapons of Our Adversaries': Georges Bataille's Analysis of Fascism and Community." *Third Text*, *33*, 3, 337-353. [UofR]

RR1224.   Zenck, Martin: "'Y A-T-Il une Musique Érotique?'": Überlegungen auf der Grundlage Unveröffentlichter Dokumente von Georges Bataille und René Leibowitz im Umfeld der Französischen Philosophie und Anthropologie." *Archiv Für Musikwissenschaft*, *76*, 1, 56-77. [WC]

BAUCHAU, Henry.
See also 431, 679.

RR1225.   Lambert, Jérémy: "L'Écriture en Chantier. Les Projets Dramaturgiques d'Henry Bauchau (1950-1970)." *Revue Internationale Henry Bauchau. L'Écriture à l'Écoute*, 7, 141-160. [WC]

RR1226.   Meurée, Christophe: "Des Fenêtres sur l'Infini? Usages du Cahier dans la Construction de la Posture chez Henry Bauchau." *Études Littéraires*, 48, 103-118. [UaB]

RR1227.   Watthee-Delmotte, M.: "La 'Parole Profonde' d'Henry Bauchau, entre Littérature et Psychanalyse. Éléments de Sémiologie du Spirituel." *Rivista di Storia e Letteratura Religiosa*, *55*, 3, 531-543. [UofR]

BAUDRILLARD, Jean.
RR1228.   ● Baudrillard, Jean: *Entretiens: 1968-2008*. Paris: PUF. 426p. [Cor]

RR1229.   ● *Dossier Zu: Sprache - Poesie, Baudrillard*. [Köln]: [Performance-Archiv "Die Schwarze Lade"]. 1 vol. [WC]

RR1230.   ● Guillaume, Marc: *La Philosophie Poétique de Jean Baudrillard*. Paris: Descartes & Cie. 91p. [Cor]

RR1231.   ● Proto, Francesco: *Baudrillard for Architects*. London: Routledge. 126p. [Syr]

RR1232.   ● Tramontana, Antonio: *I Cristalli Della Società: Simmel, Benjamin, Gehlen, Baudrillard e l'Esistenza Multiforme degli Oggetti*. Milano: Meltemi. 209p. [LoC]

RR1233.   Agbisit, G. C.: "The Poetry of Theory: Jean Baudrillard's Philosophy as Fiction." *Forum for World Literature Studies*, *11*, 3, 390-401. [UaB]

RR1234.   Athes, Haralambie: "Baudrillard, Sepultura and Steve Cutts' Animation. Dystopian Common Ground." *Hermeneia*, 22, 173-80. [PrQ]

RR1235.   Barranque, Pierre-Ulysse: "Généalogie de l'Écriture de Jean Baudrillard." *Remate de Males*, *39*, 2, 867-881. [WC]

RR1236.   Conan, Catherine, Flore Coulouma, & Julie Lecas: "Hedda Friberg-Harnesk, Reading John Banville Through Jean Baudrillard." *Études Irlandaises*, *44*, 1, 157-159. [UaB]

RR1237.   González, de R. J.: "La Muerte de Baudrillard no ha Tenido Lugar. Análisis de Obituarios en Tres Diarios Españoles." *Revista Chakiñan de Ciencias Sociales y Humanidades*, 7, 70-83. [WC]

RR1238.   Herrera-Aliaga, Eduardo: "Simulación Clínica y Jean Baudrillard." *Revista Latinoamericana de Simulación Clínica*, *1*, 2, 67-68. [WC]

RR1239.   King, Matthew J.: "Object-Oriented Baudrillard? Withdrawal and Symbolic Exchange." *Open Philosophy*, 2, 1, 75-85. [WC]

RR1240.   Miller, Paul A.: "Review: Jean Baudrillard: The Rhetoric of Symbolic Exchange, by Brian Gogan." *Rhetorica*, *37*, 3, 323-325. [Naz]

RR1241.   Mukhlis, M. I., & Naupal: "Globalization, Terrorism, and Morality: A Critique of Jean Baudrillard." *Intellectual Discourse*, *27*, 1, 89-108. [Syr]

RR1242.   Novikov, V., & S. Kovaleva: "Hyperreality, Simulacra and Simulations in Virtual Space as a Phenomenon of 'Antisocial' Theory by Jean Baudrillard." *Digital Sociology*, *2*, 1, 39-45. [WC]

RR1243.   Purwanti, S., & M. Mas'ud: "Consumption Practice in the Baudrillard Perspective." *Russian Journal of Agricultural and Socio-Economic Sciences*, *86*, 2, 40-50. [Syr]

RR1244.   Richmond, J. C., & D. V. Porpora: "Entertainment Politics as a Modernist Project in a Baudrillard World." *Communication Theory*, *29*, 4, 421-440. [RIT]

RR1245.   Slovic, Srdan: "Baudrillard's Concept of Simulation in the Era of Mass Culture." *Bastina*, 49, 167-175. [WC]

RR1246.   Tamatea, Laurence: "Compulsory Coding in Education: Liberal-Humanism, Baudrillard and the 'Problem' of Abstraction." *Research and Practice in Technology Enhanced Learning*, *14*, 1, 1-29. [Naz]

RR1247.   Tillería, Aqueveque L.: "Baudrillard. Filosofía de la Seducción." *Revista Humanidades*, *9*, 2, 1-21. [Cor]

RR1248.   Violeau, Jean-Louis: "1987: Baudrillard et les Monstres Architecturaux." *Moniteur Architecture*, 278, 18-19. [Cor]

BEAUCHEMIN, Yves.
See 494.

BEAULIEU, Victor-Lévy.
RR1249.   ● Hamel, Yan: *Les Cahiers Victor-Levy Beaulieu, Numero 7: 666-Friedrich Nietzsche*. Montréal: Nota Bene. 196p. [BAnQ]

BEAUSOLEIL, Claude.
See 263.

BEAUVOIR, Simone de.
See also 301, 313, 323, 330, 331, 766, 3164.
RR1250.   ● Badinter, Élisabeth, Laurent Greilsamer, & Nancy Huston: *Simone de Beauvoir: Les Clefs de la Liberté*. La Tour-d'Aigue: Éditions de L'Aube. 88p. [BAnQ]

RR1251.   ● Bair, Deirdre: *Parisian Lives: Samuel Beckett, Simone de Beauvoir, and Me: A Memoir*. New York: Nan A. Talese. 347p. [Syr]

RR1252.   ● Baudouin, Caroline: *Simone de Beauvoir: Philosophe et Féministe pour une Pensée de La Liberté*. Vallet: M-editer. 59. [BnF]

RR1253.   ● Bertini, Marie-Joseph, Odile Gannier, & Magali Guaresi: *Simone de Beauvoir: Les Réceptions Contemporaines de l'Œuvre de Simone de Beauvoir en Méditerranée*. Lyon: Sens Public – Puzzle. 277p. [WC]

RR1254.   ● Castellarnau, Ariadna: *Simone de Beauvoir*. Barcelona: RBA Coleccionables. 189p. [WC]

RR1255. ● González, Alicia: *Simone de Beauvoir*. [Madrid]: Prisanoticias Colecciones. 141p. [WC]

RR1256. ● Hagengruber, Ruth, & Catherine Newmark: "Philosophinnen: Eine Andere Geschichte des Denkens: Von Hypatia von Alexandrien, Hildegard von Bingen, Émilie du Châtelet, Mary Wollstonecraft, Simone Weil, Harriet Taylor Mill, Hannah Arendt, Simone de Beauvoir Bis Donna Haraway und Judith Butler." *Philosophie Magazin. Sonderausgabe.* Berlin: Philomagazin. 146p. [WC]

RR1257. ● Kirkpatrick, Kate K. Cluck: *Becoming Beauvoir: A Life*. London: Bloomsbury. 496p. [UofR]

RR1258. ● López, Rodríguez S.: *El Devenir "Mujer" en Simone de Beauvoir*. [Madrid]: Dos Bigotes. 143p. [WC]

RR1259. ● Louette, Jean-François: *Sartre et Beauvoir, Roman et Philosophie*. Genève: La Baconnière. 339p. [Cor]

RR1260. ● Naïr, Sami, & Hernández I. Clavero: *Acompañando a Simone de Beauvoir: Mujeres, Hombres, Igualdad*. Barcelona: Galaxia Gutenberg. 213p. [WC]

RR1261. ● Nya, Nathalie: *Simone de Beauvoir and the Colonial Experience: Freedom, Violence, and Identity*. Lanham, MD: Lexington Books. 99p. [Syr]

RR1262. ● Sánchez, Vegara M. I., & Christine Roussey: *Simone de Beauvoir*. Paris: Kimane. 1 vol. [WC]

RR1263. ● *Say's Who? Simone de Beauvoir*. Brooklyn: Quimby's Bookstore NYC. [24]p. [WC]

RR1264. ● Touya de Marenne, E.: *Simone de Beauvoir: Le Combat au Féminin*. Paris: Presses Universitaires de France/ Humensis. 127p. [BAnQ]

RR1265. Adams, Martin: "Simone de Beauvoir: Existential Philosophy and Human Development." *Existential Analysis*, 30, 1, 80-93. [RIT]

RR1266. Altman, Meryl: "'The Past Is an Appeal': Simone de Beauvoir Studies 1983–2014." *Simone de Beauvoir Studies*, 30, 1, 148-176. [Cor]

RR1267. Anderson, Ellie: "From Existential Alterity to Ethical Reciprocity: Beauvoir's Alternative to Levinas." *Continental Philosophy Review*, 52, 2, 171-189. [UofR]

RR1268. Bandrés, Goldáraz E.: "Survival in the Tv Series 'La Que Se Avecina' of the Stereotypes against Women Denounced by Simone de Beauvoir." *Doxa Comunicación*, 29, 75-95. [WC]

RR1269. Barroso, Carmen: "As Ideias e os Ideais Que Definem uma Vida: Simone de Beauvoir e Carmen da Silva." *Cadernos Pagu*, 56. [Naz]

RR1270. Bernard, Marion: "La Subjectivation Dominée/ Dominante: Essai de Traduction des Phénoménologies de Simone de Beauvoir et Frantz Fanon." *Symposium*, 23, 1, 56-79. [UaB]

RR1271. Bernasconi, R.: "Richard Wright as Educator: The Progressive Structure of Simone de Beauvoir's Account of Racial Hatred in the United States." *Yale French Studies*, 135-136, 151-168. [UofR]

RR1272. Bolsarin, R., & P. Pinheiro: "The Practice of Vandalism in the Collaborative Writing Process of the Wikipedia Entry 'Simone de Beauvoir'." *Educacao e Sociedade*. 40. [Syr]

RR1273. Burke, Megan M.: "Beauvoirian Androgyny: Reflections on the Androgynous World of Fraternité in *The Second Sex*." *Feminist Theory*, 20, 1, 3-18. [PrQ]

RR1274. Campagnoli, Mabel A.: "¿Hay Alguien Ahí? Simone de Beauvoir Entre 'yo' y 'nosotras'." *Zona Franca*, 27, 87. [WC]

RR1275. Charbit, Denis: "Écrivaine, Engagée, Féministe: Les Trois Cercles de la Réception de Simone de Beauvoir en Israël." *Cahiers Sens Public*, 25-26, 3, 273. [Cor]

RR1276. De Landázuri, Carlos Ortiz: "Emancipatory Thinking. Simone de Beauvoir and Contemporary Political Thought." *Anuario Filosófico*, 52, 1, 217-20. [PrQ]

RR1277. De Saint Aubert, E., & Jennifer McWeeny: "The Blood of Others: Maurice Merleau-Ponty and Simone de Beauvoir." *Simone de Beauvoir Studies*, 30, 1, 33-65. [Cor]

RR1278. Dean, Jodi: "Politics with Beauvoir: Freedom in the Encounter." *Politics & Gender*, 15, 1. [Naz]

RR1279. Devi, Gayatri: "A Companion to Simone de Beauvoir, by Laura Hengehold and Nancy Bauer, Eds." *Simone de Beauvoir Studies*, 30, 1, 200-206. [Cor]

RR1280. Elsner, Anna M.: "Beyond Medical Paternalism: Undoing the Doctor-Patient Relationship in Simone de Beauvoir's *A Very Easy Death.*" *Literature and Medicine*, 37, 2, 420-441. [UaB]

RR1281. Esposti, Chiara D.: "Wandering Women: Feminist Urban Experiences in Simone de Beauvoir and Elena Ferrante." *Annali D'Italianistica*, 37, 153-176. [UofR]

RR1282. Evans, Mary: "Becoming Beauvoir: A Life: By Kate Kirkpatrick, London and New York, Bloomsbury, 2019, xiv + 476pp., £20.00 (Hardback), ISBN 978-1-3500-4717-4." *Women's History Review*, 17 December, 1-2. [UaB]

RR1283. Falantin, Flavien: "Le Privilège de Simone de Beauvoir by Geneviève Fraisse." *The French Review*, 92, 4, 200-201. [RIT]

RR1284. Frouard, Hélène: "Simone de Beauvoir. L'Aventure d'Être Soi." *Sciences Humaines*, 318, 10, 35. [BAnQ]

RR1285. Gianoncelli, Ève: "We're Not Beauvoirians, But: Conservative (Anti)Feminist Intellectuals and the Rejection and Appropriation of Simone de Beauvoir, Her Thought, and Her Legacy." *Cahiers Sens Public*, 25-26, 3, 251. [Cor]

RR1286. Giovanini, V.: "Alterity in Simone de Beauvoir and Emmanuel Levinas: From Ambiguity to Ambivalence." *Hypatia*, 34, 1, 39-58. [PrQ]

RR1287. Hubert, Marie-Claude: "Réception Croisée du Deuxième Sexe de Simone de Beauvoir Par la Philosophe Geneviève Fraisse et Annie Ernaux." *Cahiers Sens Public*, 25-26, 3, 149. [Cor]

RR1288. "International Simone de Beauvoir Society." *Simone de Beauvoir Studies*, 30, 1, 210. [Cor]

RR1289. Jeannelle, Jean-Louis: "Simone de Beauvoir et l'Autobiographie Existentialiste': Une Réévaluation." *Simone de Beauvoir Studies*, 30, 1, 67-86. [Cor]

RR1290. Jones, Janine: "When Black Female Presence in Beauvoir's *L'Invitée* Is (Seemingly) Not Invited to the Second Sex." *Simone de Beauvoir Studies*, 30, 1, 87-109. [Cor]

RR1291. Kail, Michel: "Mémoires, t. I. et t. II, by Simone de Beauvoir." *Simone de Beauvoir Studies*. 30, 1, 181-192. [Cor]

RR1292. Knowles, Charlotte: "Beauvoir on Women's Complicity in Their Own Unfreedom." *Hypatia*, 34, 2, 242-265. [UofR]

RR1293.   Kruks, Sonia: "Book Review: Politics with Beauvoir: Freedom in the Encounter, by Lori Jo Marso." *Political Theory*, 47, 1, 121-126. [UofR]

RR1294.   Kryvoruchko, S., & T. Fomenko: "The Image of Laurence in the Novel Simone de Beauvoir 'Magic Pictures'." *Journal of Social Sciences Research*, 5, 2, 400-407. [WC]

RR1295.   La Caze, M.: "Note from the Book Review Editor / Note de la Responsable des Recensions." *Simone de Beauvoir Studies*, 30, 1, 177-179. [Cor]

RR1296.   Le Bon, B. S., Margaret A. Simons, Julie Augras, & Alice Schwarzer: "Simone de Beauvoir (Dossier)." *Emma*, 342, Jan-Feb, 60-80. [WC]

RR1297.   Lennon, K., & A. Wilde: "Alienation and Affectivity: Beauvoir, Sartre and Levinas on the Ageing Body." *Sartre Studies International*, 25, 1, 35-51. [UaB]

RR1298.   Lombardi, Jamie: "Becoming Beauvoir: a Life." *The Philosophers' Magazine*, 87, 115-116. [Cor]

RR1299.   Luz, Karime S. O.: "The Death of the Other, the Death of the Self: A New Reading of Simone de Beauvoir's Novel *She Came to Stay*." *Taller de Letras*, 235-244. [Naz]

RR1300.   Mali, Mason Q.: "Politics with Beauvoir: Freedom in the Encounter, by Lori Jo Marso." *Simone de Beauvoir Studies*, 30, 1, 193-199. [Cor]

RR1301.   Mano, M. K.: "The Woman Destroyed: From Simone de Beauvoir to 'Gender Ideology'." *Cadernos Pagu*, 56. [Naz]

RR1302.   Masclanis, François: "Le Deuxième Sexe: Représentations Socio-Politiques des Critiques de l'Ouvrage de Simone de Beauvoir." *Cahiers Sens Public*, 25-26, 3, 37. [Cor]

RR1303.   Mathur, Isha: "From Ghoonghat to de Beauvoir." *Journal of Big History*, 3, 1, 165-178. [LoC]

RR1304.   Moricheau-Airaud, Bérengère: "La Manière dont Annie Ernaux Parle de Simone de Beauvoir dans Ses Récits." *Cahiers Sens Public*, 25-26, 3, 175. [Cor]

RR1305.   Moynagh, Patricia: "Appeals for Freedom: Lori Jo Marso's Politics with Beauvoir and Elaine Stavro's Emancipatory Thinking." *Theory & Event*, 22, 3, 772-8. [RIT]

RR1306.   Mussett, Shannon M.: "Simone de Beauvoir's Ethics." *The Philosophers' Magazine*, 84, 63-70. [Cor]

RR1307.   Nogueira, Caroline F., & Georges D. J. B. Boris: "Envelhecimento na Perspectiva Fenomenológico-Existencial de Sartre e de Beauvoir." *Revista de Psicología*, 28, 2. [Naz]

RR1308.   Nunn, E. N.: "Simone de Beauvoir: Le Combat au Féminin by Éric Touya de Marenne." *Women in French Studies*, 27, 1, 227-229. [Cor]

RR1309.   Pardina, Teresa L.: "El Bagaje Filosófico de Beauvoir." *Cadernos Pagu*, 56. [Naz]

RR1310.   Pettersen, Tove: "A Word from the President of the Society / Le Mot de la Présidente de La Société." *Simone de Beauvoir Studies*, 30, 1, 27-31. [Cor]

RR1311.   Pichova, D.: "Simone de Beauvoir: 'The Second Sex' - and the Curse of Translation." *Filosoficky Casopis*, 67, 2, 241-250. [UaB]

RR1312.   Popa, Elena: "Beauvoir's Ethics, Meaning, and Competition." *Human Affairs*, 29, 4, 425-433. [RIT]

RR1313.   Riding, Alan: "Parisian Lives Samuel Beckett, Simone de Beauvoir and Me: A Memoir by Deirdre Bair." *New York Times Book Review*, *124*, 49, 52. [UofR]

RR1314.   Rodgers, Catherine: "Simone de Beauvoir et Son Père: Un 'Amour de Tête' Déçu." *Nottingham French Studies*, *58*, 1, 28-43. [Syr]

RR1315.   Rodrigues, C.: "Being and Becoming: Butler Reads de Beauvoir." *Cadernos Pagu*, 56. [Naz]

RR1316.   Sanos, Sandrine: "Lori Jo Marso, Politics with Beauvoir: Freedom in the Encounter. Elaine Stavro, Emancipatory Thinking: Simone de Beauvoir and Contemporary Political Thought." *Perspectives on Politics*, *17*, 3, 861-862. [UofR]

RR1317.   Scrimieri, Maria G.: "Domestic Life and Food Practices: Simone de Beauvoir & Rossana Campo." *Cahiers Sens Public*, *25-26*, 3, 197. [Cor]

RR1318.   Seethaler, Ina C.: "Writing Feminist Lives: The Biographical Battles Over Betty Friedan, Germaine Greer, Gloria Steinem, and Simone de Beauvoir." *Life Writing*, *16*, 2, 297-300. [WC]

RR1319.   Simons, Margaret A.: "Beauvoir and the Second Sex: The Turning Point." *Simone de Beauvoir Studies*, *30*, 1, 127-147. [Cor]

RR1320.   Simons, Margaret A.: "Beauvoir's Long March." *Yale French Studies*, *135*, 63. [PrQ]

RR1321.   Strasser, Anne: "Simone de Beauvoir et Ses Lecteurs: De Personne à Personne." *Simone de Beauvoir Studies*. *30*, 1, 110-126. [Cor]

RR1322.   Stauder, Thomas: "Beauvoir, Simone de, (2018) Mémoires." *Thélème*, *34*, 1, 303-308. [Naz]

RR1323.   Vintges, K.: "Zur Ethik Bei Simone de Beauvoir." *Aus Politik und Zeitgeschichte*, *51*, 16, 30-33. [UofR]

BECKETT, Samuel.
See also 563, 717, 850, 1190, 1251, 1313, 2137, 2156.

RR1324.   ● Baetens, Jan, Géraldine David, Olivier Deprez, & Roby Comblain: *"Construction et Définition de la Noise Gravure", d'Après Film de Samuel Beckett.* Brussel: Uitg. Wittockiana en FRMK. 34p. [WC]

RR1325.   ● Beloborodova, Olga: *The Making of Samuel Beckett's Play/ Comédie and Film.* Brussel: UP Antwerp. 351p. [Cor]

RR1326.   ● Boulter, Jonathan: *Posthuman Space in Samuel Beckett's Short Prose.* Edinburgh: Edinburgh UP. 222p. [Syr]

RR1327.   ● Brown, Llewellyn: *Beckett, Lacan and the Gaze.* Stuttgart: Ibidem Verlag. 625p. [WC]

RR1328.   ● Crépu, Michel: *Beckett, 27 Juillet 1982, 11h30.* Paris: Arléa. 83p. [Cor]

RR1329.   ● Crosara, Davide: *Il Buco nel Cielo di Carta: Samuel Beckett e il Monodramma.* Canterano (RM): Aracne. 229p. [LoC]

RR1330.   ● Damas, Xavier: *Samuel Beckett, "Oh Les Beaux Jours" (1963).* Paris: Hatier. 79p. [WC]

RR1331.   ● Gesvret, Guillaume: *Beckett en Écho. Rapprochements Arts et Littérature.* Paris: Classiques Garnier. 401p. [WC]

RR1332.   ● Libera, Antoni, & Janusz Pyda: *Dialogues on Beckett: Whatever Happened to God?* London: Anthem Press. 182p. [Syr]

RR1333.   ● McNaughton, James: *Beckett's Political Aesthetic on the Interna-*

tional Stage =: *L'Esthétique Politique de Beckett sur la Scène Internationale*. Leiden: Brill. 329p. [WC]

RR1334. ● Mével, Yann, Patrick Marot, & Philippe Antoine: *Samuel Beckett et la Culture Française*. Paris: Classiques Garnier. 384p. [Cor]

RR1335. ● Montfort, Nick, & Hannes Bajohr: *Megawatt: Ein Deterministisch-Computergenerierter Roman, Passagen aus Samuel Beckett Watt Erweiternd*. Berlin: Frohmann/ 0x0a. 378p. [WC]

RR1336. ● Oppenheim, Lois, & Geneviève Chevallier: *En Compagnie de Samuel Beckett: In the Company of Samuel Beckett / Edited by Lois Oppenheim; Translated by Geneviève Chevallier*. Caen: Passage(s). 452p. [WC]

RR1337. ● Popovici-Toma, Cosmin: *Neutraliser l'Absolu:: Blanchot, Beckett et la Chose Littéraire*. Paris: Hermann. 371p. [WC]

RR1338. ● Rabaté, Jean-Michel: *The New Samuel Beckett Studies*. Cambridge: Cambridge UP. 269p. [UofR]

RR1339. ● Stewart, Paul: *Pop Beckett: Intersections with Popular Culture*. Stuttgart: Ibidem. 308p. [WC]

RR1340. Anghel, Camelia: "Reading Samuel Beckett's Endgame as a Tale of War." *Philologica Jassyensia*, *15*, 1, 15-24. [PrQ]

RR1341. Aryan, Arya: "The Late Style of Borges, Beckett, and Coetzee as Postmodernist Cynics." *Journal of Modern Literature*, *42*, 4, 192-195. [Naz]

RR1342. Barlow, Richard: "'Celticism, Ballad Transmission, and the Schizoid Voice: Ossianic Fragments in Owenson, Yeats, Joyce, and Beckett'." *Irish Studies Review*, *27*, 4, 473-492. [UaB]

RR1343. Campbell, Edward: "Samuel Beckett, Repetition and Modern Music. By John Mcgrath." *Music and Letters*, *100*, 3, 567-570. [UaB]

RR1344. Castaldo, Achille: "Beyond the Suffering of Being. Desire in Giacomo Leopardi and Samuel Beckett." *Italian Studies*, *74*, 1, 103-105. [Syr]

RR1345. Charliac, Lucile, & Geneviève Morel: "Introduction. Franz Kaltenbeck, Lecteur de Beckett." *Savoirs et Clinique*, *26*, 1, 7. [Cor]

RR1346. Chattopadhyay, A.: "'Before the Door That Opens on My Story': Samuel Beckett and Narrative as Detritus." *Language and Psychoanalysis*, *8*, 1, 69-82. [WC]

RR1347. Chattopadhyay, Arka: "Christopher Langlois Samuel Beckett and the Terror of Literature." *Modernism/ Modernity*, *26*, 1, 228-229. [UofR]

RR1348. Chiang, Michelle: "Samuel Beckett and Modernist Film Culture: Review of Samuel Beckett and Cinema." *Journal of Modern Literature*, *42*, 4, 189-191. [UofR]

RR1349. Clements, Charlie: "'Logoclasm in the Name of Beauty': Bersani and Beckett's Enigmatic Sociability." *Lit: Literature Interpretation Theory*, *30*, 4, 247-264. [Cor]

RR1350. Clerici, F. A.: "Encounters, in Spite of All Samuel Beckett and Paul Celan." *Enthymema*, 24, 375-389. [Syr]

RR1351. Coffey, Michael: "Conor Carville, Samuel Beckett and the Visual Arts." *Journal of Beckett Studies*, *28*, 2, 249-254. [Syr]

RR1352. Curran, Daniel: "Samuel Beckett and Europe: History, Culture, Tradition." *Irish Studies Review*, *27*, 2, 292-294. [UaB]

RR1353. Elhalawani, A.: "Beckett as Muse for Egyptian Playwrights." *Samuel Beckett Today - Aujourd'hui*, *31*, 2, 219-233. [UaB]

RR1354.　Esslin-Peard, Monica: "Book Review: John Mcgrath. Samuel Beckett, Repetition and Modern Music." *Psychology of Music*, *47*, 4, 615-617. [RIT]

RR1355.　Faziani, Peter: "Arthur Rose. Literary Cynics: Borges, Beckett, Coetzee. Bloomsbury, 2017." *Studies in 20th & 21st Century Literature*, 43, 2. [UofR]

RR1356.　Felner, Mira, & Di Brandt: "Beckett Meets Tourette." *Performing Arts Journal*, 121, 8-21. [WC]

RR1357.　Ferrini, Jean-Pierre: "Samuel Beckett Premier Amour." *Quinzaines*, *1209*, 24. [UaB]

RR1358.　Furlani, André: "Book Review: Samuel Beckett and the Terror of Literature." *The Comparatist*, 43, 382-385. [Naz]

RR1359.　Gardner, Colin: "Anthony Paraskeva Samuel Beckett and Cinema." *Modernism/ Modernity*, *26*, 1, 225-227. [UofR]

RR1360.　Germoni, K.: "La Dilution du Point ou le Travail du Point 'Cassant' dans l'Œuvre de Beckett." *Samuel Beckett Today - Aujourd'hui*, *31*, 1, 21-36. [RIT]

RR1361.　Girdwood, Megan: "'Danced through its Seven Phases': Samuel Beckett, Symbolism, and Stage Choreographies." *Journal of Modern Literature*, *42*, 4, 74-92. [PrQ]

RR1362.　Gouvard, Jean-Michel: "Beckett and French War Propaganda: A New Source for Waiting for Godot." *Journal of Romance Studies*, *19*, 1, 1-22. [Naz]

RR1363.　Gouvard, Jean-Michel: "Samuel Beckett Lecteur de l'Étranger." *Irish Journal of French Studies*, *19*, 1, 186-206. [WC]

RR1364.　Heffer, B.: "Beckett's Queer Atavism." *Estudios Irlandeses*, Special Issue, 78-91. [RIT]

RR1365.　Hensbergen, Rosa: "Dance X Fase X Quad: Choreographic Seeing in Lucinda Childs, Anne Teresa de Keersmaeker, and Samuel Beckett." *Tdr*, *63*, 3. [WC]

RR1366.　Hovind, Jacob: "Langlois, Christopher. Samuel Beckett and the Terror of Literature." *French Review*, *92*, 3, 215. [UofR]

RR1367.　Hulle, D. V.: "Beckett's Art of the Commonplace: the 'Sottisier' Notebook and Mirlitonnades Drafts." *Journal of Beckett Studies*, *28*, 1, 67-89. [Syr]

RR1368.　Hutchings, William: "The Importance of Cinema to Samuel Beckett." *James Joyce Literary Supplement*, *33*, 2, 4-5. [Naz]

RR1369.　Imbert, Claude: "Pourquoi Beckett?" *Critique*, *75*, 869, 852-858. [UaB]

RR1370.　Ionescu, Arleen: "The 'Differend' of Shoes: Van Gogh, Beckett, Wiesel, Levi, and Holocaust Museums." *Partial Answers*, *17*, 2, 255-277. [UaB]

RR1371.　Jeantroux, M.: "Samuel Beckett's Translations of Latin American Poets for Unesco." *Samuel Beckett Today - Aujourd'hui*, *31*, 1, 66-81. [UaB]

RR1372.　Jejcic, Marie: "Samuel Beckett, de Chutes en Saut. Tropologie et Topologie." *Journal Français de Psychiatrie*, *48*, 2, 83. [Cor]

RR1373.　Kaltenbeck, Franz: "La Psychanalyse depuis Samuel Beckett." *Savoirs et Clinique*, *26*, 1, 16. [Cor]

RR1374.　Kennedy, S.: "Beckett, Censorship and the Problem of Parody." *Estudios Irlandeses*, 104-114. [RIT]

RR1375.　Kennedy, Seán: "Mothering Molloy, or Beckett and Cutlery." *Journal of Beckett Studies*, *28*, 1, 35-51. [Syr]

RR1376.　Kho, Younghee: "Humans in the Food Economy: The Famine, Biopower, and Beckett's Imagination of Post-Colonial State in Watt." *English Studies*, *100*, 1, 75-89. [Naz]

RR1377. Kincaid, Andrew: "Beckett's Political Imagination by Emilie Morin." *Modernism/ Modernity*, *26*, 2, 447-450. [Naz]

RR1378. Le, Moal-Sommaire A.: "Regards Croisés Entre Beckett et Bion." *Revue Française de Psychanalyse*, *83*, 1, 181. [Syr]

RR1379. Lucas, Kevin: "Samuel Beckett and the Politics of Aftermath." *Textual Practice*, *33*, 4, 695-697. [UofR]

RR1380. Marchisotto, Jennifer: "Surreal Beckett: Samuel Beckett, James Joyce, and Surrealism by Alan Warren Friedman." *James Joyce Quarterly*, *55*, 3-4, 465-467. [UaB]

RR1381. McTighe, Trish: "Everyday Catastrophes: Gender, Labour and Power in Beckett's Theatre." *Journal of Beckett Studies*, *28*, 1, 19-34. [Syr]

RR1382. Mihálycsa, Erika: "Beckett and Modernism: Edited by Olga Beloborodova, Dirk van Hulle and Pim Verhulst, New York, Palgrave Macmillan, 2018, 295 pp., 103,99 € (Hardback), ISBN: 978-3-319-70373-2." *Textual Practice*, August, 1-5. [UaB]

RR1383. Milaneschi, F.: "Beckett Translator of Joyce: Anna Lyvia Pluratself." *Revue Italienne d'Études Francaises*, 9. [Cor]

RR1384. Mooney, Sinéad: "'Delirium of Interpretation': Surrealism, the Possessions, and Beckett's Outsider Artists." *Translation Studies*, *12*, 1, 47-63. [Cor] (Éluard)

RR1385. Nadel, Ira: "Beckett's Fizzles: De-Creating the Short Story." *Short Fiction in Theory & Practice*, *9*, 2, 103-116. [LoC]

RR1386. Nixon, M.: "Introduction 'Never Neglect the Little Things in Life': Beckett and the Everyday." *Journal of Beckett Studies*, *28*, 1, 1-4. [Syr]

RR1387. O'Dwyer, N., & N. Johnson: "Exploring Volumetric Video and Narrative Through Samuel Beckett's Play." *International Journal of Performance Arts and Digital Media*, *15*, 1, 53-69. [UaB]

RR1388. Pavithra, R., & M. A., Be: "Satire and Irony in Samuel Beckett's Waiting for Godot." *Language in India*, *19*, 5, 439. [PrQ]

RR1389. Piette, Adam: "Revisioning Beckett: Samuel Beckett's Decadent Turn. By S. E. Gontarskibeckett's Political Imagination, by Emilie Morin." *French Studies*, *73*, 3, 479-480. [UofR]

RR1390. Posse, Bernard-Olivier: "Éluard en Résidu Surréaliste dans l'Œuvre de Samuel Beckett." *Samuel Beckett Today/ Aujourd'hui*, *31*, 1, 98-113. [RIT]

RR1391. Quinney, Laura: "The Bewilderment of the Self in Beckett and the Romantics." *European Romantic Review*, *30*, 3, 323-330. [UofR]

RR1392. Rabaté, Jean-Michel: "Postface. En Lisant Beckett avec Franz Kaltenbeck." *Savoirs et Clinique*, *26*, 1, 124. [Cor]

RR1393. Roberts, Trask: "Samuel Beckett's Disruptive Translations of 'Je Voudrais Que Mon Amour Meure'." *Journal of Beckett Studies*, *28*, 2, 163-178. [UaB]

RR1394. Schleifer, Ronald: "Modernism as Gesture: The Experience of Music, Samuel Beckett, and Performed Bewilderment." *Criticism*, *61*, 1, 73-96. [Naz]

RR1395. Simpson, Hannah: "Kinesthetic Empathy, Physical Recoil: The Conflicting Embodied Affects of Samuel Beckett's Quad." *Journal of Modern Literature*, *42*, 2, 132-148. [RIT]

RR1396. Simpson, Hannah: "Rhys Tranter, Beckett's Late Stage: Trauma, Language, and Subjectivity." *Journal of Beckett Studies*, *28*, 1, 102-106. [UaB]

RR1397.   Tang, Y.: "Atmospheric Violence: Samuel Beckett's Aesthetics of Respiration." *Lit, 30*, 2, 103-119. [Cor]

RR1398.   Therrien, Eve I.: "Beckett and Québec: 'Je Me Souviens'?" *Theatre Research in Canada, 20*, 2. [Cor]

RR1399.   Tranter, Rhys: "Beckett and Modernism." *James Joyce Literary Supplement, 33*, 1, 16-17. [Naz]

RR1400.   Tsushima, Michiko: "The Powerlessness to Imagine at the Heart of Imagination in Beckett." *Journal of Irish Studies*, 34, 90-101. [Cor]

RR1401.   Vashisht, Jivitesh: "Beckett, Happy Days, Royal Exchange Theatre, Manchester." *Journal of Beckett Studies, 28*, 1, 118-124. [Syr]

RR1402.   Whitmarsh, Patrick: "'So it is I Who Speak': Communicating Bodies in Samuel Beckett's Happy Days and the Unnamable." *Journal of Modern Literature, 42*, 4, 111-28. [RIT]

BEGAG, Azouz.
See also 390.

RR1403.   ● Begag, Azouz: *One, Two, Free: Viva l'Algérie: Les Algériens de la Diaspora au Service du Hirak dans Leur Pays d'Origine: Manifeste Politique.* Paris: Erick Bonnier. 112p. [BAnQ]

RR1404.   Luna, Alvaro: "The Way of the Majority's World: Language as a Bildung Lesson in Tomás Rivera's . . . Y No Se lo Tragó la Tierra and Azouz Begag's Le Gone du Chaâba." *Symposium, 73*, 3, 172-184. [Naz]

BEIGBEDER, Frédéric.
See also 479, 490.

RR1405.   ● Beigbeder, Frédéric, & Silvia Ballestra: *Una Vita Senza Fine.* Milano: Bompiani. 296p. [WC]

RR1406.   ● Beigbeder, Frédéric, & Marianne Kaas: *Een Leven Zonder Einde.* Amsterdam: De Geus 333p. [WC]

RR1407.   ● Beigbeder, Frédéric, & Gabriella Montanari: *Memorie di un Giovane Disturbato: Romanzo.* Torino: Vague. 105p. [WC]

RR1408.   Durand, Alain-Philippe: "La Partie Émergée de l'Iceberg : Frédéric Beigbeder." *Contemporary French and Francophone Studies, 23*, 1, 47-56. [RIT]

RR1409.   Olena, Ianytska: "Concept Faith in the Work of Jean-Michel di Falco and Frédéric Beigbeder 'Je Crois – Moi Non Plus'." *Scientific Bulletin of Kherson State University. Series Linguistics*, 35, 30-35. [WC]

BEKRI, Tahar.
See 219, 886.

BELGHOUL, Farida.
See 419.

BÉNABOU, Marcel.
See 4, 3779.

BENDA, Julien.
RR1410.   Luque, David: "La Traición a la Democracia. Ensayo Sobre las

Relaciones entre Universidad, Democracia y Ciudadanía desde la Idea de Traición."
Educatio Siglo XXI, *37*, 1, 21-40. [PrQ]

RR1411.   Zvi Ben-Dor Benite: "Facing the Ruler, Facing the Village: On the Roads to Complicity Following Mengzi and Benda." *CLCWeb*, *21*, 3. [PrQ]

BEN JELLOUN, Tahar.
See also 208, 695, 789.

RR1412.   ● Ben, Jelloun T.: *L'Amicizia e l'Ombra del Tradimento*. Milano: La Nave di Teseo. 103p. [WC]

RR1413.   ● Ben, Jelloun T.: *L'Hammam*. Milano: La Nave di Teseo. 60p. [WC]

RR1414.   ● Ben, Jelloun T., & Fabbri B. Buscaroli: *Tahar Ben Jelloun - La Pittura: 16.04.-7.05.2019, Forni Galleria d'Arte = Tahar Ben Jelloun - The Paintings*. Milano: La Nave di Teseo. 57p. [WC]

RR1415.   ● Ben, Jelloun T., & Thomas Dhellemmes: *Jour Bleu*. Paris: Éditions Cercle d'Art. [70]p. [BnF]

RR1416.   ● Chakkour, Naïma, & T. Ben Jelloun: *Ma Résistance: Contre la Sclérose Latérale Amyotrophique*. Paris: Seuil. 123p. [BnF]

RR1417.   ● Galerie Ptrice Trigano: *Tahar Ben Jelloun, Ville Méditerranée: [Exposition, Paris, Galerie Patrice Trigano, 4 Décembre 2019-1er Février 2020]*. Paris: Le Livre d'Art. 31p. [BnF]

RR1418.   Barbier, Clarisse: "'Une Maison Abandonnée, C'est Comme une Histoire Inachevée.' Espace, Corps et Récit dans la Nuit Sacrée de Tahar Ben Jelloun." *Présence Francophone*, *92*, 121-139. [UaB]

RR1419.   Benoit, James: "L'Espace d'Un Écho." *L'Œil*, 11, 135. [PrQ]

RR1420.   El Guabli, B.: "La Punition: By Tahar Ben Jelloun, Paris, Gallimard, 2018, 160 pp., €16 (Paperback), ISBN 978-2-07017-8513." *The Journal of North African Studies*, *24*, 6, 1051-1054. [Syr]

RR1421.   Hamon-Porter, Brigitte: "Mapping the Tunisian Uprising in Tahar Ben Jelloun's Par le Feu and Leyla Bouzid's À Peine J'ouvre les Yeux." *French Review*, *93*, 1, 79-91. [Naz]

BENOIT, Pierre.
RR1422.   ● *Les Cahiers des Amis de Pierre Benoit*. Gramat: Les Amis de Pierre Benoit. *Les Cahiers des Amis de Pierre Benoit*, 29. 312p. [WC]

BENSOUSSAN, Albert.
See also 52, 694.

RR1423.   ● Vargas, Llosa M., & Albert Bensoussan: *Les Contes de la Peste*. [Paris]: Gallimard. 162p. [BnF]

RR1424.   ● Vargas, Llosa M., Albert Bensoussan, & Daniel Lefort: *Aux Cinq Rues, Lima*. Paris: Gallimard. 307p. [BAnQ]

RR1425.   ● Vargas, Llosa M., Zuzanna Celej, Albert Bensoussan, & Daniel Lefort: *Le Navire des Enfants*. Paris: Gallimard Jeunesse. 97p. [BnF]

BÉRAUD, Henri.
See 411.

BERGOUNIOUX, Pierre.
See also 59.
RR1426. ● Bergounioux, Pierre: *Enfantillages*. Paris: L'Herne. 53p. [WC]
RR1427. ● Bergounioux, Pierre: *Faute d'Égalité*. Paris: Gallimard. 29p. [BnF]
RR1428. ● Bergounioux, Pierre: *Hôtel du Brésil*. [Paris]: Gallimard. 68p. [BAnQ]
RR1429. ● Bergounioux, Pierre: *Lundi*. Paris: Galilée Editions. 64p. [BnF]
RR1430. ● Bergounioux, Pierre, & Maurice Borne: *L'Ordre, Pour Mémoire, les Morutiers*. Montreuil: L'Œil. 112p. [WC]
RR1431. ● Demanze, Laurent: *Pierre Bergounioux: Le Présent de l'Invention*. Caen: Passage(s). 282p. [Cor]
RR1432. ● Michel, Jean-Paul, & Pierre Bergounioux: *Pierre Bergounioux*. Paris: L'Herne. 254p. [Cor]
RR1433. Gado, Rania: "La Voie Géologique vers l'Être au Monde: Géologies de Pierre Bergounioux." *Revue d'Histoire Littéraire de la France, 119*, 1, 163-182. [RIT]

BERGSON, Henri.
RR1434. ● Bergson, Henri: *L'Idée de Temps: Cours au Collège de France, 1901-1902*. Paris: Puf. 255p. [Cor]
RR1435. ● Berr, Karsten, & Jürgen H. Franz: *Zukunft Gestalten - Digitalisierung, Künstliche Intelligenz (ki) und Philosophie*. Berlin: Frank & Timme. 246p. [WC]
RR1436. ● Pitts, Andrea J., & Mark W. Westmoreland: *Beyond Bergson: Examining Race and Colonialism Through the Writings of Henri Bergson*. Albany: State University of New York Press. 255p. [Syr]
RR1437. ● Vergoossen, M. P. D.: *Montageprinzipien des Surrealismus Unter dem Einfluss von Henri Bergson*. Berlin: Epubli. 68p. [WC]
RR1438. Astore, Rocco A.: "Arguments Contrary to Spinoza's View of Time and Free-Will through the Philosophy of Henri Bergson." *Journal of Comparative Literature and Aesthetics, 42*, 1, 130-49. [PrQ]
RR1439. Atkinson, Paul: "Book Review: Henri Bergson." *Symploke¯, 27*, 1-2, 516-518. [UaB]
RR1440. Cortina, Urdampilleta A.: "El Problema de la Técnica: El Homo Faber, la Mística y la Decadencia. Cultura Maquinista en Oswald Spengler y Henri Bergson." *Pensamiento, 75*, 283, 425-434. [UaB]
RR1441. Dolbeault, Joël: "Henri Bergson, l'Idée de Temps. Cours au Collège de France 1901-1902. Paris, Presses Universitaires de France, 2019, 256 pages." *Philosophiques, 46*, 2, 444. [UaB]
RR1442. Gewehr, Rodrigo B.: "O Problema da Personalidade: Conferências de Henri Bergson na Universidade de Edimburgo (1914)." *Revista Filosófica de Coimbra, 28*, 56, 461-490. [Cor]
RR1443. Maryniak, Bogusław: "Memory of Matter. Henri Bergson and Material Bases of Remembrance." *Philosophical Discourses*, 1, 223-242. [WC]
RR1444. Moravec, Matyás: "Perpetual Present: Henri Bergson and Atemporal Duration." *European Journal for Philosophy of Religion, 11*, 3, 197. [WC]
RR1445. Solís, Castro S.: "Una Lectura Hipermoderna de la Risa de Henri Bergson: De la Risa Como Pequeño Enigma Malicioso a Su Comprensión Como Ethos de las Sociedades." *Areté, 31*, 1, 235-245. [Naz]

RR1446.   Souza, José P. M., & Gabriel K. Rocha: "'A Gênese da Ideia de Tempo', de Henri Bergson." *Voluntas*, *10*, 3, 254. [WC]

BERL, Emmanuel.
See 703.

BERNANOS, Georges.
See also 362, 363, 371, 376, 430.
RR1447.   ● Bernanos, Georges: *La Gioia*. Milano: San Paolo. 286p. [WC]
RR1448.   ● Bernanos, Georges, & Gérard Bocholier: *Georges Bernanos: Dits et Maximes de Vie*. Orbey: Arfuyen. 149p. [BAnQ]
RR1449.   ● Bernanos, Georges, & Romain Debluë: *Scandale de la Vérité: Essais, Pamphlets, Articles et Témoignages*. Paris: Robert Laffont. 1336p. [WC]
RR1450.   ● Estève, Michel: *Bernanos au Cinéma*. Paris: L'Harmattan. 173p. [WC]
RR1451.   ● Magdalena, Padberg: *Das Romanwerk von Georges Bernanos als Vision des Untergangs*. Berlin/ Boston: Walter de Gruyter. 112p. [UaB]

BERNHARDT, Sarah.
See also 310, 320, 338, 447, 504, 635.
RR1452.   ● Rebeck, Theresa: *Bernhardt/ Hamlet*. [New York]: Samuel French. 95p. [WC]
RR1453.   Duckett, Victoria, Rebecca Kastleman, Kevin Riordan, & Claire Warden: "Performing Art Nouveau: Sarah Bernhardt and the Development of Industrial Modernism." *Modernism/ Modernity*, 4, 3. [WC]
RR1454.   Foss, Colin: "Sarah Bernhardt's Bodies: Feminine Fame During Wartime in Her Memoirs and Henry Céard's La Saignée." *Dix-neuf*, *23*, 2, 136-150. [UaB]
RR1455.   Horner, Nadège: "Une Sculpture De Sarah Bernhardt En Phèdre Redécouverte." *Sculptures*, 6, 83-89. [WC]
RR1456.   Martinek, Jason: "The Diva and the Socialist: Sarah Bernhardt, *Camille*, and Eugene Debs's Crusade to Save the Fallen Woman." *Indiana Magazine of History*, *115*, 2, 146. [UofR]
RR1457.   Merck, Mandy: "Sarah Bernhardt's Posthumous Celebrity." *Women*, *30*, 4, 387-410. [Naz]

BESPALOFF, Rachel.
See also 13.
RR1458.   Cicero, Bruce: "Reading the Iliad in the Light of Eternity." *Modern Age*, *48*, 1, 48-58. [PrQ] (Simone Weil)
RR1459.   Osborn, Ronald: "Geometries of Force in Homer's Iliad: Two Readings." *Humanitas*, *21*, 1, 168-78. [PrQ] (Simone Weil)

BESSETTE, Gérard.
See 272.

BESSORA.
See also 309.

RR1460. ● Barroux, Stéphane-Yves, Bessora, & Mirna Šimat: *Alpha: Od Abidjana do Gare du Norda*. Zagreb: V.B.Z. 125p. [WC]

RR1461. Mouflard, Claire: "The Digital Griotte: Bessora's Para/ Textual Discourses on Identity Politics and Neocolonialism in Contemporary France." *Humanities, 8*, 1, 2. [Naz]

BETI, Mongo.
See also 192, 228, 271, 281, 570, 664.

RR1462. ● Owono-Kouma, Auguste: *Les Essais et les Romans de Mongo Beti: Thèmes - Intertextualité - Réécriture*. Paris: L'Harmattan. 287 p. [UofR]

RR1463. ● Samaké, Adama: *Roman Africain et Idéologie: L'Identité dans le Jeu Scripturaire de Mongo Beti*. Paris: Complicités. 236p. [BnF]

RR1464. Amossy, Ruth: "À la Croisée de l'Analyse du Discours et de l'Argumentation Rhétorique: Le Cas d'Israël." *Essais Francophones, 6*, 125, 138, 183. [PrQ]

RR1465. Onana, Pierre Suzanne Eyenga: "Insurrections Populaires et Démystification d'un Ordre Sociopolitique Alternatif dans Deux Fictions." *Estudios Románicos, 28*, 191-203. [RIT]

BEY, Maïssa.
See also 194.

RR1466. ● Bonn, Charles, & Houda Hamdi: *Maissa Bey: Deux Décennies de Créativité*. Paris: L'Harmattan. 239p. [UofR]

RR1467. Breen, Gina M.: "Do You Hear in the Mountains . . . and Other Stories by Maïssa Bey (Review)." *Women in French Studies, 27*, 239-240. [UaB]

RR1468. Chouiten, Lynda: "Maïssa Bey Nulle Autre Voix." *Quinzaines*, 1214, 15. [Syr]

RR1469. Détrez, Christine: "Maïssa Bey: Lettres d'Algérie." *Travail, Genre et Sociétés, 43*, 3, 35. [Cor]

RR1470. Fermi, Elena: "Maïssa Bey, Nulle Autre Voix." *Studi Francesi, 63*, 2, 398. [UaB]

RR1471. Harzoune, Mustapha: "Maïssa Bey, Nulle Autre Voix: La Tourd'Aigues, Éd. de L'Aube, 2018, 248 pages, 19, 90 €." *Hommes & Migrations, 1325*, 2, 208. [Cor]

RR1472. Horner, Lavinia A.: "Literary Arabic and Islamic Values as the New Conditioned Stimuli for the Good Citizen Status in Maissa Bey's *Bleu Blanc Vert*." *Romance Notes, 59*, 2, 395-406. [Naz]

RR1473. McIllvaney, Siobhán: "À Contre-Silence: Articulating a Taxonomy of Maternal Grief in Maïssa Bey's *Puisque Mon Cœur Est Mort* (2010)." *Women in French Studies, 27*, 172-181. [UaB]

BEYALA, Calixthe.
See also 292, 334, 350, 541, 704.

RR1474. Allogho, Mantwani C.: "'La Mémoire au Féminin: Lecture de C'est le Soleil Qui M'a Brûlée de Calixthe Beyala et de Déchoucaj' Œuvre Photographique de Myriam Mihindou'." *Mouvances Francophones*, 4, 1. [WC]

RR1475. Fadily, Noureddine: "L'Errance Identitaire dans les Romans de Calixthe Beyala." *Les Cahiers du Centre des Études Doctorales*, 7, 33-40. [WC]

BIANCIOTTI, Hector.
See 211, 641.

BLAIS, Marie-Claire.
See also 340.

RR1476. ● Nardout-Lafarge, Élisabeth, & Daniel Letendre: *Lectures de Marie-Claire Blais*. Montréal: Les Presses de l'Université de Montréal. 249p. [Syr]

RR1477. Blais, Marie-Claire, Julie Trudel, & Caroline Monnet: "Outer Limits." *Canadian Art*, Fall, *36*, 3, 92-5. [RIT]

RR1478. "*Soifs* Matériaux, l'Œuvre de Marie-Claire Blais Passe au Théâtre." *Chatelaine (Online)*, May 29. [PrQ]

BLANCHOT, Maurice.
See also 56, 483, 727, 745, 752, 1157, 1212, 1337, 3682.

RR1479. ● Blanchot, Maurice, Éric Hoppenot, Arthur Cools, & Vivian Liska: *Traduire Kafka*. Paris: Kimé. 353p. [WC]

RR1480. ● *Cahiers Maurice Blanchot. Vol. 6: Ecriture et Pouvoir. Automne 2019*. Dijon: Presses du Réel Editions. 136p. [WC]

RR1481. ● Espinosa, Proa S.: *El Enigma Diurno: La Escritura Neutra de Maurice Blanchot*. Madrid: Arena Libros. 129p. [WC]

RR1482. ● Filser, Barbara, & Kristin Marek: *Blanchot und das Bild: Bilder und Begriffe Nach Maurice Blanchot*. Paderborn: Wilhelm Fink. 200p. [BnF]

RR1483. ● Kuzma, Joseph D.: *Maurice Blanchot and Psychoanalysis*. Boston: Brill/ Rodopi. 231p. [Syr]

RR1484. ● Lisse, Michel, & Woo Choi: *Quatre Essais sur Maurice Blanchot*. Orange: Éditions le Retrait. 133p. [BnF]

RR1485. ● Potts, Adam: *Sonic Encounters with Blanchot*. London: Routledge. 202p. [Cor]

RR1486. ● Yang, I-Ning: *Blanchot-Lao Tseu: L'Acte de Nomination*. Paris: L'Harmattan. 215p. [LoC]

RR1487. Angelis, Zoe: "Maurice Blanchot: Literature as the Space of Politics." *Contemporary French and Francophone Studies*, *23*, 2, 154-162. [Naz]

RR1488. Arce, Álvarez M. L.: "Translation as Influence: A Dialogue between Maurice Blanchot's Literary Theory and Lydia Davis' Short Fiction." *Short Fiction in Theory & Practice*, *9*, 2, 89-101. [LoC]

RR1489. Bey, Facundo N.: "Berlín. Maurice Blanchot." *Discusiones Filosóficas*, *20*, 34, 187-190. [UaB]

RR1490. Cambria, Domenico: "Le Texte à l'Épreuve du Récit: Maurice Blanchot et Jacques Derrida." *Divus Thomas*, *122*, 1, 330-349. [UaB]

RR1491. Cools, Arthur, & M. N. de Van: "Narration and the Experience of Estrangement in the Fiction of Franz Kafka and Maurice Blanchot." *The German Quarterly*, *92*, 1, 19-34. [UofR]

RR1492. Correia, Tyler: "C. Bident, Maurice Blanchot." *Phenomenological Reviews*, 5, 47. [WC]

RR1493. Langstaff, Holly: "Uncontrollable Mechanisms: Maurice Blanchot's Inorganic Writing." *French Studies*, *73*, 3, 401-415. [UofR]

RR1494. Pimentel, D. A.: "The Impossibility of Death in Literature: Lygia

Fagundes Telles and Maurice Blanchot." *Estudos de Literatura Brasileira Contemporanea*, 56. [Cor]

RR1495.   Reuber, Alexandra: "The (Silent) Articulation of Otherness: Maurice Blanchot's Double Parole in Death Sentence, Awaiting Oblivion, and Madness of the Day." *Athens Journal of Philology*, 6, 4, 235-254. [WC]

RR1496.   Stockwell, C.: "The Life of the Night: Bolaño, Blanchot, and the Impoverishment of Openness." *Critique*, *60*, 3, 342-356. [UofR]

RR1497.   Torres, Sánchez R. D.: "La Retirada de la Presencia. Lenguaje y Negatividad en la Filosofía de Maurice Blanchot." *Ideas y Valores*, *68*, 169, 255-278. [UaB]

RR1498.   Turner, Ben: "From Resistance to Invention in the Politics of the Impossible: Bernard Stiegler's Political Reading of Maurice Blanchot." *Contemporary Political Theory*, *18*, 1, 43-64. [PrQ]

BLOCH, Jean-Richard.
See also 772.

RR1499.   ● Bloch, Jean-Richard, Marguerite Bloch, Rachel Mazuy, Lûdmila Štern, & Christophe Prochasson: *Moscou, Caucase, Été 1934: Lettres du Voyages en URSS*. Paris: CNRS. 292p. [Cor] (Nizan)

RR1500.   ● Rolland, Romain, Jean-Richard Bloch, Roland Roudil, & Antoinette Blum: *Romain Rolland et Jean-Richard Bloch: Correspondance (1919-1944)*. Dijon: Editions Universitaires de Dijon. 582p. [Cor]

RR1501.   ● Zweig, Stefan, Jean-Richard Bloch, & Claudine Delphis: *Stefan Zweig et Jean-Richard Bloch: Correspondance (1912-1940)*. Dijon: Éditions Universitaires de Dijon. 266p. [Cor]

BLOCH, Marc.
See also 382, 729, 835.

RR1502.   Al-Matary, Sarah, & Michel Prat: "The Refusal to Make a Career in One of Marc Bloch's Letters (1941): About A.-V. Jacquet's Refus de Parvenir." *Mil Neuf Cent*, *37*, 1, 171. [Cor]

RR1503.   Broich, John: "The Studious Resistance of Marc Bloch in Occupied France, a Medieval Historian Turned His Professional Eye on His Native Country and Made the Ultimate Sacrifice for His Ideals." *History Today*, *69*, 12, 40-49. [RIT]

RR1504.   Fabiani, Jean-Louis: "Comptes Rendus. Thomas Hirsch. Le Temps des Sociétés. D'Émile Durkheim à Marc Bloch. Paris, Éd. de L'EHESS, 2016, 470 p." *Annales. Histoire, Sciences Sociales*, *74*, 2, 464. [Naz]

RR1505.   Głowacka-Sobiech, Edyta: "L'Anniversaire des 'Annales.' The Year 2014 as the Time of French Anniversaries of Marc Bloch, Philipp Aries and Jacques Le Goff." *Biuletyn Historii Wychowania*, 38, 319-324. [LoC]

RR1506.   Pugh, Anthony Cheal: "La Défaite de Mai 1940: Claude Simon, Marc Bloch et l'Écriture du Désastre." *Cahiers Claude Simon*, 14, 113-132. [UaB]

RR1507.   Tondini, R. "Paul Collomp: Tra Marc Bloch e Giorgio Pasquali." *Eikasmos*, 30, 327-354. [Cor]

BLONDEL, Maurice.
See also 721, 751.

RR1508.   ● Jiménez, Domínguez C.: *La Muerte, El Acto por Excelencia, Según Maurice Blondel*. Madrid: Ediciones Universidad San Dámaso. 383p. [LoC]

RR1509. Bocken, I.: "God in Acting (l'Action) - Mysticism, Philosophy and Theology in Maurice Blondel's Work." *Tijdschrift Voor Theologie*, *59*, 3, 257-280. [Cor]

RR1510. Ciraulo, Jonathan M.: "Koerpel, Robert C.: Maurice Blondel: Transforming Catholic Tradition." *Theological Studies*, *80*, 3, 720. [UaB]

RR1511. Conway, Michael A.: "Book Review: Maurice Blondel on the Supernatural in Human Action: Sacrament and Superstition." *Irish Theological Quarterly*, *84*, 2, 212-218. [RIT]

RR1512. Dougherty, Jude P.: "Maurice Blondel: Transforming Catholic Tradition by Robert C. Koerpel (Review)." *The Review of Metaphysics*, *72*, 4, 798-799. [UofR]

RR1513. Fontaine, José: "L'Action et 'Histoire et Dogme' de Maurice Blondel Chez Joseph Malègue." *Nouvelle Revue Théologique*, *141*, 3, 430. [UaB]

RR1514. Garcia, Mourelo S.: "The Mystical Dinamism in M. Blondel's Thought." *Scripta Theologica*, *51*, 2, 395-417. [Naz]

RR1515. Henrici, Peter, S. I.: "L'Action (1893) di Maurice Blondel, Radice Feconda di Nuove Idee. Un Resoconto Filosofico." *Gregorianum*, *100*, 3, 585-598. [UaB]

RR1516. Rowland, Tracey: "Maurice Blondel: Transforming Catholic Tradition, Robert C. Koerpel, University of Notre Dame Press, 2019 (ISBN 978-0-268-10477-1), xii + 268 pp., Hb $55." *Reviews in Religion and Theology*, *26*, 4, 660-661. [UofR]

RR1517. Sullivan, John: "Book Review: Maurice Blondel." *Irish Theological Quarterly*, *84*, 3, 325-326. [Naz]

BLOY, Léon.
See also 78.

RR1518. ● Bloy, Léon, & Jean-Jacques Nuel: *Chroniques du 'Chat Noir'*. Salornay-sur-Guye: Éditions: Le Pont du Change. 108p. [BnF]

RR1519. ● Frigerio, Vittorio: *"On N'Arrêtera Pas le Progrès" et Autres Vérités Discutables: 50 Lieux Communs Revus et Commentés; Précédé de: "Léon Bloy et Gérard de Lacaze-Duthiers: Deux Consciences Contre La Bêtise"; Et Suivi d'un, "Petit Lexique d'Expression Utiles."* Liège: Presses Universitaires de Liège. 261p. [BAnQ]

RR1520. ● Glaudes, Pierre: *Léon Bloy*. Paris: Lettres Modernes Minard. 224p. [WC]

RR1521. Amadieu, Jean-Baptiste: "Interprétation Judiciaire vs Interprétation Littéraire: Le Paraclétisme de Léon Bloy Vu par les Censeurs Romains et par la Critique Littéraire." *Revue Droit & Littérature*, *3*, 1, 147. [BnF]

RR1522. Chaumeil, Yoann: "'L'Homme à Qui Je Devais le Plus Après Mon Père et Ma Mère': Léon Bloy Disciple de Jules Barbey d'Aurevilly." *Quêtes Littéraires*, 9. [WC]

RR1523. Glaudes, Pierre: "Dans la Postérité de Chateaubriand: L'Apologétique dans les Récits de Barbey d'Aurevilly et de Léon Bloy." *Rivista di Letterature Moderne e Comparate*, *72*, 1, 39-52. [UofR]

RR1524. Millet-Gerard, D.: "Le Paradis des Animaux: De Leon Bloy a Francis Jammes." *Bulletin de Litterature Ecclesiastique*, *120*, 3, 79-96. [Cor]

RR1525. Pego, Puigbo A.: "Pierre Glaudes, Léon Bloy, la Littérature et la Bible. París: Les Belles Lettres, 2017, 453 Pàg." *Comprendre*, *21*, 1, 122-125. [WC]

BOBIN, Christian.

See also 834, 836.

RR1526. ● Bobin, Christian: *Pierre*. [Paris]: Gallimard. 95p. [UofR]

RR1527. ● Dattas, Lydie, & Christian Bobin: *Le Livre des Anges: Suivi de la Nuit Spirituelle; Et de Carnet d'une Allumeuse*. [Paris]: Gallimard. 271p. [WC] (Grosjean)

RR1528. ● Tiévant, Claire, Lydie Dattas, & Christian Bobin: *Christian Bobin*. Paris: Éditions de L'Herne. 287p. [UofR]

BON, François.

See 224, 492.

RR1529. ● Bon, François, Isabelle Crevecoeur, & Aurore Callias: *Sapiens à l'Œil Nu*. Paris: CNRS. 165p. [WC]

RR1530. ● Crenn, Antonin, & François Bon: *Je Connaîtrai Luçon: Journal de Résidence, Mars Avril, Mai 2019*. Luçon: Médiathèques Sud Vendée Littoral. 146p. [BnF]

RR1531. Bernard, Isabelle: "Histoire et Paysages dans Quelques Écritures de Terrain Contemporaines: Jean-Christophe Bailly, François Bon, Patrick Deville et Marie Richeux." *Arcadia*, *54*, 2, 231-256. [UofR]

RR1532. Bernard, Isabelle: "L'Atelier d'Écriture dans l'Enseignement du Français Langue Étrangère en Jordanie. Pour une Approche Renouvelée de la Didactique de la Littérature." *Synergies Algérie*, 27, 71-82. [PrQ]

BONI, Tanella.

See also 333.

RR1533. Carlson, Nancy Naomi: "Book Review: The Future Has an Appointment with the Dawn." *World Literature Today*, *93*, 1, 79-80. [Naz]

BONNEFOY, Yves.

See also 468, 507, 787, 788, 789, 796, 807, 874.

RR1534. ● Mussapi, Roberto: *Compassione e Mistero: Heaney, Luzi, Bonnefoy*. Catania: Algra. 94p. [WC]

RR1535. Mascarou, Alain: "Ce Qui A 'Traversé les Temps de l'Éphémère': Yves Bonnefoy, Correspondance I, Édition Établie par Odile Bombarde et Patrick Labarthe." *La Revue des Revues*, *61*, 1, 8. [Cor]

RR1536. Roesler, L. M.: "'La Déclaration d'Intention': Paratext as Method in Yves Bonnefoy's 'Dédicace' to l'Improbable." *Forum for Modern Language Studies*, *55*, 2, 227-243. [UofR]

RR1537. Roesler, Layla: "Poetry as Place: the 'Vrai Lieu' in the Work of Yves Bonnefoy." *At the Interface/ Probing the Boundaries*, 119, 90-98. [Naz]

RR1538. Scotto, Fabio: "Yves Bonnefoy, Correspondance I." *Studi Francesi*, 187, 193-194. [UaB]

RR1539. Scotto, Fabio: "Yves Bonnefoy, sous la Direction de Michèle Finck." *Studi Francesi*, 187, 194-195. [UaB]

BORDUAS, Paul Émile.

RR1540. Bloom, Myra: "Suzanne and Victoria." *Canadian Literature*, 238, 113, 114, 183. [RIT]

BOSCO, Henri.
RR1541. ● Bosco, Henri: *Cahiers Henri Bosco*. Arras: Artois Presses Université. 215p. [WC]
RR1542. ● Bosco, Henri, & Alain Tassel: *Lettres à Quelques Amis Écrivains*. Paris: Classiques Garnier. 135p. [Cor]
RR1543. ● Morzewski, Christian: *Un Voyage en Provence, Vol. 2: Récit Inédit d'Henri Bosco*. Arras: Artois Presses Université. 236p. [WC]

BOSCO, Monique.
See 647.

BOSQUET, Alain.
See 614.

BOUALEM, Sansal.
RR1544. ● Cheboub, Aziz: *Utopie et Dystopie: Étude Comparative de Deux Textes: Soumission de Michel Houellebecq et 2084 de Boualem Sansal*. Saint-Denis: Édilivre. 126p. [WC]
RR1545. Cloonan, William: "Sansal, Boualem. Le Train d'Erlingen ou la Métamorphose de Dieu." *French Review*, 93, 2, 229. [UofR]
RR1546. Sansal, Boualem: "Réponse à l'Invitation d'Écrire." *Cahiers Critiques de Thérapie Familiale et de Pratiques de Réseaux*, 63, 2, 15. [Cor]

BOUCHARD, Michel Marc.
See also 259.
RR1547. Coto-Rivel, Sergio, F. C. de Fourrel, Jennifer Houdiard, & Stefano Genetti: "La Scène, l'Écran: Questionnements Identitaires et Tensions du Désir dans Tom à la Ferme de Michel Marc Bouchard et de Xavier Dolan." *Itinéraires*, 2019-2. [WC]
RR1548. "'Las Musas Huérfanas' Llegan con Humor Negro al Teatro." *Notimex*, May 25 2019. [WC]

BOUDJEDRA, Rachid.
See 288, 666.

BOURAOUI, Hédi.
See also 19.
RR1549. ● Beggar, Abderrahman: *Hédi Bouraoui: Poaimer Autrement*. Toronto: CMC Éditions. 1 vol. [WC]
RR1550. ● Bouraoui, Hédi: *Dossier de Poète: Athanas Daltchev; Suivi de, Dossier d'Artiste: Le Frère Sculpteur le Professeur Lubomir Daltchev*. Toronto: CMC Éditions. 1 vol. [BAnQ]

BOURAOUI, Nina.
See also 255, 581.
RR1551. Marchi, Lisa: "A Dark, Inner Life and a Society in Crisis: Nina Bouraoui's Standard." *Humanities*, 8, 1, 41. [PrQ]

24080

BOURDIEU, Pierre.

RR1552. ● Ames, Patricia: *La Construcción de Teoría en Pierre Bourdieu a Partir de Sus Obras en Torno a la Desigualdad y la Educación*. Lima: Pontificia Universidad Católica del Perú, Departamento de Ciencias Sociales. 17p. [WC]

RR1553. ● D'Alessandro, Ruggero: *Gusti di Classe: Pierre Bourdieu Sociologo delle Pratiche Culturali*. Castel: Manifestolibri. 156p. [LoC]

RR1554. ● De Feo, A., Mirella Giannini, & Marco Pitzalis: *Scienza e Critica del Mondo Sociale: La Lezione di Pierre Bourdieu*. Milano: Mimesis. 154p. [LoC]

RR1555. ● Desanti, Raphaël: *Pierre Bourdieu Expliqué à Mon Fils*. Saint-Denis: Edilivre. 67p. [BnF]

RR1556. ● García, Linera A.: *La Etnicidad Como Capital Simbólico: Estructura Social, Clase y Dominación Simbólica en la Obra de Pierre Bourdieu*. La Paz: Plural. 95p. [WC]

RR1557. ● Gromala, Lisa: *Kämpfe von Schulen um Selbstbehauptung: Eine Analyse Mit Pierre Bourdieu und der Grounded Theory*. Wiesbaden: Springer. 301p. [WC]

RR1558. ● Hernández, Carlos A., Gomero S. Ortega, & Figueroa M. Salazar: *Derecho, Norma y Habitus: La Sociología (Anti)Jurídica de Pierre Bourdieu*. Bogotá: Nueva Jurídica. 223p. [WC]

RR1559. ● Jourdain, Anne, & Sidonie Naulin: *La Sociologie de Pierre Bourdieu*. Malakoff: Armand Colin. 191p. [BAnQ]

RR1560. ● Kaelblen, Pascal: *Bourdieu et la Musique: Enjeux et Perspectives*. Sampzon: Delatour France. 132p. [WC]

RR1561. ● Kouvouama, Abel: *(Re)Lire les Écrits de Pierre Bourdieu: Pour une Démarche Socio-Anthropologique Critique et Créatrice*. Paris: PUPPA. 113p. [BnF]

RR1562. ● Mu, Guanglun M., & Bonnie Pang: *Interpreting the Chinese Diaspora: Identity, Socialisation, and Resilience According to Pierre Bourdieu*. Abingdon: Oxon. 165p. [Syr]

RR1563. ● Pérez, Amin: *Faire de la Politique avec la Sociologie: Adelmalek Sayad et Pierre Bourdieu dans la Guerre d'Algérie*. Marseille: Agone. 1 vol. [WC]

RR1564. ● Prennig, Thomas: *Pfarrerskinder in der Ddr: Zwischen Privilegierung und Diskriminierung. Eine Habitustheoretische Analyse Im Anschluss an Norbert Elias und Pierre Bourdieu*. Bielefeld: Transcript. 288p. [WC]

RR1565. ● Schultheis, Franz: *Unternehmen Bourdieu: Ein Erfahrungsbericht*. Bielefeld: Transcript. 104p. [LoC]

RR1566. ● Wacquant, Loïc J. D., & Claude Javeau: *Retour sur Pierre Bourdieu*. Bruxelles: Ed. de l'Institut de Sociologie de l'ULB. 159p. [WC]

RR1567. Brisset, Nicolas: "Anthropologie Économique. Cours au Collège de France, 1992-1993, Pierre Bourdieu: Paris, Seuil, 2017." *Revue de Philosophie Économique, 20*, 1, 247. [Cor]

RR1568. Bucholc, Marta: "Das Rechtsdenken Pierre Bourdieus." *Zeitschrift für Rechtssoziologie, 39*, 2, 332. [PrQ]

RR1569. Cavalcanti, Cláudio J. H., Nathan W. Lima, Matheus M. Nascimento, & Fernanda Ostermann: "Cultura Política, Desempenho Escolar e a Educação em Ciências: Um Estudo Empírico à Luz de Pierre Bourdieu." *Ciência & Educação (Bauru), 25*, 2, 431-447. [Naz]

RR1570. Díaz, Jaramillo J. A.: "Un Arte al Servicio del Pueblo: La Obra de

Clemencia Lucena Desde la Sociología de Pierre Bourdieu." *Revista Colombiana de Sociología*, *42*, 1, 271-291. [Naz]

RR1571.   Ducourant, Hélène, & Jeanne Lazarus: "Luc Boltanski and Jean-Claude Chamboredon, Under the Supervision of Pierre Bourdieu, the Bank and Its Customers: Elements for a Sociology of Credit (1963): Presentation of Extracts from a Document." *Les Études Sociales*, *169*, 1, 241. [Cor]

RR1572.   Dufal, Blaise: "L'État Comme Crypto-Église dans les Cours de Pierre Bourdieu." *Revue de l'Histoire des Religions*, 236, 429-452. [UofR]

RR1573.   García, García E. P.: "Pierre Bourdieu y Abdelmalek Sayad. El Desarraigo: La Violencia del Capitalismo en una Sociedad Rural." *Revista Mexicana de Sociología*, *81*, 4, 935-938. [UaB]

RR1574.   Giry, Johan: "Unthought Issues in Sociological Common Sense: On Marc Joly's Pour Bourdieu, & Jean-Louis Fabiani, Pierre Bourdieu. Un Structuralisme Héroïque." *Revue Française de Sociologie*, *60*, 2, 239. [Naz]

RR1575.   Go, J.: "Pierre Bourdieu, Algeria and Postcolonial Sociology." *Sotsiologicheskie Issledovaniia*, 4, 86. [PrQ]

RR1576.   Grau-Grau, Marc: "Pierre Bourdieu, Manet: A Symbolic Revolution." *International Sociology*, *34*, 2, 161-163. [RIT]

RR1577.   Grignard, Guillaume: "Catch Politique du Dimanche: L'Émission C'est Pas Tous les Jours Dimanche Analysée sous l'Œil de Pierre Bourdieu." *La Revue Nouvelle*, *1*, 1, 71. [UaB]

RR1578.   Guareschi, Massimiliano: "Pierre Bourdieu: L'Empirico, Il Contingente e Il Trascendentale nella Critica Sociale del Gusto." *Etnografia e Ricerca Qualitativa*, *12*, 3, 447-56. [PrQ]

RR1579.   Guay, Emanuel: "Pierre Bourdieu. L'Insoumission en Héritage sous la Direction de Édouard Louis, Presses Universitaires de France, Paris, 2016, pp. 157." *Canadian Journal of Political Science*, *52*, 1, 222-223. [UofR]

RR1580.   Hinojosa, Ramon, Melanie Sberna Hinojosa, & Jenny Nguyen: "Military Service and Physical Capital: Framing Musculoskeletal Disorders among American Military Veterans Using Pierre Bourdieu's Theory of Cultural Capital." *Armed Forces and Society*, *45*, 2, 268-90. [PrQ]

RR1581.   Holthaus, Leonie: "Pierre Bourdieu und die Möglichkeiten der Kritik in der Praxistheorie." *Zeitschrift für internationale Beziehungen*, *26*, 2, 67–87. [PrQ]

RR1582.   Kozlov, S. V.: "Social Magic: On an Unnoticed Concept of Pierre Bourdieu." *Sociology of Power*, *31*, 4, 139-154. [LoC]

RR1583.   Machado, Pedro H. B.: "Prolongamentos Críticos a Pierre Bourdieu: a Sociologia 'À Escala Individual' de Bernard Lahire." *Sociologias Plurais*, 5, 1. [WC]

RR1584.   Martinovich, Viviana: "Revistas Científicas Argentinas de Acceso Abierto y Circulación Internacional: Un Análisis desde la Teoría de los Campos de Pierre Bourdieu." *Información, Cultura y Sociedad*, 40, 93-116. [RIT]

RR1585.   Mustofa, Mustofa: "Undisciplined Reviewed from the Habitus Pierre Bourdieu Theory." *The Journal of Society and Media*, *3*, 2, 142. [WC]

RR1586.   O'Neill, Brian F.: "The Oral Tradition of Pierre Bourdieu: Classification Struggles, on the State, and Manet." *International Sociology*, *34*, 5, 526-535. [UofR]

RR1587.   Pilmis, Olivier: "Pierre Bourdieu, Anthropologie Économique. Cours

au Collège de France 1992-1993: Le Seuil et Raisons d'Agir, Paris, 2017, 352 p."
Sociologie du Travail, 61, 1. [UaB]

RR1588. Piotrowska, M.: "Pierre Bourdieu on Art as Social Practice. The Defense of the Concept of the Autonomous Field of Cultural Production." *Art Inquiry*, 21, 69-83. [Cor]

RR1589. Pop, Andrei: "Manet: A Symbolic Revolution, by Pierre Bourdieu. Translated by Peter Collier and Margaret Rigaud-Drayton.Cambridge: Polity Press, 2017. pp. xiv+586. $45.00." *The Journal of Modern History*, 91, 1, 196-197. [UofR]

RR1590. Quemin, Alain, & Ana P. C. Simionil: "A Contribuição de Pierre Bourdieu Para a Sociologia da Arte (França e Brasil)." *Revista Brasileira de Informação Bibliográfica em Ciências Sociais*, 89, 1-27. [LoC]

RR1591. Reed-Danahay, Deborah: "Thomas Medvetz and Jeffrey J. Sallaz, Eds. The Oxford Handbook of Pierre Bourdieu." *Contemporary Sociology*, 48, 6, 680. [RIT]

RR1592. Rodrigues, Lidiane S.: "O 'Pierre Bourdieu' de Marxistas e Anti-marxistas." *Arquivos do Cmd*, 5, 2. [WC]

RR1593. Rugy, Anne: "Pierre Bourdieu, Anthropologie Économique. Cours au Collège de France 1992-1993, Seuil, 2017, 337p. Claire Pignol La Théorie de l'Équilibre Général, Presses Universitaires du Septentrion, Les Savoirs Mieux, 2017, 121p: L'Homo Oeconomicus A-T-Il Vécu? Dialogue Imaginaire entre Pierre Bourdieu et une Économiste." *Terrains/ Théories*, 10. [WC]

RR1594. Sapiro, Gisèle: "Pierre Bourdieu Manet: A Symbolic Revolution." *Contemporary Sociology*, 48, 3, 286-287. [UofR]

RR1595. Swartz, David L.: "The Heavy Hands of the State Pierre Bourdieu on the State: Lectures at the Collège de France, 1989—1992; Kimberly J. Morgan and Ann Shola Orloff the Many Hands of the State: Theorizing Political Authority and Social Control." *Contemporary Sociology*, 48, 1, 12-18. [RIT]

RR1596. Tichavakunda, Antar A.: "An Overdue Theoretical Discourse: Pierre Bourdieu's Theory of Practice and Critical Race Theory in Education." *Educational Studies*, 55, 6, 651-666. [Naz]

RR1597. Truong, Fabien: "Ensinar Pierre Bourdieu No 9-3: O Que Falar Quer Dizer." *Política & Sociedade*, 18, 41, 280-291. [Naz]

RR1598. Vater, Katie J.: "Ignacio M. Sánchez Prado, Editor. Pierre Bourdieu in Hispanic Literature and Culture. Palgrave Macmillan, 2018." *Studies in 20th & 21st Century Literature*, 43, 2. [UaB]

RR1599. Voigt, Lucas: "Uma Análise do Desenvolvimento Conceitual da Sociologia de Pierre Bourdieu a Partir da Obra 'Os Herdeiros'." *Novos Rumos Sociológicos*, 6, 10. [WC]

BOURGET, Paul.
See also 325, 493.

RR1600. Ancelet-Netter, Dominique: "Paul Bourget Avant et Après le Disciple. Figures du Professeur et de l'Élève dans Mensonges et l'Étape." *Quêtes Littéraires*, 9. [UaB]

BOUSQUET, Joë.
RR1601. ● Weil, Simone, Florence Lussy, Michel Narcy, & Joë Bousquet:

Correspondance 1942: 'Quel Est Donc Ton Tourment?'. Paris XIIe: Claire Paulhan. 198p. [WC]

BOUVIER, Nicolas.
See also 31, 228, 471.

RR1602. ● Bouvier, Nicolas, & Alexandre Chollier: *Du Coin de l'Œil: Écrits sur la Photographie*. [Genève]: Héros-Limite. 217p. [BnF]

RR1603. ● Bouvier, Nicolas, & Alexandre Chollier: *Genève =: Geneva; La Suisse Est Folle: Proposition Déraisonnable Assortie de Quelques Images; Switzerland Is Crazy: An Unreasonable Proposition Coupled with a Few Images*. Genève: Héros-Limite. 107p. [WC]

RR1604. ● Bouvier, Nicolas, & Robyn Marsack: *So It Goes: Travels in the Aran Isles, Xian and Places in Between*. London: Eland. 182p. [WC]

RR1605. ● Lugon, Olivier: *Nicolas Bouvier Iconographe*. Genève: Bibliothèque de Genève. 159p. [BnF]

RR1606. ● *Sur les Pas de Nicolas Bouvier*. Fribourg: Sept. 195p. [WC]

RR1607. Dupuis, Sylviane: "Georges Haldas et Nicolas Bouvier: Le Poète, l'Œil, la Ville, le Moi." *Poème et le Territoire: Promenades Littéraires en Suisse Romande*, 164. [WC]

RR1608. Le Breton, David: "Nicolas Bouvier or the Travel as an Art of the Senses." *Estudios de Teoría Literaria*, *8*, 16, 158-165. [WC]

BOVE, Emmanuel.
See 14.

BRASILLACH, Robert.
See also 320, 371.

RR1609. ● Brasillach, Robert, & Cécile Dugas: *Journal d'un Homme Occupé: Mémoires*. Grez-sur-Loing: Pardès. 324p. [BAnQ]

BRASSENS, Georges.
RR1610. ● Allix, Guy, & Michel Baglin: *Je Suis . . . Georges Brassens*. Lyon: Jacques André. 94p. [WC]

RR1611. ● Brassens, Georges, & Jean-Paul Liégeois: *Je Suis Une Espèce de Libertaire: Brassens Par Lui-Même*. Paris: Cherche Midi. 167p. [BAnQ]

BRETON, André.
See also 71, 507, 731, 824, 825, 827.

RR1612. ● Audoin, Philippe, Jean-Claude Silbermann, Claude Courtot, & Jérôme Duwa: *Les Capucines aux Lèvres d'Émail: Sur André Breton*. Caen: Le Grand Tamanoir. 84p. [BnF]

RR1613. ● B., David: *Nick Carter et André Breton: Une Enquête Surréaliste*. Toulon: Soleil. 56p. [BnF]

RR1614. ● Breton, André, Paul Éluard, & Etienne-Alain Hubert: *Correspondance: 1919-1938*. [Paris]: Gallimard. 457p. [Cor]

RR1615. ● Chénieux-Gendron, Jacqueline, Olivier Wagner, & André Breton: *Nadja en Silence: L'Histoire du Manuscrit d'André Breton et de Ses Éditions: Une Lecture*. [Paris]: Gallimard. 61p. [WC]

RR1616. ● Debout-Oleszkiewicz, Simone, Florent Perrier, & Agnès Chekroun: *Correspondance 1958-1966: Suivi de, 'Mémoire. d'André Breton à Charles Fourier: La Révolution Passionnelle' & de 'Rétrospections'*. Paris: Claire Paulhan. 286p. [WC]

RR1617. Aubert, Nathalie: "Enchanted Ground: André Breton, Modernism and the Surrealist Appraisal of Fin-de-Siècle Painting." *French History*, *33*, 1, 148-150. [UaB]

RR1618. Delibasic, Spomenka: "The Fascination of André Breton for the Arithmosophic Calculation in Arcane 17 (the Number 1713 and Gérard de Nerval)." *International Journal of Literature and Arts*, *7*, 5, 98. [WC]

RR1619. Fortaleza, de A. J. E.: "'Os Fins Lógicos Nos Escapam': A Crítica da Alienação em André Breton." *Revista Limiar*, *6*, 12, 70-87. [WC]

RR1620. Hidalgo, Marian Panchón: "André Breton Bajo la Dictadura Franquista: Censura Institucional y Traducción de Entretiens: Revista de Estudios Franceses." *Çédille*, 15, 477-95. [PrQ]

RR1621. Laxton, Susan: "Enchanted Ground: André Breton, Modernism and the Surrealist Appraisal of Fin-de-Siècle Painting by Gavin Parkinson." *Modernism/ Modernity*, *26*, 4, 900-902. [Naz]

RR1622. Panchon, Hidalgo M.: "André Breton Bajo la Dictadura Franquista: Censura Institucional y Traducción de Entretiens." *Cedille*, 15, 477-495. [Syr]

RR1623. Raffi, Maria Emanuela: "'Les États Généraux' d'André Breton à l'Épreuve du Temps. Repères pour une Traversée." *Studi Francesi*, *63*, 1, 69-86. [UofR]

RR1624. Régnier, Marie-Clémence: "Nadja, Ou André Breton en Ses 'Maisons de Verre'." *Littérature*, *195*, 3, 17. [Syr]

BROSSARD, Nicole.
See also 259, 811.

RR1625. ● Gaudet, Gérald: *Nicole Brossard: L'Enthousiasme, Une Résistance Qui Dure*. Montréal: Noroît. 106p. [BAnQ]

RR1626. Marchand, Aline, Pascale Roux, & Angelo Vannini: "La Traduction-Fiction chez Nicole Brossard." *Recherches & Travaux*, 95. [WC]

BUGUL, Ken.
See also 26.

RR1627. ● Bugul, Ken, & Svenja Plaas: *Plus d'Autre Choix?* [Zurich]: OSL. 23p. [WC]

RR1628. Chilembwe, Maxwell: "L'Hégémonie Sexuelle dans Riwan ou le Chemin de Sable et Mes Hommes À Moi de Ken Bugul." *French Studies in Southern Africa*, 49, 38-58. [Cor]

RR1629. Febles, Isabel Pascua, & Alba Rodríguez-García: "Traducir las Identidades Africanas: Una Mirada Mujerista." *Clina*, *5*, 1, 95-112. [PrQ]

RR1630. Kuete, Roger Fopa: "Identity, Languages and Knowledge in Ken Bugul's Riwan ou le Chemin de Sable." *Tydskrif vir Letterkunde*, *56*, 2, 46-53. [UaB]

RR1631. Kwente, Danielle V.: "Récit de Soi et Latence Langagière dans Mes Hommes à Moi de Ken Bugul." *International Journal of Language & Literature*, 7, 1. [WC]

RR1632. Moneyang, P.: "Le Maraboutage dans La Folle et la Mort de Ken Bugul." *French Review*, *93*, 2, 89-100. [UofR]

RR1633. Sacharewicz, Edyta: "The Role of Music in Ken Bugul's Novels." *Literatūra*, *61*, 4, 44-53. [Syr]

RR1634. Tricoire, Marion: "Trajectoires Urbaines: Dakar au Prisme d'Aller et Retour de Ken Bugul." *French Review*, *92*, 3, 139-152. [UofR]

BUTOR, Michel.
See also 187, 526, 705.

RR1635. ● Butor, Michel: *Le Musée Imaginaire de Michel Butor: 105 Œuvres Décisives de la Peinture Occidentale.* Paris: Flammarion. 365p. [BAnQ]

RR1636. ● Butor, Michel, Cauchy C. Giraud, & Daniel Leuwers: *L'Or Pauvre.* Manosque: Ségust. 43p. [BnF]

RR1637. ● Calle-Gruber, Mireille, Jean-Paul Morin, & Adèle Godefroy: *Compagnonnages de Michel Butor.* Paris: Hermann. 238p. [BnF]

RR1638. ● Coste, Marion: *Votre Faust, la Création en Partage: Étude de la Mise en Scène d'Aliénor Dauchez: Votre Faust d'Henri Pousseur et Michel Butor.* Besançon: Presses Universitaires de Franche-Comté. 309p. [WC]

RR1639. ● Salini, Dominique: *Webern, Fourier et Butor Selon Pousseur: Un Voyage en Utopie.* Paris: L'Harmattan. 312p. [WC]

RR1640. ● Stiefel, Viola: *Raumerkundungen: Michel Butors Romane Im Kontext des 'Spatial Turn'.* Heidelberg: Universitätsverlag Winter. 183p. [WC]

RR1641. Bosseur, Jean-Yves: "'Michel Butor Avait le Talent de Musicaliser le Temps du Texte'." *Annales Littéraires de l'Université de Besançon*, 99. [WC]

RR1642. Ferrari, Nicola: "Marion Coste, Une Leçon de Musique Donnée aux Mots. Les Collaborations de Michel Butor avec Ludwig van Beethoven et Henri Pousseur." *Studi Francesi*, *63*, 1, 195-196. [UaB]

RR1643. Koyano, Amayi L. S.: "A Co-Construção da Imagem de Michel Butor: Argumentação em Entrevistas Literárias." *Filologia e Linguística Portuguesa*, *21*, 1, 115-138. [Syr]

RR1644. Koyano, Amayi L. S.: "Michel Butor, Voz(es)." *Magma*, 15, 235-256. [LoC]

RR1645. Labbé, Mathilde: "'Nécessité de Procéder Obliquement': Shaping Michel Butor's Image." *Nottingham French Studies*, *58*, 3, 315-331. [Syr]

RR1646. Rostamipour, S., & F. Khanmohamadi: "Analyzing Spatiotemporality in Textual Space of La Modification (A Change of Heart by Michel Butor Based on Geographical Discourse)." *Language Related Research*, *10*, 3, 47-69. [WC]

CADIOT, Olivier.
See also 515, 781.

RR1647. Chevilley, Philippe: "Pinter en un Carré Magique aux Bouffes du Nord." *Les Echos*, Mar 07. [PrQ]

RR1648. Sainsbury, Daisy: "Language and Statelessness in the Poetry of Olivier Cadiot." *Modern Languages Open*, 1. [WC]

CADOU, René Guy.
RR1649. ● Lavoué, Jean: *René Guy Cadou: La Fraternité au Coeur.* Hennebont: L'Enfance des Arbres. 299p. [WC]

CAHUN, Claude.

See also 291, 293, 296, 322, 353.

RR1650. ● Cahun, Claude, Ottonella Mocellin, Fabiola Naldi, & Maura Pozzati: *Body Configurations: Claude Cahun, Valie Export, Ottonella Mocellin.* Mantova: Corraini. 158p. [WC]

RR1651. ● Le Ru, V., Fabrice Bourlez, & Claude Cahun: *Claude Cahun entre Art et Philosophie.* Reims: Éditions et Presses Universitaires de Reims. 153p. [WC]

RR1652. ● Soto, Vila E, & Gonzalo Puerto: *Claude Cahun: La Aventura Invisible.* Madrid: Prisa Noticias. 141p. [WC]

RR1653. Baldacchino, Adeline: "Claude Cahun: Aucune Femme N'Est Une Île." *Ballast,* 7, 1, 114. [BnF]

RR1654. Bowes, Simon: "Dirt in the Lens." *Performance Research,* 24, 6, 38-46. [PrQ]

RR1655. Gianoncelli, Ève: "'Gunpowder and Lighted Wick': Claude Cahun (Pseud. Lucy Schwob) and Marcel Moore (Pseud. Suzanne Malherbe), an Avant-Garde Female Couple." *Les Études Sociales,* 170, 2, 179. [UofR]

RR1656. Meneses, Emerson S., & Martin Jayo: "Queer Avant la Lettre: Moda e Performance de Gênero Nos Autorretratos de Claude Cahun." *Dobra[s],* 12, 27, 147-164. [LoC]

RR1657. Murray, Yxta M.: "I Will Be Like Claude Cahun." *Georgia Review,* 73, 4, 985. [UofR]

RR1658. Oberhuber, Andrea, & Houde S.-J. Beauchamp: "Figures Troubles: La New Woman et La Femme Nouvelle dans 'La Dame à la Louve' de Renée Vivien et 'Héroïnes' de Claude Cahun." *Captures,* 4, 1. [WC]

RR1659. Rim, Hye-Song: "Imitation and Subversion of Gender: Claude Cahun's Self-Portrait Photography." *Journal of the Association of Western Art History,* 50, 175-198. [WC]

RR1660. Sabiá, Ana P.: "A Fotografia Performática de Claude Cahun." *Revista Digital do Lav,* 12, 1, 55. [WC]

CAILLOIS, Roger.

See also 775, 828.

RR1661. ● Heiden, Anne, & Sarah Kolb: *Logik Des Imaginären. Diagonale Wissenschaft Nach Roger Caillois. Band 2: Spiel/Raum/ Kunst/ Theorie.* Berlin: August. 300p. [WC]

RR1662. ● Petel-Rochette, Nicolas: *Carisma sin Líderes: Ensayo sobre Mímesis, Arte y Naturaleza en Roger Caillois.* Madrid: Escolar y Mayo. 213p. [LoC]

RR1663. Kwon, Min-ji, & Su-jeung Kim: "A Study on Correlation between Economy-Based Board Game's Properties and Its Design - Focused on Roger Caillois' Play Theory." *Journal of Communication Design,* 67, 7-22. [WC]

RR1664. Lévi-Strauss, Claude: "Grand Article: 'Diogène Couché'." *Cités,* 81, 137-68. [PrQ]

RR1665. Torre, C.: "La Trottola Cosmica: Da Manilio (Astronomica 3, 356-61) a Roger Caillois." *Enthymema,* 23, 461-482. [Syr]

CALAFERTE, Louis.

RR1666. ● Villard, Ludovic: *Pourquoi Je Lis "Septentrion" de Louis Calaferte.* [Lyon]: Le Feu Sacré. 65p. [BnF]

CALET, Henri.
See also 183.
RR1667. ● Calet, Henri, & Cazorla V. García: *El Todo por el Todo: París, Calle a Calle.* Madrid: Errata Naturae. 290p. [WC]
RR1668. ● Calet, Henri, & Michel P. Schmitt: *Mes Impressions d'Afrique.* Lyon: Presses Universitaires de Lyon. [WC]
RR1669. Corona, René: "Henri Calet, Mes Impressions d'Afrique." *Studi Francesi, 63,* 3, 606-607. [UaB]

CALLE, Sophie.
See also 291, 307, 315, 322, 343, 446, 610, 631, 632.
RR1670. ● Calle, Sophie: *Sophie Calle et des Visiteurs du Musée de la Chasse et de la Nature: Que Faites-Vous de vos Morts?* Arles: Actes Sud. 263p. [LoC]
RR1671. ● Calle, Sophie, & Xavier Barral: *Because.* Paris: Xavier Barral. [35]p. [BnF]
RR1672. ● Calle, Sophie, & Sabine Erbrich: *Das Adressbuch.* Berlin: Suhrkamp. 105p. [WC]
RR1673. ● Calle, Sophie, Tillman Kaiser, Ivana Ivković, Marilies Seyler, & Valter Ventura: *In Focus: 40 Years of Ars Electronica: Sophie Calle, Tillman Kaiser, Ivana Ivković, Marielis Seyler, Valter Ventura.* Wien: Österreichisches Institut für Photographie und Medienkunst. 100p. [WC]
RR1674. ● Hwamin, Shin: *Sophie Calle: Regard sur Autrui: Du Déséquilibre à l'Imaginaire.* Paris: L'Harmattan. 109p. [BnF]
RR1675. Baraona, Isabel: "Sophie Calle & Paul Auster: Doubles-Jeux." *Palíndromo, 11,* 23, 78-83. [WC]
RR1676. "Sophie Calle." *RPS Journal, 159,* 9, 606. [PrQ]

CAMUS, Albert.
See also 1, 31, 376, 451, 529.
RR1677. ● *Albert Camus: Un Extranjero en Buenos Aires: Agosto 2019 - Marzo 2020.* [Ciudad Autónoma de Buenos Aires]: Biblioteca Nacional Mariano Moreno. 95p. [WC]
RR1678. ● Auroy, Carole, & Anne Prouteau: *Albert Camus et les Vertiges du Sacré.* Rennes: Presses Universitaires de Rennes. 311p. [UofR]
RR1679. ● Basset, Guy: *De l'Ombre vers le Soleil: Albert Camus Face à la Violence.* La Roque-Alric: Éditions des Offray. 165p. [Cor]
RR1680. ● Berger, Thomas: *"Inmitten der Europäischen Nacht ...": Erneuerung der Sozialdemokratie aus dem Geist des "Mittelmeerischen Denkens" (Albert Camus).* Frankfurt am Main: Federleicht. 33p. [WC]
RR1681. ● Bousenna, Youness: *Albert Camus: L'Éternité Est Ici.* Paris: Première Partie. 122p. [LoC]
RR1682. ● Brocas, Alexis, Marylin Maeso, & Aurélie Marcireau: "Albert Camus: La Révolte et la Justice: Penser Contre la Haine et pour l'Homme Encore et Toujours." *Nouveau Magazine Littéraire,* 24, 26. [WC]
RR1683. ● Camus, Albert: *Dossier Spécial: Albert Camus ; Une Icône Francçaise.* Paris: Groupe Express. *L'Express / Edition Internationale,* 3573/3574. 114p. [WC]

RR1684. • Camus, Albert, Louis Bénisti, Jean-Pierre Bénisti, Martine Mathieu-Job, Virginie Lupo, & Guy Basset: *Albert Camus, Correspondance avec Ses Amis Bénisti, 1934-1958*. Saint-Pourçain-sur Sioule: Bleu Autour. 191p. [WC]

RR1685. • Camus, Albert, Nicola Chiaromonte, & Samantha Novello: *Albert Camus, Nicola Chiaromonte: Correspondance, 1945-1959*. [Paris]: Gallimard. 232p. [WC]

RR1686. • Catelli, Giovanni, & Danielle Dubroca: *La Mort de Camus*. [Paris]: Balland. 280p. [BnF]

RR1687. • Coande, Nicolae: *Mansarda Europa: (din Casa "Heinrich Böll" în Camera "Albert Camus")*. Piteşti: Paralela. 303p. [Cor]

RR1688. • Dehoux, Amaury, & Vincent Engel: *Les Manipulations Multiples chez Albert Camus*. Turnhout: Brepols. 297p. [WC]

RR1689. • Jahanbegloo, Ramin: *Albert Camus: The Unheroic Hero of Our Time*. New Delhi: Routledge India. 80p. [Syr]

RR1690. • Nash, Woods: *The Health Humanities and Camus's the Plague*. Kent, OH: The Kent State UP. 194p. [Syr]

RR1691. • Santos, Saínz M., & Edwy Plenel: *Albert Camus, Journaliste: Reporter à Alger, Éditorialiste à Paris*. Rennes: Apogée. 297p. [BAnQ]

RR1692. • Vanney, Philippe: *Albert Camus au Fil des Rencontres: Littérature, Théâtre, Politique*. Caen: Lettres Modernes Minard. 254p. [WC]

RR1693. Ait-Chaalal, Amine: "Albert Camus et la Guerre d'Algérie: L'Étrange Équation. Prolégomènes, Rétroactes et Regard(s)." *Les Lettres Romanes*, *73*, 1-2, 177-196. [Syr]

RR1694. Barreira, Marcelo: "O Mito de Sísifo de Albert Camus e Sua Relevância no Processo de Ensino-Aprendizagem de Filosofia." *Conjectura Filosofia e Educação*, *24*, 0, 1-16. [WC]

RR1695. Birchall, Ian: "Reading Camus Carefully? A Review of L'Ordre Libertaire: La Vie Philosophique d'Albert Camus by Michel Onfray." *Historical Materialism*, *27*, 1, 306-318. [RIT]

RR1696. Breen, Gina M.: "Neither Algerian, nor French: Albert Camus's Pied-Noir Identity." *Mediterranean Studies*, *27*, 2, 210-233. [UaB]

RR1697. Brocas, Alexis: "Albert Camus: La Révolte et la Mesure: Dossier." *Nouveau Magazine Littéraire*, *24*, 26-41. [WC]

RR1698. Brown, Jennifer S.: "The Memory of the Medieval, the Vichy Regime, and Albert Camus's La Peste." *French Review*, *92*, 3, 92-103. [Naz]

RR1699. De Wilde, T. "Albert Camus Face à la Manipulation Politique." *Les Lettres Romanes*, *73*, 1-2, 159-176. [UaB]

RR1700. Dean, Paul: "Albert Camus: Humanism and Tragedy." *The Hopkins Review*, *12*, 1, 45-59. [UofR]

RR1701. Fauré-Bellaïche, Clémentine: "Le Sourire d'Albert Camus: Actes du Colloque d'Aix-en-Provence 8–11 Novembre 2017." *Modern Language Review*, *114*, 2, 380. [PrQ]

RR1702. Garcia, L. G.: "Nihilism and Antiheroism in Albert Camus Literary Work." *Nueva Revista del Pacífico*, 70, 1-17. [UaB]

RR1703. González, García L.: "Antiheroísmo y Nihilismo en la Obra Literaria de Albert Camus." *Nueva Revista del Pacífico*, 70, 1-17. [WC]

RR1704. Haber, Darren: "Intimate Strangers: Albert Camus and Absurdity in Psychoanalysis." *Psychoanalysis, Self and Context*, *14*, 4, 349-366. [Cor]

RR1705. Lund, Hans P.: "Albert Camus Face à l'Allemagne: Réactions et Lectures." *Revue d'Histoire Littéraire de la France, 119*, 1, 125-144. [RIT]

RR1706. Lyotard, D.: "Au Versant du Jour, Les Carnets d'Albert Camus." *Revue des Sciences Humaines*, January, 335, 73-104. [Syr]

RR1707. Mahdi, Iman: "Emotional Detachment in Albert Camus' The Stranger: A Happy Man Drawn into Misery." *Journal of Humanistic and Social Studies, 10*, 2, 37-44. [PrQ]

RR1708. Malan, Charles: "Die Buitestaander (Albert Camus, Vertaal Deur Jan Rabie)." *Tydskrif Vir Letterkunde*, 43, 2. [UaB]

RR1709. Matisson, Vivien: "Albert Camus et Brice Parain: De la Manipulation du Logos." *Les Lettres Romanes, 73*, 1-2, 91-114. [Syr]

RR1710. Mezzetti, Monia: "Le Sourire d'Albert Camus, sous la Direction de David H. Walker." *Studi Francesi, 63*, 1, 190. [UaB]

RR1711. O'Leary, Catherine: "Censoring the Outsider: The Theatre of Albert Camus in Franco's Spain." *Modern Drama, 62*, 3, 292-319. [UofR]

RR1712. Orme, Mark: "Albert Camus et 'l'État de Siège': Genèse d'un Spectacle." *French Studies, 73*, 1, 140-141. [UaB]

RR1713. Orme, Mark: "Le Sourire d'Albert Camus: Actes du Colloque d'Aix en Provence, 8–11 Novembre 2017." *French Studies, 73*, 1, 141-142. [UaB]

RR1714. Pausch, M.: "Democracy Needs Rebellion: A Democratic Theory Inspired by Albert Camus." *Theoria (United Kingdom), 66*, 161, 91-107. [RIT]

RR1715. Samuels, Andrew, & Agnès Blondel: "'Je Me Révolte, Donc Nous Sommes' (Albert Camus): Nouvelle Réflexion Politique sur la Responsabilité Individuelle pour le Groupe, la Société, la Culture et la Planète." *Actualités en Analyse Transactionnelle, 166*, 2, 25. [WC]

RR1716. Sellès-Lefranc, Michèle: "Dickow (Alexander), Malela (Buata), Dir., Albert Camus, Aimé Césaire: Poétiques de la Révolte. Paris: Hermann, 2018, 365 p. – ISBN 978-2-7056-9750-1." *Études Littéraires Africaines*, 48, 243. [WC]

RR1717. Spicer, Michael W.: "Towards the Meridian: Albert Camus, Democracy, and Public Administration." *Public Integrity, 21*, 4, 378-393. [Naz]

RR1718. Thesz, Nicole: "The Existentialist Legacy: Sisyphean Struggles in Albert Camus' La Peste and Günter Grass's Die Rättin." *Oxford German Studies, 48*, 3, 404-419. [UofR]

CAMUS, Renaud.

RR1719. ● Camus, Renaud, & Saune M. Du: *Le Petit Remplacement*. Paris: Pierre-Guillaume de Roux. 485p. [Cor]

RR1720. Leconte, Cécile: "La Carrière Militante du 'Grand Remplacement' au Sein du Milieu Partisan de l'Alternative pour l'Allemagne (afd)." *Politix, 126*, 2, 111. [Cor]

RR1721. Stefanoni, Pablo: "El Futuro Como 'Gran Reemplazo': Extremas Derechas, Homosexualidad y Xenofobia." *Nueva Sociedad*, 283, 95-110. [PrQ]

CANGUILHEM, Georges.

See also Simondon.

RR1722. ● Canguilhem, Georges, Camille Limoges, & Jean-François Braunstein: *Oeuvres Complètes: Tome 3*. Paris: Vrin. 1055p. [WC]

RR1723. ● Elden, Stuart: *Canguilhem*. Medford, MA: Polity Press. 215p. [Syr]

RR1724. ● Talcott, Samuel: *Georges Canguilhem and the Problem of Error*. Cham: Springer Nature. 294p. [Syr]

CARCO, Francis.

RR1725. Dubosson, Fabien: "L'Esthète et le 'Mauvais Garçon.' La Correspondance entre William Ritter et Francis Carco (1914-1917)." *Versants*, 1, 66. [Syr]

CARDINAL, Marie.

See also 49, 55.

RR1726. Tremblay, David: "Chronique d'Archives." *Revue d'Histoire de l'Amérique Française*, *72*, 3, 131, 134, 131A. [PrQ]

CARRÈRE, Emmanuel.

See also 64, 756.

RR1727. ● Carrère, Emmanuel: *97,196 Words: Essays*. London: Jonathan Cape. 294p. [UaB]

RR1728. ● Nacache, Jacqueline, & Régis Salado: *Emmanuel Carrère: Un Écrivain au Prisme du Cinéma*. Paris: Hermann. 300p. [UofR]

RR1729. ● Zufferey, Pauline: *Emmanuel Carrère et l'Écriture Intrusive: Étude Comparative de "La Classe de Neige", "L'Adversaire", "Un Roman Russe", "D'Autres Vies Que Les Miennes"*. Neuchâtel: [Éditeur Non Identifié]. 66p. [WC]

RR1730. Boblet, Marie-Hélène, & Anne Gourio: "Des Faillites et des Failles: Ce Que Juger Veut Dire: D'Autres Vies Que La Mienne d'Emmanuel Carrère et Article 353 du Code Pénal de Tanguy Viel." *Elfe XX-XXI*, 9. [Cor]

RR1731. Gottlieb, Robert: "97, 196 Words Essays by Emmanuel Carrère." *New York Times Book Review*, *124*, 51, 1. [WC]

RR1732. Köpf, Gerhard: "Der Widersacher: Ein Tatsachenroman Von Emmanuel Carrère." *Neurotransmitter*, 30, 58-61. [WC]

RR1733. Poncelet, Dominique: "Le Livre Comme Tombeau Littéraire: Franz et François de François Weyergans et D'Autres Vies Que La Mienne d'Emmanuel Carrère." *French Review*, *93*, 2, 51-63. [Naz]

RR1734. Reda, Vonita R., & Alice Armini: "La Condition Psychologique du Personnage Principal de Roman L'Adversaire d'Emmanuel Carrère." *Digital Press Social Sciences and Humanities*, 3, 45. [WC]

RR1735. Thirion, Nicolas: "Ce Que La Littérature Fait au Droit: Le Cas Emmanuel Carrère." *Contextes*, 22. [Syr]

CARRIER, Roch.

See also 195, 254, 332.

RR1736. ● Carrier, Roch: *Leçons Apprises et Parfois Oubliées*. Montréal: Libre Expression. 309p. [BAnQ]

RR1737. Dopp, Jamie: "Rethinking Hockey." *Canadian Literature*, *238*, 141, 142, 183. [RIT]

CASSOU, Jean.

See 412.

CAVAILLÈS, Jean.

See also 714.

RR1738. ● Benis, Sinaceur H.: *Jean Cavaillès: Philosophie Mathématique.* Paris: J. Vrin. 192p. [WC]

CAYROL, Jean.

See also 84, 373.

RR1739. ● Cayrol, Jean, & Ulrike J. Betz: *Schattenalarm (1944-1945): Mit dem Essay "Lazarenische Träume."* Wien: Hamburg New Academic Press. 115p. [WC]

RR1740. ● Pollock, Griselda, & Maxim Silverman: *Concentrationary Art: Jean Cayrol, the Lazarean and the Everyday in Post-War Film, Literature, Music and the Visual Arts.* Oxford: Berghahn Books. 259p. [UofR]

RR1741. Baker, Emily-Rose: "Concentrationary Art: Jean Cayrol, the Lazarean and the Everyday in Post-War Film, Literature, Music and the Visual Arts." *Textual Practice*, May 25, 1-4. [UofR]

CÉARD, Henry.

See 677, 1454.

CÉLINE, Louis-Ferdinand.

See also 373, 397, 627.

RR1742. ● Benedetti, Riccardo D.: *Il Dossier "Bagatelle": La Polemica Su Céline in Francia e in Italia.* Milano: Medusa. 154p. [LoC]

RR1743. ● Céline, Louis-Ferdinand, & Jean-Paul Louis: *Cahiers de Prison: Février-Octobre 1946.* [Paris]: Gallimard. 226p. [BAnQ]

RR1744. ● Faurisson, Robert: *Ecrits Céliniens. Pour une Pleine Réhabilitation de Céline.* Saint Genis Laval: Akribeia. 184p. [BnF]

RR1745. ● Fleury, Jean L.: *L'Affaire Céline, ou, Cendres au Crique-à-la-Roche / Jean Louis Fleury.* Lévis, PQ: Alire. 335p. [BnF]

RR1746. ● Grouix, Pierre, François Marchetti, & Jean-Michel Wittmann: *Ferme du Bois Clair: Céline, Danemark, 1948-1951.* Montrouge: Bourg. 252p. [LoC]

RR1747. ● Hanrez, Marc: *Céline et Ses Classiques: & Autres Essais.* Paris: Paris-Max Chaleil. 188p. [BnF]

RR1748. ● Richard, Jean-Pierre, & Daniele Gorret: *Nausea di Céline: La Condizione Umana Nell'Immaginario e nelle Opere di Louis-Ferdinand Céline.* Firenze: Passaggio al Bosco. 63p. [WC]

RR1749. ● Tettamanzi, Régis: *La Parole au Scalpel: Médecine et Littérature chez L.-F. Céline et Quelques-Uns de Ses Contemporains.* Nanterre: Presses Universitaires de Paris Nanterre. 190p. [Cor]

RR1750. Auxéméry, Yann: "Le Trauma de Guerre Comme Moteur d'Écriture: Analyse Patho-Littéraire et Psycholinguistique de Louis-Ferdinand Céline." *L'Évolution Psychiatrique, 84*, 3, 451-467. [RIT]

RR1751. Coulibaly, Daouda: "Regard Stylistique et Comparatif des Pratiques Diglossiques dans Féerie Pour une Autre Fois de Louis-Ferdinand Céline et Le Lieutenant de Kouta de Massa Makan Diabaté: Deux Romans d'Expression Française." *Nordic Journal of Francophone Studies/ Revue Nordique des Études Francophones, 2*, 1, 1-11. [Naz]

RR1752.   Saguin, Emeric, & Yoann Loisel: "Le Style Littéraire Comme Solution au Traumatisme de Guerre? L'Exemple de Louis-Ferdinand Céline." *Annales Médico-Psychologiques*, *177*, 8, 829-834. [PrQ]

CENDRARS, Blaise.
See also 804.
RR1753.   ● Cendrars, Blaise, & Francesco Pilastro: *Sarajevo*. Trieste: Nonostante. 124p. [WC]
RR1754.   ● *Constellation Cendrars. Vol. 3 (2019). Le Primitivisme Littéraire.* Paris: Classiques Garnier. 192p. [WC]
RR1755.   ● Le Quellec, C. C.: *Blaise Cendrars: Un Homme en Partance.* Lausanne: Presses Polytechniques et Universitaires Romandes. 191p. [BnF]
RR1756.   ● Leroy, Claude: *Blaise Cendrars & L'Homme Foudroyé.* Paris: Presses Universitaire de Paris Nanterre. 179p. [UofR]
RR1757.   Feinsod, Harris: "Canal Zone Modernism: Cendrars, Walrond, and Stevens at the 'Suction Sea'." *English Language Notes*, *57*, 1, 116-128. [Naz]
RR1758.   Le Quellec, C. C.: "Blaise Cendrars, Suivre Les Vents." 196. In 804.

CERTEAU, Michel de.
See also 382, 716, 1160.
RR1759.   ● Bauer, Christian, & Marco A. Sorace: *Gott, Anderswo?: Theologie im Gespräch mit Michel de Certeau.* Ostfildern: Matthias Grünewald. 444p. [WC]
RR1760.   Alves, Marilia, Ricardo B. Cavalcante, Hosana F. Rates, & Regina C. Santos: "Everyday Life in Nursing Work Under the Michel de Certeau's Perspective." *Revista Brasileira de Enfermagem*, *72*, 1, 341-345. [RIT]
RR1761.   Belcher, Jodi L. A.: "Unseeing the Body with Bodies on the Move: An Epistemology for Bodies Through Certeau and Holy Week Processions." *Anglican Theological Review*, *101*, 3, 407-426. [Naz]
RR1762.   De Araujo, H. N., & Elda C. A. Bussinger: "Michel de Certeau e as Microressistências do Herói Comum: Uma Possibilidade de Compreender o Cotidiano No Direito a Partir do Murmúrio da Sociedade." *Revista Eletrônica Direito e Sociedade – Redes*, *7*, 3, 79. [WC]
RR1763.   Fabre, Pierre-Antoine: "Comptes Rendus. Diana Napoli. Michel de Certeau. Lo Storico 'Smarrito.' Brescia, Morcelliana, 2014, 248 p." *Annales. Histoire, Sciences Sociales*, *74*, 2, 474. [UofR]
RR1764.   Gilbert, Paul: "Michel de Certeau and Theology: Finding God and Seeking God Again." *La Civiltà Cattolica, 3*, 8, 1-13. [WC]
RR1765.   González-Sanz, Juan, Ana Abreu-Sánchez, & Margarita Rodríguez-Pérez: "El Lugar Social del Conocimiento Enfermero: Los Editoriales Científicos Como Artefactos Lingüísticos desde la Perspectiva de Michel de Certeau." *Enfermería: Cuidados Humanizados*, *8*, 2, 66-84. [WC]
RR1766.   Marcelino, Douglas A.: "Tempo do Evento, Poética da História: Maio de 1968 Segundo Michel de Certeau e Cornelius Castoriadis." *História da Historiografia: International Journal of Theory and History of Historiography*, 12, 30. [Naz]
RR1767.   Momège, Philippe: "Daniel Poitras, Expérience du Temps et Historiographie au XXe Siècle — Michel de Certeau, François Furet et Fernand Dumont."

RR1768.   Sobrero, Alberto M.: "La Macchina Atropologica. Michel de Certeau: L'Invenzione del Quotidiano (Parte Seconda)." *Lares*, 85, 1, 17. [PrQ]

RR1769.   Vidal, Diana G., Maria A. B. Salvadori, & Ana L. J. Costa: "Cultura e História da Educação: Diálogos com Michel de Certeau E. E. P. Thompson." *Revista Histedbr On-Line*, 19. [Cor]

RR1770.   Westerink, H. "Foucault, Certeau und die Bausteine für eine Theorie der Kritischen Spiritualität." *Coincidentia*, 10, 385-412. [WC]

CÉSAIRE, Aimé.

See 192, 546, 549, 596, 798.

RR1771.   • Balla, Bonaventure: *Aimé Césaire et les Porteurs de Lumière*. Saint-Denis: Edilivre. 169p. [WC]

RR1772.   • Césaire, Aimé, & Edouard Lépine: *Aimé Césaire: Écrits Politiques: 1935-2008*. Paris: Nouvelles Éditions Jean-Michel Place. 5 vols. [WC]

RR1773.   • Corinus, Véronique: *Aimé Césaire*. Paris: PUF. 183p. [WC]

RR1774.   • Mankassa, Côme: *Aimé Césaire, ou l'Illusion de la Liberté: Essai*. Namur: Le Lys Bleu. 171p. [WC]

RR1775.   Aguirre, Aguirre C. S.: "Humanismo y 'Calibanismo' en Aimé Césaire." *Estudios de Filosofía Práctica e Historia de las Ideas*, 21, 2, 1-22. [Naz]

RR1776.   Arnold, Albert J.: "Genèse et Histoire Éditoriale d'un Manuscrit Inconnu d'Aimé Césaire: Destiné à l'Exposition 'Wifredo Lam - Caracas, Venezuela, Mai 1955'." *Continents Manuscrits*, 12. [Cor]

RR1777.   Célestine, Audrey: "Ta-Nehisi Coates in the Land of Aimé Césaire. About the Reception of between the World and Me and We Were Eight Years in Power: An American Tragedy." *Revue Française d'Études Américaines*, 158, 1, 132. [UaB]

RR1778.   Douaire-Banny, Anne: "Théâtre Dialectique Postcolonial: Aimé Césaire et Derek Walcott." *French Studies*, 73, 2, 331-332. [UaB]

RR1779.   Galbo, Sebastian C.: "'Lands That Spit and Spew': Aimé Césaire's Vegetal Poetry." *The Journal of Commonwealth Literature*, 54, 2, 143-159. [UofR]

RR1780.   Gonzalez Seligmann, Katerina: "Cabrera's Césaire: The Making of a Trans-Caribbean Zone." *Mln*, 134, 5, 1037-58. [RIT]

RR1781.   Graham, Shane: "'It Cancels the Slave Ship!': Africa, Slavery, and the Haitian Revolution in Langston Hughes's Emperor of Haiti and Aimé Césaire's The Tragedy of King Christophe." *Modern Drama*, 62, 4, 458-482. [Naz]

RR1782.   Hel-Bongo, Olga: "Poétique du Carnet dans Cahier d'un Retour au Pays Natal d'Aimé Césaire." *Études Littéraires*, 48, 119-135. [Syr]

RR1783.   Noland, Carrie: "Translating Césaire." *Modernism/ Modernity*, 26, 2, 419-26. [RIT]

RR1784.   Palenzuela, Lucía: "Algunas Palabras Desconocidas de Jorge Cáceres y Aimé Césaire en el Contexto Internacional del Surrealismo." *Revista de Filología de la Universidad de la Laguna*, 39, 275-286. [Syr]

RR1785.   Sánchez, Gonzalo S. R.: "Encuentros y Desencuentro en la Noción de Negritud de Aimé Césaire en el Ambiente Cultural del Siglo XX." *Revista Nordestina de História do Brasil*, 1, 2, 163-176. [WC]

RR1786.   Véron, Kora: "Réponse à l'Article d'Albert James Arnold: 'Genèse et Histoire Éditoriale d'un Manuscrit Inconnu d'Aimé Césaire,' Continents Manuscrits N° 12, Février 2019." *Continents Manuscrits*, 12. [Cor]

CÉSAIRE, Ina.
See 857.

CHAILLOU, Michel.
See also 535.
RR1787.   Berquin, François: "Mémoires d'un Âne (Michel Chaillou)." *Revue des Sciences Humaines*, 335, 191-202. [Syr]
RR1788.   Bruley, Pauline: "'Autant de Départs, Autant de Styles'? L'Écriture de la Phrase chez Michel Chaillou." *Faux Titre*, 434, 163-186. [UofR]

CHAMOISEAU, Patrick.
See also 207, 210, 214, 216, 247, 260, 265, 496, 515, 541, 680, 4760.
RR1789.   Altergott, Renée: "Parasitic Reproduction: Recording the Female in the Early Works of Patrick Chamoiseau." *Women in French Studies*, 27, 203-213. [UaB]
RR1790.   Couti, Jacqueline: "Slave Old Man: A Novel: Patrick Chamoiseau Translated by Linda Coverdale New York: The New Press, 2018." *Review: Literature and Arts of the Americas*, 52, 1, 155-157. [UofR]
RR1791.   De Vriese, Hannes: "Dans les Cuisines Créoles de Patrick Chamoiseau, La Prodigieuse Nourriture de Survie." *Elfe XX-XXI*, 7. [Cor]
RR1792.   Jadli, Souad: "A La Recherche de l'Identité Culturelle et Linguistique dans 'Solibo Magnifique' de Patrick Chamoiseau." *Les Cahiers du Centre des Études Doctorales*, 27-31. [WC]
RR1793.   Kana, Nguetse P.: "Le Maître dans l'Œil du Disciple. À Propos de l'Apprentissage ou de l'Initiation Écologique dans Les Neuf Consciences du Malfini de Patrick Chamoiseau." *Quêtes Littéraires*, 9. [WC]
RR1794.   Kopf, M.: "The Footprint as an Accelerator for Individualisation and Relation: Patrick Chamoiseau's L'Empreinte à Crusoé." *Porownania*, 25, 211-228. [LoC]
RR1795.   Lloze, E.: "L'Enquête Visionnaire de Patrick Chamoiseau." *Revue des Sciences Humaines*, 334, 123-132. [Syr]
RR1796.   Mason, Bethany: "An Ecocritical Approach to Identity Representation in Patrick Chamoiseau's Chronique des Sept Misères." *Alternative Francophone*, 2, 4, 25-41. [Syr]

CHAPPAZ, Maurice.
RR1797.   ● Bille, Stéphanie C., Maurice Chappaz, & Lis Künzli: *Ich Werde das Land Durchwandern, Das du Bist: Briefwechsel 1942-1979*. [Zürich]: Blau Belletrislik im Rotpunktverlag. 399 p. [WC]

CHAR, René.
See also 535, 806, 1093.
RR1798.   ● Camus, Albert, René Char, Franck Planeille, & Ana Nuño: *Correspondancia, 1946-1959*. Madrid: Alfabeto. 324p. [LoC]
RR1799.   ● Galantaris, Christian, & Louise-Mirabelle Biheng-Martinon: *René Char: Hommage à André Rodocanachi, l'Ami des Poètes*. Paris: Pierre Rodocanachi. 441p. [BnF]

RR1800. ● Hoss, Marwan: *Jours: Textes 1969-2019: Avec Quatre Lettres Inédites de René Char*. Paris: Arfuyen. 246p. [WC]

RR1801. ● Leclair, Danièle: *René Char: Sources et Chemin de la Poésie: 14 Juin - 29 Septembre 2019*. Montricher: Fondation Jan Michalski pour l'Écriture et la Littérature. 1 vol. [WC]

RR1802. Ergenekon, Gökçe: "'La Chimère d'un Âge Perdu.' Présence du Passé dans la Poésie de René Char." *Cahiers Erta*, 18, 75-90. [WC]

RR1803. Thonnerieux, Stéphanie: "Désengagement Surréaliste et Dégagement d'un Style chez René Char." *Faux Titre*, 434, 90-107. [UofR]

CHARDONNE, Jacques.

RR1804. Dantal, Didier: "À Propos de Jacques Chardonne et de la Clarté." *Revue d'Histoire Littéraire de la France*, 119, 4, 947-958. [RIT]

RR1805. Moniz, Isabel Ana: "Utopia e (Des)Encanto em Vivre à Madère de Jacques Chardonne." *Carnets*, 25 April, 289-297. [Cor]

CHAREF, Mehdi.
See 232, 432, 4731, 4734.

CHAURETTE, Normand.
See 838, 849.

CHAUVET, Marie.
See 656.

CHAWAF, Chantal.
See also 294.

RR1806. ● Chawaf, Chantal: *Relégation*. Paris: Des Femmes-Antoinette Fouque. 149p. [UofR]

CHAZAL, Malcolm de.
See also 673.

RR1807. ● "Malcolm de Chazal: Léon-Gontran Damas." *Europe*, 97, 1081, 313p. [WC]

CHEDID, Andrée.
See also 209, 664.

RR1808. ● Chedid, Andrée, & Ghearbhuigh A. Ní: *Danta Andree Chedid*. Baile Átha Cliath: Cois Life. 53p. [LoC]

RR1809. ● Haggag, Yasmine: *'L'Autre' d'Andrée Chédid. Une Éthique de l'Altérité*. München: GRIN. 56p. [WC]

RR1810. ● Kobeissi, Hossein J.: *Andrée Chedid*. Casablanca: Centre Culturel du Livre. 136p. [WC]

CHEN, Ying.
RR1811. Hebouche, Nadra: "Humain/ Animal: Rupture, Contiguïté et Perméabilité dans Espèces de Ying Chen." *Studies in Canadian Literature*, 39, 1. [UaB]

RR1812. Robu, Cristina: "L'Espace Diégétique Comme Espace d'Exil dans L'Ingratitude de Ying Chen." *Quebec Studies*, 68, 121-140. [Naz]

RR1813. Rodgers, Julie: "The Emergent Posthuman Landscape in Ying Chen's La Rive Est Loin." *Quebec Studies*, 68, 101-120. [Naz]

CHENG, François.
See also 209, 641, 653, 783, 877, 4209.

RR1814. Bertaud, Madeleine: "Book Review: François Cheng Entre Orient et Occident. 'Poétiques et Esthétiques XXe / XXIe Siècles'." *Revue d'Histoire Littéraire de la France*, *119*, 1, 240-242. [UofR]

RR1815. Bertaud, Madeleine: "François Cheng 'Poète de l'Être'." *Revue d'Histoire Littéraire de la France*, *119*, 4, 887-900. [RIT]

RR1816. Sanchez, Jorge: "Echos du Silence (François Cheng, Patrick Le Bescont)." *Critique d'Art*, 14 juin. [WC]

RR1817. Scherrer, Ferdinand: "De la Calligraphie Chinoise à l'Écriture du Nœud Borroméen." *Ligeia*, *32*, 173-176, 185, 204, 236. [RIT]

RR1818. Tuduri, Claude: "François Cheng and the Hinterland of Writing." *Études*, 93, 5. [UofR]

RR1819. Tuduri, Claude: "François Cheng ou l'Arrière-Pays de l'Écriture." *Études*, 4260, 93-104. [UofR]

RR1820. Yuan, Li: "François Cheng Entre Orient et Occident par Véronique Brient (Review)." *French Studies*, *73*, 3, 482-483. [UaB]

CHESSEX, Jacques.
See also 372, 804.

RR1821. ● Capone, Carine, & Caecilia Ternisien: *Maylis de Kerangal: Corniche Kennedy, Naissance d'un Pont, Réparer les Vivantst: Jacques Chessex, Maurice Renard.* Vimy: Société Roman 20-50. 179p. [WC]

RR1822. ● Chessex, Jacques: *Passage de l'Ombre: Et Autres Nouvelles.* Paris: Bernard Grasset. 118p. [UofR]

RR1823. Senff, Boris: "Jacques Chessex: La Construction d'une Idole." *24 Heures*, 21-22 Sept, 21. [WC]

CHEVILLARD, Eric.
See also 2716, 366, 560.

RR1824. ● Chevillard, Éric: *L'Autofictif et Les Trois Mousquetaires: Journal 2017-2018.* [Talence]: L'Arbre Vengeur. 213p. [UofR]

RR1825. ● Chevillard, Éric, & Jean-François Martin: *Prosper à l'Œuvre.* [Paris]: Noir sur Blanc. 111p. [BAnQ]

RR1826. Bertrand, Jean-Pierre, Frédéric Claisse, Justine Huppe, & Estelle Mouton-Rovira: "Le 'Dedans' et le 'Dehors': Mises en Scènes de l'Interprétation et Poétiques de la Lecture dans l'Auteur et Moi d'Éric Chevillard, Comment Faire Disparaître La Terre? D'Emmanuelle Pireyre et Je Suis Une Aventure d'Arno Bertina." *Contextes*, 22. [Syr]

RR1827. Jouanno, Corinne: "Zoologie et Autobiographie dans Du Hérisson d'Éric Chevillard (2002)." *Revue d'Histoire Littéraire de la France*, *119*, 2, 397-414. [UofR]

RR1828. Maziarczyk, Anna: "Politiques Narratives d'Éric Chevillard: Pour une Littérature Littéraire." *Lublin Studies in Modern Languages and Literature*, *43*, 1, 69. [Cor]

RR1829. Morin, Maxime: "De la Rigidité à la Souplesse: Étude de l'Imaginaire du Mouvement dans l'Œuvre Romanesque d'Éric Chevillard." *Roman 20-50*, *67*, 1, 155. [Cor]

CHRAÏBI, Driss.
See also 228.
RR1830. Drumsta, Emily: "An Epic of the Body and of Memory: Atavism and the Critique of Enlightenment in Driss Chraïbi's Une Enquête au Pays." *Research in African Literatures*, *50*, 2, 198-218. [RIT]
RR1831. Zgani, M. R.: "Driss Chraïbi the Misunderstood: Itinerary of a Commitment." *Studii Si Cercetari Fliologice, Seria Limbi Romanice*, 25, 131-140. [Cor]

CINGRIA, Charles-Albert.
RR1832. ● Corbellari, Alain: *Cingria, Le Vagabond des Neumes*. Gollion: Infolio. 59p. [BnF]

CIORAN, Émile-Michel.
See also 1130.
RR1833. Bolea, Ştefan: "Antihumanism in the Works of E. M. Cioran and Thomas Bernhard." *Philobiblon*, *24*, 1, 79-89. [RIT]
RR1834. Brad, Rodica M.: "Cioran–Éliade, La Correspondance de Jeunesse." *French Cultural Studies*, *30*, 4, 281-293. [UofR]

CIXOUS, Hélène.
See also 547, 584, 586, 593, 602, 743, 757, 875.
RR1835. ● Gyssels, Kathleen, & Christa Stevens: *Écriture des Origines, Origines de l'Écriture: Hélène Cixous*. Leiden: Brill Rodopi. 158p. [WC]
RR1836. ● Segarra, Marta: *Hélène Cixous, Corrollaires d'une Écriture*. Saint Denis: PU Vincennes. 288p. [WC]
RR1837. Al-Mahfedi, Mohammed: "The Laugh of the Medusa and the Ticks of Postmodern Feminism: Helen Cixous and the Poetics of Desire." *International Journal of Language and Literary Studies*, *1*, 1, 54-63. [WC]
RR1838. Beavan, K.: "(Re)Writing Woman: Unshaming Shame with Cixous." *Management Learning*, *50*, 1, 50-73. [UofR]
RR1839. Boutin, Aimée, Julia Frengs, & Reinier Leushuis: "Editors' Preface: Introduction. Le Bruit des Femmes: From Hélène Cixous to #metoo." *Women in French Studies*, 27, 14-24. [Cor]
RR1840. Bowler, A. L.: "'Killing Romance' by 'Giving Birth to Love': Hélène Cixous, Jane Campion and the Language of in the Cut (2003)." *Feminist Theory*, *20*, 1, 93-112. [UaB]
RR1841. Cano, Marina: "A Woman's Novel: Olive Schreiner, Mona Caird, and Hélène Cixous's Écriture Féminine." *Victoriographies*, *9*, 1, 1-18. [Syr]
RR1842. Erlingsdottir, Irma J.: "Le Lien entre Mémoire et Histoire dans l'Histoire Terrible Mais Inachevée de Norodom Sihanouk, Roi du Cambodge d'Hélène Cixous." *Bergen Language and Linguistics Studies*, *10*, 1, 14. [WC]

RR1843. Garnier, Marie-Dominique: "Body Non-Count: Counter-Counting in Hélène Cixous' Défions l'Augure." *Parallax*, *25*, 1, 25-41. [Syr]

RR1844. Gramlich, Naomie, & Annika Haas: "Situiertes Schreiben Mit Haraway, Cixous und Grauen Quellen." *Zeitschrift für Medienwissenschaft*, *11*, 20-1, 39-52. [WC]

RR1845. Haensler, Philippe P.: "Stealing Styles: Goldsmith and Derrida, Place and Cixous." *Orbis Litterarum*, *74*, 3, 173-190. [RIT]

RR1846. Kolk, Mieke: "Tragedy and the Hero in Intercultural Perspective. King Oedipus Rewritten by Tawfiq – Al-Hakim and Hélène Cixous." *Documenta*, *22*, 4, 387-398. [WC]

RR1847. Milesi, L.: "De-Monstrating Monsters: Unmastering (in) Derrida and Cixous." *Parallax*, *25*, 3, 269-287. [UaB]

RR1848. Peral, Crespo A.: "Identité Narrative et Intertextualité dans l'Écriture Autofictionnelle d'Hélène Cixous et d'Annie Cohen." *Cuadernos de Investigación Filológica*, 46, 129. [Syr]

RR1849. Robson, Kathryn: "After the End: The Death of a Child in Marie Darrieussecq's Tom Est Mort and Héléne Cixous's Le Jour où Je N' Étais Pas Là." *Irish Journal of French Studies*, *19*, 1, 70-86. [WC]

CLAUDEL, Paul.

See also 371, 509, 719, 1131.

RR1850. ● *Bulletin de la Société Paul Claudel, Vol. 229 (2019-3). Paul Claudel Face aux Philosophes*. Paris: Classiques Garnier. 96p. [WC]

RR1851. ● Mayaux, Catherine: *Bulletin de la Société Paul Claudel, Vol. 226 (3-2018): Claudel à la Mesure du Monde*. Paris: Classiques Garnier. 147p. [WC]

RR1852. ● Nantet, Marie-Victoire: *Bulletin de la Société Paul Claudel Vol.2019-1: Claudel, Questions de Dramaturgie. Claudel, Questions de Dramaturgie*. Paris: Classiques Garnier. 124p. [WC]

RR1853. Arons, Wendy: "Kurt Hirschfeld and the Visionary Internationalism of the Schauspielhaus Zurich." *Theatre Survey*, *60*, 3, 385-413. [PrQ]

RR1854. Averseng, Hélène: "La Passion Christique au Théâtre: Réinterprétations des Symboles Sacrés dans Le Mystère de la Passion d'Arnoul Gréban et Partage de Midi de Paul Claudel." *Trans-*, 24. [Syr]

RR1855. Cavaillé, Fabien, Myriam Juan, Claire Lechevalier, & Yvan Daniel: "Paul Claudel et les Arts de la Scène en Chine: Le Spectateur-Dramaturge." *Double Jeu*, 167-181. [Cor]

RR1856. Mazis, Glen A.: "Merleau-Ponty's and Paul Claudel's Overlapping Expression of Poetic Ontology." *Chiasmi International*, 21, 167-185. [Cor]

RR1857. Servais, Jacques: "L'Événement Paul Claudel dans la Vie et l'Œuvre de H. U. Von Balthasar." *Communio*, *265*, 5, 113. [WC]

RR1858. Shalygina, Olga: "'Golden Heads' in Marina Tsvetaeva's Dramatic Works and Her Unfulfilled Translation of Paul Claudel's 'Tête d'Or'." *Literary Fact*, 13, 270-289. [LoC]

RR1859. Yee, Jennifer: "Paul Claudel et l'Indochine." *French Studies*, *73*, 2, 333-334. [UaB]

COCTEAU, Jean.

See also 391, 4661, 5040.

RR1860. ● Caizergues, Pierre: *Douze Ans de Journal Posthume: 'Le Passé Dégini' de Jean Cocteau*. Montpellier: Presses Universitaires de la Méditerranée. 155p. [Cor]

RR1861. ● Cocteau, Jean, Christian Briend, & Anne Lemonnier: *Jean Cocteau: Dessins d'une Vie: de Milly-la-Forêt au Centre Pompidou*. Paris: Centre Pompidou. 167p. [Cor]

RR1862. ● Cocteau, Jean, & David Gullentops: *Jean Cocteau: Correspondances 1910-1920: (Marie Scheikévitch - Tristan Tzara - Julien Lanoë)*. Paris: Non Lieu. 151p. [LoC]

RR1863. ● Collomb, Michel, David Gullentops, & Pierre-Marie Héron: *Cocteau, d'une Guerre à l'Autre*. Rennes: Presses Universitaires de Rennes. 257p. [UofR]

RR1864. ● Debray, Quentin: *Giraudoux, Cocteau, Giono: Un Réalisme Multifocal*. Paris: Orizons. 200p. [Cor]

RR1865. ● Hyza, Carole, & Ioannis Kontaxopoulos: *Jean Cocteau: L'Empreinte d'un Poète: Exposition, Alès, Musée-Bibliothèque Pierre-André Benoit, du 20 Juin au 6 Octobre 2019*. La Garenne-Colombes: Couleurs Contemporaines, B. Chauveau. 136p. [WC]

RR1866. ● Lévy, André N.: *Charlie Chaplin: Tout Sauf Un Charlot & Jean Cocteau*. [Vevey]: Fondation Archéographie Lévy Stelle. 76p. [WC]

RR1867. ● *Littérature: Jean Cocteau*. Paris: Drouot Estimations. 159p. [WC]

RR1868. ● Obadia, Paul: *La Belle et la Bête de Jean Cocteau, 1946. Une Affaire de Genre*. Paris: L'Harmattan. 146p. [LoC]

RR1869. ● Rasimi, Olivier: *Cocteau sur le Rivage*. Paris: Arléa. 163p. [Cor]

RR1870. Anderson, Laura: "Sonic 'Detheatricalization': Jean Cocteau, Film Music, and 'Les Parents Terribles'." *Music and Letters*, *100*, 4, 654-684. [Naz]

RR1871. Berge, Jos: "Zwischen Skylla und Charybdis: Opiate in Leben Und Werk von Ernst Ludwig Kirchner, Jean Cocteau und Andreas Walser." *Expressionismus*, 9, 13-30. [WC]

RR1872. Dotremont, C.: "Jean Cocteau." 63-64. In 2197.

RR1873. Gullentops, David: "La Partie d'Échecs chez Jean Cocteau." *Ligeia*, *32*, 169-172, 171. [PrQ] (Sachs)

RR1874. Kessel, Joseph: "Images de Jean Cocteau." *Historia*, 869, 44-45. [WC]

RR1875. Klimenok, Alexandr V.: "The 'Boulevard' Theatre of Jean Cocteau." *Izvestiya of Saratov University. New Series. Series: Philology. Journalism*, *19*, 1, 67-72. [WC]

RR1876. Mezzetti, Monia: "Jean Cocteau, sous la Direction de S. Linarès et S. Winter." *Studi Francesi*, *63*, 3, 608. [UaB]

RR1877. Noh, Shi-Hun: "A Study on the Change of Metamorphosis Motifs Represented in the Beauty and the Beast: Focused on the Film of Jean Cocteau." *The Journal of Literature and Film*, *20*, 2, 245-268. [WC]

RR1878. Pueo, Juan C.: "El Misterio de la Escritura en la Sangre de un Poeta (Le Sang d'un Poète, Jean Cocteau, 1932)." *Secuencias*, 48, 59. [WC]

RR1879. Yvan, Frédéric: "Les Enfants Terribles (1929) de Jean Cocteau. Élisabeth, La 'Vierge de Fer'." *Savoirs et Clinique*, *27*, 2, 75. [Cor]

COHEN, Albert.
See also 407, 772.

RR1880. ● Cabot, Jérôme: *Cahiers Albert Cohen, Vol.27: Albert Cohen, les Arts et la Création*. Paris: Le Manuscrit. 234p. [WC]

RR1881. De Pas, P.: "Albert Cohen le Livre de ma Mère." *Quinzaines*, 1220, 18. [UaB]

RR1882. Schaffner, Alain: "Le Banquet des Valeureux (Albert Cohen, Mangeclous)." *Elfe XX-XXI*, 7. [WC]

RR1883. Vicens-Pujol, Carlota: "S'Engager par le Rire. Autour de Quelques Textes Mineurs d'Albert Cohen." *Lublin Studies in Modern Languages and Literature*, *43*, 1, 95. [Cor]

RR1884. Zilliox, Alexia: "Albert Cohen on Screen." *Thélème. Revista Complutense de Estudios Franceses*, *34*, 1, 277-292. [Naz]

COLETTE, Sidonie Gabrielle.
See also 316, 336, 347.

RR1885. ● Klein, Charles-Armand: *Colette: À Paris, en Bretagne et au Bas de la France*. Saint-Raphaël: Campanile. 264p. [BAnQ]

RR1886. ● Maget, Frédéric: *Les 7 Vies de Colette*. Paris: Flammarion. 229p. [BAnQ]

COLLOBERT, Danielle.
RR1887. ● Collobert, Danielle, & Nathanaël: *In the Environs of a Film*. Berkeley, CA: Small Press Distribution. 102p. [UofR]

COMMÈRE, Pascal.
RR1888. ● Commère, Pascal, & Jean-Marie Queneau: *Ter*. Vezelay: Éditions de la Goulotte. [20]p. [BnF]

COMTE-SPONVILLE, André.
See also 746, 754.

RR1889. ● Comte-Sponville, André: *Contre la Peur: Et Cent Autres Propos*. Paris: Albin Michel. 422p. [Cor]

RR1890. Machulskaya, O. I.: "The Conception of André Comte-Sponville: Ego-Philosophy as a First-Person Meditation." *Russian Journal of Philosophical Sciences*, 12, 127-143. [Syr]

CONAN, Laure.
See 213.

CONDÉ, Maryse.
See also 190, 687.

RR1891. Asunción, Alonso M.: "De Mujeres y Músicas Transatlánticas en el Universo Narrativo de Maryse Condé." *Cadernos de Literatura Comparada*, 40, 161-175. [WC]

RR1892. Bavuidi, Bodia: "Interroger le Présent et Penser Notre Modernité dans En Attendant la Montée des Eaux de Maryse Condé." *Présence Francophone*, 93, 24-38. [Cor]

RR1893. Cissé, Mouhamadou: "Maryse Condé devant les Événements Africains Troublants: Entre Représentation et Discours." *Présence Francophone*, 93, 9-23. [UofR]

RR1894.   Connell, Lisa: "Carvigan-Cassin, Laura, Éd. Sans Fards, Mélanges en l'Honneur de Maryse Condé." *French Review. 93*, 2, 257. [Naz]

RR1895.   De la Fuente, D. D., & A. Szyman: "Natural Elements and Their Interaction in the Caribbean Writing of Maryse Condé." *Estudios Romanicos*, 28, 219-232. [Naz]

RR1896.   Druckman, Charlotte: "Of Morsels and Marvels by Maryse Condé." *New York Times Book Review, 124*, 51, 17. [WC]

RR1897.   Duquet, Valentin: "Victoire: La Vie Fardée de Maryse Condé." *French Forum, 44*, 2, 257-271. [Naz]

RR1898.   Gbouablé, Edwige: "La Dynamique d'un Engagement 'Poélitique': Le Cas du Théâtre de Maryse Condé." *Présence Francophone*, 93, 73-86. [UofR]

RR1899.   Gendron, Karine: "De l'Actualité à l'Actualisation dans Traversée de la Mangrove et La Vie Sans Fards de Maryse Condé." *Présence Francophone*, 93, 54-72. [UaB]

RR1900.   Ghosh, William: "Caribbean Travel and the 'Realistic Shock': Lamming, Naipaul, Condé." *Research in African Literatures, 50*, 2, 177-197. [Naz]

RR1901.   Hwang, Junghyun: "Rupturing Salem, Reconsidering Subjectivity: Tituba, the Witch of Infinity in Maryse Condé's *Tituba, Black Witch of Salem*." *American Studies in Scandinavia, 51*, 1, 43-59. [UaB]

RR1902.   Ildem, Arzu: "Sœurs de Solitude: Maryse Condé et Simone Schwarz-Bart." *Études Caribéennes*, 3. [WC]

RR1903.   Kwok, Gloria: "Sans Fards, Mélanges en l'Honneur de Maryse Condé Dir. by Laura Carvigan-Cassin (Review)." *Women in French Studies*, 27, 233-234. [UaB]

RR1904.   Makward, Christiane: "Nouveaux Entretiens avec Maryse Condé, Écrivain et Témoin de Son Temps by Françoise Pfaff (Review)." *Women in French Studies*, 27, 236-237. [Cor]

RR1905.   N'Guessan Larroux, Béatrice: "Mets et Merveilles Littéraires de Maryse Condé." *Elfe XX-XXI*, 7. [Cor]

RR1906.   Pagán, López A.: "Regards sur l'Image dans l'Écriture de Maryse Condé." *Thélème, 34*, 2, 411-422. [Naz]

RR1907.   Szyman, Alexandra: "Les Éléments Naturels et Leur Interaction dans l'Œuvre de Maryse Condé: The Natural Elements and Their Interaction in Maryse Condé's Work." *Estudios Románicos*, 28, 219-232. [Naz]

RR1908.   Ugwu, Evaristus N., & Vincent N. Obidiegwu: "Repenser sur l'Environnement: Une Étude Écocritique dans Gouverneurs de la Rosée de Jacques Roumain, Moi, Tituba Sorcière . . . Noire de Salem de Maryse Condé et l'Exil selon Julia de Gisèle Pineau." *International Journal of Francophone Studies, 22*, 3, 299-310. [RIT]

RR1909.   Ward, Catherine: "'A False Sister. A False Foreigner': Space, Sexuality, and Identity in Condé's Heremakhonon." *Journal of the African Literature Association, 13*, 1, 96-111. [Syr]

RR1910.   Zahir, Mourad: "Immigration et Problématique Identitaire chez Maryse Condé." *Les Cahiers du Centre des Études Doctorales*, 7, 41-45. [WC]

CONFIANT, Raphaël.
See also 546, 579.

RR1911.   ● Lovatiana, Juliana: *Intertexte de la Réfutation: Jean-Luc Rahari-*

manana et Raphaël Confiant: L'Investigation et l'Assignation de la Récriture Postco-loniale. Saarbrücken: Éditions Universitaires Européennes. 260p. [WC]

RR1912.   Marchand, Aline, Pascale Roux, & Anaïs Stampfli: "Raphaël Confiant et l'Auto-Traduction, de la Traduction-Outil à la Création Littéraire." *Recherches & Travaux*, 95. [Cor]

CONSTANT, Paule.

RR1913.   Ben Soussan, P.: "La Maladie Imaginaire de Paule Constant." *Cancer(s) Et Psy(s)*, *4*, 1, 149. [WC]

RR1914.   Willging, Jennifer: "Strange Bedfellows: Paule Constant, Michel Houellebecq, and Political Correctness." *Australian Journal of French Studies*, *56*, 1, 75-90. [RIT]

COPEAU, Jacques.

See also 62, 638, 845.

RR1915.   ● Copeau, Jacques, Maria I. Aliverti, & Marco Consolini: *Les Dernières Batailles (1929-1949)*. Paris: Gallimard. 627p. [BnF]

RR1916.   Carponi, C.: "Jacques Copeau's Influence in Michel Saint-Denis' Actor Training. from the École du Vieux-Colombier to the Compagnie Des Quinze." *Slovenske Divadlo*, *67*, 4, 322-334. [Cor]

RR1917.   Genetti, Stefano: "Clara Debard, Jacques Copeau et le Théâtre du Vieux-Colombier. Dictionnaire des Créations Françaises (1913-1924)." *Studi Francesi*, *63*, 1, 188. [UaB]

RR1918.   McCready, Susan: "Jacques Copeau et le Théâtre du Vieux-Colombier: Dictionnaire des Créations Françaises (1913–1924)." *French Studies*, *73*, 2, 315-316. [UofR]

RR1919.   Teixeira, Evandro L.: "Jacques Copeau: Uma Vida Dedicada à Renovação do Teatro." *Dapesquisa*, *2*, 4, 62-68. [WC]

RR1920.   Thomaz, Juliano F., & José R. Faleiro: "Jacques Copeau E O Espaço Teatral." *Dapesquisa*, *2*, 4, 69-76. [WC]

COPPÉE, François.

See also 861.

RR1921.   Robert, L.: "Se Marier (ou Pas): Le Mariage dans Rayons Perdus de Louisa Siefert et Les Humbles de François Coppée." *Lettres Romanes*, 73, 459-473. [Syr]

CREVEL, René.

RR1922.   ● Otmezguine, Jane, & René Crevel: *René Crevel: Peintre, Architecte, Décorateur*. Nice: Main d'Œuvre. 663p. [WC]

CROMMELYNCK, Fernand.

RR1923.   Lefèvre, Claire: "Monsieur Larose Est-Il l'Assassin?" Textyles, 1 Mars, 141-154. [WC]

CROS, Charles.

See 851.

DADIÉ, Bernard.

See also 192.

RR1924. ● Ueto, Viviane, & Papé M. Adoux: *Hommage à Bernard Dadié, Père-Fondateur de la Littérature Ivoirienne d'Expression Française. Gloire à l'Ancêtre Vivant.* Paris: L'Harmattan. 380p. [WC]

RR1925. Riesz, János: "Unité et Hétérogénéité d'une Œuvre: À la Mémoire de Bernard Dadié (1916–2019)." *Nouvelles Études Francophones, 34*, 1, 1-5. [UaB]

DAENINCKX, Didier.
See also 175.

RR1926. Cabral, Maria J., Carlos Carreto, Maria J. Brilhante, & José Domingues de Almeida: "La Génération Mai 68 Revisitée dans Deux Romans Français Contemporains: Les Images d'Alain Rémond et Camarades de Classe de Didier Daeninckx." *Carnets*, deuxième série, 16. [Cor]

RR1927. Daeninckx, Didier: "Le Forcené du Boulot." *Mouvements, 100*, 4, 59. [PrQ] (Manchette)

RR1928. Loriol, Marc: "Écrire à Propos du Travail [Dossier]." *Mondes du Travail, 22*, 13. [WC]

RR1929. Thénault, Sylvie: "Meurtres Pour Mémoire. Une Enquête de l'Inspecteur Cadin, and: Meurtres Pour Mémoire by Didier Daeninckx (Review)." *Le Mouvement Social, 269*, 1, 234-236. [UaB]

DAIGLE, France.
RR1930. Cormier, Pénélope: "Les Encyclopédies de France Daigle et d'Herménégilde Chiasson: Un Rapprochement Historique et Formaliste de la Littérature Acadienne et de la World Literature." *Journal of Canadian Studies/ Revue d'Études Canadiennes, 53*, 3, 514-534. [UofR]

DAMAS, Léon-Gontran.
See also 498, 817, 1807.

RR1931. ● Cissé, Idrissa: *Léon-Gontran Damas et le Défi de Vivre.* Paris: L'Harmattan. 195p. [UofR]

RR1932. Ferraroni, Roberto: "Antonella Emina, Léon-Gontran Damas. Les Détours vers la Cité Neuve." *Studi Francesi, 63*, 3, 616. [UaB]

RR1933. "Léon-Gontran Damas. Les Détours vers la Cité Neuve, Antonella Emina." *French Studies in Southern Africa, 49*, 243-247. [Cor]

DAOUD, Kamel.
See also 64, 219, 518, 589, 704.

RR1934. Algeri, V.: "The Intertextual Vertigo. A Reading of Meursault, Contre-Enquête by Kamel Daoud." *Revue Italienne d'Études Francaises, 9*. [Syr]

RR1935. "Algérie Rencontre avec Kamel Daoud, Écrivain et Journaliste." *Jeune Afrique, 59*, 3050, 40-44. [Syr]

RR1936. Alkyam, Sami: "Lost in Reading: The Predicament of Postcolonial Writing in Kamel Daoud's The Meursault Investigation." *Journal of Postcolonial Writing, 55*, 4, 459-471. [Naz]

RR1937. Boblet, Marie-Hélène: "Meursault, Contre-Enquête, Un 'Premier' Roman?" *Littérature, 194*, 2, 62. [Syr]

RR1938. Fiorentino, Francesco, & Veronic Algeri: "Le Vertige Intertextuel.

Une Lecture de Kamel Daoud, Meursault, Contre-Enquête." *Revue Italienne d'Études Françaises*, 6. [Syr]

RR1939.   Goellner, Sage: "Spectres Insistants: Primary and Secondary Hauntings in Kamel Daoud's Meursault, Contre-Enquête." *Australian Journal of French Studies*, *56*, 3, 221-233. [Naz]

RR1940.   Ji, Young-Rae: "Penser l'Autre dans les Romans Algériens de Langue Française - De Kateb Yacine à Kamel Daoud." *Société d'Études Franco-Coréennes*, 90, 133-161. [WC]

RR1941.   Lachman, Kathryn: "The Meursault Investigation: Literature and the Disappeared." *Yale French Studies*, 135, 189. [PrQ]

RR1942.   Poteau-Tralie, Mary: "Fictionalizing Fiction Through the Metaphor of (De)Construction in Kamel Daoud's Meursault, Contre-Enquête." *Studies in 20th & 21st Century Literature*, 43, 2. [UofR]

RR1943.   Quaghebeur, Marc: "Revisitation d'un Cadavre Anonyme: Enquête sur la Contre-Enquête de Kamel Daoud." *Les Lettres Romanes*, *73*, 1-2, 215-237. [UaB]

RR1944.   Ségal, Élodie: "El Extranjero: Albert Camus vs. Kamel Daoud. Por un Postexistencialismo Libertario." *Historia y Grafía*, 53, 53-78. [Cor]

RR1945.   Yilmaz, A. T.: "The Master-Slave Dialectic in Kamel Daoud's Novel Entitled Meursault, Contre-Enquête." *Folklor/ Edebiyat*, *99*, 3, 623-634. [Cor]

DARD, Frédéric.
See also 367.

RR1946.   ● Galli, Hugues: *Les Cahiers Frédéric Dard. Vol. 3: Chemins de Traverse*. Dijon: EUD - Éditions Universitaires Dijon. 250p. [WC]

RR1947.   Frigerio, Vittorio: "Hugues Galli, Thierry Gautier et Dominique Jeannerod (dir.), Les Cahiers Frédéric Dard. 'Récits d'Enfance.' *Belphégor*, 17, 1. [Syr]

DARIEN, Georges.
RR1948.   Lorig, Aurélien: "1870. A Literary Representation of the Bruised French Nation, Rlc xciii, N° 4, Oct.-Dec. 2019, p. 409-422." *Revue de Littérature Comparée*, *372*, 4, 409. [Naz]

DARRIEUSSECQ, Marie.
See also 253, 326, 454, 484, 667.

RR1949.   ● Germoni, Karine, Sophie Milcent-Lawson, & Cécile Narjoux: *L'Écriture 'Entre Deux Mondes' de Marie Darrieussecq*. Dijon: Éditions Universitaires de Dijon. 196p. [Cor]

RR1950.   Carraro, Chiara: "La Frontière: Limen et Paysage chez Marie Darrieussecq et Maylis de Kerangal." *Les Lettres Romanes*, *73*, 3-4, 495-518. [Syr]

RR1951.   Keltoum, Soualah: "Je Autofictionnel/ Jeux Intertextuels: Cosmopolitisme et/ ou Narcissisme? Dans le Pays de Marie Darrieussecq." *Anales de Filología Francesa*, 27, 1, 155-178. [Naz]

RR1952.   Shirland, Jonathan: "Being Here is Everything: The Life of Paula Modersohn-Becker by Marie Darrieussecq." *Journal of International Women's Studies*, *20*, 2, 426-31. [PrQ]

RR1953.   Versini, Dominique C.: "Excès et Métamorphoses de la Peau dans Truismes de Marie Darrieussecq." *Women in French Studies*, 27, 170-186. [UaB]

RR1954.   Vredenburgh, Amanda: "The Fantastic Bestialization of the Biopoliti-
cal Subject in Marie Darrieussecq's Truismes." *Romance Notes*, *59*, 1, 163-172. [UofR]

DAUDET, Alphonse.
See also 16, 452, 493.
RR1955.   • Dufief, Anne-Simone, Gabrielle Melison-Hirchwald, & Roger
Ripoll: *Dictionnaire Alphonse Daudet*. Paris: Honoré Champion. 500p. [WC]
RR1956.   • Zammit, Audrey, Patricia Avdjian, Christian Lacour-Ollé, &
Pedro Madrigal: *Vida y Cronología de las Obras de Alphonse Daudet Por Medio de
una Exposición*. Nîmes: C. Lacour. 63p. [BnF]
RR1957.   Bai, Y.: "World Literature and Nationalism: Tibetan Translations of
Alphonse Daudet's Short Story 'La Dernière Classe'." *Archiv Orientalni*, *87*, 3, 509-
535. [Naz]
RR1958.   Dufief, Anne S.: "Book Review: Alphonse Daudet Interviewé.
'Textes de Littérature Moderne et Contemporaine'." *Revue d'Histoire Littéraire de la
France*, *119*, 4, 994-995. [UofR]

DAUDET, Léon.
See also 627.
RR1959.   • Daudet, Léon, & Sébastien Lapaque: *Écrits d'Exil*. Paris: Séguier.
301p. [BAnQ]

DAUMAL, René.
See also 803.
RR1960.   McAuliffe, Samuel: "Precarious Ascent: Trace and Terrain in René
Daumal's Mount Analogue." *Mln*, *134*, 4, 783-805. [PrQ]

DEBORD, Guy.
See also 28, 731, 786, 4735.
RR1961.   • Fuente, Manuel: *Cine, Imagen y Representación en Guy Debord*.
Valencia: Tirant lo Blanch. 200p. [WC]
RR1962.   • Penner, Devin: *Rethinking the Spectacle: Guy Debord, Radical
Democracy, and the Digital Age*. Vancouver: UBC Press. 241p. [Cor]
RR1963.   • Rappl, Werner: *Guy Debord: Das Filmische Gesamtwerk*. Wien:
Synema - Gesellschaft für Film und Medien. 2 vols. [BnF]
RR1964.   • Trier, James: *Guy Debord, The Situationist International, and the
Revolutionary Spirit*. Leiden: Koninklijke Brill NV. 453p. [WC]
RR1965.   Englén, Pehr: "The Construction of an International: Debord, Jorn,
and Situationist Praxis." *History of European Ideas*, *45*, 6, 884-900. [UofR]
RR1966.   Gonçalves, Glauco R.: "Espetáculo, Alienação Espacial e Queda
Tendencial do Valor de Uso Na Obra de Guy Debord." *Geousp Espaço e Tempo
(Online)*, *23*, 1, 59-75. [WC]
RR1967.   Lucchesi, Jennifer S., & Mara Rovida: "Vida e Obra de Guy Debord:
Da Militância Política à Escrita do Livro a Sociedade do Espetáculo." *Temática*, 15, 5.
[WC]
RR1968.   Matos, Olgária C. F.: "Guy Debord." *Revista Limiar*, *1*, 1, 1-11. [WC]
RR1969.   Nunn, Emilie: "Social Media as an Extension of Guy Debord's The
Society of the Spectacle (1967)." *Journal of Arts Writing by Students*, *5*, 1, 79-91. [LoC]

DEBRAY, Régis.

See also 755, 4422.

RR1970. ● Debray, Régis: *Comment Peut-on Être Européen?* Paris: Babylone. 319p. [WC]

RR1971. ● Debray, Régis: *Du Génie Français.* Paris: Gallimard. 128p. [WC]

RR1972. ● Debray, Régis: *Fenomenologia del Terrore: Lo Sguardo Cieco dell'Occidente.* Milano: Mimesis. 71p. [WC]

RR1973. ● Debray, Régis: *L'Europe Fantôme.* Paris: Gallimard. 44p. [WC]

RR1974. ● Debray, Régis: *Le Siècle Vert: Un Changement de Civilisation.* Paris: Gallimard. 56p. [Cor]

RR1975. ● Debray, Régis: *Notre Adn Culturel.* La Tour-d'Aigue: Éditions de l'Aube. 78p. [BnF]

RR1976. Cucchetti, H.: "Régis Debray, Intellectuel Engagé. De Révolutionnaire Professionnel à Conseiller d'État." *Canadian Journal of Latin American and Caribbean Studies, 44,* 1, 83-104. [UofR]

RR1977. Syon, Guillaume de: "Régis Debray, Civilisation. Comment Nous Sommes Devenus Américains: Paris, Gallimard, Coll. blanche, 2017, 233 pages." *Questions de Communication, 35,* 1, 369. [Cor]

DEGUY, Michel.

See 588, 783, 4942.

DELARUE-MARDRUS, Lucie.

See also 324.

RR1978. ● Morhange, Elie: *Psautier du XIIIe Siècle et Livres Anciens, Archives Littéraires de Myriam Harry et Lucie Delarue-Mardrus, Curiosa, Illustrés Modernes et Éditions Originales avec Envoi: Vente, Paris, Hôtel Drouot, Mercredi 13 Février 2019.* Paris: Kâ-Mondo. 108p. [WC]

DELAY, Florence.

See 4241.

DELBO, Charlotte.

See also 373, 375.

RR1979. ● Dunant, Ghislaine: *Charlotte Delbo, Résistante, Écrivain de la Déportation.* Paris: Cercle d'Étude de la Déportation et de la Shoah. 91p. [WC]

RR1980. Delbo, Charlotte, & Cynthia Haft: "February." *The Massachusetts Review, 60,* 1, 17-27. [UofR]

RR1981. Dunant, Ghislaine: "Charlotte Delbo: Writing the Deportation." *The Massachusetts Review, 60,* 4, 601-18. [PrQ]

RR1982. Dunant, Ghislaine, & Kathryn Lachman: "Charlotte Delbo: Writing the Deportation." *The Massachusetts Review, 60,* 4, 601-618. [UofR]

RR1983. Vidor, Amy: "Repurposing l'Art Épistolaire: Letter-Writing as Civil Disobedience in Charlotte Delbo's Les Belles Lettres." *Women in French Studies, 27,* 236-246. [UaB]

DELERM, Philippe.

See also 5, 600.

RR1984. ● Delerm, Philippe: *Les Petites Phrases de Philippe Delerm*. Paris: Éditions Points. 3 vols. [BnF]

DELEUZE, Gilles.
See also 206, 521, 645, 722, 746, 753, 1089, 1110, 1194, 4735, 5001.

RR1985. ● Assis, Paulo, & Paolo Giudici: *Aberrant Nuptials: Deleuze and Artistic Research 2*. Leuven: Leuven UP. 478p. [Syr]

RR1986. ● Bennett, Michael, & Tano S. Posteraro: *Deleuze and Evolutionary Theory*. Edinburgh: Edinburgh UP. 240p. [WC]

RR1987. ● Berressem, Hanjo: *Gilles Deleuze's Luminous Philosophy*. Edinburgh: Edinburgh UP. 272p. [WC]

RR1988. ● Bogue, Ronald: *Thinking with Deleuze*. Edinburgh: Edinburgh UP. 454p. [WC]

RR1989. ● Bohlmann, Markus P. J., & Anna Hickey-Moody: *Deleuze and Children*. Edinburgh: Edinburgh UP. 224p. [Syr]

RR1990. ● Braidotti, Rosi, & Simone V. N. V. Bignall: *Posthuman Ecologies: Complexity and Process After Deleuze*. New York: Rowman & Littlefield. 294p. [Syr]

RR1991. ● Collett, Guillaume: *Deleuze, Guattari, and the Problem of Transdisciplinarity*. London: Bloomsbury Academic. 280p. [WC]

RR1992. ● Colson, Daniel, & Jesse Cohn: *A Little Philosophical Lexicon of Anarchism from Proudhon to Deleuze*. Brooklyn, NY: Autonomedia. 272p. [WC]

RR1993. ● Glowczewski, Barbara: *Indigenising Anthropology with Guattari and Deleuze*. Edinburgh: Edinburgh UP. 296p. [UofR]

RR1994. ● Hickey-Moody, Anna: *Deleuze and Masculinity*. Cham: Palgrave Macmillan. 194p. [UaB]

RR1995. ● Jones, Graham, & Jon Roffe: *Deleuze's Philosophical Lineage II*. Edinburgh: Edinburgh UP. 367p. [UofR]

RR1996. ● Kisser, Thomas, & Katrin Wille: *Spinozismus als Modell: Deleuze und Spinoza*. Paderborn (Germany): Wilhelm Fink. 332p. [Cor]

RR1997. ● Kleinherenbrink, Arjen: *Against Continuity: Gilles Deleuze's Speculative Realism*. Edinburgh: Edinburgh UP. 313p. [Syr]

RR1998. ● Kolisnyk, Nataliya: *Kinematografische Spiegelwelten: Mit Gilles Deleuze Ins Kino*. Würzburg: Königshausen & Neumann. 248p. [LoC]

RR1999. ● Lazo, Briones P.: *Gilles Deleuze: Las Políticas Minoritarias en Resistencia*. Ciudad de México: Universidad Iberoamericana. 175p. [LoC]

RR2000. ● Murphy, Justin: *Based Deleuze: The Reactionary Leftism of Gilles Deleuze*. [Erscheinungsort nicht Ermittelbar]: Other Life. 133p. [WC]

RR2001. ● Nedoh, Boštjan: *Ontology and Perversion: Deleuze, Agamben, Lacan*. Lanham, MD: Rowman & Littlefield International. 204p. [Cor]

RR2002. ● Núñez, Amanda: *Gilles Deleuze: Una Estética del Espacio para una Ontología Menor*. Madrid: Arena Libros. 232p. [BnF]

RR2003. ● Pérez, Bernal R.: *Escritura y Resistencia: Entre Elena Garro, Hannah Arendt y Gilles Deleuze*. Ciudad de México: Juan Pablos. 130p. [LoC]

RR2004. ● Querrien, Anne, Anne Sauvagnargues, & Arnaud Villani: *Agencer les Multiplicités avec Deleuze*. Paris: Hermann. 411p. [WC]

RR2005. ● Sholtz, Janae, & Cheri L. Carr: *Deleuze and the Schizoanalysis of Feminism: Alliances and Allies*. London: Bloomsbury Academic. 292p. [UofR]

RR2006. ● Simonetti, Alberto: *Il Penultimo del Pensiero: Gilles Deleuze Storico della Filosofia*. Udine: Mimesis. 238p. [LoC]

RR2007. ● Slama, Paul: *Marx, Deleuze, Derrida*. Paris: Presses Universitaires de France. *Revue Philosophique de la France et de l'Étranger, 144* (209, 4), [435]-587p. [WC]

RR2008. ● Sonna, Valeria: *El Platón de Gilles Deleuze*. Buenos Aires (Argentina): Prometeo Libros. 194p. [WC]

RR2009. ● Van, Heerden C., & Aragorn Eloff: *Deleuze and Anarchism*. Edinburgh: Edinburgh UP. 263p. [Syr]

RR2010. ● Zdebik, Jakub: *Deleuze and the Map-Image: Aesthetics, Information, Code, and Digital Art*. New York: Bloomsbury Visual Arts. 214p. [Syr]

RR2011. Allar, N. A.: "Rhizomatic Influence: the Antigenealogy of Glissant and Deleuze." *Cambridge Journal of Postcolonial Literary Inquiry, 6*, 1, 1-13. [Cor]

RR2012. Cazeaux, Clive: "Art, Philosophy and the Connectivity of Concepts: Ricœur and Deleuze and Guattari." *Journal of Aesthetics and Phenomenology, 6*, 1, 21-40. [UaB]

RR2013. Cimatti, Felice: "Deleuze and Italian Thought." *Deleuze and Guattari Studies, 13*, 4, 495-507. [Naz]

RR2014. Cole, David R.: "The Designation of a Deleuzian Philosophy for Environmental Education and Its Consequences." *Australian Journal of Environmental Education, 35*, 3, 173-182. [RIT]

RR2015. Davis, Colin: "Cracking Gilles Deleuze's Crystal: Narrative Space-Time in the Films of Jean Renoir." *French Studies, 73*, 2, 313. [UofR]

RR2016. Deamer, D.: "Deleuze's Three Syntheses Go to Hollywood: The Tripartite Cinema of Time Travel, Many Worlds and Altered States." *Film-Philosophy, 23*, 3, 324-350. [Syr]

RR2017. Duvernoy, Russell J.: "A Genesis of Speculative Empiricisms: Whitehead and Deleuze Read Hume." *The Southern Journal of Philosophy, 57*, 4, 459-482. [RIT]

RR2018. Ferreyra, Julián: "La Doble Vida de la Luz: Envolvimiento y Creación en Fichte y Deleuze." *Anales del Seminario de Historia de la Filosofía, 36*, 3, 725-45. [RIT]

RR2019. Gleyzon, Francois-Xavier: "Minoring Shakespeare: Deleuze's Storm - Caliban or the Last of the Palestinians." *Journal for Cultural Research, 23*, 1, 80-96. [RIT]

RR2020. Gutiérrez, Espinoza A. E., & Bernal A. M. R. Pérez: "Narración, Resistencia y Sentido en Hannah Arendt y Gilles Deleuze." *Valenciana, 12*, 23, 175-189. [Cor]

RR2021. Hanley, C.: "Thinking with Deleuze and Guattari: An Exploration of Writing as Assemblage." *Educational Philosophy and Theory, 51*, 4, 413-423. [Naz]

RR2022. Heron, Kai: "Lacan and Deleuze: A Disjunctive Synthesis: Boštjan Nedoh and Andreja Zevnik (eds.) Edinburgh UP, 2016, 240 pp., $105 Hardback, ISBN: 9781474408295." *Psychoanalysis, Culture & Society, 24*, 2, 230-233. [UofR]

RR2023. Hurst, A.: "Thinking Through Thinking: Deleuze and "The Dogmatic Image of Thought"." *South African Journal of Philosophy, 38*, 4, 392-407. [Naz]

RR2024. Jeong, Sun-Baek: "Milieu chez Deleuze, Comme Milieu Philosophique." *Journal of the Society of Philosophical Studies, 125*, 7-30. [WC]

RR2025. Kaluža, Jernej: "Anarchism in Deleuze." *Deleuze and Guattari Studies, 13*, 2, 267-292. [Naz]

RR2026. Kapelchuk, K.: "Deleuze and (anti)dialectics." *Stasis, 7*, 1, 340-362. [WC]

RR2027. Kent, L.: "Nihilism on the Metaphysical Screen: The Fate of Gilles Deleuze's Cinematic Ethics." *Cinema*, 11, 27-41. [PrQ]

RR2028. Lambert, G.: "The Joy of Surfing with Deleuze and Guattari." *Deleuze and Guattari Studies, 13*, 1, 128-135. [UaB]

RR2029. Landolfi, C.: "Beyond the Society of Judgement: Deleuze and the Social Transitivity of Affects." *Deleuze and Guattari Studies, 13*, 4, 541-551. [UaB]

RR2030. Lypka, Celiese: "Hannah Stark (2016) Feminist Theory After Deleuze." *Deleuze and Guattari Studies, 13*, 2, 293-297. [Naz]

RR2031. Maeng, Hyeyoung: "Deleuze's Aesthetics of Transcendental Realism and the Aesthetics of Following Tao." *Journal of Research in Art Education, 20*, 3, 21-42. [WC]

RR2032. Martín, Facundo N.: "Especificidad Histórica y Crítica Inmanente. Las Teorías del Capitalismo de Postone y Deleuze/ Guattari." *Escritos, 27*, 58, 95-118. [Naz]

RR2033. Martínez Quintanar, Miguel Ángel: "Concepto, Método y Sistema de 'Différence et Répétition' de Gilles Deleuze." *Anales del Seminario de Historia de la Filosofía, 36*, 3, 759-79. [RIT]

RR2034. Martinez, V. S.: "An Approach to the Genesis of the Power of the False in Gilles Deleuze." *Endoxa*, 43, 269-291. [WC]

RR2035. McLean, Bradley H.: "Deleuze's Interpretation of Job as a Heroic Figure in the History of Rationality." *Religions, 10*, 3. [RIT]

RR2036. Medien, Kathryn: "Palestine in Deleuze." *Theory, Culture & Society, 36*, 5, 49-70. [RIT]

RR2037. Moreira, Felipe G. A.: "Deleuze's Left-Wing Approach to Metaphysics." 455. In 2007.

RR2038. Murris, Karin, & Vivienne Bozalek: "Diffraction and Response-Able Reading of Texts: The Relational Ontologies of Barad and Deleuze." *International Journal of Qualitative Studies in Education, 32*, 7, 872-886. [UaB]

RR2039. Pendakis, A.: "In Medias Res: Deleuze and the Politics of Middleness." *Stasis, 7*, 1, 14-36. [WC]

RR2040. Prati, Renata: "Trabajo y Pasiones Tristes. El Sentido de lo Negativo en Gilles Deleuze." *Praxis Filosófica*, 48, 119-134. [Naz]

RR2041. Quintanar, M. A. M.: "Concept, Method and System in Différence et Répétition by Gilles Deleuze." *Anales del Seminario de Historia de la Filosofia, 36*, 3, 759-779. [RIT]

RR2042. Regev, Y.: "The Wellspring of Vessels Is Higher Than the Wellspring of Light (Gilles Deleuze and Materialist Dialectics)." *Stasis, 7*, 1, 294-316. [WC]

RR2043. Reynolds, B., & G. Zimmerman: "A Strange Lobster Tale of Self-Sacrificial Transversality: Or, Transversal Poetics Flourishes in the Spectral Ether of Deleuze, Bataille, and Shakespeare." *Journal for Cultural Research, 23*, 1, 97-117. [RIT]

RR2044. Roberts, Tom: "Resituating Post-Phenomenological Geographies: Deleuze, Relations and the Limits of Objects." *Transactions of the Institute of British Geographers, 44*, 3, 542-554. [RIT]

RR2045.   Rødje, Kjetil: "Book Review: Media After Deleuze by Tauel Harper and David Savat." *Journalism & Mass Communication Quarterly*, *96*, 2, 639-641. [UofR]

RR2046.   Sainsbury, Daisy: "Towards a Minor Poetry: Reading Twentieth-Century French Poetry with Deleuze-Guattari and Bakhtin." *Paragraph*, *42*, 2, 135-153. [UaB]

RR2047.   Schönher, Mathias: "Gilles Deleuze's Philosophy of Nature: System and Method in What Is Philosophy?" *Theory, Culture & Society*, 36, 89-107. [PrQ]

RR2048.   See, Tony: "Deleuze and Buddhism: Two Concepts of Subjectivity?" *Deleuze and Guattari Studies*, *13*, 1, 104-122. [UaB]

RR2049.   Shim, Wooil: "The Meanings of the Body and Sensation As Represented Through Park Chan-Wook's Films-by Focusing on Gilles Deleuze's Semiotics." *The Journal of Language & Literature*, 78, 323-350. [WC]

RR2050.   Sim, Gerald: "Review of David Martin-Jones's Deleuze and World Cinemas (Continuum, 2011)." *Sub-stance*, 148, 102-106. [Naz]

RR2051.   Spindler, Fredrika: "'All Philosophy Starts with Misosophy', or on Love, Trickery and Treason: Deleuze and the History of Philosophy." *Deleuze and Guattari Studies*, *13*, 3, 435-444. [Cor]

RR2052.   Swarbrick, Steven: "Nature's Queer Negativity: Between Barad and Deleuze." *Postmodern Culture*, *29*, 2. [RIT]

RR2053.   Syutkin, A., & Y. Regev: "For Deleuze: Political Economy, Materialistic Dialectics and Speculative Philosophy." *Stasis*, 7, 1, 6-8. [WC]

RR2054.   Thornton, Edward: "Deleuze and Guattari's Absent Analysis of Patriarchy." *Hypatia*, *34*, 2, 348-368. [UofR]

RR2055.   Vignola, P.: "The Transcendental Side of Gilles Deleuze's "Becoming Minor"." *Metodo*, 85-102. [WC]

RR2056.   Villani, Tiziana: "Gilles Deleuze: Philosophy and Nomadism." *Deleuze and Guattari Studies*, *13*, 4, 516-527. [Cor]

RR2057.   Weeks, Samuel: "A Politics of Peripheries: Deleuze and Guattari as Dependency Theorists." *Deleuze and Guattari Studies*, *13*, 1, 79-103. [Naz]

RR2058.   Wiley, Stephen B. C., & J. M. Wise: "Guattari, Deleuze, and Cultural Studies." *Cultural Studies*, *33*, 1, 75-97. [RIT]

RR2059.   Won, Ha: "A Study on the Projection Installation Convergence Design Based on the Logic of Sensation of Gilles Deleuze - Focused on Analyizing the Works of Kryzysztof Wodiczko." *The Korean Society of Science & Art*, 37, 5, 227-238. [WC]

DELTEIL, Joseph.

RR2060.   Bonord, A.: "'Seriez-vous Dadaïste, Monsieur?' Regards Croisés sur la Querelle de la Poésie Pure et la Poétique de Joseph Delteil." *Romanic Review*, 109, 307-319. [Naz]

DÉON, Michel.

RR2061.   ● Al, Fararguy F.: *Michel Déon et le Roman de Formation*. Saarbrücken: Éditions Universitaires Européennes.228p. [WC]

RR2062.   ● Alavoine, Bernard: *Michel Déon et la Méditerranée: À la Recherche d'un Art de Vivre*. Dijon: Éditions Universitaires de Dijon. 188p. [Cor]

DEPESTRE, René.
See also 876, 884.

RR2063. Couti, Jacqueline, & Jason C. Grant: "Man Up! Masculinity and (Homo)Sexuality in René Depestre's Transatlantic World." *Humanities*, 8, 3, 150. [RIT]

RR2064. Perisic, Alexandra: "A Secret Love Affair." *Transition*, *128*, 108, 118, 164. [RIT]

DERRIDA, Jacques.
See also 753, 927, 1048, 1056, 1163, 1490, 1845, 1847, 2007, 3508, 3665, 4250, 4254.

RR2065. ● Bernardo, Fernanda: *Derrida, O Dom da Différance: (Descon-strução, Pensamento, Literatura)*. Coimbra: Palimage. 256p. [WC]

RR2066. ● Bizzozero, Andrea: *"Fare La Verità": Una Rilettura di Jacques Derrida*. Roma: Antonianum. 176p. [LoC]

RR2067. ● Cahen, Didier: *Trois Pères: Jabès, Derrida, Du Bouchet*. Latresne: Le Bord de l'Eau. 163p. [LoC]

RR2068. ● Cohen-Levinas, Danielle, & Giuseppe Pintus: *Il Divenir-Ebreo del Poema: Doppio Invio: Celan e Derrida*. Roma: Inschibboleth. 115p. [WC]

RR2069. ● Derrida, Jacques, Geoffroy Bennington, Marc Crépon, Thomas Dutoit, & Markus Sedlaczek: *Todesstrafe*. Wien: Passagen. 1 vol. [WC]

RR2070. ● Derrida, Jacques, Pascale-Anne Brault, & Peggy Kamuf: *La Vie la Mort: Séminaire (1975-1976)*. Paris: Seuil. 363p. [WC]

RR2071. ● Evink, Eddo, & Shailoh Phillips: *Transcendence and Inscription: Jacques Derrida on Ethics, Religion and Metaphysics*. Nordhausen: Traugott Bautz. 334p. [WC]

RR2072. ● Facioni, Silvano: *Ritmografie: Derrida, la Letteratura, la Cenere*. Genova: Il Melangolo. 158p. [LoC]

RR2073. ● Freytag, Philip: *Die Rahmung des Hintergrunds: Eine Untersu-chung Über die Voraussetzungen von Sprachtheorien am Leitfaden der Debatten Derrida - Searle und Derrida - Habermas*. Frankfurt am Main: Vittorio Klostermann. 542p. [Cor]

RR2074. ● Gaston, Sean: *Jacques Derrida and the Challenge of History*. New York: Rowman et Littlefield. 339p. [Syr]

RR2075. ● Geraci, Silvia: *Tra Una Riva e l'Altra: Jacques Derrida e il Medi-terraneo*. Messina: Mesogea. 116p. [LoC]

RR2076. ● Gildea, Niall: *Jacques Derrida's Cambridge Affair: Deconstruc-tion, Philosophy and Institutionality*. Blue Ridge Summit: Rowman & Littlefield. 228p. [WC]

RR2077. ● Goodrich, Peter, & Michel Rosenfeld: *Administering Interpreta-tion. Derrida, Agamben, and the Political Theology of Law*. Bronx: Fordham UP. 352p. [Cor]

RR2078. ● Häseler, Verena: *Momente der Verantwortung bei Jacques Der-rida*. Nordhausen: Traugott Bautz. 125p. [WC]

RR2079. ● Marinas, José M., Rubén C. Fasolino, & José L. Villacañas: *Espectros de Derrida: Sobre Derrida y el Psicoanálisis*. Madrid: Guillermo Escolar. 168p. [WC]

RR2080. ● McCance, Dawne: *The Reproduction of Life Death: Derrida's La Vie la Mort*. New York: Fordham UP. 191p. [Syr]

RR2081. ● Nancy, Jean-Luc, & Düttmann A. García: *Derrida, Suppléments.* Paris: Galilée. 198p. [Cor]

RR2082. ● Orbán, Jolán, & Anikó Radvánszky: *Dons et Resistances: Études sur Jacques Derrida.* Paris: L'Harmattan. 282p. [LoC]

RR2083. ● Pimentel, Dror: *Heidegger with Derrida: Being Written.* Cham: Palgrave Macmillan. 297p. [WC]

RR2084. ● Rabaté, Jean-Michel: *Understanding Derrida, Understanding Modernism.* Sydney: Bloomsbury Academic. 314p. [Syr]

RR2085. ● Richter, Gerhard: *Ästhetische Eigenzeiten und die Zeit des Bewahrens: Heidegger mit Arendt, Derrida und Kafka.* Hannover: Wehrhahn. 149p. [Cor]

RR2086. ● Rottenberg, Elizabeth: *For the Love of Psychoanalysis. The Play of Chance in Freud and Derrida.* Bronx: Fordham UP. 272p. [Syr]

RR2087. ● Scapini, Marco A. A.: *Derrida, Desconstrução e Democracia Por Vir: Por uma Crítica da Violência para Além do Medo.* Porto Alegre: Zouk. 234p. [WC]

RR2088. ● Tosolini, Tiziano: *Paolo e i Filosofi: Interpretazioni del Cristianesimo da Heidegger a Derrida.* Bologna: Marietti 1820. 174p. [LoC]

RR2089. ● Wetzel, Michael: *Derrida: Eine Einführung.* Ditzingen: Reclam. 196p. [WC]

RR2090. ● Wolf, Markus: *Gerechtigkeit als Dekonstruktion: Zur Kulturellen Form von Recht und Demokratie Nach Jacques Derrida.* [Konstanz]: Konstanz UP. 374p. [WC]

RR2091. Boyer, Patricio: "Erin Graff Zivin, Ed. The Marrano Specter: Derrida and Hispanism." *Comparative Literature Studies, 56,* 3, 639-640. [Naz]

RR2092. Bretz, Thomas H.: "Eco-Deconstruction: Derrida and Environmental Philosophy." *Ethics and the Environment, 24,* 1, 121-30. [RIT]

RR2093. Briggs, R.: "Derrida's Nonpower — from Writing to Zoopower." *Sub-stance, 48,* 2, 23-40. [UaB]

RR2094. Castaño, Héctor G.: "A Worldless Flesh: Derrida, Merleau-Ponty and the Body in Transcultural Perspective." *Parallax, 25,* 1, 42-57. [Syr]

RR2095. De Ville, J.: "On Crime and Punishment: Derrida Reading Kant." *Law and Critique, 31,* 1, 93-111. [Naz]

RR2096. De Ville, J.: "Perpetual Peace: Derrida Reading Kant." *International Journal for the Semiotics of Law, 32,* 2, 335-357. [Syr]

RR2097. De Ville, J.: "The Moral Law: Derrida Reading Kant." *Derrida Today, 12,* 1, 1-19. [Naz]

RR2098. Derrida, Jacques, & Évelyne Grossman: "The Truth That Hurts, or the Corps À Corps of Tongues: An Interview with Jacques Derrida." *Parallax, 25,* 1, 8-24. [UaB]

RR2099. Dews, Peter, & Jean-Marc Durand-Gasselin: "Habermas et Derrida: Modernité, Justice et Religion." *Cités, 78,* 2, 89. [UaB]

RR2100. Evans, Mihail: "Derrida and Europe Beyond Identity." *Journal for Cultural Research, 23,* 3, 288-305. [UofR]

RR2101. Evink, E.: "Donner l'Amour. Le Don et le Sacrifice chez Derrida et Patočka." 491-510. In 2007.

RR2102. Forrest, Kayla: "Witnessing and Truth: A Heartbreaking Work of Staggering Genius and Jacques Derrida's 'Poetics and Politics of Witnessing'." *Cea Critic, 81,* 3, 240-247. [UofR]

RR2103.   Fouéré, Marie-Aude: "L''Effet Derrida' en Afrique du Sud: Jacques Derrida, Verne Harris et la Notion d'Archive(s) dans l'Horizon Post-Apartheid." *Annales. Histoire, Sciences Sociales*, 74, 3, 745. [UofR]

RR2104.   François-David Sebbah, & Paula Marchesini: "Girard/ Derrida: Difference on Difference." *Mln*, 134, 5, 967-81. [PrQ]

RR2105.   Hamdan, Mohammed: "'Every Sperm Is Sacred': Palestinian Prisoners, Smuggled Semen, and Derrida's Prophecy." *International Journal of Middle East Studies*, 51, 4, 525-545. [Naz]

RR2106.   Haubrich, Rebecca: "Between Towers and Giants-: Kafka, Celan, and Derrida in Babel and Prague." *Mosaic*, 52, 4, 37-54. [RIT]

RR2107.   Hinz, Ole: "Hier und Anderswo. Zum Stellenlesen bei Franz Kafka, Samuel Beckett, Theodor W. Adorno und Jacques Derrida." *Mln*, 134, 3, 661-4. [PrQ]

RR2108.   Hoa, Jen Hui Bon: "Ghosts, Fictions, and the Rule of Chance: Rancière on Derrida's Dissemination." *Mosaic*, 52, 4, 149-70. [RIT]

RR2109.   Jones-Katz, G.: "(An Illustration of) Jacques Derrida at the Limits of the Historicist Chronotype." *Rethinking History*, 23, 4, 474-499. [Naz]

RR2110.   Kasimis, Demetra: "Response to Yarbakhsh Elisabeth. Reading Derrida in Tehran: Between an Open Door and an Empty Sofreh. Humanities, 2018, 7, 21." *Humanities*, 8, 3, 140. [RIT]

RR2111.   Kingston, Andrew: "Derrida's Relevance: A Review of Clayton Crockett, Derrida After the End of Writing: Political Theology and New Materialism." *Postmodern Culture*, 29, 2. [UofR]

RR2112.   La Caze, M.: "'I've Never Met a Me': Identity and Philosophy in D'Ailleurs, Derrida." *Derrida Today*, 12, 2, 152-170. [UaB]

RR2113.   Lisse, Michel: "Scènes Primitives des Exils de Jacques Derrida." *Les Lettres Romanes*, 73, 3-4, 407-417. [Syr]

RR2114.   Loewen, Nathan R. B.: "Review of Crockett Clayton, *Derrida and the End of Writing: Political Theology and New Materialism*." *Sophia*, 58, 1, 99-101. [PrQ]

RR2115.   Mertens, Mark: "Le Jeu des Places, le Désaveu-Exclusion et le Pas Tout à Fait: La Systémique Confrontée à Mes Lectures de Derrida, de Lacan et de Žižek." *Thérapie Familiale*, 40, 3, 337. [Naz]

RR2116.   Meylahn, Johann-Albrecht: "Non-Philosophy and Derrida." *HTS Teologiese Studies / Theological Studies*, 75, 4. [UaB]

RR2117.   Morgan, N.: "Laws of Forgiveness: Obama, Mandela, Derrida." *Journal of Transnational American Studies*, 10, 2, 266-281. [Syr]

RR2118.   Nielsen, Cynthia R.: "Eco-Deconstruction: Derrida and Environmental Philosophy." *The Review of Metaphysics*, 72, 3, 600-2. [PrQ]

RR2119.   Nouzille, Philippe: "Coré et Khôra, Agamben et Derrida." *Divus Thomas*, 122, 1, 350-367. [UaB]

RR2120.   Nguyen, Duy L.: "Stupidity and the Threshold of Life, Language and Law in Derrida and Agamben." *Derrida Today*, 12,1, 41-58. [UaB]

RR2121.   Plante, Maxime: "Derrida, la Différance: Une Contribution à une 'Anthropologie Phénoménologique'." 473. In 2007.

RR2122.   Plotnitsky, Arkady: "Structure, Sign, and Play and the Discourse of the Natural Sciences: After the Hyppolite-Derrida Exchange." *Mln*, 134, 5, 953-66. [RIT]

RR2123.   Prado, de O. L. E.: "La Lettre Volée, Moments de l'Histoire de la

Psychanalyse: Poe, Borges, Lacan, Derrida, Johnson, Irwin, Etc." *Figures de la Psychanalyse*, *38*, 2, 239. [Cor]

RR2124. Senatore, Mauro: "Teleotheology: Derrida and the Aristotelian Foundations of Structuralism." *Philosophy Today*, *63*, 1, 175-94. [RIT]

RR2125. Shaul, Dylan: "Jacques Derrida, Advances." *Dialogue*, *58*, 4, 786-787. [UofR]

RR2126. Shaul, Dylan: "Faith In/ As the Unconditional: Kant, Husserl, and Derrida on Practical Reason." *Derrida Today*, *12*, 2, 171-191. [Naz]

RR2127. Shenhav, Ghilad: "The Motif of the Messianic: Law, Life, and Writing in Agamben's Reading of Derrida: By Arthur Willemse, Lanham, Lexington Books, 2017, Hardback, ISBN 9781498544115." *Political Theology*, *20*, 8, 708-709. [UaB]

RR2128. Smith, Claude: "Around Derrida's Intervention in Baltimore: 'Decentering' as a Marker of Poststructural Displacement?" *Mln*, *134*, 5, 982-91. [RIT]

RR2129. Stavo-Debauge, Joan: "Pourquoi le 'Don' de Derrida Ne Résiste Pas à l'Épreuve de l'Hospitalité." *Revue du Mauss*, *53*, 1, 217. [Cor]

RR2130. Terzi, Pietro: "The Relevance of Fink's Notion of Operative Concepts for Derrida's Deconstruction." *Journal of the British Society for Phenomenology*, *50*, 1, 50-67. [Naz]

RR2131. Therezo, Rodrigo: "From Neutral Dasein to a Gentle Twofold: Sexual Difference in Heidegger and Derrida." *Philosophy Today*, *63*, 2, 491-511. [PrQ]

RR2132. Toporisic, T.: "Is Art Itself a Criticism? Linking Wilde to Derrida, Rancière and Badiou." *Filozofski Vestnik*, *40*, 3, 261-276. [Naz]

RR2133. Yoshimatsu, Satoru: "Auto-Affective and Self-Referential Structure of Life in Derrida." *CR: The New Centennial Review*, *19*, 3, 201. [PrQ]

DESAUTELS, Denise.

See also 343, 655.

RR2134. López, Martínez M.: "Cuerpos Poéticos de un Océano a Otro: Cristina Peri Rossi, Ana Rossetti (Hispanas); Denise Desautels y Louise Dupré (Quebequesas)." *Romanica Silesiana*, *15*, 1. [Cor]

DESBIOLLES, Maryline.

RR2135. Clamens-Nanni, Frédéric, Maryline Desbiolles, Johan Faerber, & Ryoko Sekiguchi: "'La Mangeaille et le Vaporeux'. 'Parlons la Bouche Pleine!': Entretiens avec Maryline Desbiolles et Ryoko Sekiguchi." *Elfe XX-XXI*, 7. [Cor]

RR2136. Schwerdtner, Karin: "Maryline Desbiolles en Toutes Lettres: Entretien." *Women in French Studies*, 27, 213-222. [UaB]

DES FORÊTS, Louis-René.

RR2137. Kaltenbeck, Franz: "À Partir de Louis-René des Forêts et Samuel Beckett, Écrits de Vieillesse et Vieillesses Écrites." *Savoirs et Clinique*, *26*, 1, 80. [Cor]

RR2138. Wall, Anthony: "Le Bavard et le Pinailleur: À Partir de Louis-René des Forêts." *Cahiers Sens Public*, *23-24*, 1, 71. [Cor]

DESNOS, Robert.

See also 3, 807.

RR2139. ● Streletz, Werner: *Der Streletz-Schuber: Unterwegs mit Georg Trakl, Robert Desnos und Edgar Allan Poe: Eine Trilogie*. Bochum: Freiburg Projekt. 66p. [WC]

RR2140. Benjamin, Elizabeth: "Robert Desnos and the Play of Popular Culture by Charles A. Nunley (Review)." *French Studies*, 73, 3, 477-478. [UofR]

RR2141. Kuta, Małgorzata: "Sous les Vents Nocturnes . . . Les Échos Apollinariens dans l'Œuvre de Robert Desnos." *Romanica Cracoviensia*, 19, 4, 235-245. [Naz]

RR2142. Lima, Liane A. M., & Filho E. A. Almeida: "Traduzir 'Le Cactus Délicat', de Robert Desnos: Um Jean Valjean Sertanejo." *Revista Graphos*, 20, 1, 190. [WC]

RR2143. Steele, Stephen: "Nunley, Charles A. Robert Desnos and the Play of Popular Culture." *Dalhousie French Studies*, 114, 138. [Syr]

DETAMBEL, Régine.
See also 615.

RR2144. Moon, Hye-Young: "Étude Sur La Bibliothérapie De La France Et Régine Detambel." *Studies in Humanities*, 62, 315-340. [WC]

RR2145. Synn, Jinbeom: "Bibliotherapy in France Encompassing the Healing Effect of Recitation and the Writing That Serves As a Band-Aid. Review of Regine Detambel's Les Livres Prennent Soin de Nous." *Korean Association of Bibliotherapy*, 11, 2, 221-224. [WC]

DEVI, Ananda.
See also 480, 869.

RR2146. Damle, A.: "Fasting, Feasting: The Resistant Strategies of (not) Eating in Ananda Devi's Le Voile de Draupadi and Manger l'Autre." *International Journal of Francophone Studies*, 22, 3, 179-211. [UaB]

RR2147. Priya, T.: "Reducing the Female Body to Ashes: Domestic Violence in Ananda Devi's Le Sari Vert." *Language in India*, 19, 6, 252. [PrQ]

DEVILLE, Patrick.
See also 63, 608, 692.

RR2148. ● Hertrampf, Marina O. M., & Rabadi I. Bernard: *Création(s) et Réception(s) de Patrick Deville*. München: AVM.Édition. 206p. [WC]

DHAINAUT, Pierre.
RR2149. ● Dhainaut, Pierre, & Isabelle Lévesque: *Transferts de Souffles: Premières Approches, 1960-1979; Suivi de Perpétuelle, La Bienvenue*. Paris: L'Herbe qui Tremble. 263p. [BnF]

RR2150. Watine, Marie-Albane, Ilias Yocaris, & Michèle Monte: "Quand l'Écrivain Reprend Son Texte: Réécritures de Pierre Dhainaut dans l'Anthologie dans La Lumière Inachevée." *Cahiers de Narratologie*, 35. [Naz]

DHÔTEL, André.
See also 469.

RR2151. ● Dhôtel, André, Suzanne Briet, & Roland Frankart: *Cahiers André Dhôtel*. Haguenau: Association des Amis d'André Dhotel. 219p. [WC]

RR2152.   • Tellier, Denis: *Lettre à André Dhôtel: Suivie de Un Torrentueux Quadrille: Nouvelle.* Vannes: L'Œil de la Méduse. 47p. [BnF]

RR2153.   Navarette, Pierre-Antoine: "Les Fonctions Structurales de la Fenêtre dans Le Mont Damion d'André Dhôtel." *Annales Littéraires de l'Université de Besançon,* 999, 203-216. [WC]

DIB, Mohammed.
See also 234, 288, 328, 674.

RR2154.   • Ali-Benali, Zineb: *Mohammed Dib: Écrire, sur les Traces du Signe.* Casablanca: Centre Culturel du Livre. 127p. [WC]

RR2155.   Collière-Whiteside, Christine, Karine Meshoub-Manière, & Guy Dugas: "Genèse du Récit Maghrébin pour Enfants. Le Cas de Mohammed Dib." *Genesis,* 48, 81-92. [UaB]

RR2156.   Doshi, Neil: "Written in Sand: Beckett, Aesthetics, and Postcoloniality in Mohammed Dib's Le Désert Sans Détour." *Samuel Beckett Today/Aujourd'hui, 31,* 2, 234-249. [RIT]

RR2157.   Dualé, Christine, Anne Garrait-Bourrier, Wassila Latroch, & Nassima Kacimi: "Mémoire d'un Lieu dans Tlemcen ou les Lieux de l'Écriture de Mohammed Dib." *Babel,* 40, 393-410. [Syr]

DIOP, Birago.
See 205, 817, 846.

DIOP, Boubacar Boris.
See also 247, 250, 360, 414, 690.

RR2158.   • Semujanga, Josias: *L'Œuvre de Boubacar Boris Diop.* Montréal: Les Presses de l'Université de Montréal. 198p. *Études Françaises,* 55, 3. [WC]

RR2159.   "Boubacar Boris Diop. Trente-Cinq Ans de Bibliographie Critique: 1985-2019." *Études Françaises,* 55, 3, 131. [UofR]

RR2160.   Diop, Cheikh M. S.: "Boubacar Boris Diop: Auteur, Traducteur et Éditeur en Wolof." *Études Françaises,* 55, 3, 109. [UofR]

RR2161.   Diouf, Mbaye: "Boubacar Boris Diop et le Roman Total." *Études Françaises,* 55, 3, 43. [UaB]

RR2162.   Harchi, Kaoutar: "'Nos Langues Devraient Avoir Leur Chance': Modalités de Pratique d'un Nationalisme Linguistique Wolof chez Boubacar Boris Diop." *Cahiers du Cap / Laboratoire d'Excellence Création, Arts et Patrimoine,* 7, 185-201. [WC]

RR2163.   "Le Match Boubacar Boris Diop vs Souleymane Bachir Diagne." *Jeune Afrique,* 59, 3063, 16-17. [Syr]

RR2164.   Ndiaye, C.: "Monstres, Princesses et Justicières: Du Féminin Pluriel chez Boubacar Boris Diop." *Études Françaises,* 55, 3, 57-72. [UofR]

RR2165.   Seye, Serigne: "Les Écrits Journalistiques de Boubacar Boris Diop: Un Métadiscours sur la Littérature Africaine." *Études Littéraires Africaines,* 48, 149. [WC]

RR2166.   Uwe, Christian: "De La Question Littéraire à l'Œuvre: Aspects Métapoétiques de l'Œuvre Romanesque de Boubacar Boris Diop." *Études Françaises,* 55, 3, 27. [UaB]

DIOP, Cheikh Anta.
See also 204, 476.
RR2167.   Diop, Cheikh M'Backé: "Recherche Historique et Approche Métho-
dologique dans l'Œuvre de Cheikh Anta Diop." *Tumultes*, 52, 69. [PrQ]

DJAOUT, Tahar.
See 244, 290.

DJEBAR, Assia.
See also 239, 288, 302, 328, 750.
RR2168.   ● Ali-Benali, Zineb: *Assia Djebar: Écrire entre Voix et Corps: His-
toire de Soi, Histoire des Siens*. Casablanca: Centre Culturel du Livre. 143p. [WC]
RR2169.   ● Muratore, M. J.: *The Weave of Fragmentation: Discursive Strug-
gle in Novels of Assia Djebar, Sabiha Khemir, Rachida Madani*. Paris: L'Harmattan.
118p. [BnF]
RR2170.   Achheb, Loubna, & Fatsiha Touati: "Le Thème du Retour, Une
Source Créatrice d'une Écriture Paratopique dans La Disparition de la Langue Fran-
çaise d'Assia Djebar." *Cahiers Erta*, 17. [WC]
RR2171.   Baaqeel, Nuha A.: "Decolonising Language: Towards a New Femi-
nist Politics of Translation in the Work of Arab Women Writers, Ahlam Mosteghanemi,
Nawal Al Sadawim, and Assia Djebar." *International Journal of Comparative Litera-
ture and Translation Studies*, 7, 3, 39. [WC]
RR2172.   Bouchelta, Amal: "Figures de l'Altérité dans Les Nuits de Stras-
bourg d'Assia Djebar." *Revue de la Faculté des Lettres et des Sciences Humaines
(Fès)*, *26*, 17-26. [WC]
RR2173.   Boudjadja, M.: "On Miscegenation and Writing in the Novels of
Assia Djebar." *Studii Si Cercetari Fliologice, Seria Limbi Romanice*, 25, 23-34.
[Cor]
RR2174.   Brozgal, Lia N.: "Book Review: Approaches to Teaching the Works
of Assia Djebar." *Research in African Literatures*, *50*, 2, 264-265. [UofR]
RR2175.   Campos Ruiz, Ilse Daniela: "Memoria y Narración en los Cuentos
de Assia Djebar y Ama Ata Aidoo." *Synergies Mexique*, *9*, 31, 38, 119. [RIT]
RR2176.   Cheref, Abd-el-Kader: "Cultural Memory and Resistance in Assia
Djebar's Vaste Est la Prison." *Romance Studies*, 37, 3-4. 134-148. [WC]
RR2177.   El Guabli, B.: "Writing against Mourning: Memory in Assia Djeb-
ar's Franco-Graphie." *The Cambridge Journal of Postcolonial Literary Inquiry*, 6, 1,
14-29. [Cor]
RR2178.   El-Nossery, Névine: "*Approaches to Teaching the Works of Assia
Djebar* Ed. by Anne Donadey (Review)." *African Studies Review*, *62*, 3, E1-E4. [Naz]
RR2179.   Galmiche, Julia: "Au-Delà des Frontières: La Représentation de la
Femme dans L'Amour, La Fantasia d'Assia Djebar et La Joueuse de Go de Shan Sa."
Mouvances Francophones, *4*, 1. [WC]
RR2180.   Gueydan-Turek, Alexandra: "*Assia Djebar et la Transgression des
Limites Linguistiques, Littéraires et Culturelles* by Wolfgang Asholt, et Lise Gauvin,
and: *Approaches to Teaching the Works of Assia Djebar* Ed. by Anne Donadey
(Review)." *Nouvelles Études Francophones*, *34*, 1, 210-216. [UaB]
RR2181.   Harchi, Kaoutar: "L'Entrée d'Assia Djebar à l'Académie Française:
Réception Politique d'un Discours." *Opus*, *27-28*, 109-127. [WC]

RR2182.　Hazel, Alexa: "The Politics of Form in Assia Djebar's L'Amour, La Fantasia." *The Cambridge Journal of Postcolonial Literary Inquiry*, 6, 3, 347-365. [Cor]

RR2183.　Ivey, Beatrice: "Book Review: Approaches to Teaching the Works of Assia Djebar." *Modern Language Review*, *114*, 1, 148-149. [Naz]

RR2184.　Jordan, Shirley: "Approaches to Teaching the Works of Assia Djebar." *French Studies*, *73*, 1, 155-156. [UaB]

RR2185.　Kim, Jihyun: "Étude sur la Composition Fragmentaire dans L'Amour, La Fantasia d'Assia Djebar." *Société Coréenne d'Enseignement de Langue et Littérature Françaises*, *66*, 125-148. [WC]

RR2186.　Meyer, E. N.: "Approaches to Teaching the Works of Assia Djebar Ed. by Anne Donadey (Review)." *The French Review*, *92*, 3, 191-192. [UofR]

RR2187.　Nuha, Ahmad Baaqeel: "Decolonising Language: Towards a New Feminist Politics of Translation in the Work of Arab Women Writers, Ahlam Mosteghanemi, Nawal Al Sadawim, and Assia Djebar." *International Journal of Comparative Literature & Translation Studies*, *7*, 3, 39-49. [PrQ]

RR2188.　Tindira, Jessica: "La Fille de Son Père: Secrecy, Love, and Writing in Assia Djebar's Nulle Part dans la Maison de Mon Père." *French Review*, *92*, 4, 67-76. [UofR]

DJIAN, Philippe.
See 611, 4716.

DOLTO, Françoise.
RR2189.　● *Françoise Dolto, Aujourd'hui*. Monfort-sur-Meu: AFPEN. 97p. [WC]

RR2190.　● Saint-Onge, Kathleen: *Discovering Françoise Dolto: Psychoanalysis, Identity and Child Development*. New York: Routledge Taylor & Francis. 259p. [Cor]

RR2191.　● Vidal, Séverine, Françoise Dolto, Abellán A. Jaraba, & Catherine Dolto-Tolitch: *L'Onde Dolto: D'Après 'Lorsque l'Enfant Paraît' de Françoise Dolto*. [Paris]: Delcourt. 147p. [BnF]

RR2192.　Bates, R.: "Democratic Babies? Françoise Dolto, Benjamin Spock and the Ideology of Post-War Parenting Advice." *Journal of Political Ideologies*, *24*, 2, 201-219. [Naz]

RR2193.　Kammerer, Mariette: "Dolto, Toujours Là: Trente Ans Après la Mort de la Psychanalyste Françoise Dolto, Comment Sa Pensée et Ses Théories Sont-Elles Encore Enseignées aux Étudiants en Travail Social?" *Lien Social*, 1246, 16. [WC]

RR2194.　Mansuy, Marie-Pierre: "Caroline Eliacheff. Françoise Dolto, Une journée Particulière." *Figures de la Psychanalyse*, *37*, 1, 207. [Cor]

RR2195.　Ohayon, Annick: "Françoise Dolto. Le Sacre de l'Enfant." *Les Grands Dossiers des Sciences Humaines*, *54*, 3, 23. [BAnQ]

DONGALA, Emmanuel.
See also 355, 505.
RR2196.　Anyinefa, Koffi: "Méréana et Ses Sœurs: Féminisme Quotidien dans Photo de Groupe au Bord du Fleuve d'Emmanuel Dongala." *Lendemains*, 44, 106-116. [Cor]

DORGELÈS, Roland.
See 386.

DORION, Hélène.
See 72.

DOTREMONT, Christian.
See also 73.

RR2197.   ● Para, Jean-Baptiste, & Stéphane Massonet: *Christian Dotremont.* Paris: Europe. *Europe,* 1079. 355p. [WC]

RR2198.   ● Vanhoegaerden, Samuel, & M. Draguet: *Christian Dotrmont: Peintre de l'Écriture - Les Logogrammes (1962-1979).* Knokke: Samuel Vanhoegaerden Gallery. 242p. [WC]

RR2199.   Bertramd, G. A.: "Photo/Graphies dans l'Œuvre de Christian Dotremont." 179-189. In 2197.

RR2200.   Bonnefoy, Y.: "Les Logogrammes de Christian Dotremont." 77-78. In 2197.

RR2201.   González, Arantxa R.: "Photography as a Writing Machine: Notes on Christian Dotremont's Logoneiges." *Matlit Revista do Programa de Doutoramento em Materialidades da Literatura,* 7, 1, 81-93. [WC]

RR2202.   Jorn, A.: "Deux Lettres et Demie d'Asger Jorn a Christian Dotremont." 27-31. In 2197.

RR2203.   Martin, S.: "Les Eclaboussures d'Encre de Ma Voix et Ecouter Encore et Encore Christian Dotremont." 150-156. In 2197.

RR2204.   Massonet, S.: "Les Lieux de Christian Dotremont." 3-7. In 2197.

RR2205.   Nicolas-Teboul, L.: "Vers la Vie Quotidienne et la Vie Collective Christian Dotremont et La Main à Plume." 9-20. In 2197.

RR2206.   Vandevoorde, H.: "Amour et Maladie, un Roman de Hugo Claus et Christian Dotremont." 35-44. In 2197.

DOUBROVSKY, Serge.
See also 616, 622, 636.

RR2207.   ● Doubrovsky, Serge, & Isabelle Grell: *Parcours Critique: II.* Grenoble: UGA Éditions. 1 vol. [WC]

RR2208.   Hanania, Cécile: "Un Homme de Passage de Serge Doubrovsky: La Tentation de L'Odyssée." *Cahiers Erta,* 17, 53-68. [WC]

RR2209.   Pezzullo, Viviana: "Claudia Jacobi. Proust Dixit? Réceptions de *La Recherche* dans l'Autofiction de Serge Doubrovsky, Carmen Martín Gaite et Walter Siti. Bonn Up, 2016." *Studies in 20th & 21st Century Literature,* 43, 2. [UofR]

DRIEU LA ROCHELLE, Pierre.
See also 400.

RR2210.   Demurger, Lucas: "1927: Drieu La Rochelle Publie la Lettre 'Sur l'Amitié et la Solitude'." *Littérature, 193,* 1, 60. [Syr]

DRUON, Maurice.
RR2211.   Tsunehisa, Tanaka: "Les Plantes Malfaisantes Dans Tistou Les Pouces Verts de Maurice Druon." *The Sapporo University Journal, 47,* 3, 51-60. [WC]

DUBOIS, Jean-Paul.

RR2212. • Dubois, Jean-Paul: *Tous les Hommes N'Habitent Pas le Monde de la Même Façon.* Paris: L'Olivier. 245p. [WC]

DU BOS, Charles.

RR2213. • Du Bos, C, Johann W. Goethe, & Jean Lacoste: *Œuvres Complètes: Goethe.* Paris: Honoré Champion. 458p. [WC]

DU BOUCHET, André.

See also 887.

RR2214. Créac, H. M.: "Les Premiers Cahiers d'André du Bouchet (1949-1952). Carnets de Poète ou Cahiers de Peintre?" *Revue des Sciences Humaines,* 335, 133-148. [Syr]

RR2215. Julian, Johannes I. K.: "Translation as Poetics in the Works of André du Bouchet." *Modern Language Review,* 114, 1, 35-51. [Naz]

RR2216. Linarès, Serge: "André du Bouchet et Ses Éditeurs." *Revue d'Histoire Littéraire de la France,* 119, 1, 145-162. [RIT]

DUCHARME, Réjean.

RR2217. Vianna, Neto A. R.: "Como Plagiar Sem Perder a Originalidade. O Discurso Dialógico de Bakhtin e o Estatuto do Bastardo - Em Memória de Réjean Ducharme." *Bakhtiniana,* 14, 1, 125-149. [Cor]

DUHAMEL, Georges.

See 642.

DUMÉZIL, Georges.

RR2218. • Castrucci, Emanuele: *La Teoria Indoeuropea Delle Tre Funzioni in Georges Dumézil e Altri Saggi: Ricognizioni per una Critica della Cultura.* Milano: Giuffrè Francis Lefebvre. 221p. [WC]

RR2219. • Poitevin, Michel: *Georges Dumézil, l'Enchanteur Érudit.* Rennes: Apogée. 81p. [BAnQ]

RR2220. Abeijón, Matías: "Historia, Estructura y Experiencia. Relaciones Metodológicas entre Michel Foucault y Georges Dumézil." *Ideas y Valores,* 68, 169, 153-179. [Naz]

DUPIN, Jacques.

See 71, 789, 795.

DUPRÉ, Louise.

See 259, 513, 2134.

DURAS, Marguerite.

See also 301, 310, 316, 329, 373, 434, 535, 666, 689.

RR2221. • Ammour-Mayeur, Olivier, Florence Chalonge, Yann Mével, & Catherine Rodgers: *Marguerite Duras: Passages, Croisements, Rencontres.* Paris: Classiques Garnier. 482p. [UofR]

RR2222. • Cassirame, Brigitte: *Autour du 'Vice-Consul' de Marguerite Duras: Étude Littéraire.* Saint-Denis: Publibook. 166p. [Cor]

RR2223.	● Cléder, Jean: *Duras*. Paris: François Bourin. 142p. [UofR]
RR2224.	● Duras, Marguerite: *Me & Other Writing*. [St. Louis, MO]: Dorothy. 185p. [Syr]
RR2225.	● Garric, Henri: *Solitude et Communauté dans le Roman: Carson Mccullers, Le Coeur est un Chasseur Solitaire; Marguerite Duras, le Vice-Consul; Christa Wolf, Médée. Voix*. Neuilly-sur-Seine: Atlande. 271p. [Cor]
RR2226.	● July, Joël, & Najet Limam-Tnani: *Le Marin de Gibraltar de Marguerite Duras: Lectures Critiques*. Aix-en-Provence: Presses Universitaires de Provence. 142p. [LoC]
RR2227.	● Royer, Michelle: *The Cinema of Marguerite Duras: Multisensoriality and Female Subjectivity*. Edinburgh: Edinburgh UP. 133p. [Syr]
RR2228.	● Royer, Michelle, & Lauren Upadhyay: *Marguerite Duras à la Croisée des Arts*. Wien: P.I.E. Peter Lang. 301p. [WC]
RR2229.	Angelini, Eileen M.: "Hanania, Cécile, Ed. Marguerite Duras. Le Rire dans Tous Ses Éclats." *Dalhousie French Studies*, 114, 141-142. [UofR]
RR2230.	Blair, Anna K.: "Marguerite Duras at the Tepid Baths." *Landfall*, 238, 138-142. [UaB]
RR2231.	Buonomo, Leonardo: "Henry James's Feminist Afterlives: Annie Fields, Emily Dickinson, Marguerite Duras by Kathryn Wichelns." *The Henry James Review*, *40*, 3, E11-E13. [UaB]
RR2232.	Cabral, Maria J., Carlos Carreto, Maria J. Brilhante, & Ana Fernandes: "Yes, Peut-Être de Marguerite Duras: Réécriture de l'Histoire." *Carnets*, deuxième série, 16. [Cor]
RR2233.	Chnaiderman, Beatriz S.: "Marguerite Duras, Femme de Lettres." *Revista de Psicanálise Stylus*, 38, 179-185. [WC]
RR2234.	Dothas, Juan M.: "La Fenêtre dans Moderato Cantabile de Marguerite Duras: Une Analyse Sémiotique." *Annales Littéraires de l'Université de Besançon*, 999, 25-40. [WC]
RR2235.	Downing, Lisa: "Aesthetics, Values and Autobiography in the Works of Willa Cather and Marguerite Duras, by Erna Cooper." *French Studies*, *73*, 4, 646-647. [UaB]
RR2236.	Feng, Qing: "Une Légende de 50 Ans: La Traduction et l'Introduction de Marguerite Duras en Chine." *Synergies Chine*, *14*, 29, 39, 249. [PrQ]
RR2237.	Ferreira-Meyers, Karen: "Henry James's Feminist Afterlives— Annie Fields, Emily Dickinson, Marguerite Duras by Kathryn Wichelns." *Women in French Studies*, *27*, 1, 229-230. [UaB]
RR2238.	Kocevar, Savannah: "La Crise de la Théâtralité dans L'Eden Cinéma de Marguerite Duras: Entre Éclatement des Codes Dramaturgiques et Mise en Pièce du Corps Vieillissant, le Corps Jeune comme Signe d'un Renouveau Théâtral." *Anales de Filología Francesa*, *27*, 1, 501-514. [Naz]
RR2239.	Mema, Laureta: "Un Nouveau Langage pour Peupler le Corps dans L'Amant, Marguerite Duras / A New Language to Inhabit the Body in The Lover, Marguerite Duras." *Caligrama*, *24*, 3, 87. [Syr]
RR2240.	Monroy, Ortiz L. J.: "Literatura, Memoria y Recordación: Una Lectura de la Intertextualidad entre Hiroshima Mon Amour, de Marguerite Duras; y 'Jabalya Mon Amour', de Rocío Cerón." *La Palabra*, 35. [UaB]
RR2241.	Monterrubio, Ibanez L.: "La Evolución de la Materia Epistolar en la

Obra Literaria de Marguerite Duras: Aurélia Steiner, La Destrucción de La Misiva." *Cedille*. 15, 423-457. [Syr]

RR2242.   Sack, Daniel: "The Malady of Film in the Theatre Katie Mitchell Stages Marguerite Duras." *Paj*, 123, 52-61. [UofR]

RR2243.   Shulyatyeva, Dina V.: "Silence as Literary Device in Marguerite Duras's Novels." *Philological Sciences*, 2, 62-68. [Cor]

RR2244.   Silva, Lara R.: "A Experiência Literária em o Caminhão, de Marguerite Duras: Questões Sobre a Cultura e a Arte." *Revista Limiar*, 6, 12, 196-218. [WC]

RR2245.   Vaudrey-Luigi, Sandrine: "La Prose de Marguerite Duras: Des Styles à l'Idiolecte." *Faux Titre*, 434, 129-146. [UofR]

RR2246.   Watine, Marie-Albane, Ilias Yocaris, & Sandrine Vaudrey-Luigi: "L'Amant de Marguerite Duras: De l'Écriture Novatrice au Non-Événement de Style." *Cahiers de Narratologie*, 35. [Cor]

RR2247.   Zafiropoulos, M.: "Erik Porge, le Ravissement de Lacan. Marguerite Duras à la Lettre." *Figures de la Psychanalyse*, 37, 1, 217-219. [Cor]

DURKHEIM, Émile.
See also 725, 733, 1504.

RR2248.   ● Béra, Matthieu, & Nicolas Sembel: *Les Formes Élémentaires de la Vie Religieuse, Cent Ans Après: Émile Durkheim et la Religion: [Actes du Colloque du 11 au 13 Juin 2012, Bordeaux, Talence et Pessac]*. Paris: Classiques Garnier. 449p. [WC]

RR2249.   ● Juan, Salvador: *Durkheim et la Sociologie Française: D'Hier à Aujourd'hui*. Auxerre: Sciences Humaines Éditions. 280p. [WC]

RR2250.   ● Lezama, José L.: *La Naturaleza ante la Tríada Divina: Marx, Durkheim, Weber*. Ciudad de México, México: El Colegio de México, Centro de Estudios Demográficos, Urbanos y Ambientales. 235p. [WC]

RR2251.   ● Rawls, Anne W.: *"De la Division du Travail Social" Revisited: Vers une Théorie Sociologique de la Justice: Émile Durkheim*. Lormont: Le Bord de l'Eau. 289p. [WC]

RR2252.   ● Stoczkowski, Wiktor: *La Science Sociale comme Vision du Monde: Émile Durkheim et le Mirage du Salut*. [Paris]: Gallimard. 629p. [Cor]

RR2253.   ● Tuomivaara, Salla: *Animals in the Sociologies of Westermarck and Durkheim*. Cham: Palgrave Macmillan. 261p. [WC]

RR2254.   Abbott, A.: "Living One's Theories: Moral Consistency in the Life of Émile Durkheim." *Sociological Theory*, 37, 1, 1-34. [Naz]

RR2255.   Bender, Mateus: "Da Regra Moral ao Desvio: Aproximações Teóricas de Émile Durkheim Nas Obras de Erving Goff Man e Howard S. Becker." *Diálogo*, 41, 17. [WC]

RR2256.   Béra, Matthieu: "Four Unpublished Letters from Durkheim to Bouglé (1897)." *L'Année Sociologique*, 69, 1, 43. [UofR]

RR2257.   Carls, P.: "Modern Democracy as the Cult of the Individual: Durkheim on Religious Coexistence and Conflict." *Critical Research on Religion*, 7, 3, 292-311. [Syr]

RR2258.   Chairul, Basrun U. M., M. Yulisvestra, K. K. Oki, W. Mulyasari, & R. Ridwan: "The Thought of Emile Durkheim in the Contestation of Development in Indonesia." *International Journal of Scientific and Technology Research*, 8, 8, 1881-1885. [WC]

RR2259.   Connor, Brian T.: "Émile Durkheim and the Birth of the Gods: Clans, Incest, Totems, Phratries, Hordes, Mana, Taboos, Corroborees, Sodalities, Menstrual Blood, Apes, Churingas, Cairns, and Other Mysterious Things." *Social Forces*, *98*, 2, 1-3. [UofR]

RR2260.   Denunzio, F., & I. Gjergji: "L'Indice Segreto. Origine e Sviluppo del Rapporto di Merton con Durkheim." *Sociologia e Ricerca Sociale*, 119, 38-52. [Naz]

RR2261.   Eckert, Julia: "Durkheim in World Society: Roger Cotterrell's Concept of Transnational Law." *Ratio Juris*, *32*, 4, 498-508. [UaB]

RR2262.   Fernandes, Freire A. T.: "Émile Durkheim e a Crítica do Capitalismo em da Divisão do Trabalho Social." *Mediações*, *24*, 2, 154-78. [Naz]

RR2263.   Gaede, Neto R., & João H. Stumpf: "O Suicídio e o Público Jovem na Sociedade Contemporânea. Subsídios para Grupos de Juventudes a Partir de Émile Durkheim." *Revista Eclesiástica Brasileira*, *78*, 311, 566. [WC]

RR2264.   Horii, M.: "Historicizing the Category of 'Religion' in Sociological Theories: Max Weber and Emile Durkheim." *Critical Research on Religion*, 7, 1, 24-37. [Syr]

RR2265.   Ibrahim, Muhammad F., Zebari T. Hesso, & Ahmad Muhammadpour: "The Factors of Social Anomie According to Durkheim's Theory." *Twejer*, *2*, 4, 217-254. [WC]

RR2266.   Kostyło, Piotr: "Émile Durkheim and the Longing for Community Life." *Yearbook of Pedagogy*, *42*, 1, 37-54. [WC]

RR2267.   Lebow, Richard N.: "Durkheim et les Relations Internationales." *Études Internationales*, *50*, 2, 221. [Cor]

RR2268.   Lemert, Charles: "Durkheim's Ghost: The Century After His Death: France, Germany, Turkey." *İstanbul Üniversitesi Sosyoloji Dergisi*, *39*, 1. [Naz]

RR2269.   Liagouras, George: "Economic Growth, Happiness and Socialism: Durkheim's Critique of Economic Reason and Beyond." *New Political Economy*, *24*, 5, 659-677. [UaB]

RR2270.   Marson, S. M., & J. P. Lillis: "Durkheim's Greatest Blunder." *Journal of Sociology and Social Welfare*, *46*, 2, 155-177. [Naz]

RR2271.   Møen, Atle: "Democracy and Public Communication: A Durkheimian Lens on Habermas." *Acta Sociologica*, *62*, 1, 20-33. [PrQ]

RR2272.   Moosbrugger, Mathias: "Historian in Disguise: On Derrida, Durkheim and the Intellectual Ambition of René Girard." *Forum Philosophicum*, *24*, 1, 5-24. [UaB]

RR2273.   Mustofa, Farrid: "Religion, Identity and Solidarity: Emile Durkheim's Perspective." *Jurnal Penelitian*, 20 May, 65. [WC]

RR2274.   Navarre, Maud: "Livres: 'Durkheim Aujourd'hui'." *Sciences Humaines*, 310. [PrQ]

RR2275.   Paunescu, M.-O.: "Socrates and Durkheim: Paradox and Common Sense Logic." *Studii de Lingvistica*, *9*, 1, 207-230. [Syr]

RR2276.   Prus, R.: "Redefining the Sociological Paradigm: Emile Durkheim and the Scientific Study of Morality." *Qualitative Sociology Review*, *15*, 1, 6-34. [RIT]

RR2277.   Rivaya, Benjamín: "Las Formas Elementales del Derecho (El Pensamiento Jurídico de Emile Durkheim)." *Dereito*, *28*, 2. [PrQ]

RR2278.   Sanchis, Pierre: "Durkheim e o Mito." *Revista Caminhos*, *12*, 1, 143. [WC]

RR2279.   Sanzhenakov, A. A.: "On the Difference of the Approaches of Searle and Durkheim to the Description of Social Reality." *Siberian Journal of Philosophy*, *17*, 2, 189-198. [Cor]

RR2280.   Serrano, Maíllo A.: "Una Reconstrucción de la Idea de Sutherland de Patrones y Procesos Delictivos a Partir del Primer Durkheim." *Estudios Penales y Criminológicos*, 39. [WC]

RR2281.   Shin, Dong-Joon: "Crime and Inequality: Anomie Theory's Limitations and Durkheim's Insights." *Journal of Korean Criminological Asscciation*, *13*, 2, 111-132. [WC]

RR2282.   Silva, Rodolfo F.: "Durkheim e Bourdieu: Aproximações e Distanciamentos." *Sociologias Plurais*, 5, 1. [WC]

RR2283.   Sohrabi, Hadi: "A Durkheimian Critique of Contemporary Multiculturalism." *Ethnic and Racial Studies*, *42*, 8, 1283-304. [PrQ]

RR2284.   Trophimov, S. V.: "Emile Durkheim on the Role of Religion in Public Life. Substantiation of the Choice of Elementary Religion." *Moscow State University Bulletin. Series 18. Sociology and Political Science*, *25*, 3, 173-197. [UaB]

RR2285.   Vallera, Farah L.: "Durkheim Said What?: Creating Talking Textbooks with Augmented Reality and Project-Based Activities." *Journal of Research on Technology in Education*, *51*, 3, 290-310. [UaB]

RR2286.   Wawrzyniak, J.: "From Durkheim to Czarnowski: Sociological Universalism and Polish Politics in the Interwar Period." *Contemporary European History*, *28*, 2, 172-187. [Naz]

DUTOURD, Jean.

RR2287.   Chaker Mohamed, Ben Ali: "Reading Ernest Hemingway in Algeria." *The Hemingway Review*, *39*, 1, 128-33. [RIT]

EBERHARDT, Isabelle.

See also 442.

RR2288.   Ben, Rejeb A.: "Le Vagabondage ou la Flânerie Subversive chez Isabelle Eberhardt." *Voix Plurielles*, *16*, 1, 57-64. [Syr]

RR2289.   Chaix, Benjamin: "Des Écrits Originaux d'Isabelle Eberhardt Parlent Pour Elle à la Maison Tavel." *Tribune de Genève*, 6 February. [WC]

RR2290.   Pitteloud, Anne: "Isabelle Eberhardt, à la Rencontre de l'Autre." *Courrier de Genève*, 25 January. [WC]

RR2291.   Sokołowicz, Małgorzata: "'Lâ Illâha Illa-Llâh'. L'Islam d'Isabelle Eberhardt et les Transformations du Religieux." *Romanica Wratislaviensia*, 66, 81-92. [WC]

ECHENOZ, Jean.

See also 357, 506, 689, 692.

RR2292.   ● Delisle, Guy, & Jean Echenoz: *Ici ou Ailleurs*. Montréal: Pow Pow. 1 vol. [BAnQ]

RR2293.   Cloonan, William: "American Culture's Impact on Postwar France: A Positive Report." *Contemporary French and Francophone Studies*, *23*, 1, 38-46. [PrQ]

RR2294.   Ieven, Émilie: "Les Lignes Utopiques de l'Équipée Malaise. Sur l'Espace et le Mouvement chez Jean Echenoz." *Littérature*, *195*, 3, 52. [UofR]

RR2295.   Maziarczyk, Anna: "L'Intertextualité et l'Intermédialité au Service du Roman (Doublement) Dialogique. Le Cas d'Échenoz et de Laurrent." [PrQ] (Toussaint)

EEKHOUD, Georges.
See 356.

ÉLIADE, Mircea.
See 1834.

EL MALEH, Edmond Amran.
See also 604.
RR2296.   ● Sacré, James, & Philippe Hélénon: *Dans la Parole de l'Autre: Lorand Gaspar: Edmond Amram El Maleh.* Soligny-la-Trappe: Rougier V. 44p. [WC]
RR2297.   Ben, Msila A.: "Edmond Amran El Maleh: Culture et Écriture." *Littératures Maghrébines au Cœur de la Francophonie Littéraire,* 2, [139]-154. [WC]

ÉLUARD, Paul.
See also 462, 548, 1384.
RR2298.   ● Boudrot, Pierre: *Minuit au Cœur, au Cœur de Minuit: Le Coffret Éluard: Histoire d'un Exemplaire.* Paris: Métamorphoses. 61p. [BnF]
RR2299.   ● Éluard, Paul, & Ray Man: *Facile: Poèmes de Paul Eluard; Photographies de Man Ray.* Paris: RMN. 36p. [WC]
RR2300.   ● Guigon, Emmanuel, Malén Gual, & Cristina Vila: *Pablo Picasso, Paul Eluard: Una Amistad Sublime.* Barcelona: Fundació Museu Picasso de Barcelona. 231p. [LoC]
RR2301.   ● Kulin, Katja: *Gala Éluard: Muse der Surrealisten und die Große Liebe Salvador Dalís Romanbiografie.* Freiburg: Herder. 221p. [WC]
RR2302.   Créac'h, Martine: "Les Couleurs du Devoir (Paul Eluard)." *Littérature,* 195, 3, 5. [UofR]
RR2303.   Dotremont, C.: "Paul Eluard, Le Poète de la Résistance." 61-62. In 2197.

EMAZ, Antoine.
See also 783.
RR2304.   ● Emaz, Antoine, & Fabio Pusterla: *Sulla Punta della Lingua: Dieci Movimenti Poetici; Seguiti dalla Meditazione Lirismo Critico?* Milano: Marcos y Marcos. 185p. [WC]
RR2305.   ● Saint-Roch, Florence: *Antoine Emaz de A à Z.* Saint-Omer: Les Venterniers. 27p. [BnF]
RR2306.   Irati, Fernández E.: "Antoine Emaz: Le Lyrisme de la Sobriété." *Çédille,* 15, 139-165. [Syr] (Maulpoix)
RR2307.   Lévesque, Isabelle: "Antoine Émaz d'Écrire, Un Peu." *Quinzaines,* 1212, 20-21. [UaB]

ERNAUX, Annie.
See also 2, 224, 298, 299, 301, 343, 492, 501, 535, 610, 1287, 1304.

RR2308. ● Deneubourg, Jérôme: *Qui a Peur d'Annie Ernaux?* Vitré: Lunatique. 116p. [LoC]

RR2309. Berton, Jacques: "'Ici, Je Ne Suis Pas à Ma Place': Rapport aux Savoirs et Lutte des Places en Formation." *VST*, *143*, 3, 106. [Cor]

RR2310. Ernaux, Annie, & Dominique Viart: "Repas de Famille. Entretien avec Annie Ernaux." *Elfe XX-XXI*, 7. [Cor]

RR2311. Fortier, Corinne: "Inceste Gémellaire, Deuil et Mélancolie Créatrice: De la Transidentité à l'Œuvre de Pierre Molinier et d'Annie Ernaux." *L'Autre*, *20*, 1, 51. [WC]

RR2312. Lindsay, Gabriella: "Hazy Analogies: Sexual and Colonial Complicities in Annie Ernaux's Mémoire de Fille." *Comparative Literature Studies*, *56*, 4, 787-806. [Naz]

RR2313. Mhainnín, Máire A. N.: "'Il Aurait Peut-Être Préféré Avoir une Autre Fille': Paternal Mourning in the Work of Annie Ernaux." *Irish Journal of French Studies*, *19*, 1, 107-122. [WC]

ESTEBAN, Claude.
See 797.

ÉTIENNE, Gérard.
RR2314. ● Étienne, Gérard, & Nolwenn Henaff: *Inégalités en Perspectives.* Paris: Archives Contemporaines. 231p. [WC]

RR2315. Grossman, Simone: "Gérard Étienne et Hervé Lebreton: Une Rencontre Artistique." *Nouvelles Études Francophones*, *34*, 1, 151-161. [Syr]

RR2316. Satyre, Joubert: "*La Reine Soleil Levée* de Gérard Étienne, ou le Pacte entre Vodou et Dictature." *Nouvelles Études Francophones*, *34*, 1, 162-174. [UaB]

FALL, Aminata Sow.
See also 675, 690, 750.
RR2317. Diop, Ibou C.: "Aminata Sow Fall, Un Humanisme au Féminin." *Lendemains*, 44, 138-147. [Cor]

RR2318. Kuhn, Helke: "'Yalla Yalla Bey Sa Toll' — La Force Féminine dans l'Œuvre Romanesque de Aminata Sow Fall." *Lendemains*, 44, 148-158. [Cor]

FANON, Frantz.
See also 226, 395, 509, 798, 1270.
RR2319. ● Bernini, Lorenzo: *Il Sessuale Politico: Freud con Marx, Fanon, Foucault.* Pisa: ETS. 303p. [LoC]

RR2320. ● Chaulet-Achour, Christiane: *Dans le Sillage de Frantz Fanon.* Alger: Casbah. 142p. [WC]

RR2321. ● Haddour, Azzedine: *Frantz Fanon, Postcolonialism and the Ethics of Difference.* Manchester: Manchester UP. 271p. [Naz]

RR2322. ● Kipfer, Stefan: *Le Temps et l'Espace de la (Dé)colonisation: Dialogue entre Frantz Fanon et Henri Lefebvre.* Paris: Eterotopia France. 257p. [BAnQ]

RR2323. ● Manoharan, Karthick R., & Allen Hibbard: *Frantz Fanon: Identity and Resistance.* Hyderabad (India): Orient BlackSwan. 118p. [WC]

RR2324. ● Mokhtefi, Elaine: *Algers, Capitale de la Révolution: De Fanon aux Black Panthers.* Paris: La Fabrique. 279p. [WC]

RR2325. Abdulqadir, Dizayi S.: "Locating Identity Crisis in Postcolonial Theory: Fanon and Said." *Journal of Advanced Research in Social Sciences*, *2*, 1. [WC]

RR2326. Agathangelou, A. M.: "A Conversation with Emma Hutchison and Frantz Fanon on Questions of Reading and Global Raciality." *Millennium*, *47*, 2, 249-262. [UaB]

RR2327. Aguirre, Aguirre C.: "Apuntes para una Corpo-Política desde las Escrituras Aimé Césaire y Frantz Fanon." *Universum (Talca)*, *34*, 1, 15-38. [Naz]

RR2328. Allan, M.: "Old Media/ New Futures: Revolutionary Reverberations of Fanon's Radio." *Pmla*, *134*, 1, 188-193. [UofR]

RR2329. Beyers, Jaco: "Reconstructing Black Identity: The Black Panther, Frantz Fanon and Achilles Mbembe in Conversation." *Hts Teologiese Studies/ Theological Studies*, *75*, 4. [RIT]

RR2330. Bose, Anuja: "Frantz Fanon and the Politicization of the Third World as a Collective Subject." *Interventions*, *21*, 5, 671-689. [UaB]

RR2331. Bugbee, Teo: "Frantz Fanon: Black Skin, White Mask." *Film Comment*, *55*, 2, 75. [RIT]

RR2332. Davis, Danielle: "Fanon, Violence, Racism and Embodiment: Making Raced Bodies and Practising a New Dialogue of Raced Bodies in Situation?" *Social Alternatives*, *38*, 4, 5-15. [RIT]

RR2333. Do, Nascimento R.: "Frantz Fanon No Brasil: Uma Releitura da Sua Recepção Pelo Pensamento Negro Feminista." *Revista Ártemis*, *27*, 1, 158-181. [Naz]

RR2334. Duarte, Diego E. S.: "Novos Caminhos a Partir de Frantz Fanon." *Geografia em Atos (Online)*, *5*, 12, 158-165. [WC]

RR2335. Farhan, Sara: "On Frantz Fanon: Key Concepts." *Left History*, *22*, 2. [Cor]

RR2336. Fink, Ann E.: "Fanon's Police Inspector." *Ajob Neuroscience*, *10*, 3, 137-144. [UaB]

RR2337. Georgis, D.: "Freud, Fanon and the Difference Desire Makes." *Emotion, Space and Society*, 31, 105-107. [UaB]

RR2338. Harris, J. W.: "Domestic Imperialism: The Reversal of Fanon." *Stance*, 12, 64-73. [Naz]

RR2339. Harris, Katharine A.: "Review: Living Fanon: Global Perspectives." *Excursions Journal*, *3*, 1, 108-112. [WC]

RR2340. Hassett, Dónal: "Translating Frantz Fanon Across Continents and Languages." *Translation Studies*, *12*, 3, 375-378. [UaB]

RR2341. Hook, Derek: "*Frantz Fanon, Psychiatry and Politics* by Nigel C. Gibson and Roberto Beneduce (Review)." *Critical Philosophy of Race*, *7*, 2, 400-404. [Cor]

RR2342. Izwaini, Sattar: "The Re-Presentation of Fanon's Les Damnés de la Terre in Arabic Translation." *Interventions*, *21*, 2, 151-171. [UofR]

RR2343. Kullberg, Christina: "New Perspectives on Frantz Fanon." *New West Indian Guide / Nieuwe West-Indische Gids*, 93, 279-285. [Naz]

RR2344. Le Jeune, J.: "Revolutionary Terror and Nation-Building: Frantz Fanon and the Algerian Revolution." *Journal of the Study of Radicalism*, *13*, 2, 1-44. [UaB]

RR2345. Lee, Taek-Gwang: "Decolonizing Madness: Fanon and Lacan." *The Criticism and Theory Society of Korea*, *24*, 2, 35-50. [WC]

RR2346.   Maldonado-Torres, Nelson, Mireille F. M. France, Jeong E. A. We, & Zandisiwe Radebe: "Editorial Introduction: Frantz Fanon, Decoloniality, and the Spirit of Bandung." *Bandung*, 6, 2, 153-161. [Naz]

RR2347.   Maranga-Musonye, M.: "The Fanon Factor in Ngũgĩ Wa Thiong'o's Children's Fiction." *Research in African Literatures*, 50, 3, 51-69. [Naz]

RR2348.   Mcgregor, Rafe: "Frantz Fanon, Psychiatry and Politics, Nigel C. Gibson & Roberto Beneduce, 2017. London: Rowman & Littlefield International, 322 Pp, £80 (hb), £24.99 (ebook)." *Journal of Applied Philosophy*, 36, 2, 348-349. [UofR]

RR2349.   Meaney, Thomas: "Frantz Fanon and the CIA Man." *The American Historical Review*, 124, 3, 983-995. [UofR]

RR2350.   Moustapha, Diop E. H.: "Translating Frantz Fanon Across Continents and Languages." *Journal of the African Literature Association*, 13, 2, 283-285. [Syr]

RR2351.   Munro, Martin: "Frantz Fanon, Alienation and Freedom. Edited by Jean Khalfa and Robert J. C. Young. Translated by Steven Corcoran." *French Studies*, 73, 2, 329-330. [UofR]

RR2352.   Newlove, Chris J.: "The Wretched of the Earth and Strategy: Fanon's 'Leninist' Moment?" *Review of African Political Economy*, 46, 159, 135-142. [UofR]

RR2353.   Opperman, R.: "A Permanent Struggle against an Omnipresent Death: Revisiting Environmental Racism with Frantz Fanon." *Critical Philosophy of Race*, 7, 1, 57-80. [UaB]

RR2354.   Paris, William Michael: "Gender and Technology in Frantz Fanon: Confrontations of the Clinical and Political." *Philosophy Compass*, 14, 9. [PrQ]

RR2355.   Sánchez-Grobet, Andrea: "Fanon, el Cuerpo y la Colonialidad: Una Lectura Feminista." *Entrediversidades*, 6, 2, 137-170. [Cor]

RR2356.   Shilliam, Robbie: "From Ethiopia to Bandung with Fanon." *Bandung*, 6, 2, 163-189. [Naz]

RR2357.   Siani, Alberto L.: "Stefan Bird-Pollan. Hegel, Freud and Fanon. The Dialectic of Emancipation. London-New York: Rowman & Littlefield, 2015. ISBN 978-1-78348-301-3. Pp. 262. £29.95." *Hegel Bulletin*, 40, 3, 523-527. [Cor]

RR2358.   Ureña, Carolyn: "Fanon's Idealism: Hopeful Resignation, Violence, and Healing." *Bandung*, 6, 2, 233-251. [Naz]

RR2359.   Whitney, Shiloh: "From the Body Schema to the Historical-Racial Schema." *Chiasmi International*, 21, 305-320. [Cor]

RR2360.   Wood, Dan: "Fanon and the Underside of Commodity Fetishism." *Phaenex*, 13, 1, 1-45. [Syr]

RR2361.   Worthy, Jay: "On the Place of Resistance in Ontology." *Chiasmi International*, 21, 321-334. [Cor]

FARGUE, Léon-Paul.
See 634.

FÉNÉON, Félix.
RR2362.   ● Cahn, Isabelle, & Philippe Peltier: *Félix Fénéon: Critique, Collectionneur, Anarchiste*. Paris: Musée d'Orsay. 317p. [WC]

RR2363.   ● Fénéon, Félix: *Les Arts Lointains Iront-Ils au Louvre?* Paris: Espaces et Signes. 94p. [BnF]

RR2364.   ● Fénéon, Félix: *Les Impressionnistes en 1886*. Bègles: L'Esprit du Temps. 63p. [BnF]

RR2365. ● Fénéon, Félix, & Jean Paulhan: *Correspondance 1917-1944: Il Vous Aura Fallu, Pour Mon Lustre, Faire de Cent Personnages des Fantômes*. Paris: C. Paulhan. 243p. [WC]

RR2366. ● Fénéon, Félix, John Rewald, Sébastien Chauffour, & Maurice Imbert: *Correpondance. 27 Février 1937-23 Janvier 1941*. Tusson: Du Lerot. 165p. [WC]

RR2367. ● Henoch, Julie, & Félix Fénéon: *Volte-face aux Nouvelles en Trois Lignes de Félix Fénéon*. Vevey: Hélice Hélas. 1 dépliant. [WC]

RR2368. ● Pommereau, Claude, Sandrine Rosenberg, Aude Adrien, Daphné Bétard, Marion Guyonvarch, Joséphine Kraft, Pierre Pinchon, & Félix Fénéon: *Félix Fénéon (1861-1944): Les Temps Nouveaux, De Seurat à Matisse: Musée de l'Orangerie*. Issy-les-Moulineaux: Beaux-Arts Éditions. 64p. [BAnQ]

RR2369. "Arrêt Sur Image Portrait de M. Félix Fénéon." *Œil*, 726, 82-87. [UaB]

RR2370. Goppelsroder, F.: "Tweets Avant la Lettre? Félix Fénéon's Novels in Three Lines." *Zeitschrift fur Franzosische Sprache und Literatur*, *128*, 23, 166-186. [UofR]

RR2371. Gutiérrez, José I.: "La Construcción de 'Faits Divers' en los 'Microrrelatos' de Félix Fénéon." *Cuadernos de Investigación Filológica*, *45*, 3. [Syr]

RR2372. Kerr, Greg: "Shattering the Middle Ground: Violence and the Imperative of Reportage in Félix Fénéon's Nouvelles en Trois Lignes." *Contemporary French Civilization*, *44*, 4, 311-332. [Syr]

RR2373. Mugnier, Hé: "Culture: Rencontrer Fénéon." *Esprit*, 458. [PrQ]

RR2374. Peltier, Philippe, Isabelle Cahn, & Elena Martínez-Jacquet: "Félix Fénéon: Art from Distant Places." *Tribal Art*, *23*, 92, 54-59. [WC]

RR2375. Schira, Etienne: "Félix Fénéon: Critique, Collectionneur, Anarchiste." *Critique d'Art*, 5 December. [Cor]

FERAOUN, Mouloud.
See also 328.

RR2376. Desjarlais, Robert: "And Other Deaths Have Followed . . . (with Mouloud Feraoun)." *Comparative and Continental Philosophy*, *11*, 2, 198-213. [Cor]

RR2377. Kaci-Mohamed, Salah: "At Literary Altitude: Albert Camus's and Mouloud Feraoun's Discourses on Identity." *The Journal of North African Studies*, *10*, 1080, 1-23. [WC]

FERNANDEZ, Dominique.
RR2378. ● Moreau, Gustave, Julián, Casal, Dominique Fernandez, & Rivas R. Herrera. *Aux Lumières Pourprées du Crépuscule: Correspondance Croisée: Suivi de Mi Museo Ideal*. Paris: Hermann. 129p. [BnF]

RR2379. Fernandez, Dominique: *Ramon Fernandez*. Mexico: Fondo de Cultura Economica. 1 vol. [WC]

FERRÉ, Léo.
See 459, 847.

FERRON, Jacques.
RR2380. ● Ferron, Jacques, Madeleine Ferron, Robert Cliche, Marcel Ols-

camp, & Lucie Joubert: *Le Monde A-T-Il Fait la Culbute?*: *Correspondances 3, 1966-1985*. Montréal: Leméac. 589p. [BAnQ]

RR2381.   Bérubé, Renald: "La Part du Diable. Le Saint-Élias de Jacques Ferron by Jacques Cardinal (Review)." *University of Toronto Quarterly*, *88*, 3, 403-406. [UofR]

FERRY, Luc.

RR2382.   Ferreira, Douglas W.: "A Ética em Luc Ferry: Um Humanismo Fundamentado Nos Valores Cristãos." *Sapere Aude*, *10*, 19, 294-309. [WC]

RR2383.   Ferreira, Douglas W.: "Da Modernidade em Luc Ferry à Pós-Modernidade de Vattimo: As Diferentes Concepções de Niilismo." *Griot*, *19*, 2, 87-107. [Syr]

FÉVAL, Paul.

RR2384.   • Altairac, Joseph: *Pinchon, Bécassine et co*. Amiens: AARP. 352p. [WC]

FEYDEAU, Georges.

RR2385.   • Schaubühne, am Lehniner Platz: *Champignol Wider Willen, von Georges Feydeau*. Berlin: Schaubühne am Lehniner Platz. 65p. [WC]

FINKIELKRAUT, Alain.

See also 626.

RR2386.   • Finkielkraut, Alain: *À la Première Personne*. [Paris]: Gallimard. 121p. [Cor]

RR2387.   Prod'homme, Lucie: "Agression d'Alain Finkielkraut: Réflexion sur l'Antisémitisme en France Aujourd'hui." *La Revue Nouvelle*, 7, 7, 11. [UaB]

FONDANE, Benjamin.

RR2388.   • Fondane, Benjamin, Francesco Testa, & Luca Orlandini: *Tra Gerusalemme e Atene: Scritti Sull'Ebraismo*. Firenze: Giuntina. 301p. [WC]

RR2389.   • Fondane, Benjamin, & Gonzalo Torné: *El Lunes Existencial y el Domingo de la Historia*. Madrid: Hermida. 230p. [WC]

RR2390.   • Freedman, Eric A.: *Bibliographie de l'Œuvre de Benjamin Fondane: Volume 2*. Paris: Non-Lieu. 253p. [BnF]

RR2391.   Bondor, George: "Benjamin Fondane et la Philosophie de la Crise." *Hermeneia*, *23*, 223-8. [RIT]

RR2392.   Dur, Ion: "Benjamin Fondane – True from Aesthetic Discourse." *Advances in Sciences and Humanities*, *5*, 6, 138. [WC]

RR2393.   Mindra, Mihai: "Benjamin Fondane's Ulysses." *Journal of Modern Jewish Studies*, *18*, 2, 249-50. [PrQ]

RR2394.   Petrescu, Radu I.: "Fondane. Dialogues au Bord du Gouffre." *Philologica Jassyensia*, *15*, 2, 328-31. [RIT]

FOUCAULT, Michel.

See also 10, 521, 732, 747, 749, 1770, 2220, 2319, 3541, 4570, 4835.

RR2395.   • Abraham, Tomás: *La Máscara Foucault: De París a la Argentina*. C. A. B. A.: Paidós. 379p. [LoC]

RR2396. • Bert, Jean-François, & Sourish Datta: *Michel Foucault*. Calcutta: Sampark. 152p. [WC]

RR2397. • Brigaglia, Marco: *Potere: Una Rilettura di Michel Foucault*. Napoli: Editoriale Scientifica. 366p. [LoC]

RR2398. • Castilla, Cerezo A., & Miguel Morey: *Una Extraña Triangulación: Lenguaje, Obra y Literatura en Michel Foucault*. Granada: Comares. 112p. [LoC]

RR2399. • Catucci, Stefano: *Introduzione a Foucault*. Bari: Laterza. 217p. [WC]

RR2400. • Camargo, Ricardo: *Parrhesía en Foucault*. Santiago de Chile: RiL Editores. 190p. [WC]

RR2401. • Cazeneuve, Nathan, Tristan Duval-Cos, & Etienne Lauret: *Où Est le Pouvoir?: Réflexions autour de Michel Foucault*. 257p. [WC]

RR2402. • Dean, Mitchell, & Daniel Zamora: *Le Dernier Homme et la Fin de la Révolution: Foucualt Après Mai 68*. Montréal: Lux. 224p. [BAnQ]

RR2403. • Dufaux, Jean, & Martin Jamar: *Foucault: Une Tentation dans le Désert*. [Bruxelles]: Dargaud Benelux. 57p. [BnF]

RR2404. • Fernández, Agis D., & López D. J. García: *Poder, Derecho y Justicia: Reflexiones Desde el Espacio Discursivo de Michel Foucault*. Santa Cruz de Tenerife: HH Ediciones. 150p. [WC]

RR2405. • Foucault, Michel, Thierry Voeltzel, & Santiago A. Sánchez: *Veinte Años y Después: Conversaciones con Michel Foucault; Seguido de Letzlove: Anagrama de un Encuentro*. Adrogué (Argentina): La Cebra. 168p. [WC]

RR2406. • Fuentes, Megías F.: *El Filósofo, el Psicagogo y el Maestro: Filosofía y Educación en Pierre Hadot y Michel Foucault*. Madrid: Miño y Dávila. 296p. [WC]

RR2407. • Gutting, Gary: *Foucault: A Very Short Introduction*. Oxford: Oxford UP. 130p. [UofR]

RR2408. • Lamy, Jérôme: *Politique des Savoirs: Michel Foucault, Les Éclats d'une Œuvre*. Paris: Éditions de la Sorbonne. 180p. [WC]

RR2409. • Larrauri, Maite, & Max: *La Sexualidad Según Michel Foucault*. [Madrid]: Libros de Fronterad. 108p. [WC]

RR2410. • López, Cristina, Marcelo Raffin, & Agustín Colombo: *Pensar con Foucault Hoy: Relecturas de las Palabras y las Cosas y la Voluntad de Saber*. 197p. [WC]

RR2411. • Lugo, Vázquez M.: *Foucault y la Crítica a la Concepción Moderna de la Locura*. Buenos Aires: Editorial Biblos. 344p. [WC]

RR2412. • Marchart, Oliver, & Renate Martinsen: *Foucault und das Politische: Transdisziplinäre Impulse für die Politische Theorie der Gegenwart*. Wiesbaden: Springer. 384p. [Cor]

RR2413. • Negri, Antonio, Fernando Venturi, & Diego A. Sztulwark: *Marx y Foucault*. Buenos Aires (Argentina): Cactus. 255p. [WC]

RR2414. • Nouailles, Bertrand, & Alain Petit: *Foucault Hérétique: Les Mots et les Choses*. Clermont-Ferrand: Presses Universitaires Blaise-Pascal. 234p. [WC]

RR2415. • Ribard, Dinah: *1969: Michel Foucault et la Question de l'Auteur: "Qu'Est-Ce Qu'un Auteur?"*. Genève: Slatkine. 110p. [WC]

RR2416. • Royo, Simón: *El Sujeto Anárquico: Reiner Schürmann y Michel Foucault*. Madrid: Arena Libros. 165p. [BnF]

RR2417. • Sawyer, Stephen W., & Daniel Steinmetz-Jenkins: *Foucault, Neoliberalism, and Beyond*. Lanham, MD: Rowman & Littlefield. 203p. [Cor]

RR2418. • Schönherr-Mann, Hans-Martin: *Michel Foucault als Politischer Philosoph*. Innsbruck: Innsbruck UP. 183p. [LoC]

RR2419. • Sforzini, Arianna: *Michel Foucault: Un Pensiero del Corpo*. Verona: Ombre Corte. 138p. [WC]

RR2420. • Skorucak, Thomas: *Le Courage des Gouvernés: Michel Foucault, Hannah Arendt*. Paris: CNRS Éditions. 378p. [Cor]

RR2421. • Voyce, Malcolm: *Foucault and Family Relations. Governing from a Distance in Australia*. Lexington, MA: Lexington Books. 260p. [LoC]

RR2422. • Vuillemin, Jean-Claude: *Foucault l'Intempestif*. Paris: Hermann. 353p. [Cor]

RR2423. • Wade, Simeon: *Foucault in California: [A True Story-Wherein the Great French Philosopher Drops Acid in the Valley of Death]*. Berkeley, CA: Heyday. 131p. [UaB]

RR2424. Agrazar, Jesuán: "El Problema de la Causa Patógena en la Psicopatología Sexual: Entre Krafft-Ebing y Foucault." *Acta Psiquiátrica y Psicológica de América Latina*, 65, 2, 130-40. [PrQ]

RR2425. Aitchison, Guy: "Foucault, Democracy and the Ambivalence of Rights." *Critical Review of International Social and Political Philosophy*, 22, 6, 770-785. [Cor]

RR2426. Baek, Seung J.: "Butler, Foucault and Alexina." *The Journal of Modern British & American Language & Literature*, 37, 3, 45-61. [WC]

RR2427. Ben, Pablo: "Foucault, Capitalismo y Sexualidad: Tensiones Conceptuales circa 1976." *Mora (Buenos Aires)*, 25, 2, 1-10. [Syr]

RR2428. Benavides-Franco, Tulio A.: "El Cuerpo como Espacio de Resistencia: Foucault, las Heterotopías y el Cuerpo Experiencial." *Co-Herencia*, 16, 30, 247-272. [Naz]

RR2429. Blanco, Azucena González: "La Hermenéutica Literaria de Michel Foucault." *Revista de Literatura*, 81, 161, 7. [PrQ]

RR2430. Boulé, Éric, & Emanuel Guay: "The Powers of Sensibility. Aesthetics Politics Through Adorno, Foucault and Rancière, de Michael Feola, Evanston, Northwestern UP, 2018, 168 p." *Politique et Sociétés*, 38, 3, 156. [Cor]

RR2431. Calder-Dawe, O., & N. Gavey: "Feminism, Foucault, and Freire: A Dynamic Approach to Sociocultural Research." *Qualitative Psychology*, 6, 3, 216-231. [Naz]

RR2432. Camelo, Perdomo D. F.: "Historia y Poder: Los(Des)Usos de Marx en Foucault." *Revista Filosofía Uis*, 18, 2, 125-141. [WC]

RR2433. Castro, E.: "The Notion of Police in the Works of Michel Foucault: Object, Boundaries, Antinomies." *Anuario Colombiano de Historia Social y de la Cultura*, 46, 2, 185-206. [RIT]

RR2434. Catonne, J.-P.: "Michel Foucault et la Prison." *Pratiques en Santé Mentale*, 64, 4, 47-51. [WC]

RR2435. Choque, Aliaga O. D.: "Foucault: Biopolítica y Discontinuidad." *Praxis Filosófica*, 49, 191-218. [Naz]

RR2436. Dalmau, Iván G.: "Ciencias Humanas y Objetivación: Reflexiones en Torno a la Crítica Política del Saber Elaborada por Michel Foucault." *Valenciana*, 12, 24, 163-182. [Cor]

RR2437.   Dos Santos, Rômulo Ballestê Marques, & Francisco Teixeira Portugal: "O Panóptico e a Economia Visual Moderna: Do Panoptismo ao Paradigma Panóptico na Obra de Michel Foucault." *Revista Psicologia Política*, *19*, 44, 34. [PrQ]

RR2438.   Duperut, Carelí: "Tras lo Singular: Foucault y el Ejercicio del Filosofar H." *Estudios de Filosofía Práctica e Historia de las Ideas*, *21*, 1, 1-7. [Cor]

RR2439.   Fabre, A., & P. Labardin: "Foucault and Social and Penal Historians: The Dual Role of Accounting in the French Overseas Penal Colonies of the Nineteenth Century." *Accounting History Review*, *29*, 1, 1-37. [Syr]

RR2440.   Fajardo, Christian: "Política y Biopolítica: Una Aproximación desde Foucault, Agamben y Rancière." *Ciencia Política*, *14*, 28, 197-222. [PrQ]

RR2441.   Fokiceva, Elina: "Foucault on Painting." *Visual Studies*, *34*, 2, 201-202. [RIT]

RR2442.   Franco, Tulio Alexander Benavides: "El Cuerpo como Espacio de Resistencia: Foucault, las Heterotopías y el Cuerpo Experiencial." *Co-Herencia*, *16*, 30, 247-72. [PrQ]

RR2443.   Frost, Tom: "The Dispositif between Foucault and Agamben." *Law, Culture and the Humanities*, *15*, 1, 151-171. [UaB]

RR2444.   Garland, David: "Reading Foucault: An Ongoing Engagement." *Journal of Law and Society*, *46*, 4, 640-661. [UofR]

RR2445.   Gefen, Alexandre: "Review of Michel Foucault, Les Aveux de la Chair, Vol. 4 of Histoire de la Sexualité." *Critical Inquiry*, *45*, 2, 558. [Naz]

RR2446.   Hardy, Nick: "Integrating Archer and Foucault." *Journal of Critical Realism*, *18*, 1, 1-17. [UaB]

RR2447.   Kawashima, Ken C.: "The Hidden Area between Marx and Foucault." *Positions: Asia Critique*, *27*, 1, 115-144. [Syr]

RR2448.   Keck, Charles S.: "Radical Educations in Subjectivity: The Convergence of Psychotherapy, Mysticism and Foucault's 'Politics of Ourselves'." *Ethics and Education*, *14*, 1, 102-115. [UofR]

RR2449.   Kelly, M. G. E.: "Discontinuity in Poststructuralist Epistemology Foucault Contra Deleuze and Derrida." *Cosmos and History*, *15*, 1, 324-349. [Syr]

RR2450.   Kim, Joohwan: "For the Reconstruction of the Late Foucault's Project on Aesthetics of Existence: Focusing on Technique, Repetition and Force." *Korean Journal of Sociology*, *53*, 3, 129-174. [Cor]

RR2451.   Konoval, B.: "From Sexuality to Governmentality: The Oedipus Complex of Michel Foucault." *Modern Intellectual History*, *16*, 1, 217-249. [UofR]

RR2452.   Krakus, Anna, & Cristina Vatulescu: "Foucault in Poland: A Silent Archive." *Diacritics*, *47*, 2, 72-105. [Naz]

RR2453.   Lais, D.: "Foucault as an Ethical Philosopher: The Genealogical Discussion of Antiquity and the Present." *Foucault Studies*, *27*, 27, 69-95. [Syr]

RR2454.   Legg, S.: "Subjects of Truth: Resisting Governmentality in Foucault's 1980s." *Environment and Planning D: Society and Space*, *37*, 1, 27-45. [UaB]

RR2455.   Luna, W.: "Re-thinking Thought: Foucault, Deleuze, and the Possibility of Thinking." *Foucault Studies*, *27*, 27, 48-68. [Syr]

RR2456.   Martins, C. J., & Munoz J. A. Jimenez: "Modernity and the Regulation of Bodies: Elias Meets Foucault." *Motriz*, *25*, 1. [Syr]

RR2457.   Mason, Lance E.: "The Self & Political Possibilities in Dewey & Foucault: Comparative Implications for School & Society." *Journal of Thought*, *53*, 3-20. [RIT]

RR2458.   Masquelier, Charles: "Bourdieu, Foucault and the Politics of Precarity." *Distinktion*, 20, 2, 135-155. [Cor]

RR2459.   Maxwell, Lida: "The Politics and Gender of Truth-Telling in Foucault's Lectures on Parrhesia." *Contemporary Political Theory*, 18, 1, 22-42. [Naz]

RR2460.   Medien, Kathryn: "Foucault's Orient: The Conundrum of Cultural Difference, from Tunisia to Japan." *Journal of Middle East Women's Studies*, 15, 2, 229-231. [RIT]

RR2461.   Milani, Baptiste: "Parler Pour Ne Pas Entrer en Tentation: La Rechute dans le Salut, selon Michel Foucault." *Communio*, 261, 1, 82. [WC]

RR2462.   Moosavinia, S. R., S. T. Sarokolaei, & K. Racevskis: "Edward Said and Michel Foucault: Representation of the Notion of Discourse in Colonial Discourse Theory." *Journal of Research in Applied Linguistics*, 10, 2, 182-197. [WC]

RR2463.   Morris, Freja: "Foucault As Educator." *British Journal of Educational Studies*, 67, 1, 142-144. [UaB]

RR2464.   Murcia, Ángela Patricia Rincón: "La Sociedad Normalizadora en Foucault. A Propósito de los Sujetos y Sujetas al Poder." *Cuadernos de Filosofía Latinoamericana*, 40, 121, 95-108. [RIT]

RR2465.   Ohaneson, Heather C.: "Voices of Madness in Foucault and Kierkegaard." *International Journal for Philosophy of Religion*, 87, 1, 27-54. [UofR]

RR2466.   O'Meara, Lucy: "After Foucault: Culture, Theory, and Criticism in the 21st Century. Edited by Lisa Downing." *French Studies*, 73, 3, 500-501. [UaB]

RR2467.   Öz, Yusuf: "Grammar and Power in Wittgenstein and Foucault / Wittgenstein Ve Foucault'Da Gramer Ve Iktidar." *Humanitas*, 7, 14, 423-36. [PrQ]

RR2468.   Páez, Guzmán E. R.: "Foucault." *Cuestiones de Filosofía*, 4, 23. [WC]

RR2469.   Papastephanou, Marianna: "Of(f) Course: Michel Foucault, the Mobile Philosopher and His Dreamworlds." *Critical Horizons*, 20, 1, 1-19. [Naz]

RR2470.   Peters, Michael A., & Danilo Taglietti: "Deleuze's Rhizomatic Analysis of Foucault: Resources for a New Sociology?" *Educational Philosophy and Theory*, 51, 12, 1187-1199. [Naz]

RR2471.   Petit, J.-F.: "Michel Foucault, Patrologue et Éthicien? M. Foucault, les Aveux de la Chair (2018)." *Nouvelle Revue Théologique*, 141, 1, 105-113. [UaB]

RR2472.   Poncela, Pierrette: "Problématiser les Pratiques Pénales avec et Après Michel Foucault." *Délibérée*, 6, 1, 6. [WC]

RR2473.   Prozorov, Sergei: "Why Is There Truth? Foucault in the Age of Post-Truth Politics." *Constellations*, 26, 1, 18-30. [Syr]

RR2474.   Rago, Margareth: ""Estar Na Hora do Mundo": Subjetividade e Política em Foucault e Nos Feminismos." *Interface*, 23. [RIT]

RR2475.   Rahli, Hocine: "Faire Parler le Corps: Foucault Passe aux Aveux." *Critique*, 869, 10, 900. [UofR]

RR2476.   Rosalen, Eloisa: "Between Practices and Criticisms: Michel Foucault, Feminisms and the Subject." *Estudos Feministas*, 27, 1. [PrQ]

RR2477.   Sabot, P.: "De Foucault à Butler, en Passant par Sartre: L'Impossibilité du 'Nous'?" *Aurora*, 31, 52, 8-31. [WC]

RR2478.   Sanchez, Santiago A.: "The Governmentality as a Power at a Distance: Foucault and the Crisis of Disciplines." *Daimon*, 76, 155-170. [Cor]

RR2479.   Scasserra, José I.: "Butler y Foucault en Simultáneo. Disputas sobre el Sujeto, de Isabel Lorey." *Mora (Buenos Aires)*, 25, 1, 1-2. [Syr]

RR2480.   Schultz, Daniel J.: "Elephants, Dreams, and Sex: Reading Religion in Foucault's Ethics." *The Journal of Religion, 99*, 2, 173-193. [UofR]

RR2481.   Schutijser, D.: "The Modern Attitude According to Michel Foucault: Subjectivation at the Limits." *Eidos*, 225-251. [Naz]

RR2482.   Scull, Andrew, & Pauline Toulet: "Michel Foucault: Que Reste-T-Il de l'Idole?" *Books, 100*, 9, 97. [BAnQ]

RR2483.   Sforzini, Arianna: "Michel Foucault Va Au Cinéma / Foucault at the Movies." *Le Foucaldien*, 5, 1. [Cor]

RR2484.   Sheldahl-Thomason, Strand: "Foucault and the Use of Exposure: Discipline, Ethics, and Self-Writing." *Review of Communication, 19*, 3, 225-240. [RIT]

RR2485.   Sherman, David: "Foucault's Neoliberal Ideology." *European Journal of Philosophy, 27*, 2, 500-514. [UaB]

RR2486.   Velasquez, M. M., & F. T. Serrano: "The Last Lesson of Michel Foucault: A Vitalism for a Future Philosophy." *Athenea Digital, 19*, 2. [Naz]

RR2487.   Vuillerod, Jean-Baptiste: "Coupure Épistémologique ou Coupure Politique? Sur un Dialogue de Jeunesse entre Foucault et Althusser." *Actuel Marx, 66*, 2, 152. [Cor]

RR2488.   Wheatley, Lance: "Following Foucault: The Trail of the Fox." *Journal of Critical Realism, 18*, 5, 529-534. [RIT]

RR2489.   Zamora, Vargas D.: "Foucault, The End of a Decade." *Contemporary European History, 28*, 2, 262-272. [UaB]

RR2490.   Zhao, Weili: "'Observation' as China's Civic Education Pedagogy and Governance: An Historical Perspective and a Dialogue with Michel Foucault." *Discourse: Studies in the Cultural Politics of Education, 40*, 6, 789-802. [UofR]

RR2491.   Zouggari, Najate: "Foucault, Bourdieu et la Question Néolibérale." *Schweizerische Zeitschrift für Soziologie, 45*, 1, 130. [PrQ]

FOURCADE, Dominique.
RR2492.   ● Fourcaut, Laurent: *L'Œuvre Poétique de Dominique Fourcade. Ed. Reliée. Un Lyrisme Lessivé à Mort du Réel.* Paris: Classiques Garnier. 311p. [WC]

RR2493.   Petterson, James: "Dominique Fourcade: Recalculations." *Studies in 20th & 21st Century Literature, 43*, 1. [Naz]

FRANCE, Anatole.
See also 815.
RR2494.   Rey, Pierre-Louis: "Book Review: Proust et Anatole France. 'Recherches Proustiennes'." *Revue d'Histoire Littéraire de la France, 119*, 3, 734-736. [UofR]

RR2495.   Tchoshanov, Mourat, Olga Kosheleva, & Vladik Kreinovich: "Anatole France's Statement on Education Transformed into a Theorem." *Russian Digital Libraries Journal, 22*, 6, 769-772. [WC]

RR2496.   Teixeira, Alanna D. J.: "Literatura, História e Representação do Passado em Anatole France." *História em Revista*, 23. [LoC]

FRANKÉTIENNE.
See also 54.
RR2497.   Franklin, Jocelyn: "Dézafi by FranKétienne." *Journal of Haitian Studies, 25*, 2, 282-284. [Syr]

RR2498. Waite, Genevieve: "Légende Haïtien, Créateur Translingue: Un Entretien avec Frankétienne." *Journal of Haitian Studies*, 25, 2, 260-267. [UaB]

FRÉNAUD, André.
See also 709.
RR2499. ● *André Frénaud et Ses Livres: Catalogue 19*. Paris: Librairie-Galerie Emmanuel Hutin. 1 vol. [BnF]
RR2500. ● Froye, Marianne, Jean-Yves Debreuille, & André Frénaud: *André Frénaud, Poétique de la Subversion*. Paris: Honoré Champion. 747p. [Cor]

GALLAIRE, Fatima.
See 292.

GARY, Romain.
See also 407, 772.
RR2501. ● Coquant, Valéry G.: *De Gary à Ajar, Le Voyage de Romain: Biographie*. Plombières les Bains: Ex Aequo. 233p. [WC]
RR2502. ● Decout, Maxime: *Album Romain Gary*. [Paris]: Gallimard. 242p. [WC]
RR2503. ● Désérable, François-Henri: *Romain Gary: Le Visionnaire*. La Tour-d'Aigue: Éditions de L'Aube. 53p. [WC]
RR2504. ● Gary, Romain, & Mireille Sacotte: *Romans et Récits*. Paris: Gallimard. 2 vols. 1447, 1688 p. [UofR]
RR2505. ● Hangouët, Jean-François: *Picaros et Pédoncules: Romain Gary et l'En-Avant de l'Humanité selon Pierre Teilhard de Chardin*. Genève: Droz. 224p. [Cor]
RR2506. Cabral, Maria J., Carlos Carreto, Maria J. Brilhante, & Jacques Isolery: "Romain Gary et Mai 68. Mots d'Ordre et de Désordre." *Carnets*, deuxième série, 16. [Cor]
RR2507. Genetti, Stefano: "Romain Gary, une Voix dans le Siècle, sous la Direction de J. Roumette, A. Schaffner et A. Simon." *Studi Francesi*, 63, 3, 608-609. [UaB]
RR2508. Koziej, Alicja J.: "Pris au Piège. Les Idéalistes dans 'Les Racines du Ciel' de Romain Gary." *Lublin Studies in Modern Languages and Literature*, 43, 1, 39. [Cor]
RR2509. Lee, Yehoon: "A Study on Avoiding the Reality of Romain Gary." *The Journal of Humanities and Social Sciences*, 21 (10, 6), 983-992. [WC]
RR2510. Mercier, Christophe: "Romain Gary: Un Cas Unique dans l'Histoire Littéraire." *Commentaire*, 167, 3, 677. [Cor]
RR2511. Schoolcraft, Ralph: "L'Œuvre de Romain Gary. Notre Folie N'Est Jamais Celle Que Nous Racontons." *Journal Français de Psychiatrie*, 48, 2, 54. [Cor]

GASPAR, Lorand.
See also 569, 797, 2296.
RR2512. Scotto, Fabio: "Lorand Gaspar, Archives et Genèse de l'Œuvre, A. Gourio et D. Leclair." *Studi Francesi*, 63, 2, 396-397. [UofR]

GATTI, Armand.
RR2513. ● Coudray, Sophie: *Armand Gatti: La Traversée des Possibles: Essai Collectif*. Nice: Marsa. 154p. [WC]

RR2514. ● Gatti, Armand, & Michel Séonnet: *Comme Battements d'Ailes: Poésie 1961-1999*. Paris: Gallimard. 215p. [WC] (Yacine)

RR2515.   O'Neill, E.: "El Otro Cristdbal d'Armand Gatti." *Positif*, 705, 82-83. [Syr]

GENET, Jean.

See also 316, 367, 509, 558, 564, 840, 4719.

RR2516.   ● Gallmeier, Heike: *When I First Heard About Jean Genet I Thought Hilarious: Mahdad Alizadeh, Viiri Linnéa Broo Andersson, Judith Beyer, Dominique Buege, Stainer Chindebvu, Alexandra Ellerbrock, Malina Heinemann, Jann Holstein, Rikako Kashima, Maximilian Klawitter, Paul GÜnther Köstner, Emma Kucharzik, Lorenz Lang, Maria Martini, Paula Matheis, Katharina Michalsky, Laurine Michon, Atli Pálsson, Linh Lida Pham, Maira Schmerder, Felix Schröder, Julia Selle, Emma Sylten*. Berlin: Universität der Künste. 78p. [WC]

RR2517.   ● Hervé, Martin, Patrick Autréaux, & Mathieu Riboulet: *Mathieu Riboulet sur les Grands Chemins de Jean Genet: [Treizièmes Rencontres de Chaminadour, Guéret, Septembre 2018]*. Guéret: Association des Lecteurs de Marcel Jouhandeau et des Amis de Chaminadour. 341p. [WC]

RR2518.   Agerup, Karl: "Action for Art's Sake: Rethinking Jean Genet's Political Turn." *Interlitteraria*, *23*, 2, 399-413. [Cor]

RR2519.   Agerup, Karl: "Saïd et Genet. La Représentation des Palestiniens et la Question de l'Orientalisme chez Jean Genet." *Bergen Language and Linguistics Studies*, *10*, 1, 9. [WC]

RR2520.   Bonnet, Valérie, Chloé Gaboriaux, Marie Plassart, & Thomas Liano: "Jean Genet et le Black Panther Party: Une Danse des Pronoms." *Mots*, *121*, 3, 55. [Cor]

RR2521.   Brueton, Joanne: "Une Rose des Vents Politique: The Southern Winds of Jean Genet's Poetic Compass." *Artl@s Bulletin*, *8*, 2, 44. [PrQ]

RR2522.   Coto-Rivel, Sergio, F. C. de Fourrel, Jennifer Houdiard, & Jean-Christophe Corrado: "Les Amours d'Hitler et de Jeanne d'Arc: Les Représentations Sexualisées de la France et de l'Allemagne dans Pompes Funèbres de Jean Genet." *Itinéraires*, 2019-2-3. [WC]

RR2523.   Crockarell, Sarah: "The Maids by Jean Genet." *Theatre Journal*, *71*, 3, 386-388. [UofR]

RR2524.   Dumont, Lucile, Quentin Fondu, Laélia Véron, & Laurie Rousseville: "Le Marxisme de Lucien Goldmann et le 'Théâtre de la Révolte' de Jean Genet." *Contextes*, 25. [Syr]

RR2525.   Piret, Pierre: "L'Exil et la Honte. Jean Genet et les Palestiniens." *Les Lettres Romanes*, *73*, 3-4, 377-391. [Syr]

RR2526.   Preston, Carrie J.: "Blackfaced at the Blacks: Audience Participation in Jean Genet's Lessons on Race." *Modern Drama*, *62*, 1, 1-22. [RIT]

RR2527.   Rousseville, Laurie: "Le Marxisme de Lucien Goldmann et le 'Théâtre de la Révolte' de Jean Genet." *Contextes*, 25. [PrQ]

RR2528.   Silva, Pedro H. R.: "A Violência como Destino em Jean Genet." *Revista de Estudos Acadêmicos de Letras*, *12*, 1, 162-170. [WC]

RR2529.   Tarnowski, Stefan: "Does Revolution Still Resonate?: On Jean Genet and Failure." *Artasiapacific*, 116, 50-51. [Naz]

RR2530.   Yoon, Jeongim: "L'Éthique de la Blessure: Les Écrits sur l'Art de Jean Genet." *Études de Langue et Littérature Françaises*, 119, 105-133. [WC]

GENETTE, Gérard.

See also 587.

RR2531. • Bourgatte, Michaël, & Daniel Jacobi: *Gérard Genette, Théoricien de la Communication?* Paris: PUF. 166p. [WC]

RR2532. • Charles, Michel: *Gérard Genette.* Paris: Seuil. *Poétique*, 185. 190p. [WC]

RR2533. Bonaccorsi, Julia, & Yves Jeanneret: "Genette and Information and Communication Sciences: A Paradoxical Filiation?" *Communication & Langages*, *202*, 4, 49. [UaB]

RR2534. Bourgatte, Michaël, & Daniel Jacobi: "Le Devenir des Concepts de Gérard Genette dans la Recherche en Communication." *Communication & Langages*, *202*, 4, 39. [UaB]

RR2535. Lindemann, C.: "Dialogue and the Limits of Narrative Discourse: Gérard Genette, Gertrude Stein." *Word and Text*, 9, 107-124. [WC]

RR2536. Pardo, Jiménez P.: "Gérard Genette de Bardadrac a Postscript." *Anales de Filología Francesa*, 27, 1, 243-256. [Naz]

RR2537. Soulez, Guillaume: "Genette, a Counter-Investigation: Pragmatics, Forms, and Diachrony in the 'Narrative Voice'." *Communication & Langages*, *202*, 4, 115. [UaB]

GENEVOIX, Maurice.

RR2538. • Fidelin, Benoît: *Genevoix, Mon Ami.* Montrouge: Bayard. 160p. [LoC]

RR2539. • Luneau, Aurélie, Jacques Tassin, & Maurice Genevoix: *Maurice Genevoix: Biographie.* [Paris]: Flammarion. 301p. [WC]

RR2540. • Tassin, Jacques: *Au-devant de Maurice Genevoix.* Orléans: Corsaire. 124p. [BnF]

RR2541. Thébaud, Jean-Loup: "À Plusieurs Voix: Il Faut Sauver le Soldat Genevoix." *Esprit*, 451, 26-9. [PrQ]

GERMAIN, Sylvie.

See 679, 696.

GEVERS, Marie.

See also 79, 698.

RR2542. Brogniez, Laurence, David Martens, & Jean-Marie Klinkenberg: "Marie Gevers au Pays des Merveilles: Images d'un Jeu de l'Oie." *Textyles*, 56, 77-96. [Cor]

GHELDERODE, Michel de.

See also 774.

RR2543. Niedokos, Judyta: "Théâtre de Michel de Ghelderode – Un Retour aux Œuvres 'Mineures'?" *Cahiers Erta*, 19, 117-134. [WC]

GHÉON, Henri.

See 844.

GIDE, André.

See also 376, 776, 1168.

RR2544. ● Bompaire, François: *Définir l'Ironie en France Entre 1800 et 1950: Construction Théorique et Mémoire Gidienne*. Paris: Classiques Garnier. 488p. [Cor]

RR2545. ● Della, Casa M.: *André Gide, l'Européen: Avec un Texte Inédit d'André Gide*. Paris: Classiques Garnier. 349p. [BnF]

RR2546. ● Gide, André, Pierre Masson, & Olivier Monoyez: *André Gide et les Peintres: Lettres Inédites*. [Paris]: Gallimard. 202p. [Cor]

RR2547. ● Gide, André, & Patrick Pollard: *Gide et le Mythe Grec: Suivi de Fragments du 'Traité des Dioscures' et Autres Textes Inédits*. Paris: Classiques Garnier. 262p. [LoC]

RR2548. ● Haroche-Bouzinac, Geneviève: *André Gide dans Ses Lettres*. Paris: Honoré Champion. *Epistolaire*, 45. 411p. [WC]

RR2549. ● Perrier, Jean-Claude: *L'Univers d'André Gide*. [Paris]: Flammarion. 223p. [BAnQ]

RR2550. ● Philippe, Ambre: *André Gide autour du Monde. Un Carnet de Voyage Gidien*. Paris: Orizons. 366p. [BnF]

RR2551. ● Rougemont, Denis, & Jonathan Wenger: "L'Œuvre et l'Influence d'André Gide (Inédit)." *Études de Lettres: Bulletin de la Faculté des Lettres de l'Université de Lausanne et de la Société des Études de Lettres*. Etudes de Lettres: Bulletin de la Faculté des Lettres de l'Université de Lausanne et de la Société des Études de Lettres, 2019, *311*, 11. 1 vol. [WC]

RR2552. Al-Yassiry, Mohamed Yaser: "À la Recherche de la Sainteté et de l'Amour Céleste dans 'La Porte Étroite' d'André Gide. The Search for Sanctity and Divine Love 'The Narrow Door' André Gide." *Journal of the College of Languages*, 40, 139-154. [WC]

RR2553. Bertrand, Stéphanie: "Book Review: André Gide, Une Question de Décence. 'Bibliothèque Gidienne'." *Revue d'Histoire Littéraire de la France*, *119*, 2, 482-483. [UofR]

RR2554. Codazzi, Paola: "Book Review: André Gide, André Malraux. L'Amitié à l'Œuvre (1922-1951)." *Revue d'Histoire Littéraire de la France*, *119*, 1, 232-233. [RIT]

RR2555. Corbellari, Alain, Nicolas Stenger, Denis Rougemont, & Jonathan Wenger: "L'Œuvre et l'Influence d'André Gide (Inédit)." *Études de Lettres*, 311, 11-30. [UaB]

RR2556. Fiorentino, Francesco, & Guillaume Bridet: "L'Immoraliste d'André Gide Au-Delà des Études Postcoloniales." *Revue Italienne d'Études Françaises*, 9. [Syr]

RR2557. Gardini, Michela: "Stéphanie Bertrand, André Gide et l'Aphorisme. Du Style des Idées." *Studi Francesi*, *63*, 3, 606. [UaB]

RR2558. Geisler, Eberhard: "André Gide, mit Ludwig Hohl Gelesen. Zum 150. Geburtstag des Französischen Dichters." *Lendemains*, *44*, 174-175, 196-204. [Cor]

RR2559. Pollard, Patrick: "André Gide et l'Aphorisme: Du Style des Idées. Par Stéphanie Bertrand." *French Studies*, *73*, 3, 476-477. [UofR]

RR2560. Quentin, de G. M. G.: "De l'Effondrement de l'Étalon-Or au Crépuscule des Idoles dans 'Les Faux-Monnayeurs' d'André Gide." *Lublin Studies in Modern Languages and Literature*, *43*, 1, 27. [Cor]

RR2561. Reeck, Matt: "The Paradoxes of Description in André Gide's Voyage au Congo and Le Retour du Tchad." *South Central Review*, *36*, 1, 82-103. [Naz]

RR2562.   Schnyder, P.: "'Il Faut Travailler avec Acharnement...' André Gide: Regards sur Sa Morale de l'Effort." *Romanic Review*, 109, 221-232. [Naz]

GILSON, Étienne.
See also 406, 708, 736, 744, 765.

RR2563.   ● Gilson, Étienne, & Florian Michel: *Oeuvres Complètes: 1908-1943*. Paris: Vrin. 818p. [BnF]

RR2564.   Brilli, Elisa: "Some Metamorphoses of the Civitas Terrena. Augustine in Étienne Gilson and Robert Markus." *Revue de l'Histoire des Religions*, 236, 2, 243. [UaB]

RR2565.   Serra, Perez M. A.: "Esse or Existence? The Real Distinction between Lawrence Dewan and Étienne Gilson." *Revista Espanola de Filosofia Medieval*, 26, 2, 135-160. [Naz]

RR2566.   Trémolières, François: "Florian Michel, Étienne Gilson, une Biographie Intellectuelle et Politique: Paris, Vrin, 2018, 458 p." *Archives de Sciences Sociales des Religions*, 188, 4, 386. [Syr]

GIONO, Jean.
See also 664, 848.

RR2567.   ● Chougnet, Jean-François, Bérangère Huguet, & Laure Lane: *Lucien Jacques: Le Sourcier de Giono*. Arles: Actes Sud. 127p. [WC]

RR2568.   ● Huguet, Alexandra: "Le Hussard sur le Toit, de Jean Giono." *Nrp. Lettres Lycée. Hors-Série*, 32, 1. [WC]

RR2569.   ● Le Clézio, J.-M. G., Emmanuelle Lambert, & Jacques Mény: *Giono*. Marseille: Mucem. 315p. [Cor]

RR2570.   ● Leclere, Damien, Delphine Martin-Orts, & Paul Benarroche: *Jean Giono (1895-1970): Livres, Manuscrits et Photographies: Collection du Docteur Roger Sailles: Vente, Marseille, Vendredi 26 Avril 2019*. Paris: Leclere. 243p. [WC]

RR2571.   ● Mény, Jacques: *Revue Giono, Vol. 12: 2019*. Manosque: Amis de Jean Giono. 272p. [WC]

RR2572.   ● Meurant, Jack: *Jean Giono et le Pacifisme: 1934-1944: De la Paix à la Guerre*. Artignosc-sur-Verdon: Parole. 143p. [BnF]

RR2573.   Lopes, da C. L.: "Jean Giono e a Reinvenção da Odisseia na Literatura Francesa do Pós-Guerra." *História: Questões & Debates*, 67, 2, 199. [WC]

RR2574.   McLauchlan, Laura: "A Multispecies Collective Planting Trees: Tending to Life and Making Meaning Outside of the Conservation Heroic." *Cultural Studies Review*, 25, 1, 135-53. [RIT]

RR2575.   Pramuk, Christopher: "A Task Worthy of God Remembering Jean Giono's 'The Man Who Planted Trees'." *America*, 12, 9, 24-29. [Naz]

GIRARD, René.
See also 526, 711, 2104, 2272, 3620, 4085.

RR2576.   ● Casini, Federica: *Un Senso Invincibile e Inespugnabile: René Girard Critico Letterario*. Firenze: Le Cáriti. 230p. [LoC]

RR2577.   ● Dubouchet, Paul: *Brève Philosophie de la Constitution: De Cicéron à René Girard: Analyse et Psychanalyse des Systèmes Constitutionnels*. Paris: L'Harmattan. 157p. [LoC]

RR2578.   Antonello, Pierpaolo: "Sacrificing 'Homo Sacer'." *Forum Philosophicum, 24,* 1, 145-182. [RIT]

RR2579.   Antonello, Pierpaolo, & Alessandra Diazzi: "Introduction: Intersubjectivity, Desire, and Mimetic Theory: René Girard and Psychoanalysis." *Contagion,* 26, 1-8. [Naz]

RR2580.   Bandera, Cesáreo, & Adam Ericksen: "René Girard, Friendship, and Battling to the End: A Conversation with Cesáreo Bandera." *Contagion,* 26, 195-208. [UaB]

RR2581.   Borenovic, M.: "René Girard's Scapegoating and Stereotypes of Persecution in the Divine Battle between Veles and Perun." *Bogoslovni Vestnik, 79,* 4, 1039-1052. [WC]

RR2582.   Brito, Ênio J. D. C.: "Da Violência ao Apocalipse na Obra de René Girard." *Rever, 19,* 1, 221-228. [Syr]

RR2583.   Checchi, Tania: "Myth and Il Y A: A Convergent Reading of René Girard and Emmanuel Levinas." *Forum Philosophicum, 24,* 1, 127-144. [UaB]

RR2584.   Dadosky, John D.: "Grant Kaplan's René Girard, Unlikely Apologist: Mimetic Theory and Fundamental Theology." *Pro Ecclesia, 28,* 4, 446-454. [Naz]

RR2585.   Darcy, Michael: "Personalism As Interpersonalism: John Paul II and René Girard." *Quaestiones Disputatae, 9,* 2, 126-148. [UaB]

RR2586.   Dickinson, Colby: "Polarized Readings of René Girard: Utilizing Girardian Thought to Break a Theological and Philosophical Impasse." *Forum Philosophicum, 24,* 1, 25-42. [RIT]

RR2587.   Duns, Ryan G.: "Cowdell, Scott: René Girard and the Nonviolent God." *Theological Studies, 80,* 4, 999. [UaB]

RR2588.   Duyndam, J.: "De Fenomenologie van René Girard." *Tijdschrift Voor Filosofie,* 81, 233-253. [Syr]

RR2589.   Gans, Eric: "René Girard and the Deferral of Violence." *Forum Philosophicum, 23,* 2, 155-170. [UaB]

RR2590.   Garcia-Duran, X.: "Hommage to René Girard." *Comprendre, 21,* 1, 91-104. [WC]

RR2591.   Gutierrez, Lozano C.: "Ángel Barahona. René Girard: De la Ciencia a la Fe." *Xiphias Gladius Revista Interdisciplinar de Teoría Mimética,* 2, 85-87. [WC]

RR2592.   Harding, Brian: "Sacred Violence in Mimetic Theory and Levinasian Ethics." *Journal for Cultural Research, 23,* 4, 396-410. [PrQ]

RR2593.   Hughes, Kevin L.: "The Providential Failure of Christianity: René Girard, Ivan Illich, and the Renewal of Apocalyptic Theology." *Pro Ecclesia, 28,* 4, 432-445. [Naz]

RR2594.   Kaplan, Grant: "Cynthia L. Haven, Evolution of Desire: A Life of René Girard." *Pro Ecclesia, 28,* 2, 214-217. [Naz]

RR2595.   Lebreton, Christian, Damien Richard, & Helene Cristini: "Mimetic Desire and Mirror Neurons: The Consciousness of Workplace Bullying." *Problems and Perspectives in Management, 17,* 1, 103-16. [PrQ]

RR2596.   Lee, Kang-Woo, & Je-Seung Lee: "Sports Violence and the Birth of Victory Desire: Focusing on Rene Girard's Desire Theory." *The Korean Journal of Physical Education, 58,* 5, 11-20. [WC]

RR2597.   Lefler, Nathan: "Two Kinds of Unanimity: St. Benedict, René Girard, and Modern Democratic Governance." *Contagion,* 26, 273-286. [UaB]

RR2598.   Miguel, Maiara R.: "A Vingança e o Sagrado no Filme 'Abril Despedaçado': Uma Análise Segundo o Teórico René Girard." *Numen*, *21*, 1. [Cor]

RR2599.   "Mimetic Wisdom: René Girard and the Task of Christian Philosophy." *Forum Philosophicum*, *23*, 2. [RIT]

RR2600.   Pieper, Frederico: "Crise Mimética e Vítima Sacrificial. Contribuição de René Girard para as Teorias da Religião." *Estudos Teológicos*, *59*, 1, 14. [Syr]

RR2601.   Quevedo, A.: "René Girard and the Oath of Herod." *Topicos (Mexico)*, 57, 149-175. [Syr]

RR2602.   "René Girard and the Epistemology of Revelation." *Forum Philosophicum*, *23*, 2, 189-200. [RIT]

RR2603.   Reveley, James, & John Singleton: "Mimesis, Scapegoating and Financial Crises: A Critical Evaluation of René Girard's Intellectual Legacy." *Science & Society*, *83*, 4, 469-494. [UofR]

RR2604.   Romejko, Adam: "Cynthia L. Haven, Evolution of Desire. A Life of René Girard, East Lansing 2018, pp. 317." *Historia I Polityka*, *28*, 35, 145. [Cor]

RR2605.   Sánchez, Villalón I.: "Etiología y Naturaleza de los Trastornos Alimentarios desde la Teoría Mimética de René Girard." *Xiphias Gladius Revista Interdisciplinar de Teoría Mimética*, 2, 65-81. [WC]

RR2606.   Sbardella, Ellton L., & Clélia Peretti: "Cristianismo e Violência. Contribuições Teológicas a Partir de René Girard." *Estudos Teológicos*, *59*, 1, 47. [Syr]

RR2607.   Sitch, B.: "Bog Bodies and Sacrificial Theory." *Journal of Wetland Archaeology*, 19, 154-171.

RR2608.   "Thinking with René Girard." *Forum Philosophicum*, *24*, 1. [RIT]

RR2609.   Wilmes, Andreas: "Demystifying the Negative René Girard's Critique of the 'Humanization of Nothingness'." *Forum Philosophicum*, *24*, 1, 91-126. [RIT]

RR2610.   Youngs, Samuel J.: "Mimesis and Atonement: René Girard and the Doctrine of Salvation, Michael Kirwan and Sheelah Treflé Hidden (eds), Bloomsbury, 2017 (ISBN 978-1-5013-2542-7), xvi + 186 pp., Hb £88." *Reviews in Religion & Theology*, *26*, 3, 448-452. [UofR]

RR2611.   Zhernokleyev, Denis: "Mimetic Desire in Dostoevsky's The Idiot with Continual Reference to René Girard." *The Dostoevsky Journal*, *20*, 1, 77-95. [Cor]

RR2612.   Zink, Michel: "Le Professeur Michel Zink A Été Élu le 14 Décembre 2017 à l'Académie Française au Fauteuil de René Girard: Il A Prononcé Son Discours de Réception le 18 Octobre 2018." *La Lettre du Collège de France*, 45, 58-59. [BnF]

GIRAUDOUX, Jean.
See also 463, 497, 791.

RR2613.   ● Brémond, Mireille: *Cahier Jean Giraudoux, Vol. 47: Giraudoux à la Scène Hier et Aujourd?hui*. Paris: Classiques Garnier. 296p. [WC]

RR2614.   ● Job, André: *Giraudoux: L'Humanisme Républicain à l'Épreuve*. Paris: Michalon. 122p. [UofR]

RR2615.   Brémond, Mireille: "Dictionnaire Jean Giraudoux. Publié sous la Direction d'André Job et Sylviane Coyault. Avec la Collaboration de Pierre d'Almeida." *French Studies*, *73*, 2, 308. [UaB]

RR2616.   Bridet, Guillaume: "Book Review: Dictionnaire Jean Giraudoux. 'Dictionnaires & Références'." *Revue d'Histoire Littéraire de la France*, *119*, 1, 234-236. [UofR]

RR2617.   Buyse, Kris: "Jean Giraudoux." *Documenta, 8,* 4, 196-203. [WC]
RR2618.   Guérin, Jeanyves: "Le Capitaliste sur la Scène des Spectacles du Groupe Octobre à la Folle de Chaillot de Giraudoux." *The Tocqueville Review, 40,* 2, 221-233. [UofR]

GLISSANT, Édouard.
See also 202, 207, 224, 225, 227, 251, 278, 496, 541, 549, 798, 810, 2011.
RR2619.   ● Drabinski, John E.: *Glissant and the Middle Passage: Philosophy, Beginning, Abyss.* Minneapolis: University of Minnesota Press. 243p. [Syr]
RR2620.   Alvarado-Borgoño, Miguel: "El Ansia por la Comunicación de Édouard Glissant y de la Literatura Antropológica Chilena." *Cinta de Moebio,* 64, 31-42. [Naz]
RR2621.   Britton, Celia: "Édouard Glissant: L' Identité Généreuse, by François Noudelmann." *New West Indian Guide,* 93, 152-153. [UaB]
RR2622.   Cailler, Bernadette: "Promenoir(s) de la Mort Seule: Quand Michaël Ferrier Revient vers Édouard Glissant Lecteur de Tristan L'Hermite." *Dalhousie French Studies,* 113, 123-132. [UofR]
RR2623.   Coombes, S.: "Glissant and Diaspora Studies." *Journal of Postcolonial Writing,* 55, 6, 769-781. [RIT]
RR2624.   Davis, Benjamin P.: "The Politics of Édouard Glissant's Right to Opacity." *The Clr James Journal,* 25, 1, 59-70. [Cor]
RR2625.   Kowalewski, Daniele, et al.: "Mobilidades Contemporâneas no Contexto Pós-Colonial: Mbembe, Glissant e Mattelart." *Lua Nova,* 108, 137. [PrQ]
RR2626.   März, Moses: "Imagining a Politics of Relation: Glissant's Border Thought and the German Border." *Tydskrif Vir Letterkunde,* 56, 1, 49-61. [Naz]
RR2627.   Pessini, Elena: "Édouard Glissant Lecteur de Claudel." *Il Tolomeo,* 1. [WC]
RR2628.   Philippe, Maxime: "La Littérature-Monde: La Leçon d'Édouard Glissant." *Synergies Chine,* 14, 159, 166, 251. [PrQ]
RR2629.   Pinto, Simone R., & Aristinete Bernardes: "Caribbean Identities: Creolization in Édouard Glissant." *Sociedade e Estado,* 34, 3, 637-660. [UaB]
RR2630.   Ramirez, M. G.: "Transversality as Disruption and Connection: on the Possibilities and Limits of Using the Framework of Trauma in Glissant's Philosophy of Caribbean History." *Philosophical Readings,* 11, 3, 152-162. [WC]
RR2631.   Reeck, Matt: "Édouard Glissant: L'Identité Généreuse by François Noudelmann (Review)." *The French Review,* 92, 4, 207-208. [UofR]
RR2632.   Robillard, Guillaume: "Strategies of Resistance in 'French Caribbean Cinema'." *Contemporary French and Francophone Studies,* 23, 5, 636-643. [Naz]
RR2633.   Rocha, Vanessa M.: "Paroles d'Antan et Devoir de Mémoire dans le Quatrième Siècle, d'Édouard Glissant." *Matraga,* 26, 48. [WC]
RR2634.   Sago, Kylie: "Beyond the Headless Empress: Gabriel Vital Dubray's Statues of Josephine, Edouard Glissant's Tout-Monde, and Contested Monuments of French Empire." *Nineteenth-century Contexts,* 41, 5, 501-519. [Syr]

GODBOUT, Jacques.
See also 236.
RR2635.   ● Emiroglou, Patrick: *Salut l'Écrivain!* [Montréal]: Del Busso. 167p. [BAnQ]

RR2636.   Diercie, Dwyarie R., & Joesana Tjahjani: "Intercultural Concepts in Place Cliché by Jacques Godbout." *The Southeast Asian Journal of English Language Studies*, *25*, 3, 137-149. [Syr]

GOFFETTE, Guy.
See 31, 805.

GOLDSCHMIDT, Georges-Arthur.
See also 602.

RR2637.   • Asholt, Wolfgang, Catherine Coquio, & Jürgen Ritte: *Traverser les Limites: Georges-Arthur Goldschmidt: Le Corps, l'Histoire, la Langue*. [Paris]: Hermann. 226p. [LoC]

RR2638.   • Goldschmidt, Georges-Arthur: *Une Langue Pour Abri*. Chambéry: Fondation Facim. 138p. [BnF]

RR2639.   • Handke, Peter, & Georges-Arthur Goldschmidt: *Kali: Une Histoire d'Avant-Hier*. Paris: Gallimard. 117p. [WC]

RR2640.   Brown, Heidi: "Trauma, Language, and Literature: Psycholinguistic Dynamics in Georges-Arthur Goldschmidt's Autobiographical Writing in Response to World War II." *French Forum*, *44*, 3, 389-404. [UofR]

RR2641.   Woywode, Felix: "Andreas B. Kilcher: Poetik und Politik des Witzes bei Heinrich Heine (Franz Hessel Lecture), Èditions de l'Éclat, Paris 2014, 108 S.: Daniel Weidner: Übersetzen und Überleben. Walter Benjamin Liest Marcel Proust, 2015, 119 S. Andrea Schatz: Die Damaskus-Affäre (1840). Französisch-Deutsche Perspektiven, 2017, 105 S. Anne-Kathrin Reulecke: Poetik der Zweisprachigkeit. Autobiographie und Übersetzung bei Georges-Arthur Goldschmidt, 2018, 107 S." *Zeitschrift für Germanistik*, *29*, 3, 682-683. [UaB]

GONCOURT, Edmond de.
See also 436, 465, 525.

RR2642.   • Goncourt, Edmond, Jules Goncourt, & Jean-Louis Cabanès: *Journal des Goncourt, Vol. 4: 1865-1868*. Paris: Honoré Champion. 774p. [WC]

RR2643.   • Goncourt, Edmond, Jules Goncourt, Catherine Thomas, & Pierre-Jean Dufief: *Portraits Intimes du XVIIIe Siècle*. Paris: Honoré Champion. 592p. [WC] (Goncourt)

RR2644.   Phenix, S.: "Suture Self: Constructing Femininity in Edmond de Goncourt's Chérie." *Romance Notes*, *59*, 1, 185-195. [Naz]

RR2645.   Raffi, Maria Emanuela: "Michael Tilby, Flaubert, Edmond de Goncourt, and Gavarni's ' 'Immoral' Débardeurs." *Studi Francesi*, *63*, 3, 598. [UaB]

GOSCINNY, René.
See also 58.

RR2646.   • Bernière, Vincent: *Astérix le Gaulois: La Naissance d'un Mythe*. Paris: Vagator. 144p. [BnF]

RR2647.   • Catel: *Le Roman des Goscinny: Naissance d'un Gaulois*. Paris: Bernard Grasset. 340p. [BAnQ]

RR2648.   • Crespo, Tomás: *El Diccionario de Astérix: (De Abraracourcix a Zurix)*. Pineda de Mar (Barcelona): Editorial California. 221p. [WC]

RR2649. ● Goscinny: *Les Trésors Retrouvés de René Goscinny: Et Ses Inédits*. Grenoble: Glénat. 97p. [WC]

RR2650. ● Kastelnik, Christian: *René Goscinny et la Brasserie des Copains*. Caudebec-en-Caux: La Déviation. 99p. [BnF]

RR2651. ● Molin, Bernard-Pierre: *Astérix: Le Coffret Veni Vedi Vici*. Vanves: EPA. 2 vols. 159p., 159p. [BnF]

RR2652. Rahmayanti, Mela: "L'Acte de Parole Directif dans la Bande-Dessinee (bd) Asterix Chez Les Helvètes par Rene Goscinny et Albert Uderzo. Mémoire." *Lingua Litteratia Journal*, *6*, 1, 76-83. [WC]

GOURMONT, Rémy de.

RR2653. ● Gourmont, Remy, & Christian Buat: *Dialogues des Amateurs sur les Choses du Temps: Suivi de Nouveaux Dialogues des Amateurs*. Paris: Classiques Garnier. 632p. [LoC]

GRACQ, Julien.
See also 460, 469, 480, 689.

RR2654. Boislève, Jacques: "Julien Gracq Joueur d'Échecs du Petit Théâtre au Grand Jeu." *Ligeia*, *169-172*, 1, 208. [UofR]

RR2655. Daunais, Isabelle: "Les Carnets de Julien Gracq: 'La Promenade entre Toutes Préférée'." *Études Littéraires*, *48*, 1-2, 75-85. [UaB]

RR2656. Masseron, Caroline, Jean-Marie Privat, & Émile Bordeleau-Pitre: "Perdre Ses Lettres en République Décadente: D'une Poétique de l'Internat dans le Rivage des Syrtes de Julien Gracq." *Pratiques*, December, 183-184. [Cor]

RR2657. Modiano, Patrick: "Zu Julien Gracq." *Sinn und Form*, *71*, 1, 125. [Syr]

GRANDBOIS, Alain.

RR2658. ● Moreau, Patrick: *La Prose d'Alain Grandbois ou Lire et Relire les Voyages de Marco Polo*. Montréal: Nota Bene. 206p. [BAnQ]

GREEN, Julien.
See also 713.

RR2659. ● Auroy, Carole: *Le Journal Vespéral de Julien Green*. Clamart: Calliopées. 117p. [WC]

RR2660. ● Green, Julien, Guillaume Fau, & Alexandre Vitry: *Journal Intégral: 1*. Paris: Robert Laffont. 1330p. [BAnQ]

RR2661. ● Kostis, Nicholas: *The Exorcism of Sex and Death in Julien Green's Novels*. Berlin: De Gruyter Mouton. 1 vol. [WC]

RR2662. Waite, Genevieve: "Julien Green: 'L'Écrivain Double' in Self-Translation." *French Forum*, *44*, 3, 361-376. [Naz]

GREIMAS, Algirdas Julien.
See also 574, 701.

RR2663. ● Ben, Msila A.: *Greimas Aujourd'hui: Du Sens et des Langages: Actes du Colloque International 22 et 23 Novembre 2016*. Meknès: Faculté des Lettres et des Sciences Humaines de Meknès. 254p. [WC]

RR2664. ● Greimas, Algirdas J., Stefano Bartezzaghi, & Giuditta Bassano: *La Semiotica del Testo in Esercizio*. Milano: Bompiani. 448p. [WC]

RR2665. • Hermans, Paul: *A. J. Greimas, Maître de la Fiducie: Accommoder Sens et (Con)science*. Delft: Semiosis. 134p. [BnF]

RR2666. Demuru, Paolo: "De Greimas a Eric Landowski. A Experiência do Sentido, o Sentido da Experiência: Semiótica, Interação e Processos Sócio-Comunicacionais." *Galáxia (São Paulo)*, 2, 85-113. [Cor]

RR2667. Imbert, P.: "Concepts of Narrative, Founding Violence, and Multiculturalism in the Americas: Greimas, Girard, and Kymlicka." *Semiotica*, 227, 245-259. [UofR]

RR2668. Jeong, Youyeon, & Taegu Lee: "Narrative Analysis Using Greimas Semiotics - Focusing on 'The Suicide Shop'." *The Journal of Image and Cultural Contents*, 16, 309-323. [WC]

RR2669. Jo, Eunjin, & Hyeong-Yeon Jeon: "A Suggestion of Narrative Generation Basic Model for Scenario Creation: Focused on the Function Theory of Propp and Narrative Theory of Greimas." *Humanities Contents*, 52, 191-222. [WC]

RR2670. Jonkus, D.: "Greimas's Semiotics: Between Structuralism and Phenomenology." *Problemos*, 96, 83-95. [Naz]

RR2671. Han, Ji-Young: "A Study on the Medium-Replacement of Dance and Cinema Through the Dance Film 'Black Swan' (2010) - Focused on Greimas Semiotics." *Dance Research Journal of Dance*, 77, 1, 269-293. [WC]

RR2672. Kim, Eun H.: "Semiotic Analysis of Outdoor Brand Tv Commercials: Focusing on Actant Model of Greimas." *Studies in Linguistics*, 50, 289-306. [WC]

RR2673. Levina, J.: "Greimas's Three Aesthetics." *Colloquia*, 42, 113-134. [LoC]

RR2674. Marillaud, Pierre: "Greimas' Semiotic Thinking and Its Evolution between 'Structural Semantics' (1970) and 'Semiotics of Passions' (1991)." *Tyumen State University Herald. Humanities Research. Humanitates*, 5, 4, 6-37. [LoC]

RR2675. Marsciani, Francesco: "Greimas e o Desenvolvimento Gerativo da Imanência Semiótica." *Galáxia (São Paulo)*, 2, 163-173. [Cor]

RR2676. Migliore, Tiziana, & Ramunė Brundzaitė: "The Mixed Category of Human/ Animal in Greimas' Mythologies. Transl. by Ramunė Brundzaitė." *Semiotika*, 14, 11-23. [UaB]

RR2677. Moraes, Lima L., & Ivã C. Lopes: "Texto e Corpus em Semântica Estrutural, de Greimas." *Acta Semiótica et Lingvistica*, 24, 2, 2-12. [UaB]

RR2678. Petitot, Jean: "Memórias e Percursos Semióticos do Lado de Greimas." *Galáxia (São Paulo)*, 2, 114-136. [Cor]

RR2679. Rodríguez, Blanca A., & Ramírez V. A. Ruiz.: "Noticias del Fondo Greimas de Semiótica." *Tópicos del Seminario*, 42, 235-246. [WC]

RR2680. Schulz, Michael: "De Greimas a Jacques Geninasca. Por uma Semiótica da Fala." *Galáxia (São Paulo)*, 2, 64-84. [Cor]

RR2681. So, Pil-gyun: "A Cognitive Study on the Aphoristic Statement Shown at 'Only with One Leaf' by Hyun Chong Jeong - Focusing on Application of Greimas' Semiotic Square Model." *Korean Language and Literature*, 109, 121-147. [LoC]

GRENIER, Jean.
RR2682. Machielsen, Jan: "The Making of a Teen Wolf: Pierre de Lancre's Confrontation with Jean Grenier (1603–10)." *Folklore*, *130*, 3, 237-257. [UofR]

GROSJEAN, Jean.
See 1527.

GROULX, Lionel.
RR2683.   Dorais, Francois-Olivier: "'Lionel Groulx: Le Penseur le Plus Influent de l'Histoire du Québec' by Charles-Philippe Courtois (Review)." *The Canadian Historical Review*, *100*, 2, 288-290. [Naz]
RR2684.   Laberge, Yves: "Lionel Groulx: Le Penseur le Plus Influent de l'Histoire du Québec by Charles-Philippe Courtois (Review)." *British Journal of Canadian Studies*, *32*, 12, 139-140. [UaB]

GUATTARI, Félix.
See 753, 1991, 1993, 2012, 2013, 2021, 2025, 2028, 2032, 2046, 2054, 2057, 2058, 4735.
RR2685.   ● Berressem, Hanjo: *Felix Guattari's Schizoanalytic Ecology*. Edinburgh: Edinburgh UP. 272p. [WC]
RR2686.   ● Jellis, Thomas: *Why Guattari? A Liberation of Cartographies, Ecologies and Politics*. London: Routledge. 251p. [Syr]
RR2687.   ● Olkowski, Dorothea E., Eftichis Pirovolakis, Constantin V. Boundas, & Andrew Goffey: *Deleuze and Guattari's Philosophy of Freedom: Freedom's Refrains*. London: Routledge. 232p. [Syr]
RR2688.   Brown, Grant C.: "Schizoanalytical Theology: Deleuze and Guattari's Ecological Spirituality and Glissant's Postcolonial Critique." *Alternative Francophone*, *2*, 4, 6-24. [Syr]
RR2689.   Joff, P. N. Bradley: "From the Exterminating Angel to Guattari's Scarecrow." *The Journal of English Language and Literature*, *65*, 3, 409-424. [UaB]
RR2690.   Park, Mincheol, & Jin A. Choi: "Felix Guattari's Ecophilosophy: Chaosmose, the Production of Ecological Subjectivity and Eco-Democracy." *Journal of the Society of Philosophical Studies*, 127, 233-258. [WC]
RR2691.   Parry, Jason: "Philosophy as Terraforming: Deleuze and Guattari on Designing a New Earth." *Diacritics*, *47*, 3, 108-38. [PrQ]
RR2692.   Ribeiro, Vladimir M. L.: "O Paradigma Estético de Félix Guattari." *Griot*, *19*, 1, 1-24. [Syr]
RR2693.   Simonini, E., & R. C. Romagnoli: "Machine and Reality: Cybernetics, Autopoiesis and Production of Subjectivity in Félix Guattari." *Psicologia em Estudo*, 24. [RIT]
RR2694.   Varas, Paulina E.: "Transversal Polyphonies: A Reflection with Miguel D. Norambuena on Félix Guattari's Trip to Chile." *Deleuze and Guattari Studies*, *13*, 3, 377-394. [Naz]

GUÉHENNO, Jean.
RR2695.   ● Guéhenno, Jean, & Jean-Marie Guéhenno: *Je Vous Écris d'Europe: Chroniques du "Figaro", 1946-1977*. Paris: L'Ours. 92p. [BnF]

GUENTCHEV, Lubomir.
See 17.

GUÉRIN, Raymond.
See 648.

GUÈVREMONT, Germaine.
See also 231.
RR2696. Lord, Michel: "Le Cycle du Survenant I. Édition Critique. En Pleine Terre et Autres Textes par Germaine Guèvremont." *University of Toronto Quarterly*, *88*, 3, 396-398. [Naz]
RR2697. Lord, Michel: "Œuvres de Fiction I. Édition Critique. Tu Seras Journaliste et Autres Œuvres sur le Journalisme par Germaine Guèvremont." *University of Toronto Quarterly*, *88*, 3, 393-396. [Naz]

GUIBERT, Hervé.
See also 316.
RR2698. ● Berger, Hans G., Hervé Guibert, & Boris Brauchitsch: *Hans Georg Berger, Hervé Guibert: Un Amour Photographique*. Paris: Michel de Maule. 207p. [WC]
RR2699. ● Cavallo, Christopher: *Les Voix d'Accès d'Hervé Guibert: Étude du Dialogisme dans le Mausolée des Amants*. Paris: L'Harmattan. 276p. [UofR]
RR2700. ● Guibert, Hervé, & María Millán: *Hervé Guibert: [Exposición]*. Madrid: Fundación Loewe. 24p. [WC]
RR2701. Porumb, Anca: "La Mise à Nu du Moi Malade chez Hervé Guibert." *Anales de Filología Francesa*, *27*, 1, 277-289. [Naz]
RR2702. Sábado, Novau M.: "Representation of the Self and Disease: Writing, Photography and Video in Hervé Guibert." *Humanities*, *8*, 4, 181. [Naz]

GUILLAUMIN, Émile.
See 85.

GUILLEVIC, Eugène.
See also 57, 513.
RR2703. ● Guillevic, Eugène, & Michael Brophy: *Écrits Intimes: Carnet, Cahier, Feuillets, 1929-1938*. Strasbourg: L'Atelier Contemporain-François-Marie Deyrolle. 139p. [LoC]

GUILLOUX, Louis.
See also 361, 492.
RR2704. ● Legavre, Jean-Baptiste: *Louis Guilloux dans les Médias: Les Réceptions de l'Œuvre*. Rennes: Presses Universitaires de Rennes. 272p. [UofR]

GUITRY, Sacha.
See also 320, 492, 526.
RR2705. ● Gavory, Antoine: *Rendez-Nous Sacha Guitry!* Nice: Ovadia. 341p. [Cor]

GUITTON, Jean.
RR2706. ● Guitton, Jean, & Albero J. L. Calvo: *Pensamiento y Guerra*. Madrid: Encuentro S. A. 251p. [WC]
RR2707. ● Poli, Paolo: *Il Pensiero di Jean Guitton: L'Uomo, il Tempo, Dio*. Lecce: Youcanprint 'Self-Publishing.' 329p. [LoC]

GUYOTAT, Pierre.

See also 70.

RR2708. ● Fédida, Pierre, & Jean Guyotat: *Œuvres Complètes: Tome 2.* Paris: MJW. 224p. [BnF]

RR2709. ● Guyotat, Pierre: *Divers: Textes, Interventions, Entretiens: 1984-2019.* Paris: Les Belles Lettres. 495p. [LoC]

RR2710. Levesque, Simon, et al.: "Idiotie de Pierre Guyotat." *Spirale,* 270, 75-77. [WC]

RR2711. Levesque, Simon, Sébastien Dulude, & Eftihia Mihelakis: "Pierre Guyotat Politique: Mesurer la Vie à l'Aune de l'Histoire de Julien Lefort-Favreau." *Spirale,* 268, 73-75. [WC]

HADDAD, Malek.

See also 252.

RR2712. ● Haddad, Safia: *Malek Haddad, Le Poète Blessé.* Alger: Sedia. 147p. [WC]

HALÉVY, Daniel.

See also 426, 429.

RR2713. ● Halévy, Daniel, & Valentina d'Anna: *Nietzsche.* Milano: Oaks. 562p. [WC]

HAMELIN, Louis.

See also 738.

RR2714. Hubner, Patrick, José García-Romeu, & David Laporte: "'Thar She Blows!': Imaginaire de la Fin et Quête de la Nouvelle Jérusalem dans Le Soleil des Gouffres de Louis Hamelin." *Babel,* 39, 171-188. [Syr]

HAMPÂTÉ BÂ, Amadou.

See also 190, 208, 216, 277, 591, 690.

RR2715. Camara, Mohamed: "Syntagme Nominal Expansif ou l'Expression de l'Hétérogénéité et/ou de l'Homogénéité dans Petit Bodiel de Hampaté Bâ." *Multilinguales,* 11. [WC]

HARPMAN, Jacqueline.

RR2716. Pagacz, Laurence: "Chute et Éveil du Corps dans les Dystopies: Moi Qui N'ai Pas Connu Les Hommes de Jacqueline Harpman et Choir d'Éric Chevillard." *Études Littéraires,* 48, 3, 37. [UaB]

RR2717. Resende, Marcelo B.: "Espectros da Alteridade na Obra de Jacqueline Harpman." *Fronteiraz. Revista do Programa de Estudos Pós-Graduados em Literatura e Crítica Literária,* 22, 151-166. [WC]

HÉBERT, Anne.

See also 196.

RR2718. ● Lamontagne, Marie-Andrée: *Anne Hébert, Vivre Pour Écrire: Biographie.* Montréal: Boréal. 558p. [BAnQ]

RR2719. Carrier-Lafleur, Thomas: "Le Temps d'Anne Hébert au Cinéma: Mémoire et Altérité dans Kamouraska et Le Torrent." *Nouvelles Vues,* 20, 1. [WC]

RR2720. Gendron, Karine: "La Fenêtre dans Les Fous de Bassan d'Anne Hébert: Ambiguïté de l'Événement aux Récits." *Annales Littéraires de l'Université de Besançon*, 999, 87-102. [WC]

RR2721. Lord, Michel: "Œuvres Complètes. V. Théâtre, Nouvelles et Proses Diverses: Le Temps Sauvage, La Mercière Assassinée, Les Invités au Procès by Anne Hébert et Annie Tanguay, And: La Cage, Suivi de l'Île de la Demoiselle by Patricia Godbout, And: Textes Dramatiques Parus dans des Périodiques ou Inédits by Annie Tanguay, And: Le Torrent by Annie Tanguay, And: Contes et Nouvelles Parus dans des Périodiques ou Inédits by Nathalie Watteyne, And: Proses Diverses Parues dans des Périodiques, des Ouvrages ou Inédites by Annie Tanguay et Nathalie Watteyne (Review)." *University of Toronto Quarterly*, 88, 3, 399-403. [Naz]

HELLENS, Franz.
See also 698.

RR2722. ● Hellens, Franz, & Michel Gilles: *Le Double: Et Autres Contes Fantastiques: Fantastique*. Bruxelles: Espace Nord. 317p. [WC]

RR2723. Brogniez, Laurence, David Martens, & Marcela Scibiorska: "Regards Croisés sur 'La Plaque Tournante de l'Europe': Belgique, Pays de Plusieurs Mondes (La Guilde du Livre) de Franz Hellens et Maurice Blanc." *Textyles*, 59-76. [Cor]

HELLO, Ernest.
RR2724. ● Hello, Ernest: *Contes Extraordinaires: 1879*. S.l.: ThéoText. 281p. [BnF]

HÉMON, Louis.
RR2725. ● Bélanger, David, & Thomas Carrier-Lafleur: *Il S'est Écarté: Enquête sur La Mort de François Paradis*. Montréal: Nota Bene. 223p. [BAnQ]

RR2726. Lapointe, Gilles: "Post-colonialisme et Modernité chez Louis Hémon: Nicole Deschamps et le Mythe de Maria Chapdelaine." *Études Françaises*, 55, 2, 159. [UofR]

RR2727. Sostaric, S.: "Maria Chapdelaine: On the Reception of Hemon's Tale of French Canada." *Knjizevna Smotra*, 51, 192, 29-39. [LoC]

HENEIN, Georges.
See 274.

HENRY, Michel.
See also 721, 724, 767, 4715.

RR2728. ● Henry, Michel, Scott Davidson, & Frédéric Seyler: *The Michel Henry Reader*. Evanston, IL: Northwestern UP. 266p. [Syr]

RR2729. ● Henry, Michel, Stephan Grätzel, & André Hansen: *Das Wesen des In-Erscheinung-Tretens*. München: Karl Alber. 884p. [WC]

RR2730. ● Palma, Ramírez M.: *Michel Henry: Ser-hijo: La Incesante Experiencia de la Vida*. Madrid: Ciudad Nueva. 214p. [WC]

RR2731. Al-Charif, Mangala: "De la 'Dératisation' Comme Phénoménologie à Propos du 'Jeune Officier' de Michel Henry." *Hawliyat*, 8, 185-208. [LoC]

RR2732. Bowen, Amber: "How to Cross the Rubicon Without Falling In: Michel Henry, Søren Kierkegaard, and New Phenomenology." *International Journal of Philosophy and Theology*, 80, 465-481. [UaB]

RR2733.   Canullo, Carla: "Michel Henry as a Philosopher of Religion." *Contributions to Phenomenology*, 103, 257-270. [UaB]

RR2734.   Ferrer, Urbano: "La Donación del Cuerpo en la Cuarta Dimensión del Abandono del Límite. En Diálogo con Michel Henry." *Studia Poliana*, 21, 55-71. [Naz]

RR2735.   Grzibowski, Silvestre D.: "Fenomenologia do Corpo em Michel Henry: Uma Leitura a Partir da Imanência Subjetiva." *Voluntas*, *10*, 1, 53. [WC]

RR2736.   Inverso, H.: "Los Principios de la Fenomenología y la Fenomenología de lo Inaparente. Aspectos del Método en las Filosofías de Michel Henry y Jean-Luc Marion." *Arete*, *31*, 2, 349-376. [Naz]

RR2737.   Joe, Tegu: "Descartes, Husserl and Henry - Michel Henry's Interpretation of the Cartesian Cogito and Material Phenomenology -." *Phenomenology and Contemporary Philosoph*, 80, 1-32. [WC]

RR2738.   Llorente, Cardo J.: "Spinoza Como Ontoteólogo: Un Paso Más Allá de la Interpretación de Michel Henry." *Praxis Filosófica*, 48, 97-118. [Naz]

RR2739.   Maciel, Diego.: "O Papel da Afetividade No Ensino de Filosofia: Um Estudo a Partir de Martin Heidegger a Michel Henry." *Revista Digital de Ensino de Filosofia – Refilo*, *5*, 2. [WC]

RR2740.   Ramella, L.: "The Philosophical Matrices of New Barbarism. The Parallel Perspectives of Michel Henry and Jean-François Mattéi." *Rivista di Filosofia Neo-Scolastica*, 3, 539-554. [UaB]

RR2741.   Sackin-Poll, A.: "Michel Henry and Metaphysics: An Expressive Ontology." *Open Theology*, *5*, 1, 405-419. [Cor]

RR2742.   Sales Souto, S.: "Vida Enquanto Absoluto Incondicionado: Sobre a Materialidade da Essência da Manifestação Na Fenomenologia de Michel Henry." *Griot*, *19*, 3, 105-114. [Syr]

RR2743.   Schaefer, Max: "Bonds of Trust: Thinking the Limits of Reciprocity with Heidegger and Michel Henry." *Studia Phaenomenologica*, 19, 289-309. [Syr]

RR2744.   Vlieghe, Joris: "'Éducation Sentimentale'? Rethinking Emotional Intelligence with Michel Henry: From Incarnation to Education." *Ethics and Education*, *14*, 3, 367-382. [Naz]

HERGÉ.

See also 117.

RR2745.   ● Garcia, Bob: *Tintin: Du Cinéma à la Bd*. Paris: Desclée de Brouwer. 273p. [WC]

RR2746.   ● Mérand, Patrick: *La Faune et la Flore dans l'Œuvre d'Hergé*. Paris: Sépia. 102p. [WC]

RR2747.   ● Roberge, Jean-Michel: *Milou, Une Vie de Chien: La Condition Animale dans Les Aventures de Tintin et Milou: Hergé et les Animaux de 1942 à 1976*. Mont-Saint-Aignan: Jean-Michel Roberge. 105p. [BnF]

RR2748.   Bidaud, Samuel: "Proust et Hergé: De Quelques Points Communs entre À la Recherche du Temps Perdu et Les Aventures de Tintin." *Interlitteraria*, *23*, 2, 414-426. [Cor]

RR2749.   Marchand, A. B.: "Hergé et le Papier Troué." *Europe*, 97, 1085-1086, 60-65. [Syr]

RR2750.   Rime, Jean: "Tintin Face à l'Actualité: La Transposition de l'Affaire Lindbergh dans Tintin en Amérique." *Contextes*, 24. [PrQ]

RR2751. Robert, Pascal: "Incommunication et Ironie de l'Objet chez Hergé." *Hermès*, *84*, 2, 194. [UofR]

RR2752. Vohlidka, John M.: "The Comics of Hergé: When the Lines Are Not So Clear." *Journal of Graphic Novels & Comics*, *10*, 1, 184-185. [Cor]

HOCQUARD, Emmanuel.
See also 37, 409, 781.

RR2753. Magno, Luigi: "Emmanuel Hocquard, Le Cours de Pise." *Studi Francesi*, *63*, 2, 395-396. [UaB]

HOCQUENGHEM, Guy.
See also 342.

RR2754. ● Hocquenghem, Guy, Hauke Betzler, Lukas Betzler, & Hauke Branding: *Das Homosexuelle Begehren: Nautilus Flugschrift*. Hamburg: Nautilus. 200p. [WC]

RR2755. Gérard, Brieuc: "Sous les Pavés, l'Hiver: Hocquenghem, Transparence, et Politiques Queers Radicales dans le Sillage de Mai 68." *Contemporary French and Francophone Studies*, *23*, 2, 208-215. [Naz]

HOUELLEBECQ, Michel.
See 22, 358, 611, 667, 684, 1189, 1544, 1914, 3937.

RR2756. ● Cucchi, Silvia, & Valentina Sturli: *Estremi Occidenti: Soggetto, Conflitto e Mutazione in Walter Siti e Michel Houellebecq*. Pisa: Fabrizio Serra. 118p. [WC]

RR2757. ● Dissaux, Nicolas: *Houellebecq, Un Monde de Solitudes: L'Individu et le Droit*. Paris: L'Herne. 81p. [Cor]

RR2758. ● Godo, Emmanuel: *Conversation Avenue de France, Paris 13e, Entre Michel Houellebecq, Écrivain et Évagre le Pontique, Moine du Désert*. Paris: Les Éditions du Cerf. 140p. [Cor]

RR2759. ● Houellebecq, Michel: *Michel Houellebecq, Oswald Spengler und der 'Untergang des Abendlandes': Reden Anlässlich der Verleihung des Oswald-Spengler-Preises an Michel Houellebecq, Brüssel, 19. Oktober 2018*. Berlin: Manuscriptum Verlagsbuchhandlung. 149p. [WC]

RR2760. ● Houellebecq, Michel, Agathe Novak-Lechevalier, & Fabrizio Ascari: *Michel Houellebecq: Cahier*. Milano: La Nave di Teseo. 390p. [WC]

RR2761. ● Jurga, Antoine, & Sabine Wesemael: *La Carte et le Territoire et Soumission de Michel Houellebecq: Dossier Critique*. Vimy: Société Roman 20-50. *Roman 20-50*, 66. 185p. [WC]

RR2762. ● Novak-Lechevalier, Agathe: *Houellebecq, l'Art de la Consolation*. [Paris]: Stock. 304p. [Cor]

RR2763. ● Novak-Lechevalier, Agathe, & Stephan Kleiner: *Michel Houellebecq*. Köln: DuMont Buchverlag. 432p. [WC]

RR2764. ● Vacca, Paul: *Michel Houellebecq, Phénomène Littéraire: Essai*. Paris: Robert Laffont. 157p. [UofR]

RR2765. ● Williams, Russell: *Pathos, Poetry and Politics in Michel Houellebecq's Fiction*. Leiden: Brill Rodopi. 299p. [Syr]

RR2766. Agerup, Karl: "The Political Reception of Michel Houellebecq's Submission." *European Review*, *27*, 4, 615-635. [Naz]

RR2767. Amores Füster, Miguel: "Le Paradoxe du Reality: Une Réflexion sur la Posture Littéraire de Michel Houellebecq: Revista de Estudios Franceses." *Çédille*, 16, 153-71. [PrQ]

RR2768. Azeez, Govand K.: "Decoding Islamophobia in Contemporary Society: The Case of Houellebecq." *Continuum*, 33, 6, 717-728. [Syr]

RR2769. Baggesgard, M. A., & J. L. Stephensen: "Making Off with Michel Houellebecq - Adaptational Strategies and La Carte et le Territoire." *Australian Journal of French Studies*, 56, 1, 91-113. [UaB]

RR2770. Baranlloni, Lagos M. C.: "Fotografía y Representación en la Novela el Mapa y el Territorio de Michel Houellebecq." *Letrônica*, 12, 3, 34991. [RIT]

RR2771. Betty, Louis: "Who's Afraid of Michel Houellebecq? The Answer: Almost Everyone." *Australian Journal of French Studies*, 56, 1, 37-52. [UaB]

RR2772. Bousquet, Louis: "L'Islam dans les Romans de Michel Houellebecq." *Romanica Wratislaviensia*, 66, 93-108. [WC]

RR2773. Bowd, Gavin: "The Anti-Sartre? Michel Houellebecq and Politics." *Australian Journal of French Studies*, 56, 1, 8-23. [Naz]

RR2774. Buzay, Emmanuel: "Le Monde selon Google dans le Roman d'Aurélien Bellanger *La Théorie de l'Information*." *Contemporary French and Francophone Studies*, 23, 4, 480-9. [PrQ]

RR2775. Carrara, G.: "Il Gioco e l'Érotismo: David Foster Wallace, Michel Houellebecq e Walter Siti." *Enthymema*, 496-508. [Syr]

RR2776. Cerniuvienė, Liucija, & Rūta Jakutytė: "Michel Houellebecq in Lithuanian: The Paradoxes of Translation." *Literatūra*, 61, 4, 122-137. [UaB]

RR2777. Crowley, Martin: "Houellebecq's France." *Australian Journal of French Studies*, 56, 1, 24-36. [RIT] (Angot)

RR2778. De Jonghe, M.: "'Jouer Son Propre Rôle': Michel Houellebecq dans l'Enlèvement de Michel Houellebecq." *Captures*, 2, 1. [WC]

RR2779. Faria, Dominique, & Ferdinand Laignier: "Les Possibilités d'une Île: Escale chez Marcu Biancarelli, Michel Houellebecq et Angelo Rinaldi." *Carnets*, deuxième série, 17. [Cor]

RR2780. Fassin, Eric: "Houellebecq Antilibéral, du Sexe à l'Islam." *Modern & Contemporary France*, 27, 1, 11-26. [Naz]

RR2781. Godefroy, Cyrille: "Michel Houellebecq Sérotonine." *Quinzaines*, 1207, 10. [UaB]

RR2782. Godo, Emmanuel: "Michel Houellebecq and Us: 'Hitting Where It Hurts'." *Études*. 11, 93. [Syr]

RR2783. Hawley, John: "Jean Raspail, Michel Houellebecq, & Jenny Erpenbeck: Acknowledging the Barbarian Within." *Litera*, 29, 1, 1-18. [WC]

RR2784. Laignier, Ferdinand: "What Irony and Humour Reveal About Our Thoughts: The Example of Marcu Biancarelli, Michel Houellebecq, and Angelo Rinaldi." *Romanica Olomucensia*, 30, 2, 299-314. [WC]

RR2785. Lemaitre, Clément: "Les Mécanismes de l'Humour dans Plateforme de Michel Houellebecq." 169. In 1829.

RR2786. Loussier, Hemlata Giri: "Une Rupture Post-Sentimentale: La Crise de la Modernité. Étude sur les Œuvres de Michel Houellebecq." *Synergies Inde*, 8, 119, 128, 155. [PrQ]

RR2787. Malinovska, Z., & J. Zivcak: "A Bitter Diagnostic of the Ultra-Liberal

Human: Michel Houellebecq on Some Ethical Issues." *Ethics and Bioethics (in Central Europe)*, 9, 3-4, 190-196. [WC]

RR2788.   Malvestio, M.: "Trading Butterflies: The Representation of Asian Sex Workers in Vollmann and Houellebecq." *Enthymema*, 23, 57-72. [WC]

RR2789.   Mcglynn, Sean: "Marine Le Pen—Somewhere between George Orwell and Michel Houellebecq." *Political Quarterly*, 90, 2, 319-321. [Naz]

RR2790.   Nilsson, Per-Erik: "Fuck Autonomy: Neo-Orientalism and Abjection in Michel Houellebecq's Soumission." *European Review*, 27, 4, 600-614. [Naz]

RR2791.   Novak-Lechevalier, Agathe: "Comment Habiter le Monde? Michel Houellebecq Architecte." *Modern & Contemporary France*, 27, 1, 111-128. [Naz]

RR2792.   Petcu, Carmen: "Democratic Metaphysics and Political Anxieties in Houellebecq's Novels." *Review of Contemporary Philosophy*, 18, 140-6. [RIT]

RR2793.   Qadiri, S.: "Notions of a Postsecular Nation Michel Houellbecq's Soumission and Sabri Loutah's Les Sauvages I-IV." *Journal of Romance Studies*, 19, 1, 115-133. [Naz]

RR2794.   Roux, Alwyn: "'Tussen die Abjekte en die Eteriese': 'n Belangrike Toevoeging Tot Afrikaanse Literêre Vertalings - Tussen die Abjekte en die Eteriese: 'n Keur uit Die Poësie van Michel Houellebecq." *Literator*, 40, 1, 1-2. [Naz]

RR2795.   Ruiz, Ugo: "Montée aux Médias sur Fond de Scandale: Le Cas de Soumission de Michel Houellebecq." *Bergen Language and Linguistics Studies*, 10, 1, 11. [WC]

RR2796.   Song, Taemi: "'Le Moi Dissocié' dans La Possibilité d'une Île de Michel Houellebecq." *Société d'Études Franco-Coréennes*, 90, 67-97. [WC]

RR2797.   Sweeney, Carole: "'Le Mot Déclin est Presque Trop Doux': Michel Houellebecq's (Euro)Déclinisme." *Modern & Contemporary France*, 27, 1, 45-59. [UaB]

RR2798.   Van den Brandt, H. P.: "Religion, Gender, Race, and Conversion: 'Soumission' by Michel Houellebecq and 'Onderworpen' by Johan Simons and Chokri Ben Chikha." *Tijdschrift Voor Genderstudies*, 22, 2. [Cor]

RR2799.   Van Wesemael, S.: "Sérotonine de Michel Houellebecq: Prédiction du Destin Tragique de la Civilisation Occidentale." *Relief*, 13, 1, 54. [Syr]

RR2800.   Verga, Aron: "Lectures Croisées de l'Œuvre de Michel Houellebecq, sous la Direction d'Antoine Jurga et Sabine Van Wesmael." *Studi Francesi*, 63, 1, 196-197. [UaB]

RR2801.   Viard, Bruno: "Houellebecq Romancier Catholique et Socialiste." *Australian Journal of French Studies*, 56, 1, 70-4. [RIT]

RR2802.   Vigier, Luc: "Michel Houellebecq: S'Excentrer pour Se Sauver." *Quinzaines*, 1218, 8. [Syr]

RR2803.   Wampole, Christy: "Conceptual Botany: Michel Houellebecq and a Burgeoning Vegetal Interest." *French Forum*, 44, 2, 207-223. [UofR]

RR2804.   Williams, Russell: "Michel Houellebecq: Google, Plagiarism, and Postproduction." *Contemporary French and Francophone Studies*, 23, 4, 414-24. [PrQ]

RR2805.   Williams, Russell: "Uncomfortable Proximity. Literary Technique, Authorial Provocations and Dog Whistles in Michel Houellebecq's Fiction." *Modern & Contemporary France*, 27, 1, 61-76. [PrQ]

RR2806.   Wodianka, Stephanie: "Sommes-Nous François?: Literatur und Vanitas bei Michel Houellebecq." *Paragrana*, 27, 2, 291-312. [Cor]

HUSTON, Nancy.

See also 196, 304, 298.

RR2807. ● Huston, Nancy: *Des Espoirs*. Lausanne: Tribune Psychanalytique. 267p. [WC]

RR2808. ● Huston, Nancy: *Rien d'Autre Que Cette Félicité: Monologue*. Montréal: Leméac. 57p. [BAnQ]

RR2809. Alves, Ana M.: "L'Empreinte de Roland Barthes sur l'Univers Frontalier Hustonien." *Quêtes Littéraires*, 9. [WC]

RR2810. Averis, Kate: "Eco-ficciones Americanas: Crisis Ambiental y Social en La Novia Oscura (1999) de Laura Restrepo y Le Club des Miracles Relatifs (2016) de Nancy Huston." *Estudios de Literatura Colombiana*, 45, 105-122. [Syr]

RR2811. Averis, Kate: "Nancy Huston's Translingual Literary Universe." *Esprit Créateur*, *59*, 4, 109-123. [UofR]

RR2812. Cros, Laurence, Anika Falkert, & Chantal Arlettaz: "Mobilité Géographique et Créativité: Le Parcours Singulier de Deux Romancières Originaires de la Prairie Canadienne, Margaret Laurence (1926-1987) et Nancy Huston (1953-)." *Études Canadiennes / Canadian Studies*. *86*, 1, 113-132. [Syr]

RR2813. De Viveiros, G.: "Paroles de Femmes: La Citation Comme Archive chez Nancy Huston." *Women in French Studies*, 27, 151-161. [UaB]

RR2814. Galis, Polly: "Mus(e)ing Bodies in Nancy Huston and Guy Oberson's Poser Nue." *Women in French Studies*, 27, 187-198. [Cor]

RR2815. Holmes, Diana: "Bad Sex/Good Sex: Nancy Huston and the Boundaries of Erotic Writing." *Esprit Créateur*, *59*, 3, 60-72. [Naz]

RR2816. Sabljo, M. S.: "History and Memory in Nancy Huston's Fault Lines." *Knjizevna Smotra*, *51*, 192, 53-61. [LoC]

HUYSMANS, Joris-Karl.

RR2817. ● Ameille, Brice, Romain Enriquez, Stéphane Guégan, & André Guyaux: *Joris-Karl Huysmans Critique d'Art: Musée d'Orsay*. Dijon: Faton. 50p. [WC]

RR2818. ● Brunel, Pierre, & André Guyaux: *Joris-Karl Huysmans*. Paris: L'Herne. 318p. [BnF]

RR2819. ● Dottin-Orsini, Mireille, Daniel Grojnowski, Stéphane Guégan, Franscesca Guglielmi, André Guyaux, Aude Jeannerod, Estelle Pietrzyk, & Pierre Vaisse: *Joris-Karl Huysmans: de Degas à Grünewald*. Paris: Musée d'Orsay. 226p. [WC]

RR2820. ● Huysmans, Joris-Karl, Pierre Glaudes, & Jean-Marie Seillan: *Œuvres Complètes: Tome 4*. Paris: Classiques Garnier. 1128p. [BnF]

RR2821. ● Huysmans, Joris-Karl, & André Guyaux: *Les Rêveries d'un Croyant Grincheux: Suivi de Joris-Karl Huysmans; Biographie*. Paris: L'Herne. 118p. [BnF]

RR2822. ● Huysmans, Joris-Karl, Daniel Grojnowski, & Maylis Kerangal: *À Rebours*. Paris: Flammarion. 405p. [Naz]

RR2823. Abud, Filho R. M.: "Administração da Morte: A Aposentadoria de Senhor Bougran, de J.-K. Huysmans e a Morte de Ivan Ilitch, de Lev Tolstoi." *Scriptorium*, 5, 1, 33211. [WC]

RR2824. Cooke, Roderick: "Le Schopenhauer de Huysmans et Céard: Deux Avatars Littéraires de la Résignation." *Studi Francesi*, *63*, 1, 56-68. [UofR]

RR2825.   Creasy, M.: "'A Sort of Breviary': Arthur Symons, J. K. Huysmans and British Decadence." *Cahiers Victoriens and Edouardiens*, 9. [Naz]

RR2826.   Fournier, Jean-François: "Épiphanies: Explosions de Clarté Obscure dans Là-Bas de Huysmans." *French Forum*, 44, 3, 345-360. [Naz]

RR2827.   Leono, Massimo: "Huysmans Gastronome: Une Sémiotique des Gastromanies Contemporaines à Partir d'à Rebours." *Epistémè*, 22, 120-145. [WC]

RR2828.   Mercier, Christophe: "Huysmans Romancier?" *Commentaire*, 168, 4, 931. [Cor]

RR2829.   Smeets, M. H. G.: "Dix Lettres Retrouvées de J.-K. Huysmans à Son Oncle Constant." *Revue d'Histoire Littéraire de la France*, 119, 671-694. [UofR]

IONESCO, Eugène.

RR2830.   ● Chmiel-Bożek, Halina: *Marionnettes Douloureuses: Analyse Qualificative et Fonctionnelle des Personnages dans Les Drames d'Eugène Ionesco.* Kraków: Wydawnictwo Naukowe UP. 311p. [WC]

RR2831.   ● Ferbers, Jutta, Eugène Ionesco, Jacqueline Seelmann-Eggebert, Ulrich Seelmann-Eggebert, Claus Peymann, Leander Haußmann, & Gilles Taschet: *Dieæ Stühle, eine Tragische Farce, Eugène Ionesco: Deutsch von Jacqueline Seelmann-Eggebert und Ulrich Seelmann-Eggebert.* Wien: Burgtheater. 75p. [WC]

RR2832.   ● Hodgson, Simon, Elspeth Sweatman, Joy Meads, & Annie Sears: *Words on Plays: Insights into the Play, the Playwright and the Production [of] Rhinoceros by Eugène Ionesco; Translated by Derek Prouse; Directed by Frank Galati.* San Francisco: American Conservatory Theater. 48p. [WC]

RR2833.   Camassa, Edoardo: "Variants of Estrangement in Julio Cortázar's Historias de Cronopios y de Famas (and a Comparison with Eugène Ionesco's L'Œuf Dur)." *Trans-*, 24. [Syr]

RR2834.   Constantinou, M.: "Humour et Jeux de Mots dans l'Œuvre d'Eugène Ionesco et Ses Traductions en Grec." *Intralinea*, 21, 1-10. [Syr]

RR2835.   Feng, Wei: "The Chairs by Eugène Ionesco." *Theatre Journal*, 71, 2, 227-229. [UofR]

RR2836.   Gopika, Raja A., & B. Indu: "Navigating the Mechanics of Secondary Imagination in the Select Works of Eugene Ionesco and Harold Pinter." *International Journal of Innovative Technology and Exploring Engineering*, 8, 12, 4337-4340. [WC]

RR2837.   Hubert, Marie-Claude: "Book Review: Eugène Ionesco en Ses Réécritures. Le Travail de la Répétition." *Revue d'Histoire Littéraire de la France*, 119, 1, 236-238. [UofR]

RR2838.   Stanislav, O.: "Cohesion in the Syntax of the 'Absurd of the Theater' as a Representation of the Language and Cultural Picture of the World of the French People (Based on the Play by E. Ionesco's 'Rhinoceros')." *International Humanitarian University Herald. Philology*, 5, 43, 139-141. [WC]

IRIGARAY, Luce.

See also 593, 728, 4729, 4752.

RR2839.   ● Hadjioannou, Christos, Luce Irigaray, & Mahon O'Brien: *Towards a New Human Being.* Cham: Palgrave Macmillan. 253p. [WC]

RR2840.   ● Hamley, Isabelle M., & David G. Firth: *Unspeakable Things Unspoken: An Irigarayan Reading of Otherness and Victimisation in Judges 19-21.* Eugene, OR: Pickwick. 250p. [WC]

RR2841. • Irigaray, Luce: *Sharing the Fire: Outline of a Dialectics of Sensitivity*. Cham: Palgrave Macmillan. 111p. [Syr]

RR2842. • Roberts, Laura: *Irigaray and Politics: A Critical Introduction*. Edinburgh: Edinburgh UP. 187p. [Syr]

RR2843. • Söderbäck, Fanny: *Revolutionary Time: On Time and Difference in Kristeva and Irigaray*. Albany: State University of New York Press. 398p. [Syr]

RR2844. Anel, Ara A.: "Confluencias entre la Tesis Posmoderna de 'La Muerte del Sujeto' y el Pensamiento de Luce Irigaray = Convergences between Postmodern Thesis on 'The Death of the Subject' and the Thought of Luce Irigaray." *Femeris*, *4*, 3, 203. [WC]

RR2845. Biro, L. S.: "Disrupting Symmetry: Jean-Luc Nancy and Luce Irigaray on Myth and the Violence of Representation." *Eidos*, *3*, 2, 62-74. [Cor]

RR2846. Cossi, Rafael K.: "Luce Irigaray e a Psicanálise: Uma Crítica Feminista." *Gerais*, *12*, 2, 319-337. [Syr]

RR2847. Fusco, Nicola V.: "Amor a La Diferencia/ Amor en la Diferencia. Reflexiones Acerca del 'Espacio del Silencio' en la Obra de Luce Irigaray." *Dossiers Feministes*, 27-41. [WC]

RR2848. Galea, Simone: "A Place Called Home. Women and Philosophy of Education." *Educational Philosophy and Theory*, *51*, 7, 702-708. [RIT]

RR2849. Heil, Johanna: "Dancing Contact Improvisation with Luce Irigaray: Intra-Action and *Elemental Passions*." *Hypatia*, *34*, 3, 485-506. [PrQ]

RR2850. Hekman, Susan: "Divine Women? Irigaray, God, and the Subject." *Feminist Theology*, *27*, 2, 117-125. [UaB]

RR2851. Lajoie, Corinne: "Luce Irigaray and Michael Marder, Through Vegetal Being: Two Philosophical Perspectives." *Dialogue*, *58*, 2, 396-397. [UofR]

RR2852. Tolstov, I. V., & V. M. Petrushov: "The Antropology of Gender by Vasil Rosanov and the Ethics of Sexual Difference by Luce Irigaray." *Anthropological Measurements of Philosophical Research*, 15, 145-154. [Cor]

RR2853. Zolkos, Magdalena: "Bereft of Interiority: Motifs of Vegetal Transformation, Escape and Fecundity in Luce Irigaray's Plant Philosophy and Han Kang's *The Vegetarian*." *Substance*, *48*, 2, 102-118. [Naz]

ISTRATI, Panaït.
See also 442.

RR2854. • Schmidt, Birgit: *Ich Bin Kein Theoretiker, Aber Ich Verstehe den Sozialismus Ganz Anders: Leben, Arbeit und Revolte des Rumänischen Schriftstellers Panaït Istrati*. Bodenburg: Édition AV. 108p. [WC]

RR2855. Burta-Cernat, B. A.: "The 'Vagabond' Typology in Panait Istrati's Books." *Transylvanian Review*, 28, 114-122. [Cor]

RR2856. Chiau, L.: "Identity and Universality in the Work of Panait Istrati." *Transylvanian Review*, 28, 101-112. [Cor]

IZZO, Jean-Claude.

RR2857. • Matalon, Jean-Marc: *Jean-Claude Izzo: Les Vies Multiples du Créateur de Fabio Montale*. Monaco: Éditions du Rocher. 169p. [BnF]

RR2858. • Nardini, Stefania, Jérôme Nicolas, & Ivana Stoyanova: *Jean-Claude Izzo: Histoire d'un Marseillais*. Marseille: Les Éditions des Fédérés—La Marseillaise. 140p. [BnF]

JABÈS, Edmond.
See also 427, 2067.
RR2859. ● Frank-Wygoda, Tsivia: *Edmond Jabès and the Archeology of the Book: Text, Pre-Texts, Contexts.* Berlin: De Gruyter. 250p. [WC]
RR2860. ● Tacik, Przemysław, & Patrycja Poniatowska: *The Freedom of Lights: Edmond Jabès and Jewish Philosophy of Modernity.* New York: Peter Lang. 403p. [Cor]

JACCOTTET, Philippe.
See also 783, 795, 804.
RR2861. ● Díaz, Rafael-José: *Al Borde del Abismo y Más Allá: Gustave Roud, Anne Perrier, Philippe Jaccottet.* Rivas-Vaciamadrid (Madrid): Mercurio Editorial. 124p. [WC]
RR2862. Hani, Georges: "De la Douceur Mise en Discours: Perception et Énonciation dans Cahier de Verdure de Philippe Jaccottet." *Écho des Études Romanes,* *15*, 1, 103. [PrQ]

JACOB, Max.
RR2863. ● Jacob, Max, Julien Lanoë, & Anne S. Kimball: *Lettres (1925-1944): Avec, Poèmes et Textes Inédits de Max Jacob.* Genève: Droz. 715p. [UaB]
RR2864. ● Lachgar, Lina, Pierre Colle, & Max Jacob: *Max Jacob dans Tous Ses États: Avec 15 Croquis Inédits de Max Jacob.* Paris: Éditions du Canoë. 77p. [BnF]
RR2865. ● *Max Jacob et les Arts de la Scène: Correspondances Inédites, Documents Iconographiques, Hommages & Comptes Rendus.* Toulouse: Association des Amis de Max Jacob. *Les Cahiers Max Jacob,* 19, 20. 501p. [WC]

JACOB, Suzanne.
See 65.

JAMMES, Francis.
See 1524.

JARRY, Alfred.
See 531, 829, 852, 848.
RR2866. ● Bevan, Sheelagh, Jennifer N. Johnson, Julien Schuh, Linda K. Stillman, & Alfred Jarry. *Alfred Jarry - The Carnival of Being.* New York: The Morgan Library et Museum. 170p. [WC]
RR2867. ● Jarry, Alfred, & Henri Béhar: *Œuvres Complètes: Tome V.* Paris: Classiques Garnier. 856p. [BnF]
RR2868. ● Stillman, Linda K., & Antonio Castronuovo: *Alfred Jarry in America.* Imola: Babbomorto. [12]p. [WC]
RR2869. Kor, Y.: "Ubu, Jarry et Gémier: Entre Anti-Mâle et Sur-Mâle." *European Drama and Performance Studies,* 12, 253-271. [LoC]

JAURÈS, Jean.
See also 392, 552.
RR2870. ● *1914-1918, de Jaurès au Soldat Inconnu: Exposition Philatélique, Cartophile et Variée . . . [Melun, l'Espace Saint-Jean, 13 Octobre-1er Décembre 2018].* Melun: Société Melunaise de Timbrologie. 300p. [BnF]

RR2871. ● Belser, Christophe: *Pourquoi Toi? Jaurès*. Clermont-Ferrand: De Borée. 231p. [WC]

RR2872. ● Dozoir, Claire: *Jean Jaurès*. Paris: Quelle Histoire. [40]p. [BnF]

RR2873. ● Jaurès, Jean: *Voici le XXe Siècle: Le Socialisme, la République et la Guerre (Décembre 1905-Septembre 1907)*. Paris: Fayard. 683p. [BnF]

RR2874. ● *Jean Jaurès: L'Icône du Socialisme Français*. Vanves: Hachette Collections. 53p. [BnF]

RR2875. ● Morvan, Jean-David, Frédérique Voulyzé, Vincent Duclert, & Rey Macutay: *Jean Jaurès*. Levallois-Perret: Hachette Filipacchi Associés. 46p. [BnF]

RR2876. Ceballos, Cuadrado A.: "El Combate por la Paz de Jean Jaurès: Análisis de Sus Textos en l'Humanité." *Ámbitos*, 45, 53-74. [WC]

RR2877. Huard, Raymond: "Jean Jaurès, Œuvres, Tome 5, Le Socialisme en Débat, 1893-1897." *Revue d'Histoire du XIX*, 58, 1, 284. [UofR]

RR2878. Jaurès, Jean: "The Political Ideas of Jean-Jacques Rousseau: An Unpublished Text of Jean Jaurès." *Cahiers Jaurès*, 231-232, 1, 193. [Cor]

RR2879. Monchablon, Alain: "Notes de Lecture: 'Jaurès Contemporain'." *Hommes & Libertés*, 185, 60. [PrQ]

JOUET, Jacques.
See 54, 784.

RR2880. ● Jouet, Jacques, Marc Lapprand, & Natali Leduc: *Kobé*. Bourges: Les Mille Univers. 85p. [BnF]

RR2881. Poiana, Peter: "The Hyperbolic Logic of Constraint in the Poetic Works of Jacques Jouet." *Substance*, 48, 2, 65-80. [RIT]

JOUHANDEAU, Marcel.
RR2882. Ornella, Tajani: "Autobiographie d'un Pécheur Habitué. Sur Marcel Jouhandeau." *Revue Italienne d'Études Françaises*, 6. [Syr]

JOUVE, Pierre Jean.
See also 299, 804.

RR2883. ● Le Colleter, T.: *La Matière Ensorcelée: Poétiques et Représentations de la Musique au XXe Siècle (Federico García Lorca, Pierre Jean Jouve, Giorgio Caproni)*. Paris: Classiques Garnier. 751p. [UofR]

RR2884. ● Rezgui-Guetat, Yosr: *Pierre Jean Jouve: Aspects de la Dualité dans 'Hécate' et 'Paulina 1880.'* Paris: L'Harmattan. 293p. [Cor]

RR2885. Catoen-Cooche, Dorothée: "Pierre Jean Jouve et Arras: Confessions d'un Enfant Malheureux." *Nord'*, 73, 1, 113. [Cor]

RR2886. Fos-Falque, S.: "Lecture: Le Labyrinthe du Désir Variation autour de Pierre Jean Jouve." *Carnet/Psy*, 229, 8, 34-38. [Cor]

RR2887. Kelly, Michael G.: "La Musique et la Forme dans l'Œuvre Poétique de Pierre Jean Jouve." *French Studies*, 73, 2, 309. [UaB]

JULIET, Charles.
RR2888. ● Boucher, Fanny, Charles Juliet, & Eric Chenal: *La Lumière en Héritage: Précédé d'une Rencontre-Entretien avec Charles Juliet; Photographies: Éric Chenal*. [Paris]: Aux Éditions des Cendres.91p. [WC]

RR2889. ● Peyrin, Marie-Thérèse: *Fraternellement, Charles Juliet: Textes de Lectrices et de Lecteurs à Propos de Son Œuvre*. Lyon: Jacques André. 345p. [LoC]

KANE, Cheikh Hamidou.
See 248, 289, 541.

KAPLAN, Nelly.
RR2890. Killian, Nellie: "Burn It All Down." *Film Comment, 55*, 4, 54-7. [RIT]
RR2891. Killian, Nellie: "Nelly Kaplan One of the Most Overlooked French Filmmakers of the '60s and '70s (and Beyond) Made Mercurial, Unapologetically Screwball Portraits of Self-Possessed Women That Take No Prisoners." *Film Comment, 55*, 4, 54-57. [Naz]

KATTAN, Naïm.
See also 741.
RR2892. Malinovich, Nadia: "Growing Up in Interwar Iraq: The Memoirs of Naim Kattan and Heskel Haddad." *Journal of Jewish Identities, 12*, 1, 19-36. [UaB]

KESSEL, Joseph.
See also 393.
RR2893. ● Kessel, Joseph: *Reportages*. Paris: Tallandier. 2 vols. [WC]
RR2894. ● Weber, Olivier, & Alain Bouldouyre: *Dictionnaire Amoureux de Joseph Kessel*. Paris: Plon. 1073p. [Cor]
RR2895. Cecilia, Juan Herrero: "El Testimonio del Escritor Joseph Kessel sobre la Insurrección de Cataluña en Octubre de 1934: Revista de Estudios Franceses." *Çédille, 15*, 283-318. [RIT]

KHADRA, Yasmina.
See also 288, 491.
RR2896. ● Khadra, Yasmina, & Johannes W. Röhrig: *Khalil: Roman: Avec un Dossier sur l'Auteur, les Attentats de Paris et de Bruxelles et la Terreur Islamiste*. Ditzingen: Reclam. 327p. [WC]
RR2897. Boraso, Silvia: "Yasmina Khadra. Khalil." *Il Tolomeo*, 1. [WC]
RR2898. Senoussi, Mohammed, & Mortad I. Serir: "Plotting the Unspeakable in Khadra's Wolf Dreams." *Critique: Studies in Contemporary Fiction, 60*, 4, 501-513. [Naz]
RR2899. Watson, Julianna B.: "Auto-Destruction or Auto-Reproduction?: Post/ Colonial Legacies of Violence in Yasmina Khadra's À Quoi Rêvent les Loups." *Francosphères, 8*, 1, 57-72. [Cor]

KHAÏR-EDDINE, Mohammed.
See also 239.
RR2900. ● Bouju, Emmanuel, Yolaine Parisot, & Charline Pluvinet: *Pouvoir de la Littérature: De l'Energeia à l'Empowerment*. Rennes: Presses Universitaires de Rennes. 360p. [WC]
RR2901. Diab-Duranton, Salam, Abdenbi Lachkar, & Mohammed E. Fakkoussi: "Le Merveilleux et le Refoulement de la Violence: Une Écriture Névrotique du Mésocosmos dans Une Odeur de Mantèque de Mohammed Khaïr-Eddine." *Ilcea*, 37. [Cor]

KHATIBI, Abdelkébir.

See also 214, 539, 759.

RR2902.　Benabdelali, Abdesslam: *Abdelkebir Khatibi, l'Étranger Profession-nel.* Casablanca: Centre Culturel du Livre. 127p. [WC]

RR2903.　Boraso, Silvia: "Atmane Bissani. 'Abdelkébir Khatibi: Le Penser-Écrire d'un Intellectuel Perspectiviste'." *Il Tolomeo*, 1. [WC]

RR2904.　El Kechouri, G.: "Abdelkébir Khatibi, La Mémoire Tatouée." *Zamane: Le Maroc d'Hier et d'Aujourd'hui*, 103, 56-59. [WC]

RR2905.　Hamil, M.: "Abdelkebir Khatibi: From Regional Postcolonialism to Global Cosmopolitanism." *Cincinnati Romance Review*, 46, 41-57. [Cor]

RR2906.　Winston, Shannon K.: "The Blink and the Bilangue: Interstices of the Textual/ Visual in Abdelkebir Khatibi's Moroccan Mediterranean." *French Studies*, *73*, 1, 67-83. [UaB]

RR2907.　Zaganiaris, Jean: "Le Cauchemar d'Abdelkébir Khatibi: 'Aujourd'hui, Nous Faisons Pas Partie d'un Monde Commun'." 149-162. In 759.

KHOURY-GHATA, Vénus.

See also 31, 789.

RR2908.　● Tumia, Francesca: *Venus Khoury-Ghata: Pour une Pratique Métaphorique du Monde.* Rennes: Presses Universitaires de Rennes. 234p. [UofR]

RR2909.　● Zubiate, Jean-Pierre: *Vénus Khoury-Ghata Poète.* Toulouse: Presses Universitaires du Midi. *Littératures*, 80. 216p. [UaB]

KLOSSOWSKI, Pierre.

RR2910.　● Augieri, Aldo: *Eterotopia dell'Identità nelle Scene Narrative di Pierre Klossowski.* Lecce: Milella. 215p. [LoC]

RR2911.　● Klossowski, Pierre: *Sur Proust.* [Paris]: Serge Safran. 125p. [Cor]

RR2912.　● Klossowski, Pierre, & Greco G. Girimonti: *Nietzsche, Il Politeismo e la Parodia.* Milano: Adelphi. 116p. [WC]

RR2913.　● Pfersmann, Andreas, & Georges Bataille: *P. K. (Pierre Klossowski).* Madrid: Arena Libros. 197p. [WC]

RR2914.　Collière-Whiteside, Christine, Karine Meshoub-Manière, & Thibaut Vaillancourt: "Pierre Klossowski, du Signe Unique. Feuillets Inédits, Édition de Guillaume Perrier, Paris, Les Petits Matins." *Genesis*, 48, 188-190. [UaB]

RR2915.　Perrier, Guillaume: "Pierre Klossowski, le Signe Unique et le Sous-Venir." *Tangence*, 120, 65. [Cor]

KOFMAN, Sarah.

See also 402, 756.

RR2916.　Kubissa, Posada, L.: "Crítica Feminista, Universalismo Ético Kantiano y una Lectura de Sarah Kofman." *Revista Portuguesa de Filosofia*, *75*, 1, 145-158. [UaB]

RR2917.　Mitsou, Marilisa, Maria C. Chatziioannou, & Isabelle Ullern: "La Philosophie 'Biographée' selon Sarah Kofman." *L'Atelier du Crh*, 21. [Syr]

RR2918.　Szendy, Peter: "Derivative Shakespeare: The Merchant of Venice and Dividual Capitalism." *Diacritics*, *47*, 1, 62-79. [RIT]

KOJÈVE, Alexandre.

See also 737.

RR2919. Armon, A.: "Between the End of History and the Last Man: World History and the Dialogue between Leo Strauss and Alexandre Kojève." *Telos*, 186, 8-24. [UofR]

RR2920. Autant-Mathieu, Marie-Christine, Aleksandr Lavrov, & Dimitri Tokarev: "L'Histoire, la Politique et la Mort dans Le Journal d'un Philosophe (1917-1920) d'Alexandre Kojève." *Revue des Études Slaves*, *90*, 1-2, 271-284. [Syr]

RR2921. Karkov, Nokolay: "The Black Circle: a Life of Alexandre Kojève, by Jeff Love. New York: Columbia UP, 2018. xiv, 360 pp. Notes. Bibliography. Index. Photographs. $40.00, Hard Bound." *Slavic Review*, *78*, 3, 870-872. [Naz]

RR2922. McIlwain, D.: "Leo Strauss and Alexandre Kojève on Tyranny and Theory." *Recovering Political Philosophy*, 117-134. [WC]

RR2923. McIlwain, D.: "Michael Oakeshott and Alexandre Kojève on Play and Practice." *Recovering Political Philosophy*, 135-152. [WC]

RR2924. Nichols, James H.: "Atheism by Alexandre Kojève (Review)." *The Review of Metaphysics*, *73*, 1, 142-143. [Naz]

KOLTÈS, Bernard-Marie.

See also 848.

RR2925. ● Limon, Hans: *Dans la Nuit de Koltès*. Paris: Les Cygnes. 88p. [BnF]

RR2926. ● Petitjean, André: *Bernard-Marie Koltès: Portrait d'un Dramaturge en Écrivain*. Dijon: Éditions Universitaires de Dijon. 173p. [Cor]

RR2927. ● Sarrazac, Jean-Pierre, & Grande F. Gómez: *Poética del Drama Moderno: De Henrik Ibsen a Bernard Marie Koltès*. Bilbao: Artezblai. 377p. [WC]

RR2928. Lepsoo, Tanel: "Roberto Zucco de Bernard-Marie Koltès: L'Histoire d'une Insupportable Fascination de l'Ordinaire." *Synergies Pays Riverains de la Baltique*, 13, 73, 84, 123. [PrQ]

KOUROUMA, Ahmadou.

See also 190, 192, 206, 208, 219, 235, 247, 275, 664, 798.

KRISTEVA, Julia.

See also 33, 56, 407, 605, 712, 764, 1140, 2843.

RR2929. ● Ivizate, González D. M.: *Poesía y Género: Indagación Retrospectiva: Una Aproximación a Julia Kristeva*. Vigo: Academia del Hispanismo. 86p. [WC]

RR2930. ● Ivizate, González D. M.: *Una Aproximación a Julia Kristeva: Poesía y Género: Indagación Retrospectiva*. Vigo: Editorial Academia del Hispanismo. 88p. [WC]

RR2931. Angelova, Emilia: "New Forms of Revolt: Essays on Kristeva's Intimate Politics, Eds. Sarah K. Hansen and Rebecca Tuvel." *Philosophia*, *9*, 1, 159-165. [UaB]

RR2932. Espino, T.: "The Eloquence of Polyglots: Julia Kristeva's Bilingualism and Intercultural Hermeneutics." *Rilce*, 1, 117-136. [Naz]

RR2933. Kastowo, Aryo I.: "La Relation Intertextuelle des Trois Contes dans Histoires ou Contes du Temps Passé par Charles Perrault et dans le Conteur Amoureux par Bruno de la Salle: Une Étude Intertextuelle selon la Pensée de Julia Kristeva. Mémoire." *Lingua Litteratia Journal*, 6, 1, 15-26. [WC]

RR2934.　Kristeva, Julia, Georges Nivat, & Olivier Mongin: "La Personne au Centre." *Esprit*, 7, 159. [UofR]

RR2935.　Lucas, Cássio B., & Alexandre R. Silva: "Kristeva e Butler: Significância, Performatividade e Produção Como Parâmetros para uma Semiótica Crítica." *Galáxia (São Paulo)*, 41, 89-100. [Cor]

RR2936.　Nikolchina, Miglena: "Noncoinciding Coincidences: Tzvetan Stoyanov with Julia Kristeva and Georgi Markov." *History of Humanities*, 4, 2, 341-356. [Cor]

RR2937.　Spassova, Kamelia: "Dual Codes: Text Within a Text in Lotman and Kristeva." *Prace Filologiczne. Literaturoznawstwo*, 8, 11, 13-28. [Cor]

RR2938.　Wu, M.-H.: "Kristevan Herethics in Emily Brontë's Wuthering Heights." *Bronte Studies*, 44, 4, 376-391. [UaB]

KRISTOF, Agota.
See also 602.

RR2939.　● Balsi, Sara: *Agota Kristof: Écrivaine Translingue*. Saint-Denis: Presses Universitaires de Vincennes. 300p. [UofR]

RR2940.　Andricikova, M., & P. Getlik: "'The Notebook' by Ágota Kristóf and Its Film Adaptation: Testimony of (In)Voluntary Anaesthesia." *World Literature Studies*, 11, 3, 89-101. [Cor]

KRYSINSKA, Marie.
See 324, 811, 812.

RR2941.　Coppo, Elena: "Alle Origini del Vers Libre: Il Caso Marie Krysinska." *Studi Francesi*, 63, 3, 455-470. [UaB]

KWAHULÉ, Koffi.
See also 199, 455, 855.

RR2942.　● Chalaye, Sylvie: *Koffi Kwahulé*. Paris: Classiques Garnier. 323p. [UofR]

RR2943.　● Kwahule, Koffi: *Les Africains: Koffi Kwahulé*. Montreuil: Éditions Théâtrales. 78p. [WC]

LABOU TANSI, Sony.
See also 247, 257, 541, 664, 675, 797.

RR2944.　● Gahungu, Celine: *Sony Labou Tansi: Naissance d'un Écrivain*. Paris: CNRS. 284p. [UofR]

RR2945.　Desquilbet, Alice: "Gahungu Céline, 2019, Sony Labou Tansi. Naissance d'un Écrivain: Paris, CNRS Éditions, 'Planète Libre,' 288 p." *Journal des Africanistes*, 89, 1, 185-187. [UaB]

RR2946.　Hulstyn, Michaela: "Djibril Diop Mambéty, Sony Labou Tansi, and the Recourse to the Imaginary." *Contemporary French and Francophone Studies*, 23, 2, 180-187. [Naz]

RR2947.　Won, Jong-Ik: "Writing of Violence, Violence of Writing - Sony Labou Tansi's La Vie et Demie." *Study of Humanities*, 31, 207-237. [WC]

LACAN, Jacques.
See also 827, 944, 1103, 1105, 1203, 1327, 2001, 2022, 3014, 2123, 2247, 2345, 3541, 3542, 3549.

RR2948. ● Balaska, Maria: *Wittgenstein and Lacan at the Limit: Meaning and Astonishment.* Cham: Palgrave Macmillan. 171p. [Syr]

RR2949. ● Baudrand, Gabriel: *Des Discours Contemporains à la Lumière de Lacan.* Paris: L'Harmattan. 129p. [BnF]

RR2950. ● Bazzanella, Emiliano: *Eros e Thanatos: Senso, Corpo e Morte nel Seminario XX di Jacques Lacan.* Trieste: Asterios. 174p. [WC]

RR2951. ● Benmansour, Maryan: *Lacan Avec Spinoza: Actes du Colloque Organisé à Paris, les 21 et 22 Mai 2016.* Paris: Association de la Lysimaque. 689p. [LoC]

RR2952. ● Benvenuto, Sergio: *Conversations with Lacan: Seven Lectures for Understanding Lacan.* London: Routledge. 186p. [Cor]

RR2953. ● Bernard, David: *Lacan avec Wedekind. Une Autre Lecture de l'Adolescence.* Rennes: PU Rennes. 264p. [BnF]

RR2954. ● Bousseyroux, Michel, Rithée Cevasco, & Jorge Chapuis: *Pensar el Psicoanálisis con Lacan: Caminar Derecho sobre un Cabello.* [Barcelona]: Ediciones S. & P. 433p. [WC]

RR2955. ● Cavallari, Claudio: *Foucault con Lacan: La Produzione Discorsiva del Soggetto.* [Giulianova]: Galaad Edizioni. 261p. [LoC]

RR2956. ● Clarke, Matthew: *Lacan and Education Policy: The Other Side of Education.* Sydney: Bloomsbury. 180p. [Cor]

RR2957. ● Colombo, Luigi: *Da Lolita a Lacan.* Roma: Alpes Italia. 107p. [WC]

RR2958. ● Gambini, Fabrizio, & Mauro Milanaccio: *Perché la Topologia: Lacan, la Psicoanalisi e la Topologia.* [Giulianova]: Galaad. 223p. [BnF]

RR2959. ● Hulak, Fabienne: *Lire Lacan au XXIe Siècle.* Nîmes: Champ Social. 265p. [BnF]

RR2960. ● Julien, Philippe, & Hans-Peter Jäck: *Jacques Lacan Lesen: Zurück zu Freud.* Wien: Turia + Kant. 240p. [BnF]

RR2961. ● Lacan, Jacques, Jacques-Alain Miller, & Bruce Fink: *Desire and Its Interpretation: The Seminar of Jacques Lacan, Book VI.* Medford, MA: Polity. 529p. [WC]

RR2962. ● Le Gaufey, G.: *Lacan and the Formulae of Sexuation: Exploring Logical Consistency and Clinical Consequences.* London: Routledge. 115p. [Cor]

RR2963. ● Leguil, Clotilde: *L'Essere e il Genere: Uomo/ Donna Dopo Lacan.* Torino: Rosenberg & Sellier. 156p. [WC]

RR2964. ● Leoni, Federico: *Jacques Lacan, Una Scienza di Fantasmi.* Napoli: Orthotes. 178p. [LoC]

RR2965. ● Maudet, Emmanuel: *Lacan Pas à Pas.* Paris: Ellipses. 187p. [WC]

RR2966. ● Mercier, Claude: *En un Éclair: La Troisième Proposition d'Octobre de Jacques Lacan.* Paris: L'Unebévue. 224p. [WC]

RR2967. ● Meyer, Matthew P.: *Archery and the Human Condition in Lacan, the Greeks, and Nietzsche. The Bow with the Greatest Tension.* Lexington: Lexington Books. 234p. [Cor]

RR2968. ● Pagel, Gerda: *Jacques Lacan zur Einführung.* Hamburg: Junius. 163p. [WC]

RR2969. ● Palombi, Fabrizio: *Jacques Lacan*. Roma: Carocci. 322p. [WC]

RR2970. ● Previtali, A. Russo: *Zanzotto / Lacan: L'Impossibile e il Dire*. Milano: Mimesis. 191p. [LoC]

RR2971. ● Rillaer, Jacques: *Freud & Lacan, des Charlatans?: Faits et Légendes de la Psychanalyse*. Bruxelles: Mardaga. 276p. [BAnQ]

RR2972. ● Rousselle, Duane: *Jacques Lacan and American Sociology: Be Wary of the Image*. Cham: Palgrave Macmillan. 97p. [Syr]

RR2973. ● Ruti, Mari, & Amy Allen: *Critical Theory between Klein and Lacan. A Dialogue*. London: Bloomsbury Academic. 272p. [Syr]

RR2974. ● Tombras, Christos: *Discourse Ontology: Body and the Construction of a World, from Heidegger Through Lacan*. Basingstoke: Palgrave Macmillan. 232p. [WC]

RR2975. ● Vanheule, Stijn, Derek Hook, & Calum Neill: *Reading Lacan's Écrits: From 'Signification of the Phallus' to 'Metaphor of the Subject.'* New York: Routledge. 327p. [Cor]

RR2976. ● Ver Eecke, W.: *Breaking Through Schizophrenia: Lacan and Hegel for Talk Therapy*. Lanham: Rowman & Littlefield. 269p. [WC]

RR2977. ● Vincent, Bruno: *Lacan, Style des Écrits*. Lormont: Le Bord de l'Eau. 186p. [LoC]

RR2978. ● Wolf, Bogdan: *Anxiety between Desire and the Body: What Lacan Says in Seminar X*. New York: Routledge, Taylor et Francis. 198p. [Syr]

RR2979. ● Zafiropoulos, Markos: *Les Mythologiques de Lacan*. Toulouse: Erès. 167p. [WC]

RR2980. ● Zafiropoulos, Markos, Vincenzo Rapone, & Michele G. Bianchi: *Lacan e le Scienze Sociali: Il Declino del Padre (1938-1953)*. Roma: Alpes Italia. 210p. [WC]

RR2981. Alfandary, Isabelle: "Identity between Sex and Gender in Freud and Lacan." *Rue Descartes*, *95*, 1, 22. [UaB]

RR2982. Askofaré, Sidi: "With Lacan . . . or to Be Contemporary." *Essaim*, *42*, 1, 123. [Cor]

RR2983. Assoun, Paul-Laurent: "La Structure et l'Idiolecte. Expérimenter le Symptôme de Freud à Lacan." *Figures de la Psychanalyse*, *38*, 2, 53. [Cor]

RR2984. Blanco-Paredes, Hilda: "S. Freud & J. Lacan 'Estructuras Clínicas'." *Boletín Científico de la Escuela Superior Atotonilco de Tula*, *6*, 11, 58-60. [WC]

RR2985. Bousseyroux, Michel: "Où Va la Psychanalyse, Aujourd'hui? Celan Contre Mallarmé et avec Lacan: Pourquoi N'Y A-T-Il Pour Lacan d'Identité de Fin d'Analyse Que Poématique?" *L'En-je Lacanien*, *33*, 2, 7. [Cor]

RR2986. Castanet, Didier: "Avec Lacan . . . 'Ce Que Parler Veut Dire'." *L'En-je Lacanien*, *32*, 1, 125. [Cor]

RR2987. Cavanagh, Sheila L.: "Queer Theory, Psychoanalysis, and the Symptom: A Lacanian Reading." *Studies in Gender and Sexuality*, *20*, 4, 226-30. [PrQ]

RR2988. Cléro, Jean-Pierre: "Lacan et le Discrédit Qu'Il Subit de la Part d'un Grand Nombre de Philosophes." *Essaim*, *42*, 1, 49. [Cor]

RR2989. Coble, Richard: "Struggling with Our Racism: White Progressive Christians and Lacan." *Pastoral Psychology*, *68*, 5, 561-574. [Naz]

RR2990. Dalzell, Thomas: "On God in Lacan: A Response to Tina Beattie." *New Blackfriars*, *100*, 1089, 538-553. [UaB]

RR2991.   Dias, Brendali, & Isaías G. Ferreira: "A Lógica da Interpretação em Lacan: Entre o Significante-Mestre e o Há Um." *Revista de Psicanálise Stylus*, 38, 125-136. [WC]

RR2992.   Dulsster, Dries, & Stijn Vanheule: "On Lacan and Supervision: A Matter of Super-Audition: On Lacan and Supervision." *British Journal of Psychotherapy*, 35, 1, 54-70. [UaB]

RR2993.   Feys, Jean-Louis: "La Psychologie Discursive et les Discours Lacaniens." *L'Évolution Psychiatrique*, 84, 4, 617-30. [PrQ]

RR2994.   Gascuel, Nils: "Lacan au Lycée." *Essaim*, 42, 1, 141. [Cor]

RR2995.   Greenshields, Will: "Lacan Contra the Surrealists." *Nottingham French Studies*, 58, 1, 64-81. [UofR]

RR2996.   Guillen, Fabienne: "Symptôme Et Sinthome, 7e Partie. Lacan, 1957-1960." *Psychanalyse*, 43, 1, 113. [WC]

RR2997.   Johnston, A.: "Working-through Christianity: Lacan and Atheism." *Filozofski Vestnik*, 40, 1, 109-138. [Naz]

RR2998.   Joos, de Ter Beerst, A.: "Marie Pesenti-Irrmann, Lacan à l'École des Femmes, Toulouse, Érès, Coll. 'Point Hors Ligne?,' 2017." *La Revue Lacanienne*, 20, 1, 217. [Cor]

RR2999.   Kaltenbeck, F.: "L'Attention de Lacan." *Savoirs et Clinique*, 25, 2, 107-111. [Cor]

RR3000.   Kœrner, Emmanuel: "La Mort dans la Vie: Du 'Maître Absolu' à l'Objet du Désir. Un Parcours avec Freud et Lacan." *Essaim*, 43, 2, 101. [Cor]

RR3001.   Krinski, Sthefan, Manoel Madeira, & Simone Moschen: "A Noção de Semblante em Jacques Lacan: Contribuição às Identidades Contemporâneas." *Revista Latinoamericana de Psicopatologia Fundamental*, 22, 4, 803-27. [PrQ]

RR3002.   Kruse, Meridith: "Realizing a Different Lacan?" *Glq: A Journal of Lesbian and Gay Studies*, 25, 1, 202-205. [UaB]

RR3003.   Lacan, Jacques: "Conclusions du IX." *La Cause du Désir*, 103, 3, 21. [WC]

RR3004.   Lacan, Jacques: "'Le Jouir de l'Être Parlant S'Articule'." *La Cause du Désir*, 101, 1, 11. [WC]

RR3005.   Lacan, Jacques: "'L'Ombilic du Rêve Est un Trou': Jacques Lacan Répond à une Question de Marcel Ritter." *La Cause du Désir*, 102, 2, 35. [WC]

RR3006.   Le Gaufey, G.: "Lacan 73." *Figures de la Psychanalyse*, 38, 2, 33. [Cor]

RR3007.   Lenormand, Marie: "'Pas Sans Lacan'. De la Peur à l'Uneasiness." *Essaim*, 42, 1, 127. [Cor]

RR3008.   Lepoutre, Thomas, Isabel V. Fernandez, Fanny Chevalier, Marie Lenormand, & Nicolas Guérin: "Les Frontières Psychanalytiques du Moi: Freud, Klein, Winnicott, Lacan." *L'Évolution Psychiatrique*, 84, 1, 69-101. [UaB]

RR3009.   Lorenzatti, Joel J.: "De Lacan a Darwin." *Revista de Psicología*, 18, 1, 77-96. [WC]

RR3010.   Martinez, Ana, & Jose Monseny: "The School of Lacan: an Interpretation of the Analyst's Desire." *Analysis*, 22, 91-102. [WC]

RR3011.   Maruani, G.: "La Vérité Est-Elle un Concept Psychanalytique? Le Débat entre Lacan et Green." *Psychotherapies*, 39, 2, 79-83. [Naz]

RR3012.   McSherry, Tony: "A Phenomenology of Love, Thanks to Lacan,

Miller, and Jellybean." *European Journal of Psychotherapy, Counselling, and Health*, *21*, 3-4, 231-243. [RIT]

RR3013.   Meraz, Gabriel: "Faire Trou: Lacan / Fontana / Soury." *Ligeia, 173-176*, 2, 153. [WC]

RR3014.   Mertens, Mark: "Le Jeu des Places, le Désaveu-Exclusion et le Pas Tout à Fait: La Systémique Confrontée à Mes Lectures de Derrida, de Lacan et de Žižek." *Thérapie Familiale*, *40*, 3, 337. [Naz]

RR3015.   Monnier, David: "Lacan et l'Amour au Temps du Capitalisme." *Nouvelle Revue de Psychosociologie*, *27*, 1, 197. [Cor]

RR3016.   Newirth, Joseph: "Review of the Lacan Tradition." *Psychoanalytic Psychology*, *36*, 2, 203-205. [UofR]

RR3017.   Ohayon, Annick: "Jacques Lacan, 'La Psychiatrie Anglaise et la Guerre'." *Nouvelle Revue de Psychosociologie*, *27*, 1, 209. [Cor]

RR3018.   Pavón-Cuéllar, David: "Lacan and Althusser on Psychology: The Political Ethos of Serving Ideals and Justifying Ideology." *Psychotherapy and Politics International*, *17*, 2. [RIT]

RR3019.   Penot, Bernard: "What I Found with Lacan." *Essaim*, *42*, 1, 85. [Cor]

RR3020.   Perman, Gerald P.: "Lacan on Psychosis: From Theory to Praxis." *Journal of the American Psychoanalytic Association*, *67*, 6, 1072-1076. [UaB[

RR3021.   Pickmann, Claude-Noële: "Sublimation with Lacan: From the Act Creating the Woman to the Tickling of Das Ding." *Figures de la Psychanalyse*, *37*, 1, 41. [Cor]

RR3022.   Schreiber, Ephraim, Gabriel Schreiber, Sofia Avissar, & Demian Halperin: "Genesis Through Lacan: A Shift in God's Discourse Toward Therapeutic Management." *International Journal of Applied Psychoanalytic Studies*, *16*, 3, 181-194. [UaB]

RR3023.   Sédat, Jacques: "Lacan 1951: Une Interprétation du Transfert." *Figures de la Psychanalyse*, *38*, 2, 87. [Cor]

RR3024.   Sharpe, Matthew: "Killing the Father, Parmenides: On Lacan's Anti-Philosophy." *Continental Philosophy Review*, *52*, 1, 51-74. [Naz]

RR3025.   Sokolowsky, Laura: "À Propos de la Réponse de Jacques Lacan à Marcel Ritter." *La Cause du Désir*, *102*, 2, 33. [WC]

RR3026.   Sokolowsky, Laura: "La Déclaration de Jacques Lacan en Juillet 1973." *La Cause du Désir*, *101*, 1, 10. [WC]

RR3027.   Sous, Jean-Louis: "Du Tressage Rouan/ Lacan." *Ligeia, 173-176*, 2, 125. [WC]

RR3028.   Stephen, James B.: "The Autonomy of the Symbolic: On Lacan's Cybernetic Seminar." *The Journal of Contemporary Psychoanalysis*, *21*, 1, 157-194. [WC]

RR3029.   Terral-Vidal, Marie: "Si Lacan M'Était Conté." *Figures de la Psychanalyse*, *38*, 2, 173. [Cor]

RR3030.   Tigre, Andréa B., & Maria H. C. Cunha: "Freud Leitor, Lacan Leitor." *Trivium: Estudos Interdisciplinares*, *11*, 1. [WC]

RR3031.   Wang, Quan: "A Posthumanist Reading of Knowledge in Zhuangzi and Jacques Lacan." *Asian Philosophy*, *29*, 1, 65-78. [Naz]

RR3032.   Welty, William G.: "Lacan, Psychoanalysis, and Comedy: Patricia Gherovici and Manya Steinkoler (eds.) Cambridge UP, New York, NY, 1st Ed., 2016,

247 pp., \$99.99 Hardcover, ISBN: 978-1-107-08617-3." *Psychoanalysis, Culture & Society*, 24, 1, 91-94. [Naz]

RR3033.   Zafiropoulos, Markos: "Les Mythologiques de Lacan : Fantasme et Passe (La Marche de l'Écrevisse)." *Figures de la Psychanalyse*, 38, 2, 119. [Cor]

LACOUE-LABARTHE, Philippe.
See also 415, 568, 3322.

RR3034.   Prestía, Martín: "Filosofía, Poesía y Política en Carlos Astrada: Notas para una Lectura de el Mito Gaucho (1948)." *Boletín de Estética*, 48, 28-38. [WC]

RR3035.   Trüb, Simon D.: "Philippe Lacoue-Labarthe's Interpretation of Walter Benjamin in Heidegger and the Politics of Poetry." *Angelaki*, 24, 6, 95-110. [UofR]

RR3036.   Ustun, Berkay: "Antinomies of Metaphysical Experience between Theodor Adorno and Philippe Lacoue-Labarthe." *Open Philosophy*, 2, 1, 428-446. [WC]

LADRIÈRE, Jean.
RR3037.   ● Kalindula, Norbert: *Exigence Critique, Rationalité et Méthodologie des Sciences: Penser avec Jean Ladrière*. Louvain-la-Neuve: Académia L'Harmattan. 203p. [LoC]

RR3038.   ● Leclercq, Jean, Thierry Scaillet, & Oraa J. M. Aguirre: *Lire Jean Ladrière: Une Introduction à Son Œuvre*. [Louvain-La-Neuve]: Presses Universitaires de Louvain. 376p. [BnF]

RR3039.   Oliveira, Thadeu L. M.: "O Estudo Performativo das Palavras da Revelação e da Fé na Filosofia de Jean Ladrière." *Pesquisas em Teologia*, 2, 3, 1-13. [WC]

LAFERRIÈRE, Dany.
See also 196, 209.

RR3040.   ● Laferrière, Dany: *Vers d'Autres Rives*. La Tour d'Aigues: Éditions de L'Aube. 106p. [UofR]

RR3041.   Asibong, Andrew: "Beyond a Carnival of Zombies: The Economic Problem of 'Aliveness' in Laurent Cantet's *Vers Le Sud.*" *Studies in French Cinema*, 19, 4, 279-293. [Naz]

RR3042.   Choplin, Olivia J.: "Remembering and Forgetting the Duvaliers: Grappling with Haitian Memory in the Works of Marie-Célie Agnant and Dany Laferrière." *Journal of Haitian Studies*, 25, 1, 154-177. [UaB]

RR3043.   Ferraroni, Roberto: "Marie Joqueviel-Bourjea, Dany Laferrière Écrirevoir." *Studi Francesi*, 63, 1, 204-205. [UaB]

RR3044.   Flores, Larisa P.: "Sexo en las Antillas: Diáspora, Tragedia y Subversión un Estudio Comparado desde el Punto de Vista de la Intersección de las Opresiones." *Caribbean Studies*, 47, 2, 25-57. [UofR]

RR3045.   Idiatha, Wilfried, Aurélie Journo, Magali Nachtergael, & Emmanuel Mbégane Ndour: "Le Visage de l'Autre Comme Écotone dans Tout Ce Qu'On Ne Te Dira Pas, Mongo de Dany Laferrière." *Itinéraires*, 2019-1. [WC]

RR3046.   Kakish, Shereen: "Entre Quete Identitaire et Fragmentation Textuelle: Etude des Enjeux Generiques et Narratifs dans 'L'Odeur du Café' de Dany Laferriere." *Australian Journal of French Studies*, 56, 3, 234-248. [Naz]

RR3047.   Kakish, Shereen: "*Je Suis un Écrivain Japonais* de Dany Laferrière:

À Tous Ceux Qui Voudraient Être Quelqu'un d'Autre." *Contemporary French and Francophone Studies*, *23*, 5, 662-70. [PrQ]

RR3048.   Pillet, Fabien: "La Question de l'Éthnoréception dans Comment Faire l'Amour avec un Nègre Sans Se Fatiguer de Dany Laferrière." *Studies in Canadian Literature*, *44*, 1, 47-65. [UofR]

LAFORGUE, Jules.
See also 525, 644.
RR3049.   Eynard, Marc: "Pascal en Marge du Sanglot de la Terre de Jules Laforgue?" *Revue d'Histoire Littéraire de la France*, *119*, 2, 347-368. [UofR]
RR3050.   Marangoni, Alessandra: "Laforgue et le Sacré-Cœur." *Romantisme*, *185*, 3, 108. [UaB]

LAMKO, Koulsy.
See 360, 856.

LANSON, Gustave.
See also 223.
RR3051.   ● Lanson, Gustave, & Eva Sládková: *O Metodě Literární Historie.* Praha: Ústav Pro Českou Literaturu AV ČR. 162p. [WC]

LAPLANCHE, Jean.
See also 598.
RR3052.   ● Laplanche, Jean, & Alberto Luchetti: *Nuovi Fondamenti per la Psicoanalisi: La Seduzione Originaria: 1987.* Milano: Mimesis. 189p. [WC]
RR3053.   ● Laplanche, Jean, & Alberto Luchetti: *Sexuale: La Sessualità Allargata nel Senso Freudiano, 2000-2006.* Milano: Mimesis. 308p. [WC]
RR3054.   ● Laplanche, Jean, & Alberto Luchetti: *Tra Seduzione e Ispirazione, l'Uomo: 1992-1999.* Milano: Mimesis. 294p. [WC]
RR3055.   Ashtor, Gila: "Sex Instead of Shattering: A Critical Exploration of Bersani and Laplanche." *Studies in Gender and Sexuality*, *20*, 4, 249-262. [Naz]
RR3056.   Ribeiro, S. D., & Belo F. R. Rodrigues: "Rethinking the Lefebvre Case with Jean Laplanche." *Psicologia Clinica*, *31*, 3, 557-576. [Syr]
RR3057.   Rizq, Rosemary: "At the Queen's Hall with E. M. Forster and Jean Laplanche." *British Journal of Music Therapy*, *33*, 2, 83-86. [UaB]
RR3058.   Wyatt, Jean: "Laplanche, Freud, Leonardo: Sustaining Enigma." *American Imago*, *76*, 2, 183-206. [UofR]

LARBAUD, Valery.
See also 299.
RR3059.   ● Connell, Allison: *The Translations of Valery Larbaud: A Model of Literary Exploration.* Woodstock, NB: Chapel Street Editions. 215p. [WC]
RR3060.   ● Gerling, Vera E.: *Cahiers Valery Larbaud.* Paris: Classiques Garnier. *Cahier Valéry Larbaud*, 55. 250p. [WC]
RR3061.   Evans, David E.: "Rhythm Across Borders: Free Verse between Cosmopolitanism and Statelessness in Valery Larbaud's Les Poésies de A. O. Barnabooth." *Modern Languages Open*, 1. [WC]

LAURENT, Jacques.
See 15.

LAYE, Camara.
RR3062. ● Engel, Anna: *Koba! Aye Koba, Lama! Über die Bedeutung Laye Camara's Kulturell Interner Perspektive auf die Malinké in 'L'Enfant Noir'*. München: GRIN. 13p. [WC]
RR3063. Simpore, Karim: "Camara Laye et J. M. G. Le Clézio dans la Quête Épistémologique de la Nature par le Mythe d'Origine." *French Cultural Studies, 30,* 3, 248-255. [UofR]

LE, Linda.
See also 602.
RR3064. Bacholle, Michèle: "Les Lettres d'Hommage de Linda Lê." *Études Françaises, 55,* 1, 105-120. [UaB]

LEBLANC, Maurice.
See also 433.
RR3065. ● Barkawitz, Martin: *Arsène Lupin und der Automatenmensch.* Dettenhausen: Belle Époque. 280p. [WC]
RR3066. Vilariño, Andrea Diana: "La Revista Sherlock Holmes y la Configuración del Lector de Policial." *Orbis Tertius,* 24, 29. [PrQ]

LE BRAZ, Anatole.
RR3067. Giraudon, Daniel: "La Mort de Trois Prêtres en Trégor au XVIII: De la Véracité des Chants Populaires en Langue Bretonne." *Annales de Bretagne et des Pays de l'Ouest, 126,* 3, 117. [UaB]

LE BRIS, Michel.
See also 223, 265, 287.
RR3068. ● Le Bris, M.: *Pour l'Amour des Livres.* Paris: Grasset. 262p. [Cor]

LE CLÉZIO, Jean-Marie Gustave.
See also 445, 462, 473, 478, 487, 535, 553, 566, 585, 3063.
RR3069. ● Armel, Aliette: *Le Clézio, l'Homme du Secret.* Paris: Le Passeur. 154p. [UofR]
RR3070. ● Feyereisen, Justine: *Les Cahiers J.-M. G. Le Clézio.* Caen: Passage(s). 214p. [WC]
RR3071. Akromov, Ulugbek S.: "'Characteristics of the Motivation of Travel' in Jean-Marie Gustave Le Clezio Works." *Theoretical & Applied Science, 72,* 4, 382-386. [LoC]
RR3072. Arma, Park: "Étude des Espaces Narratifs de la Quarantaine de Le Clézio." *Association Culturelle Franco-Coréenne, 40,* 1, 27-54. [WC]
RR3073. Constant, Isabelle: "Alma: Le Regard Engagé de J.-M. G. Le Clézio." *Mouvances Francophones,* 4, 1. [WC]
RR3074. Franceschi, Solenne: "Mondo et Autres Histoires de J.-M. G. Le Clézio." *Nrp. Lettres Collège. Hors-Série, 663,* 5, 24. [WC]

RR3075.   Kıran, Ayşe Eziler: "Désert, Espace Poétique des Contradictions." *Synergies Turquie*, 12, 121-37. [PrQ]

RR3076.   Liao, Banglei: "Musicality of Le Clézio's Novels." *Sino-US English Teaching*, 16, 12. [LoC]

RR3077.   Moser, Keith: "Deconstructing Seductive Images and Valorizing the Contributions of Working-Class Heroes: The Forgotten Music of Sixto Rodriguez and the Fiction of J. M. G. Le Clézio." *Dalhousie French Studies*, 113, 89-98. [Syr]

RR3078.   Moser, Keith: "J. M. G. Le Clézio and Gérard Gouesbet's Cosmic, Ecocentric Framework for Understanding the Nature of Human Violence." *French Cultural Studies*, 30, 3, 232-247. [UofR]

RR3079.   Moser, Keith: "Jean-Marie Pelt and J. M. G. Le Clézio's Invitation to Think and Live Otherwise in the Anthropocene." *French Review*, 93, 1, 63-78. [Naz]

RR3080.   Nielipowicz, Natalia: "La Restitution des Voix Disparues dans Alma de J. M. G. Le Clézio." *Cahiers Erta*, 20, 20, 39-52. [WC]

RR3081.   Oh, Bobae: "Deux Soulèvements de 1968 dans Révolutions de J.-M. G. Le Clézio: 'La Nuit de Tlatelolco' et 'Mai 68'." *Société d'Études Franco-Coréennes*, 88, 49-69. [WC]

RR3082.   Petropoulou, Zoé: "Le Clézio, Jean-Marie Gustave. Alma." *French Review*, 92, 3, 259. [Naz]

RR3083.   Thibault, Bruno: "Changer de Style, Changer de Décor, Changer de Peau: Les Mutations Narratives dans l'Œuvre de J. M. G. Le Clézio." *Faux Titre*, 434, 204-216. [UaB]

LE DŒUFF, Michèle.
RR3084.   Power, Ian: "The New Musical Imaginary: Description as Distraction in New Music." *Tempo*, 73, 289, 6-20. [RIT]

LEDUC, Violette.
See also 316, 343, 614.

RR3085.   ● Frantz, Anaïs: *Violette Leduc: Genèse d'une Œuvre Censurée*. Paris: Presses Sorbonne Nouvelle. 247p. [UofR]

RR3086.   ● Leduc, Violette, & Marina Marchesiello: *Odio I Dormienti e Altre Prose Inedite*. Pistoia: Via del Vento. 43p. [WC]

RR3087.   ● Tarabella, Eleonora, & Violette Leduc: *La Donna Brutta: Vita e Scrittura di Violette Leduc*. Milano: Società per l'Enciclopedia delle Donne. 437p. [WC]

LEFEBVRE, Henri.
See also 2322, 3056.

RR3088.   ● Andy, Merrifield: *Henri Lefebvre: Eine Kritische Einführung*. Wien: Bahoe Books. 250p. [WC]

RR3089.   ● Biagi, Francesco, & Henri Lefebvre: *Henri Lefebvre: Una Teoria Critica dello Spazio*. Milano: Jaca Book. 252p. [WC]

RR3090.   ● Borelli, Guido: *Henri Lefebvre: Un Marxista Nello Spazio* =: *Henri Lefebvre: A Marxist in Space*. Milano: F. Angeli. 191p. [WC]

RR3091.   ● Leary-Owhin, Michael E., & John P. McCarthy: *The Routledge*

Handbook of Henri Lefebvre, the City and Urban Society. London: Routledge. 556p. [Cor]

RR3092.   Alvarez, Isabel P.: "A Noção de Mobilização do Espaço em Henri Lefebvre." *Geousp Espaço e Tempo (Online), 23*, 3, 494-505. [WC]

RR3093.   Amendola, Giandomenico: "Ricordo di Henri Lefebvre." *Sociologia Urbana e Rurale*, 118, 10-11. [LoC]

RR3094.   Borelli, Guido: "Henri Lefebvre: La Rivoluzione Come Festa." *Sociologia Urbana e Rurale*, 118, 86-113. [LoC]

RR3095.   Borelli, Guido: "Henri Lefebvre: Un Marxista nello Spazio. 'Ravi de Vous Revoir en Italie, M. Lefebvre'." *Sociologia Urbana e Rurale*, 118, 7-9. [LoC]

RR3096.   Carlos, Ana F.: "Henri Lefebvre: A Problemática Urbana em Sua Determinação Espacial." *Geousp Espaço e Tempo (Online), 23*, 3, 458-477. [WC]

RR3097.   Espinosa, Zepeda H.: "Bitter, Sabine y Weber, Helmut (eds.). (2018). Autogestion or Henri Lefebvre in New Belgrade. Berlín: Sternberg Press." *Estudios Demográficos y Urbanos, 35*, 1, 269. [Naz]

RR3098.   Ferro, Rodrigo R.: "Interpretando a Função Social da Propriedade Urbana com Base no Pensamento de Henri Lefebvre." *Revista de Direito da Cidade, 11*, 2. [Naz]

RR3099.   Fuchs, Christian: "Henri Lefebvre's Theory of the Production of Space and the Critical Theory of Communication." *Communication Theory, 29*, 2, 129-150. [UofR]

RR3100.   Gardiner, Michael E.: "Henri Lefebvre e la Sociologia della Noia." *Sociologia Urbana e Rurale*, 118, 63-85. [LoC]

RR3101.   Ghulyan, H.: "Lefebvre's Production of Space in the Context of Turkey: A Comprehensive Literature Survey." *Sage Open, 9*, 3. [Naz]

RR3102.   Goonewardena, Kanishka, & Sinéad Petrasek: "Henri Lefebvre e il Diritto alla Città: Storia, Teoria, Politica." *Sociologia Urbana e Rurale*, 118, 12-29. [LoC]

RR3103.   Gray, Patrick, & Maurice Samely: "Shakespeare and Henri Lefebvre's 'Right to the City': Subjective Alienation and Mob Violence in Coriolanus, Julius Caesar, and 2 Henry VI." *Textual Practice, 33*, 1, 73-98. [UaB]

RR3104.   Hassan, Naglaa: "The Production of Heterotopic Spaces between Theory and Practice: Tahrir Square in Light of Michel Foucault's and Henri Lefebvre's Theories." *Cairo Studies in English*, 1, 102-118. [WC]

RR3105.   Mansilla, López J. A., & Sergi Yanes: "Review of 'Hacia Una Arquitectura del Placer' by Henri Lefebvre." *Perifèria. Revista d'Investigació I Formació en Antropologia, 24*, 1, 215. [WC]

RR3106.   Santos, César S.: "Henri Lefebvre e a Morfologia de Uma Dialética Espacial." *Geousp Espaço e Tempo (Online), 23*, 3, 525-550. [WC]

RR3107.   Santos, César S., Carlos A. F. Alessandri, & Glória D. A. Alves: "O Dossiê Henri Lefebvre e a Problemática Urbana na Geousp." *Geousp Espaço e Tempo (Online), 23*, 3, 453-457. [WC]

RR3108.   Santos, Julyanne C. B. M., Daniella M. S. Dias, & Paula R. Arruda: "Capitalismo, Globalização e a Proposta de Direito à Cidade de Henri Lefèbvre." *Revista de Direito da Cidade, 11*, 3. [Naz]

RR3109.   Taveira, Valéria C. B., Victor H. D. O. Marques, Flávia P. Machado, & Paulo C. L. Oliveira: "A Privatização do Espaço e Suas Implicações desde a Produção do Espaço de Henri Lefebvre." *Multitemas, 24*, 57, 119. [Cor]

RR3110.   Vazquez, Pizzi D.: "Henri Lefebvre e la Critica Marxista dell'Abi-
tare." *Sociologia Urbana e Rurale*, 118, 114-130. [LoC]
RR3111.   Volochko, Danilo: "Henri Lefebvre: Totalidade, Radicalidade e Dialética Espacial." *Geousp Espaço e Tempo (Online)*, *23*, 3, 506-524. [WC]

LEIRIS, Michel.
See 216, 438, 665.
RR3112.   ● Côté, Sébastien: *L'Ethnologie Détournée: Carl Einstein, Michel
Leiris et la Revue Documents*. Paris: Classiques Garnier. 304p. [WC]
RR3113.   Bernasek, Lisa: "Colonial, Popular, and Scientific? The *Exposition
du Sahara* (1934) and the Formation of the Musée de l'Homme." *Museum Anthropol-
ogy*, *42*, 2, 89-108. [UaB]
RR3114.   Poiana, P.: "Choses d'Apparat: The Poetics of Dress in Michel Lei-
ris's L'Afrique Fantôme." *International Journal of Francophone Studies*, *22*, 3, 213-
231. [RIT]
RR3115.   Reeck, Matt: "Michel Leiris (Translated by Brent Hayes Edwards).
Phantom Africa." *Contemporary French Civilization*, *44*, 1, 128-129. [Syr]

LEMAIRE, Jean-Pierre.
See also 31.
RR3116.   ● Clairambault, François, & Jean-Pierre Lemaire: *Les Anges Sont
Transparents*. Hennebont: L'Enfance des Arbres. 131p. [BnF]
RR3117.   ● Léna, Marguerite, Roselyne Feraudy, & Jean-Pierre Lemaire: *Une
Secrète Lumière: Méditations pour l'Année Liturgique, Visions de Patmos*. Les Plans-
sur-Bex (Suisse): Parole et Silence. 77p. [BnF]

LEMONNIER, Camille.
See also 422.
RR3118.   ● Saenen, Frédéric, & Myriam Watthee-Delmotte: *Camille Lemon-
nier, Le 'Zola Belge': Déconstruction d'un Poncif Littéraire*. Bruxelles: Académie
Royale de Belgique. 97p. [WC]
RR3119.   Catharina, Pedro P. G. F., & Rubens V. M. Pedrosa: "Quadros de
Quermesse em Un Mâle, de Camille Lemonnier: Um Topos Naturalista." *Revista
Scripta Uniandrade*, *17*, 1. [WC]

LEPAGE, Robert.
See also 77, 4704.
RR3120.   ● *Coriolan, de Shakespeare, Traduction et Adaptation Michel Gar-
neau, Mise en Scène Robert Lepage*. [Montréal]: TNM. 1 vol. [BAnQ]
RR3121.   ● *La Face Cachée de la Lune, Conception et Mise en Scène, Robert
Lepage, Interprétation, Yves Jacques*. Montréal: Duceppe. 15p. [BAnQ]
RR3122.   Bardou, Mathilde: "Robert Lepage: Kanata." *Art Press*, 463, 25. [WC]
RR3123.   D'Arienzo, Grazia: "La Questione Autoctona e l'Eredità Coloniale
del Canada: Appunti Su Kanata, di Robert Lepage." *Mimesis Journal*, 8, 167-174.
[Cor]
RR3124.   Dundjerovic, Aleksandar: "Melissa Poll. Robert Lepage's Sceno-
graphic Dramaturgy: The Aesthetic Signature at Work." *Modern Drama*, *62*, 4, 574-
576. [Naz]

RR3125.   Gagnon, Jean: "L'Œuvre Disqualifiée - Robert Lepage, l'Appropriation Culturelle et la Liberté Artistique." *Inter*, 132, 20-1. [PrQ]

RR3126.   Hotte, Caroline Nepton: "Kanata . . . Appropriation ou Effacement?" *Esse*, 97, 74-9. [RIT]

RR3127.   Khoury, Camille: "Kanata: Les Enjeux de la Controverse: Kanata – Episode I – La Controverse, Robert Lepage/ Théâtre du Soleil, Cartoucherie de Vincennes, dans Le Cadre de la 47e Édition du Festival d'Automne." *Agôn*, 26 janvier. [WC]

RR3128.   Reynolds, James. "Intermediality and Spectatorship in the Theatre Work of Robert Lepage: The Solo Shows." *International Journal of Performance Arts and Digital Media*, 15, 1, 120-122. [Cor]

RR3129.   Reyns-Chikuma, Chris: "Le Dragon Bleu: Adapter le Cadre de la Peinture au Théâtre de Robert Lepage et de Ce Théâtre à la Bande Dessinée de Fred Jourdain, Cosmopolitiquement et Ludiquement." *Canadian Review of Comparative Literature*, 46, 3, 446-469. [UaB]

RR3130.   Vaïs, Michel: "Lepage and Mnouchkine Collide with Cultural Appropriation." *PAJ*, 41, 3, 71-74. [PrQ]

LEROUX, Gaston.
See also 187.

RR3131.   ● Fontaine, Gérard: *Le Fantôme de l'Opéra. Légendes et Mystères au Palais Garnier*. Paris: Monum - Éditions du Patrimoine. 192p. [BnF]

RR3132.   ● Gaudin, Jean-Charles, & Christophe Picaud: *Le Fantôme de l'Opéra: Une Aventure de Rouletabille d'après Gaston Leroux*. Toulon: Soleil. 59p. [BnF]

LEVINAS, Emmanuel.
See also 376, 1267, 1286, 1297, 2068, 2583, 2592, 3393, 3468, 3966.

RR3133.   ● Armengaud, Françoise, Johannes Bennke, Dieter Mersch, Richard Cohen, & Brian Alkire: *Emmanuel Levinas: On Obliteration: An Interview with Franoise Armengaud Concerning the Work of Sacha Sosno*. Zürich: Diaphanes. 80p. [WC]

RR3134.   ● Atterton, Peter, & Tamra Wright: *Face-to-face with Animals: Levinas and the Animal Question*. Albany: State University of New York Press. 230p. [UofR]

RR3135.   ● Bianchi, Gianluca: *Lévinas e la Difesa dell'Interiorità*. Milano: Mimesis. *Filosofie*, 614. 148p. [LoC]

RR3136.   ● Brinnich, Max: *Über Sinn und Bedeutung bei Kant und Levinas*. München: Karl Alber. 185p. [WC]

RR3137.   ● Fischer, Norbert, Peter Reifenberg, & Jakub Sirovátka: *Das Antlitz des Anderen: Zum Denken von Emmanuel Levinas*. München: Karl Alber. 118p. [WC]

RR3138.   ● Grabher, Gudrun: *Levinas and the Other in Narratives of Facial Disfigurement: Singing Through the Mask*. New York: Routledge. 212p. [Syr]

RR3139.   ● Gutiérrez, Velasco C. A.: *Parole et Dialogue: De la Pronominalité à l'Engagement Étique: Rosenzweig, Buber, Levinas*. Milano: Mimésis. 492p. [WC]

RR3140.   ● Molinaro, Nina L.: *The Art of Time: Levinas, Ethics, and the Contemporary Peninsular Novel*. Lewisburg, PA: Bucknell UP. 223p. [UofR]

RR3141.   ● Pierron, Jean-Philippe, Bernard N. Schumacher, & Agata Zielinski: *Levinas et le Soin*. Paris: Classiques Garnier. 157p. [WC]

RR3142. ● Ponzio, Augusto: *Con Emmanuel Levinas: Alterità e Identità.* Milano: Mimesis. 369p. *Filosofie*, 618. [LoC]

RR3143. ● Sugarman, Richard I.: *Levinas and the Torah: A Phenomenological Approach.* Albany: State University of New York Press. 376p. [Cor]

RR3144. ● Valori, Furia: *Heidegger e Levinas: Percorsi Antropologici Tra Ontologia e Etica.* Lanciano: Carabba. 209p. [LoC]

RR3145. ● Zambrano, Borjabad M.: *Levinas y el Otro.* [Madrid]: Faber & Sapiens. 64p. [WC]

RR3146. ● Zegarra, Felipe: *El Pobre y el Otro: Reflexiones en Torno a Emmanuel Levinas.* Lima (Peru): Fondo Editorial de la PUCP. 207p. [WC]

RR3147. Balbontin-Gallo, C.: "Levinas et la Question du Politique de Quel État S'Agit-Il?" *Revue Philosophique de Louvain*, *116*, 3, 365-396. [UofR]

RR3148. Bell, N.: "Political Justice: Levinas Contra Aristotle." *Religions*, *10*, 2. [Syr]

RR3149. Belmer, S.: "Emmanuel Levinas and Theodor Adorno on Ethics and Aesthetics." *Angelaki*, *24*, 5, 29-43. [UaB]

RR3150. Bennke, J.: "Testimonial Image Practices As a Politics of Aesthetics After Levinas." *Religions*, *10*, 3. [Syr]

RR3151. Berenpas, M.: "Unsaying the Said: Emmanuel Levinas and the Zhuangzi on Linguistic Scepticism." *Empedocles*, *10*, 1, 87-99. [LoC]

RR3152. Bernasconi, Robert: "Emmanuel Levinas on Surrender and Self-Sacrifice: A Response to Simone Drichel." *Psychoanalysis, Self and Context*, *14*, 1, 29-35. [Cor]

RR3153. Calin, Rodolphe: "The Notion of Accomplishment in Levinas." *Levinas Studies*, 13, 69-83. [UaB]

RR3154. Chehayed, Nibras: "Nietzsche and Levinas on Time." *Continental Philosophy Review*, *52*, 4, 381-395. [RIT]

RR3155. Ciaramelli, Fabio: "L'Humanisme Levinassien et les Droits d'Autrui." *Revue d'Éthique et de Théologie Morale*, *303*, 3, 39. [Cor]

RR3156. Cohen-Levinas, D.: "Vers une Phénoménologie du Bien. Platonisme et Hébraïsme chez Emmanuel Levinas." *Philosophie*, *141*, 2, 112-122. [UaB]

RR3157. Cohoon, C.: "Human Edibility, Ecological Embodiment: Plumwood and Levinas." *Environmental Ethics*, *41*, 2, 143-163. [RIT]

RR3158. Cruz, M. A.: "Beyond Atheism and Atheology: The Divine Humanism of Emmanuel Levinas." *Religions*, *10*, 2. [Syr]

RR3159. Daves, Seth: "Book Review of Rafael Winkler's *Philosophy of Finitude: Heidegger, Levinas, and Nietzsche.*" *Continental Philosophy Review*, *52*, 4, 415-8. [PrQ]

RR3160. Davies, Paul: "Levinas's Restlessness: "God and Philosophy" Without Consolation." *Levinas Studies*, 13, 141-174. [Naz]

RR3161. De Broca, A. "La Rencontre d'un Clinicien avec la Pensée de Levinas." *Ethique et Santé*, *16*, 4, 153-157. [WC]

RR3162. Drichel, Simone: "Emmanuel Levinas and the 'Specter of Masochism': A Cross-Disciplinary Confusion of Tongues." *Psychoanalysis, Self and Context*, *14*, 1, 3-22. [Cor]

RR3163. Froese, Robert: "Levinas and the Question of Politics." *Contemporary Political Theory*, *19*, 1, 1-19. [RIT]

RR3164.   Giovanini, Valerie: "Alterity in Simone de Beauvoir and Emmanuel Levinas: From Ambiguity to Ambivalence." *Hypatia*, *34*, 1, 39-58. [PrQ]

RR3165.   Glendinning, Simon: "Levinas's Ethical Politics, by Michael L. Morgan." *Mind*, 128, 510, 584-588. [Naz]

RR3166.   Hammerschlag, S.: "Lévinas and Sartre: Existentialism After the Stalag." *Yale French Studies*, 135-136, 209-229. [UofR]

RR3167.   Irom, B.: "Mediating Syria's Strangers Through Levinas: Communication Ethics and the Visuals of Children." *Communication Theory*, *29*, 4, 441-462. [UofR]

RR3168.   Keisuke, Tokita: "Emmanuel Levinas: Faire avant d'Entendre." *Cahiers d'Études Françaises*, 24, 33-50. [WC]

RR3169.   Kim, Do-Hyung: "The Dialogue between Emmanuel Levinas and Feminism - The Feminism's Understanding and Misunderstanding of Levinas." *Journal of the New Korean Philosophical Association*, 96, 145-165. [WC]

RR3170.   King, Christopher: "Gadamer, Levinas, and the Hermeneutic Ontology of Ethics." *Philosophies*, *4*, 3, 48. [Naz]

RR3171.   Klun, B.: "Alterity and Understanding a Hermeneutical Approach to Levinas." *Synthesis Philosophica*. *34*, 1, 141-156. [Cor]

RR3172.   Kosky, Jeffrey L.: "Levinas and the Trauma of Responsibility: The Ethical Significance of Time." *The Review of Metaphysics*, *73*, 2, 359-61. [PrQ]

RR3173.   Kotegawa, Shojiro: "Truth and Sincerity: The Concept of Truth in Levinas' Philosophy." *Contributions to Phenomenology*, 101, 163-172. [Cor]

RR3174.   Larios, Joe: "Levinas and the Primacy of the Human." *Ethics and the Environment*, *24*, 2, 1-22. [Naz]

RR3175.   Larios, Joe: "Levinas and the Problem of Predation: From Fraternity to Kinship." *Sub-stance*, 148, 26-41. [UaB]

RR3176.   Lawrence, Sean: "'I'm a Pacifist': Peace in the Thought of Emmanuel Levinas." *Religions*, *10*, 2, 84. [Syr]

RR3177.   Lorelle, Paula: "Sensibility and the Otherness of the World: Levinas and Merleau-Ponty." *Continental Philosophy Review*, *52*, 2, 191-201. [RIT]

RR3178.   Losada-Sierra, M.: "Levinas' Ethics as Naturalization of Jewish Messianism." *Theologica Xaveriana*, *69*, 188, 1-25. [Naz]

RR3179.   Louis, Agnès: "Une Critique Juive de l'Occident Chrétien. Lecture d'Emmanuel Lévinas et de Benny Lévy." *Le Philosophoire*, *51*, 1, 97. [Cor]

RR3180.   Loumansky, Amanda: "Levinas's Contribution to the Law of Hospitality." *Liverpool Law Review*, *41*, 1, 67-78. [Naz]

RR3181.   Mao, Xin: "Religion's Ambivalent Relation with Violence: From Scott Appleby to Emmanuel Levinas." *Religions*, *10*, 11, 632. [Naz]

RR3182.   Meihuizen, N.: "Hamlet, Levinas, Relationship, and Otherness." *English Studies in Africa*, *62*, 2, 124-133. [Naz]

RR3183.   Morgan, Michael L.: "Plato, Levinas, and Transcendence." *Levinas Studies*, 13, 85-102. [Naz]

RR3184.   Mumford, James: "The Experience of Obligation: The Enduring Promise of Levinas for Theological Ethics." *Studies in Christian Ethics*, *32*, 3, 352-369. [Naz]

RR3185.   Nordmann, Sophie: "Rationalité Philosophique et Pensée Religieuse: Levinas et la Possibilité d'une Philosophie Juive." *Le Philosophoire*, *51*, 1, 79. [Cor]

RR3186.   Pendola, A.: "Levinas, Bureaucracy, and the Ethics of School Lead-
ership." *Educational Philosophy and Theory*, *51*, 14, 1528-1540. [UaB]
    RR3187.   Podolsky, Robin: "Sumud Freedom Camp: Levinas' Face-to-Face in
Praxis." *Religions*, *10*, 4, 256. [Naz]
    RR3188.   Portella, Elizabeth: "Mediation and Its Shadow." *Philosophy Today*,
63, 2, 427-445. [UofR]
    RR3189.   Rapport, Nigel: "Anthropology Through Levinas (Further Reflec-
tions): On Humanity, Being, Culture, Violation, Sociality, and Morality." *Current
Anthropology*, *60*, 1, 70-90. [WC]
    RR3190.   Reed, R. C.: "Spiritual Trial in Kierkegaard: Religious Anxiety and
Levinas's Other." *International Journal of Philosophy and Theology*, 80, 495-509.
[UaB]
    RR3191.   Römer, Inga: "La Raison Pure Pratique, Au-Delà de l'Être. Levinas
Lecteur de Kant." *Philosophie*, *142*, 3, 12. [UaB]
    RR3192.   Saldukaityte, J.: "The Place and Face of the Stranger in Levinas."
Religions, *10*, 2. [Naz]
    RR3193.   Severson, Eric R.: "Levinas and the Trauma of Responsibility.
Review of Levinas and the Trauma of Responsibility: The Ethical Significance of
Time, by Cynthia D. Coe." *Research in Phenomenology*, *49*, 1, 119-125. [RIT]
    RR3194.   Simmons, J. A., & K. Carnahan: "When Liberalism Is Not Enough:
Political Theology After Reinhold Niebuhr and Emmanuel Levinas." *Religions*, *10*,
7. [Syr]
    RR3195.   Tajalli, P., & S. Segal: "Levinas, Weber, and a Hybrid Framework for
Business Ethics." *Philosophy of Management*, *18*, 1, 71-88. [Naz]
    RR3196.   Van Eeden, R.: "Levinas's Political Chiasmi: Otherwise Than Being
as a Response to Liberalism and Fascism, Humanism and Antihumanism." *Religions*,
10, 3. [Syr]
    RR3197.   Yampolskaya, A.: "Prophetic Subjectivity in Later Levinas: Sober-
ing Up from One's Own Identity." *Religions*, *10*, 1. [Naz]

LÉVI-STRAUSS, Claude.
    See also 10, 1664, 3457, 4148, 4195.
    RR3198.   ● Anghelescu, Adrian I.: *Oamenii Aceia: Ultima Înhumare la But-
tenheim, Satul Lui Levi Strauss*. Braşov: Libris. 181p. [WC]
    RR3199.   ● D'Onofrio, Salvatore: *Lévy-Strauss e la Catastrofe: Nulla è Per-
duto, Possiamo Riprenderci Tutto*. Milano: Mimesis. 90p. [WC]
    RR3200.   ● Journet, Nicolas: *Claude Lévi-Strauss: L'Homme, l'Œuvre, Son
Héritage*. Auxerre: Sciences Humaines. 157p. [WC]
    RR3201.   Brandi, Felipe: "Francine Iegelski Astronomia das Constelações
Humanas. Reflexões Sobre Claude Lévi-Strauss e a História São Paulo, Humanitas,
2016, 422 p." *Annales. Histoire, Sciences Sociales*, 74, 2, 450-452. [RIT]
    RR3202.   Cléro, Jean-Pierre: "Y A-T-Il Trace d'Éthique chez Lévi-Strauss?"
Revue d'Études Benthamiennes, 16. [Cor]
    RR3203.   Désveaux, Emmanuel: "Les Carnets Nambikwara de Lévi-Strauss."
Journal de la Société des Américanistes, *105*, 2, 9-14. [UaB]
    RR3204.   Erikson, Philippe: "Claude Lévi-Strauss (1908-2009), in Memo-
riam." *Journal de la Société des Américanistes*, 105, 7-8. [Syr]

RR3205.   Erikson, Philippe: "Entretien de Claude Lévi-Strauss." *Journal de la Société des Américanistes*, 105, 15-42. [Syr]

RR3206.   Fauvel, Aude, Jean-Christophe Coffin, Thibaud Trochu, & Frédéric Keck: "Roman Jakobson, Claude Lévi-Strauss, Correspondance. 1942-1982: Préfacé, Édité et Annoté par Emmanuelle Loyer et Patrice Maniglier, Paris, Seuil (La Librairie du XXIe Siècle), 2018, 448 pages." *Revue d'Histoire des Sciences Humaines*, 35, 271-272. [Syr]

RR3207.   Fuglestvedt, Ingrid: "The Mythical Mind of the Older Stone Age – A Lévi-Straussian Reappraisal." *Time and Mind*, 12, 3, 187-195. [RIT]

RR3208.   Guister, Marina A.: "The Spectre of Formalism: Polemics between Propp and Levi-Strauss as a Communicative Failure." *Folklore*, 2, 4, 155-169. [WC]

RR3209.   Harkin, Michael E.: "Lévi-Strauss: Two Lives." *Reviews in Anthropology*, 48, 2, 88-102. [UofR]

RR3210.   Hidayat, Herry N.: "United Nations of Rendang: Meme Dalam Perspektif Strukturalisme Lévi-Strauss." *Jurnal Lingua Idea*, 10, 2, 115. [WC]

RR3211.   Imbert, Claude: "Book Review: Lévi-Strauss Face à la Catastrophe. Rien N'Est Joué, Nous Pouvons Tout Reprendre ('Philosophie' 55)." *L'Homme*, 230, 195-198. [Syr]

RR3212.   Konersmann, Ralf, Dirk Westerkamp, & M. van Vliet: "Morphologie, Transformation und Übersetzbarkeit: Eine Gegenüberstellung der Ästhetischen Konzepte von Cassirer und Lévi-Strauss." *Zeitschrift für Kulturphilosophie*, 1, 21-43. [WC]

RR3213.   Laberge, Yves: "Penser Global: Internationalisation et Globalisation des Sciences Humaines et Sociales sous la Direction de Michel Wieviorka, Laurent Lévi-Strauss, Gwenaëlle Lieppe Éditions de la Maison des Sciences de l'Homme Paris, 2015, pp. 478." *Canadian Journal of Political Science*, 52, 2, 416-417. [UofR]

RR3214.   "Levi Strauss Going Public." *Asian Textile Journal*, 28, 4, 40. [WC]

RR3215.   Monin, M. A., V. A. Terekhova, & E. V. Ledeneva: "V. Y. Propp and C. Lévi-Strauss on the Myth and Folktale." *European Journal of Science and Theology*, 15, 3, 167-175. [WC]

RR3216.   Piguet, Raphaël: "Lévi-Strauss Révolutionnaire: Pour une Critique Structuraliste." *Contemporary French and Francophone Studies*, 23, 2, 188-197. [Naz]

RR3217.   Prado, Entretien J.: "'Dans la Gueule du Loup': Entretien avec Monique Lévi-Strauss. (Versão em Francês)." *Ponto Urbe*, 25. [WC]

RR3218.   Rouse, Carolyn M.: "Claude Lévi-Strauss's Contribution to the Race Question: *Race and History*." *American Anthropologist*, 121, 3, 721-4. [PrQ]

RR3219.   Saidah, Saidah: "The Myth of Sandekala in Novel Senjakala by Risa Saraswati Based on Lévi-Strauss' Structuralism Approach." *Aksis*, 3, 1, 209-218. [WC]

RR3220.   Santos, Josefa A. D. S.: "Da Observação Participante à Pesquisa de Campo - As Contribuições de Claude Lévi-Strauss para a Ciência Antropológica." *Revista Ibero-Americana de Humanidades, Ciências e Educação*, 5, 3. [WC]

RR3221.   Schlösser, Lioba: "Claude Lévi-Strauss (1908-2009), La Pensée Sauvage (1962)." *Kulturpoetik*, 19, 1, 179-185. [Naz]

RR3222.   Testenoire, Pierre-Yves: "Compléments à la Correspondance Jakobson - Lévi-Strauss." *Acta Structuralica*, 4, 2. [WC]

24179

RR3223. Thomas, Loer: "Lévi-Strauss. Eine Biographie." *Sozialer Sinn, 20,* 2, 389-411. [Cor]

RR3224. Xie, Jing: "From Mauss to Lévi-Strauss: 'Mana' and the Translatability of Practical Ideas." *She Hui, 39,* 5, 106-126. [UaB]

RR3225. Yamaguchi, Liesl: "Correspondances: La Couleur des Voyelles chez Lévi-Strauss, Jakobson, Rimbaud et Banville." *Parade Sauvage,* 30, 121-142. [UaB]

RR3226. Zerkowski, M.: "Claude Lévi-Strauss, Jacques Lacan and Sorcery." *Lud,* 103, 319-355. [Syr]

LÉVY, Bernard-Henri.

RR3227. ● Lévy, Bernard-Henri: *Looking for Europe =: Cercando L'Europa: Contro Il Montare dei Populismi.* Milano: La Nave di Teseo. 91p. [WC]

LIKING, Werewere.
See 352, 846, 878.

LILAR, Suzanne.
See also 698.

RR3228. Lenina, Nataliya: "'Grâce Poétique' et Œuvre d'Art: Méditations Phénoménologiques dans le Journal de l'Analogiste de Suzanne Lilar." *Interfaces,* 42, 73-98. [WC]

LIMBOUR, Georges.
See 658.

LITTELL, Jonathan.
See also 398, 457, 645, 652.

RR3229. ● Gries, Britta: *Der Holocaust in Deutschsprachigen Publizistischen Diskursen: Eine Sprachwissenschaftliche Analyse am Beispiel der Diskussion um den Roman 'Die Wohlgesinnten' von Jonathan Littell.* Bern: Peter Lang. 1 vol. [WC]

RR3230. ● Littell, Jonathan: *Les Récits de Fata Morgana: Etudes; Récit sur Rien; En Pièces; Une Vieille Histoire.* Paris: Gallimard. 230p. [BAnQ]

RR3231. Catani, Damian: "From Victims to Perpetrators: The Banality of Evil in Jonathan Littell's The Kindly Ones." *At the Interface/Probing the Boundaries,* 103, 7-30. [Naz]

RR3232. Martelli, M.: "The Image's Resistance. Text, Image and Event in Giorgio Vasta's Absolutely Nothing and Jonathan Littell's Carnets de Homs." *Studi Culturali, 16,* 2, 257-272. [WC]

RR3233. Oliveira, Rafael T.: "In the Belly of the Behemoth: A Study of Law and Nonlaw in the Context of 'The Kindly Ones', by Jonathan Littell." *Anamorphosis, 5,* 1, 277-316. [WC]

LOPES, Henri.
See also 81, 505.

RR3234. ● Diène, Babou, Modou F. Thiam, & Khadimou R. Thiam: *Henri Lopes, Une Écriture de Butinage: Pour une Approche Sociologique des Littératures Africaines.* Paris: L'Harmattan. 301p. [Cor]

RR3235. ● Nganga-Mienanzambi, Mathusalem: *Écriture et Intermédialité dans les Fictions Narratives de Henri Lopes*. Saarbrücken: Éditions Universitaires Européennes. 308p. [WC]

LORRAIN, Jean.
See also 34, 245, 465.
RR3236. ● Lorrain, Jean, & Angela Calaprice: *Colloquio Sentimentale e Altre Prose Inedite*. Pistoia: Via del Vento. 39p. [WC]
RR3237. Rickard, Mathew: "Jean Lorrain, Le Sang des Dieux: Poèmes. Établissement des Textes, Préface, Notes et Bibliographie par Alexandre Burin et Pascal Noir." *French Studies*, *73*, 2, 302-303. [UaB]

LOTI, Pierre.
See also 395.
RR3238. ● Fraile, Álex: *El Soñador Errante: De Viaje con Pierre Loti*. Madrid: La Linea del Horizonte. 247p. [WC]
RR3239. ● Loti, Pierre, Alain Quella-Villéger, & Bruno Vercier: *Loti en Oléron*. Saint-Pourçain-sur-Sioule: Bleu Autour. 246p. [BnF]
RR3240. ● Pradines, Stéphane, & Claude Stéfani: *La Collection d'Armes Orientales de Pierre Loti: [Exposition, Rochefort, Musée Hèbre, 23 Juin 2018-27 Avril 2019]*. Paris: Les Indes Savants. 157p. [LoC]
RR3241. ● Quella-Villéger, Alain: *Pierre Loti: Une Vie de Roman*. Paris: Calmann-Lévy. 435p. [BAnQ]
RR3242. ● Quella-Villéger, Alain, Bruno Vercier, & Pierre Loti: *Pierre Loti Dessinateur: Une Œuvre au Long Cours*. Saint-Pourçain-sur-Sioule: Bleu Autour. 289p. [BnF]
RR3243. ● Vercier, Bruno: *Pierre Loti*. La Crèche: Geste. 177p. [BnF]
RR3244. Donzelli, Xavier: "Pierre Loti, un Aspirant Écrivain au Pays des Moais." *Historia*, 867, 58-63. [BAnQ]
RR3245. Jones, Christa C.: "Pierre Loti." *French History*, *33*, 3, 484-485. [UofR]
RR3246. Kawakami, Akane: "Pierre Loti by Richard M. Berrong (Review)." *French Studies*, *73*, 4, 641. [UaB]

LOUIS-COMBET, Claude.
RR3247. ● Louis-Combet, Claude: *Marie Madeleine: Anthologie de Textes*. Grenoble: Millon. 181p. [WC]

LOUYS, Pierre.
See also 400.
RR3248. Lampela, Laurel: "Jeanne Mammen: Paris, Bruxelles, Berlin." *Studies in Art Education*, *60*, 1, 54-7. [RIT]

LUBAC, Henri de.
RR3249. ● Lubac, Henri, & Juan Costa: *Catolicismo: Aspectos Sociales del Dogma*. Madrid: Encuentro. 403p. [WC]
RR3250. ● Lubac, Henri, Denis Dupont-Fauville, & Georges Chantraine: *Les Églises Particulières dans l'Église Universelle*. Paris: Les Éditions du Cerf. 402p. [WC]

RR3251. ● Stern, Jean: *Le Lien Entre Catholicisme et Israël d'après le Cardinal Henri de Lubac.* Paris: L'Harmattan. 161p. [BnF]

RR3252. ● Wood, Jacob W.: *To Stir a Restless Heart: Thomas Aquinas and Henri de Lubac on Nature, Grace, and the Desire for God.* Washington, DC: The Catholic University of America Press. 472p. [Syr]

RR3253. ● Zwitter, Alek: *L'Histoire en Présence de l'Éternel: L'Eschatologie d'Henri de Lubac.* Paris: Les Éditions du Cerf. 379p. [BAnQ]

RR3254. Almeida, Antônio José: "O Que Está em Jogo Teologicamente no Debate sobre a Ordenação de Homens Casados?" *Horizonte, 17*, 53, 1120-69. [PrQ]

RR3255. Ferkolj, J.: "Love Towards God and the Church in the Life of Cardinal Henri de Lubac." *Bogoslovni Vestnik, 79*, 1, 105-114. [WC]

RR3256. Flynn, Gabriel: "The Church in a Pluralistic World: The Public Vision of Ressourcement." *Religions, 10*, 11. [RIT]

RR3257. Komonchak, J. A.: "Henri de Lubac et Le Concile Vatican II (1960-1965) by L. Figoureux." *Cristianesimo nella Storia, 40*, 3, 741-750. [Cor]

RR3258. Mikhaylov, Petr B.: "Henri de Lubac in the Theological Discussions about Religious and Religion at the Second Vatican Council." *Philosophy of Religion: Analytic Researches, 4*, 1, 72-89. [LoC]

RR3259. Prevot, Andrew: "T & T Clark Companion to Henri de Lubac, Edited by Jordan Hillebert." *Journal of Jesuit Studies, 6*, 3, 548-549. [Cor]

LUCA, Gherasim.
See also 379, 519.

RR3260. ● Martin, Serge, & Michel Scognamillo: *Ghérasim Luca: Tourbillon d'Être: [Exposition, Paris, Librairie Métamorphoses 21 Janvier-22 Février 2019].* Paris: Librairie Métamorphoses. 205p. [WC]

RR3261. ● Răileanu, Petre: *Gherasim Luca Poezie Ontofonie: Urmat de Gherasim Luca Este o Femeie.* Bucuresti: Tracus Arte. 315p. [WC]

RR3262. Clonts, Charlene: "'Le Funambule Apatride ou la Question du Rythme chez Gherasim Luca'." *Modern Languages Open*, 1. [WC]

RR3263. Lambert, C.: "Inflexions Politiques et Trajectoires Poétiques: Les Exils de Gherasim Luca et Radovan Ivsic." *Lettres Romanes, 73*, 3-4, 393-406. [UaB]

RR3264. Martin, Serge: "'Avec Ghérasim Luca (1913–1994), Extension du Domaine des Apatrides'." *Modern Languages Open*, 1. [WC]

RR3265. Tigirlas, L. C.: "Gherasim Luca - Son Double, Son Dé-Z'écroué." *Psychologie Clinique*, 48, 158-172. [WC]

LYOTARD, Jean-François.
See also 550, 760, 4729.

RR3266. ● Birnbaum, Daniel, & Sven-Olov Wallenstein: *Spacing Philosophy: Lyotard and the Idea of the Exhibition.* Berlin: Sternberg Press. 251p. [Cor]

RR3267. ● Boudinet, Gilles: *Un Art de l'Enfance. Lyotard et l'Éducation.* Paris: Hermann. 188p. [BnF]

RR3268. ● Vilar, Gerard: *Jean-François Lyotard: Estètica I Política.* Barcelona: Gedisa. 174p. [WC]

RR3269. Balibar, Étienne, & Walker Gavin: "Politics and Translation: Reflections on Lyotard, Derrida, and Said." *Positions, 27*, 1, 99-114. [UofR]

RR3270. Damião, Abraão P.: "A Condição Pós-Moderna de Jean-François Lyotard e Suas Consequências Epistemológicas." *Fênix*, *16*, 2. [Syr]

RR3271. Ionescu, Vlad: "Jean-François Lyotard." *The European Legacy*, *24*, 5, 574-577. [UofR]

RR3272. La Salvia, A. L.: "Sobre a Tradução de o Curso Filosófico, de Jean François Lyotard." *Revista Digital de Ensino de Filosofia – Refilo*, *4*, 2. [WC]

RR3273. Li, Elizabeth, & Katie Crabtree: "Listening for Kierkegaardian Echoes in Lyotard: The Paradox of Faith and Lyotard's Ethical Turn." *International Journal of Philosophy and Theology*, 80, 374-389. [UaB]

RR3274. Scheerlinck, Ryan: "Kiff Bamford: Jean-François Lyotard (Critical Lives), Reaktion Books, London, 2017, 176 S., 29 Abb." *Philosophische Rundschau*, *66*, 2, 188. [Syr]

RR3275. Trimçev, Rieke: "Kiff Bamford: Jean-François Lyotard." *Zeitschrift für Philosophische Literatur*, *7*, 1, 96-100. [WC]

RR3276. Woodward, Ashley: "Dispositif, Matter, Affect, and the Real: Four Fundamental Concepts of Lyotard's Film-Philosophy." *Film-Philosophy*, *23*, 3, 303-323. [Naz]

RR3277. Woodward, Ashley: "Lesson of Darkness: Phenomenology and Lyotard's Late Aesthetics." *Journal of the British Society for Phenomenology*, *50*, 2, 104-119. [UofR]

MAALOUF, Amin.
See also 209.

RR3278. Dakroub, Fida: "Étude Dialogique du Couple Orient/ Occident Chez Amin Maalouf." *French Review*, *92*, 3, 114-124. [Naz]

RR3279. El Jably, F.: "Les Origines et les Représentations de l'Immigration dans 'Les Désorientés' d'Amin Maalouf." *Les Cahiers du Centre des Études Doctorales*, *7*, 69-72. [WC]

RR3280. "Littérature Entretien Avec Amin Maalouf, Écrivain Franco-Libanais." *Jeune Afrique*, *59*, 3046, 82-86. [Syr]

MABANCKOU, Alain.
See also 229, 268, 287, 541, 548, 682.

RR3281. ● Mabanckou, Alain: *Huit Leçons sur l'Afrique*. Paris: Grasset. 217p. [UofR]

RR3282. Bokemper, Daniel: "Broken Glass." *World Literature Today*, *93*, 1, 78. [PrQ]

RR3283. Cacchioli, Emanuela: "Alain Mabanckou, Les Cigognes Sont Immortelles." *Studi Francesi*, *63*, 2, 402-403. [UaB]

RR3284. Idiatha, Wilfried, Aurélie Journo, Magali Nachtergael, & Josefina Bueno Alonso: "Nouvelles Expressivités Littéraires Pour l'Afrique Qui Vient: Alain Mabanckou et Léonora Miano." *Itinéraires*, 1. [WC]

RR3285. Kim, Yong H.: "Alain Mabanckou, Espace et Écriture dans Verre Cassé." *Société Coréenne d'Enseignement de Langue et Littérature Françaises*, 65, 69-93. [WC]

RR3286. Lyakhovskaya, Nina D.: "On the Path to Self-Discovery. New Meanings in the Novels of the Congolese Writer Alain Mabanckou 'Blue White Red' and 'Memoirs of a Porcupine'." *Vestnik of Kostroma State University*, 3, 127-132. [WC]

RR3287.   Mabanckou, Alain: "Our Guest: The Mobile Africas of Alain Mabanckou." *The Unesco Courier*, 2, 51-53. [UaB]

RR3288.   Ngetcham: "De l'Ici à l'ailleurs. De l'Écriture du Terroir à la Quête d'une Identité Pluriculturelle dans Le Ventre de l'Atlantique de Fatou Diome." *French Studies in Southern Africa*, 49, 181-202. [Cor]

RR3289.   Stern, Kristen: "Between France and Me: Ta-Nehisi Coates, Alain Mabanckou and Transatlantic Mis-Readings of Race." *Journal of the African Literature Association*, *13*, 2, 201-217. [Syr]

RR3290.   Toivanen, Anna-Leena: "Cartographies of Paris: Everyday Mobilities in Michèle Rakotoson's Elle, au Printemps and Alain Mabanckou's Tais-Toi et Meurs." *Journal of Urban Cultural Studies*, 6, 1, 59-78. [Naz]

RR3291.   Vurm, P.: "Verre Cassé by Alain Mabanckou in Search of a (Model) Reader." *Études Romanes de Brno*, *40*, 2, 159-167. [UofR]

MACÉ, Gérard.
See also 641.

RR3292.   ● *Gérard Macé: Écrivain et Colporteur*. Paris: Minuit. 96p. [BnF]

RR3293.   ● Macé, Gérard: *Et Je Vous Offre le Néant*. Paris: Gallimard. 141p. [Cor]

RR3294.   ● Macé, Gérard: *Le Goût de l'Homme*. Paris: Gallimard. 120p. [BAnQ]

RR3295.   Coste, C.: "Lire et Relire Gérard Macé." *Critique*, *870*, 11, 915-916. [UaB]

RR3296.   Coste, Claude: "Qui Dévore Qui? Gérard Macé, Le Goût de l'Homme." *Critique*, *870*, 11, 928-936. [UaB]

RR3297.   Coste, Claude, & Yves Hersant: "Gérard Macé: 'L'Imagination N'Est Pas l'Apanage des Romanciers'." *Critique*, *870*, 11, 957. [Syr]

RR3298.   Demanze, Laurent: "Pensées et Passages Baudelairiens Gérard Macé, Baudelaire." *Critique*, *870*, 11, 937-946. [UaB]

RR3299.   Ferrini, Jean-Pierre: "Poésies de Gérard Macé." *Quinzaines*, 1208, 20-21. [Syr]

RR3300.   Kim, Hyeona: "La Figuration de la Photo Mentale dans la Photographie Sans Appareil de Gerard Mace." *Études de Langue et Littérature Françaises*, 119, 81-104. [WC]

RR3301.   Lapeyre, Chantal: "Le Baroque Sans le Nom Gérard Macé, Rome Éphémère." *Critique*, 75, 870, 947-956. [UofR]

RR3302.   Macé, Gérard: "Comment Devenir William Kentridge." *Les Cahiers du Musée National d'Art Moderne / Centre Georges Pompidou*, 146, 3-7. [BnF]

RR3303.   "Présentation: Lire et Relire Gérard Macé." *Critique*, *870*, 11, 915-916. [UaB]

RR3304.   Romagné, Thierry: "Gérard Macé Colportage." *Quinzaines*, 1209, 3. [Syr]

RR3305.   Romagné, Thierry: "Gérard Macé et Je Vous Offre le Néant." *Quinzaines*, 1222, 21. [Syr]

MAC ORLAN, Pierre.
See also 357.

RR3306.   *Lectures de Mac Orlan, Vol. 7. Mac Orlan Critique Littéraire*. Paris: Le Bretteur. 207p. [WC]

MAETERLINCK, Maurice.
See also 850, 852.
RR3307.   Avram, Cristi: "Pelléas and Mélisande – Maurice Maeterlinck and the Opera Performance. 2018 Retrospective." *Theatrical Colloquia*, 9, 1, 163-171. [Naz]
RR3308.   Bondaruk, L. V.: "Author's Methods of Symbolic Image Reproduction in the Dramatic Text: Lesya Ukrainka/ Maurice Maeterlinck." *Scientific Notes of Taurida National V. I. Vernadsky University, Series Philology. Social Communications*, 3, 2, 155-159. [WC]
RR3309.   Czerska, Karolina: "La Marionnette et le Mannequin à la Lisière de la Mort: Kantor, Ghelderode, Maeterlinck." *Synergies Pologne*, 16, 43, 54, 148. [PrQ]
RR3310.   De Vos, J.: "Nicolas Maeterlinck & André Capiteyn, Maurice Maeterlinck. Wonen in Dromen." *Documenta*, 30, 1, 69-70. [WC]
RR3311.   Dubois, Françoise Paulet: "Regards, Frayeurs et Points de Suspension dans L'Oiseau Bleu de Maurice Maeterlinck." *Anales de Filología Francesa*, 27, 533-53. [RIT]
RR3312.   Emery, Elizabeth: "'Un Déjeuner Avec M. Maeterlinck': Intermedial Experimentation in Adolphe Brisson's *Portraits Intimes*." *Esprit Créateur*, 59, 1, 95-110. [UofR]
RR3313.   Engelberts, Matthijs: "Christian Janssens, Maurice Maeterlinck, Un Auteur dans le Cinéma des Années Dix et Vingt. Berne: Peter Lang, 2016." *Relief*, 13, 2, 94. [Syr]
RR3314.   Friede, Susanne: "Écriture(s) du Fantastique dans le Drame Symboliste. Le 'Premier Théâtre' de Maurice Maeterlinck." *Archiv Für das Studium Der Neueren Sprachen Und Literaturen*, 2. [UaB]
RR3315.   Valke, S. S.: "Post-Symbolist Irony on the Latvian Stage: The Staging of Van Charles Lerberghe's Pan and Maurice Maeterlinck's Le Miracle de Saint Antoine." *Forum for World Literature Studies*, 11, 1, 63-80. [Naz]

MAILLET, Antonine.
See also 196.
RR3316.   Greco, M. C.: "La Réécriture, ou Renverser la Perspective: Évangéline Deusse d'Antonine Maillet." *Studies in Canadian Literature*, 44, 2, 157-177. [UaB]

MAKINE, Andreï.
See also 276.
RR3317.   Obergöker, Timo: "Makine, Un Postmoderne Face à l'Histoire World War II in Andreï Makine's Historiographic Metafiction. 'No One Is Forgotten, Nothing Is Forgotten', par Helena Duffy, Brill, Leiden–Boston 2018." *Romanica Wratislaviensia*, 66, 210-211. [LoC]
RR3318.   Pirvu, S.: "The Nostalgia of the Place of Birth in Andreï Makine's The French Will and in Sorin Titel's The Aloof Country." *Swedish Journal of Romanian Studies*, 2, 1, 34-41. [WC]

MALAQUAIS, Jean.
RR3319.   Godard, Henri: "Jean Malaquais, Une Étoile Filante de la Littérature." *Revue Italienne d'Études Françaises*, 6. [Syr]

MALET, Léo.
See also 475.
RR3320.   ● Barral, Nicolas: *Corrida auf den Champs-Élysées: Nach Dem Roman Von Léo Malet und den Figuren von Tardi*. [Hamburg]: Schreiber & Leser. 96p. [WC]
RR3321.   ● Marmin, Michel: *Où Nestor Burma Rencontre l'Aristo. Avec Deux Collages Inédits de Léo Malet et une Acrylique Originale de Pascal Marmin*. Toulouse: Auda Isarn. 101p. [WC]

MALLARMÉ, Stéphane.
See also 534, 552, 793, 806, 808, 852, 986, 3381.
RR3322.   ● Badiou, Alain, Philippe Lacoue-Labarthe, & Jacques Rancière: *Mallarmé, das Theater, der Stamm*. Wien: Passagen. 67p. [WC]
RR3323.   ● Bohac, Barbara, & Pascal Durand: *Mallarmé au Monde: Le Spectacle de la Matière*. Paris: Hermann. 304p. [Cor]
RR3324.   ● *Mallarmé et Tournon, 1863-2013*. Tournon-sur-Rhône: Sauvegarde du Patrimoine du Lycée Gabriel Faure. 103p. [BnF]
RR3325.   ● Milner, Jean-Claude: *Profils Perdus de Stéphane Mallarmé*. Lagrasse: Verdier. 135p. [BAnQ]
RR3326.   ● Ricardou, Jean, & Erica Freiberg: *'Salut'Aux Quatre Coins: Mallarmé à la Loupe*. [Bruxelles]: Les Impressions Nouvelles. 476p. [WC]
RR3327.   Ardrey, Caroline: "Book Review: Le Double Discours de Mallarmé: Une Initiation à la Fiction." *Modern Language Review*, *114*, 1, 147-148. [Naz]
RR3328.   Bellocq, S.: "Sartre's Lecture on Mallarmé: Critic Poetry as Pure Negation." *Contrastes*, *24*, 3, 7-23. [WC]
RR3329.   Castillo, Nicolas A.: "Imagination, Intellect et Espace dans le 'Coup de dés' de Mallarmé." *Australian Journal of French Studies*, *56*, 3. [RIT]
RR3330.   Dubois, Alexandre: "La Poésie Délivrée: Le Livre en Question du Parnasse à Mallarmé. Par Nicolas Valazza." *French Studies*, *73*, 4, 638-639. [UofR]
RR3331.   Ettlin, Annick: "La Religion de Mallarmé. Nouvelle Édition Revue et Corrigée, par Bertrand Marchal." *French Studies*, *73*, 4, 639-640. [UofR]
RR3332.   Gotman, Kélina: "Mallarmé's 'Livre': Notes Towards a Schizotheatre." *Textual Practice*, *33*, 1, 175-194. [RIT]
RR3333.   Guilhen, Ellen: "Mallarmé Redivivo Em Eduardo Guimaraens." *Revista Texto Poético*, *15*, 28, 338. [WC]
RR3334.   Hempfer, K. W.: "Differentiating 'Lyric Poetry' and 'Poetry of Circumstance': Mallarmé as Paradigm." *Zeitschrift fur Franzosische Sprache und Literatur*, *128*, 23, 187-211. [UofR]
RR3335.   Hopkins John, Arnold Falcon: "From Shipwreck to Constellation: Rethinking Meillassoux on Mallarmé from a Semiotic Perspective." *Semiotica*, 231, 57-86. [PrQ]
RR3336.   Illouz, Jean-Nicolas: "Mallarmé, Une Poétique du Don (À Propos des 'Loisirs de la Poste' et Autres 'Récréations Postales')." *Revista Texto Poético*, *15*, 28, 168. [WC]

RR3337.   Illouz, Jean-Nicolas: "Un Poème Typo-Litho-Graphique: Mallarmé, Redon, Un Coup de Dés." *Romantisme*, *184*, 2, 21. [UaB]

RR3338.   Kenny, Thomas J.: "The Image of Mallarmé in 'Scylla and Charybdis'." *Joyce Studies Annual*, 2019, 241-245. [Naz]

RR3339.   Lubecker, Nikolaj: "Mallarmé's Instruments: The Production of the Individu-Livre." *French Studies*, *73*, 3, 367-383. [UaB]

RR3340.   Lukes, Alexandra: "Dictionary and Divination: Mallarmé Translating, Back-Translating, and Not Translating." *MLN*, *134*, 4, 745-763. [Naz]

RR3341.   Merello, Ida: "Nicolas Valazza, la Poésie Délivrée. Le Livre en Question du Parnasse à Mallarmé." *Studi Francesi*, 188 (*63*, 2), 379. [UofR]

RR3342.   Micaelia, Caroline: "A Poesia de Mallarmé Encontra a Pintura de Manet." *Revista Criação & Crítica*, 25, 48-67. [WC]

RR3343.   Raffi, Maria Emanuela: "Mallarmé à Tournon et Au-Delà, Sous la Direction de Gordon Millan." *Studi Francesi*, *187*, 182-183. [UaB]

RR3344.   Scott, David: "The Madness of Translating Mallarmé." *Translation Studies*, *12*, 1, 36-46. [UaB]

RR3345.   Souchard, Flora: "Le Souffle d'une Aile: Poétiques de l'Éventail Chez Mallarmé et Claudel." *Romantisme*, *184*, 2, 116. [Cor]

RR3346.   Stroparo, Sandra M.: "Endereçamento e Epistolaridade: Poesia e Circunstância em Mallarmé." *Caligrama*, *24*, 1, 111. [Syr]

RR3347.   Urbano, Karolina: "Martínez y Mallarmé: El Libro Total en la Nueva Novela." *Revista Anales*, *1*, 376, 393-408. [WC]

RR3348.   Varley-Winter, R.: "Colouring Écriture Féminine in Peter Manson's Translations of Mallarmé." *Journal of British and Irish Innovative Poetry*, 11, 1. [UaB]

RR3349.   Villalobos, Alberto: "Los Golpes de Dados de Nietzsche y Mallarmé." *Logos Revista de Filosofía*, 133, 81-98. [Cor]

RR3350.   Wehle, Winfried: "Au Seuil d'une Éthique de la Jouissance Mentale: Mallarmé, Un Coup de Dés." *Revue d'Histoire Littéraire de la France*, *119*, 4, 851-864. [RIT]

RR3351.   Werth, Margaret. "Mallarmé and Impressionism in 1876." *Nonsite*, 27. [PrQ]

MALLET-JORIS, Françoise.

RR3352.   Bizek-Tatara, Renata: "Difficulté de Se Dire. Sur l'Écriture Autobiographique de Françoise Mallet-Joris." *Anales de Filología Francesa*, *27*, 1, 7-22. [Naz]

RR3353.   Bizek-Tatara, Renata: "Du Récit de l'Autre au Récit de Soi. La Double Confidence de Françoise Mallet-Joris." *Cahiers Erta*, *20*, 20, 85-98. [WC]

MALOT, Hector.

RR3354.   ● Delahaye, Christa, & Jean-Paul Delahaye: *Hector Malot, l'Écrivain Instituteur*. Arras: Artois Presses Université. 199p. [WC]

RR3355.   ● Frayssinet, Sylvie: *Sans Famille: Guide Pédagogique*. Paris: Belin Education. 40p. [WC]

RR3356.   Berutu, Duma L.: "L'Autoritarisme et la Liberté Positive de Personnage Principal dans le Roman Sans Famille d'Hector Malot (une Étude Psychologie d'Erich Fromm)." *Lingua Litteratia Journal*, 6, 1, 1-6. [WC]

RR3357.   Compoint, Hélène: "Fictions d'Être Orphelin au Cours de la Phase de Latence. Les Trois Brigands, Harry Potter, Sans Famille." *Cliniques Méditerra-néennes*, *99*, 1, 111. [WC]

RR3358.   Pouliot, Suzanne: "Cahiers Robinson by Hector Malot (Review)." *Nouvelles Études Francophones*, *34*, 2, 215-218. [UaB]

MALRAUX, André.
See also 371, 523, 2554.

RR3359.   ● Aubert, Stéphane, Pierre-Alain Weydert, Filippo Passadore, & Mathilde Neuve-Eglise: *La Collection Intime d'André Malraux: Vente, Paris, Artcurial, Mercredi 19 Juin 2019*. Paris: Artcurial. 92p. [WC]

RR3360.   ● Marion, Hervé: *Malraux et le Samouraï*. Paris: Magellan. 126p. [Cor]

RR3361.   Bordignon, Giulia: "Walter Grasskamp, The Book on the Floor: André Malraux and the Imaginary Museum. Los Angeles: Getty Publications, 2016. pp. 232. US $45.00 (Cloth)." *History of Humanities*, *4*, 1, 204-207. [UaB]

RR3362.   Cambon, Pierre: "Maitreya, le Buddha à Venir, le 'Génie Gothico-Bouddhique' d'André Malraux." *La Revue des Musées de France*, 4, 99-109, 116, 118. [WC]

RR3363.   Real López, I.: "El Musée d'Art Moderne André Malraux: El Museo-Tipo de la Modernidad Francesa." *Diferents. Revista de Museus*, 4, 84-97. [WC]

MAN, Paul de.
See also 417, 420, 424, 572, 577, 715, 868.

RR3364.   Bókay, Antal: "The Lyric and Its Reading – Paul de Man's Theory of Lyric." *Transcultural Studies*, *15*, 1, 72-80. [Syr]

RR3365.   Cometa, Michele: "Incomprensibilità e Ironia. Filosofia e Lettera-tura in Friedrich Schlegel e Paul de Man." *Rivista di Estetica*, 70, 31-48. [UaB]

MANCHETTE, Jean-Patrick.
See also 689, 1927.

RR3366.   ● Cabanes, Max, Doug Headline, & Jean-Patrick Manchette: *Nada: Nach Einem Roman Von Jean-Patrick Manchette*. Bielefeld: Splitter 10. 187p. [WC]

MARCEL, Gabriel.
See also 60, 761, 839.

RR3367.   ● Marcel, Gabriel, Brendan Sweetman, Maria Traub, & Geoffrey Karabin: *The Invisible Threshold: Two Plays by Gabriel Marcel*. South Bend, IN: St. Augustine's Press. 265p. [UofR]

RR3368.   ● Mathei, Peter, & Robert Spaemann: *Leben Sie Wohl, Lieber Pfarrer!: Philosoph Robert Spaemann, Pfarrer Peter Mathei - Briefe 1980-2017: Mit 13 Briefen Zum Thema Hoffnung Bei Gabriel Marcel und Ernst Bloch*. Zug: Österreichische Literaturgesellschaft. 222p. [WC]

RR3369.   De Freitas, S. C. A.: "Gabriel Marcel, Nietzsche e o Niilismo." *Princípios*, *26*, 50, 397-402. [Cor]

RR3370.   "Homo Viator vs. Rooted Human in the Catholic Existentialism of Gabriel Marcel." *Scientific Yearbook 'History of Religions in Ukraine'*, 29, 85-94. [WC]

RR3371.   Ramírez, Agudelo y. A.: "Del Problema de la Muerte al Misterio de la Muerte en Gabriel Marcel." *Daímon*, 76, 189-204. [Naz]

RR3372.   Silva, Ezir G.: "Compêndio Gabriel Marcel: Homenagem aos 90 Anos de Publicação do Diário Metafísico." *Princípios*, 26, 50, 403-415. [Cor]

RR3373.   Stryzhyk, Ihor: "Gabriel Marcel's Notion of Incarnate Being: The Anthropology of the Body as a Zone between Matter and Spirit." *Visnyk of the Lviv University Series Philosophical Sciences*, 23, 59-68. [WC]

RR3374.   Tunstall, Dwayne A.: "Book Review: Gabriel Marcel and American Philosophy: The Religious Dimension of Experience." *American Journal of Theology & Philosophy*, 40, 1, 75-79. [Naz]

MARIN, Louis.
See also 380, 477, 500, 516.

RR3375.   ● Marin, Louis, & Pierre-Antoine Fabre: *La Traversée des Signes*. Paris: Éditions de l'École des Hautes Études en Sciences Sociales. 94p. [LoC]

RR3376.   Marie-Castanet, Cécile: "A Force de Signes: Travailler Avec Louis Marin (sous la Dir. d'Alain Cantillon, Pierre Antoine Fabre, Bertrand Rougé)." *Critique d'Art*, 13 juin. [Cor]

RR3377.   Vizzini, Giuseppe: "La Lecture de Louis Marin des Fables de la Fontaine et des Contes de Perrault. La Prise de Parole du Faible Comme Subversion du Pouvoir Politique." *Trans-*, 30 novembre. [Syr]

MARINETTI, Filippo Tommasso.
See also 554, 578.

RR3378.   ● Agnese, Gino: *Marinetti/ Majakovskij: 1925. I Segreti di un Incontro*. Soveria Mannelli: Rubbettino. 110p. [Cor]

RR3379.   ● Pautassi, Armando, & Severina Javelli: *Severina Javelli: Lettere, 1890-1914: Marinetti, Massenet, Scarfoglio, Perivier, Ojetti, gli Uomini di una Vita tra l'Amore e il Bel Canto*. Boves: ArabAFenice. 231p. [WC]

RR3380.   ● Viviani, Alberto, Burali D. A. P. Perrone, Umberto L. Ronco, & Filippo T. Marinetti: *Volando Con Balbo e Marinetti: Anni Trenta: Aeropittura Nuovo Balzo in Avanti del Futurismo*. Milano: Nuove Edizioni Culturali Milano Museo del Futurismo Alberto Viviani Burali. 158p. [WC]

RR3381.   Borra, Antonello: "Giuseppe Gazzola (A Cura Di). Mallarmé. Versi e Prose. Traduzione Italiana di F. T. Marinetti. Seconda Stesura Inedita." *Italica*, 96, 2, 368-369. [UaB]

RR3382.   Capello, Francesco: "La Mente Orale. 'Città di Carne', Fusionalità e Cannibalismo nella Poesia del Primo Marinetti." *Annali d'Italianistica*, 37, 411-450. [Naz]

RR3383.   De Aldama, O. C.: "1936. La Pluma y la Espada. Marinetti, Puccini y Ungaretti en el Pen Club Argentino." *Anuario de Estudios Americanos*, 76, 1, 329. [Naz]

RR3384.   Ialongo, Ernest: "Filippo Tommaso Marinetti and Fascist Italy's Racial Turn: Accomodating the Regime and Legitimating Persecution." *Visual History*, 4, 113-134. [WC]

RR3385.   Metlić, Dijana: "Zenitist Cinema: Influences of Marinetti and May-akovsky." *International Yearbook of Futurism Studies*, 9, 236-268. [WC]

RR3386.   Pernice, Vincenzo: "Mafarka Il Futurista Come Romanzo Italiano dell'Avvenire. F. T. Marinetti e il Grande Concorso di Poesia." *E-scripta Romanica*, 7, 52-59. [Cor]

RR3387.   Tobin, Jordan: "Marinetti's Visit to Russia in 1914: Reportage in Russia and in Italy." *International Yearbook of Futurism Studies*, 9, 3-34. [WC]

RR3388.   Tutupary, Victor D.: "Manifesto Futurisme Filippo Tommaso Marinetti Dan Progresivisme Agresif Dalam Sejarah." *Dialektika*, *12*, 2, 158. [LoC]

RR3389.   Watine, Marie-Albane, Ilias Yocaris, & Barbara Meazzi: "Stefano Bragato, Futurismo in Nota. Studio sui Taccuini di Marinetti." *Cahiers de Narratologie*, 35. [Naz]

MARION, Jean-Luc.
See also 724, 2736.

RR3390.   ● Bonfand, Alain, Jean-Luc Marion, & Paul Klee: *Paul Klee, l'Œil en Trop*. Paris: J. Vrin. 202p. [BnF]

RR3391.   ● Kearney, Richard, René Dausner, John Caputo, Simon Critchley, Catherine Keller, Julia Kristeva, Jean-Luc Marion, Charles Taylor, David Tracy, Gianni Vattimo, Merold Westphal, James Wood, Jens Zimmermann, & Karl Pichler: *Revisionen des Heiligen: Streitgespräche zur Gottesfrage*. Wien: Herder. 340p. [WC]

RR3392.   ● Marion, Jean-Luc, & Salvatore Abbruzzese: *Breve Apologia per un Momento Cattolico*. Brescia: Scholé. 153p. [WC]

RR3393.   ● Pirktina, Lasma: *Das Ereignis: Martin Heidegger, Emmanuel Levinas, Jean-Luc Marion*. München: Karl Alber. 500p. [Cor]

RR3394.   ● Vinolo, Stéphane: *Jean-Luc Marion, Apologie de l'Inexistence*. Paris: L'Harmattan. 2 vols. [Cor]

RR3395.   Barreto, Marco H.: "Sobre a Natureza do Argumento de Anselmo. Uma Crítica à Interpretação de Jean-Luc Marion." *Síntese: Revista de Filosofia*, *46*, 145, 141. [UaB]

RR3396.   Benjamins, Jacob: "Are We Living in an Era of Nihilism? Jean-Luc Marion and Reading the Signs of the Times." *Literature and Theology*, *33*, 4, 476-491. [UofR]

RR3397.   Brower, Virgil W.: "Advent of Auto-Affection: Possibility, Givenness and Reception in Jean-Luc Marion." *Auc Theologica*, *9*, 1, 31-44. [Syr]

RR3398.   García, Labrador J., & Stéphane Vinolo: "Hannah Arendt y Jean-Luc Marion. El Acontecimiento y los Márgenes de la Metafísica." *Tópicos, Revista de Filosofía*, 57, 207-234. [Syr]

RR3399.   Grinfelde, M.: "Illness as the Saturated Phenomenon: The Contribution of Jean-Luc Marion." *Medicine, Health Care, and Philosophy*, *22*, 1, 71-83. [Naz]

RR3400.   Jan Gresil S. Kahambing: "Jean-Luc Marion's Phenomenology of the Icon as an Apologia for Quiapo's Black Nazarene Traslacíon." *Prajña Vihara*, *20*, 2, 13. [RIT]

RR3401.   Katz, A.: "Jean-Luc Marion: ¿Fenomenólogo?" *Arete*, *31*, 2, 377-395. [Syr]

RR3402.   Kim, Dong-Kyu: "Revelation and Knowledge in Jean-Luc Marion's Phenomenology: A Phenomenological-Epistemic Approach to Revelation and Its Hermeneutical Problem." *Study of Humanities*, 31, 341-374. [WC]

RR3403.   Kondyuk, Denis: "Jean-Luc Marion. L'Égo ou l'Adonne." *Theological Reflections: Euro-Asian Journal of Theology*, 23, 159-160. [WC]

RR3404.   Moati, Raoul: "Jean-Luc Marion. On Descartes' Passive Thought:

The Myth of Cartesian Dualism. Trans. Christina M. Gschwandtner. Chicago: University of Chicago Press, 2018. 304 pp." *Critical Inquiry*, *45*, 4, 992-994. [UofR]

RR3405.   Ocampo, Fernanda: "Ser, Esencia y Atributos Divinos: El Conocimiento de Dios en la Metafísica Tomasiana Según la Interpretación de Jean-Luc Marion." *Areté*, *31*, 1, 155-190. [Syr]

RR3406.   Oltvai, K.: "Another Name for Liberty: Revelation, 'Objectivity,' and Intellectual Freedom in Barth and Marion." *Open Theology*, *5*, 1, 430-450. [Cor]

RR3407.   Pizzi, Matías I.: "Roggero, J-L. (ed.), Jean Luc Marion. Límites y Posibilidades de la Filosofía y de la Teología, Buenos Aires, Sb Editorial, 2017, 231 pp." *Tópicos. Revista de Filosofía de Santa Fe*, 37, 187-192. [Naz]

RR3408.   Roggero, Jorge: "El Problema de la Donación En la Fenomenología de J.-L. Marion." *Areté*, *31*, 1, 191-215. [Syr]

RR3409.   Şandru, Adrian R.: "The Trinitarian Manifestation of God in Jean-Luc Marion's Phenomenology." *Contributions to Phenomenology*, 103, 245-256. [Cor]

RR3410.   Teixeira, William D. J.: "As Naturezas Simples e a Metafísica Cartesiana: Uma Crítica a Jean-Luc Marion." *Cadernos Espinosanos*, 41, 321-338. [LoC]

RR3411.   Van Ruler, H.: "Descartes for Philosophers: Review of Jean-Luc Marion's on Descartes' Passive Thought: The Myth of Cartesian Dualism." *Graduate Faculty Philosophy Journal*, *40*, 1, 211-224. [UaB]

RR3412.   Vinolo, S.: "Contemporary Subjectivations: Alain Badiou and Jean-Luc Marion." *Eidos*, 31, 252-279. [Naz]

MARITAIN, Jacques.
See also 371, 723, 3419.
RR3413.   ● Maritain, Jacques, & Florian Michel: *L'Engagement Chrétien: Pour le Bien Commun; Lettre Sur l'Indépendance*. Paris: Salvator. 104p. [BAnQ]

RR3414.   ● Miclea, Ioan: *Jacques Maritain: Vol. 2*. Baia Mare: Surorilor Lauretane. 623p. [WC]

RR3415.   ● Pinna, Samuele, & Sergio Ubbiali: *Il Mistero di Dio e l'Abisso del Male: Charles Journet e Jacques Maritain Alla Scuola di San Tommaso d'Aquino*. Roma: Ateneo Pontificio Regina Apostolorum: If Press. 398p. [LoC]

RR3416.   ● *Souvenir de Pierre Villard: Carnet de Jacques Maritain: Journal de 1935*. Evry: Cercle d'Études Jacques et Raïssa Maritain. *Cahiers Jacques Maritain*, 78. 112p. [WC]

RR3417.   De Souza, R. L.: "The Ideas of Jacques Maritain and Emmanuel Mounier on the Brazilian Catholic Field and the Liberation Education of Paulo Freire." *Revista Brasileira de Historia*, *39*, 82, 177-198. [Syr]

RR3418.   Taylor, Patrick O'Neill: "Jacques Maritain and Reginald Garrigou-Lagrange on the Permission of Evil." *Heythrop Journal*, *60*, 5, 699-710. [PrQ]

MARITAIN, Raïssa.
See also 730.
RR3419.   Hikota, Riyako C.: "The Wisdom of Youth: Essays Inspired by the Early Works of Jacques and Raïssa Maritain, Travis Dumsday (ed.), Catholic University of America Press, 2016 (ISBN 978-0-9827119-8-9), xviii + 355 pp., Pb $36.95." *Reviews in Religion & Theology*, *26*, 3, 415-418. [UofR]

RR3420.   Lamb, Matthew L.: "Theological Indebtedness to Jacques and Raïssa

Maritain: A Testimony to Their Contribution to My Theological Vocation." *Nova et Vetera*, *17*, 3, 617-623. [Syr]

MARLEAU, Denis.
See also 859.
RR3421.   Popovic, Pierre: "L'Album du Théâtre Ubu. Mises en Scène de Denis Marleau, 1982-1994." *Theatre Research in Canada*, *17*, 1. [Naz]

MAROH, Julie.
See 354.

MARS, Kettly.
See also 876.
RR3422.   ● Mars, Kettly, & Ingeborg Schmutte: *Der Engel des Patriarchen*. Trier: Litradukt. 252p. [WC]
RR3423.   Alcott, Linda S.: "Hidden in Plain Sight: Post-Quake Portraits of the Disenfranchised in the Writings of Emmelie Prophéte and Kettly Mars." *Women in French Studies*, 27, 20-33. [UaB]

MARTEAU, Robert.
RR3424.   ● Casanòva, Joan-Ives: *Robert Marteau: Mesure du Ciel et de la Terre*. Paris: Éditions Léo Scheer. 298p. [LoC]
RR3425.   Gugelot, Frédéric, Cécile Vanderpelen-Diagre, Denis Saint-Jacques, & Gérard Fabre: "Robert Marteau ou la Résistance Catholique en Poésie." *Contextes*, 23. [Syr]

MARTIN DU GARD, Roger.
See also 357, 699.
RR3426.   Baty-Delalande, H.: "Comment Se Désintéresser? Roger Martin du Gard et les 'Petites Histoires' du Romancier." *Romanic Review*, *109*, 1-4, 245-258. [UofR]

MASPERO, François.
See 317, 413.

MATZNEFF, Gabriel.
See also 8.
RR3427.   ● Matzneff, Gabriel: *L'Amante de l'Arsenal. Journal 2016-2018*. Paris: Gallimard. 432p. [Cor]
RR3428.   Legraverand, Anne: "Gabriel Matzneff ou l'Inévitable Échec de Pygmalion." *Le Journal des Psychologues*, *368*, 6, 72. [BAnQ]

MAUCLAIR, Camille.
See also 523.

MAULPOIX, Jean-Michel.
See 29, 799, 806, 2306.

MAUPASSANT, Guy de.
See also 4099.

RR3429.   Bashkirova, K. A., & G. I. Galeeva: "Linguopsychological Analysis of the Characters of Guy de Maupassant on the Example of Short Story 'Pierrot'." *Journal of Research in Applied Linguistics*, 10, 732-739. [WC]

RR3430.   Benhamou, Noelle: "La Prostitution dans la Poésie de Guy de Maupassant: Genèse d'Une Notion Clé de l'Œuvre en Prose." *Anales de Filología Francesa*, 27, 403-17. [PrQ]

RR3431.   Bordeleau-Pitre, Émile: "M. Caravan ou l'Homme-Pendule: L'Oppression de la Ligne et de la Lettre dans En Famille de Maupassant." *Captures*, 2, 2. [WC]

RR3432.   Canavan, Brendan: "Tourism-in-literature: Existential Comfort, Confrontation and Catastrophe in Guy de Maupassant's Short Stories." *Annals of Tourism Research*, 78. [RIT]

RR3433.   Chouiten, L.: "Colonial Conflict in Maupassant's Mes Voyages en Algérie." *Nineteenth Century Prose*, 46, 2, 71-92. [Naz]

RR3434.   Färnlöf, Hans: "Enjeux de l'Espace — Lecture Croisée de la Fenêtre et du Signe de Maupassant." *Annales Littéraires de L'université de Besançon*, 999, 71-84.[WC]

RR3435.   Färnlöf, Hans: "L'Essence ou les Sens d'un Thème? Étude de la Femme Combattante dans Quelques Nouvelles de Maupassant." *Romantisme*, 184, 2, 106. [Cor]

RR3436.   Farsian, M. R., & S. N. Alavi: "Emotionalization of Words in the Story of Horla by Guy de Maupassant." *Language Related Research*, 10, 2, 123-145. [WC]

RR3437.   Francesco, Bono: "Bel-Ami from the Page to Film—Notes on the First Transposition of Maupassant's Novel to the Screen." *Journal of Literature and Art Studies*, 9, 10. [LoC]

RR3438.   Horne, Philip: "Strings of Pearls: James, Maupassant, and 'Paste'." *Literary Imagination*, 21, 2, 137-157. [UaB]

RR3439.   Indriyanto, Kristiawan: "The Comparative Analysis of Guy de Maupassant's Two Friends and Arturo Arias' Toward Patzun." *Lire Journal*, 3, 1, 53-59. [WC]

RR3440.   Sai, B. S., & P. S. Reddy: "Somerset Maugham: Emulating Maupassant's Pursuit of the Truth." *Language in India*, 19, 2, 482. [PrQ]

RR3441.   Scuro, Giulia: "Noëlle Benhamou, Dossier Guy de Maupassant. Clinique de Passy 1892-1893." *Studi Francesi*, 188 (*63*, 2), 383-384. [UaB]

RR3442.   White, Nicholas: "Between Men and Women: Making Friends in Guy de Maupassant's Bel-Ami." *Romanic Review*, 110, 1-4, 203-21. [PrQ]

RR3443.   Yadav, Shubham: "Character Analysis of 'Mathilde Loisel' in the Maupassant's 'The Necklace'." *International Journal of English Literature and Social Sciences*, 4, 3, 647-649. [WC]

MAURIAC, Claude.
See 662, 705.

MAURIAC, François.
See also 537.

RR3444.　● Casseville, Caroline, & Jean Touzot: *Dictionnaire François Mauriac*. Paris: Honoré Champion. 1204p. [Cor]

RR3445.　● Mauriac, François: *Bordeaux, Une Enfance Provinciale*. Bègles (Gironde): L'Esprit du Temps. 61p. [BnF]

RR3446.　Delbrel, Yann: "L'Écriture Contre les Excès de l'Épuration: La 'Vraie Justice' dans les Chroniques de François Mauriac (1944-1946)." *Revue Droit & Littérature*, 3, 1, 285. [BnF]

RR3447.　Flower, John: "Book Review: Caroline Casseville and Jean Touzot (eds): Dictionnaire François Mauriac." *Journal of European Studies*, 49, 3-4, 499-501. [UofR]

RR3448.　Lewallen, Jason: "Interpreting Conversion: Hermeneutic Training in François Mauriac's Le Nœud de Vipères." *Christianity & Literature*, 68, 2, 213-232. [Naz]

MAURRAS, Charles.
See also 98, 364, 383, 776,

RR3449.　● Dard, Olivier: *Charles Maurras: Le Nationalisme Intégral*. Malakoff (Hauts-de-Seine): Dunod. 376p. [BnF]

RR3450.　● Tisserand, Axel: *Actualité de Charles Maurras: Introduction à Une Philosophie Politique Pour Notre Temps*. Paris: Pierre Téqui. 453p. [Cor]

RR3451.　Fillon, Catherine: "Le Procès de Charles Maurras (24-27 Janvier 1945)." *Histoire de la Justice*, 29, 1, 315. [WC]

RR3452.　Molodiakov, Vasili E.: "Charles Maurras, 'Action Française' and the Problem of War and Peace in Europe: From the 'Anschluss' of Austria Up to Nazi Invasion into Poland." *Almanac 'Essays on Conservatism,'* 60, 374-388. [WC]

MAUSS, Marcel.
See also 729, 3224.

RR3453.　● Caillé, Alain: *Extensions du Domaine du Don: Demander, Donner, Recevoir, Rendre: Essai*. [Arles]: Actes Sud. 329p. [BAnQ]

RR3454.　● Mallard, Grégoire: *Gift Exchange: The Transnational History of a Political Idea*. Cambridge: Cambridge UP. 293p. [Cor]

RR3455.　Godelier, Maurice: "Acerca de Las Cosas Que Se Dan, de las Cosas Que Se Venden y de las Que No Hay Que Vender Ni Dar Sino Que Hay Que Guardar. Una Reevaluación Crítica del Ensayo Sobre el Don de Marcel Mauss." *Hispania*, 60, 204, 11. [Syr]

RR3456.　Pelletier, Caroline, Vasiliki Chrysikou, Will Gibson, Sophie Park, & Fiona Stevenson: "The Gift in A & E: Re-Framing the Medical Case Presentation Through Mauss." *Social Theory & Health*, 17, 4, 389-406. [Naz]

RR3457.　Redaelli, E.: "The Institution as Expression and Differential System: Marcel Mauss from Durkheim to Lévi-Strauss." *Discipline Filosofiche*, 29, 2, 51-70. [LoC]

RR3458.　Rosa, Vitor: "As Técnicas do Corpo em Marcel Mauss e o Campo Desportivo." *Estudos de Sociologia*, 24, 47, 341. [PrQ]

RR3459.　Schlanger, Nathan: "Marcel Mauss (1872-1950): Socializing the Body Through Techniques." *History of Humanities*, 4, 2, 313-317. [Cor]

RR3460.　Schrauwers, Albert: "The Spirit of the Gift, the Price of Potency: A

Maussian Model of the Southeast Asian State of Luwu." *Journal of the Royal Anthropological Institute*, 25, 4, 738-759. [Naz]

MAXIMIN, Daniel.
See also 219, 693.
RR3461. Nguetse, Paul K.: "Cataclysmes Naturels, Enjeux Écologiques et Poétique de la Résistance dans Soufrières (1987) et L'Île et Une Nuit (1995) de Daniel Maximin." *French Studies in Southern Africa*, 49, 203-244. [Cor]

MEDDEB, Abdelwahab.
See also 255.
RR3462. ● Kabbal, Maati: *Abdelwahab Meddeb: Traverser les Symboles, Transgresser les Règles*. Casablanca: Central Culturel du Livre. 103p. [WC]
RR3463. ● Kiwan, Nadia: *Secularism, Islam and Public Intellectuals in Contemporary France*. Manchester: Manchester UP. 182p. [Syr]
RR3464. Hajji, Adil: "À Plusieurs Voix: Relire Meddeb." *Esprit*, 459, 23-7. [PrQ]
RR3465. Marchand, Aline, Pascale Roux, & Ridha Boulaâbi: "De Tayeb Salih à Abdelwahab Meddeb: Saison de la Migration Vers le Nord ou Vers l'Orientalisme?" *Recherches & Travaux*, 95. [Cor]

MEMMI, Albert.
See also 527, 740, 3466.
RR3466. ● Memmi, Albert, & Guy Dugas: *Journal de Guerre 1939-1943: Suivi de, Journal d'un Travailleur Forcé; et Autres Textes de Circonstance*. Paris: CNRS. 302p. [LoC]
RR3467. Kałuża, Maciej: "Rethinking Camus's Truce Appeals: Neither Colonizer nor Colonized in Relation to Memmi's Colonial Dichotomy." *Interventions: International Journal of Postcolonial Studies*, 21, 2, 219-234. [UofR]
RR3468. Kranz, Mendel: "Postcolonial Zionism: Theological-political Paradigms in Levinas and Memmi." *Hebrew Studies*, 60, 293-322. [Naz]
RR3469. Sanson, Hervé: "Albert Memmi-André Schwarz-Bart, Écrivains à Vif." *Études Caribéennes*, 3. [Cor]

MENDÈS, Catulle.
See 34, 525.

MERLEAU-PONTY, Maurice.
See 1146, 1277, 1856, 2094, 3177.
RR3470. ● Alloa, Emmanuel, Frank Chouraqui, & Rajiv Kaushik: *Merleau-Ponty and Contemporary Philosophy*. Albany: SUNY Press. 312p. [Syr]
RR3471. ● Amoroso, Prisca: *Pensiero Terrestre e Spazio di Gioco: L'Orizzonte Ecologico dell'Esperienza a Partire da Merleau-Ponty*. Milano: Mimesis. 238p. [LoC]
RR3472. ● Andrews, Jorella: *Question of Painting: Re-thinking Thought with Merleau-Ponty*. London: Bloomsbury Academic. 344p. [WC]
RR3473. ● Apostolopulos, Demetres G.: *Merleau-Ponty's Phenomenology of Language*. New York: Rowman et Littlefield. 313p. [WC]

RR3474. ● Barbaras, Renaud: *Lectures Phénoménologiques: Merleau-Ponty, Sartre, Patocka et Quelques Autres*. Paris: Beauchesne. 296p. [WC]

RR3475. ● Dalmasso, Anna C.: *L'Œil et l'Histoire: Merleau-Ponty et l'Historicité de la Perception*. [Sesto S. Giovanni, Italie]: Mimésis. 221p. [WC]

RR3476. ● Faettini, Barbara: *Le Emozioni Nei Sogni: Merleau-Ponty e la Psicoanalisi Post-Bioniana*. Milano: Mimesis. 234p. [LoC]

RR3477. ● Gill, Jerry H.: *Words, Deeds, Bodies: L. Wittgenstein, J. L. Austin, M. Merleau-Ponty, and M. Polanyi*. Leiden: Brill Rodopi. 94p. [WC]

RR3478. ● Johnson, Galen A.: *Merleau-Ponty: Un Extrait du Cours Inédit sur le Problème de la Parole = An Excerpt from the Unpublished Course on the Problem of Speech = Un Estratto dal Corso Inedito su il Problema della Parola*. [Milan]: Mimesis. 411p. [WC]

RR3479. ● Kaushik, Rajiv: *Merleau-Ponty between Philosophy and Symbolism: The Matrixed Ontology*. Albany: SUNY Press. 171p. [Syr]

RR3480. ● Lisciani-Petrini, Enrica, & Raoul Kirchmayr: *Sartre/ Merleau-Ponty: Un Dissidio Produttivo*. Milano: Il Saggiatore. 203p. [WC]

RR3481. ● Loughnane, Adam: *Merleau-Ponty and Nishida. Artistic Expression as Motor-Perceptual Faith*. Albany: SUNY Press. 442p. [Syr]

RR3482. ● McDonald, Mary Catherine: *Merleau-Ponty and a Phenomenology of PTSD: Hidden Ghosts of Traumatic Memory*. Lanham, MD: Lexington Books. 139p. [LoC]

RR3483. ● Mercury, Jean-Yves: *Chemins Avec et Autour de Merleau-Ponty*. Paris: L'Harmattan. 185p. [LoC]

RR3484. ● Merleau-Ponty, Maurice, & Vigna P. Dalla: *La Prosa del Mondo Merleau-Ponty, Maurice Numeri*. Milano: Mimesis. 184p. [WC]

RR3485. ● Nunzella, Angela: *Coscienza Tattile: Maurice Merleau-Ponty e l'Essere Nell'arte*. Firenze: Polistampa. 77p. [LoC]

RR3486. ● Roux, Jean-Marie: *Les Degrés du Silence: Du Sens Chez Austin et Merleau-Ponty*. Louvain-la-Neuve: Peeters. 474p. [Cor]

RR3487. ● Sallis, John, & Richard Rojcewicz: *The Logos of the Sensible World: Merleau-Ponty's Phenomenological Philosophy*. Bloomington, IN: Indiana UP. 175p. [Cor]

RR3488. ● Zaietta, Lucia: *Une Parenté Étrange: Repenser l'Animalité avec la Philosophie de Merleau-Ponty*. Milano: Mimésis. 306p. [BnF]

RR3489. Allen, K.: "Merleau-Ponty and Naive Realism." *Philosophers Imprint*, *19*, 2. [Syr]

RR3490. Alloa, Emmanuel: "Le Premier Livre de Merleau-Ponty, Un Roman." *Chiasmi International*, 21, 253-268. [Cor]

RR3491. Andén, Lovisa: "Literature and the Expressions of Being in Merleau-Ponty's Unpublished Course Notes." *Journal of the British Society for Phenomenology*, *50*, 3, 208-219. [UofR]

RR3492. Antich, Peter: "Perceptual Experience in Kant and Merleau-Ponty." *Journal of the British Society for Phenomenology*, *50*, 3, 220-233. [UaB]

RR3493. Balay, Joe: "Seeing with a Mountain: Merleau-Ponty and the Landscape Aesthetics of Mont. Sainte-Victoire." *Environment, Space, Place*, *11*, 1, 38-56. [Cor]

RR3494. Bobant, Charles: "Compte Rendu de Anna Caterina Dalmasso, Le

Corps, C'est l'Écran. La Philosophie du Visuel de Merleau-Ponty." *Chiasmi International*, 21, 379-388. [Cor]

RR3495. Bobant, Charles: "Merleau-Ponty et l'Art: Un Itinéraire Philosophique." *Chiasmi International*, 21, 337-354. [Cor]

RR3496. Boccali, Renato: "Sur l'Intercorporéité et l'Interanimalité Merleau-Ponty et la Chair Primordiale." *Revue de Métaphysique et de Morale*, 101, 1, 39. [UaB]

RR3497. Cañas, Patricia M.: "The Understanding of the Body and Movement in Merleau-Ponty." *Trans/form/ação*, 42, 1, 201-226. [Cor]

RR3498. Carbone, Mauro: "La Surface Obscure." *Chiasmi International*, 21, 103-115. [Cor]

RR3499. Cash, Conall: "Politique Symbolique et Expression. 'L'Expérience Prolétarienne' Entre Merleau-Ponty et le Post-Marxisme." *Rue Descartes*, 96, 2, 117. [UaB]

RR3500. Contensou, Olivier: "Jérôme Mélançon, la Politique dans l'Adversité. Merleau-Ponty aux Marges de la Philosophie. Métispresses, 2018, 284 Pages." *Philosophiques*, 46, 2, 468. [UaB]

RR3501. Diprose, Rosalyn: "Merleau-Ponty's Ontology of Sound: How Hearing Loss and 'Trump Talk' Disable Communication and Intersubjectivity." *Philosophy Today*, 63, 1, 1-20. [RIT]

RR3502. Dodeman, Claire: "Claude Lefort Lecteur de Merleau-Ponty: De 'L'expérience Prolétarienne' à la 'Chair du Social'." *Rue Descartes*, 96, 2, 108. [UaB]

RR3503. Ferrada-Sullivan, Jorge: "Sobre la Noción de Cuerpo en Maurice Merleau-Ponty." *Cinta de Moebio*, 65, 159-166. [UofR]

RR3504. Furukawa, Marques D.: "Communauté et Subjectivité Politiques: La Mística du Mouvement des Travailleurs Ruraux Sans-Terre (MST) et la Phénoménologie Politique de Maurice Merleau-Ponty." *Politique et Sociétés*, 38, 3, 27. [Cor]

RR3505. Hayes, Shannon: "Merleau-Ponty's Melancholy: On Phantom Limbs and Involuntary Memory." *Epoché*, 24, 1, 201-219. [Cor]

RR3506. Lemanek, K.: "Habit, Bodyhood, and Merleau-Ponty." *Diametros*, 16, 60, 52-60. [Syr]

RR3507. Morris, David: "Merleau-Ponty and Mexica Ontology: On Time as Contingent Templacement and the Beginnings of Philosophy." *Chiasmi International*, 21, 289-303. [Cor]

RR3508. Potestà, Andrea: "El Silencio y la Palabra Merleau-Ponty, Derrida y Los Márgenes del Lenguaje." *Trans/form/ação*, 42, 1, 227-244. [Cor]

RR3509. Puc, Jan: "Bad Habit and Bad Faith. The Ambiguity of the Unconscious in the Early Merleau-Ponty." *Studia Universitatis Babeş-Bolyai.Philosophia*, 64, 1, 7. [PrQ]

RR3510. Robert, Franck: "Merleau-Ponty, l'Origine de la Géométrie et la Littérature." *Chiasmi International*, 21, 149-165. [Cor]

RR3511. Rudd, Anthony: "On Painting and Its Philosophical Significance." *International Philosophical Quarterly*, 59, 2, 137-154. [RIT]

RR3512. Somers-Hall, Henry: "Merleau-Ponty's Reading of Kant's Transcendental Idealism." *The Southern Journal of Philosophy*, 57, 1, 103-131. [Naz]

RR3513. Verano, Leonardo: "Dialéctica Negativa En Merleau-Ponty." *Kriterion: Revista de Filosofia*, 60, 142, 127-142. [Syr]

RR3514.   Vicente, Vânia: "On Ethics, Merleau-Ponty and Phenomenology: Echoes of a Dialogue with Renaud Barbaras." *Revista da Abordagem Gestáltica, 25,* 2, 185-95. [PrQ]

RR3515.   Walsh, Philip J.: "Intercorporeity and the First-Person Plural in Merleau-Ponty." *Continental Philosophy Review, 53,* 1, 21-47. [RIT]

RR3516.   Zaietta, L.: "Mélodie, Essence et Espèce. Thématisme et Variations entre Raymond Ruyer et Maurice Merleau-Ponty." *Revue de Métaphysique et de Morale, 101,* 1, 79-90. [Syr]

MERTENS, Pierre.
See also 422.

RR3517.   Roland, Hubert: "Exil Historique, 'Exil Intérieur' et Création. Réflexion Inspirée par la Construction du Personnage de Gottfried Benn dans les Éblouissements de Pierre Mertens." *Les Lettres Romanes, 73,* 3-4, 419-434. [Syr]

MESCHONNIC, Henri.
See also 630, 853, 865.

RR3518.   ● Eyriès, Alexandre: *Poétique de la Communication: Lectures Critiques de l'Œuvre d'Henri Meschonnic.* Paris: L'Harmattan. 176p. [BnF]

RR3519.   ● Meschonnic, Henri, Marko Pajevic, & John E. Joseph. *The Henri Meschonnic Reader: A Poetics of Society.* Edinburgh: Edinburgh UP. 336p. [WC]

RR3520.   Banon, David: "Henri Meschonnic: Traduire le Chant, Traduire les Paroles." *Tsafon,* 77, 93-104. [Cor]

RR3521.   Barreto, Matheus: "Ritmo em Massaud Moisés e Henri Meschonnic: Uma Apresentação e um Contraste." *Pandaemonium Germanicum, 22,* 38, 142-167. [Cor]

MIANO, Léonora.
See also 287, 334, 682, 3284.

RR3522.   ● Ducournau, Claire, Ecker M. Unter, & Catherine Mazauric: *Awa: La Revue de la Femme Noire. Léonora Miano-Déranger le(s) Genre(s).* Metz: Association pour l'Étude des Littératures Africaines: Centre Écritures. 270p. [WC]

RR3523.   Biondi, Carminella: "Marianne et le Garçon Noir, Sous la Direction de Léonora Miano." *Studi Francesi, 63,* 2, 202-203. [Syr]

RR3524.   Boblet, Marie-Hélène, Anne Gourio, & Marion Coste: "Vulnérabilité, Puissance d'Agir et Care dans Contours du Jour Qui Vient (2006) de Léonora Miano." *Elfe XX-XXI,* 9. [Cor]

RR3525.   Eddahbi, Bouchra: "Immigration et Question de l'Identité dans 'Tels des Astres Éteints' de Léonora Miano." *Les Cahiers du Centre des Études Doctorales,* 7, 19-25. [WC]

RR3526.   Fusaro, Anaïs: "*Marianne et le Garçon Noir* by Léonora Miano (Review)." *French Studies, 73,* 1, 160-161. [UaB]

RR3527.   Gehrmann, Susanne, Ronit Frenkel, & Pamila Gupta: "Emerging Afro-Parisian 'Chick-Lit' by Lauren Ekué and Léonora Miano." *Feminist Theory, 20,* 2, 215-228. [Naz]

RR3528.   Idiatha, Wilfried, Aurélie Journo, Magali Nachtergael, & Pierre-Yves Dufeu: "À Quel Prix Vêt-On la Terre Ou le Vent? Regards Mulongo Sur le Vêtement dans La Saison de l'Ombre de Léonora Miano." *Itinéraires,* 2019-1. [WC]

RR3529. "Impériale Léonora Miano." *Français dans le Monde*, 426, 8. [Syr]

RR3530. "Littérature Entretien Avec Léonora Miano." *Jeune Afrique*, 59, 3063, 68-72. [UofR]

RR3531. Messay, Marda: "'Des Voix Refuseront de Se Taire': Women's Voices in Léonora Miano's Contours du Jours Qui Vient." *Women in French Studies*, 27, 182-191. [UaB]

RR3532. Miller, Robert, & Gloria Onyeoziri: "La Forêt Comme Lieu de Mémoire et d'Oubli dans Les Aubes Écarlates (2009) et La Saison de l'Ombre (2013) de Léonora Miano." *Voix Plurielles*, 16, 2, 59-73. [Syr]

RR3533. Montlouis-Gabriel, Johanna: "Reading 'Hairstories' and 'Hairitages' in Léonora Miano's and Rokhaya Diallo's Works." *Études Littéraires Africaines*, 47, 85. [WC]

RR3534. Murray, Thomas: "La Masculinité à Travers l'Atlantique: Enjeux Identitaires et Musicaux dans Crépuscule du Tourment 1 et 2 de Léonora Miano." *Études Littéraires Africaines*, 47, 147. [WC]

RR3535. Ndi, Etondi V.: "Africana Womanism et Homosexualité dans Crépuscule du Tourment 1 de Léonora Miano." *Études Littéraires Africaines*, 47, 117. [WC]

RR3536. Peñalver, Vicea M.: "Termes d'Adresse et Pulsion Invocante Chez Léonora Miano." *Çédille*, 16, 381-406. [Syr]

RR3537. Unter, Ecker M.: "Léonora Miano et Virginie Despentes: Lectures Croisées des Masculinités 'Désaxées'." *Études Littéraires Africaines*, 47, 131. [WC]

RR3538. Vandendorpe, Chloé: "L'Intermédialité dans l'Art Romanesque de Léonora Miano." *Études Littéraires Africaines*, 47, 163. [WC]

RR3539. Vottero, Constance: "Réseaux de Genres: Relationnalité et Intersectionnalité dans Americanah de Chimamanda Ngozi Adichie et Blues Pour Élise de Léonora Miano." *Études Littéraires Africaines*, 47, 101. [WC]

MICHAUX, Henri.
See also 381, 471, 719, 801.

RR3540. ● *Henri Michaux, Max Ernst, Jacques Prévert: Ancienne Collection René Bertelé, Collection Bernard Loliée.* Paris: Binoche et Giquello. 80p. [WC]

RR3541. ● Kadi, Barbara U., & Gerhard Unterthurner: *Macht - Knoten - Fleisch: Topographien des Körpers bei Foucault, Lacan und Merleau-Ponty.* Stuttgart: J. B. Metzler. 300p. [WC]

RR3542. ● Melenotte, George-Henri, Yan Pélissier, & Claire Salles: *Le Geste du Pinceau: Jacques Lacan, François Rouan, Henri Michaux.* Paris: Ligeia. 255p. [WC]

RR3543. ● Michaux, Henri: *Henri Michaux.* Lyon: Fage. 64p. [BnF]

RR3544. ● Peyre, Yves: *Henri Michaux: Dans la Ferveur d'une Complicité.* Gerpinnes: Tandem. 163p. [WC]

RR3545. ● Peyré, Yves: *Joseph Sima-Henri Michaux: Lumière, Autre Terre: Catalogue de l'Exposition du 18 Octobre au 21 Décembre 2019 à la Galerie Orbis Pictus, Paris.* Paris: Orbis Pictus. 119p. [BnF]

RR3546. Arantxa Romero González: "Escritos Sobre Pintura. Henri Michaux." *Arte, Individuo y Sociedad*, 31, 1, 225-6. [RIT]

RR3547. Bacharach, Jeanne: "Henri Michaux de Misérable Miracle à Émergences-Résurgences: Écritures de 'L'Insupportable Trouble'." *Ligeia*, 173-176, 2, 113. [UofR]

RR3548. Calleja, M.: "The Sublime in Lutoslawski's Three Poems of Henri Michaux (1961-63)." *Aisthesis (Italy)*, *12*, 1, 165-173. [Naz]

RR3549. Depelsenaire, Yves: "'Entre Centre et Absence': Une Double Référence de Jacques Lacan à Henri Michaux." *Ligeia*, *173-176*, 2, 101. [UofR]

RR3550. Dieterle, Bernard: "Forschung im Rausch: Henri Michaux' Erkundung der Innenwelt." *Kulturpoetik*, *19*, 1, 124-141. [Naz]

RR3551. Etienne-Raynal, Clément: "Poteaux d'Angle, Structure Aveugle. Sublime Henri Michaux." *Imaginaire & Inconscient*, *43*, 1, 87. [Cor]

RR3552. Gillain, Nathalie: "Charlot, une Source d'Inspiration Pour Henri Michaux: De la Figuration de Mouvements à la Subversion des Genres Littéraires." *Études Françaises*, *55*, 2, 95. [UaB]

RR3553. Hoggard, Lynn: "A Certain Plume: Henri Michaux. Translated by Richard Sieburth. New York: New York Review Books, 2018. 223 pp." *Translation Review*, *104*, 1, 99-102. [UaB]

MICHON, Pierre.

RR3554. ● Benoteau-Alexandre, Marie-Eve: *Pierre Michon, la Littérature et le Sacré*. Paris: Manuscrit. 396p. [UofR]

RR3555. ● Mavrakis, Annie: *L'Atelier Michon*. Saint-Denis: Presses Universitaires de Vincennes. 185p. [UofR]

RR3556. ● Rezgui-Turki, Asma: *Pierre Michon: Création Romanesque et Écriture (Auto)Biographique*. Paris: L'Harmattan. 401p. [Cor]

RR3557. Hanhart-Marmor, Yona: "Le Sifflet de Makoko. Pierre Michon et la Littérature Seconde." *Littérature*, 195, 33-51. [Syr]

RR3558. Proulx, Gabriel: "Hagiographie Profane et Contemporanéité dans Vies Minuscules de Pierre Michon." *Contemporary French and Francophone Studies*, *23*, 5, 653-661. [Naz]

RR3559. Scotto, Fabio: "L'Herne. Pierre Michon, A. Castiglione et D. Viart." *Studi Francesi*, *63*, 2, 397-398. [UaB]

RR3560. Séguy, Mireille: "'L'Os et l'Or et le Texte Mêlés.' Pierre Michon ou la Réinvention des Reliques." *Littérature*, 196, 99-112. [Syr]

MILLET, Catherine.
See also 294, 297, 327, 342, 348, 472, 473.

MILLET, Richard.

RR3561. ● Millet, Richard: *Étude Pour un Homme Seul: Récit*. Paris: Pierre-Guillaume de Roux. 111p. [Cor]

RR3562. ● Millet, Richard: *Huppert et Moi*. Paris: Pierre-Guillaume de Roux. 82p. [LoC]

RR3563. ● Millet, Richard: *Journal: Tome II*. Paris: Léo Scheer. 275p. [BnF]

RR3564. Koffeman, Maaike: "Bettina Full & Michelle Lecolle (dir), Jeux de Mots et Créativité. Langue(s), Discours et Littérature; Annelies Schulte Nordholt & Paul J. Smith (dir), Jeux de Mots – Enjeux Littéraires, de François Rabelais à Richard Millet." *Relief*, *13*, 1, 178. [Syr]

MIMOUNI, Rachid.

RR3565. Ali, Ahmed A.: "Le Transgressif Comme Pratique Textuelle Politique dans l'Œuvre de Rachid Mimouni." *Convergences Francophones*, *6*, 1, 18-32. [WC]

MINYANA, Philippe.

RR3566. ● Sakr, Mountajab: *Action, Silence, Figures dans le Théâtre de Philippe Minyana.* Paris: L'Harmattan. 224p. [WC]

MIRBEAU, Octave.

See also 525, 547, 673.

RR3567. ● Barouh, Claude: *Octave Mirbeau: Les Années Cheverchemont.* Triel-sur-Seine: Triel, Mémoire & Histoire. 68p. [BnF]

RR3568. ● Bat, Marie-Bernard: *Les Paradoxes d'Octave Mirbeau. Ed. Reliée.* Paris: Classiques Garnier. 335p. [WC]

RR3569. ● Michel, Pierre: *Cahiers Octave Mirbeau.* Angers: Société Octave Mirbeau, 26. 368p. [WC]

RR3570. Dzene, Edzegue J. B.: "Octave Mirbeau, the Unclassifiable: Criticism of the Triptych 'Family - School-Church'." *Studii Si Cercetari Fliologice, Seria Limbi Romanice, 1,* 26, 108-120. [Cor]

RR3571. Fartas, Nadia: "'Derrière Un Grillage' d'Octave Mirbeau et l'Hommage des Artistes à Picquart." *Interfaces,* 42, 165-188. [BnF]

MIRON, Gaston.

See also 508, 557.

RR3572. Pribiag, Ioana V.: "Amironner: Notes on Worlding the Local." *Journal of Canadian Studies, 53,* 3, 535-554. [UofR]

MISTRAL, Frédéric.

See also 885.

RR3573. ● Baudin, Gérard: *Les Grandes Heures du Mas du Juge, Berceau du Poète Provençal Frédéric Mistral.* Marseille: Des Chevalets et Un Poète. 37p. [WC]

RR3574. ● Mathis, Suzy, André Gaudelette, & Gérard Baudin: *Frédéric Mistral en Bande Dessinée.* Marseille: Des Chevalets et Un Poète. [13]p. [WC]

RR3575. Bauer, Dominique: "Text, Topos, and the Awareness of History in Frédéric Mistral's Poème du Rhône." *Dix-neuf,* 23, 254-264. [UaB]

RR3576. Casanova, Jean-Yves: "Les 'Traductions' Françaises de Frédéric Mistral: Déplacements et Occultations." *Littératures,* 80, 167-183. [Syr]

MNOUCHKINE, Ariane.

See also 592, 862, 1125, 3130.

RR3577. Armani, Nora: "Cultures Are Not Anyone's Property Ariane Mnouchkine in Conversation with Joëlle Gayot Translated from the French with an Introduction." *Performing Arts Journal,* 123, 65-70. [Naz]

MODIANO, Patrick.

See also 64, 566, 585, 689, 2657.

RR3578. ● Blanckeman, Bruno: *Patrick Modiano, ou, l'Écriture Comme un Nocturne: Des Noirceurs de l'Histoire aux Ténèbres du Temps.* Caen: Passage(s). 157p. [Cor]

RR3579. ● Schlesser, Gilles: *Paris dans les Pas de Patrick Modiano.* Paris: Parigramme. 157p. [BAnQ]

RR3580. Chouvier, Bernard: "Modiano Face aux Impasses du Temps." *Cahiers de Psychologie Clinique*, *53*, 2, 13. [Cor]

RR3581. Cooke, Dervila: "La Part du Féminin dans l'Œuvre de Patrick Modiano: Fonctions et Attributs des Personnages Féminins Modianiens." *French Studies*, *73*, 1, 143-144. [UaB]

RR3582. Goloborodko, Iaroslav, & Anastasiia Lepetiukha: "Virages des Visions de Patrick Modiano." *Neophilologus*, *104*, 2, 165-176. [RIT]

RR3583. Hanif, Fauzan: "L'Influence du Genre à la Transmission de la Mémoire: Cas de Dora Bruder de Patrick Modiano." *Digital Press Social Sciences and Humanities*, 3, 22. [WC]

RR3584. Holm, Helge V.: "Voyance, Chronotopie et Intertextualité dans Dora Bruder de Patrick Modiano." *Bergen Language and Linguistics Studies*, *10*, 1, 8. [WC]

RR3585. Mamedkhanova, Naida J.: "Comparison of the Past and Present in Works of Patrick Modiano." *Homeros*, *1*, 1, 1-8. [WC]

RR3586. Morris, Alan: "Shadow Play: Patrick Modiano and the Legacy of the Holocaust." *French Forum*, *44*, 1, 13-28. [Naz]

RR3587. Zaparart, María J.: "Patrick Modiano en Español: El Caso de Dora Bruder." *Belas Infiéis*, *8*, 2, 129-138. [WC]

MOKEDDEM, Malika.
See also 655.

RR3588. Masseron, Caroline, Jean-Marie Privat, & Simon Lanot: "'On Lui Acheta un Cartable et des Sandales': Une Ethnocritique du Roman de Malika Mokeddem Les Hommes Qui Marchent." *Pratiques*, 183-184. [Cor]

MONÉNEMBO, Tierno.
See also 219, 360, 414.

RR3589. ● Le Quellec, Christine Cottier: *'Le Terroriste Noir' de Tierno Monénembo*. Gollion [Suisse]: Infolio 129p. [UofR]

RR3590. Gefen, Alexandre, Claude Perez, & Bernard D. Meyer: "Le Global Turn ou Comment Lire les Coqs Cubains Chantent à Minuit de Tierno Monénembo." *Elfe XX-XXI*, 8. [WC]

RR3591. Monénembo, Tierno: "Nos Amis Dictateurs Sortis des Urnes." *Manière de Voir*, *165*, 6, 48. [Naz]

RR3592. Tsakeu, Mazan S. D.: "Tierno Monénembo: Un Engagement de Biais. Une Lecture de L'Aîné des Orphelins." *Mouvances Francophones*, *4*, 1. [WC]

MONNIER, Adrienne.
See also 353.

RR3593. ● Verrax, Éric: *Adrienne Monnier et Edmond Charlot, Pour l'Amour des Livres: Avec Quatorze Fixés Sous Verre de Chanath: Autour de l'Exposition 2019 Au Musée du Revard-Musée du Fixé Sous Verre, [Pugny-Chatenod]*. Lyon: Éditions du Musée du Revard. 165p. [BnF]

MONTHERLANT, Henry de.
RR3594. Cauvin, Gaëlle: "Henry de Montherlant, Rhadidja Suivi de Sur Une Belle Lépreuse, Alger, El Kalima, 'Les Petits Inédits Maghrébins,' 2018, 103 p." *Continents Manuscrits*, 26 septembre. [Cor]

RR3595.   Coto-Rivel, Sergio, de F. C. Fourrel, Jennifer Houdiard, & Pierre Damamme: "L'Horreur du Féminin dans le Cycle des Jeunes Filles d'Henry de Montherlant, ou Comment On Émascule la France." *Itinéraires*, 2. [WC]

MORAND, Paul.
See also 299, 458.
RR3596.   ● Morand, Paul, Olivier Aubertin, & Estienne N. d'Orves: *Bains de Mer, Bains de Rêve et Autres Voyages*. Paris: Robert Laffont. 1057p. [BAnQ]
RR3597.   ● Proust, Marcel, & Massimo Carloni: *Il Visitatore della Sera: Lettere a Paul Morand e a Madame Soutzo*. Torino: Nino Aragno. 335p. [WC]
RR3598.   Bértolo, José: "'A Arte Do Evento': Acidente, Narrativa e Forma em la Glace à Trois Faces, entre Jean Epstein e Paul Morand." *Cadernos de Literatura Comparada*, 41, 13-35. [WC]
RR3599.   Cazentre, Thomas: "Du Boy à la Chouette: Dessins Épistolaires de Paul Morand (1916-1922)." *Revue de la Bnf*, 58, 1, 148. [Cor]
RR3600.   Miller, Paul B.: "Caribbean Winter: by Paul Morand, Translation and Introduction by Mary Gallagher, Oxford, Signal Books, 2018, 171 pp., £12.99 (paperback), ISBN 978-1909930681." *Studies in Travel Writing*, 23, 2, 211-214. [UaB]

MORIN, Edgar.
See also 686, 4705.
RR3601.   ● Abbé Pierre, Jean Rousseau, & Edgar Morin: *La Force des Infiniment Petits*. Paris: Cherche Midi. 223p. [LoC]
RR3602.   ● Barroux, Martine Lani-Bayle, & Edgar Morin: *Apprendre la Vie: Barroux Dessine Edgar Morin et Martine Lani-Bayle*. Marseille: L'Initiale. [24]p. [BnF]
RR3603.   ● Dortier, Jean-François: *Edgar Morin: L'Aventure d'Une Pensée*. Auxerre: Sciences Humaines. 191p. [Cor]
RR3604.   ● Égoué, Casimir: *Pertinence et Critique du Concept de Paradigmatologie, Introduit par Edgar Morin*. Saint-Ouen: Les Éditions du Net. 216p. [BnF]
RR3605.   ● Fontanella, Magda, & Andrea Millul: *L'Identità Umana Come Sistema Complesso: Da Edgar Morin alla Filosofia in Reparto*. Cargeghe: Documenta. 221p. [WC]
RR3606.   ● Lani-Bayle, Martine, & Adélaïde Ronxin: *Dis, Raconte, Comment Ça Marche?: Découvrir et Penser le Monde Avec Edgar Morin*. Cholet: Pourpenser. 47p. [BnF]
RR3607.   ● Morin, Edgar: *La Fraternité Pourquoi: Résister à la Cruauté du Monde*. Arles: Actes Sud. 61p. [BAnQ]
RR3608.   ● Morin, Edgar, Alberto M. Cacopardo, & Augusto Cavadi: *Pensare il Mediterraneo, Mediterraneizzare il Pensiero: Da Luogo di Conflitti a Incrocio di Sapienze*. Trapani: Il Pozzo di Giacobbe. 75p. [WC]
RR3609.   ● Morin, Edgar, Denis Lafay, & Pascal Lemaître: *Pour Changer de Civilisation: Dialogue Avec Denis Lafay*. La Tour d'Aigues: Éditions de l'Aube. 101p. [BAnQ]
RR3610.   ● Nsonsissa, Auguste, & Gévi A. Ampini: *Edgar Morin ou la Nouvelle Épistémologie*. Paris: L'Harmattan. 260p. [Cor]
RR3611.   Aguiar, Ricardo O. G., Daniel L. Soares, Renata F. Toledo, & Arnaldo Rocha: "Os Sete Saberes de Edgar Morin São Necessários Também à Comunicação." *Conexão Comunicação e Cultura*, 18, 35, 57-75. [LoC]

RR3612.   Almeida, Rogério, & Juliana M. S. Oliveira: "As Máquinas de Complexidade: Diálogo Com Edgar Morin." *Educação e Pesquisa*, 45. [Naz]

RR3613.   Andrade, Salazar J. A.: "The Brain in Light of Edgar Morin's Paradigm of Complexity: El Cerebro a la Luz del Paradigma de la Conmplejidad." *Archivos de Medicina, 20*, 1, 226-241. [Naz]

RR3614.   Arnoldy, Édouard: "Edgar Morin, le Cinéma, un Art de la Complexité. Articles et Inédits – 1952-1962." *1895*, 176-180. [Cor]

RR3615.   Baraldi, Victoria: "Leer a Morin. Notas Para Comprender Nuevos y Viejos Problemas." *Intercambios, 6*, 2, 3-11. [WC]

RR3616.   Da Silva, O. J. M., & R. de. Almeida: "Machines of Complexity: Dialogues with Edgar Morin." *Educacao e Pesquisa*, 45. [Naz]

RR3617.   Demirel, Funda: "The Role of Education in Human Nature and Future Human Design According to Edgar Morin." *New Trends and Issues Proceedings on Humanities and Social Sciences, 6*, 6, 18-29. [WC]

RR3618.   Dicks, Henry: "Physics, Philosophy and Poetics at the End of the Groupe des Dix: Edgar Morin and Michel Serres on the Nature of Nature." *Natures Sciences Sociétés, 27*, 2, 169. [Syr]

RR3619.   Dortier, Jean-François: "Edgar Morin - Mes Amis, Mes Amours, Mes Idées." *Sciences Humaines, 319*, 11, 32. [BAnQ]

RR3620.   Fernandez, A. M.: "Demystification and Revaluation of Freedom Through Girard and Morin." *Revista de Humanidades*, 38, 117-134. [Syr]

RR3621.   Fougerouse, Marie-Christine: "Enseigner à Vivre! Edgar Morin et l'Éducation Innovante." *Synergies France, 13*, 219, 220, 226-227. [RIT]

RR3622.   Garim, Luize C., & Rafael Montoito: "A Literatura Como Potencializadora de Discussões No Campo da Educação: Os Saberes de Edgar Morin em Discussão No Livro Holy Cow: Uma Fábula Animal." *Revista Thema, 16*, 2, 381. [Syr]

RR3623.   Hallal, R., N. A. M. Pinheiro, R. Oliveira, & A. P. Falcao. "Teaching Mathematics in the Light of Edgar Morin Theory: An Approach to Teaching-Learning Differencial and Integral Calculus I." *Espacios, 40*, 29. [Naz]

RR3624.   Laberge, Yves: "L'Unité d'un Homme. Par Edgar Morin." *French Studies, 73*, 3, 480-481. [UofR]

RR3625.   Lemos, Pedro B. S., Francisco J. A. Aquino, Solonildo A. Silva, Sandro C. S. Jucá, Francisco E. M. Silva, & Saulo R. Freitas: "O Conceito de Paradigma em Thomas Kunh e Edgar Morin: Similitudes e Diferenças." *Research, Society and Development, 8*, 10. [WC]

RR3626.   Lifshitz, A.: "Edgar Morin and the Medical Education of the Future." *Medicina Interna de Mexico, 35*, 2, 187-189. [UaB]

RR3627.   Marks, John: "Biology and Complexity: Edgar Morin and Henri Atlan." *Natures Sciences Sociétés, 27*, 2, 159. [Syr]

RR3628.   Martinazzo, Celso J.: "O Sentido do Ato de Educar em Edgar Morin." *Educação e Filosofia*, 33, 67. [LoC]

RR3629.   Morin, Edgar, Éric Fourreau, & Emmanuel Négrier: "Edgar Morin." *Nectart, 9*, 2, 12. [WC]

RR3630.   Morin, Edgar, René Passet, Franck-Dominique Vivien, & Henry Dicks: "Edgar Morin et René Passet: Les Passeurs du Groupe des Dix." *Natures Sciences Sociétés, 27*, 2, 225. [Syr]

RR3631.   Moser, Keith: "Edgar Morin's 'Complex Thought': A Blueprint for

Reconstituting our Ecological Self in the Anthropocene Epoch?" *Journal of Comparative Literature and Aesthetics, 42,* 2, 20-32. [RIT]

RR3632. Péquignot, Julien: "La Jeunesse et le Yé-Yé Vus par Edgar Morin: Culture de Masse Mondialisée versus Particularismes Français, ou la Résistance Télévisuelle à l'Américanisation Musico-Visuelle (1963)." *Parlement[s], Revue d'Histoire Politique, 29,* 1, 107. [Cor]

RR3633. Pinto, Anaísa C, Sônia Barros, Mara L. Garanhani, Lara S. M. Floriano, & Suellen V. Skupien: "Conceito de Ser Humano de Professores do Curso de Enfermagem à Luz do Homo Complexus de Edgar Morin." *Brazilian Journal of Development, 5,* 9, 14543-14555. [WC]

MOUAWAD, Wajdi.

See also 835, 838, 848.

RR3634. ● Kerlin, Alexander, Wajdi Mouawad, Itai Ṭiran, & Florian Etti: *Vögel, Wajdi Mouawad: In Deutscher, Englischer, Hebräischer und Arabischer Sprache Mit Deutschen und Englischen Übertiteln: Übersetzung Jalal Altawil (Arabisch), Eli Bijaoui (Hebräisch), Linda Gaboriau (Englisch), Uli Menke (Deutsch).* Wien: Burgtheater. 46p. [WC]

RR3635. ● Mouawad, Wajdi, Hakan S. Mican, & Sylvia Rieger: *Vögel: Von Wajdi Mouawad.* Hamburg: Thalia Theater. 1 vol. [WC]

RR3636. ● Valenti, Simonetta: *Rencontre: Le Nouvel Humanisme de Wajdi Mouawad.* Bruxelles: P. I. E. Peter Lang. 183p. [WC]

RR3637. Chi-Woon, Ahn: "Une Étude Sur Incendies de Wajdi Mouawad par l'Analyse de Langues Poétiques dans les Narratives des Personnages." *Journal of Korean Theatre Studies Association, 1,* 70, 81-114. [LoC]

RR3638. Jakubczuk, Renata: "Deux Versions Modernes de l'Histoire d'Œdipe: Au Retour des Oies Blanches de Marcel Dubé et Incendies de Wajdi Mouawad." *Cahiers Erta,* 17, 9-23. [WC]

RR3639. Khordoc, Catherine: "Visibility Graphs and Blindspots: Wajdi Mouawad's Incendies and Its Mathematical Poetics." *French Cultural Studies, 30,* 4, 307-316. [RIT]

RR3640. Khordoc, Catherine: "Worlded Literature in Quebec: Wajdi Mouawad's Le Sang des Promesses Cycle." *Journal of Canadian Studies, 53,* 3, 495-513. [Naz]

RR3641. Mouawad, Wajdi, & Nathalie Sarthou-Lajus: "'Le Théâtre Est Une Forme d'Attentat'." *Études,* 93. [UofR]

RR3642. "Rencontre Wajdi Mouawad, Metteur en Scène et Comédien." *Œil,* 719, 142-145. [UaB]

RR3643. Vacher, Pascal: "Des Chemins de Traverse Qui Ne Mènent Pas Nulle Part: Forêts, de Wajdi Mouawad, ou l'Entrelacs de l'Histoire et de l'Intime, du Politique et du Psychique." *Voix Plurielles, 16,* 2, 106-116. [Syr]

MOUFFE, Chantal.

RR3644. ● Randeria, Shalini, Ludger Hagedorn, Katharina Hasewend, Peter Engelmann, Nancy Fraser, Janos Kis, Ivan Krastev, Mark Lilla, Chantal Mouffe, Jan-Werner Müller, Claus Offe, Jacques Rupnik, & Nadia Urbinati: *An Den Grenzen der Demokratie: Beiträge von Nancy Fraser, Janos Kis, Ivan Krastev, Mark Lilla, Chantal Mouffe, Jan-Werner Müller, Claus Offe, Jacques Rupnik, Nadia Urbinati.* Wien: Passagen. 200p. [WC]

RR3645.   Capasso, Verónica: "Arte, Política y Espacio: Una Propuesta de Análisis Desde la Teoría de Chantal Mouffe." *Alpha*, 47, 253-268. [Naz]

RR3646.   Cervera-Marzal, Manuel: "Une 'Démocratie Radicale' Pas Si Radicale?: Chantal Mouffe et la Critique Immanente du Libéralisme." *Raisons Politiques*, 75, 3, 13. [Cor]

RR3647.   De Almeida, L. M. C.: "Diferença Ontológica, Pós-Fundacionismo e Exterioridade Constitutiva: Reflexões Sobre o Fundamento Autoestabelecido Na Teoria do Discurso de Ernesto Laclau e Chantal Mouffe." *Revista Sul-Americana de Ciência Política*, 5, 2, 215. [WC]

RR3648.   Demir, Gökhan: "For a Left Populism: by Chantal Mouffe. London: Verso, 2018." *Rethinking Marxism*, 31, 4, 541-545. [Naz]

RR3649.   Dreyfus, Alain: "Chantal Mouffe (Belgique, 1943)." *Le Nouveau Magazine Littéraire*, 13, 1, 55. [UofR]

RR3650.   Duclos, Pierre, & Charlotte Régnier: "Chantal Mouffe, Pour Un Populisme de Gauche: Albin Michel, 2018, 132 p., 14 €." *Projet*, 368, 1, 95a. [UaB]

RR3651.   Goldstein, P.: "Ernesto Laclau and Chantal Mouffe: The Evolution of Post-Marxism." *Global Discourse*, 9, 2, 351-363. [WC]

RR3652.   Inston, Kevin: "Chantal Mouffe: Hegemony, Radical Democracy and the Political." *European Legacy*, 24, 2, 238-240. [UaB]

RR3653.   Jesse, Eckhard: "Chantal Mouffe: Für Einen Linken Populismus." *Das Historisch-Politische Buch*, 67, 2, 230-231. [Cor]

RR3654.   Van Den, A. G.: "Challenges for a Left Populism: A Response to Chantal Mouffe." *Global Discourse*, 9, 2, 439-443. [LoC]

RR3655.   Vega, Fernández, J.: "Chantal Mouffe. 2018. For a Left Populism. Londres: Verso." *Nóesis*, 28, 108-111. [Naz]

RR3656.   Yamanaka, Sho: "Rethinking of the Significance of Passions in Political Education: A Focus on Chantal Mouffe's 'Agonistic Democracy'." *Educational Studies in Japan: International Yearbook*, 13, 13, 111-121. [Cor]

MOUNIER, Emmanuel.
See also 3417.

RR3657.   ● Corigliano, Filippo: *Personalismo: Saggio Su Emmanuel Mounier*. Milano: Mimesis. 109p. [LoC]

RR3658.   ● Dunaj, Cyril: *Penser la Relation Avec Emmanuel Mounier*. Les Plans-sur-Bex (Suisse): Parole et Silence. 99p. [BnF]

RR3659.   ● Parente, Lucia: *Sfumature di Pensiero su Emmanuel Mounier*. Milano: Mimesis. 115p. [WC]

RR3660.   Dias, Gilmar L.: "Emmanuel Mounier e a Filosofia Personalista No Brasil." *Horizontes*, 37. [LoC]

RR3661.   Lucas, Marie-Odile: "Le Corps Personnel. Étude du Rôle du Corps dans l'Élaboration de l'Être Personnel dans le Traité du Caractère et le Personnalisme d'Emmanuel Mounier." *Transversalités*, 148, 1, 155. [Cor]

RR3662.   Petit, Jean-François: "Un 'Retour en Grâce' de la Philosophie d'Emmanuel Mounier?" *Transversalités*, 148, 1, 143. [Cor]

MUDIMBE, Valentin.
See also 214, 661, 675, 771, 777.

RR3663.   Madureira, Luís: "Chronicles from the 'Vulture Kingdom': The Postcolonial State in Question in Ungulani Ba Ka Khosa's Historical Fiction." *Research in African Literatures*, *50*, 1, 150-73. [PrQ]

RR3664.　Ripert, Yohann C.: *"The Mudimbe Reader* Ed. by Pierre-Philippe Fraiture and Daniel Orrells (Review)." *African Studies Review*, *62*, 3, E8-E10. [Naz]

NANCY, Jean-Luc.

See also 2081, 2845.

RR3665.　● Derrida, Jacques, & Simon Hantai: *Toccare, Jean-Luc Nancy.* 401p. [WC]

RR3666.　● Laügt, Elodie: *Figures de l'Intrusion Chez Jean-Luc Nancy.* Paris: L'Harmattan. 171p. [WC]

RR3667.　● Meister, Carolin, Carolin Meister, & Jean-Luc Nancy: *Jean-Luc Nancy. Wozu Braucht Man Kunst?: Staatliche Akademie der Bildenden Künste Karlsruhe. Riemschneider Lectures 2017.* Köln: König, Walther. 36p. [WC]

RR3668.　● Nancy, Jean-Luc, & Aniko Adam: *Entre Nous: Études Sur Jean-Luc Nancy.* Paris: L'Harmattan. 116p. [WC]

RR3669.　Alvaro, Daniel: "Apuntes Sobre la Ontología Relacional de Jean-Luc Nancy." *Castalia*, 32, 37-52. [WC]

RR3670.　Breton, M., & F. Nault: "Sortir de la Théologie? Jean-Luc Nancy et la Déconstruction du Christianisme." *Revue Théologique de Louvain*, *50*, 2, 224-256. [Cor]

RR3671.　Bulo, Vargas V.: "Desde el Cuerpo a la Materialidad. Contribuciones de Jean Luc-Nancy." *Revista de Filosofía*, 76, 29-37. [Naz]

RR3672.　Chamberlain, James A.: "Motivating Cosmopolitanism: Jürgen Habermas, Jean-Luc Nancy, and the Case for Cosmocommonism." *Contemporary Political Theory*, *19*, 1, 105-126. [Naz]

RR3673.　Cohen, Rona: "Jean-Luc Nancy and the Extension of the Mind." *Philosophy Today*, *63*, 2, 347-362. [Naz]

RR3674.　Collins, Ashok: "Testifying to the Truth: Paul Ricœur and Jean-Luc Nancy on the Theological Turn." *Australian Journal of French Studies*, *56*, 2, 170-183. [RIT]

RR3675.　Collins, Ashok: "The Virtue of Joy: Spinoza in Jean-Luc Nancy's Deconstruction of Christianity." *Research in Phenomenology*, *49*, 2, 143-162. [Naz]

RR3676.　Crowley, Martin: "The Many Worlds of Jean-Luc Nancy." *Paragraph*, *42*, 1, 22-36. [RIT]

RR3677.　Ferrada, Jorge: "Sobre la Noción de Excritura en Jean-Luc Nancy." *Cinta de Moebio*, 64, 123-131. [UofR]

RR3678.　Goh, Irving: "Exscription, or the Sense of Failure: Jean-Luc Nancy, Tecuciztecatl, and Édouard Levé." *MLN*, *134*, 5, 1080-1097. [Naz]

RR3679.　Griffith, James: "Jean-Luc Nancy, Ego Sum: Corpus, Anima, Fabula, Translated by Marie-Eve Morin." *Derrida Today*, *12*, 1, 106-112. [UaB]

RR3680.　Hanke, Bob: "Roy Andersson's Living Trilogy and Jean-Luc Nancy's Evidence of Cinema." *Film-Philosophy*, *23*, 1, 72-92. [Syr]

RR3681.　Listik, Yonathan: "Jean-Luc Nancy's Notion of Singularity." *Ekstasis: Revista de Hermenêutica e Fenomenologia*, *7*, 2. [Naz]

RR3682.　Martínez, Olguín J. J.: "La Communauté Déplacée. Écriture et Communauté dans le Dialogue Entre Maurice Blanchot et Jean-Luc Nancy." *Agora*, *38*, 2.

RR3683.   Masterson, Mark: "Coming. By Jean-Luc Nancy. Translated by Charlotte Mandell." *Journal of the History of Sexuality*, *28*, 2, 313-315. [UofR]

RR3684.   Saidel, Matías Leandro: "Reinvenciones de lo Común: Hacia una Revisión de Algunos Debates Recientes." *Revista de Estudios Sociales*, 70, 10-24. [PrQ]

RR3685.   Sullivan, J. F.: "On the Notion of Concealed Thinking in Jean-Luc Nancy." *Cinta de Moebio*, 64, 123-131. [RIT]

RR3686.   Vargas, V. B.: "From the Body to Materiality. From Jean-Luc Nancy." *Revista de Filosofía (Chile)*, 76, 29-37. [UaB]

N'DIAYE, Marie.
See also 294, 295, 305, 668, 697.

RR3687.   Benoit, Malyoune: "Dire la Migration, 'Khady Demba' dans Trois Femmes Puissantes de Marie Ndiaye." *Journal of the African Literature Association*, *13*, 2, 218-230. [Syr]

RR3688.   Gallagher, Mary: "Shirley Jordan, Marie Ndiaye: Inhospitable Fictions (Cambridge: Legenda, 2017) 131 pp." *Irish Journal of French Studies*, *19*, 1, 216-218. [WC]

RR3689.   Jensen, Laura: "'Ce Noir Qui Aurait Pu Être Mon Frère': Race and Fraternité in Marie Ndiaye's Fiction." *Contemporary French and Francophone Studies*, *23*, 3, 324-332. [Naz]

RR3690.   "Jordan, Shirley. Marie Ndiaye: Inhospitable Fictions." *Forum for Modern Language Studies*, *55*, 1, 118-119. [UofR]

RR3691.   Kersting, Philippe: "Perspectives Postcoloniales Sur Marie Ndiaye et Son Œuvre." *Lendemains*, *44*, 173, 100-110. [Cor]

RR3692.   Khajavi, B.: "The Daily Life and Its Disturbing Strangeness in Marie Ndiaye's Self-Portrait in Green." *Research in Contemporary World Literature*, *24*, 1, 69-94. [WC]

RR3693.   Parks, Iona W.: "Justi-Fiction Exposed: Marie Ndiaye and Olivia Rosenthal's Animal Effect in Trois Femmes Puissantes and in Que Font les Rennes Après Noël?" *French Review*, *93*, 1, 154-167. [UofR]

RR3694.   Still, Judith: "Refusing Consumption and Querying Genre: A Partial Reading of Marie Ndiaye." *Parallax*, *25*, 3, 288-303. [UaB]

RR3695.   Tabakh, Hajer: "La Souffrance Amoureuse Chez Marie Ndiaye." *Dacoromania Litteraria*, 5, 73-81. [WC]

RR3696.   Turin, Gaspard: "Accommodements en Régime Magique. Fonctions de la Nourriture Chez Marie Ndiaye." *Elfe XX-XXI*, 7. [Cor]

NELLIGAN, Émile.
See also 213, 883..

RR3697.   Vovk, Svetlana: "An Eminent French-Canadian Poet Emile Nélligan." *USA & Canada: Economics – Politics – Culture*, 7, 117-126. [Syr]

NÉMIROVSKY, Irène.
See also 320.

RR3698.   ● Samama, Guy: *Irène Némirovsky*. Paris: Centre Documentation Recherche. 220p. [WC]

RR3699.   Cenedese, M. L.: "The Rhythm of Unity: Irène Némirovsky's Suite

Française and Leo Tolstoy's War and Peace." *Comparative Literature*, *71*, 1, 64-85. [Naz]

RR3700.   Fiorentino, Francesco, & Teresa M. Lussone: "Prendre à 'Contre-Pied la Psychanalyse': Le Maître des Âmes d'Irène Némirovsky." *Revue Italienne d'Études Françaises*, 9. [Syr]

NEPVEU, Pierre.
RR3701.   ● Nepveu, Pierre: *L'Espace Caressé par Ta Voix*. Montréal: Noroît. 109p. [BAnQ]
RR3702.   ● Nepveu, Pierre: *Kilomètre Zéro*. Trois-Rivières: Art le Sabord. 58p. [BAnQ]

NGAL, Georges.
RR3703.   Mukenge, Arthur, & Emmanuel Kayembe: "Giambattista Viko de Georges Ngal: Une Théorie Clandestine du Champ Littéraire Africain." *French Studies in Southern Africa*, 49, 140-161. [Cor]

NGANDU NKASHAMA, Pius.
See 289.

NIMIER, Roger.
See 421.

NIZAN, Paul.
See 1499.

NOAILLES, Anna de.
See also 324.
RR3704.   ● Breuillaud-Sottas, Françoise, Jean-Marc Hovasse, & François Maillet: *Goûter au Paradis: Anna de Noailles Sur les Rives du Léman =: Tasting Paradise. Anna de Noailles on the Shores of Lake Geneva*. Cinisello Balsamo (Milano): Silvana. 127p. [Cor]
RR3705.   Lafarga, Francisco: "Traducciones Españolas de la Obra de Anna de Noailles." *Transfer*, 15, 351-370. [WC]

NOBÉCOURT, Lorette.
See also 615.
RR3706.   Zurawska, Anna: "Hildegarde de Bingen, une Sainte Post-Séculière? La Clôture des Merveilles de Lorette Nobécourt." *Romanica Wratislaviensia*, 66, 121-132. [WC]

NOËL, Bernard.
See also 66, 782, 783, 1001.
RR3707.   ● Tatarka, Dominik, Bernard Noël, & Mateusz Chmurski: *Le Démon du Consentement et Autres Textes*. Paris: Eur'Orbem. 186p. [WC]

NOTHOMB, Amélie.
See also 326.

RR3708. ● Chaillan, Marianne: *Ainsi Philosophait Amélie Nothomb*. Paris: Albin Michel. 205p. [Cor]

RR3709. ● Robert, Michel, Amélie Nothomb, & Sara M. Cacioppo: *La Bocca Delle Carpe: Conversazioni con Amélie Nothomb*. Roma: Voland. 104p. [WC]

RR3710. Crespi, Patrizia: "Métaphysique des Tubes d'Amélie Nothomb: Une Vie Racontée à Travers l'Intensité Linguistique." *Anales de Filología Francesa*, *27*, 1, 97-117. [Syr]

RR3711. Demeule, Fanie: "Se Nourrir de Mots: Poétique Alimentaire dans l'Écriture Autofictionnelle de l'Anorexie Chez Amélie Nothomb." *Captures*, *1*, 2. [WC]

RR3712. Ferreira-Meyers, Karen: "Identité, Mémoire, Lieux. Le Passé, le Présent et l'Avenir d'Amélie Nothomb, Mark D. Lee & Ana de Medeiros (dirs.)." *French Studies in Southern Africa*, 49, 250-252. [Cor]

RR3713. Golutvina, Anastasiya V., & Lyudmila V. Babina: "Precedent Phenomena Use in Works of the Modern French Writers Guillaume Musso, Amelie Nothomb and Bernard Werber." *Philological Sciences. Issues of Theory and Practice*, 1, 74-79. [LoC]

RR3714. Hazim, Jawad: "L'Intertextualité entre Réminiscences et Signifiance dans le Récit de Voyage d'Amélie Nothomb." *Litera*, 25 décembre, 193-206. [WC]

RR3715. Intan, Tania: "Mythe de Beauté et Image de Soi Chez une Adolescente dans 'Robert des Noms Propres' d'Amélie Nothomb." *Francisola*, *3*, 2, 153. [WC]

RR3716. Klinkenberg, Jean-Marie, & Catherine Rodgers: "Lee (Mark D.) et Medeiros (Ana de), Dir., Identité, Mémoire, Lieux. Le Passé, le Présent et l'Avenir d'Amélie Nothomb: Paris, Classiques Garnier, Coll. Rencontres, N° 353, Série Littérature des XXe et XXIe siècles, N° 276, 2018, 33p." *Textyles*, 54, 207-210. [Cor]

RR3717. Locic, Simona: "Reinventing the Fairy Tale's Heroine in the Novel 'Barbe Bleue' of Amélie Nothomb." *Thélème*, *34*, 2, 377-392. [Naz]

RR3718. Myronova, N.: "Individual Characteristics of the French Ethnocultural Code Amour (on the Material of Amélie Nothomb 'Mercury')." *International Humanitarian University Herald. Philology*, *3*, 43, 12-15. [WC]

RR3719. Sourieau, Marie-Agnès: "Lee, Mark D., et Ana de Medeiros, Éd. Identité, Mémoire, Lieux: Le Passé, le Présent et l'Avenir d'Amélie Nothomb." *French Review*, *93*, 2, 263. [Naz]

RR3720. Tynan, Avril: "Please Watch Responsibly: The Ethical Responsibility of the Viewer in Amélie Nothomb's *Acide Sulfurique*." *French Forum*, *44*, 1, 133-147. [UofR]

NOUGÉ, Paul.
See also 558.

RR3721. Dotremont, C.: "Histoire de Ne Pas Rire de Paul Nougé." *Europe*, *97*, 1079, 69-71. [Syr]

RR3722. Kukuryk, Agnieszka: "La Transgression des Normes par le Surréalisme Bruxellois Selon Paul Nougé." *Synergies Pologne*, *16*, 113, 122, 147. [RIT]

NOVARINA, Valère.
See also 514, 850.

RR3723. Thomasseau, J.-M.: "Le Salut au Théâtre ou Comment S'en Sortir?: Un Entretien Avec Valère Novarina." *European Drama and Performance Studies*, 12, 167-181. [LoC]

NYS-MAZURE, Colette.
See also 241.
RR3724.   Roussel-Gillet, Isabelle: "Colette Nys-Mazure, la Plus Que Présence: Resemencer la Poésie Avec le Livre d'Artistes." *Nouvelles Études Francophones, 34,* 2, 154-164. [UaB]

O., Rachid.
See 345, 611.

OLLIER, Claude.
See also 649, 666.
RR3725.   Laaouinat, Radouane: "Mise en Scène de l'Espace dans Marrakch Medine de Claude Ollier." 179-190. In 649.

OLLIVIER, Émile.
RR3726.   Berthiaud, Emmanuelle: "'Travailler Au Bonheur de [son] Compagnon': Marie-Thérèse Gravier et Émile Ollivier (Décembre 1868-Août 1870)." *Parlement[s], Revue d'Histoire Politique, 14,* 2, 79. [Cor]
RR3727.   Kunesová, Kvetuse: "The Migrant Memory: Les Urnes Scellées by Emile Ollivier." *Romanica Olomucensia, 31,* 1, 79-89. [LoC]
RR3728.   Modenesi, M.: "Passages di Émile Ollivier Viaggiare e Migrare tra il Tempo e lo Spazio." *Altre Modernita,* 21, 228-235. [Syr]
RR3729.   Paillard, M.: "Embodied Explorations and Migrants' Agency: Movements, Memory and Solidarity in Passages by Émile Ollivier." *International Journal of Francophone Studies, 22,* 3, 311-330. [UaB]

OSTER, Christian.
RR3730.   Faria, Dominique: "L'île Chez Christian Gailly et Christian Oster: Reconnaissance ou Méconnaissance du Territoire Insulaire?" *Carnets,* 17. [Cor]

OULIPO.
See also 397.
RR3731.   ● Bary, Cécile , & Alain Schaffner: *L'Oulipo et les Savoirs: (Formules 21/2018).* New Orleans: UP of the South. 1 vol. [WC]
RR3732.   ● Duncan, Dennis: *The Oulipo and Modern Thought.* Kettering: Oxford UP. 192p. [Syr] (Queneau)
RR3733.   ● Lebrec, Caroline: *Combinatoires Ludiques: Littérature, Contrainte et Mathématique.* New York: Peter Lang. 245p. [LoC] (Queneau)
RR3734.   ● Liitoja, Hillar: *The Oulipo Challenge.* Buffalo: Guernica Editions. 196p. [UofR]
RR3735.   ● Tahar, Virginie: *La Fabrique Oulipienne du Récit: Expérimentations et Pratiques Narratives Depuis 1980.* Paris: Classiques Garnier. 756p. [UofR]
RR3736.   ● Terry, Philip: *The Penguin Book of Oulipo.* [London]: Penguin Books. 531p. [Cor] (Queneau)
RR3737.   Berkman, Natalie: "Raconter L'Oulipo (1960–2000): Histoire et Sociologie d'un Groupe, par Camille Bloomfield." *French Studies, 73,* 2, 322-323. [UaB]

RR3738. Brignoli, Laura: "Camille Bloomfield, Raconter l'Oulipo (1960-2000). Histoire et Sociologie d'un Groupe." *Studi Francesi*, *63*, 1, 196. [UofR]

RR3739. Ciarcià, Paola, & Mauro Speraggi: "Oulipo: L'Opificio delle Parole." *Rivistadada*, 53, 4-49. [WC]

RR3740. Duncan, Dennis: "'All that is Evident is Suspect: Readings from the Oulipo, 1963-2018', by Edited by Ian Monk and Daniel Levin Becker - Review." *The Spectator*, Apr 27 2019. [RIT]

OUOLOGUEM, Yambo.
See also 690, 798.

RR3741. Devevey, Éléonore: "Contrefaire, Subvertir. Portrait de Frobenius / Shrobénius dans le Devoir de Violence de Yambo Ouologuem." *Continents Manuscrits*, 12. [Cor]

RR3742. Nyela, Désiré: "Ouologuem, l'Insolent." *Dalhousie French Studies*, 113, 133-146. [Syr]

OYONO, Ferdinand.
See also 286.

RR3743. Bezari, Christina, Riccardo Raimondo, Thomas Vuong, & El-Shaddai Deva: "D'un Imaginaire Colonial à Un Autre: Ferdinand Oyono en Traduction Allemande." *Itinéraires*, 2018-2. [WC]

PAGNOL, Marcel.
See also 4716, 4753.

RR3744. ● Brun, Marion: *Marcel Pagnol, Classique-Populaire. Ed. Brochée. Réflexions sur les Valeurs d'une Œuvre Intermédiale*. Paris: Classiques Garnier. 840p. [WC]

RR3745. Lestari, Ristiani A.: "La Transformation des Personnages et des Fonds dans le Roman la Gloire de Mon Pere de Marcel Pagnol au Film: Une Etude d'Écranisation de Pamusuk Eneste." *Lingua Litteratia Journal*, *6*, 1, 27-34. [WC]

RR3746. Pataki, Elvira: "Vergilius Provence-Ban: Marcel Pagnol Bucolica-Fordítása." *Antikvitás & Reneszánsz*, 3, 111-127. [BnF]

PARANT, Jean-Luc.
RR3747. ● Parant, Jean-Luc: *Sens et Non-Sens*. Barjols: Plaine Page. [32]p. [BnF]

RR3748. ● Parant, Jean-Luc, Mark Brusse, Marielle Macé, & Kristell Loquet: *Nous Sommes Tous des Migrants*. [Strasbourg, France]: L'Atelier Contemporain. 92p. [Cor]

PAULHAN, Jean.
See also 10, 84, 526, 791, 2365.

RR3749. ● Paulhan, Jean, Henri Pourrat, Claude Dalet, Michel Lioure, & Anne-Marie Lauras: *Correspondance: 1920-1959*. Paris: Gallimard. 816p. [WC]

RR3750. ● *Petit Bestiaire de Jean Paulhan*. Paris: Société des Lecteurs de Jean Paulhan. *Jean Paulhan et Ses Environs: Lettre de la Société des Lecteurs de Jean Paulhan*. 143p. [WC]

RR3751. ● Rilke, Rainer M., & Bernard Baillaud: *Vergers: Suivi des Quatrains Valaisans et de Treize Lettres à Jean Paulhan*. Paris: Le Bruit du Temps. 184p. [BnF]

RR3752. ● Wenger, Jonathan: *De la Plus Tendre Correction: 'Addenda Minora' aux 'Œuvres Complètes' et à la Bibliographie de Jean Paulhan*. Neuchâtel: Chez l'Amiral D.-G. [17]p. [WC]

RR3753. Kechichian, P.: "Autoportrait de Jean Paulhan." *Nouvelle Revue Française*, 637, 132-137. [UofR]

RR3754. Koskas, Camille: "Un Grand Roman des Années 1950? Les Deux Étendards Selon Jean Paulhan." *Revue d'Histoire Littéraire de la France, 119*, 3, 653-670. [UofR]

RR3755. Koskas, Camille, et al.: "Traces du Grand Meaulnes dans Le Pont Traversé (1921) de Jean Paulhan." *Tangence*, 79-93. [Cor]

PÉGUY, Charles.
See also 1, 56, 68, 381, 396, 510, 733.

RR3756. ● *Barrès et Péguy: Si Loin, Si Près*. Paris: L'Amitié Charles Péguy. 243p. [WC]

RR3757. ● Collonges, Julien, & Tatiana Victoroff: *La Lyre et les Armes: Poètes en Guerre: Péguy, Stadler, Owen, Etc*. Paris: Classiques Garnier. 510p. [BnF]

RR3758. ● *Le Cinéma et Péguy*. Paris: L'Amitié Charles Péguy. 66p. [WC]

RR3759. ● Maguire, Matthew W.: *Carnal Spirit. The Revolutions of Charles Peguy*. Philadelphia: University of Pennsylvania Press. 296p. [Syr]

RR3760. ● Pailloux, Louis: *Lettre à Charles Péguy Sur l'Amour Humaine [sic]*. Trocy-en-Multien: Éditions Conférence. 50p. [BnF]

RR3761. ● Péguy, Charles: *Mes Pensées*. Paris: BoD. 125p. [BnF]

RR3762. ● Vélikanov, Marie: *La Sainteté Chez Charles Péguy*. Paris: Les Éditions du Cerf. 346p. [LoC]

RR3763. Aubron, Hervé: "Péguy par le Bas-Côté." *Le Nouveau Magazine Littéraire, 21*, 9, 76. [UaB]

RR3764. Bauwelinck, Egon: "Charles Péguy's Flu: The Metaphor of Diagnosis on the Crossroads of Historical, Sociological and Philosophical Discourses in 1900." *Tempo, 25*, 3, 673-692. [Naz]

RR3765. Labouret, Denis: "Charles Péguy - Choosing Adventure." *Mil Neuf Cent. Revue d'Histoire Intellectuelle, 37*, 1, 53. [Cor]

RR3766. Molenti, Agostino: "El Método de Pensamiento Cívico-Anárquico de Charles Péguy." *Universum (Talca), 34*, 2, 197-222. [Naz]

PÉLADAN, Josephin.
RR3767. ● Péladan, Joséphin, & K. K. Albert: *How to Become a Mage: A Fin-de Siècle French Occult Manifesto*. Woodbury, MN: Llewellyn Worldwide. 1 vol. [WC]

RR3768. ● Peladan, Joséphin, & Palmira Feixas: *Sobre el Andrógino: Teoría Plástica*. Terrades (Girona): Wunderkammer. 76p. [WC]

RR3769. Kayanidi, Leonid G.: "'La Prométhéide' by Josephin Péladan and 'Prometheus' by Vyacheslav Ivanov: Rosicrucian Subtexts of the Symbolic Tragedy." *Vestnik Tomskogo Gosudarstvennogo Universiteta*, 439, 5-10. [WC]

RR3770. Slavkin, Mary: "Fairies, Passive Female Sexuality, and Idealized Female Archetypes at the Salons of the Rose + Croix." *RACAR, Canadian Art Review, 44*, 1, 64. [PrQ]

PENNAC, Daniel.
See also 597.
RR3771. Kim, Annabel L.: "The Excremental Poetics of Daniel Pennac's Journal d'un Corps." *French Studies*, *73*, 3, 416-433. [UofR]

PEREC, Georges.
See also 56, 446, 544, 566, 585, 756.
RR3772. ● Decout, Maxime, & Yû Maeyama: *Cahiers Georges Perec. Vol. 13. La Disparition*. Saint Omer: Les Venterniers. 244p. [WC]
RR3773. ● Delemazure, Raoul: *Une Vie dans les Mots dans les Autres. Ed. Reliée. Le Geste Intertextuel dans l'Œuvre de Georges Pérec*. Paris: Classiques Garnier. 465p. [WC]
RR3774. ● Forsdick, Charles, Andrew N. Leak, & Richard Phillips: *Georges Perec's Geographies: Material, Performative and Textual Spaces*. London: UCL Press. 258p. [Syr]
RR3775. ● Guichard, Françoise, Georges Perec, & Camille Bloomfield: *54 Véritables Cartes Postales Adressées à Georges Perec: Une Sélection*. Paris: Caractères. 93p. [BnF]
RR3776. ● Perec, Georges, & Mireille Ribière: *Georges Perec: Entretiens, Conférences, Textes Rares, Inédits*. Nantes: Joseph K. 1081p. [WC]
RR3777. ● Roumette, Julien: *Récits d'Ellis Island de Georges Perec et Robert Bober au Miroir Contemporain*. Paris: Lettres Modernes Minard. 1 vol. [WC]
RR3778. ● Ruiz, de S. A.: *La Ciudad Desnuda: Variaciones en Torno a Un Hombre Que Duerme de Georges Perec*. Madrid: Abada. 284p. [WC]
RR3779. Brauer, Matthew: "Perec's Arabic: Producing Translingualism in *Les Revenentes*." *Esprit Créateur*, *59*, 4, 54-67. [PrQ] (Bénabou)
RR3780. Díaz-Velázquez, Yunuen E.: "'Me Acuerdo de Malet e Isaac', de Georges Perec. Memoria, Historia y Reescritura." *La Colmena*, 104, 45. [WC]
RR3781. Fiorentino, Francesco, & Daniela Tononi: "De l'Effet Transformatif de l'Imaginaire: W ou le Souvenir d'Enfance de Georges Perec au Prisme des Genres." *Revue Italienne d'Études Françaises*, 9. [Syr]
RR3782. Gabel, Aubrey: "'L'Utopie Serait-Elle Institutionnalisée?': Georges Perec at the Moulin d'Andé." *Contemporary French and Francophone Studies*, *23*, 2, 171-179. [Naz]
RR3783. Motte, Warren: "Original Copies in Georges Perec and Andy Warhol by Priya Wadhera." *Esprit Créateur*, *59*, 1, 155. [UaB]
RR3784. Salceda, Hermes: "Clés Pour La Disparition de Georges Perec." *Faux Titre*, 423. [UaB]
RR3785. Wadhera, Priya: "An Omnipresent Absence: Georges Perec's Silent Protest of the Holocaust in La Disparition." *Contemporary French and Francophone Studies*, *23*, 5, 576-583. [Naz]

PÉRET, Benjamin.
See also 625.
RR3786. ● *Cahiers Benjamin Peret*. Lyon: Association des Amis de Benjamin Péret. 152p. [WC]
RR3787. Delille, Emmanuel: "Librairie: 'Correspondance (1920-1959)'." *Esprit*, 458. [PrQ]

PERGAUD, Louis.

RR3788. ● Bigorgne, Jean-Jacques: *Je Suis Louis Pergaud.* Lyon: Jacques André. 86p. [BnF]

RR3789. ● Chappez, Gérard: *Louis Pergaud: De l'École Buissonnière au Champ d'Honneur.* Bière: Cabédita. 169p. [Cor]

PERRET, Jacques.
See 657.

PHILIPPE, Charles-Louis.

RR3790. ● *Les Amis de Charles-Louis Philippe: Bulletin.* Soumans: Association des Amis de Charles Louis Philippe. *Bulletin - Amis de Charles-Louis Philippe,* 75. 67p. [WC]

PIAGET, Jean.

RR3791. ● Bossé, Michel: *Le Legs de F. de Saussure: Tremplin ou Boulet?: Analyse Épistémologique des Positions Linguistiques de Lev S. Vygotski, Jean Piaget et Jean-Pierre Changeux.* Saint-Lambert, PQ: Cursus Universitaire. 1 vol. [WC]

RR3792. ● Da Rocha, Orandes C., Junior: "Didática Psicológica. Aplicação à Didática da Psicologia de Jean Piaget." *Schème,* *10,* 2, 188-202. [WC]

RR3793. ● De Andrade, Mayara: "A Relação Entre a Crítica de Jean Piaget às Epistemologias Clássicas e a Explicação do Processo de Produção de Novidade." *Schème,* *11,* 1, 4-21.

RR3794. ● Montangero, Jacques, & Danielle Maurice-Naville: *Piaget ou l'Intelligence en Marche: Les Fondements de la Psychologie du Développement.* Bruxelles: Mardaga. 268p. [WC]

RR3795. Enloe, Walter: "The Development of Hiroshima International School: The Influence of Jean Piaget." *Schools: Studies in Education,* 16, 2, 218-235. [RIT]

RR3796. Ferracioli, Laércio: "Aprendizagem, Desenvolvimento e Conhecimento na Obra de Jean Piaget: Uma Análise do Processo de Ensino-Aprendizagem em Ciências." *Revista Brasileira de Estudos Pedagógicos,* 80, 194. [Cor]

RR3797. Fournier, Martine: "Jean Piaget. Comment l'Intelligence Se Développe-T-Elle?" *Les Grands Dossiers des Sciences Humaines,* 54, 3, 12. [BAnQ]

RR3798. Stoltz, Tania, & Angelika Wiehl: "Das Menschenbild als Rätsel Für Jeden: Anthropologische Konzeptionen von Jean Piaget und Rudolf Steiner im Vergleich." *Pädagogische Rundschau,* 73, 253-264. [WC]

RR3799. Zorzi, Analisa: "A Construção da Autonomia Intelectual dos Sujeitos em Jean Piaget: Uma Síntese Teórica." *Schème,* *11,* 1, 50-72. [WC]

PIEYRE DE MANDIARGUES, André.
See 299.

PINEAU, Gisèle.
See also 267, 280, 863, 1908.

RR3800. Auma, Rose: "Le Picaresque: Analyse du Roman Chair Piment de Gisele Pineau." *European Scientific Journal,* 15, 14. [WC]

RR3801. Boblet, Marie-Hélène, Anne Gourio, & Marion Labourey: "Fragilités

Contemporaines et Trauma Colonial. Le Réalisme Magique Pour Dire les Vulnérabilités Sociales dans Cent Vies et des Poussières de Gisèle Pineau." *Elfe XX-XXI*, 9. [Cor]

RR3802.   Ferraroni, Roberto: "Gisèle Pineau, le Parfum des Sirènes." *Studi Francesi*, *63*, 2, 404-405. [UaB]

RR3803.   Gras, Delphine: "Revisiting the Past in the Age of Posts: Rememory in Toni Morrison's God Help the Child and Gisèle Pineau's Femmes des Antilles." *Contemporary Women's Writing*, *13*, 3, 270-286. [UaB]

RR3804.   Mangerson, Polly T.: "Que Peut la Littérature Pour Changer le Monde? Entretien Avec Gisèle Pineau." *French Review*, *93*, 1, 168-176. [Naz]

RR3805.   Obidiegwu, Vincent N.: "De L'exil à la Désillusion dans Un Papillon dans la Cité, L'Exil Selon Julia et Chair Piment de Gisèle Pineau." *International Journal of Francophone Studies*, *22*, 1, 127-145. [RIT]

RR3806.   Panaïté, Oana: "'Je Cherche de l'Or dans Cette Terre Qu'Est l'Écriture": Correspondance Avec Gisèle Pineau." *Nouvelles Études Francophones*, *34*, 2, 116-119. [Syr]

PINGET, Robert.
See 660, 666, 872.

PINSON, Jean-Claude.
See also 780, 783, 789.

RR3807.   Fernández, Erquicia I.: "Jean-Claude Pinson: Une 'Poéthique' du 'Poétariat'." *Cuadernos de Investigación Filológica*, 45, 151. [Syr]

PLEYNET, Marcelin.
See 691.

PLISNIER, Charles.
See 640.

PONGE, Francis.
See also 512, 532, 782.

RR3808.   ● Auclerc, Benoît, & Pauline Flepp: *Présences et Absences de Ponge dans le Paysage Littéraire Contemporain*. Paris: Classiques Garnier. 228p. [WC]

RR3809.   ● Cuillé, Lionel, Jean-Marie Gleize, Bénédicte Gorrillot, & Marie Frisson: *Francis Ponge, Ateliers Contemporains: Actes du Colloque Cerisy 'Francis Ponge: Ateliers Contemporains' Organisé du 24 au 31 Août 2015*. Paris: Classiques Garnier. 659p. [WC]

RR3810.   ● Frisson, Marie: *Francis Ponge, Ateliers Contemporains. Ed. Reliée*. Paris: Classiques Garnier. 664p. [WC]

RR3811.   ● Met, Philippe: *Ponge et le Cinéma*. Paris: Nouvelles Éditions Jean-Michel Place. 128p. [LoC]

RR3812.   Batt, Noëlle: "Philosophical Language Games. Poetic Language Games. Wittgenstein and Ponge." *Revue de Métaphysique et de Morale*, *104*, 4, 323. [UofR]

RR3813.   Cuillé, Lionel: "La Fabrique du Printemps: Francis Ponge et Mai 68." *Contemporary French and Francophone Studies*, *23*, 2, 163-170. [Naz]

RR3814.   Hancock, Austin: "The Protestant Ethic and Structures of Materialist

Salvation in Francis Ponge's Le Parti Pris des Choses." *French Studies*, *73*, 3, 384-400. [UaB]

RR3815.　Perius, Cristiano: "Epistemologia e Arte: a Questão do Conhecimento Estético em Francis Ponge." *Porto Arte*, 24, 41. [WC]

POULAILLE, Henry.
See 492.

POULIN, Jacques.
See 230, 254, 259, 867, 871.

POURRAT, Henri.
See also 3749.
RR3816.　● Taverdet, Gérard: *Parlures de 'Gaspard des Montagnes', Henri Pourrat*. Fontaine-lès-Dijon: Taverdet. 1 vol. [BnF]

POZZI, Catherine.
See also 318.
RR3817.　● Jaëll, Marie, Catherine Pozzi, Lisa Erbès, Catherine Guichard, Christiane Turckheim, Daniel Bornemann, Michèle Finck, & Mathieu Schneider: *Je Suis un Mauvais Garçon: Journal d'une Exploratrice des Rythmes et des Sons; Suivi de Correspondances Avec Catherine Pozzi*. Paris: Arfuyen. 251p. [WC]

PRÉVERT, Jacques.
See also 12, 462, 471, 563.
RR3818.　● Aurouet, Carole: *Jacques Prévert, Détonations Poétiques*. Paris: Classiques Garnier. 357p. [Cor]

RR3819.　● Kouadio, N'guessan A.: *La Poésie de Jacques Prévert: Un Langage Générateur de Liberté*. Saarbrücken: Éditions Universitaires Européennes. 432p. [WC]

RR3820.　● Zilahy, Mirko, Angelo Maggi, Christian Iansante, & Elia Iezzi: *Io Ti Amo: Le Più Belle Poesie d'Amore di Jacques Prevert, Pablo Neruda e Federico Garcia Lorca*. Roma: Dante Alighieri. 227p. [WC]

RR3821.　"Le Roi et l'Oiseau de Paul Grimault et Jacques Prévert: [Dossier]." *Popcorn*, *19*, 9, 10. [WC]

RR3822.　Trunel, Lucile: "Jacqueline Duhême: Une Vie en Couleurs, de Matisse à Prévert." *Art & Métiers du Livre*, 332, [40]-47. [WC]

PRÉVOST, Jean.
RR3823.　● Para, Jean-Baptiste: *Jacques Rivière: Jean Prévost; 1919, Le Traité de Versailles*. Paris: Europe. Europe, *97*, 1082-1083-1084 (juin-juillet-août), 378 p. [WC]

PRIGENT, Christian.
RR3824.　● Prigent, Christian: *Point d'Appui: 2012-2018*. Paris: POL. 463p. [LoC]

RR3825.　● Santi, Sylvain, & Michel Surya: *Cerner le Réel: Christian Prigent à l'Œuvre*. Lyon: ENS. 366p. [UofR]

PROULX, Monique.

RR3826.   Arseneau, Véronique: "The Reverse Irony of Monique Proulx's Le Sexe des Étoiles." *Romanica Olomucensia, 30*, 2, 217-229. [LoC]

PROUST, Marcel.

See also 671, 2209, 2494, 2641, 2748, 2911, 3597.

RR3827.   ● Ampoulié, Marie-Noëlle: *Marcel Proust, Prix Goncourt 1919: Catalogue de l'Exposition, 24 Avril au 25 Août 2019, Maison de Tante-Léonie, Musée Marcel-Proust, Illiers-Combray.* Illiers-Combray: Maison de Tante Léonie, Maison Marcel Proust. 47p. [BnF]

RR3828.   ● Assouline, Pierre: *Proust par Lui-Même* Paris: Tallandier. 660p. [BnF]

RR3829.   ● Bongiovanni, Bertini M.: *À l'Ombre de Vautrin: Proust et Balzac.* Paris: Classiques Garnier. 209p. [Cor]

RR3830.   ● Bubel, Sylvester: *Poetiken der Epiphanie in der Europäischen Moderne: Studien zu Joyce, Proust, Benjamin und Ponge.* Würzburg: Königshausen u. Neumann. 500p. [WC]

RR3831.   ● *Bulletin Marcel Proust.* Illiers-Combray: Societé des Amis de Marcel Proust et des Amis de Combray. 259p. [WC]

RR3832.   ● Chaudier, Stéphane: *Proust ou le Démon de la Description.* Paris: Classiques Garnier. 533p. [UofR]

RR3833.   ● Daubigny, Fanny, & Bruce Whiteman: *Proust in Black: Los Angeles, A Proustian Fiction = Proust au Noir.* San Diego, California: Hyperbole Books. 105p. [WC]

RR3834.   ● De Botton, A.: *Come Proust Può Cambiarvi la Vita.* Milano: U. Guanda. 195p. [WC]

RR3835.   ● Desanges, Gérard: *Marcel Proust au Café-Concert.* Paris: L'Harmattan. 161p. [LoC]

RR3836.   ● Desanges, Gérard: *Marcel Proust et la Politique. Une Conscience Française. Ed. Brochée.* Paris: Classiques Garnier. 488p. [WC]

RR3837.   ● Enthoven, Jean-Paul, Raphaël Enthoven, & Alain Bouldouyre: *Dictionnaire Amoureux de Marcel Proust.* Paris: Plon-Grasset. 744p. [BnF]

RR3838.   ● Fallois, Bernard, & Luc Fraisse: *Proust Avant Proust: Essai Sur les Plaisirs et les Jours.* Paris: Les Belles Lettres. 187p. [Cor]

RR3839.   ● Fallois, Bernard, & Luc Fraisse: *Sept Conférences Sur Marcel Proust: Bernard de Fallois; Édition Établie, Annotée et Préfacé par Luc Fraisse.* Paris: Fallois. 310p. [WC]

RR3840.   ● Felten, Uta, & Volker Roloff: *Revue d'Études Proustiennes, Vol. 9 (2019-1): Proust et la Philosophie: Regards de la Critique Allemande.* Paris: Classiques Garnier. 266p. [WC]

RR3841.   ● Ferrière, Jean: *Et Si 'À la Recherche du Temps Perdu' Nous Était Conté?: Ou Marcel Proust par les Textes.* Lèves: Ella. 294p. [BnF]

RR3842.   ● Foschini, Lorenza: *Il Vento Attraversa le Nostre Anime: Marcel Proust e Reynaldo Hahn: Una Storia d'Amore e d'Amicizia.* Milano: Mondadori. 169p. [LoC]

RR3843.   ● Foschini, Lorenza, & Nathalie Bauer: *Plaisirs d'Amour, Jours d'Amitié: De Marcel Proust et Reynaldo Hahn.* [Paris]: Busclats. 267p. [BnF]

RR3844. ● Fraisse, Luc, & Gérard Bensussan: *Proust et Kant: Hommage à Anne Henry*. Paris: Classiques Garnier. 349p. [WC]

RR3845. ● Friedkin, William, Nicolas Ragonneau, & Jérôme Prieur: *Dans les Pas de Marcel Proust*. Droue-sur-Drouette: La Pionnière. 21p. [BnF]

RR3846. ● Grande, Per B.: *Desire: Flaubert, Proust, Fitzgerald, Miller, Lana Del Rey*. East Lansing, MI: Michigan State UP. 264p. [Cor]

RR3847. ● Hartley, Julia C.: *Reading Dante and Proust by Analogy*. Cambridge: Legenda. 143p. [WC]

RR3848. ● Hiramitsu, Ayano: *Les Chambres de la Création dans l'Œuvre de Marcel Proust*. Paris: Honoré Champion. 237p. [Cor]

RR3849. ● Iven, Mathias, & Angelika Fischer: *Das Paris des Marcel Proust*. Berlin: Edition A. B. Fischer. 63p. [BnF]

RR3850. ● Jany, Christian: *Scenographies of Perception: Sensuousness in Hegel, Novalis, Rilke, and Proust*. Cambridge: Legenda. 253p. [Cor]

RR3851. ● Laget, Thierry: *Proust, Prix Goncourt: Une Émeute Littéraire*. [Paris]: Gallimard. 262p. [UofR]

RR3852. ● Launet, Édouard, & Saraï Delfendahl: *Proust d'une Main: Chefs-d'Œuvres Inédits de la Littérature Érotique*. Paris: Exils. 180p. [WC]

RR3853. ● Mounic, Anne: *Marcel Proust à la Recherche du Temps Perdu. Considérer la Vie Comme Digne d'Être Vécue*. Latresne: Bord de l'Eau. 120p. [WC]

RR3854. ● Muller, Marcel N., Sòstero G. Henrot, & Léonore M. Gerstein: *Le Masque d'Abraham: Essais et Articles Sur À la Recherche du Temps Perdu*. Paris: Classiques Garnier. 364p. [UofR]

RR3855. ● Proust, Marcel, Ricardo Bloch, & Daniel Pennac. *À la Recherche du Texte Perdu: Marcel Proust, du Côté de Chez Swann, Page 1*. Paris: Philippe Rey. 111p. [WC]

RR3856. ● Proust, Marcel, Laurence Grenier-Kaufman, & Olivier Brabois: *Du Côté de Chez Proust: Invitation à Lire l'Œuvre de Marcel Proust*. Paris: First Éditions. 139p. [BnF]

RR3857. ● Roditi, Edouard, & Karl Orend: *The Quest for the Lost Proust*. Paris: Alyscamps Press. 22p. [WC]

RR3858. ● Roloff, Volker: *Marcel Proust - Lektüre Und Intermedialität*. Tübingen: Stauffenburg. 220p. [BnF]

RR3859. ● Tadié, Jean-Yves: *Marcel Proust: Croquis d'une Épopée*. Paris: Gallimard. 384p. [Cor]

RR3860. ● Vendeuvre, Isabelle: *Satire et Fiction dans les Œuvres de Marcel Proust et de Henry James. Ed. Reliée*. Paris: Classiques Garnier. 364p. [WC]

RR3861. ● Vendôme, Maurice: *Proust, Commercy 1915*. Droue-sur-Drouette: Pionnière. 23p. [WC]

RR3862. ● Vinken, Barbara, & Ulrike Sprenger: *Marcel Proust und die Frauen*. Berlin: Insel. 237p. [WC]

RR3863. ● Volpilhac, Aude: *Scènes de Lecture: De Saint Augustin à Proust*. Paris: Gallimard. 530p. [BnF]

RR3864. ● Wickers, Olivier: *Proust Face à l'Énigme Léonard. Une Saison au Louvre*. Paris: Exils. 120p. [UofR]

RR3865. ● Willemart, Philippe: *Les Processus de Création dans À l'Ombre des Jeunes Filles en Fleurs de Marcel Proust*. Paris: Les Éditions du Cerf. 195p. [WC]

RR3866. Andén, Lovisa, & Franck Robert: "Introduction." *Chiasmi International*, 21, 25-28. [Cor]

RR3867. Bayard, Pierre: "Et Si Proust N'Avait Pas Existé?" *Littérature*, *196*, 4, 113. [Syr]

RR3868. Bergez, Daniel: "Marcel Proust À l'Ombre des Jeunes Filles en Fleurs." *Quinzaines*, 1221, 13-14. [UaB]

RR3869. Bidaud, S.: "Lire Marcel Proust à la Lumière de Gustave Guillaume: Mémoire Involontaire, Temps Opératif et Tenseur Binaire." *Information Grammaticale*, 160, 16-23. [UofR]

RR3870. Denis, Anne, & Jean Capiaux: "Anamorphoses et Atemporalité dans l'Œuvre de Proust." *Revue Française de Psychosomatique*, *55*, 1, 111. [Cor]

RR3871. Didier, Béatrice: "Book Review: Marcel Proust et Reynaldo Hahn. Une Création à Quatre Mains. 'Bibliothèque Proustienne'." *Revue d'Histoire Littéraire de la France*, *119*, 1, 230-231. [RIT]

RR3872. Fraisse, L.: "La Parole Intérieure Constitutive de la Vie Spirituelle: La Mystique de la Pensée Chez Proust." *Rivista di Storia e Letteratura Religiosa*, 55, 3, 505-518. [UofR]

RR3873. Fraisse, L.: "Proust ou la Lecture Comme Expérience du Temps." *Studi Francesi*, 189, 485-495. [Syr]

RR3874. Harder, Hollie: "On the Beach and in the Boudoir: Albertine as a Classical Amazon Figure in Marcel Proust's À la Recherche du Temps Perdu." *French Forum*, *44*, 2, 289-303. [PrQ]

RR3875. Hecquet, Vincent: "Yuri Cerqueira dos Anjos, Marcel Proust et la Presse de la Belle Époque: Paris, H. Champion, Coll. Recherches Proustiennes, 2018, 343 pages." *Questions de Communication*, *36*, 2, 321. [Cor]

RR3876. Kato, Yasué: "Proust et Ruskin: La Naissance de l'Écrivain Critique-Traducteur et le Projet Jean Santeuil." *Roman 20-50*, *67*, 1, 75. [Cor]

RR3877. Maghia, R., & F. Corgibet: "Imaginons Proust Dermatologue! Son Questionnaire Revisité par la Fédé." *Dermato Mag*, 7, 3, 173-174. [BnF]

RR3878. Marinčič, Katarina: "Divini Elementa Poetae: Les Lieux et Leurs Noms dans l'Œuvre de Jeunesse de Marcel Proust." *Prostor*, *13*, 2, 102-118. [WC]

RR3879. Mercier, Christophe: "Proust Avec Fallois." *Commentaire*, *165*, 1, 199. [Cor]

RR3880. Pradeau, C.: "Rivifre, Proust et le Nouveau Monde." *Europe*, *97*, 1082, 61-70. [Syr]

RR3881. Proulx, François: "Proust Lecteur d'Emerson à l'Époque de Jean Santeuil." *Roman 20-50*, *67*, 1, 89. [Cor]

RR3882. Quaranta, Jean-Marc: "Proust Apprenti: Retour(s) Sur Jean Santeuil." *Roman 20-50*, *67*, 1, 101. [Cor]

RR3883. "Questionnaire de Proust." *Revue Droit & Littérature*, *3*, 1, 21. [BnF]

RR3884. Slavtscheva, Maria: "Die Bedeutung des Gelesenen: Eine Komparatistische Studie Über Rainer Maria Rilke Und Marcel Proust." *Arcadia*, *54*, 2, 196. [PrQ]

RR3885. Srbinovska, Slavica: "Memory, Time and Space in the Hybrid Structures: Marcel Proust and Orhan Pamouk." *Journal of Contemporary Philology*, *2*, 2, 105, 105-118. [PrQ]

RR3886. Treilhou-Balaudé, Catherine: "Comptes Rendus. Sophie Lucet et

Sophie Proust (dir.). Mémoires, Traces et Archives en Création dans les Arts de la Scène. Rennes, Pur, 2017, 406 p." *Annales. Histoire, Sciences Sociales*, *74*, 3, 842. [Naz]

RR3887.   Van Montfrans, M.: "[Review Of: N. Mauriac Dyer (2017) Bulletin d'Informations Proustiennes. - No. 47]." *Marcel Proust Aujourd'hui*, 15, 180-183. [UaB]

RR3888.   Wood, Michael: "An Absolutely Different Life: Michael Wood Reviews 'Sept Conférences Sur Marcel Proust' by Bernard de Fallois, 'Proust Avant Proust' by Bernard de Fallois and 'Le Mystérieux Correspondant' et 'Autres Nouvelles Inédites' by Marcel Proust, Edited by Luc Fraisse." *The London Review of Books*, Nov 07 2019, 21-6. [PrQ]

PRUDHOMME, Sylvain.

RR3889.   Chatelet, Cécile: "Révoltes et Débâcles dans la Fiction Contemporaine Française. Images Réfléchies des Soulèvements dans Rue des Voleurs de Mathias Énard et les Grands de Sylvain Prudhomme." *Contemporary French and Francophone Studies*, *23*, 3, 342-350. [Naz]

PSICHARI, Ernest.
See 364.

QUENEAU, Raymond.
See also 683, 3733, 3732, 3736.

RR3890.   ● Gosling, James P.: *Raymond Queneau's Dubliners: Bewildered by Excess of Love*. Newcastle upon Tyne: Cambridge Scholars Publisher. 219p. [Syr]

RR3891.   ● Tononi, Daniela: *Génétiqueneau: Sur la Genèse de "Pierrot Mon Ami", "Les Fleurs Bleues" et "Le Vol d'Icare"*. Grenoble: UGA Éditions, Université Grenoble Alpes. 168p. [Cor]

RR3892.   Blin-Rolland, Armelle: "Adaplastics: Forming the Zazie dans le Métro Network." *Modern & Contemporary France*, *27*, 4, 457-473. [UaB]

RR3893.   McAuliffe, Sam: "Black Dust: Raymond Queneau and the Encyclopedia of the Inexact Sciences." *Paragraph*, *42*, 2, 154-169. [Naz]

RR3894.   McCaffrey, Enda: "Zazie's Enduring Legacy: A Philosophical Reflection." *Modern & Contemporary France*, *27*, 4, 505-518. [Naz]

RR3895.   Morrey, Douglas: "'La Nouvelle Vague, Elle T'emm-!' Louis Malle, Zazie dans le Métro and the French New Wave." *Modern & Contemporary France*, *27*, 4, 493-503. [Naz]

RR3896.   Wardle, M.: "A Worldwide Web of Words: Queneau Redux." *Forum (Netherlands)*, *17*, 1, 62-76. [WC]

QUIGNARD, Pascal.
See also 461, 646, 673, 806.

RR3897.   ● Quignard, Pascal: *La Vie N'Est Pas Une Biographie*. Paris: Galilée. 180p. [UofR]

RR3898.   Álvares, Cristina: "Penser la Différence Anthropologique: Une Lecture Croisée de Quignard et Bimbenet." *French Forum*, *44*, 3, 423-435. [UofR]

RR3899.   Alvares, C.: "Jadis, dans le Commencement la Parole N'Était Pas. Sacré, Anthropogenèse et Animalité Humaine Chez Pascal Quignard." *Cedille*, 15, 41-53. [Syr]

RR3890.   Bekhedidja, Nabila: "La Technique du Collage: Une Stratégie Esthétique et Un Procédé Littéraire dans 'Terrasse à Rome' de Pascal Quignard." *Francisola*, *3*, 2, 105. [WC]

RR3891.   Brandolini, M. C.: "De A Jusqu'à Z": Le Dictionnaire Sauvage Pascal Quignard." *Rivista di Letterature Moderne e Comparate*, *72*, 2, 211-219. [UaB]

RR3892.   Calle-Gruber, Mireille: "Carpe Diem. Cueille, Extirpe, Arrache le Jour. Pourquoi Songer à Cueillir le Jour?: Une Journée de Voyage dans les Langues de Pascal Quignard." *Littera*, 4, 7-15. [Cor]

RR3893.   Kim, Ko Woon: "L'Étude Sur la Lieuité des Minoritaires Chez Pascal Quignard - Au Travers de Villa Amalia et Les Solidarités Mystérieuses." *Études de Langue et Littérature Françaises*, 118, 37-70. [WC]

RR3894.   Kuwada, Kohei: "L'Inquiétante Quotidienneté: Le Motif de l'Eau dans l'Œuvre de Pascal Quignard." *Littera*, 4, 39-48. [Cor]

RR3895.   Martin, Xavier: "La Littérature à l'Épreuve du Réel: Les Jeux de Pascal Quignard Avec les Lettres." *Bergen Language and Linguistics Studies*, *10*, 1, 11. [WC]

RR3896.   Schilling, Derek: "Vuong, Léa. Pascal Quignard: Towards the Vanishing Point." *French Review*, *92*, 3, 224-224. [Naz]

RR3897.   Vuong, Léa: "Pascal Quignard: Vies, Œuvres par Agnès Cousin de Ravel (Review)." *French Studies*, *73*, 3, 485. [UaB]

RR3898.   Yoo, Jae-Hwa: "Sur la Métaphore et l'Aphasie de Pascal Quignard." *The Journal of Contemporary Psychoanalysis*, *21*, 1, 79-118. [WC]

RABEMANANJARA, Jacques.
See 200, 256.

RACHILDE.
See 387, 465.

RADIGUET, Raymond.
RR3899.   Legoy, Covinne. "'Comme une Foule de Vieux Amis': À la Lueur des Bals Masqués, une Histoire de l'Amitié Est-Elle Possible?" *Romanic Review*, *110*, 1-4, 31-52. [RIT]

RAMUZ, Charles-Ferdinand.
RR3900.   ● Pétermann, Stéphane: *C. F. Ramuz: Sentir Vivre et Battre le Mot.* Lausanne: Presses Polytechniques et Universitaires Romandes. 159p. [BnF]

RANCIÈRE, Jacques.
See also 1096, 2108, 2132, 2430, 2440.
RR3901.   ● Bassas, Javier: *Jacques Rancière: Ensayar la Igualdad.* Barcelona: Gedisa. 142p. [WC]

RR3902.   ● Cowden, Stephen, & David Ridley: *The Practice of Equality: Jacques Rancière and Critical Pedagogy.* New York: Peter Lang. 192p. [Cor]

RR3903.   ● Fernández, Polanco A., et al.: *#Re-visiones: Conversaciones: Susan Buck-Morss, Suely Rolnik, Jacques Rancière, Marina Garcés, Pablo Lafuente, Aura Cumes, Iritt Rogoff, Kristin Ross, Lucía Egaña.* Madrid: Brumaria. 288, 302p. [WC]

RR3904.   • Mayer, Ralf, Alfred Schäfer, & Steffen Wittig: *Jacques Rancière: Pädagogische Lektüren*. Wiesbaden: Springer VS. 291p. [BnF]

RR3905.   • Ramond, Charles: *Jacques Rancière: L'Égalité des Intelligences*. Paris: Belin. 208p. [Cor]

RR3906.   • Rancière, Jacques, Katia Genel, & Axel Honneth: *Reconnaissance ou Mésentente: Un Dialogue Critique*. Paris: Éditions de la Sorbonne. 152p. [WC]

RR3907.   • Vogt, Erik M.: *Zwischen Sensologie und Ästhetischem Dissens: Essays zu Mario Perniola und Jacques Rancière*. Wien: Turia + Kant. 241p. [Cor]

RR3908.   Allerkamp, Andrea, Katia Genel, & Mariem Hazoume: "What to Do with Adorno's Aesthetic Theory? An Interview with Jacques Rancière." *Journal of French and Francophone Philosophy*, 27, 2, 127-141. [WC]

RR3909.   Almeida, Leonardo M. C.: "Jacques Rancière e a Política dos Direitos dos Animais: A Estética da Subjetividade Jurídica e a Politização do Social." *Revista da Faculdade de Direito Ufpr*, 64, 2, 161. [WC]

RR3910.   Burgos, Adam: "Jacques Rancière and Critical Theory: Issue Introduction." *Journal of French and Francophone Philosophy*, 27, 2, 1-7. [WC]

RR3911.   Chowdhury, Dwaipayan: "Disruptions: An Interview with Jacques Rancière." *Lateral*, 8, 1. [WC]

RR3912.   Claviez, Thomas: "Where are Jacques and Ernesto when You Need them? Rancière and Laclau on Populism, Experts and Contingency." *Philosophy & Social Criticism*, 45, 9-10, 1132-43. [PrQ]

RR3913.   Flatscher, Matthias, & Sergej Seitz: "Of Citizens and Plebeians: Postnational Political Figures in Jürgen Habermas and Jacques Rancière." *European Law Journal*, 25, 5, 502-507. [Naz]

RR3914.   González, Blanco A.: "Política de la Ficción / Ficción de la Política en Jacques Rancière." *Signa*, 28, 733. [UaB]

RR3915.   Hussak, van V. R. P.: "Dentro da Sala Escura. Algumas Reflexões em Torno a Questão do Espectador a Partir de Silvia Schwarzböck e Jacques Rancière." *Revista Limiar*, 6, 12, 88-100. [WC]

RR3916.   Karapetrovic, Milena: "Ontology and Politics: From Disagreement to Absence the Political Philosophy of Jacques Rancière and Slavoj Zizek." *Politeia*, 9, 18, 51-65. [WC]

RR3917.   Lamy, Jérôme: "Gabriel Gauny, le Philosophe Plébéien: Textes Rassemblés et Présentés par Jacques Rancière, Paris, La Fabrique, 2017, 276 p." *Cahiers d'Histoire*, 143. [UaB]

RR3918.   Lloyd, Moya: "Whose Names Count? Jacques Rancière on Alfredo Jaar's Rwanda Project." *Contemporary Political Theory*, 18, 3, 311-330. [Naz]

RR3919.   Nickleson, Patrick: "Translator's Introduction: Jacques Rancière, 'Autonomy and Historicism: The False Alternative'." *Perspectives of New Music*, 57, 1-2, 325-327. [UaB]

RR3920.   Nino, D. M. P.: "Reflections on Intellectual Emancipation from Jacques Rancière's 'The Ignorant Schoolmaster'." *Topicos (Mexico)*, 56, 339-364. [Syr]

RR3921.   Osvaldo, Fontes F.: "Jacques Rancière e a Modernidade do Movimento." *Moringa*, 10, 2. [Syr]

RR3922.   Pember, Alice: "James Harvey (2018) Jacques Rancière and the Politics of Art Cinema." *Film-Philosophy*, 23, 2, 223-226.[Syr]

RR3923.   Perica, I.: "The Archipolitics of Jacques Rancière." *Krisis*, 1, 15-26. [Naz]

RR3924.   Pribiag, Ioana V.: "Politics and Its Others: Jacques Rancière's Figures of Alterity." *Philosophy Today*, *63*, 2, 447-470. [Naz]

RR3925.   Rancière, Jacques, & Patrick Nickleson: "Autonomy and Historicism: The False Alternative (on the Regimes of Historicity of Art)," *Perspectives of New Music*, *57*, 1, 329-351. [UaB]

RR3926.   Ross, Alison: "Acting Through Inaction: The Distinction between Leisure and Reverie in Jacques Rancière's Conception of Emancipation." *Journal of French and Francophone Philosophy*, *27*, 2, 76-94. [WC]

RR3927.   Quintana, Laura: "Jacques Rancière and the Emancipation of Bodies." *Philosophy & Social Criticism*, *45*, 2, 212-238. [RIT]

RR3928.   Santos, Priscilla C., & Luiz H. U. Cademartori: "Por uma Democracia: Entre a Democracia Liberal e a Prática Política em Jacques Rancière." *Seqüência*, *42*, 83, 220-246. [Naz]

RR3929.   Steimbreger, Lautaro: "¿Autoridad Emancipatoria? Una Aproximación desde el Maestro Ignorante de Jacques Rancière." *Análisis*, 51, 94, 57-79. [WC]

RR3930.   Tavakkoli, Amirpasha: "Jacques Rancière, Modernité, Événement Inachevé: Les Temps Modernes. Art, Temps, Politique." *Relief*, *13*, 1, 183. [Syr]

RR3931.   Vogt, Erik: "Aesthetics Qua Excess: Mario Perniola and Jacques Rancière." *Am Journal of Art and Media Studies*, *20*, 1. [WC]

RR3932.   Voigt, André F.: "O Conceito de 'Cena' na Obra de Jacques Rancière: A Prática do 'Método da Igualdade'." *Kriterion*, *60*, 142, 23-41. [RIT]

RAY, Jean.
See also 698.

RR3933.   ● Bekaert, Jean-Louis, Jean-Louis Etienne, & Michel Oleffe: *Jean Ray Illustré*. Kuurne: L'Amicale Jean Ray/ Vriendenkring Jean Ray. 2 vols. [WC]

RR3934.   Jiménez, Murillo J. C.: "El Juego Conflictivo del Desdoblamiento en 'Yo Maté a Alfred Heavenrock' de Jean Ray: Una Paradoja Identitaria Entre el Héroe y su Doppelgänger." *Letras*, 65, 61-92. [Cor]

RÉAGE, Pauline.
RR3935.   Tremblais, Mathilde: "Une Fille Amoureuse de Pauline Réage, ¿Una Autoficción Avant la Lettre?" *Anales de Filología Francesa*, *27*, 1, 365-384. [Naz]

REBATET, Lucien.
See 320.

RÉDA, Jacques.
See also 224, 624, 802.

RR3936.   Germain, Marie O.: "De la Physique Amusante: Entretien Avec Jacques Réda." *Revue de la Bnf*, *58*, 1, 94. [Cor]

RR3937.   Parenteau, Olivier: "Deux Poètes Font les Courses: L'Hypermarché Chez Jacques Réda et Michel Houellebecq." *Captures*, *1*, 2. [WC]

RÉGNIER, Henri de.
See also 535.

RR3938.   ● Jaloux, Edmond, Henri, Régnier, & Pierre Lachasse: *Correspondance Avec Henri et Marie de Régnier (1896-1939). Ed. Reliée*. Paris: Classiques Garnier. 400p. [LoC]

RR3939.　● Regnier, Henri: *Henri de Régnier, Témoin de Son Temps. Ed. Reliée. Anthologie.* Paris: Classiques Garnier. 816p. [BnF]

RR3940.　Cabello Andrés, Nuria: "La Poetica del Agua en Henri de Régnier." *Epos*, 35, 63-79. [RIT]

RR3941.　Dufour, Élodie: "Henri de Régnier: Moderne, Classique, Moderne Classique?" *Faux Titre*, 434, 217-228. [UaB]

RR3942.　Javourez, Franck: "'Imaginer le Visage Absent de la Déesse.' Une Visite au Palais des Choses d'Henri de Régnier." *Revue d'Histoire Littéraire de la France*, *119*, 3, 553-566. [RIT]

RR3943.　Perrin, Jean-François: "La Scène de Réminiscence Comme Instrument Compositionnel: La Double Maîtresse d'Henri de Régnier." *Revue d'Histoire Littéraire de la France*, *119*, 1, 103-112. [UofR]

RENARD, Jules.
See also 439.

RR3944.　Ciobaca, C.-E.: "Translation Norms and Children's Literature: (Re) Translating Poil de Carotte." *Studii Si Cercetari Fliologice, Seria Limbi Romanice*, *1*, 26, 71-93. [Cor]

REVERDY, Pierre.
See also 507, 825.

RR3945.　Barrientos, R. R.: "María Eugenia Silva. Vicente Huidobro y Pierre Reverdy Frente al Creacionismo. Santiago: Mago Editores, 2018: 168 p." *Anales de Literatura Chilena*, *19*, 31, 281-283. [WC]

REZA, Yasmina.
See also 53, 854.

RR3946.　● Evers, Lisa, Candy Welz, Theresa Beranek, Swaantje L. Kleff, & Yasmina Reza: *Der Gott des Gemetzels: Yasmina Reza.* Weimar: Deutsches Nationaltheater und Staatskapelle Weimar Weimar Buch - und Kunstdruckerei Keßler. 41p. [WC]

RR3947.　● Théâtre du Rideau Vert: *'Art', Une Pièce de Yasmina Reza, Mise en Scène Marie-France Lambert.* [Montréal]: Théâtre du Rideau Vert. 10p. [BAnQ]

RR3948.　Torrisi, Valentina: "Puestas en Escena de Obras de Draturgas en la Cartelera de ABC de Madrid (2006-2009)." *Signa*, 28, 1453-97. [RIT]

RR3949.　Villamia, Luis: "L'Empire des Nerfs: L'Échec de la Civilisation et la Violence Postmoderne dans l'Œuvre de Yasmina Reza." *French Forum*, *44*, 3, 437-452. [Naz]

RICARDOU, Jean.
See also 691.

RR3950.　● Boissieu, Emmanuel: *Paul Ricœur: Un Inconditionnel de l'Amour.* [Toulouse]: Domuni-Press. 116p. [LoC]

RR3951.　● Ricardou, Jean, Erica Freiberg, & Marc Avelot: *Les Lieux-Dits: Et Autres Écrits.* [Bruxelles]: Les Impressions Nouvelles. 297p. [BnF]

RR3952.　Hill, Leslie: "Un Aventurier de l'Écriture: Entretiens Avec Jean Ricardou. Propos Recueillis par Amir Biglari." *French Studies*, *73*, 3, 483-484. [UofR]

RICŒUR, Paul.

See also 2012, 3674.

RR3953. • Furia, Paolo: *Rifiuto, Altrove, Utopia: Una Fenomenologia Estetica del Riconoscimento Nell'opera di Paul Ricœur*. Milano: Mimesis. 384p. [LoC]

RR3954. • Gillies, Robert A.: *Guilt and Forgiveness: A Study in the Thought and Personality of Paul Ricœur*. [Haddington, Scotland]: Handsel Press. 116p. [WC]

RR3955. • Linden, Phillip J.: *Slavery, Religion and Regime: The Political Theory of Paul Ricœur as a Conceptual Framework for a Critical Theological Interpretation of the Modern State*. [Bloomington, IN]: Xlibris. 319p. [LoC]

RR3956. • Ricœur, Paul, & Pierre-Olivier Monteil: *Écrits et Conférences: 4*. Paris: Seuil. 340p. [WC]

RR3957. • Weiland, Marc: *Mensch und Erzählung: Helmuth Plessner, Paul Ricœur und die Literarische Anthropologie*. Stuttgart: J. B. Metzler. 343p. [BnF]

RR3958. Benjamins, J.: "Metaphorical Bridges: Paul Ricœur's Theory of the Interanimation of Discourses for Phenomenology of Religion." *Research in Phenomenology*, *49*, 3, 403-424. [Naz]

RR3959. Clorinda, Vendra M. C.: "Paul Ricœur on Collective Memory: The Cohesion of Social Life." *Voluntas*, *10*, 3, 87. [WC]

RR3960. Costa, Gilmário G.: "Acerca da Questão do Trágico na Filosofia Prática de Paul Ricœur." *O Que Nos Faz Pensar*, *28*, 44, 239. [WC]

RR3961. Dahl, Darren E.: "The Origin in Traces: Diversity and Universality in Paul Ricœur's Hermeneutic Phenomenology of Religion." *International Journal for Philosophy of Religion*, *86*, 2, 99-110. [PrQ]

RR3962. Daughton, Amy: "Hope and Tragedy: Insights from Religion in the Philosophy of Paul Ricœur." *European Journal for Philosophy of Religion*, *11*, 3, 135. [WC]

RR3963. Du Toit, L.: "Introduction: Paul Ricœur's Question." *Philosophy & Rhetoric*, *52*, 3, 227-231. [RIT]

RR3964. Fischer, Pacheco M. P., & Tassiana B. Santos: "Direito, Anista e Perdão: A Partir da Perspectiva de Paul Ricœur." *Revista Brasileira de Sociologia do Direito*, *6*, 1. [WC]

RR3965. Freysteinson, Wyona M.: "A Synopsis of Ricœur's Phenomenology of the Will: Implications for Nursing Practice, Research, and Education." *Journal of Holistic Nursing*, *37*, 1, 87-93. [PrQ]

RR3966. Galabru, Sophie: "Paul Ricœur et Emmanuel Levinas: Vulnérabilité, Mémoire et Narration: Peut-On Raconter la Vulnérabilité?" *Études Ricoeuriennes / Ricœur Studies*, *10*, 1, 125-139. [Syr]

RR3967. Hawkins, Spencer: "Theory of a Practice: A Foundation for Blumenberg's Metaphorology in Ricœur's Theory of Metaphor." *Thesis Eleven*, *155*, 1, 91-108. [PrQ]

RR3968. Houle, Jean-François: "Estime de Soi et Reconnaissance Chez Paul Ricœur." *Symposium*, *23*, 2, 202-218. [UaB]

RR3969. Jani, Anna: "Guilt, Confession, and Forgiveness: From Methodology to Religious Experiencing in Paul Ricœur's Phenomenology." *The Journal of Speculative Philosophy*, *33*, 1, 8-21. [UofR]

RR3970. Katz-Gilbert, Muriel: "Note Sur la Conception Narrative de l'Identité Personnelle Chez Paul Ricœur et Ses Limites dans le Champ de la Psychanalyse." *Cahiers de Psychologie Clinique*, *52*, 1, 225. [Cor]

RR3971.   Naugrette-Fournier, Marion, Bruno Poncharal, & Michèle Leclerc-Olive: "Temps et Récit de Paul Ricœur (1983-1985): Un Ouvrage Majeur de la Philosophie Française dans le Monde Anglophone?" *Palimpsestes*, 33, 44-52. [Naz]

RR3972.   Oldfield, J.: "Geoffrey Dierckxsens: Paul Ricœur's Moral Anthropology—Singularity, Responsibility, and Justice: Lexington Books, 2018, ISBN: 978-1-4985-4520-4." *Continental Philosophy Review*, *52*, 3, 327-333. [UofR]

RR3973.   O'Mathúna, Dónal P. & Matthew R. Hunt: "Ethics and Crisis Translation: Insights from the Work of Paul Ricœur." *Disaster Prevention and Management*, *29*, 2, 175-186. [Naz]

RR3974.   Quinceno, Osorio J. D.: "Memoria y Mismidad. Análisis desde la Fenomenología-Hermenéutica de Paul Ricœur." *Humanidades (Montevideo. En Línea)*, 5, 60-83. [Naz]

RR3975.   Rebok, María G.: "Paul Ricœur: O el Reconocimiento Como Experiencia de Donación Mutua." *Tópicos. Revista de Filosofía de Santa Fe*, 30, 88-103. [Naz]

RR3976.   Salles, Walter F.: "Paul Ricœur e a Lógica do Perdão." *Horizonte*, *17*, 52, 414-435. [Naz]

RR3977.   Sands, Justin: "Hermeneutics, History, and D'où Parlez-Vous? Paul Ricœur and Tsenay Serequeberhan on How to Engage African Philosophy from a Western Context." *South African Journal of Philosophy*, *38*, 4, 371-382. [Naz]

RR3978.   Sanfelice, Vinicius Oliveira: "L'Œuvre de la Métaphoricité Chez Paul Ricœur: Entre 'Esthétique' et 'Figurabilité' Psychanalytique." *Revista Portuguesa de Filosofia*, *75*, 4, 2329-2344. [UaB]

RR3979.   Seo, Hyejeong: "A Study of Paul Ricœur's View on the Salvation of the Society." *The Bible & Theology*, 92, 219-249. [WC]

RR3980.   Singsuriya, P.: "Ricœur's Method and Theological Self-Understanding." *Acta Theologica*, *39*, 1, 222-40. [PrQ]

RR3981.   Tell, Maria Belen: "Filosofía y 'Plus de Sentido' en Franz Rosenzweig y Paul Ricœur." *Cuadernos Judaicos*, 36, 2-18. [PrQ]

RR3982.   Todorovic, T.: "Interpreting the Selfhood Paul Ricœur." *Filozofska Istrazivanja*, *39*, 1, 17-31. [Cor]

RR3983.   Travaglini, G.: "Imagination and Knowledge in the Metaphorology of Paul Ricœur." *Theoria (Sweden)*, *85*, 5, 383-401. [UofR]

RR3984.   Valldecabres, D. V.: "Paul Ricœur's Hermeneutics and Audiovisual Narrative: Mimesis and Self-Knowledge." *Rilce*, 1, 295-309. [Naz]

RR3985.   Vidam, Teodor, & Marius Pop: "Sketch on Paul Ricœur's Life and Writings." *Sæculum*, *47*, 1, 121-132. [Syr]

RR3986.   Waldenfels, Bernhard: "Paul Ricœur: Raconter, Se Souvenir et Oublier." *Études Ricoeuriennes / Ricœur Studies*, *10*, 1, 10-26. [Naz]

RR3987.   Weichert, Katarzyna: "The Role of Image and Imagination in Paul Ricœur's Metaphor Theory." *Eidos*, *3*, 1, 64-77. [WC]

RR3988.   White, Grant: "Liturgical Theology After Schmemann: An Orthodox Reading of Paul Ricœur by Brian A. Butcher." *Journal of Orthodox Christian Studies*, *2*, 1, 117-119. [Cor]

RR3989.   White, Nathan H.: "The Mediated Nature of Knowledge: Paul Ricœur's Philosophy as a Means of Teaching Students About Science and Religion." *Contemporary Trends and Issues in Science Education*, 48, 63-76. [WC]

RIMBAUD, Arthur.
See also 57, 795, 984, 3225.

RR3990. ● Blaineau, Alexandre: *Les Chevaux de Rimbaud*. Arles: Actes Sud. 180p. [BAnQ]

RR3991. ● Cavallaro, Adrien: *Rimbaud et le Rimbaldisme: XIXe-XXe Siècles*. Paris: Hermann. 495p. [UofR]

RR3992. ● Cornu, Jean-Michel: *L'Abyssinienne de Rimbaud: Et Autres Études*. Caen: Lurlure. 290p. [Cor]

RR3993. ● Cotellessa, Silvio: *L'Europa del Futuro Passato: L'Integrazione Europea e la 'Sindrome di Rimbaud'*. Soveria Mannelli: Rubbettino. 123p. [LoC]

RR3994. ● Fontaine, Hugues: *Arthur Rimbaud Photographe*. Paris: Textuel. 215p. [BnF]

RR3995. ● Gaitet, Richard: *Rimbaud Warriors: Rhapsodie Pour Bohémiens*. Paris: Paulsen. 237p. [Cor]

RR3996. ● Gauthier, Jean-Marie: *L'Œuvre et le Destin d'Arthur Rimbaud: Un Regard Clinique*. Louvain-la-Neuve: EME Éditions. 202p. [LoC]

RR3997. ● Kramer, Max: *Poésie Moderne et Inversion: Les Stratégies Queer Chez Arthur Rimbaud, Stefan George et Federico Garcia Lorca*. Paris: L'Harmattan. 279p. [Cor]

RR3998. ● Murphy, Steve, & Jean-Jacques Lefrère: *Rimbaud, Verlaine et Zut: À la Mémoire de Jean-Jacques Lefrère*. Paris: Classiques Garnier. 606p. [Cor]

RR3999. ● Oberlé, Philippe: *Arthur Rimbaud et Henry de Monfreid en Éthiopie: La Disparition d'un Poète, l'Annonce d'un Romancier*. Nîmes: Mondial Livre. 242p. [WC]

RR4000. ● Perrin, Raymond: *Rimbaud et la Rimbaldo-Fiction: Chance ou Malchance Pour la Rimbaldie*. Paris: L'Harmattan. 178p. [UofR]

RR4001. ● Pichon, Fanny: *Rimbaud en un Clin d'Œil!: L'Histoire de Sa Vie, Ses Plus Beaux Textes, le Mythe Rimbaud*. Paris: First. 160p. [BnF]

RR4002. ● Rimbaud, Arthur, Alfred Wolfenstein, & Hermann Haarmann: *Rimbaud: Leben - Werk - Briefe*. Marburg: Büchner-Verlag. 300p. [WC]

RR4003. ● Thomas, Frédéric: *Rimbaud Révolution*. Montreuil: L'Echappée. 103p. [LoC]

RR4004. Acquisto, Joseph: "Poetry, Politics, and the Body in Rimbaud: Lyrical Material, by Robert St. Clair." *French Studies*, *73*, 4, 642. [UofR]

RR4005. Chambert-Loir, Henri: "Jean Rocher, Arthur Rimbaud dans L'Herbe d'Où l'On Ne Peut Fuir; Pourquoi S'Engager Pour Déserter." *Archipel*, 98, 270-272. [Cor]

RR4006. Chevrier, Alain: "Book Review: Arthur Rimbaud." *Parade Sauvage*, 30, 283-285. [UaB]

RR4007. Connolly, Thomas C.: "Poetry, Politics & the Body in Rimbaud: Lyrical Material by Robert St. Clair, And: Arthur Rimbaud by Seth Whidden." *French Forum*, *44*, 3, 456-465. [RIT]

RR4008. Fouquet, Marie: "Rimbaud Warrior." *Le Nouveau Magazine Littéraire*, *18*, 6, 75. [UaB]

RR4009. Ginsburgh, Victor, & Stamos Metzidakis: "On Rimbaud's 'Vowels,' Again: Vowels or Colors?" *Athens Journal of Philology*, 6, 4, 225-234. [WC]

RR4010. Gouvard, Jean-Michel: "Rimbaud, Brecht, Benjamin: Une 'Histoire Splendide'." *Parade Sauvage*, 30, 191-202. [UaB]

RR4011.   Harrow, Susan: "Critical Lives: Arthur Rimbaud." *Modern & Contemporary France*, 27, 3, 406-407. [RIT]

RR4012.   Jesi, Furio: "A Reading of Rimbaud's *'Bateau Ivre'*." *Theory & Event*, 22, 4, 1003-1017. [Naz]

RR4013.   Kinsella, John: "From Aftering Delmore Schwartz's A Season in Hell [Rimbaud] Translation." *New England Review*, 40, 3, 28-36. [UaB]

RR4014.   O'Dell, Emily J.: "Geographies of Disability in the Letters of Rimbaud: Mapping Colonialism and Disablement in Yemen and Ethiopia." *Journal of Literary & Cultural Disability Studies*, 13, 4, 445-460. [Naz]

RR4015.   Pollin-Dubois, Karl: "L'Appel du Bleu: Godard Sur les Traces de Rimbaud." *French Review*, 93, 2, 122-134. [Naz]

RR4016.   Raffi, Maria Emanuela: "Walid Hamdi, l'Adjectif dans la Poésie de Rimbaud." *Studi Francesi*, 187 (*63*, 1), 180. [UaB]

RR4017.   Rauer, Selim: "Book Review: L'Adjectif dans la Poésie de Rimbaud." *Parade Sauvage*, 30, 288-294. [UaB]

RR4018.   Reverte, M.: "Le Sonnet du Trou du Cul: Paul Verlaine et Arthur Rimbaud." *Dermato Mag*, 7, 2. [BnF]

RR4019.   Richter, Mario: "Frédéric Thomas, Rimbaud Révolution." *Studi Francesi*, 189 (*63*, 3), 598. [UaB]

RR4020.   Rogghe, Simon: "Le Cri du Papillon: The Doors et Rimbaud." *Parade Sauvage*, 30, 229-248. [UaB]

RR4021.   Rogghe, Simon: "'Ni dans le Monde Sensible, Ni Sensiblement En Dehors de Ce Monde": The Occultation of Surrealism and Rimbaud's Assassins." *The French Review*, 93, 2, 64-76. [RIT]

RR4022.   Sangsue, Daniel: "Le Fantôme de Rimbaud." *Parade Sauvage*, 30, 259-266. [UaB]

RR4023.   Schellino, Andrea: "Yalla Seddiki, Rimbaud Is Rimbaud Is Rimbaud Is Rimbaud Is Rimbaud. Rien de Nouveau Chez Rimbaud." *Studi Francesi*, 187 (*63*, 1), 180-181. [UaB]

RR4024.   Unwin, Timothy: "Arthur Rimbaud, by Seth Whidden." *French Studies*, 73, 3, 470-471. [UofR]

RR4025.   Vaillant, Alain: "Le Phénomène Rimbaud." *Parade Sauvage*, 30, 97-120. [UaB]

RR4026.   "Whidden, Seth. Arthur Rimbaud." *Forum for Modern Language Studies*, 55, 4, 500-501. [UofR]

RR4027.   Whidden, Seth: "Le Sieur Rimbaud, Marinier." *Parade Sauvage*, 30, 275-278. [UaB]

RR4028.   Yakubovich, Yauheniya: "Rimbaud en Bélarusse: Tradition Traductologique et Étude de Cas." *Synergies Europe*, 14, 103, 118, 195. [PrQ]

RINGUET.
See 1.

RIVAZ, Alice.
RR4029.   Barthelmebs-Raguin, Hélène: "Construire l'Auctorialité: Les Correspondances d'Alice Rivaz: Building Auctoriality: The Correspondence of Alice Rivaz." *Estudios Románicos*, 28, 31-45. [Naz]

RIVIÈRE, Jacques.

See also 387, 3823.

RR4030. ● "Cahiers Jacques Rivière Alain-Fournier: 4 (2019)." *Cahiers Jacques Rivière Alain-Fournier*, 4. 1 vol. [WC]

ROBBE-GRILLET, Alain.

RR4031. Brignoli, Laura: "Alain Robbe-Grillet, Entretiens Complices." *Studi Francesi*, 188 (*63*, 2), 393-394. [UaB]

RR4032. Fulka, J.: "Affect and Exteriority: Sartrian Inspiration of Alain Robbe-Grillet." *Svet Literatury*, 59, 135-146. [Cor]

RR4033. Grossi, B.: "Entre la Imagen y el Concepto. Alain Robbe-Grillet y el Discurso Angelical de la Teoría." *Cedille*, 15, 219-239. [Syr]

RR4034. Günday, Rifat: "The Effect of Cinema in the Novel of Labyrinth of Alain Robbe-Grillet." *International Journal of Languages Education*, 7, 4, 392-400. [WC]

ROBLÈS, Emmanuel.

See also 868.

RR4035. Guy, Dugas: "Le Père/ Méditerranée dans l'Œuvre Romanesque d'Emmanuel Roblès." *Babel*, 2, 87-91. [Syr]

ROCHE, Denis.

See also 781.

RR4036. ● Cassegrain, Guillaume: *Vanishing Point (Approches de Denis Roche)*. Lyon: Fage. 96p. [BnF]

RR4037. ● Gleize, Jean-Marie: *Denis Roche: Éloge de la Véhémence*. Paris: Seuil. 290p. [UofR]

RR4038. ● Roche, Denis: *Temps Profond: Essais de Littérature Arrêtée 1977-1984*. [Paris]: Seuil. 385p. [BAnQ]

RR4039. Clonts, Charlène: "Exopoétique de Denis Roche Pour Une Pratique Iconotextuelle." *Intercâmbio*, 12, 32-45. [PrQ]

RR4040. Martens, David: "Une Supercherie Collaborative: Claude Bonnefoy et Denis Roche dans l'Ombre de Marc Ronceraille." *Nottingham French Studies*, 58, 3, 348-365. [Syr]

ROCHE, Maurice.

RR4041. Molly, Wilkinson Johnson: "Mega-Events, Urban Space, and Social Protest: The Olympia 2000 Bid in Reunified Berlin, 1990–1993." *Central European History*, 52, 4, 689-712. [RIT]

ROCHEFORT, Christiane.

See 517.

RODENBACH, Georges.

See also 486.

RR4042. ● Quaghebeur, Marc: *L' Œuvre au Miroir des Mots/ L'Univers de Georges Rodenbach*. Brüssel: Archives et Musée de la Littérature. 90p. [WC]

ROLIN, Dominique.
See also 655.
RR4043. ● Sollers, Philippe, Dominique Rolin, & Frans Haes: *Lettres à Dominique Rolin: 1981-2008*. [Paris]: Gallimard. 327p. [Cor]
RR4044. Haes, F. D.: "Philippe Sollers, Lettres à Dominique Rolin 1981-2008." *Infini*, 44-52. [Syr]

ROLIN, Olivier.
RR4045. ● Rolin, Olivier: *Extérieur Monde*. Paris: Gallimard. 301p. [Syr]
RR4046. Armstrong, Joshua: "Spatial Stream of Consciousness." *Substance*, 48, 1, 5-25. [PrQ]
RR4047. Bezari, Christina, Riccardo Raimondo, Thomas Vuong, & Laude Ngadi Maïssa: "Cartographier l'Imaginaire d'un Écrivain-Monde: Les Traductions de l'Œuvre d'Olivier Rolin." *Itinéraires*, 2. [WC]

ROLLAND, Romain.
See also 222, 357, 376, 381, 1500.
RR4048. ● Istrati, Panaït, Romain Rolland, Daniel Lérault, & Jean Rière: *Correspondance:1919-1935*. [Paris]: Gallimard. 644p. [Cor]
RR4049. ● Lepenies, Wolf: *'Warum Singt der Franzose Anders als Er Spricht?': Deutsch-Französische Irritationen am Beispiel der Beziehung von Romain Rolland und Richard Strauss*. Winterthur: Amadeus. 40p. [Cor]
RR4050. ● Mazzoleni, Silvia: *Ostinatamente Voltaire: Un Suo Ritratto di Jean Huber Ritrovato nel Castello d'Hauteville: Synthèse en Français; Romain Rolland a Ferney*. Tesserete: Pagine d'Arte. 128p. [WC]
RR4051. ● Rolland, Romain: *Voyage en Espagne*. [Madrid]: Casimiro Livres. 125p. [BnF]
RR4052. ● Rolland, Romain, Bernard Duchatelet, & Martine Liégeois: *Voyages en Bourgogne (1913-1937)*. Dijon: Éditions Universitaires de Dijon. 128p. [BnF]
RR4053. Avery, Joseph J.: "Rethinking the Freud-Rolland Relationship: An Explication and Translation of Freud's 'Acropolis Letter'." *American Imago*, 76, 1, 99-122. [PrQ]
RR4054. Galarza, N. M.: "Above the Battle: Representations of the Anonymous Soldier in Romain Rolland's Work." *Quaderns de Filologia: Estudis Literaris*, 24, 153-167. [BnF]
RR4055. Gil, Maria D. F.: "Stefan Zweig, Romain Rolland e a Grande Guerra." *Biblos*, 5, 125-146. [UaB]
RR4056. Irvine, M.: "'Rien Ne Sera Plus Beau Que Ces Lettres': La Correspondance de Romain Rolland et de Louise Cruppi." *Études Françaises*, 55, 1, 33-49. [UofR]
RR4057. Molines, Galarza N.: "Más Allá de la Contienda: Representaciones del Soldado Anónimo en la Obra de Romain Rolland." *Quaderns de Filologia - Estudis Literaris*, 24, 24, 153. [WC]
RR4058. Ortrud, M. H. M.: "La Conmemoración Pacifista de Los Muertos. 'Krieg' (1921/22) de Käthe Kollwitz y Clerambault (1920) de Romain Rolland." *Quaderns de Filologia - Estudis Literaris*, 24, 24, 137. [BnF]

ROMAINS, Jules.

See also 678.

RR4059. ● Voegele, Augustin: *De l'Unanimisme au Fantastique: Jules Romains Devant l'Extraordinaire.* New York: Peter Lang. 360p. [LoC]

RR4060. Korkut, Ece: "La Construction d'Un Ethos Manipulateur: Knock Ou le Triomphe de la Médecine." *Synergies Turquie*, 12, 103, 119, 301. [RIT]

RR4061. Smith, Macs: "Le Groupe Fait du/ de Bruit: Communication et Communauté dans Mort de Quelqu'un de Jules Romains." *MLN*, *134*, 4, 764-782. [Naz]

ROPS, Félicien.

RR4062. ● Rops, Félicien: *Dossier Zu: Félicien Rops.* [Köln] [KMB]. 1 vol. [WC]

RR4063. ● Laoureux, Denis, Christian Pacco, & Véronique Carpiaux: *Arts Plastiques en Province de Namur: 1830-2020.* [Namur]: Le Delta. 236p. [WC]

ROSTAND, Edmond de.

RR4064. ● Calvié, Laurent: *Cyrano Avant Rostand: Mythe, Thème et Variations.* Toulouse: Anacharsis. 281p. [BnF]

RR4065. ● Ferrari, Genny: *Cyrano de Bergerac: Tratto Dalla Commedia di Edmond Rostand.* Scarperia e San Piero (FI): Kleiner Flug. 62p. [WC]

RR4066. Benkö, Rita: "Cyrano de Bergerac and His Voyages to the Moon, the Sun . . . and the Brain." *Les Dossiers du Grihl*, 2. [Cor]

RR4067. Bruno-Chomin, G.: "Utopian Redemption and the Plurality of Worlds: Tommaso Campanella and Cyrano de Bergerac." *Rinascimento*, 59, 427-446. [UaB]

RR4068. Kozyrev, A.: "Two Lives of Cyrano de Bergerac: For the 400th Anniversary." *Perm Scientific Center Journal*, *12*, 3, 116-124. [WC]

RR4069. Laplace-Claverie, Hélène: "Book Review: Cyrano de Bergerac d'Edmond Rostand. 'Un Auteur, Une Œuvre'." *Revue d'Histoire Littéraire de la France*, *119*, 2, 481-482. [RIT]

RR4070. Naugrette, Florence: "Book Review: Cyrano de Bergerac. 'Champion Classiques Littératures'." *Revue d'Histoire Littéraire de la France*, *119*, 4, 997-1000. [UofR]

RR4071. Raffi, Maria Emanuela: "Edmond Rostand, Cyrano de Bergerac." *Studi Francesi*, *63*, 2, 384-385. [Syr]

ROUART, Jean-Marie.

RR4072. ● Rouart, Jean-Marie: *Les Aventuriers du Pouvoir: De Morny à Macron.* Paris: Robert Laffont. 781p. [BnF]

ROUAUD, Jean.

See also 571, 713.

RR4073. ● Rouaud, Jean: *La Vie Poétique: 5.* Paris: Bernard Grasset. 281p. [WC]

RR4074. Ferrini, Jean-Pierre: "Jean Rouaud Kiosque." *Quinzaines*, 1214, 17-18. [Syr]

RR4075. Saulieu, Geoffroy: "Art et Religion de Lascaux à Göbekli Tepe: Rencontres au Musée de l'Archéologie Nationale à Propos de la Splendeur Escamotée de Frère Cheval Ou le Secret des Grottes Ornées de Jean Rouaud (Grasset, 2018)." *Les Nouvelles de l'Archéologie*, 155, 57-59. [Cor]

RR4076.   Siary, Gérard, & Yulia A. Kosova: "'The World, More or Less' by Jean Rouaud: Between Novel and Autofiction." *Rudn Journal of Studies in Literature and Journalism*, 24, 1, 73-83. [WC]

ROUBAUD, Jacques.
See 543, 544.

ROUD, Gustave.
See also 685, 804, 2861.

RR4077.   ● Pétermann, Stéphane, & Emilien Sermier: *Gustave Roud-Gérard de Palézieux: Correspondance 1951-1976*. [Lausanne]: Association des Amis de Gustave Roud. 229p. [WC]

ROUGEMONT, Denis de.
See also 406, 595.

RR4078.   ● Corbellari, Alain, & Victor J. Stenger: *Denis de Rougemont: Entre Littérature, Théologie et Politique*. Lausanne: Études de lettres, 3, 311. 206p. [WC]

RR4079.   ● Keller, Jennifer: *Rougemont, l'Éducation et l'Europe*. Neuchâtel: Presse et Promotion de l'Université de Neuchâtel. [16]p. [WC]

RR4080.   ● Stenger, Nicolas, François Saint-Ouen, & Jonathan Wenger: *'Union, Étude': Denis de Rougemont*. Cormondrèche: Imprimerie de L'Ouest. 145p. [WC]

RR4081.   Bondi, Damiano, & Elisa Grimaldi: "Trilogie de la Personne: La Pensée Philosophique et l'Engagement Politique de Denis de Rougemont." 163. In 4078.

RR4082.   Corbellari, Alain: "Un Humaniste Kierkegaardien à la Recherche du Sacré: Denis de Rougemont et le Collège de Sociologie." 71. In 4078.

RR4083.   Debluë, Romain: "Liberté, Responsabilité, Vocation: Denis de Rougemont et Jacques Maritain, Autour de 'La Part du Diable'." 101. In 4078.

RR4084.   Martinez, I. S. J. A.: "La Théologie Protestante de Karl Barth Comme Arrière-Plan d'une 'Théologie Existentielle' Chez Denis de Rougemont." 181. In 4078.

RR4085.   Mercerat, Benjamin: "D'une Romanesque l'Autre: Denis de Rougemont et René Girard." 147. In 4078.

RR4086.   Stenger, Nicolas: "La Responsabilité Sociale de l'Écrivain: Denis de Rougemont et le 'Pen Club' dans les Années 1970." 49. In 4078.

RR4087.   Yoon, Seock-Jun: "Denis de Rougemont, A Pioneer in the European Integration Based on Culture." *Korean Society for European Integration*, 10, 2, 29-51. [WC]

ROUMAIN, Jacques.
See also 790, 1908.

RR4088.   ● Marxsen, Patti M., & Matthew J. Smith: *Jacques Roumain: A Life of Resistance*. Pompano Beach, FL: Caribbean Studies Press. 290p. [WC]

RR4089.   Alcocer, Rudyard J.: "Looking for a Hero: Masters of the Dew, la Source, and the Quest for Water in Haiti." *Contemporary French and Francophone Studies*, 23, 5, 568-575. [Naz]

RR4090. Fernandez, Domingo E., Nathalie Ludec, & Vicente Romero: "Los Prolegómenos del Comunismo Indo-Afroamericano en Haití y Jacques Roumain: 1927-1933." *Amérique Latine Histoire et Mémoire*, 37. [WC]

RR4091. Pessini, Alba: "Jacques Roumain, Œuvres Complètes." *Studi Francesi*, *63*, 3, 619-620. [Syr]

RR4092. Roumain, Jacques: "Grievances of the Black Man." *Transition*, 128, 146, 157, 164. [RIT]

ROUSSEL, Raymond.

RR4093. ● Bazantay, Pierre: '*L'Étrange Usine': Analyse et Transcription des Manuscrits Retrouvés de 'Nouvelles Impressions d'Afrique' de Raymond Roussel (1977-1933)*. Rennes: Presses Universitaires de Rennes. 308p. [BnF]

RR4094. ● Houppermans, Sjef, Patrick Marot, & Philippe Antoine: *Raymond Roussel et la Psychanalyse*. Paris: Classiques Garnier. 280p. [UaB]

RR4095. ● Khaitzine, Richard: *La Langue des Oiseaux: Tome 3*. Paris: Dervy. 473p. [WC]

RR4096. ● Khaitzine, Richard: *Raymond Roussel, la Plus Grande Énigme Littéraire du XXe Siècle*. Paris: Dervy. 473p. [BnF]

RR4097. ● Roussel, Raymond, Patrick Besnier, Jean-Paul Goujon, & Yann Moix: *Raymond Roussel: La Doublure; La Vue; Impressions d'Afrique; Locus Solus; L'Étoile au Front; La Poussière de Soleils; Nouvelles Impressions d'Afrique; Comment J'ai Écrit Certains de Mes Livres*. Paris: Robert Laffont. 1330p. [BnF]

RR4098. Dotremont, C.: "Raymond Roussel, le Poète Extrême." *Europe*, *97*, 1079, 59-60. [UaB]

ROY, Gabrielle.
See also 21, 231, 240, 269, 311.

RR4099. Navarette, P.-A.: "Sémiotique de la/ Lumière/ et de L'/ Obscurité/ de L'Île de la Fée d'Edgar Poe, et Pierre et Jean de Guy de Maupassant, à La Route d'Altamont de Gabrielle Roy, et L'Assassinat de la Via Belpoggio d'Italo Svevo." *Semiotica*, 226, 243-269. [UofR]

SACHS, Maurice.
See 1873.

SACRÉ, James.
See also 797, 2296.

RR4100. Fernández-Erquicia, Irati: "Le Quotidien et la Poésie Française Contemporaine." *Relief*, *13*, 1, 105-116. [Syr]

SAGAN, Françoise.
See also 310, 347.

RR4101. ● Méchoulam, Ingrid: *Sous le Soleil de Sagan*. Neuilly-sur-Seine: Michel Lafont. 143p. [Cor]

RR4102. Abed-Auon, Al-Rodan S.: "L'Univers Fragile dans Bonjour Tristesse de Françoise Sagan." *Journal of the College of Languages*, 40, 71-88. [WC]

RR4103. Gardini, Michela: "Céline Hromadova, Françoise Sagan à Contre-Courant 2017." *Studi Francesi*, *63*, 1, 192. [UofR]

RR4104.   Genon, Arnaud: "Françoise Sagan à Contre-Courant." *Modern &* *Contemporary France*, 27, 2, 274-275. [Naz]
RR4105.   Telegina, N. I., & I. M. Tsiutsiak: "Functions and Means of Creating Implication in Francoise Sagan`s Novel 'The Heart Keeper'." *Lviv Philological Journal*, 5, 147-151. [WC]

SAINT-DENYS GARNEAU, Hector de.
See 269, 778.

SAINT-EXUPÉRY, Antoine de.
RR4106.   ● Saint-Exupéry, Antoine: *Le Petit Prince: En Langage Simplifié* *Avec les Aquarelles de l'Auteur.* Bière: Cabédita. 59p. [WC]
RR4107.   ● Saint-Exupéry, Antoine, Jean-Noël Sarrail, & Sabine Guerrero: *Dessine-Moi un Mouton!: Spectacle Musical en 23 Chansons d'Après Le Petit Prince* *d'Antoine de Saint-Exupéry.* Lyon: Lugdivine. 111p. [WC]
RR4108.   ● Salzmann, Birgitta: *Das Evangelium des Kleinen Prinzen: Zur* *Spiritualität von Antoine de Saint-Exupéry.* Einsiedeln: Schweiz Paulus. 94p. [WC]
RR4109.   Barai, Aneesh: "'It's Such a Small Planet, Why Do You Need Borders?': Seeing Flying in Le Petit Prince and Its Screen Adaptations." *Jeunesse: Young* *People, Texts, Cultures*, 11, 2, 225-246. [UaB]
RR4110.   Bergez, Daniel: "Antoine de Saint-Exupéry du Vent, du Sable et des Étoiles Œuvres." *Quinzaines*, 1208, 10-12. [Syr]
RR4111.   Costedoat, Caroline, et al.: "When a Lost 'Petit Prince' Meets Antoine de Saint Exupéry: An Anthropological Case Report." *Forensic Science International*, 296, 145-152. [Naz]
RR4112.   O'Meara, Melanie K.: "Activating Minor Pedagogy in an Adaptation and Staging of the Little Prince." *Text and Performance Quarterly*, 39, 1, 37-55. [Naz]
RR4113.   Sekeh, Wiesje E., Donal M. Ratu, & Ferry H. Mandang: "Character Education Values in The Little Prince by Antoine de Saint-Exupéry." *Journal of* *English Language and Literature Teaching*, 4, 1. [WC]
RR4114.   Spas, Thierry: "Antoine de Saint-Exupéry. Mission Sur Arras: La Résistance en Germe." *Nord'*, 73, 1, 135. [Cor]
RR4115.   Tolstykh, N. V.: "The Specifics of the Translation of Modern Non-Equivalent Vocabulary into Ancient Greek (Based on the Material of the Antoine de Saint-Exupéry's Philosophical Tale 'The Little Prince')." *Scientific Notes of Taurida* *National V. I. Vernadsky University, Series Philology. Social Communications*, 3, 1, 182-188. [WC]

SAINT-JOHN PERSE.
See also 227, 251, 385, 511, 785, 795.
RR4116.   ● Djailani, Nassuf: *Naître Ici: Suivi de, Épître à Saint-John Perse.* Paris: Bruno Doucey. 141p. [WC]
RR4117.   ● Levillain, Henriette, & Catherine Mayaux: *Dictionnaire Saint-John Perse.* Paris: Honoré Champion. 660p. [UofR]
RR4118.   Comte, Thibault U.: "Henriette Levillain Catherine Mayaux Dictionnaire Saint-John Perse." *Quinzaines*, 1222, 19. [Syr]
RR4119.   Kim, Siwon: "Éléments d'Écologie dans la Poésie de Saint-John Perse." *Société d'Études Franco-Coreennes*, 89, 5-21. [WC]

RR4120.   Kim, Siwon: "Saint-John Perse et le Retour de Robinson Crusoé: L'Effondrement du Mythe Ou un Nouveau Mythe." *Société Coréenne d'Enseignement de Langue et Littérature Françaises*, 64, 205-229. [WC]

RR4121.   Luo, G.: "The Epic Quality and Artistic Strategies of the Expedition by Saint-John Perse." *Foreign Literature Studies*, *41*, 6, 79-91. [Cor]

SAINT-POL ROUX.
See 32, 812.

SALMON, André.
See 391.

RR4122.   Cepero, Iliana: "Martín Fierro, Argentine Nationalism, and the Return to Order." *Modernism/ Modernity*, *26*, 1, 111-40. [RIT]

SALVAYRE, Lydie.
See also 667, 863, 875.

RR4123.   Bezari, Christina, Riccardo Raimondo, Thomas Vuong, & Marianne Braux: "Traduction et Hétérolinguisme: Une Étude Comparative de Trois Traductions de Pas Pleurer de Lydie Salvayre." *Itinéraires*, 2. [WC]

RR4124.   Grenouillet, Corinne: "La Révolution Espagnole de 1936 dans Pas Pleurer de Lydie Salvayre." *Literatura*, *60*, 4, 34-46. [Naz]

RR4125.   Servoise, S.: "La Vie Commune de Lydie Salvayre: Chronique des Dominations Ordinaires." *Études Françaises*, *55*, 3, 173-187. [UaB]

SARDOU, Victorien.
RR4126.   Sardou, Victorien, & Clément Masson: "La Perle Noire: Une Nouvelle." *Tétras Lire*, *41*, 5, 4. [WC]

SARRAUTE, Nathalie.
See also 55, 621, 666.

RR4127.   ● Jefferson, Ann, Aude Saint-Loup, & Pierre-Emmanuel Dauzat: *Nathalie Sarraute*. Paris: Flammarion. 496p. [BAnQ]

RR4128.   Gefen, Alexandre: "Nathalie Sarraute." *Le Nouveau Magazine Littéraire*, *22*, 10, 62. [UaB]

SARRAZIN, Albertine.
See also 609.

RR4129.   ● Sarrazin, Albertine: *Nouvelles de Prison*. Nolay: Les Éditions du Chemin de Fer. 112p. [BnF]

RR4130.   Wattel, Anne: "Albertine Sarrazin: L'Ôteure de Verrous." *Romanistische Zeitschrift für Literaturgeschichte*, *43*, 1-2, 89-102. [UaB]

SARTRE, Jean-Paul.
See also 463, 724, 798, 1103, 1259, 1297, 1307, 2477, 2773, 3166, 3328, 3474, 3480.

RR4131.   ● Berger, Dagmar: *Ziel, Sinn und Existenz des Künstlers Nach Jean-Paul Sartre*. Hamburg: Dr. Kovac. 104p. [BnF]

RR4132.   ● Bourton, William: *Sartre: Les Périls de la Liberté*. Paris: Michalon. 124p. [WC]

RR4133. ● Cabestan, Philippe: *La Philosophie de Sartre: Repères*. Paris: J. Vrin. 188p. [WC]

RR4134. ● Cohen-Solal, Annie: *Sartre, 1905-1980: Préface Inédite*. Paris: Gallimard. 960p. [WC]

RR4135. ● Collamati, Chiara, & Juliette Simont: *Sur les Concepts d'Histoire: Sartre en Dialogue*. Paris: Classiques Garnier. 233p. [WC]

RR4136. ● Dassonneville, Gautier: *Sartre Inédit: Le Mémoire de Fin d'Études (1927)*. Paris: Classiques Garnier. 344p. [WC]

RR4137. ● Fergnani, Franco: *Jean-Paul Sartre: La Scoperta Dell'esistenza*. Milano: Feltrinelli. 109p. [BnF]

RR4138. ● Moati, Raoul: *Sartre et le Mystère en Pleine Lumière*. Paris: Les Éditions du Cerf. 474p. [Cor]

RR4139. ● Nieweler, Andreas: *Sartre*. Hannover: Friedrich. 49p. [WC]

RR4140. Amedegnato, Ozouf S, & Ibrahim Ouattara: "'Orfeo Negro' de Jean Paul Sartre: Una Lectura Programática de la Negritud." *Revista de Estudios Africanos*, 23. [WC]

RR4141. André, Jean-Marie: "L'Analogon et les Deux Consciences de Jean-Paul Sartre . . .: À Propos de la Peinture et de la Musique." *Hegel*, *1*, 1, 69. [BnF]

RR4142. Bieger, Laura: "Jean-Paul Sartre, Richard Wright, and the Relational Aesthetics of Literary Engagement." *Real Yearbook of Research in English and American Literature*, *35*, 1, 169-188. [Syr]

RR4143. Bollaert, Charlotte: "Jean-Paul Sartre's Theatre After Communism: Perpetuating the Past Through Non-Retranslation?" *Cadernos de Tradução*, *39*, 1, 45-72. [WC]

RR4144. Bollaert, C.: "The Russian Thick Journal as a Discursive Space of Negotiation Jean-Paul Sartre's Reception in the Soviet Union During the Thaw Era." *Translation and Interpreting Studies*, *14*, 2, 198-217. [Syr]

RR4145. Coombes, Sam: "Jean-Paul Sartre, Being and Nothingness: An Essay in Phenomenological Ontology, Trans. by Sarah Richmond." *French Studies*, *73*, 4, 665-666. [UaB]

RR4146. Cotrina, Cosar J. P.: "El Acontecimiento de la Verdad en la Fenomenología Ontológica de Jean-Paul Sartre." *Estudios de Filosofía*, 17, 83-99. [WC]

RR4147. Du Graf, L.: "Existentialism's 'White Problem': Richard Wright and Jean-Paul Sartre's The Respectful Prostitute." *Yale French Studies*, January, 135-136, 134-150. [UofR]

RR4148. Frimat, François: "Dossier: Lévi-Strauss: Une Anthropologie Sans Philosophie?: L'Histoire Sans la Solitude: Claude Lévi-Strauss et Jean-Paul Sartre." *Cites*, 81, 81-93. [PrQ]

RR4149. Gasilin, Andrey: "Psychoanalytic Receptions in Baudelaire, by Jean-Paul Sartre." *Chelovek*, *30*, 5, 20-37. [Cor]

RR4150. Gilbert, D. A., & D. L. Burgin: "Jean-Paul Sartre: The Russian Teatr Interviews of 1956 and 1962." *Sartre Studies International*, *25*, 2, 1-17. [Naz]

RR4151. Kaya, H.: "A Comparative Study: Existentialism in No Exit by Jean-Paul Sartre and Shadowless by Hasan Ali Toptaş." *Folklor/ Edebiyat*, *99*, 3, 577-591. [WC]

RR4152. Mathieu, Anne: "Jean-Paul Sartre et la Guerre d'Algérie." *Manière de Voir*, *166*, 8, 44. [RIT]

RR4153. Migeot, François: "Engagement et Approche Actionnelle: Jean-Paul

Sartre Précurseur du Cecrl?" *Annales Littéraires de L'Université de Besançon*, 1002, 115-128. [WC]

RR4154.   Nielsen-Sikora, Jürgen: "Gary Cox: Jean-Paul Sartre. Existenzialismus und Exzess." *Das Historisch-Politische Buch*, *67*, 1, 36-37. [UaB]

RR4155.   Preece, Julian: "Jean-Paul Sartre's Réflexions Sur la Question Juive (1946) as Blueprint for Grass's Jewish Figures: From Hundejahre (1963) to Im Krebsgang (2002)." *Oxford German Studies*, *48*, 3, 391-403. [UofR]

RR4156.   Rendtorff, Jacob D.: "Engagement for Freedom: Jean-Paul Sartre's Concept of the Political Self." *Eco-Ethica*, 8, 93-107. [LoC]

RR4157.   Riera, M. F. G.: "An Approach to the Notions of Anxiety and Despair in Sören Kierkegaard and His Role in the Concrete Relations with the Other of Jean-Paul Sartre." *Pensamiento*, *75*, 285, 931-945. [UaB]

RR4158.   Russo, Maria: "Violenza e Generosità. L'Incontro Con l'Altro nei Quaderni per una Morale di Jean-Paul Sartre." *Notizie di Politeia*, 35, 135, 132. [PrQ]

RR4159.   Torghabeh, R. A.: "Jean Paul Sartre and 'False Belief' in Becket's Krapp's Last Tape." *Research in Contemporary World Literature*, *24*, 1, 221-232. [WC]

RR4160.   Yazbek, Andre C.: "O Estatuto da Relação Erótica No Existencialismo de Jean-Paul Sartre: Desejo, Alteridade e Consciência Encarnada em o Ser e o Nada." *Sofia*, *8*, 2, 176-187. [WC]

RR4161.   Zetterberg, Hugo: "No Exit: Arab Existentialism, Jean-Paul Sartre, and Decolonization by Yoav Di-Capua (Review)." *Journal of Colonialism and Colonial History*, *20*, 3. [RIT]

SASSINE, Williams.
See also 286.

RR4162.   De Meyer, B. "Williams Sassine N'Est Pas N'importe Qui, Florence Paravy (dir.)." *French Studies in Southern Africa*, 49, 260-262. [Cor]

RR4163.   Ferreira-Meyers, Karen: *"Williams Sassine N'Est Pas N'Importe Qui* by Florence Paravy (Review)." *Nouvelles Études Francophones*, *34*, 1, 224-226. [UaB]

RR4164.   Goerg, Odile: "Degon Élisabeth. — Williams Sassine. Itinéraires d'un Indigné Guinéen." *Cahiers d'Études Africaines*, *235*, 3, 911. [UofR]

SATRAPI, Marjane.
See also 100, 118, 339, 432, 617.

RR4165.   ● Barker, Nicholas: *Atar Notes Text Guide: Persepolis by Marjane Satrapi*. Caulfield North, Victoria: InStudent Media. 71p. [WC]

RR4166.   ● Ebrahimi, Mehraneh: *Women, Art, and Literature in the Iranian Diaspora*. Syracuse, NY: Syracuse UP. 183p. [Naz]

RR4167.   Alvim, de A. M.: "Questões de Gênero e Diáspora em Persépolis, de Marjane Satrapi." *Revista Darandina*, 23 septembre, 1-14. [WC]

RR4168.   Beigi, Leila Sadegh: "Marjane Satrapi's Persepolis and Embroideries: A Graphic Novelization of Sexual Revolution Across Three Generations of Iranian Women." *International Journal of Comic Art*, *21*, 1, 350. [PrQ]

RR4169.   Email, Azra Ghandeharion, Zhaleh Abbasi Hosseini, & Alireza Anushirvani: "From Visual to Imagined Level of Images in Comics: Representation of Marjane in Persepolis." *Global Media Journal*, *13*, 26, 207. [PrQ]

RR4170.   Ezzatikarami, Mahdiyeh, & Firouzeh Ameri: "Persepolis and Human

Rights: Unveiling Westernized Globalization Strategies in Marjane Satrapi's *Persepolis.*" *International Journal of Applied Linguistics and English Literature*, 8, 5, 122. [Cor]

RR4171. Manit, Piriyadit: "Du Ventre Maternel à la Tombe: Dynamisme de l'Espace dans Poulet aux Prunes de Marjane Satrapi." *Agathos*, 10, 2, 169-88. [RIT]

RR4172. Ryu, Hyun-Ju: "Marjane Satrapi's Persepolis and Transmedia." *The New Studies of English Language & Literature*, 72, 183-203. [WC]

RR4173. Sadegh, Beigi L.: "Marjane Satrapi's Persepolis and Ebroideries: A Graphic Novelization of Sexual Revolution Across Three Generations of Iranian Women." *International Journal of Comic Art*, 21, 1, 350-365. [WC]

SAUSSURE, Ferdinand de.
See also 1166, 1192, 1201, 3791.

RR4174. ● Caputo, Cosimo: *La Scienza Doppia del Linguaggio: Dopo Chomsky, Saussure e Hjelmslev.* Roma: Carocci. 150p. [LoC]

RR4175. ● Mejía, Quijano C. L., Giraldo D. Jaramillo, & Zapata A. Pérez: *El Primer Curso: Lingüística General de Ferdinand de Saussure, Louis Caille y Albert Riedlinger.* Medellín: Semsa. 419p. [WC]

RR4176. ● Puech, Christian, et al.: *Héritages, Réceptions, Écoles en Sciences du Langage: Avant et Après Saussure.* Paris: Presses Sorbonne Nouvelle. 371p. [WC]

RR4177. Albrecht, Jörn, & Irene Kunert: "Saussure — Encore et Toujours." *Historiographia Linguistica*, 46, 175-190. [RIT]

RR4178. Bergouioux, Gabriel: "Saussure et la Théorie de la Littérature." *Littera*, 4, 91-103. [Cor]

RR4179. Chidichimo, Alessandro: "Saussure, 1896." *Acta Structuralica*, 4, 1. [WC]

RR4180. Costa, Aline, & Luiza Milano: "A Noção de Gramática em Saussure." *Revista Leitura*, 1, 62, 107-126. [WC]

RR4181. Lima, Dayanne: "Saussure, Bréal e a Questão do Sentido." *Revista Leitura*, 1, 62, 255-275. [WC]

RR4182. Robin, Thérèse: "Ferdinand de Saussure. La Grammaire du Gotique. Deux Cours Inédits. 1. Cours de Grammaire Gotique (1890-1891). 2. Cours de Grammaire Gothique (1881-1882). Accompagnés d'Autres Articles de Saussure Sur le Gotique." *Nowele*, 72, 1, 116-118. [Cor]

RR4183. Romagnoli, Chiara: "New Developments of Chinese Interpretation of Ferdinand de Saussure's Linguistic Thought." *Histoire, Épistémologie, Langage*, 41, 1, 115. [Cor]

RR4184. Starobinski, J.: "Lettres et Syllabes Mobiles: (Pétrarque, Ronsard, Saussure)." *Lettere Italiane*, 71, 3, 67-80. [Naz]

RR4185. Surette, Leon: "Deconstruction: A Misprision of Saussure and Charles Sanders Peirce." *Philosophy and Literature*, 43, 2, 411-440. [UofR]

RR4186. Toldo, Claudia, & Débora Facin: "Saussure: A Alguns Passos da Enunciação." *Revista Leitura*, 1, 62, 296-314. [WC]

RR4187. Yamaguchi, Liesl: "Sensuous Linguistics: On Saussure's Synesthesia." *New Literary History*, 50, 1, 23-42. [UofR]

SAVITZKAYA, Eugène.
RR4188. ● Savitzkaya, Eugène: *Ode au Paillasson.* Saint-Clément: Le Cadran Ligné. 60p. [BnF]

RR4189.   Demoulin, Laurent: "Transgression Paradoxale Chez Eugène Savitz-kaya." *Synergies Pologne*, *16*, 16, 55-67. [Syr]

SCHEHADÉ, Georges.

RR4190.   ● Becker, Susanne: *Das Poetische Theater Frankreichs im Zeichen des Surrealismus: René de Obaldia, Romain Weingarten und Georges Schehadé*. Tübingen: Narr Franck Attempto. 309p. [BnF]

SCHMITT, Eric-Emmanuel.
See also 367.

RR4191.   ● Billerbeck, Jasmin: *Éric-Emmanuel Schmitt, Oscar et la Dame Rose: Interpretation*. [Hallbergmoos]: Stark. 96p. [WC]

RR4192.   Rezvantalab, Zeinab, & Babaie Z. Haji: "Migration, le Bonheur Ou un Espoir Idéalisé? dans 'Ulysse from Bagdad' d'Éric Emmanuel Schmitt." *Francisola*, *3*, 2, 185. [WC]

RR4193.   Robova, Antoaneta: "Éric-Emmanuel Schmitt et Ses Maîtres de Bonheur: À la Croisée des Voies Littéraire et Musicale." *Quêtes Littéraires*, 9. [WC]

RR4194.   Robova, Antoaneta: "Stratégies Métalittéraires et Pratiques Essayistiques dans l'Œuvre d'Éric-Emmanuel Schmitt." *Relief*, *13*, 2, 31. [Syr]

SCHWARZ-BART, André.
See also 718, 772, 798.

RR4195.   ● Moscovici, Serge, et al.: *Mon Après-Guerre à Paris: Chroniques des Années Retrouvées*. Paris: Bernard Grasset. 376p. [Cor] (Lévi-Strauss)

RR4196.   Gyssels, Kathleen: "Portrait of an Authentic Schnorrer: Abrasza Zemsz in Richard Marienstras's Memory." *Journal of Jewish Identities*, *12*, 2, 197-209. [RIT]

SCHWARZ-BART, Simone.
See also 202, 267, 693, 798.

RR4197.   ● Schwarz-Bart, Simone, & Yann Plougastel: *Nous N'Avons Pas Vu Passer les Jours*. Paris: Bernard Grasset. 198p. [UaB]

RR4198.   Menezes, Filipe A. R., & Kathleen Gyssels: "O Etno-Romance de André e Simone Schwarz-Bart." *Arquivo Maaravi*, *13*, 25, 69-83. [WC]

SCHWOB, Marcel.
See also 14, 672.

RR4199.   ● Gauthier-Villars, Henry, et al.: *Lettres à Marcel Schwob*. Tusson: Du Lérot. 94p. [LoC]

RR4200.   ● Pérez, Vernetti L.: *Las Vidas Imaginarias de Schwob*. Viladamt: Luces de Gálibo. 80p. [WC]

RR4201.   ● Schwob, Marcel, & Marcel Proust: *Lectures*. Angoulême: Marguerite Waknine. 49p. [BnF]

RR4202.   McClay, B. D.: "The Children's Crusade Marcel Schwob." *Commonweal*, *146*, 7, 37-38. [UofR]

RR4203.   Romero, F. R.: "Marcel Schwob, Collection of Letters." *Estudios Romanicos*, 28, 115-126. [Naz]

RR4204.   Romero F. Ríos: "Marcel Schwob, Illusionniste de Vies." *Anales de Filología Francesa*, *27*, 1, 291-310. [Naz]

SEBBAR, Leïla.

See also 228, 669.

RR4205. Kamecka, Małgorzata: "History and Identity According to Leïla Sebbar." *Literatura*, *61*, 4, 54-66. [Naz]

RR4206. Martinelli, L.: "Leïla Sebbar's Writing between Exile and Memory." *Studii Si Cercetari Fliologice, Seria Limbi Romanice*, 25, 84-100. [Cor]

SEGALEN, Victor.

See also 32, 389, 435, 496.

RR4207. ● Bucheli, Valérie: *Intertextualité Exotique de Victor Segalen.* Genève: Droz. 342p. [Cor]

RR4208. ● Camelin, Colette, & Muriel Détrie: *Victor Segalen: Attentif à Ce Qui N'A Pas Été Dit: [Actes du Colloque Organisé à Cerisy du 4 au 11 Juillet 2018].* Paris: Hermann. 470p. [Cor]

RR4209. ● Cheng, François: *L'Un Vers l'Autre: En Voyage Avec Victor Segalen.* [Paris]: Albin Michel. 180p. [WC]

RR4210. ● Collin, David: *La Grande Diagonale: Avec Victor Segalen.* Lyon: Hippocampe. 136p. [LoC]

RR4211. ● Poizat-Amar, Mathilde: *Dans le Sillage de Victor Segalen: Héritages, Présences, Trajectoires.* Caen: Passage(s). 162p. [Cor]

RR4212. ● Roux, Marie V. N. V.: *Victor Segalen, In a Sound World.* Cambridge, MA: The MIT Press. 1 vol. [WC]

RR4213. Choi, Min: "Victor Segalen and Humanized Nature of China." *Studies of Korean & Chinese Humanities*, 62, 139-165. [WC]

RR4214. Kukuryk, Agnieszka: "Du Disciple au Maître: Victor Segalen et Paul Gauguin." *Quêtes Littéraires*, 9. [WC]

RR4215. Kukuryk, A.: "Perception and Reading in Peintures by Victor Segalen." *Romanica Cracoviensia*, *19*, 2, 107-117. [Naz]

RR4216. Ouchari, Saïd: "Michel Onfray, Lecteur de Victor Segalen." *Intercâmbio*, 12, 96-106. [RIT]

RR4217. Sanchez, Serge: "L'Ultime Stèle de Victor Segalen." *Le Nouveau Magazine Littéraire*, *18*, 6, 72. [UaB]

SEMBÈNE, Ousmane.

See also 250, 633, 700, 860, 4693, 4714, 4721, 4737.

RR4218. ● Berty, Valérie: *Sembène Ousmane (1923-2007): Un Homme Debout: Écrivain, Cinéaste et Humaniste.* Paris: Présence Africaine Éditions. 233p. [Cor]

RR4219. Dick, Tambari O.: "Revolutionary Consciousness in Ousmane Sembene's God's Bits of Wood." *Afrrev Laligens*, 8, 2, 110. [LoC]

RR4220. Louis, Ndong: "Zeitvermittlung als Kulturtransfer am Beispiel der Deutschen Übersetzung von Ousmane Sembènes Novelle Le Mandat (die Postanweisung)." *Lebende Sprachen*, *64*, 2, 463-473. [UofR]

RR4221. Ndour, Moustapha: "Narrative Realism at the Interplay of Traditionality and Modernity in Ousmane Sembene's God's Bits of Woods and Ngugi Wa Thiong'o's The River Between." *International Journal of Comparative Literature and Translation Studies*, 7, 2, 55. [WC]

RR4222.	Nunn, Tessa: "The Screaming Mother and Silent Subaltern in Ousmane Sembene's La Noire de." *Women in French Studies*, 27, 192-202. [UaB]

RR4223.	Yoon, D. M.: "Cold War Creolization: Ousmane Sembène's Le Dernier de l'Empire." *Research in African Literatures*, 50, 3, 29-50. [Naz]

SEMPRUN, Jorge.
See also 368, 376, 398, 404, 605.

RR4224.	Fernández, Meneses J.: "Between Art and Commerce: The Semprún Decree and the New Spanish Cinema of the 1990s." *Hispanic Research Journal (Iberian and Latin American Studies)*, 20, 2, 87-103. [Naz]

RR4225.	Fernández, Pérez C.: "El Museo Imaginario de Jorge Semprún." *De Arte. Revista de Historia del Arte*, 18, 231. [WC]

RR4226.	Garduño, Gloria M. P.: "Book Review: Jorge Semprún. Frontières/Fronteras. Frankfurter Studien Zur Iberoromania und Frankophonie, 8." *Nueva Revista de Filología Hispánica*, 67, 2, 712-720. [UofR]

RR4227.	López, Vilar M.: "La Mirada Como Reconstrucción del Acontecimiento en la Escritura o la Vida de Jorge Semprún = The Gaze as Reconstruction of the Event in la Escritura o la Vida of Jorge Semprún." *Hispania Nova*, 25 avril, 264. [Cor]

RR4228.	Mariani, Maria Anna: "The Witness's Two Bodies: The Migration of the Testimonial Function After Primo Levi's Death." *MLN*, 134, 1, 143-56. [PrQ]

SÉNAC, Jean.
RR4229.	Harzoune, Mustapha: "Jean Sénac, Œuvres Poétiques: Préface de René de Ceccaty, Postface de Hamid Nacer-Khodja, Arles, Actes Sud, 2019, 836 pages, 29 €." *Hommes & Migrations*, 1326, 3, 186. [UaB]

SENGHOR, Léopold Sédar.
See also 205, 252, 846.

RR4230.	● Dièye, Massamba: *Léopold Sédar Senghor: Le Salma d'Or*. Dakar: L'Harmattan Sénégal. 143p. [LoC]

RR4231.	● Faye, Waly L.: *Comprendre Senghor: Tome 1*. Dakar: L'Harmattan Sénégal. 241p. [LoC]

RR4232.	● Niang, Aliou C.: *A Poetics of Postcolonial Biblical Criticism: God, Human-Nature Relationship, and Negritude*. Eugene, OR: Cascade Books. 217p. [WC]

RR4233.	● Senghor, Léopold S.: *La Normandité*. Caen: Lurlure. 43p. [BnF]

RR4234.	Blum, Françoise, & Constantin Katsakioris: "Leopold Sédar Senghor and the Soviet Union: The Confrontation, 1957-1966." *Cahiers d'Études Africaines*, 235, 3, 839. [UofR]

RR4235.	Bobo, Rostand S.: "Le Je Lyrique Chez Léopold Sédar Senghor." *Anales de Filología Francesa*, 27, 1, 23-34. [Naz]

RR4236.	David, Philippe: "Valantin Christian, 2016, Trente Ans de Vie Politique Avec Léopold Sédar Senghor: Paris, Belin, 208 p." *Journal des Africanistes*, 89, 2, 228. [UaB]

RR4237.	Durez, Aymeric: "L'Invention du Projet de Francophonie Intergouvernementale par Léopold Sédar Senghor: Une Tentative de Révision des Relations Franco-Africaines et Inter-Africaines." *Revue d'Histoire Diplomatique (Paris)*, 1, 17-32. [WC]

RR4238. Hogarth, Christopher: "'Causer des Migraines à Léopold Sédar Senghor': Sub-Saharan Postcolonial Translingual Writing, the Cases of Senegal and Fatou Diome." *Esprit Créateur, 59*, 4, 81-93. [UaB]

RR4239. Otata, Wilfried H.: "Roche (Christian), Léopold Sédar Senghor, Le Président Humaniste. Paris: L'Harmattan, Coll. Espaces Littéraires, 2017, 238 p. – ISBN 978-2-343-12858-7." *Études Littéraires Africaines*, 47, 246. [WC]

SERGE, Victor.
See also 50.
RR4240. ● Hoberman, J.: "Totalitarian Recall." *Bookforum*, Summer 2019. [RIT]

SERHANE, Abdelhak.
See 601.

SERRES, Michel.
See also 443, 710, 726, 732, 763, 3618.
RR4241. ● Edwards, Michael, Florence Delay, & Claude Dagens: *Hommages à M. Michel Serres Décédé le 1er Juin 2019*. Paris: Palais de l'Institut. 15p. [BnF]

RR4242. ● Serres, Michel: *Relire le Relié*. Paris: Le Pommier. 242p. [WC]

RR4243. ● Serres, Michel, Paul Fave, & Bernard Daubas: *Moralas Esberidas =: Morales Espiègles*. Paris: Le Pommier. 179p. [WC]

RR4244. Bakhtiar, Siavash: "When Meteors Vanish in Political Philosophies - Thinking with Michel Serres in Times of New Climate Regime." *European Journal of Interdisciplinary Studies, 5*, 3, 41. [WC]

RR4245. Barth, Elisa: "Provozierende Fülle: Eine Erinnerung an Michel Serres." *Zeitschrift Für Medienwissenschaft, 11*, 2, 200-202. [WC]

RR4246. Batt, Noëlle: "Michel Serres: The Written Text/ The Spoken Text." *Sub-stance*, 150, 5-6. [UofR]

RR4247. Boisvert, Raymond: "Obituary: Michel Serres." *Philosophy Now*, 134, 56-57. [Naz]

RR4248. Jonasson, Kalle: "'Sport Qua Science': Michel Serres' Ball as an Asset of Knowledge." *Sport in Society, 22*, 9, 1512-1527. [WC]

RR4249. Klein, Étienne: "Michel Serres ou la 'Science des Passerelles'." *Études*, 43. [Syr]

RR4250. Lee, Seung C.: "Impossible Gifts, Parasitic Networks: Jacques Derrida's and Michel Serres's Critiques of Reciprocity." *Cross-Cultural Studies, 25*, 2, 191-229. [WC]

RR4251. Mercier, Lucie K.-C.: "Michel Serres's Leibnizian Structuralism." *Angelaki, 24*, 6, 3-21. [UaB]

RR4252. "Michel Serres, in Memoriam." *Médium, 60-61*, 3, 2. [Cor]

RR4253. Monod, Jean-Claude: "Michel Serres. Un Conteur en Philosophie." *Sciences Humaines, 317*, 8, 33. [BAnQ]

RR4254. Moser, Keith: "Writing a Different Ending to the 'World War' Pitting Humanity against the Biosphere in Michel Serres and Jacques Derrida's Philosophy." *Substance, 48*, 2, 41-58. [Naz]

RR4255. Paláu, Castaño L. A.: "Las Tres Vueltas al Mundo. Michel Serres." *Ciencias Sociales y Educación, 8*, 15, 255-260. [WC]

RR4256.   Paláu, Castaño L. A.: "Michel Serres, Historiador de Las Ciencias."
Ciencias Sociales y Educación, 8, 16, 175-188. [WC]
RR4257.   Paláu, Castaño L. A.: "Nuestro Linaje Totemista. Michel Serres."
Ciencias Sociales y Educación, 8, 15, 261-275. [WC]
RR4258.   Pierssens, Michel: "Michel Serres: A Personal Memoir." *Sub-stance,*
150, 16-18. [Naz]
RR4259.   Serres, Michel: "Foreword. Resource and Resourcing." *Droit et
Société, 101,* 1, 5. [Cor]
RR4260.   Sialaros, Michalis: "Geometry: The Third Book of Foundations: By
Michel Serres, Translated by Randolph Burks, London, Bloomsbury, 2017, lviii + 219
pp., ISBN 9781474281416, £19.99 (Hardback)." *International Studies in the Philoso-
phy of Science, 32,* 1, 75-77. [UaB]
RR4261.   Simons, Massimiliano: "Herinneringen Aan Michel Serres (1930-
2019)." *De Uil Van Minerva, 32,* 3, 144-148. [WC]
RR4262.   Treanor, Brian: "Thinking After Michel Serres." *Sub-stance,* 150,
21-29. [UofR]
RR4263.   Watkin, Chris: "Not More of the Same: Michel Serres's Challenge to
the Ethics of Alterity." *Philosophy Today, 63,* 2, 513-534. [Naz]
RR4264.   Watkin, Christopher: "Representing French and Francophone Stud-
ies with Michel Serres." *Australian Journal of French Studies, 56,* 2, 125-40. [RIT]
RR4265.   Watkin, Christopher: "Why Michel Serres?" *Sub-stance,* 150, 30-40.
[UaB]
RR4266.   Watson, Janell: "Sexed or Sexist? the Androgynous Cosmocracy of
Michel Serres." *Sub-stance,* 150, 41-44. [Naz]

SFAR, Joann.
See also 123.
RR4267.   ● Gehrig, Anette, & Jonas Engelmann: *Joann Sfar: Sans Début Ni
Fin [Ausstellungszeitung].* Basel: Cartoonmuseum Basel. 1 vol. [WC]
RR4268.   Gasser, Christian: "Ein Papagei Spricht Durch den Kater des Rab-
biners: Ein Comic Über Jüdischen Humor und Jüdische Kultur Machte Joann Sfar in
Frankreich Zum Star." *Neue Zürcher Zeitung, 240,* 79, 43. [WC]

SIMENON, Georges.
RR4269.   ● Baronian, Jean-Baptiste: *Maigret: Docteur ès Crimes.* [Bruxelles]:
Les Impressions Nouvelles. 125p. [BnF]
RR4270.   ● Baronian, Jean-Baptiste: *Simenon, Romancier Absolu: Essai.*
Paris: Pierre-Guillaume de Roux. 183p. [Cor]
RR4271.   ● Ferrand, Jean-Paul: *Georges Simenon, Une Sensibilité Anarchiste.*
Paris: L'Harmattan. 188p. [LoC]
RR4272.   ● Fourcaut, Laurent: *Simenon: Pas de Vie Sans les Livres.* Gollion:
Infolio. 59p. [BnF]
RR4273.   ● Geat, Marina: *Simenon et Fellini: Paradoxes et Complicités
Épistolaires.* Paris: L'Harmattan. 165p. [LoC]
RR4274.   ● Wenger, Murielle: *Jules Maigret: Enquête Sur le Commissaire à
la Pipe.* Waterloo: Lucpire. 222p. [LoC]
RR4275.   Fabbri, Alexandra: "Paradoxes Judiciaires: De la Violence au Lan-
gage dans l'Œuvre de Georges Simenon." *Les Cahiers de la Justice, 2,* 2, 363. [WC]

RR4276.   O'Donoghue, H.: "Georges Simenon: The Yellow Dog." *Translation and Literature*, 28, 392-398. [UaB]

RR4277.   Sheeren, Hugues: "Véronique Rohrbach, le Courrier des Lecteurs à Georges Simenon. L'Ordinaire en Partage." *Studi Francesi*, 63, 2, 391-392. [UaB]

SIMON, Claude.
See also 371, 394, 478, 507, 528, 535, 625, 643, 673.

RR4278.   • "Cahiers Claude Simon." *Cahiers Claude Simon*, 14. 324p. [UaB]

RR4279.   • Toussaint, Jacques, & M. Van Coile: *Georges Wasterlain (1889-1963), Sculpteur et Peintre Ouvrier de la Mine à l'Ébauchoir: Donation de M. Claude Simon à l'Asbl le Bois du Cazier*. Namur: Art et Héritance. 96p. [WC]

RR4280.   Anzoumana, Sinan: "Jalons Pour une Mise en Visibilité de la Sexualité dans Triptyque de Claude Simon: Discursivité, Voies de Fait et Dispositifs." *Multilinguales*, 11. [WC]

RR4281.   Balcázar, Melina: "The Flesh of History: Mario Vargas Llosa and Claude Simon Beyond the Misunderstanding." *Revue de Littérature Comparée*, 371, 3, 325-374. [Naz]

RR4282.   Crivella, Giuseppe: "Le Sensible Est Introuvable . . . Merleau-Ponty e il Linguaggio: Da la Prose du Monde Alle Cinq Notes Sur Claude Simon." *Chiasmi International*, 21, 187-205. [Cor]

RR4283.   Gosselin, Katerine: "Souvenirs de Lecture et Souvenirs de Soi: Autobiographie et Roman en Face-à-Face dans Le Jardin des Plantes (1997) et Le Tramway (2001) de Claude Simon." *Tangence*, 120, 37. [Cor]

RR4284.   Yocaris, Ilias: "Une Rupture dans la Continuité: Claude Simon et l'Avènement du Nouveau Nouveau Roman." *Faux Titre*, 434, 147-162. [UaB]

SIMONDON, Gilbert.
RR4285.   • Bardin, Andrea, Giovanni Carrozzini, & Pablo Rodríguez: *Special Issue: The Work of Simondon*. Chicago: Philosophy Department of DePaul University. 1 vol. [WC]

RR4286.   • Ferrarato, Coline: *Philosophie Prospective du Logiciel: Une Étude Simondonienne*. London: ISTE Editions. 144p. [WC]

RR4287.   • Simondon, Gilbert, & Lina M. Gil: *Sobre la Psicología (1956-1967)*. Buenos Aires: Cactus. 479p. [WC]

RR4288.   Aguirre, Gonzalo S.: "Normatividad entre Esteticidad y Tecnicidad Según Simondon: Hacia una Estética del Derecho Como Mecanología de las Normas Jurídicas." *Ars (São Paulo)*, 17, 35, 19-42. [Syr]

RR4289.   Alombert, Anne: "How Can Culture and Technics Be Reconciled in the Digital Milieu and Automatic Societies? Political Implications of the Philosophies of Technology of Simondon and Stiegler." *Culture, Theory and Critique*, 60, 3, 315-326. [UaB]

RR4290.   Bardet, Marie: "Límite y Relación: Pensar el Contacto Desde la Filosofía de Gilbert Simondon." *Revista de Filosofía*, 76, 39-56. [UaB]

RR4291.   Bellon, Jacqueline: "Figure, Ground and the Notion of Equilibria in the Work of Gilbert Simondon and Gestalt Theory." *Gestalt Theory*, 41, 3, 293-317. [Cor]

RR4292.   Berdet, Marc, Carlos Pérez López, Meike Schmidt-Gleim, & Adolfo

Vera: "La Tecnoestética de Gilbert Simondon Frente a la Herencia de Karl Marx: Perspectivas y Confrontaciones." *Anthropology & Materialism*, 4. [WC]

RR4293.   Carrozzini, Giovanni: "Gilbert Simondon's Philosophy in the Light of Some Notions of Georges Canguilhem." *Philosophy Today*, *63*, 3, 625-642. [Naz]

RR4294.   Choi, Sung W.: "A Study on the Directionality of the Thinking for Design as Grounded on the Technology Philosophy of Gilbert Simondon." *Journal of Cultural Product & Design*, 59, 73-86. [WC]

RR4295.   Del Río, E.: "Bill Viola with Gilbert Simondon: Collective Individuation and the Subjectivity of Disaster." *Angelaki*, *24*, 6, 57-75. [UaB]

RR4296.   Guchet, Xavier: "'Technological Object' in Gilbert Simondon's Philosophy: One Word, Three Different Meanings." *Philosophy Today*, *63*, 3, 705-716. [UofR]

RR4297.   Keating, T. P.: "Pre-individual Affects: Gilbert Simondon and the Individuation of Relation." *Cultural Geographies*, *26*, 2, 211-226. [Naz]

RR4298.   Kim, Jae-Hee: "Transindividuality and Post-Labor Based on Simondon and Stiegler." *Kriterion: Revista de Filosofia*, *60*, 143, 319-338. [Syr]

RR4299.   Lindberg, Susanna: "Being with Technique-Technique as Being-With: The Technological Communities of Gilbert Simondon." *Continental Philosophy Review*, *52*, 3, 299-310. [Naz]

RR4300.   Mazzilli-Daechsel, Stefano: "Simondon and the Maker Movement." *Culture, Theory and Critique*, *60*, 3, 237-249. [UaB]

RR4301.   Montoya, Jorge W.: "From Analog Objects to Digital Devices." *Philosophy Today*, *63*, 3, 717-730. [Naz]

RR4302.   Picchi, T.: "The Dream of General Intellect: Simondon between Workerism and Post-Fordism." *Philosophy Today*, *63*, 3, 687-703. [UofR]

RR4303.   Terranova, Charissa N.: "Preindividuation, Individuation, and Bacteria: Revisiting Gilbert Simondon's Philosophy Through the Hologenome." *Public*, *30*, 59, 138-148. [Cor]

SLIMANI, Leïla.

See also 23, 303, 314, 331.

RR4304.   Starace, Lorenza: "Leïla Slimani's Chanson Douce: Paradoxes of Identity and Visibility in the Littérature-Monde Paradigm." *Francosphères*, *8*, 2, 143-165. [Cor]

RR4305.   Young, Molly: "Adèle by Leila Slimani." *New York Times Book Review*, *124*, 4, 13. [UofR]

SOLLERS, Philippe.

See also 526, 613, 717, 4043, 4044.

RR4306.   ● Rachet, Olivier: *Sollers en Peinture: Une Contre-Histoire de l'Art*. Paris: Tinbad. 214p. [LoC]

RR4307.   Sollers, P.: "La Mort des Avant-Gardes." *Infini*, 144, 24-43. [Syr]

SOUCY, Gaétan.

RR4308.   Powers, Scott M.: "'Tu N'As Pas à Te Sentir Coupable d'Être': A Multiversal Approach to Guilt in Gaétan Soucy's L'Acquittement." *Studies in Canadian Literature*, *43*, 1. [UaB]

SOUPAULT, Philippe.
See also 391.
RR4309. ● Metzner, Manfred: *Ré Soupault - Norwegen 1936.* Heidelberg: Verlag das Wunderhorn. 80p. [WC]
RR4310. Velázquez Ezquerra, José Ignacio: "Soupault, *Les Dernières Nuits de Paris* y Los Intertextos: *Georgette* y/o *Nadja*" *Thélème, 34,* 1, 245-58. [RIT]
RR4311. Wagner, B.: "Sud-Nord. Les Dernières Nuits de Paris (Philippe Soupault): Un Chronotope Surréaliste." *Revue des Sciences Humaines,* 336, 23-35. [Syr]

STAROBINSKI, Jean.
RR4312. ● Méthot, Pierre-Olivier: "Jean Starobinski et la Rationalité de la Médecine." *Bulletin du Cercle d'Études Jean Starobinski, 12,* 8. [WC]
RR4313. ● Monnet, Vincent: "Jean Starobinski Quitte la Beauté du Monde." *Campus. Université de Genève,* 137, 10. [WC]
RR4314. ● Montesquieu, Jean Starobinski, & Louis Desgraves: *Essai Sur le Goût.* Paris: Rivages Poche. 125p. [WC]
RR4315. ● Para, Jean-Baptiste: *Jean Starobinski: Jean-Pierre Richard.* Paris: Europe. *Europe, 97,* 1080. 380p. [WC]
RR4316. Barras, Vincent: "Jean Starobinski, 17 Novembre 1920-4 Mars 2019." *Gesnerus,* 76, 114-115. [UofR]
RR4317. Blaise, Mario, & Éric Corbobesse: "Portrait Iconoblaste de Jean Starobinski." *PSN, 17,* 2, 69. [Naz]
RR4318. Chitussi, Barbara: "Jean Starobinski e la Conoscibilità della Maschera." *Intersezioni, 39,* 2, 267-284. [WC]
RR4319. Delon, Michel: "Remembrance of Jean Starobinski (1920-2019)." *Dix-Huitième Siècle, 51,* 1, 7. [UofR]
RR4320. Ender, Evelyne: "Starobinski's Resistance to Theory—le Regard de l'Absent." *MLN, 134,* 5, 878-97. [PrQ]
RR4321. Grosrichard, Alain, & Judith Miller: "Entretien Avec Jean Starobinski, L'Essai et Son Éthique." *La Cause du Désir, 102,* 2, 21. [WC]
RR4322. Guillemain, Hervé: "Histoire, Littérature et Psychiatrie. Jean Starobinski (1920–2019)." *L'Évolution Psychiatrique, 84,* 3, 512-513. [UofR]
RR4323. "Hommage à Jean Starobinski: 17 Novembre 1920 - 4 Mars 2019." *Sigila, 43,* 1, 6. [UaB]
RR4324. Ossola, C.: "Ricordo di Jean Starobinski e di Michel Jeanneret." *Lettere Italiane, 71,* 2, 227-229. [UaB]
RR4325. Rodríguez, Amán R.: "Autobiografía y Yo Corporal en la Ensayística de Salvador Elizondo. Una Lectura Desde Jean Starobinski." *Romanica Cracoviensia, 19,* 4, 257-269. [Syr]
RR4326. Shum, Peter: "Jean Starobinski and the Critical Gaze." *Interdisciplinary Literary Studies, 21,* 3, 338-358. [Syr]
RR4327. Zavala, Díaz A. L.: "Sobre Jean Starobinski, la Tinta de la Melancolía." *Historia Mexicana, 68,* 4, 1917-1922. [Naz]

STÉTIÉ, Salah.
See also 541, 758, 789.
RR4328. ● Nassif, Stéphanie: *Salah Stétié, D'Ombres et de Lumière.* Paris: Hermann. 114p. [UofR]

RR4329. ● Stétié, Salah: *Poésie & Chanson*. Paris: *Europe*, 98, 1091 (Janvier-Février 2020), p. 4-372. [WC]

RR4330. ● Stétié, Salah, & Philippe Favier: *Pensées Pour Soi*. Bruxelles (Belgique): La Pierre d'Alun. 114p. [BAnQ]

RR4331. Khodr, Fadi: "Études de 'K': Yunus Emré, Dino Buzzati, Salah Stétié." *Synergies Turquie*, *12*, 139, 149, 301. [RIT]

SUARÈS, André.

RR4332. ● De Merolis, F.: *André Suarès: Coscienza Critica dell'Europa*. Ortona (Ch), Italia: Menabò. 169p. [LoC]

RR4333. ● Rosny, Antoine: *La Culture Classique d'André Suarès*. Paris: Classiques Garnier. 877p. [LoC]

RR4334. ● Suarès, André: *Fragments Manuscrits Relatifs à la Culture Classique*. Paris: Classiques Garnier. 548p. [Cor]

RR4335. Lesiewicz, Sophie: "Habent Sua(s) Res Libelli: 'L'Art du Livre' d'André Suarès." *Art & Métiers du Livre*, 333, [34]-41. [WC]

SULLY PRUDHOMME.

RR4336. Masson, Géraldine: "Georges Lafenestre, le Poète Conservateur." *Revue d'Histoire Littéraire de la France*, *119*, 3, 589-604. [UofR]

SUPERVIELLE, Jules.

RR4337. ● *Bijoux et Orfèvrerie Provenant de L'Écrain de Mme Abrami et d'Autres Écrins - Tableaux Modernes Provenant de la Collection de Jules Supervielle et Sa Descendance et d'Autres Collections Particulières - Objets d'Art et Mobilier du XXe Siècle - Jouets - Dessins - Peintures Mobilier et Objets d'Art des XVIIe, XVIIIe et XIXe Siècles: [Vente, Paris], Salle V V-Quartier Drouot, Lundi 25 Mars 2019*. Paris: Mallié-Arcelin. 102p. [BnF]

RR4338. Hubner, Patrick, José García-Romeu, & Martín Lombardo: "Creación, Otredad y Desplazamientos. Apuntes Sobre un Episodio en la Vida de un Pintor Viajero de César Aira y L'Homme de la Pampa de Jules Supervielle." *Babel*, 39, 33-47. [Syr]

RR4339. Kim, Si-Won: "L'Odyssée dans la Poésie de Jules Supervielle." *Société d'Études Franco-Coréennes*, 88, 5-23. [WC]

TADJO, Véronique.
See also 208, 257, 333, 360, 606, 704.

RR4340. ● Tadjo, Véronique: *The Culture of Dissenting Memory: Truth Commissions in the Global South*. New York: Routledge. 171p. [Cor]

RR4341. Raschi, Natasa: "Véronique Tadjo, En Compagnie des Hommes." *Studi Francesi*, *63*, 2, 399-401. [UaB]

TARDIEU, Jean.
See also 850.

RR4342. ● Pasqualicchio, Nicola: *Le Tour du Théâtre: Jean Tardieu Drammaturgo*. Verona: Fiorini. 149p. [WC]

RR4343. ● Turolla, Giacomo: *À Quelques Pas des Lignes: Correspondance 1914-1918*. Lyon: Presses Universitaires de Lyon. 209p. [WC]

TCHICAYA U TAMSI.
See also 395, 516, 695, 817.
RR4344. ● Leroux, Pierre: *Le Prêtre, le Traître et le Rebelle: Figure Christique et Messianisme dans les Œuvres de Dambudzo Marechera et Tchicaya U Tam'si.* Trier: WVT, Wissenschaftlicher. 221p. [BnF]

TEILHARD DE CHARDIN, Pierre.
See also 2505.
RR4345. ● Bèle, Guffroy R. A.: *Teilhard de Chardin: Théologien Malgré Lui.* [Chouzé-sur-Loire]: Saint-Léger. 271p. [WC]
RR4346. ● Duffy, Kathleen: *Hawking and Teilhard on Creation.* [Woodbridge, CT]: American Teilhard Association. *Teilhard Studies*, 78. 19p. [WC]
RR4347. ● Duffy, Kathleen: *Teilhard's Struggle: Embracing the Work of Evolution.* Maryknoll: Orbis Books. 148p. [LoC]
RR4348. ● Giustozzi, Gianfilippo, & Emilio P. Bossi: *Pierre Teilhard de Chardin: Da 'Gesuita Proibito' a Risorsa per il Pensiero Cristiano: Atti del Convegno di Gavirate, 6 Maggio 2017.* Canterano: Aracne. 104p. [LoC]
RR4349. ● Gonçalves, Lind A.: *Pour une Écclésiologie Écologique: L'Actualité de la Vision Teilhardienne dans l'Émergence de la Sensibilité Écologique.* Namur (Belgique): Presses Universitaires de Namur. 129p. [LoC]
RR4350. ● Lièvre, Léonard: *Les Fragiles Étincelles de Nos Feux Ardents: Du Silex à l'Internet Avec Teilhard de Chardin.* Le Coudray-Macouard: Les Acteurs du Savoir. 104p. [LoC]
RR4351. ● Misraki, Paul, & Jacques Masurel: *Pour Aimer Ce Monde en Devenir: Introduction à la Pensée de Teilhard de Chardin.* Le Coudray-Macouard: Les Acteurs du Savoir. 90p. [BnF]
RR4352. ● Sack, Susan K.: *America's Teilhard: Christ and Hope in the 1960s.* Washington, DC: The Catholic University of America Press. 324p. [Syr]
RR4353. ● Savary, Louis M.: *Teilhard de Chardin on Morality: Living in an Evolving World.* New York: Paulist Press. 188p. [LoC]
RR4354. ● Sorkhabi, Rasoul B.: *Pierre Teilhard de Chardin and Sir Julian Huxley: A Tale of Two Friends.* [Woodbridge, CT]: American Teilhard Association. 26p. [WC]
RR4355. ● Udías, Vallina A., & Marie-Anne Roger: *La Présence du Christ dans le Monde: Prières de Teilhard de Chardin.* Paris: Salvator. 151p. [BnF]
RR4356. Curran, Ian: "Theology, Evolution, and the Figural Imagination: Teilhard de Chardin and His Theological Critics." *Irish Theological Quarterly, 84,* 3, 287-304. [UaB]
RR4357. Delio, Ilia: "Teilhard de Chardin and World Religions." *Journal of Ecumenical Studies, 54,* 3, 306-327. [UofR]
RR4358. Eloe, Laura: "From Newman Through Teilhard and Beyond." *Newman Studies Journal, 16,* 1, 51-71. [UaB]
RR4359. Kemp, Kenneth W.: "Teilhard de Chardin, The 'Six Propositions,' and the Holy Office." *Zygon, 54,* 4, 932-953. [UofR]
RR4360. Grumett, David: "Cult Books Revisited: Pierre Teilhard de Chardin's The Phenomenon of Man." *Theology, 122,* 6, 404-411. [UaB]
RR4361. Grumett, D.: "Teilhard, The Six Propositions, and Human Origins: A Response: With Kenneth W. Kemp, 'Teilhard de Chardin, the 'Six Propositions,' and

the Holy Office'; and David Grumett, 'Teilhard, The Six Propositions, and Human Origins: A Response'." *Zygon*, *54*, 4, 954-964. [Naz]

RR4362. Petersen, Arthur C.: "Teilhard's Silencing, Mutual Enhancement, and Historical Europe." *Zygon*, *54*, 4, 823-825. [UofR]

RR4363. Prats, Mercè: "Le Phénomène Humain de Pierre Teilhard de Chardin, Un Mémoire Scientifique?" *Organon*, 51, 91-121. [Cor]

RR4364. Respigiani, Oreste: "2005: Aniversário de Dois Grandes Místicos Católicos do Século XX: Pierre Teilhard de Chardin e Thomas Merton." *Revista Eclesiástica Brasileira*, *66*, 261, 181. [LoC]

RR4365. Suleková, Mária, & Kevin T. Fitzgerald: "Can the Thought of Teilhard de Chardin Carry Us Past Current Contentious Discussions of Gene Editing Technologies?" *Cambridge Quarterly of Healthcare Ethics*, *28*, 1, 62-75. [Naz]

RR4366. Thackeray, J. F.: "Teilhard de Chardin, Human Evolution and 'Piltdown Man'." *Evolutionary Anthropology*, *28*, 3, 126-132. [Syr]

RR4367. Vasconcelos, Aparecida M.: "Nos Êxitos e Nos Fracassos Humanos. A Mística da Terra na Cosmovisão de Pierre Teilhard de Chardin." *Revista Eclesiástica Brasileira*, *72*, 285, 26. [WC]

RR4368. Vico, Martín J.: "La Justificación Científica y Filosófica del Respeto Hacia la Naturaleza: Teilhard de Chardin, Arne Naess y El Papa Francisco." *Contrastes*, *23*, 1. [LoC]

TENGOUR, Habib.

RR4369. ● Tengour, Habib, Regina Keil-Sagawe, & Paul Hindemith: *Der Alte vom Berge Gefolgt von Nacht mit Hassan: Habib Tengour; Aus dem Französischen Übersetzt, Kommentiert und mit Einem Nachwort von Regina Keil-Sagawe.* Bremen: Sujet. 196p. [WC]

THÉORET, France.
See also 340, 609.

RR4370. Mihelakis, Eftihia: "Prédation, Virginité et Mauvaise Foi Chez France Théoret." *Tangence*, 119, 79. [Cor]

THÉRÈSE DE LISIEUX.

RR4371. ● Baudoüin, Élisabeth, & Guzmán Carriquiry: *Thérèse et François.* Paris: Salvator. 219p. [LoC]

RR4372. ● Bouflet, Joachim: *Quand Thérèse Parlait aux Mystiques: La Sainte de Lisieux a Bouleversé Leur Vie.* Perpignan: Artège. 243p. [BnF]

RR4373. ● Caster, Gary: *The Way of Simple Love: Inspiring Words from St. Thérèse of Lisieux.* Cincinnati, OH: Franciscan Media. 181p. [WC]

RR4374. ● Ducharlet, Émile: *Du Carmel aux Tranchées: Thérèse de Lisieux.* Saint-Ouen-en-Brie: La Lucarne Ovale. 46p. [BnF]

RR4375. ● Gaucher, Guy. *Thérèse de Lisieux (1873-1897): Biographie.* Paris: Cerf. 683p. [WC]

RR4376. ● Guibert, Joël, & James H. McMurtrie: *Abandonment to God: The Way of Peace of St. Thérèse of Lisieux.* Manchester, NH: Sophia Institute Press. 173p. [WC]

RR4377. ● Piccirilli, Antonella: *Fragile Come Tutti, Felice Come Pochi: Teresa di Lisieux e le Nostre Ferite.* Cinisello Balsamo: San Paolo. 283p. [WC]

RR4378. • *St Thérèse of Lisieux in Scotland 2019*. Airdrie: Bishops' Conference of Scotland. 93p. [WC]

RR4379. Desmazières, Agnès: "Thérèse Posthume." *Archives de Sciences Sociales des Religions*, 188, 161-72. [PrQ]

RR4380. Henriet, Patrick: "Claude Langlois. Le Continent Théologique. Explorations Historiques/ Claude Langlois. Thérèse de Lisieux et la Miséricorde: Rennes, Presses Universitaires de Rennes, 2016/ Paris, Éditions du Cerf, 2016." *Revue de l'Histoire des Religions*, *236*, 1, 224. [UaB]

THÉRIAULT, Yves.
See 655, 741.

THIBODEAU, Serge Patrice.
See also 240.

RR4381. Lavoie, Carlo: "Ici le Monde: Marginalité Acadienne et Mondialisation Chez Serge Patrice Thibodeau." *Journal of Canadian Studies*, *53*, 3, 577-598. [Naz]

THOMAS, Édith.
See 426.

THOMAS, Henri.
See also 639.

RR4382. Hébert, Sophie: "Les 'Écritures Confuses' d'Henri Thomas: Perspectives Poétique, Générique, Génétique." *Études Littéraires*, 48, 87-102. [UaB]

TILLION, Germaine.
See 375, 410.

TINAN, Jean de.
RR4383. • Tinan, Jean, & Claude Sicard: *Lettres à Madame Bulteau*. Paris: Honoré Champion. 321p. [WC]

TINAYRE, Marcelle.
See also 347.

RR4384. Christiansen, Hope: "Plus Ça Change, Plus C'est la Même Chose: Léontine Zanta's La Science et l'Amour (1920)." *Symposium*, *73*, 1, 14-28. [UofR]

TITUS-CARMEL, Gérard.
RR4385. • Blanchet, Marc: *Gérard Titus-Carmel, 'Viornes & Lichens'*. Saint-Étienne-les-Orgues: Artgo & Cie. 58p. [BnF]

RR4386. • Chol, Isabelle: *Titus-Carmel. Les Actes du Colloque*. Saint-Benoît-du-Sault: Tarabuste. 218p. [WC]

RR4387. • Titus-Carmel, Gérard: *Horizon d'Attente*. Saint-Benoît-du-Sault: Tarabuste. 104p. [BnF]

RR4388. • Titus-Carmel, Gérard, & Thomas Augais: *Écrits de Chambre et d'Écho*. [Strasbourg]: Atelier Contemporain. 640p. [BnF]

TODOROV, Tzvetan.
See also 423, 706.

RR4389.   Barrozo, Naiara Martins: "O Fantástico de Todorov de Um Ponto de Vista Benjaminiano." *Cadernos de Pós-Graduação em Letras*, 19, 3. [WC]

RR4390.   Cunha, Fontes M.: "A Conquista da América: A Questão do Outro – Cap. I - Descobrir (Tzvetan Todorov)." *Revista do Instituto Histórico e Geográfico do Pará*, 6, 1. [WC]

RR4391.   Domingues, João: "Le Triomphe de l'Artiste la Révolution et les Artistes – Russie: 1917-1941 Tzvetan Todorov Paris, Flammarion/ Versilio, 2017 336 Páginas. ISBN 9782081404731." *Revista de Estudos Literários*, 8, 507-512. [LoC]

TOURNIER, Michel.
See also 542, 563.

RR4392.   ● Bouloumié, Arlette: *Dictionnaire Michel Tournier*. Paris: Honoré Champion. 458p. [WC]

RR4393.   ● Koster, Serge: *Tournier Parti*. Paris: Pierre-Guillaume de Roux. 114p. [Cor]

RR4394.   Bolukmese, E., & M. Canakci: "An Intertextuality Approach to the Works of Daniel Defoe's 'Robinson Crusoe' and Michel Tournier's 'Friday, Or, the Other Island'." *Folklor/ Edebiyat*, 97, 1, 133-151. [Cor]

RR4395.   Dalmas, Franck: "Bataillé, Mathilde. Michel Tournier: L'Écriture du Temps." *French Review*, 92, 3, 208. [Naz]

RR4396.   Lemann, N.: "Naturalisation of Power. Some Notes on the Margins of Daniel Defoe's Robinson Crusoe and Michel Tournier's Friday, or, the Other Island with the Shakespearean Tempest in the Background." *Porownania*, 25, 229-245. [LoC]

RR4397.   Van der Toorn, N.: "Sémiotique et Onomastique dans le Roi des Aulnes de Michel Tournier." *Neophilologus*, *103*, 1, 23-65. [UofR]

RR4398.   Wally, J.: "Whose Foot(print)? An Analysis of Aspects of the Implied Worldview of Daniel Defoe's Robinson Crusoe, Michel Tournier's Vendredi ou les Limbes du Pacifique and Stephen King's 'Survivor Type'." *Germanisch-Romanische Monatsschrift*, *69*, 2, 143-172. [Syr]

TOUSSAINT, Jean-Philippe.
See also 667, 2295.

RR4399.   ● Richir, Alice: *Ecriture du Fantasme Chez Jean-Philippe Toussaint et Tanguy Viel: Diffraction Littéraire de l'Identité*. Leiden: Brill. 288p. [Syr]

RR4400.   ● Toussaint, Jean-Philippe, Katia Poletti, & Félix Vallotton: *Félix Vallotton, Intimité(s): . . . et le Regard de Jean-Philippe Toussaint*. Paris: Martin de Halleux. 77p. [LoC]

RR4401.   Clamens-Nanni, Frédéric: "Images de la Femme Aimée dans le Cycle de Marie de Jean-Philippe Toussaint: Entre Roman et Cinéma." *Études Françaises*, 55, 2, 43. [UaB]

RR4402.   Czerkies, Dorota: "Une (En)Quête du Récit: Références au Genre Policier en Tant Que Moyen d'un Renouveau Romanesque dans la Réticence de Jean-Philippe Toussaint." *Studia Litteraria*, *14*, 3, 139-150. [Naz]

RR4403.   Elez, Vesna: "Articuler les Affects: Fuir de Jean-Philippe Toussaint." *Dacoromania Litteraria*, 5, 45-55. [WC]

RR4404.   Falantin, Flavien: "Richir, Alice. Écriture du Fantasme Chez Jean-Philippe Toussaint et Tanguy Viel." *French Review*, *93*, 2, 266. [UofR]

RR4405.   Kaas, Marianne: "Traduire Jean-Philippe Toussaint." *Quinzaines*, 1216, 13. [WC]

RR4406.   Olivier, Claire: "Jean-Philippe Toussaint la Clé Usb." *Quinzaines*, 1219, 6-7. [Syr]

RR4407.   Richir, Alice: "Écriture du Fantasme Chez Jean-Philippe Toussaint et Tanguy Viel Diffraction Littéraire de l'Identité." *Faux Titre*, 429. [UofR]

TRASSARD, Jean-Loup.
See also 469.

RR4408.   Bataillé, Mathilde: "Book Review: Jean-Loup Trassard ou le Paysage Empêché." *Revue d'Histoire Littéraire de la France*, *119*, 1, 238-240. [UofR]

RR4409.   Buekens, Sara: "Proximité Avec la Nature et Jeu des Genres Littéraires: L'Homme des Haies de Jean-Loup Trassard et Naissance d'un Pont de Maylis de Kerangal." *Études Littéraires*, *48*, 3, 21. [UaB]

TREMBLAY, Michel.
See also 576, 838, 867, 888.

RR4410.   ● *Enfant Insignifiant!*, Texte Michel Tremblay, Mise en Scène et *Adaptation, Michel Poirier*. Montréal: Duceppe. 3p. [BAnQ]

RR4411.   Bédard-Goulet, Sara, & Frédéric Vinot: "L'Événement de Spectature et l'Image Cinématographique dans les Vues Animées de Michel Tremblay." *Synergies Pays Riverains de la Baltique*, 13, 49, 60, 124. [PrQ]

RR4412.   Chapman, Rosemary: "Michel Tremblay: Albertine, en Cinq Temps: Genèse et Mise en Scène by Rachel Killick (Review)." *British Journal of Canadian Studies*, *32*, 12, 170-171. [Naz]

RR4413.   Khalil, Rania Rafik Mohamed: "An Examination of the Use and Production of Space in Brian Friel's Translations (1980), Michel Tremblay's Solemn Mass for a Full Moon in Summer (2009) and Emma Donoghue's Room (2017)." *Textual Turnings*, *1*, 1, 256-272. [WC]

RR4414.   Nolette, Nicole, & Dominique Louër: "La Fabrique de la Traduction, un Cadrage Queer: Michel Tremblay Traduit par John van Burek et Bill Glassco." *TTR*, *32*, 2, 159. [BAnQ]

TRIOLET, Elsa.
See also 521.

RR4415.   ● Aragon, Louis, & François Eychart: *Les Annales de la Société des Amis de Louis Aragon et Elsa Triolet*. Paris: Delga. *Annales de la Société des Amis de Louis Aragon et Elsa Triolet*, 20. 465p. [WC]

TURCOTTE, Élise.
See also 655.

RR4416.   ● Turcotte, Élise: *L'Apparition du Chevreuil*. Québec, PQ: Alto. 157p. [BAnQ]

TZARA, Tristan.
See also 531, 1862.

RR4417.   Brown, Kathryn: "Collage as Form and Idea in the Art Criticism of Tristan Tzara." *French Studies*, 73, 4, 544-560. [UofR]

RR4418.   Chereches, Lavinia: "Interpretive-Analytical Hypostases in 'Sept Fragments de Tristan Tzara' for Voice and Piano by Adrian Pop." *Studia Universitatis Babeș-Bolyai Musica*, 64, 2, 229-259. [Cor]

RR4419.   Orita-Serban, Manuela: "Le Mouvement Dadaïste: Sources, Histoire Littéraire; Précurseur du Surréalisme. La Figure Emblématique du Poète Roumain Tristan Tzara." *Studia Universitatis Babeș-Bolyai Philologia*, 64, 3, 185-196. [UaB]

VADEBONCŒUR, Pierre.
See 65, 388.

VAILLAND, Roger.
RR4420.   ● Céline, Louis-Ferdinand, & Andrea Lombardi: *Céline Contro Vailland: Due Scrittori, una Querelle, un Palazzo di una Via di Montmartre Sotto l'Occupazione Tedesca*. Massa (Massa-Carrara): Eclettica. 81p. [WC]

VALÉRY, Paul.
See also 318, 381, 441, 536, 792, 806.
RR4421.   ● Aziza, Nadir: *Paul Valéry et la Méditerranée: Journées Paul Valéry, Musée Paul Valéry, Sous le Haut Patronage de l'Académie Française*. [Sète]: Musée Paul Valéry. 458p. [Cor]

RR4422.   ● Debray, Régis: *Un Été Avec Paul Valéry*. [Sainte-Marguerite-sur-Mer]: Équateurs. 173p. [Cor]

RR4423.   ● Elder, David, & William Marx: *Paul Valéry et l'Acte de Traduire*. Paris: Classiques Garnier. 302p. [BnF]

RR4424.   ● Kocay, Victor: *Paul Valéry: Vers le Poème-Image*. Paris: L'Harmattan. 222p. [Cor]

RR4425.   ● Morim, de C. E. H.: *Contradiction et Temps dans les 'Cahiers' de Paul Valéry*. Paris: L'Harmattan. 152p. [BnF]

RR4426.   ● Ryan, Paul: *Paul Valéry, Sous le Signe de l'Art et des Artistes*. Paris: Lettres Modernes Minard. 572p. [BnF]

RR4427.   ● Sanna, Antonietta: *Paul Valéry Traducteur de Léonard de Vinci: Lecture Interprétation Création*. Paris: Éditions des Archives Contemporaines. 132p. [BnF]

RR4428.   Ahn, Joong-Eun: "T. S. Eliot and Paul Valéry: 1926-1929." *Journal of the T. S. Eliot Society of Korea*, 29, 3, 77-97. [WC]

RR4429.   Cattani, P.: "The Writings of Paul Valéry on Politics: Essays, Pamphlets, Writings of Circumstance or Literary Texts?" *Revue Italienne d'Études Françaises*, 9. [Syr]

RR4430.   Fiorentino, Francesco, & Paola Cattani: "Les Écrits Sur l'Actualité de Paul Valéry: Essais, Pamphlets, Écrits de Circonstance ou Textes Littéraires?" *Revue Italienne d'Études Françaises*, 9. [Cor]

RR4431.   López, Camila S.: "'Durtal', de Paul Valéry: Uma Tradução." *Rónai*, 7, 2, 151-159. [WC]

RR4432.   Milinkovic, Snezana, & Tobia Zanon: "'Carezze' Italiane di Paul Valéry." *Italica Belgradensia*, Spéciale, 117-125. [WC]

RR4433.   Triboulet, Jean-Pierre: "À Propos du 'Discours aux Chirurgiens' de Paul Valéry." *Hegel*, 2, 2, 164. [BnF]

RR4434.   Ustun, Berkay: "Paul Valéry's Implex, or That by Which We Remain Contingent, Conditional." *Neohelicon*, 46, 2, 623-644. [Naz]

VALLÈS, Jules.
See also 325, 369.

RR4435.   ● Léger, Céline: *Autour de Vallès: Revue de Lectures et d'Études Vallésiennes*. Montpellier: Association les Amis de Jules Vallès. 191p. [WC]

VAN LERBERGHE, Charles.
See 3315.

VARGAFTIG, Bernard.

RR4436.   ● Lefort, Régis: *Bernard Vargaftig: Esthétique du Renversement*. Boston: Brill Rodopi. 234p. [Syr]

RR4437.   ● Prevots, Aaron: *Bernard Vargaftig: Gestures Toward the Sacred*. Wien: Peter Lang. 124p. [LoC]

RR4438.   Prevots, Aaron: "Self-Awareness and Feminine Presence in the Poetry of Bernard Vargaftig: Aveu, Distance, Ouverture, Nudité." *French Review*, 93, 2, 41-50. [UofR]

VAUTHIER, Jean.
See 526, 848.

VELTER, André.
See also 18, 783, 789.

RR4439.   ● Pignon-Ernest, Ernest, & André Velter: *Annoncer la Couleur*. Arles (Bouches-du-Rhône): Actes Sud. 82p. [BnF]

RR4440.   ● Pignon-Ernest, Ernest, & André Velter: *L'Universel Cabotinage*. Paris: Société des Études Romantiques et Dix-Neuviémistes. 299p. [WC]

RR4441.   Darras, Jacques: "Cultures: André Velter: Renouveler le Pacte Avec l'Invisible." *Esprit*, 452. [PrQ]

VENAILLE, Franck.
See also 194.

RR4442.   ● Avila, Alin: *Peter Klasen: Iconographie Urbaine / La Force des Signes*. Paris: ENSBA Éditions. 200p. [WC]

VERCORS (pseud. of Jean Bruller).

RR4443.   Fiorentino, Francesco, & Roberta Sapino: "De Jean Bruller à Vercors: Texte et Images dans les 21 Recettes Pratiques de Mort Violente." *Revue Italienne d'Études Françaises*, 9. [Syr]

VERHAEREN, Émile.
See also 809.

RR4444.   ● Verhaeren, Émile, Albert Samain, Sylvain Frezzato, & Bernard Lherbier: *Les Sirènes Chantaient: Choix de Textes*. Anglet: Peigneurs de Comètes. 319p. [BnF]

RR4445.   Finch-Race, Daniel A.: "Gritty Metropoetics in Ada Cambridge's 'London' and Émile Verhaeren's 'Londres'." *Nineteenth-Century Contexts*, *41*, 1, 85-96. [Syr]

VERLAINE, Paul.
See also 3998, 4018.

RR4446.   ● Verlaine, Paul: *Écrits Sur Rimbaud*. Paris: Payot et Rivages. 145p. [BnF]

RR4447.   ● Verlaine, Paul, & Patrice Locmant: *Les Poètes du Nord: Une Conférence et un Poème Retrouvé Suivi de Deux Lettres Inédites.* [Paris]: Gallimard. 92p. [Cor]

RR4448.   ● Verlaine, Paul, Samuel N. Rosenberg, & Nicolas Valazza: *Paul Verlaine: A Bilingual Selection of His Verse*. University Park, PA: The Pennsylvania State UP. 397p. [Syr]

RR4449.   Bajrami, Bade, & Valbona Berisha: "Traduction et Négociations dans Trois Versions Albanaises de 'Gaspard Hauser Chante' de Verlaine." *Synergies Europe*, 14, 91, 101, 194-195. [PrQ]

RR4450.   Choi, In-Ryeong, J. W. Kim, & M. Y. Choi: "Emergence of Complexity in Poetry: 'Soleils Couchants' by Verlaine." *Palgrave Communications*, *5*, 1, 1-7. [Cor]

RR4451.   Creasy, Matthew: "'The Neglected, the Unutterable Verlaine': Arthur Symons, the *Saturday Review,* and French Literature in the 1890s." *Victorian Periodicals Review*, *52*, 1, 103-123. [RIT]

RR4452.   Fenko, Svetlana A.: "Poetics of Paul Verlaine's Book of Essays 'Les Poètes Maudits' ('Accursed Poets')." *Philological Sciences. Issues of Theory and Practice*, 8, 91-96. [WC]

VERNE, Jules.
See also 677.

RR4453.   ● Almeida, José D., & Maria F. Outeirinho: *Tours Verniens: Géographie, Langue et Textes Littéraires*. Paris: Le Manuscrit. 171p. [WC]

RR4454.   ● Bailleux, Nathalie: *Trophée Jules Verne: Le Record Extraordinaire: [Exposition, Brest, Musée de la Marine, 28 Juin 2019-3 Janvier 2021]*. Brest: Musée National de la Marine. 155p. [BnF]

RR4455.   ● Chapelle, Pierrette: *La Fabrique d'une Revue de Voyages Illustrée (1860-1914): Le Tour du Monde*. Paris: Classiques Garnier. 328p. [WC]

RR4456.   ● Diesbach, Ghislain: *Jules Verne Politiquement Incorrect?: Suivi de Histoire de Mon Livre*. Versailles: Via Romana. 319p. [WC]

RR4457.   ● Giton, Céline: *Voyageuses Extraordinaires: Les Femmes Rêvées par Jules Verne: Avec un Choix de 102 Gravures Originales Extraites des Éditions Hetzel*. L'Honor-de-Cos: L'Alisier Blanc. 252p. [Cor]

RR4458.   ● Gouvard, Jean-Michel: *Le Nautilus en Bouteille: Une Lecture de Jules Verne à la Lumière de Walter Benjamin*. Rennes: Pontcerq. 206p. [Cor]

RR4459.   ● Levêque, Laure: *Jules Verne: Un Lanceur d'Alerte dans le Meilleur des Mondes*. Paris: L'Harmattan. 206p. [Cor]

RR4460.   ● Louviot, Myriam, & Jérémie Dres: *Les Rêves de Jules Verne*. Paris: Didier. 45p. [WC]

RR4461.   ● Pinson, Guillaume, & Maxime Prévost: *Jules Verne et la Culture*

Médiatique: De la Presse du XIXe Siècle au Steampunk. [Québec]: Presses de l'Université Laval. 254p. [Syr]

RR4462. ● Rognon, Antoine: *Jules Verne et la Suisse/ y Suiza.* Marratxi (Islas Baleares): Paganel. 94p. [BnF]

RR4463. ● Tarrieu, Alexandre: *Dictionnaire des Personnes Citées par Jules Verne.* Marratxí (Iles Balears): Paganel. 3 vols. [BnF]

RR4464. Compère, Daniel: "Quand Jules Verne S'Inspire du Nord et de la Picardie." *Nord'*, *74*, 2, 25. [Cor]

RR4465. Crampon, Monique: "Jules Verne et la Petite Musique du Latin." *Nord'*, *74*, 2, 55. [Cor]

RR4466. Crovisier, Jacques: "Albert Badoureau, Ingénieur Fantasque et Collaborateur de Jules Verne." *Nord'*, *74*, 2, 46. [Cor]

RR4467. Dehs, Volker: "État Présent: Jules Verne." *French Studies*, *73*, 2, 266-277. [UaB]

RR4468. Dehs, Volker: "Jules Verne et la Société Industrielle d'Amiens." *Nord'*, *74*, 2, 37. [Cor]

RR4469. Elias, Ann: "Alien Harbour: Frank Hurley, Jules Verne, and the Early Dress-Divers of Underwater Sydney." *Australian Historical Studies*, *50*, 2, 212-234. [RIT]

RR4470. Ernst-Michael Stiegler: "Immer auf Achse!: Jules Verne und die Moderne Geophysik." *Physik in unserer Zeit*, *50*, 1, 24-7. [PrQ]

RR4471. Fix, Florence: "Book Review: Jules Verne et l'Invention d'un Théâtre-Monde. 'Études Sur le Théâtre et les Arts de la Scène'." *Revue d'Histoire Littéraire de la France*, *119*, 4, 995-997. [RIT]

RR4472. Kopp, Lé, et al.: "Spatialisation des Rumeurs Chez Jules Verne." *Géocarrefour*, *93*, 1. [PrQ]

RR4473. Lazos, Panagiotis: "Around the Moon. False Scientific Ideas in the Famous Book of Jules Verne." *Almagest*, *10*, 1, 92-105. [WC]

RR4474. Locmant, Patrice: "Jules Verne et la Pologne." *Revue des Études Slaves*, *90*, 3, 397-407. [Syr]

RR4475. Marcetteau-Paul, Agnès: "Jules Verne et le Roman de la Science." *Quinzaines*, *1214*, 10-11. [Syr]

RR4476. Morency, Jean: "Les Fables Canadiennes de Jules Verne. Discorde et Concorde dans Une Autre Amérique." *Revue d'Histoire de L'Amérique Française*, *73*, 1, 189, 191, 189A. [PrQ]

RR4477. Motte, Martin: "Les Espaces Communs Vus par Jules Verne." *Stratégique*, *123*, 3, 87. [Cor]

RR4478. Pike, David L.: "Armchair Undergrounds: Jules Verne and Subterranean Tourism." *Dix-neuf*, *23*, 1, 1-18. [UaB]

RR4479. Sudret, Laurence: "Jules Verne et le Mariage." *Nord'*, *74*, 2, 17. [Cor]

RR4480. Terdimou, Maria: "Elements of Mathematics and Astronomy in the Work of Jules Verne." *Almagest*, *10*, 1, 116-130. [WC]

RR4481. Vlahakis, George N.: "Political and Ideological Views of Jules Verne: A Consideration Through His Books." *Almagest*, 10, 106-115. [WC]

VIALATTE, Alexandre.
See also 438.

RR4482. • Dubuffet, Jean, & Alexandre Vialatte: *On Vous Attend: Lettres de Jean Dubuffet à Alexandre Vialatte 1951-1969: et Autres Textes, Correspondances, Évocations, Divertissements.* Paris: Association des Amis d'Alexandre Vialatte. 173p. [WC]

RR4483. Bezari, Christina, Riccardo Raimondo, Thomas Vuong, & Frances Egan: "The Translator as Literary Critic? Alexandre Vialatte's Battling Le Ténébreux Through the Eyes of the Translator." *Itinéraires*, 2-3, 2. [WC]

VIAN, Boris.

RR4484. • Bertolt, Nicole, & Alexia Guggémos: *Boris Vian, 100 Ans: Le Livre Anniversaire.* [Gennevilliers]: Heredium. 253p. [BnF]

RR4485. • Defays, Jean-Marc: *Boris Vian: Éternellement.* Paris: CLE International. 82p. [WC]

RR4486. • Pradère-Ascione, Clémentine: *Boris Vian: La Fantaisie Noire.* Paris: Presses Sorbonne Nouvelle. 301p. [Cor]

RR4487. • Seguin, Jean-Luc: *Lettres Ouvertes à l'Humanité: Comme les Auraient Aimées Boris Vian et Stéphane Hessel.* Saint-Denis: Édilivre. 108p. [BnF]

RR4488. • Sitbon, Clara: *Boris Vian, Faiseur de Hoax: Pour une Démystification de l'Affaire Vernon Sullivan.* Leiden (Pays-Bas): Brill Rodopi. 237p. [WC]

RR4489. • Spoorenberg, H. H., & Boris Vian: *Denkbeeldige Studie Over Nederland Door Boris Vian =: Rapport Sur la Découverte Que Je Fis de la Hollande.* Amsterdam: Nederlandse Academie voor 'Patafysica. 100p. [WC]

RR4490. • Vian, Boris, & Mathias Malzieu: *Boris Vian.* Paris: Le Livre de Poche. 4 vol. [BnF]

RR4491. • Vian, Boris, & Valérie Maugan-Chemin: *L'Herbe Rouge: Dossier Thématique, un Roman de la Fantaisie.* Paris: Le Livre de Poche. 251p. [WC]

RR4492. Bourderionnet, Olivier: "Jouer Avec la Forme: Politique et Poétique du Jazz dans la Prose et les Chansons de Boris Vian." *Atem Archiv Für Textmusikforschung*, 3, 2. [WC]

RR4493. Colin, Fabrice, & Hervé Aubron: "Boris Vian: Du Génie En Tube." *Nouveau Magazine Littéraire*, 18, 80-97. [WC]

RR4494. Cortijo, Talavera A.: "Revisión del 'Espacio Autobiográfico' en la Narrativa de Boris Vian." *Anales de Filología Francesa*, 27, 1, 75-95. [Naz]

RR4495. De Cabo, M., & Estefania Montecchio: "La Mujer Natural: La Influencia de Charles Baudelaire en 'L'Automne à Pekin' de Boris Vian." *Tropelías*, 31, 284-296. [WC]

RR4496. Kaczmarek, Tomasz: "Boris Vian et René de Obaldia: Enquête Sur les Résurgences de l'Expressiossisme." *Acta Philologica*, 54, 17-28. [WC]

RR4497. Montesi, Vanessa: "Las Otras Voces de Boris Vian: Traducciones Interlingüísticas e Intermediales de L'Écume des Jours y Su Recepción en el Reino Unido." *1616: Anuario de Literatura Comparada*, 9, 151. [UaB]

RR4498. Rolls, Alistair: "Boris Vian, Faiseur de 'Hoax': Pour une Démystification de l'Affaire Vernon Sullivan." *Australian Journal of French Studies*, 56, 3, 350-1. [RIT]

RR4499. Sitbon, Clara: "Boris Vian, Faiseur de Hoax Pour une Démystification de l'Affaire Vernon Sullivan." *Faux Titre*, 432. [UofR]

VILAR, Jean.
See also 10, 845.
RR4500. ● Vilar, Jean, Gérard Philipe, & Virginie Berling: *Jean Vilar-Gérard Philipe: 'J'imagine Mal la Victoire Sans Toi.'* [Paris]: TriArtis. 62p. [LoC]

VILLIERS DE L'ISLE-ADAM.
RR4501. Kılıçeri, Nedret Öztokat: "Le Tueur de Cygnes de Villiers de L'Isle-Adam: Une Analyse Sémiotique." *Synergies Turquie*, 12, 201-16. [PrQ]

VINAVER, Michel.
See also 82.
RR4502. ● Rey-Galtier, Delphine: *Michen Vinaver*. Lausanne: Ides et Calendes. 143p. [WC]
RR4503. Sant'Anna, Catarina: "Metis Grega e Simulacro em o Programa de Televisão (1990), de Michel Vinaver." *Urdimento*, 1, 20, 141-150. [WC]

VITEZ, Antoine.
See also 841, 843, 1126.
RR4504. ● Étienne, Marie, & Jacques Darras: *Antoine Vitez & la Poésie: La Part Cachée*. In'hui: Le Castor Astral. 218p. [LoC]
RR4505. ● Joinnault, Brigitte: *Antoine Vitez. La Mise en Scène des Textes Non Dramatiques (Cd Audio Inclus)*. Vic la Gardiole: L'Entretemps. 408p. [WC]
RR4506. De Gasquet, J. G.: "The Theatre Workshop According to Antoine Vitez. An Actor's Philosophy." *European Drama and Performance Studies*, 1, 13, 289-308. [LoC]

VITRAC, Roger.
See 526.

VIVIEN, Renée.
See also 294, 324, 353, 1658.
RR4507. Bristow, Joseph: "'There You Will See Your Page': Olive Custance, Alfred Douglas, and Lyrics of Sapphic Boyhood." *Victorian Poetry*, 57, 2, 265-94. [PrQ]
RR4508. Dilts, Rebekkah: "(Un)Veiling Sappho: Renée Vivien and Natalie Clifford Barney's Radical Translation Projects." *Refract*, 2, 1. [WC]
RR4509. Hawthorne, M.: "Behind the Bamboo Screen: Renée Vivien and the Rituals of Self-Destruction." *French Review*, 92, 4, 54-66. [Naz]

VOLKOFF, Vladimir.
See 526.

VOLODINE, Antoine.
RR4510. Ellis, Susannah: "Messianic Fiction in Antoine Volodine's Nuclear Catastrophe Novel Minor Angels." *Paragraph*, 42, 2, 223-237. [UaB]
RR4511. Huit, La J. N.: "Antoine Volodine. 2019. Frères Sorcières." *Glad!*, 7. [BnF]

RR4512. Patoine, Pierre L.: "Lectura Inmersiva, Lectura Encarnada: Una Aproximación Neuroestética a la Descripción del Entorno en la Obra de Antoine Volodine." *Signa*, 28, 205-235. [PrQ]

RR4513. Stamm, Gina: "Inventing a Vegetal Post-Exotic in the Work of Antoine Volodine." *Ecozon@: European Journal of Literature, Culture and Environment*, 10, 2, 42-57. [Syr]

VUILLARD, Éric.

RR4514. Boblet, Marie-Hélène, Anne Gourio, & Bernabé Wesley: "De Mémoire Vulnérable: Le Massacre des Sioux dans Tristesse de la Terre d'Éric Vuillard." *Elfe XX-XXI*, 9. [Cor]

RR4515. Bracher, Nathan: "Learning the Lessons of History and Literature: The Case of Éric Vuillard's L'Ordre du Jour." *History and Memory*, 31, 1, 3-24. [RIT]

RR4516. Toulmonde, Claudette: "Éric Vuillard, la Guerre des Pauvres: Actes Sud, Coll. 'Un Endroit Où Aller,' 2019, 68 p." *Cahiers d'Histoire. Revue d'Histoire Critique*, 143. [UaB]

WARREN, Louise.

RR4517. ● Warren, Louise: *Le Livre Caché de Lisbonne: Essai*. Montréal, PQ: Noroît. 178p. [BAnQ]

WEIL, Éric.

RR4518. Branco, J. C.: "Eric Weil e o Interesse Filosofico Pela Historia." *Kriterion (Brazil)*, 60, 144, 629-649. [Syr]

RR4519. Branco, Judikael C.: "Filosofia e Democracia em Eric Weil." *Pensando*, 9, 18, 104. [Syr]

RR4520. Branco, Judikael C., & L. F. da Rocha: "Hannah Arendt e Eric Weil: A Crise na Educação Como Problema do Nosso Tempo." *Revista Educativa*, 21, 1, 65. [LoC]

RR4521. Canivez, Patrice: "La Philosophie Comme Profession et la Participation Démocratique dans la Pensée Politique d'Éric Weil." *Eco-ethica*, 8, 109-126. [LoC]

RR4522. Perine, Marcelo: "Dios Como Categoría del Discurso Filosófico en 'Lógica de la Filosofía' de Éric Weil." *Revista Internacional de Religión y Espiritualidad en la Sociedad*, 1, 1, 43-50. [WC]

RR4523. Perine, Marcelo: "Sua Queda É Sua Dignidade: Eric Weil e Agostinho Sobre a 'Felix Culpa'." *Horizonte*, 31 August, 1021. [Naz]

RR4524. Soares, Daniel B.: "A Discussão Sobre a Democracia a Partir de Eric Weil." *Kínesis*, 11, 28, 57-75. [WC]

RR4525. Soares, Daniel B.: "Sociedade Moderna: Ciência e Sentido em Eric Weil." *Griot*, 19, 2, 171-181. [Syr]

RR4526. Valério, Uema F.: "Eric Weil e o Encontro de Um Outro Kantiano Pós-Hegeliano em Marx?" *Kínesis*, 10, 25, 296-311. [WC]

WEIL, Simone.
See also 708, 712, 721, 1256, 1458, 1459, 1601.

RR4527. ● Bart, Elisabeth: *Les Incandescentes. Simone Weil, Cristina Campo et Maria Zambrano*. Paris: Pierre Guillaume de Roux. 236p. [WC]

RR4528. ● Cappelli, Kévin: *Simone Weil, le Tournant Spirituel*. Rennes: Apogée. 80p. [BnF]

RR4529. ● Ceci, Giulia: *Disappartenere: Esistenza e Mistica in Simone Weil*. Milano: Jouvence. 288p. [LoC]

RR4530. ● Chenavier, Robert, & Thomas Pavel: *Simone Weil, Réception et Transposition. Ed. Reliée. Actes du Colloque de Cerisy-la-Salle, du 1er au 8 Août 2017*. Paris: Classiques Garnier. 382p. [WC]

RR4531. ● Doering, E. J., & Ruthann K. Johansen: *When Fiction and Philosophy Meet: A Conversation with Flannery O'Connor and Simone Weil*. Macon, GA: Mercer UP. 253p. [UofR]

RR4532. ● *Dossier Zu: Schriftsteller - Simone Weil*. [Köln]: [Performance-Archiv "Die Schwarze Lade"]. 1 vol. [WC]

RR4533. ● Fulco, Rita: *L'Europa di Simone Weil: Filosofia e Nuove Istituzioni*. Macerata: Quodlibet Giugno. 231p. [WC]

RR4534. ● García-Carpintero, María Á.: *Simone Weil Educadora: Tras los Ecos de Su Voz*. Barcelona: Claret. 328p. [WC]

RR4535. ● Guéquière, Vincent: *Simone Weil: Lutter Avec la Force*. Paris: Editions de l'École de Guerre. 145p. [BnF]

RR4536. ● *Les Premiers Écrits de Simone Weil (1925-1934): Art, Perception, Puissance*. Paris: Association pour l'Étude de la Pensée de Simone Weil. *Cahiers Simone Weil, 42*, 2. 202p. [WC]

RR4537. ● Micheletti, Gustavo: *La Sventura e la Grazia: Come Credere in un Dio Assente: Un Saggio su Simone Weil*. Trieste: Asterios. 302p. [LoC]

RR4538. ● Olsson, Karen: *The Weil Conjecture: On Maths and the Pursuit of the Unknown*. London: Bloomsbury. 214p. [Cor]

RR4539. ● Schülert, Marie: *Philosophie Mit Kindern: 'Pädagogische Einwurzelung' Bei Simone Weil*. Berlin: Münster LIT. 102p. [WC]

RR4540. ● *Simone Weil et La Littérature: La Littérature Comme Expression et/ ou Pouvoir: Un Témoignage Inédit Sur Simone Weil*. Paris: Association pour l'Étude de la Pensée de Simone Weil. *Cahiers Simone Weil, 42*, 3. 289p. [WC]

RR4541. ● *Simone Weil et La Littérature: Les Anciens, un Classique, un Contemporain*. Paris: Association pour l'Étude de la Pensée de Simone Weil. *Cahiers Simone Weil, 42*, 4. 239-432p. [WC]

RR4542. ● Spagnolo, Emanuele: *Simone Weil: Obbedire Alla Morte per Salvarsi dalla Sventura*. Villa Verucchio (RN): Pazzini. 73p. [WC]

RR4543. ● Taïbi, Nadia: *Simone Weil et Notre Temps: Philosopher, Penser, Résister*. Vallet: M-Éditer. 61p. [BnF]

RR4544. ● Weil, Simone: *Force et Malheur*. Bordeaux: Editions la Tempête. 280p. [WC]

RR4545. ● Weil, Simone, Robert Chenavier, & Jean Riaud: *Questions Politiques et Religieuses: (1942-1943)*. Paris: Gallimard. 756p. [WC]

RR4546. ● Weil, Simone, Robert Chenavier, Patrice Rolland, & Marie-Noëlle Chenavier-Jullien: *Écrits de New York et de Londres (1942-1943): Pt. 1*. Paris: Gallimard. 1 vol. [WC]

RR4547. ● Weil, Simone, Florence Lussy, Michel Narcy, & Joë Bousquet: *Correspondance 1942: 'Quel Est Donc Ton Tourment?'*. Paris XIIe: Claire Paulhan. 198p. [WC]

RR4548. Aaltola, Elisa: "Confronting Suffering with Narrative Theory, Constructed Selfhood, and Control: Critical Perspectives by Simone Weil and Buddhist Metaphysics." *Journal of Disability & Religion*, 23, 3, 227-250. [UaB]

RR4549. Adinolfi, I.: "Necessity and Freedom. Greek Thought, Gnosis and the Gospel in Simone Weil." *Cristianesimo Nella Storia*, 40, 3, 593-628. [Cor]

RR4550. Aparicio, L. C.: "Simone Weil's Notebooks: The Language of the Nuptial Chamber." *Revista Chilena de Literatura*, 99, 101-120. [Naz]

RR4551. Barros, Eduardo P.: "A Frágil Democracia: Simone Weil e o Fim dos Partidos Políticos." *Revista Internacional Interdisciplinar Interthesis*, 16, 2, 143-149. [Syr]

RR4552. Barthelet, Philippe: "Between Theodicy and Apologetics. Plato as 'A Human Preface of the Gospel': Joseph de Maistre and Simone Weil in the Wake of Cudworth." *Archives Internationales d'Histoire des Idées*, 222, 259-268. [RIT]

RR4553. Bingemer, Maria C. L.: "A Desventura e a Opção Pelos Pobres. Simone Weil e a Teologia da Libertação Latino-Americana." *Revista Eclesiástica Brasileira*, 69, 276, 772. [WC]

RR4554. Campo, Giuliano: "Simone Weil and Theatre: From Attention to the Descending Way." *Stanislavski Studies*, 7, 2, 177-200. [UaB]

RR4555. Carenini, Emma: "Simone Weil Contre les Fake News?" *Quinzaines*, 1211, 3-4. [UofR]

RR4556. Colell, Aparicio L.: "Los Cuadernos de Simone Weil: Lenguaje de la Cámara Nupcial." *Revista Chilena de Literatura*, 99, 101-120. [Naz]

RR4557. De Kesel, M.: "The Power to Say I. Reflections on the Modernity of Simone Weil's Mystical Thought." *Interdisciplinary Journal for Religion and Transformation in Contemporary Society*, 5, 1, 165-181. [WC]

RR4558. Gabellieri, Emmanuel: "Pensar a Kenosis. Filosofia e Teologia da Misericórdia em Simone Weil." *Revista Eclesiástica Brasileira*, 69, 276, 792. [WC]

RR4559. Gilbert, B.: "Simone Weil's Philosophy of History." *Journal of the Philosophy of History*, 13, 1, 66-85. [Naz]

RR4560. Jimenez, J. M. R.: "Impotence and Time in Simone Weil's Youth Writings." *Revista de Filosofia: Aurora*, 31, 52, 347-366. [WC]

RR4561. Kotva, S.: "Attention: Thomas A. Clark and Simone Weil." *Journal of British and Irish Innovative Poetry*, 11, 1. [UaB]

RR4562. Lorenzon, Alino: "Pessoa Humana, Enraizamento e Desenraizamento: A Fome e a Questão Ecológica No Pensamento de Simone Weil." *Revista Eclesiástica Brasileira*, 69, 276, 914. [WC]

RR4563. MacDonald, S.: "Simone Weil and Hannah Arendt on the Beautiful and the Just." *European Legacy*, 24, 805-818. [UofR]

RR4564. Martins, Alexandre A.: "Simone Weil's Radical Ontology of Rootedness: Natural and Supernatural Justices." *Praxis*, 2, 1, 23-35. [WC]

RR4565. Martins, Alexandre A.: "The Leftist Political Parties in Light of Simone Weil's Criticism: The Workers' Party Case." *Síntese*, 46, 145, 47. [UaB]

RR4566. Morgan, W. J.: "Simone Weil's Lectures on Philosophy: A Comment." *Rudn Journal of Philosophy*, 23, 4, 420-429. [WC]

RR4567. Muenala, Valverde G. P.: "La Praxis de la Encarnación en el Pensamiento de Simone Weil." *Cuestiones Teológicas*, 46, 105, 165-190. [Syr]

RR4568. Nogueira, M. S. M.: "Annihilation and Decreation: An Approximation of the Approaches Marguerite Porete and Simone Weil." *Trans/ Form/ Acao*, 42, Special Issue, 193-216. [Cor]

RR4569.   Ruiz, Jiménez J. M.: "Impotencia y Tiempo en los Escritos de Juventud de Simone Weil." *Revista de Filosofia Aurora*, 31, 52. [WC]

RR4570.   Rytzler, J.: "Turning the Gaze to the Self and Away from the Self-Foucault and Weil on the Matter of Education as Attention Formation." *Ethics and Education*, *14*, 3, 285-297. [Naz]

RR4571.   Simeoni, F.: "Animal e Impersonnel: Sull'umano in Simone Weil." *Etica e Politica*, *21*, 2, 155-170. [Syr]

RR4572.   Simeoni, F.: "Lavoro e Attenzione: Aspetti della Mediazione nel Pensiero di Simone Weil." *Metodo*, *7*, 2, 89-112. [WC]

RR4573.   Valle, Bortolo: "Simone Weil: O Sofrimento Como Pathos da Filosofia." *Revista de Filosofia Aurora*, 31, 53. [WC]

RR4574.   Valverde, Galo Patricio Muenala: "La Praxis de la Encarnación en el Pensamiento de Simone Weil." *Cuestiones Teológicas*, *46*, 105, 165-90. [PrQ]

RR4575.   White, J.: "In Search of Our Roots: Remembering Simone Weil's North American Emergence." *Dalhousie Review*, *99*, 3, 411-420. [UofR]

WERTH, Léon.
See also 565.

RR4576.   Bracher, Nathan: "Deposition 1940–1944: A Secret Diary of Life in Vichy France, by Léon Werth." *French Studies*, *73*, 2, 337-338. [UaB]

RR4577.   Millington, Chris: "Léon Werth, Deposition 1940–1944: A Secret Diary of Life in Vichy France." *European History Quarterly*, *49*, 2, 359-361. [UofR]

RR4578.   Perrin, Nigel: "Léon Werth (trans. and ed. David Ball), Deposition 1940–1944: A Secret Diary of Life in Vichy France." *Journal of Contemporary History*, *54*, 2, 478-480. [Naz]

WEYERGANS, François.
See also 1733.

RR4579.   ● Fernandez, Dominique, & Michael Edwards: *Hommages à M. François Weyergans: Décédé le 27 Mai 2019*. Paris: Palais de l'Institut. 12p. [BnF]

RR4580.   Jarosz, Adam: "Contre la Bible, Contre le Père ou à la Découverte de l'Univers des Références Intertextuelles Extra Bibliques dans Franz et François de François Weyergans." *Romanica Cracoviensia*, *19*, 2, 137-146. [Syr]

WIESEL, Elie.
See also 404, 522, 720, 735, 742, 748, 872, 1370.

RR4581.   ● Baron, Josef J.: *Das Holocaust-Paradoxon und das Elie-Wiesel-Dilemma: Von den Drei Phasen, Modalitäten und Szenarien des Antisemitismus, Faschismus und Holocaust und von der Unmöglichkeit Diese mit Mitteln der Herkömmlichen Aufklärung Rechtzeitig zu Erkennen und Abzuwehren*. Greiz: Frei & Herrlich. 136p. [WC]

RR4582.   ● Epstein, Nadine, Jonathan Sacks, & Ted Koppel: *Elie Wiesel: An Extraordinary Life and Legacy*. Washington, DC: MomentBooks. 176p. [WC]

RR4583.   ● Friedemann, Joë: *Élie Wiesel: Échos d'une Quête*. Paris: Orizons. 169p. [Cor]

RR4584.   ● Nesfield, Victoria, & Philip Smith: *The Struggle for Understanding: Elie Wiesel's Literary Works*. Albany: SUNY Press. 290p. [UofR]

RR4585.   ● Reich, Howard: *Art of Inventing Hope: Intimate Conversations with Elie Wiesel*. Chicago: Review Press. 192p. [Syr]

RR4586.   Ancy, Thresia N. K.: "Portrayal of Holocaust and Alienation in the Light of Trauma in Elie Wiesel's Trilogy Night, Day, Dawn." *Thematics Journal of Geography*, *8*, 8, 193-198. [WC]

RR4587.   Fisher, Eugene J.: "Elie Wiesel: Teacher, Mentor, and Friend Ed. by Alan L. Berger." *Journal of Ecumenical Studies*, *54*, 3, 467-469. [UofR]

RR4588.   Kalay, Faruk: "Elie Wiesel's Dangling Child: The Protagonist of Night." *Turan*, *11*, 41, 22-8. [RIT]

RR4589.   Potap, Olga: "Power of Memory (in Commemoration of Elie Wiesel, 1928–2016)." *Changing Societies & Personalities*, *3*, 2, 101-112. [WC]

RR4590.   Sabanci, Uzun G.: "'Paradoxical Doubleness in Elie Wiesel's Night." *Mediterranean Journal of Humanities*, *9*, 2, 453-463. [WC]

WITTIG, Monique.
See also 335, 366, 707.

RR4591.   Hernández, Piñero A.: "'Aquí y Ahora': La Noción de Contrato Social en el Lesbianismo Materialista de Monique Wittig." *Investigaciones Feministas*, *10*, 1, 27-44. [Cor]

YACINE, Kateb.
See also 244, 328, 1940, 2514.

RR4592.   Morel, Juliette: "Modélisation Spatiale du Récit Littéraire Complexe de Kateb Yacine." *Mappemonde*, 125. [Naz]

RR4593.   Sevcik, Stefanie: "Specters of Nedjma: Shifting Temporalities, Identities, and Itineraries in Kateb Yacine's Nedjma Cycle." *Research in African Literatures*, *50*, 1, 174-97. [RIT]

YOURCENAR, Marguerite.
See also 301, 318, 448, 463.

RR4594.   ● Béjaoui, Faten: *Écriture du Simulacre Masculin / Féminin dans Nouvelles Orientales de Marguerite Yourcenar*. [Manouba]: Université de Manouba. 492p. [Cor]

RR4595.   ● Brémond, Mireille: *Marguerite Yourcenar, une Femme à l'Académie. Ed. Reliée. Malgré Eux, Malgré Elle?* Paris: Classiques Garnier. 156p. [WC]

RR4596.   ● Cordonnier, Vincent: *La Sagesse d'Hadrien Selon Yourcenar*. [Paris]: Éditions du Retour. 226p. [LoC]

RR4597.   ● Diguet, Magalie: *Marguerite Yourcenar, 'Mémoires d'Hadrien': Parcours, Soi-Même Comme un Autre*. Paris: Ellipses. 101p. [BnF]

RR4598.   ● Loignon, Sylvie: *Marguerite Yourcenar, Mémoires d'Hadrien, 1951: 1re Générale: Nouveau Bac*. Paris: Hatier. 91p. [WC]

RR4599.   ● Poignault, Rémy: *Marguerite Yourcenar et le Monde des Lettres: À Simone Delcroix, in Memoriam*. Clermont-Ferrand: SIEY. 431p. [BnF]

RR4600.   ● Yourcenar, Marguerite, Bruno Blanckeman, & Elyane Dezon-Jones: *"Le Pendant des 'Mémoires d'Hadrien' et Leur Entier Contraire"*: *Correspondance 1964-1967*. [Paris]: Gallimard. 633p. [LoC]

RR4601. Blanckeman, Bruno: "Portrait d'Auteure en Démiurge Polymorphe: Marguerite Yourcenar." *Faux Titre*, 434, 45-54. [UofR]

RR4602. Brémond, Mireille: "Dictionnaire Marguerite Yourcenar." *French Studies*, 73, 1, 139-140. [UaB]

RR4603. Brochard, Cécile: "'Le Grand Pan N'est Pas Mort': La Vision de la Nature dans les Romans de Marguerite Yourcenar." *Faux Titre*, 427, 283-296. [UaB]

RR4604. Codena, Serena: "Achmy Halley, Marguerite Yourcenar. Portrait Intime." *Studi Francesi*, 63, 2, 390. [Syr]

RR4605. Genova, Pamela: "'À Chacun Son Tokyo.': Marguerite Yourcenar's Reading of Yukio Mishima as a Revolutionary Exemplar for Western Literary Art." *Contemporary French and Francophone Studies*, 23, 5, 617-624. [Naz]

RR4606. Ledez, Manon: "Des 'Fables Sur le Temps': Temps Vulgaire et Hors-Temps Poétique dans Quatre Récits de Marguerite Yourcenar." *Roman 20-50*, 67, 1, 141. [Cor]

RR4607. Peric, Katarzyna: "We Met in Paris: Grace Frick and Her Life with Marguerite Yourcenar by Joan E. Howard." *Women in French Studies*, 27, 1, 224-226. [UaB]

RR4608. Silveira, Suzane M. V.: "Autoria Feminina e Parceria Textual: O Monólogo Interior em Marguerite Yourcenar, Lygia Fagundes Telles e Katherine Mansfield." *Jangada*, 1, 14, 172-186. [WC]

RR4609. Zein, Laila F.: "Representasi Hegemoni Dalam Novel Mémoires d'Hadrien Karya Marguerite Yourcenar." *Jentera*, 8, 1, 67. [Cor]

ZOBEL, Joseph.
See also 227, 351.

RR4610. Demougin, Laure: "Joseph Zobel, d'Awa à Présence Africaine: Histoire et Géographies (Imaginaires) d'une Publication Noire." *Études Littéraires Africaines*, 47, 27. [LoC]

RR4611. Pajoul, Roxane: "Joseph Zobel: Négritude and the Novel, by Louise Hardwick." *New West Indian Guide*, 93, 365-366. [Naz]

RR4612. Scheel, Charles W.: "Retouches de la Représentation de la Femme dans Trois Éditions de la Nouvelle de Joseph Zobel 'Pionnier d'une Nuit' (ou 'Le Premier Convoi'): Simples Lissages Stylistiques, Expressions d'une Maturation Psychologique de l'Écrivain, ou Révisions Socio-Culturelles?" *Continents Manuscrits*, 13. [Cor]

ZOLA, Émile.
See also 358, 359, 383, 465, 538, 773, 3118.

RR4613. ● Chapuzet, Jean-Charles, Vincent Gravé, & Christophe Girard: *L'Affaire Zola*. Grenoble: Glénat 192p. [BnF]

RR4614. ● De Amicis, E.: *Émile Zola: L'Uomo, il Polemista, lo Scrittore*. Roma: Ecra. 110p. [WC]

RR4615. ● Grenier, Nicolas: *Petite Anthologie Sportive: & Autres Plaisirs Littéraires: d'Honoré de Balzac à Émile Zola*. Le Crest: Éditions du Volcan. 138p. [BnF]

RR4616. ● Harvey, Cynthia: *Portrait du Romancier en Bouddha: Balzac, Flaubert, Zola*. Montréal: Groupe Nota Bene. 153p. [BAnQ]

RR4617. ● Lumbroso, Olivier, Jean-Sébastien Macke, Jean-Michel Pottier, &

Alain Pagès: *Émile Zola et le Naturalisme, en Tous Genres: Mélanges Offerts à Alain Pagès*. Paris: Presses Sorbonne Nouvelle. 391p. [Cor]

RR4618. ● Minogue, Valerie, & Patrick Pollard: *Espaces et Paysages Industriels: Zola et les Réalités Sociales de Son Époque = (Landscapes of Industry: Zola and the Industrial Realities of His Time): Papers from the Lille Colloquium, 13-16 June 2018*. London: The Émile Zola Society. 240p. [WC]

RR4619. ● Munnich, Susana: *Soy Mi Deseo: (Stendhal, Balzac, Flaubert, Zola)*. Santiago [Chile]: LOM Ediciones Julio. 231p. [WC]

RR4620. ● Paine, Jonathan: *Selling the Story: Transaction and Narrative Value in Balzac, Dostoevsky, and Zola*. Cambridge, MA: Harvard UP. 344p. [Syr]

RR4621. ● Smith, Johan J., & Jaco Adriaanse: *Zola*. Cape Town: Penguin Books. 300p. [WC]

RR4622. ● Wolff, Bertrand: *De "Zola" à Zola, la Flambée du Solaire*. Chantepie: Les Éditions de Rennes en Sciences. 23p. [BnF]

RR4623. ● Zola, Émile: *Comment Écrire un Bon Roman: Les Conseils d'Émile Zola*. Paris: Éditions de la Tour Maubourg. 94p. [BnF]

RR4624. Azoulai, Juliette: "Evolutionary Time and Revolutionary Time (Michelet, Flaubert, Zola)." *Faux Titre*, 431, 327-342. [UaB]

RR4625. Behrens, Rudolf: "Life, Sex and Temporality in Zola's La Faute de L'Abbé Mouret." *Faux Titre*, 431, 140-156. [UofR]

RR4626. Budasz, Sarah: "The Bright Side of Life by Émile Zola (Review)." *French Studies*, 73, 3, 468-469. [UofR]

RR4627. Byron, Thomas: "Newtonianism, Thermodynamics, and Information Theory in Zola's Le Ventre de Paris." *Intertexts*, 23, 1, 195-222. [Naz]

RR4628. Carrico, Abbey: "Progressive Waters: Memory, Narrative and Localism in Émile Zola's L'Inondation." *Dix-neuf*, 23, 231-238. [Cor]

RR4629. Chavy, Pierre: "La Curée d'Émile Zola: L'Expropriation au Temps du Baron Haussmann." *Revue Droit & Littérature*, 3, 1, 257. [BnF]

RR4630. Cooke, Roderick: "A Paradox in the Dreyfus Affair: The Curious Case of Saint-Georges de Bouhélier." *French Cultural Studies*, 30, 1, 3-16. [RIT]

RR4631. De Viveiros, G.: "Identité Fluide dans la Correspondance de Zola et la Pratique de l'Autoportrait." *Études Françaises*, 55, 1, 51-66. [UofR]

RR4632. Färnlöf, Hans: "La Somme du Transfert: Pour une Approche Compréhensive de la Transmission de l'Œuvre de Zola en Suédois." *Orbis Litterarum*, 74, 2, 130-145. [RIT]

RR4633. François, Arnaud: "Zola, Hereditability of Character and Hereditability of Deviation: After a Remark by Bergson in L'Évolution Créatrice." *Faux Titre*, 431, 123-139. [UaB]

RR4634. Frigerio, Vittorio: "Zola, Émile. Les Mystères de Marseille." *Dalhousie French Studies*, 114, 135-135. [Syr]

RR4635. Galland, Maxime: "La Transgression en Bourse dans le Roman au XIX: (Lectures Croisées de Balzac, Stendhal et Zola)." *Revue Droit & Littérature*, 3, 1, 197. [BnF]

RR4636. Garzon, S. F.: "The Dreyfus Affair: Intellectuals and Spanish Press in 1898." *Historia y Comunicacion Social*, 24, 2, 713-726. [Naz]

RR4637. Guermès, Sophie: "Book Review: Le Langage des Sources dans les Trois Villes d'Émile Zola. La Dialectique de la Foi et de la Raison. 'Romantisme et Modernités'." *Revue d'Histoire Littéraire de la France*, 119, 4, 992-993. [UofR]

RR4638.   Heck, Adeline: "Émile Zola, His Excellency Eugène Rougon. Translated with an Introduction and Notes by Brian Nelson." *French Studies*, 73, 1, 130-131. [UofR]

RR4639.   Kociubińska, Edyta: "Paris 'Dans Tous Ses États' Selon les Chroniques d'Émile Zola (rec. Anna Kaczmarek-Wiśniewska. La Vie Quotidienne à Paris Suivant les Chroniques d'Émile Zola: Un Regard Oblique)." *Roczniki Humanistyczne*, 67, 5, 155. [Cor]

RR4640.   Lee, Junghwan: "Zola, Germinal et Pour les Lecteurs - Étude Sur la Circulation Médiatique de Germinal en Tant Que Roman-Feuilleton Entre 1884 et 1885." *Société d'Études Franco-Coréennes*, 90, 99-131. [WC]

RR4641.   Lethbridge, Robert: "Émile Zola, La Fabrique des Rougon-Macquart: Édition des Dossiers Préparatoires, VII: 'Le Rêve'. 'La Bête Humaine'. Publiés par Colette Becker." *French Studies*, 73, 2, 301-302. [UaB]

RR4642.   Lethbridge, Robert: "La Confession de Claude by Émile Zola (Review)." *French Studies*, 73, 3, 467-468. [UaB]

RR4643.   Lethbridge, Robert: "Lire Zola au XXIe Siècle. Sous la Direction d'Aurélie Barjonet et Jean-Sébastien Macke." *French Studies*, 73, 3, 469-470. [UofR]

RR4644.   López, Méndez M.: "Construction Déterministe du Personnage Féminin Chez Émile Zola et Miguel de Carrión." *Literatura: Teoría, Historia, Crítica*, 21, 1, 93-116. [Naz]

RR4645.   Melmoux-Montaubin, Marie-Françoise: "Book Review: Le Relevé des Jours. Émile Zola Écrivain-Journaliste 'Études Romantiques et Dixneuviémistes'." *Revue d'Histoire Littéraire de la France*, 119, 3, 731-733. [UofR]

RR4646.   Miranda, C. M., & M. F. Alamos: "Emilio Zola y la Influencia de la Medicina en Su Obra la Fortuna de Los Rougon-Macquart." *Revista Medica de Chile*, 147, 10, 1329-1334. [Syr]

RR4647.   Mokina, Natalia V.: "The Conquest of Plassans by Emile Zola and the Petty Demon by Fyodor Sologub: To the Issue of 'Another's Word' in a Symbolist Novel." *Izvestiya of Saratov University. New Series. Series: Philology. Journalism*, 19, 2, 198-203. [WC]

RR4648.   Niland, Richard: "Émile Zola: The Bright Side of Life, Translated by Andrew Rothwell; The Dream, Translated by Paul Gibbard." *Translation and Literature*, 28, 377-383. [UofR]

RR4649.   Pinna, Piero: "Editer et Relire la Correspondance de Zola, Sous la Direction de S. Guermès." *Studi Francesi*, 63, 3, 598-600. [UaB]

RR4650.   Rachwalska, von R. J.: "Le Geste Signifiant. La Rhétorique du Corps Paroxystique dans la Conquête de Plassans d'Émile Zola." *Cahiers Erta*, 18, 125-140. [WC]

RR4651.   Ratri, Theresia D., & Suma R. Rusdiarti: "Domination Inconscience (Id) du Personnage Principal dans le Roman de Thérèse Raquin par Émile Zola." *Digital Press Social Sciences and Humanities*, 3, 43. [WC]

RR4652.   Reymond, Adrien: "Politique et Droit Public Selon Zola." *Revue Droit & Littérature*, 3, 1, 181. [BnF]

RR4653.   Son, Kyung-Ae: "La Vie et la Mort, la Réalité et le Rêve, Analyse du Rêve de Zola." *Société d'Études Franco-Coréennes*, 87, 5-22. [WC]

RR4654.   Soranzo, Thaís: "'Minhas Impressões Sobre Zola', de George Moore." *Non Plus*, 8, 15, 83-110. [WC]

RR4655.   Souza, Raick D. J.: "Rilton Ferreira Borges, Zola e as Percepções do Tempo: Naturalismo e História em Germinal, Alameda, 2018." *Germinal: Marxismo e Educação em Debate*, *11*, 2, 257. [Syr]

RR4656.   Tardivo, André E., & Ana M. S. Zukosk: "Sauter la Clôture: Uma Leitura de Thérèse Raquin (1867), de Émile Zola." *Interfaces*, *10*, 2. [WC]

RR4657.   Valentova, K.: "Les Échos de l'Ivresse: Le Paralangage dans L'Assommoir d'Émile Zola." *Cedille*, 15, 575-606. [Syr]

RR4658.   Zhang, Chaofeng: "Comparison of Works on Dong-in Kim and Zola's Naturalism: Text Comparison Study on *The Human Beast*." *Sookmyung Research Institute of Humanities*, 3, 79-116. [WC]

ZUMTHOR, Paul.
See also 588.

RR4659.   ● Dos Santos Idelette, & Jean-René Valette: *Poétiques de Paul Zumthor (1915-2015)*. *Ed. Reliée*. Paris: Classiques Garnier. 352p. [Cor]

PART THREE

CINEMA

SECTION I

Cinema in General

See also 154, 374, 443, 654, 748, 750, 991, 1185, 1348, 1368, 1740, 2016, 2027, 2050, 2483, 2632, 2671, 3276, 3922, 4224.

RR4660. ● Abecassis, Michaël, et al.: *Le Grain de la Voix dans le Monde Anglophone et Francophone*. New York: Peter Lang. 320p. [LoC]

RR4661. ● Aillagon, Jean-Jacques: *Nice Cinémapolis: [Exposition, Nice, Musée Masséna, 17 Mai-30 Septembre 2019]*. [Paris]: In Fine Éditions d'Art. 192p. [BnF] (Cocteau, Demy, Lumière)

RR4662. ● Albera, François: *Le Cinéma au Défi des Arts*. Crisnée: Yellow Now. 224p. [LoC] (Chabrol)

RR4663. ● Altamayer, Eric, Samuel Zarka, Jean-Louis Comolli, Dominique Chateau, Emmanuel Finkiel, Clélia Zernik, Raoul Peck, Mathieu Rasoli, & Avishag Zafrani: *Penser le Cinéma, Faire le Cinéma*. Paris: PUF. 199p. [WC]

RR4664. ● Amic, Sylvain, Dominique Païni, Joanne Snrech, François Albera, Olivier Assayas, Jacques Aumont, Philippe Dagen, Chloé Ledoux, Andrej B. Nakov, Vincent Pomarède, & Véronique Souben: *Arts et Cinéma: Les Liaisons Heureuses*. Gand: Snoeck. 263p. [WC] (Assayas)

RR4665. ● Andersen, Nathan: *Film, Philosophy, and Reality: Ancient Greece to Godard*. New York: Routledge. 203p. [Syr]

RR4666. ● André, Lucie: *Être Actrice Noire en France. (Dé)jouer les Imaginaires*. Paris: L'Harmattan. 168p. [LoC]

RR4667. ● Bacqué, Bertrand, Lucrezia Lippi, Serge Margel, & Olivier Zuchuat: *Montage: Une Anthologie (1913-2018)*. Genève: Mamco, Musée d'Art Moderne et Contemporain de Genève. 574p. [WC]

RR4668. ● Baumgartner, Michael, & Ewelina Boczkowska: *Music, Collective Memory, Trauma, and Nostalgia in European Cinema After the Second World War*. Andover: Routledge. 344p. [Cor] (Clair)

RR4669. ● Birkin, Jane: *Post-Scriptum: Journal, 1982-2013*. [Paris]: Fayard. 424p. [BnF]

RR4670. ● Bouiller, Jean-Roch, et al.: *Le Panorama, un Art Trompeur*. Villeneuve-d'Ascq: Presses Universitaires du Septentrion. 226p. [Syr] (Lumière)

RR4671. ● Bovier, François, & Serge Margel: *Cinéma Ethnographique*. Lausanne: Association Décadrages. 280p. [WC] (Marker)

RR4672. ● Bubbio, Paolo D., & Chris Fleming: *Mimetic Theory and Film*. New York: Bloomsbury. 211p. [UofR]

RR4673. ● Busetta, Laura, Marlène Monteiro, & Muriel Tinel-Temple: *From Self-Portrait to Selfie: Representing the Self in the Moving Image*. Oxford: Peter Lang. 271p. [WC] (Varda)

RR4674. ● Caracalla, Laurence: *Les 100 Répliques Cultes du Cinéma Français*. Paris: Le Figaro. 206p. [WC]

RR4675. ● Cárdenas, Federico, & Frías I. León: *El Cine de los Maestros*. Lima: Pontificia Universidad Católica del Perú, Fondo Editorial. 365p. [WC] (Chabrol)

RR4676. ● Catanese, Rossella, Lavina F. Scotto, & Valentina Valente: *From Sensation to Synaesthesia in Film and New Media*. Newcastle upon Tyne: Cambridge Scholars. 264p. [WC] (Resnais)

RR4677. ● Chareyron, Romain, & Gilles Viennot: *Screening Youth: Contemporary French and Francophone Cinema*. Edinburgh: Edinburgh UP. 253p. [Syr] (Breillat, Ozon, Téchiné)

RR4678. ● Ciment, Michel: *Une Vie de Cinéma*. Paris: Gallimard. 512p. [BAnQ] (Chéreau)

RR4679. ● Conrad, Diane, & Monica Prendergast: *Teachers and Teaching on Stage and on Screen: Dramatic Depictions*. Chicago, IL: Intellect Books. 266p. [Syr] (Haneke)

RR4680. ● Dimendberg, Edward: *The Moving Eye: Film, Television, Architecture, Visual Art, and the Modern*. New York, NY: Oxford UP. 170p. [WC] (Ophuls)

RR4681. ● Dottelonde, Pierre, & Charles Masters: *Le Cinéma Francais Voyage =: French Cinema Worldwide*. Paris: Le Cherche Midi. 254p. [WC]

RR4682. ● Elarbi, Kevin: *Ma Folle Histoire du Cinéma*. Roquebrune-Cap-Martin: Éditions Ocrée. 361p. [BnF]

RR4683. ● Elsässer, Thomas: *European Cinema and Continental Philosophy: Film as Thought Experiment*. New York: Bloomsbury Academic. 341p. [UofR] (Denis)

RR4684. ● Epinoux, Estelle, Vincent Lefebvre, & Magalie Flores-Lonjou: *Fontière(s) au Cinéma*. Paris: Mare & Martin Arts. 552p. [WC] (Varda)

RR4685. ● Epstein, Jean, et al.: *Bonjour Cinéma: Le Cinématographe Vu de l'Etna et Autres Écrits*. Montreuil: Les Éditions de l'Œil. 319p. [BnF]

RR4686. ● Fallois, Bernard, & Philippe Hugues: *Chroniques Cinématographiques*. Paris: Fallois. 458p. [BnF] (Clair)

RR4687. ● Freeman, Thomas S., & David L. Smith: *Biography and History in Film*. Cham: Palgrave Macmillan. 336p. [WC] (Bresson)

RR4688. ● Gass, Lars H.: *Filmgeschichte als Kinogeschichte. Eine Kleine Theorie des Kinos*. Leipzig: Spectormag GbR. 80p. [BnF] (Ophuls)

RR4689. ● Gauville, Hervé: *Le Cinéma par la Danse*. Nantes: Capricci. 170p. [BnF] (Demy, Ophuls)

RR4690. ● Grabher, Peter: *Hier und Anderswo: Palästina-Israel im Essayistischen Film (1960-2010)*. Marburg: Schüren. 336p. [WC] (Godard, Marker)

RR4691. ● Grammont, Claudine, & Dominique Païni: *Cinématisse*. [Paris]: In Fine Éditions d'Art. 128p. [BnF] (Clair)

RR4692. ● Heuckelom, Kris: *Polish Migrants in European Film: 1918-2017*. Cham (Switzerland): Palgrave Macmillan. 283p. [Syr] (Guitry, Kieslowski)

RR4693. ● Hjort, Mette, & Eva Jørholt: *African Cinema and Human Rights*. Bloomington, IN: Indiana UP. 314p. [Naz] (Sembène)

RR4694. ● Holanda, Karla: *Mulheres de Cinema*. Rio de Janeiro: Numa. 410p. [WC] (Akerman, Varda)

RR4695. • Holland, Samantha, Steven Gerrard, & Robert Shail: *Gender and Contemporary Horror in Film*. Bingley, UK: Emerald Publishing. 261p. [Syr] (Denis)

RR4696. • Hutchinson, Pamela: *Cinéma en 30 Secondes: Les Idées, Genres, Réalisateurs et Acteurs les Plus Importants de l'Histoire du 7e Art, Expliqués en Moins d'une Minute*. Montréal: Hurtubise. 160p. [WC]

RR4697. • Jeannelle, Jean-Louis, & Mireille Brangé: *Films à Lire. Des Scénarios et des Livres*. Bruxelles: Les Impressions Nouvelles. 368p. [WC] (Renoir, Rivette)

RR4698. • Jibokji, Joséphine: *Objets de Cinéma: De Marienbad à Fantômas*. Paris: Institut National d'Histoire de l'Art. 343p. [WC] (Allain)

RR4699. • Judor, Éric: *Comédie à la Française*. Vanves: Marabout. 192p. [BnF] (Haneke)

RR4700. • King, Geoff: *Positioning Art Cinema: Film and Cultural Value*. London: I.B. Tauris. 330p. [Syr] (Dardenne, Haneke)

RR4701. • Layrac, Alain: *Une Vie de Scénariste*. [Paris]: Hémisphères. 253p. [WC] (Moreau)

RR4702. • Lemonier, Marc: *Dictionnaire Désolant du Cinéma Français*. Waterloo: Jourdan. 184p. [WC]

RR4703. • Leperchey, Sarah, & José Moure: *Filmer le Quotidien*. Bruxelles: Les Impressions Nouvelles. 253p. [BnF] (Akerman, Pialat)

RR4704. • Littschwager, Simin N.: *Making Sense of Mind-Game Films: Narrative Complexity, Embodiment, and the Senses*. New York: Bloomsbury Academic. 241p. [Syr] (Lepage)

RR4705. • Margulies, Ivone: *In Person: Reenactment in Postwar and Contemporary Cinema*. New York: Oxford UP. 336p. [UofR] (Lanzmann, Morin)

RR4706. • Margulies, Ivone, & Jeremi Szaniawski: *On Women's Films: Across Worlds and Generations*. London: Bloomsbury Academic. 397p. [UofR] (Akerman, Denis, Varda)

RR4707. • Mari, Pauline: *Hartung Nouvelle Vague: De Resnais Vers Rohmer*. [Dijon]: Les Presses du Réel. 239p. [WC] (Clouzot, Rohmer)

RR4708. • Martin-Jones, David: *Cinema against Doublethink: Ethical Encounters with the Lost Pasts of World History*. London: Routledge. 242p. [Syr]

RR4709. • Michael, Charlie: *French Blockbusters: Cultural Politics of a Transnational Cinema*. Edinburgh: Edinburgh UP. 236p. [Syr] (Besson, Jeunet)

RR4710. • Moraly, Jean-Bernard: *Revolution in Paradise: Veiled Representations of Jewish Characters in the Cinema of Occupied France*. Brighton: Sussex Academic Press. 292p. [Cor] (Carné)

RR4711. • Morrey, Douglas: *The Legacy of the New Wave in French Cinema*. New York: Bloomsbury Academic. 263p. [Syr] (Audiard, Ozon)

RR4712. • Müller, Jürgen: *Films des Années 60*. Paris: Taschen. 741p. [BnF] (Godard)

RR4713. • Mulvey, Lauren: *Afterimages: On Cinema, Women and Changing Times*. London: Reaktion Books. 286p. [Syr] (Akerman)

RR4714. • Mulvey, Laura, & Guillaume Mélère: *Fétichisme et Curiosité*. Paris: Brook. 364p. [BnF] (Sembène)

RR4715. • Nichols, David P.: *Transcendence and Film: Cinematic Encounters with the Real*. Lanham: Lexington Books. 169p. [Cor] (Henry)

RR4716. • Pettey, Homer B., & R. B. Palmer: *French Literature on Screen*. Manchester: Manchester UP. 250p. [Syr] (Djian, Pagnol)

RR4717. • Peucker, Brigitte: *Aesthetic Spaces: The Place of Art in Film*. Evanston, IL: Northwestern UP. 210p. [Syr] (Varda)

RR4718. • Rosenbaum, Jonathan: *Cinematic Encounters: 2*. Chicago: University of Illinois Press. 310p. [Cor]

RR4719. • Rothman, William: *Tuitions and Intuitions: Essays at the Intersection of Film Criticism and Philosophy*. Albany: SUNY Press. 391p. [Cor] (Genet, Rouch)

RR4720. • Sava, Laura: *Theatre Through the Camera Eye: The Poetics of an Intermedial Encounter*. Edinburgh: Edinburgh UP. 238p. [Syr] (Malle)

RR4721. • Sawadogo, Boukary: *African Film Studies: An Introduction*. New York: Routledge. 142p. [Cor] (Sembène)

RR4722. • Schmid, Marion: *Intermedial Dialogues: The French New Wave and the Other Arts*. Edinburgh: Edinburgh UP. 228p. [Syr] (Chabrol, Rivette)

RR4723. • Serceau, Michel: *Le Cinéma Fait Sa Littérature: Étude de la Réception de la Littérature par le Cinéma*. Paris: Classiques Garnier. 530p. [LoC]

RR4724. • Sircar, Ronojoy: *Remember, Repeat, Inhabit. A Study of Antonin Artaud, Krzysztof Kieslowski and Nikhil Chopra*. London: Bloomsbury Academic. 200p. [WC]

RR4725. • Smith, Ian Haydn: *Cult Filmmakers*. London: White Lion. 143p. [WC] (Denis, Jeunet)

RR4726. • Steele, Jamie: *Francophone Belgian Cinema*. Edinburgh: Edinburgh UP. 228p. [Syr] (Dardenne)

RR4727. • Steinbock, Eliza: *Shimmering Images: Trans Cinema, Embodiment, and the Aesthetics of Change*. Durham, NC: Duke UP. 231p. [Syr] (Méliès)

RR4728. • Thornham, Sue: *Spaces of Women's Cinema: Space, Place and Genre in Contemporary Women's Filmmaking*. New York: Bloomsbury. 226p. [Syr] (Denis, Serreau)

RR4729. • Want, Christopher: *Philosophers on Film from Bergson to Badiou: A Critical Reader*. New York: Columbia UP. 355p. [Cor] (Irigaray, Lyotard)

RR4730. Anderton, Abby: "The Sound of Atrocity Propaganda: Listening to the Concentration Camp in Allied Cultural Memory." *German Studies Review*, *42*, 3, 499-518. [PrQ] (Resnais)

RR4731. Barlet, Olivier: "Africultures Dossier: African Cinema of the 2010s." *Black Camera*, *10*, 2, 226-49. [PrQ] (Charef)

RR4732. Bercuci, Loredana: "Now You Hear It, Now You See It. Silence and Trauma in Autodocumentary Film." *Metacritic Journal for Comparative Studies and Theory*, *5*, 2, 91-109. [PrQ]

RR4733. Brook, Vincent: "A Wave of their Own: How Jewish Filmmakers Invented the New Hollywood." *Jewish Film & New Media*, *7*, 1, 48-80. [RIT] (Moreau)

RR4734. Brozgal, Lia: "Seeing through Race in Contemporary French Cinema." *Esprit Créateur*, *59*, 2, 12-24. [RIT] (Charef)

RR4735. Bueno, Claudio C.: "From Spectacle to Deterritorialisation: Deleuze, Debord and the Politics of Found Footage Cinema." *Deleuze and Guattari Studies*, *13*, 1, 54-78. [Naz]

RR4736. Chevalier, Léa: "Michel Marie, la Belle Histoire du Cinéma Français en 101 Films." *1895*, *88*, 2, 184. [Cor]

RR4737.   Chikafa-Chipiro, Rosemary: "The Future of the Past: Imagi(ni)ng Black Womanhood, Africana Womanism and Afrofuturism in Black Panther." *Image & Text*, *33*, 1, 1-20. [WC] (Sembène)

RR4738.   Ciment, M.: "Éditorial Cinéma Francais, Anneé Zéro?" *Positif*, 704. [Syr]

RR4739.   Cardone, Daniela: "*Urbs* and *Civitas*: Stone Order and Civil Order Collapsing in Some Cinematographic Examples." *International Journal for the Semiotics of Law*, *32*, 3, 683-697. [Naz]

RR4740.   Cohen, Margaret: "The Underwater Imagination: From Environment to Film Set, 1954–1956." *English Language Notes*, *57*, 1, 51. [PrQ] (Malle)

RR4741.   Croombs, Matthew: "In the Wake of Militant Cinema: Challenges for Film Studies." *Discourse*, *41*, 1, 68-89. [RIT] (Assayas)

RR4742.   Flood, Maria, & Florence Martin: "The Terrorist as Ennemi Intime in French and Francophone Cinema." *Studies in French Cinema*, *XIX*, 3, 171-277. [PrQ]

RR4743.   Gélinas, Melissa: "'First Comes the Ear': Paulin Soumanou Vieyra and the Politics of African Languages." *JCMS: Journal of Cinema and Media Studies*, *LVIII*, 3, 118-21. [PrQ]

RR4744.   Génin, Bernard: "Voyages à Travers le Cinéma Français de Bertrand Tavernier, un Cinéphile Épatant'." *Positif*, 700, 110-111. [Syr]

RR4745.   Gueden, Marie: "Serpentin-Lévesque Entre 1918 et 1922, un 'Comique Français' Entre Vis et Visse Comica." *1895*, *89*, 3, 42. [Cor]

RR4746.   Haacke, Paul: "The Melancholic Voice-Over in Film Noir." *Journal of Cinema and Media Studies*, *58*, 2, 46-70. [RIT]

RR4747.   Hovanec, Caroline: "Another Nature Speaks to the Camera: Natural History and Film Theory." *Modernism/ Modernity*, *26*, 2, 243-65. [PrQ]

RR4748.   Hoyler, Michael, & Allan Watson: "Framing City Networks Through Temporary Projects: (Trans)national Film Production Beyond 'Global Hollywood'." *Urban Studies*, *56*, 5, 943-959. [Naz]

RR4749.   Keefe, Anna V.: "Sarah Walkley. Cultural Diversity in the French Film Industry: Defending the Cultural Exception in a Digital Age. Palgrave Macmillan." *Studies in 20th & 21st Century Literature*, *43*, 2. [Naz]

RR4750.   Leadston, Mackenzie: "Happily Never After: The Visual Politics of Contemporary French Interracial Romantic Comedy." *Studies in French Cinema*, 19, 4, 335-352. [Naz] (Memmi, Serreau)

RR4751.   Llanos, Melussa E.: "Los Coristas. Análisis Psicoestético y Socioeducativo de Un Filme Francés." *Revista Latinoamericana de Educación Inclusiva*, *13*, 2, 227-242. [WC]

RR4752.   Marso, Lori: "Feminist Cringe Comedy: Dear Dick, The Joke Is on You." *Politics & Gender*, *15*, 1, 107-129. [Naz] (Breillat, Irigaray)

RR4753.   Martinelli, Dario: "Audiovisuality and the City of Marseille, France: Creativity, Communication, Representation." *Creativity Studies*, *12*, 1, 166-82. [RIT] (Pagnol)

RR4754.   McCallum, E. L.: "Not Your Mother's Melodrama: Three Twenty-First-Century Women's Films." *Camera Obscura*, *34*, 2, 133-61. [PrQ] (Akerman, Denis)

RR4755.   McCann, Ben: "History, Truth and (Mis)Representation in Versailles (2015-2018)." 141-55. In 253.

RR4756.　Palma, Paola: "Faux Amis? Les Travers de la Coproduction Cinématographique Franco-Italienne dans les Années 1950-1960." *Synergies Italie*, *15*, 55, 66, 114. [PrQ]

RR4757.　Powrie, Phil: "Books Published on French and Francophone Cinema in 2018." *Studies in French Cinema*, *XIX*, 4, 353-5. [PrQ]

RR4758.　Powrie, Phil: "Theses Published on French and Francophone Cinema 2016-2018." *Studies in French Cinema*, *XIX*, 4, 356-8. [PrQ]

RR4759.　Reader, Keith: "Le Cinéma Français de 1958 à 1967: De la Nouvelle Vague Aux Prémices de Mai 68, par Francis Goubel." *French Studies*, *73*, 4, 664-665. [UaB]

RR4760.　Robillard, Guillaume: "Strategies of Resistance in 'French Caribbean Cinema'." *Contemporary French and Francophone Studies*, *23*, 5, 636-643. [RIT] (Chamoiseau)

RR4761.　Rondeau, Corinne: "On Marginality as Resistance." *Moving Image Review & Art Journal*, *III*, 1-2, 132-7. [PrQ]

RR4762.　Rossi, Jerome: "Composers and 'Microgénie': A Study of the Symphonic Sound of French Cinema in the Thirties." *Music and the Moving Image*, *12*, 2, 15-39. [UaB]

RR4763.　Sharpe, Mani: "Gender and the Politics of Decolonization in Early 1960s French Cinema." *Journal of European Studies*, *49*, 2, 163-83. [PrQ] (Malle)

RR4764.　Tarjanyi, Peter: "Sexagon: Muslims, France, and the Sexualization of National Culture by Mehammed Amadeus Mack (Review)." *College Literature*, *46*, 2, 510-2. [PrQ]

RR4765.　Tkacheva, Anna N.: "Features of the Russian Localization of the French Film Titles." *Philological Sciences. Issues of Theory and Practice*, 2, 144-148. [LoC]

RR4766.　Trotignon, Yves: "L'Art Français de (Filmer) la Guerre." *Inflexions*, *42*, 3, 25. [BnF]

RR4767.　Wieviorka, Olivier: "La Résistance: Une Représentation Impossible?" *Inflexions*, *42*, 3, 133. [WC]

RR4768.　Williams, James S.: "Neoliberal Violence and Aesthetic Resistance in Abderrahmane Sissako's Bamako (2006)." *Studies in French Cinema*, *19*, 4, 294-313. [Naz]

RR4769.　Zafrani, Avishag: "Dossier: Penser le Cinéma, Faire le Cinéma: Mouvement/ Arrêt: Cinéma et Pensée." *Cites*, 77, 33-42. [PrQ]

SECTION II

Individual Directors, Cinema Authors, Cinema Theorists, and Actors

AKERMAN, Chantal.

RR4770.　● Ackerman, Chantal: *Chantal Ackerman: Tempo Expandido = Expanded Time*. [São Paulo]: Oi Futuro. 120p. [WC]

RR4771.　● Gatti, Ilaria, & Alessandro Cappabianca: *Chantal Akerman: Uno Schermo nel Deserto*. Roma: Fefè. 281p. [LoC]

RR4772.　● Hogg, Joanna, & Adam Roberts: *Chantal Akerman Retrospective Handbook*. London: A Nos Amours. 241p. [WC]

RR4773. ● Madeira, Maria J.: *Chantal Akerman*. Lisboa: Cinemateca Portuguesa-Museu do Cinema. 133p. [WC]

RR4774. ● Schmid, Marion, & Emma Wilson: *Chantal Akerman: Afterlives*. Cambridge: Legenda/ Modern Humanities Research Association. 169p. [WC]

RR4775. ● Völcker, Tine R.: *Les Rendez-Vous de Tarnów. Über Chantal Akerman und Polen*. Leipzig: Spectormag. 60p. [WC]

RR4776. ● White, Patricia: *Camera Obscura: Feminism, Culture, and Media Studies: On Chantal Akerman*. Durham, NC: Duke UP. 237p. [WC]

RR4777. Allen, Nicholas P. L., & Louise Marié Combrink: "Character (and Absence) as a Narrative Key in Installation Art." *Literator*, *40*, 1, 1-10. [UaB]

RR4778. Atherton, Claire: "Tribute to Chantal Akerman." *Camera Obscura*, 100, 91-98. [Naz]

RR4779. Bergstrom, Janet: "Disappearance in the Films of Chantal Akerman." *The Moving Image Review & Art Journal (Miraj)*, *8*, 1, 96-103. [Cor]

RR4780. Bergstrom, Janet: "With Chantal in New York in the 1970s: An Interview with Babette Mangolte." *Camera Obscura*, *34*, 1, 31-57. [PrQ]

RR4781. "Beside Chantal Akerman's NOW." *Moving Image Review & Art Journal*, *III*, 1-2, 1-192. [PrQ]

RR4782. "Chantal Akerman Filmography." *Camera Obscura*, *34*, 1, 219-231. [UofR]

RR4783. Conway, Kelley: "Lyrical Akerman." *Camera Obscura*, *34*, 1, 139-61. [PrQ]

RR4784. Fajgenbaum, Emma: "Memoirs of an Undutiful Daughter." *New Left Review*, 120. [PrQ]

RR4785. Flitterman-Lewis, Sandy: "Ephemeral, Elusive, Impossible: Chantal Akerman and the Concept of 'Home'." *The Moving Image Review & Art Journal (Miraj)*, *8*, 1-2, 106-116. [Cor]

RR4786. Fox, Albertine: "Sensory Experience, Sound and Queerness in Chantal Akerman's Maniac Shadows (2013)." *The Moving Image Review & Art Journal (Miraj)*, *8*, 1-2, 68-81. [Cor]

RR4787. Holl, U., & E. Kuhn: "On the Difficulty of Forgetting: Recollections of the Basel Symposium on Chantal Akerman." *Camera Obscura*, *34*, 1, 163-183. [UofR]

RR4788. Jacquin, Maud: "'A Matter of Skin': Chantal Akerman's 'Porous Narratives'." *The Moving Image Review & Art Journal (Miraj)*, *8*, 1, 82-95. [Cor]

RR4789. King, Gemma: "Translingualism and Race Passing in *Samba*: On Fantasies of Migrant Identity in Contemporary France." *Esprit Créateur*, *59*, 4, 84-108. [RIT]

RR4790. Le Bihan, Marion Cruza: "Papael Crítico 62." *Papeles del CEIC*, 2, 1-5. [RIT]

RR4791. Longfellow, B.: "The Matrixial Borderspace: The Complex Inscription of Trauma in Chantal Akerman's No Home Movie." *Camera Obscura*, *34*, 1, 113-137. [Naz]

RR4792. Lübecker, Nikolaj: "Landscape Memories: Akerman's Sud and the 'Spectator-Environment'." *Angelaki*, *24*, 6, 41-56. [UaB]

RR4793. Mangolte, B.: "Now, Chantal Akerman's Last Work." *Camera Obscura*, *34*, 1, 67-73. [UofR]

RR4794. Marcos, Molano M., & Ruíz P. Moreno: "'News from Home' de

Chantal Akerman: El Documental Autobiográfico en el Contexto del Documental Contemporáneo." *Fonseca, Journal of Communication*, 18, 103. [Syr]

RR4795.   Margulies, Ivone: "Our Way of Working: A Conversation with Claire Atherton About Chantal Akerman." *Camera Obscura*, 100, 13-30. [Naz]

RR4796.   Mazière, Michael: "Chantal Akerman in London." *Camera Obscura*, *34*, 1, 185-195. [Naz]

RR4797.   Min, Jinyoung: "Belgitude in Chantal Akerman's Early Films." *Yongbong Journal of Humanities*, 55, 115-151. [LoC]

RR4798.   Murari, Lucas: "Chantal Akerman: Tempo Expandido." *Aniki*, 6, 2, 223-227. [WC]

RR4799.   Païni, Dominique: "On les Rendez-Vous d'Anna and Jeanne Dielmann [Sic]." *Moving Image Review & Art Journal*, *III*, 1-2, 118-22. [PrQ]

RR4800.   Percival, Sandra: "Chantal? A Dialogue with Sonia Wieder-Atherton." *Camera Obscura*, *34*, 1, 197-217. [PrQ]

RR4801.   Pollock, Griselda: "'Akerman' On-Screen: Chantal Akerman Behind and Before the Camera, and After Cinema." *The Moving Image Review & Art Journal (Miraj)*, *8*, 1-2, 8-26. [Cor]

RR4802.   Rennebohm, Kate: "'A Pedagogy of the Image': Chantal Akerman's Ethics Across Film and Art." *The Moving Image Review & Art Journal (Miraj)*, *8*, 1, 40-53. [Cor]

RR4803.   Roberts, Adam: "Akerman the Scavenger." *Moving Image Review & Art Journal*, *III*, 1-2, 156-65. [PrQ]

RR4804.   Stein, Jane: "Hanging Out Yonkers: A Photographic Record." *Camera Obscura*, *34*, 1, 58-65. [PrQ]

RR4805.   Talu, Yonca: "Maternal Instincts." *Film Comment*, *55*, 4, 79. [RIT]

RR4806.   Turim, Maureen: "Next to Chantal Akerman: An Installation of Generations and the Shoah." *Camera Obscura*, 100, 99-112. [Naz]

RR4807.   Usiskin, J.: "Before, Between and Beyond: Chantal Akerman's Impenetrable Landscapes." *Moving Image Review and Art Journal*, *8*, 1-2, 124-131. [Cor]

RR4808.   Veiga, Roberta: "Um Gesto Político Intersticial e um Histórico Palimpséstico: A Escrita de si em d'Est e Là-Bas de Chantal Akerman." *Galáxia (São Paulo)*, 41, 75-88. [Cor]

RR4809.   White, Patricia: "Camera Obscura and Chantal Akerman." *Camera Obscura*, *34*, 1, 1-11. [UofR]

ALLOUACHE, Merzak.
See also 226.

RR4810.   Amanoua, Koffi P.: "'Brûler' Pour la Vie dans Harragas de Merzak Allouache et Sin Nombre de Cary Fukunaga." *Nouvelles Études Francophones*, *34*, 1, 198-207. [UaB]

ARCAND, Denys.
RR4811.   Vidal, Jose Antonio Cerrillo: "Nuevas Prácticas Tanatológicas y la Emergencia del Modelo Neo-Moderno de la Muerte." *Empiria*, 43, 15-37. [RIT]

ASSAYAS, Olivier.
See also 4664, 4741.

RR4812.   Bauche, Nicolas: "Doubles Vies d'Olivier Assayas." *Positif*, 695, 38-39. [Syr]

RR4813.   Flinn, Margaret C.: "Olivier Assayas' Memories of May." *Contemporary French and Francophone Studies*, *23*, 2, 216-224. [Naz]

RR4814.   "Tim Hayes on Olivier Assayas's Tech Thriller Demonlover." *Sight and Sound*, *29*, 6, 96. [UofR]

RR4815.   Uccelli, A.: "Gioco Delle Coppie di Olivier Assayas." *Cineforum*, *59*, 1, 27-29. [Cor]

AUDIARD, Jacques.
See also 4711.

RR4816.   Frasca, G.: "Jacques Audiard, Tra Volontà Surrealista e Immersion nel Genere." *Cineforum*, *59*, 5, 6-8. [UaB]

RR4817.   Jinanto, Damar: "L'Échange de Pouvoir: Un Reflet de la Vie Carcérale dans le Film Un Prophète de Jacques Audiard." *Digital Press Social Sciences and Humanities*, 3, 12. [WC]

RR4818.   Köksal, Özlem, & Rappas I. A. Çelik: "A Hand That Holds a Machete." *Third Text*, *33*, 2, 256-267. [UaB]

RR4819.   Lee, Sun: "A Study on the Relationship between Body and Power in Jacques Audiard's Rust and Bone." *Film Studies*, 82, 309-334. [WC]

BARDOT, Brigitte.

RR4820.   ● Bardot, Brigitte, & Anne-Cécile Huprelle: *Tears of Battle: An Animal Rights Memoir*. New York: Arcade. 190p. [WC]

RR4821.   ● Evin, Guillaume, François Bagnaud, & Alain Delon: *Bardot*. Malakoff: Dunod. 175p. [WC]

RR4822.   ● Goujon, Michel: *La Recluse: Le Mystère Brigitte Bardot*. Paris: Plon. 429p. [BnF]

RR4823.   ● Korterink, Hendrik J.: *De Laatste Playboy. Hein Kips, Playboy Tussen Bruinsma, Bardot en Sinatra*. Hilversum: Just Publishers. 256p. [WC]

RR4824.   ● Robinson, Jeffrey, & Jean-Paul Mourlon: *Bardot: Deux Vies*. Paris: Archipoche. 415p. [BnF]

RR4825.   ● Saura, Antonio, Jordi Mayoral, Eduard Mayoral, & Cristina Mayoral: *Brigitte Bardot et Autres Dames*. Barcelona: Mayoral. 29p. [WC]

RR4826.   ● Uribe, Matías: *Brigitte Bardot: España, Cine, Discos y Vida*. [Zaragoza]: Amazon. 264p. [WC]

RR4827.   Scheie, Timothy: "Cowboy and Alien: The Bardot Westerns." *Studies in French Cinema*, *19*, 2, 103-121. [Naz]

BAZIN, André.

RR4828.   ● Cardullo, Bert: *The Catholic Critic: André Bazin on Hollywood Movies*. Mumbai: Curato. 1 vol. [WC]

RR4829.   ● Joret, Blandine: *Studying Film with André Bazin*. Amsterdam: Amsterdam UP. 191p. [WC]

RR4830.   Albera, François: "L'Exercice Critique: André Bazin, Écrits Complets I et II." *1895*, 87, 171-176. [Cor]

RR4831.   Cine, Documental C.: "André Bazin y Farrebique." *Cuadernos de Cine Documental*, 13, 20. [LoC]

RR4832. Esqueda, Verano L.: "Cinema Beyond Signs: Revisiting Indexicality in André Bazin's Film Theory." *Signa*, 28, 599-630. [UaB]

RR4833. Esqueda, Verano L.: "El Cine Como Espejo Diferido: El Concepto de Transferencia en André Bazin y Stanley Cavell." *Palabra Clave*, 22, 3. [Naz]

RR4834. Garson, Charlotte: "Bazin Vivant!" *Études*, Juin, 6, 89. [UofR]

RR4835. Sang, Hee H.: "The Boundary of Cinema and Descriptive Methods of Cinema History: In Reference to Andre Bazin's 'The Myth of Total Cinema' and Foucault's Works of History." *Film Studies*, 81, 69-87. [WC]

RR4836. Wittusen, Cato: "Bazin, An Early Late Modernist." *The Journal of Aesthetics and Art Criticism*, 77, 3, 295-306. [Naz]

BECKER, Jacques.

RR4837. Procházka, David: "In Seach of Jean Wiéner: A Bibliographic Exploration of His Published Music." *Music Library Association Notes*, 75, 3, 409-78. [RIT]

BESSON, Luc.
See also 4709.

RR4838. ● Besson, Luc: *Enfant Terrible: Autobiographie*. S.l.: XO Éditions. 452p. [BAnQ]

RR4839. ● *Valerian und Veronique Hommage 1*. Hamburg: Carlsen. 96p. [WC]

BLIER, Bertrand.

RR4840. Krief, S.: "Starsky & Homosexuality, The Story of Puritan France." *Society*, 56, 5, 489-493. [UofR]

RR4841. Rapold, Nicolas: "Buffet Froid." *Film Comment*, 55, 6, 76. [RIT]

BREILLAT, Catherine.
See also 4677, 4752.

RR4842. ● McLennan, Matthew R.: *Philosophy and Vulnerability: Catherine Breillat, Joan Didion, and Audre Lorde*. London: Bloomsbury Academic. 183p. [WC]

RR4843. ● Wilson, Emma: *The Reclining Nude: Agnès Varda, Catherine Breillat, and Nan Goldin*. Liverpool: Liverpool UP. 235p. [RIT]

RR4844. Belot, Sophie: "Authenticity in a Real Young Girl (Catherine Breillat, 1976)." *Film Studies*, 20, 1, 21-35. [Cor]

RR4845. Doherty, Annabelle: "A Cinematic Cultural Memory of Courtship, Weddings, Marriage, and Adultery in July Monarchy France Through Heritage Films Claude Chabrol's Madame Bovary, Jean-Paul Rappeneau's The Horseman on the Roof, and Catherine Breillat's The Last Mistress." *Adaptation*, 12, 2, 118-148. [Syr]

RR4846. Dooley, Kath: "'C'Était Moi Mais Ce N'Était Pas Moi': Portrayal of the Disabled Body in Catherine Breillat's Abus de Faiblesse (2013)." *Studies in French Cinema*, 19, 2, 150-164. [Naz]

RR4847. Wilson, Emma: "The Cinema of Catherine Breillat, by Sophie Bélot." *French Studies*, 73, 1, 162-163. [UaB]

BRESSON, Robert.
See also 4687.

RR4848.   Andrew, Dudley: "This is Not Another Reading of a Master: The Invention of Robert Bresson: The Auteur and His Market, by Colin Burnett." *Senses of Cinema*, 92. [PrQ]

RR4849.   Alvim, Luíza: "Rhythms of Images and Sounds in Two Films by Robert Bresson." *Acta Universitatis Sapientiae, Film and Media Studies*, *16*, 1, 173-187. [Cor]

BUÑUEL, Luis.

RR4850.   ● Álvarez, Bravo M., Luis Buñuel, Héctor Orozco, & Javier Espada: *Nazarín: Manuel Álvarez Bravo y Luis Buñuel*. [Madrid]: Casa de México en España. 80p. [WC]

RR4851.   ● Buñuel, Luis, & Jo Evans: *Luis Buñuel: A Life in Letters*. New York: Bloomsbury Academic. 594p. [LoC]

RR4852.   ● Cristóbal, Manuel, de V. J. M. Fernandez, & José L. Agreda: *The Art of Buñuel in the Labyrinth of the Turtles*. [Extremadura, Spain]: Glow. 135p. [WC]

RR4853.   ● Galera, Albert: *La Mirada Surrealista de los Directores Luis Buñuel, David Lynch, Alejandro Jodorowsky, Guy Maddin, Peter Strickland*. Barcelona: Hermenaute. 294p. [WC]

RR4854.   ● Hadda, Sarah: *Der Schnitt als Denkfigur Im Surrealismus: Max Ernst, Man Ray, Luis Buñuel und Salvador Dalí*. Bielefeld: Transcript. 305p. [WC]

RR4855.   ● Miranda, López R., & Torres D. Mondragón: *Luis Buñuel en México*. Ciudad de México: Cineteca Nacional: Secretaría de Cultura. 71p. [WC]

RR4856.   Gijón, Pablo R.: "Julie Jones. Más Allá de la Pantalla con Luis Buñuel. Zaragoza: Prensas de la Universidad de Zaragoza, 2018. 174 pp." *Revista Canadiense de Estudios Hispánicos*, *43*, 2, 494-495. [UaB]

RR4857.   Gutiérrez, Albilla J. D.: "Los Olvidados de Luis Buñuel." *Cuadernos del Centro de Estudios de Diseño y Comunicación*, 18, 19-25. [WC]

RR4858.   Hong, Myung-Hee: "Depaysement and Its Dreams for a Hallucinative Allegory in Luis Bunuel's Films: 'The Discreet Charm of the Bourgeoisie' and 'The Phantom of Liberty'." *Journal of the Korea Entertainment Industry Association*, *13*, 6, 135-142. [WC]

RR4859.   Lincoln, Strange R. I.: "Susana (1950) y Viridiana (1961) de Luis Buñuel: Personajes y Relatos Bíblicos. El Intercambio Dialógico y la Carnavalización." *El Ojo Que Piensa. Revista de Cine Iberoamericano*, 18. [WC]

RR4860.   Moreno-Caballud, Luis: "Del Surrealismo al Subdesarrollo: Modernidad, Transgresión y Convención en el Primer Cine de Luis Buñuel." *Archivos de la Filmoteca*, 77, 159-76. [PrQ]

RR4861.   Sánchez-Navarro, Jordi: "Luis Buñuel, Animado." *Comein*, 89. [WC]

CARAX, Léos.
See also 540.

RR4862.   Martin, Adrian, Cristina Álvarez López, & Ivan Pintor Iranzo: "The Idea of a Series: Energy Vectors in Montage." *In Transition*, *1*, 4. [PrQ]

CARNÉ, Marcel.
See also 4710.

RR4863.   ● Pillard, Thomas, & Esther Pot: *Le "Quai des Brumes" de Marcel Carné*. Paris: Vendémiaire. 135p. [LoC]

RR4864.   Dima, Vlad: *"Port of Shadows*: Absence and Love." *Canadian Journal of Film Studies / Revue Canadienne d'Études Cinématographiques*, 28, 1, 44-65. [UofR]

CHABROL, Claude.
See also 4662, 4675, 4722, 4845.

RR4865.   Foster, Gwendolyn Audrey: "Women as Prey: Les Bonnes Femmes (Claude Chabrol, 1960)." *Senses of Cinema*, 90. [PrQ]

RR4866.   Frajman, Anthony: "Les Cousins (Claude Chabrol, 1959)." *Senses of Cinema*, 90. [PrQ]

RR4867.   Lapointe, Julien: "La Cérémonie (Claude Chabrol, 1995)." *Senses of Cinema*, 90. [PrQ]

CHÉREAU, Patrice.
See also 4678.

RR4868.   ● Chéreau, Patrice, & Julien Centrès: *Journal de Travail: Tome 3*. Arles: Actes Sud. 237p. [BnF]

RR4869.   ● McIntyre, Donald, & David Rees: *The Only Way Is Up: Reflections on a Life in Opera*. Christchurch (New Zealand): Quentin Wilson. 240p. [LoC]

RR4870.   ● Nattiez, Jean-Jacques: *Fidélité et Infidélité dans les Mises en Scène d'Opéra*. [Paris]: J. Vrin. 311p. [WC]

CLAIR, René.
See also 4668, 4686, 4691.

RR4871.   ● D'Amicone, Giulio: *Il Silenzio è d'Oro: (Le Silence Est d'Or, 1947): Di René Clair*. Roma: Gremese. 126p. [WC]

RR4872.   Kessler, J.: "René Clair en Amérique." *Positif*, April, 698, 74-77. [Syr]

CLOUZOT, Henri-Georges.
See 4707.

RR4873.   Andrieu, Louis: "Cultures: Portrait de la Jeune Fille En Feu." *Esprit*, 457. [PrQ]

RR4874.   Sragow, Michael: "Waiting in the Wings." *Film Comment*, 55, 1, 74. [RIT]

DARDENNE, Luc et Jean-Pierre.
See also 4700, 4726.

RR4875.   ● Dardenne, Luc, & Jean-Pierre Dardenne: *Le Jeune Ahmed: Scénario Original et Dialogues: Dossier*. [Bruxelles]: Alice. 145p. [WC]

RR4876.   ● Dardenne, Luc, Jean-Pierre Dardenne, Jeffrey Zuckerman, Jason Sommer, & Sammi Skolmoski: *On the Back of Our Images (1991-2005)*. Chicago: Featherproof Books. 369p. [WC]

RR4877.   Astrianingsih, Ari P.: "Directive Speech Acts in the L'Enfant Film by Jean Pierre and Luc Dardenne." *International Journal of Language Education and Culture Review*, 5, 2, 166-172. [WC]

RR4878.   Dardenne, Luc, & Jean-Pierre Dardenne: "Le Jeune Ahmed." *L'Avant-Scène. Cinéma*, 666, 145p. [WC]

RR4879.　Dardenne, Jean-Pierre, Luc Dardenne, Philippe Rouyer, & N. T. Binh: "Arriver à Filmer la Vie Qui Revient." *Positif*, 700, 39-43. [WC]

RR4880.　Rouyer, Philippe, & Yann Tobin: "Entretien Avec Jean-Pierre et Luc Dardenne." *Positif*, 700, 39-43. [Syr]

RR4881.　Wheatley, Catherine: "The Third City: The Post Secular Space of the Dardenne Brothers' Seraing." *Film-Philosophy, XXIII*, 3, 264-81. [PrQ]

DEMY, Jacques.

RR4882.　● Köhler, Kristina, Fabienne Liptay, & Jörg Schweinitz: *Jacques Demy*. München: Text + Kritik. 100p. [WC]

RR4883.　Ganim, Russell: "*Fleur Rebelle, Fleur Royale*: The Friendship of Lady Oscar and Marie Antoinette in *The Rose of Versailles*." *Neohelicon, 46*, 2, 767-782. [Naz]

RR4884.　Razafimbelo, Ondine: "Le Rôle de la Musique dans Peau d'Âne de Jacques Demy: L'Apport de l'Analyse Paradigmatique du Thème de la 'Recherche de l'Amour' à la Compréhension de la Relecture Filmée du Conte." *Musurgia, 26*, 3, 89. [UaB]

RR4885.　Varda, Agnès, & Jacques Demy: "Jacquot de Nantes." *L'Avant-Scène. Cinéma*, 664, 213. [WC]

DENIS, Claire.

See also 4675, 4683, 4695, 4706, 4725, 4728, 4754.

RR4886.　Hutchinson, Pamela: "Heavenly Bodies. A Crew of Death-Row Prisoners on a One-Way Mission to a Distant Galaxy Are Forced to Contemplate the Meaning of Life, Death and the Universe, in Claire Denis's First English-Language Film, High Life." *Sight and Sound, 29*, 6, 20-25. [UofR]

RR4887.　Quandt, James: "Claire Denis's High Life." *Artforum International, 57*, 8, 59-64. [Naz]

RR4888.　Wilson, Emma: "Love Me Tender: New Films from Claire Denis." *Film Quarterly, 72*, 4, 18-28. [UofR]

DESPLECHIN, Arnaud.

RR4889.　Bauche, Nicolas: "L'Illusion Amoureuse la Sentinelle d'Arnaud Desplechin." *Positif*, 700, 22-22. [UaB]

RR4890.　Cerisuelo, Marc: "Roubaix, Une Lumière d'Arnaud Desplechin." *Positif*, 703, 40-41. [Syr]

RR4891.　De Cazanove, A., & Kalyane Fejtö: "Entretien Avec Arnaud Desplechin." *Revue Française de Psychanalyse, 83*, 4, 1189. [UaB]

DIOP MAMBÉTY, Djibril.

See also 2946.

RR4892.　● Cella, Simona, & Cinzia Quadrati: *Djibril Diop Mambéty, o, il Viaggio Della Iena: La Rivoluzione Cinematografica di un Visionario Regista Senegalese*. Torino: L'Harmattan Italia. 147p. [LoC]

RR4893.　Fisher, Alexander: "Reclaiming Josephine Baker in the Filmic Ethnomusicology of Djibril Diop Mambéty." *Music and the Moving Image, 12*, 2, 3-14. [Naz]

RR4894.　Moji, P. B.: "Hyenas/ Hustlers: An Afrosur/ Realist Reading of Touki Bouki (1973)." *Journal of African Cinemas, 11*, 3, 193-205. [WC]

RR4895.   Nelson, Max: "On Film: 'I've Cooked the Pudding': On Djibril Diop Mambety." *Salmagundi*, 200-201, 51-57. [UofR]

DUVIVIER, Julien.
RR4896.   Auphan, Éric: "Analysis of a Film Scene. Julien Duvivier (1896-1967)." *Historiens et Géographes*, 445, 152-152. [UaB]
RR4897.   "Revival: David Thompson on the Range and Depth of Julien Duvivier's Films." *Sight and Sound*, 29, 3, 84-85. [WC]

GANCE, Abel.
See also 361.
RR4898.   Albera, François: "J'Accuse d'Abel Gance." *1895*, 87, 1, 186. [Cor]
RR4899.   Whalan, Mark: "The Culture of Fear in World War One." *Reviews in American History*, 47, 4, 613-21. [RIT]

GODARD, Jean-Luc.
See also 4015, 4665, 4690, 4712.
RR4900.   ● Bourgois, Guillaume: *Dialoguer Avec Ray, Godard, Visconti & Friends: Regards et Écoutes*. Paris: L'Harmattan. 182p. [LoC]
RR4901.   ● Emmelhainz, Irmgard: *Jean-Luc Godard's Political Filmmaking*. Cham (Switzerland): Springer International. 327p. [Syr]
RR4902.   ● Godard, Jean-Luc: *Le Livre d'Image*. [Genf]: Casa Azul Films. 94p. [WC]
RR4903.   ● Pouy, Jean-Bernard: *Lettre de Sergeï Eisenstein à Jean-Luc Godard: Lettre de Joseph Staline à John Wayne*. Montreuil: Éditions Folies d'Encre. 15p. [BnF]
RR4904.   ● Serrut, Louis-Albert, & Dominique Château: *Le Cinéma de Jean-Luc Godard et la Philosophie*. Paris: L'Harmattan. 171p. [LoC]
RR4905.   ● Vallín, Pedro: *Lme Cago En Godard!: Por Qué Deberías Adorar el Cine Americano (y Desconfiar del Cine de Autor) Sí Eres Culto y Progresista*. Barcelona: Arpa. 304p. [WC]
RR4906.   Baumgartner, M.: "J. S. Bach, Jean-Luc Godard, & The Reimagining of the Immaculate Conception in Hail Mary (1985)." *Bach*, 50, 2, 175-219. [UaB]
RR4907.   Carvalho, Jailson D.: "Jean-Luc Godard e a Educação: O Exemplo de la Chinoise (A Chinesa, 1967)." *Plurais*, 4, 2, 146. [LoC]
RR4908.   Fletcher, Alex: "Late Style and Contrapuntal Histories: The Violence of Representation in Jean-Luc Godard's Le Livre d'Image." *Radical Philosophy*, 204. [PrQ]
RR4909.   Gardner, C.: "'It's Not Blood, It's Red': Color as Category, Color as Sensation in Jean-Luc Godard's Le Mépris, Pierrot le Fou, Weekend, and Passion." *Criticism*, 61, 2, 245-270. [UofR]
RR4910.   Jusová, Iveta, & Dan Reyes: "Between Two Waves: Věra Chytilová and Jean-Luc Godard." *Studies in Eastern European Cinema*, 10, 1, 22-38. [UaB]
RR4911.   Knight, Douglas: "*Godard and Sound: Acoustic Innovation in the Late Films of Jean-Luc Godard* by Albertine Fox (Review)." *Music, Sound, and the Moving Image*, 13, 1, 92-98. [UaB]
RR4912.   Levis, Bilsky L.: "De Artistas, Consumidores y Críticos: Dinámicas del Cambio, El Gusto y la Distinción en el Campo Artístico Actual. Jean-Luc Godard

y Su Adiós al Lenguaje." *Cuadernos del Centro de Estudios de Diseño y Comunicación*, 62. [WC]

RR4913.   Martins, Helena: "'Resta Saber Se o Não-Pensamento Contamina o Pensamento': Citação e Invenção em Adeus à Linguagem de Jean-Luc Godard." *Cadernos de Literatura Comparada*, 41, 171-190. [WC]

RR4914.   Morrey, Douglas: "The Forest for the Trees: Political Contexts for Godard's Nature Imagery in Film Socialisme and Adieu au Langage." *Studies in French Cinema*, *19*, 1, 55-68. [UofR]

RR4915.   Park, Youngseok: "Jean-Luc Godard's Metahistory: Historical Montage and Digital Image." *The Journal of Literature and Film*, *20*, 3, 525-552. [WC]

RR4916.   Silva, Leyla T. B.: "O Sagrado Erótico em Je Vous Salue, Marie, de Jean-Luc Godard." *Numen*, *21*, 1. [Cor]

RR4917.   Utterson, Andrew: "Goodbye to Cinema? Jean-Luc Godard's Adieu au Langage (2014) as 3D Images at the Edge of History." *Studies in French Cinema*, *19*, 1, 69-84. [Naz]

RR4918.   Watt, Calum: "'Money Is a Public Good': Godard's Film Socialisme (2010) and Bernard Maris." *Studies in French Cinema*, *19*, 1, 40-54. [UofR]

HANEKE, Michael.
See also 4679, 4699, 4700.

RR4919.   ● Haneke, Michael, Philippe Rouyer, & Michel Cieutat: *Non Ho Niente da Nascondere: Interviste Sul Cinema e Sulla Vita*. Milano: Il Saggiatore. 412p. [WC]

RR4920.   Bornhauser, Niklas, & Carolina Pezoa: "Pasajes en Cinta Blanca." *Aisthesis*, 2019, 195-216. [Syr]

RR4921.   Dawney, Leila, Timothy J. Huzar, & Joanna Bourke: "Elaine Scarry, Michael Haneke's Funny Games and the Structure of Cruelty." *Body & Society*, *25*, 3, 136-152. [UaB]

RR4922.   Fulton, Dawn: "Unknown Knowns: Michael Haneke's Caché and the Failure of Allegory." *Modern Language Review*, *114*, 4, 682. [PrQ]

RR4923.   Hill, C., & J. Batcho: "An Invitation to Bear Witness: Collective Guilt and the Ethical Spectator in Haneke's Caché." *Studies in European Cinema*, 16, 2, 94-107. [Cor]

RR4924.   Hunter, Jefferson: "Film Chronicle: 1984 Dir. by Michael Radford, And: Eye in the Sky Dir. by Gavin Hood, And: The Last Enemy Dir. by Iain Macdonald, And: Hamlet Dir. by Gregory Doran, And: Hamlet Dir. by Michael Almereyda, And: You Were Never Really Here Dir. by Lynne Ramsay, And: Caché Dir. by Michael Haneke, And: The Lives of Others Dir. by Florian Henckel Von Donnersmarck." *The Hopkins Review*, *12*, 3, 437-446. [Syr]

RR4925.   Jeong, Chancheol: "Michael Haneke's Videology: Rec, Play, and Rewind/ Fast-Forward." *The Journal of Literature and Film*, *20*, 3, 659-679. [WC]

RR4926.   Kang, Hee-Won: "Child as a Possibility of Violence: Michael Haneke's The White Ribbon and William Wordsworth's 'We Are Seven'." *The Journal of Contemporary Psychoanalysis*, *21*, 2, 9-39. [WC]

RR4927.   Mikheeva, Julia V.: "Sound in the Films of Michael Haneke from the Perspective of Phenomenological Aesthetics." *Journal of Flm Arts and Film Studies*, *11*, 3, 116-127. [LoC]

RR4928.   Monteiro, Eliana: "El Amor, los Cuerpos y las Ropas en Michael Haneke." *Cuadernos del Centro de Estudios de Diseño y Comunicación*, 58. [WC]

RR4929.   Peres, Helga C., & Luiz R. Gomes: "Do Sentido Formativo ao Enigma da Frieza: Uma Análise do Filme 'A Fita Branca', de Michael Haneke." *Comunicações*, 26, 1, 181. [WC]

RR4930.   Romão, Ana: "Hospitality in Post-9/11 Representations of 'Home Invasion': Michael Haneke's Funny Games (1997/2007)." *At the Interface/ Probing the Boundaries*, 125, 114-129. [UaB]

JEUNET, Jean-Pierre.
See 4709, 4725.

KASSOVITZ, Mathieu.

RR4931.   Rykner, Arnaud: "Photographie et Mise en Scène: La Fabrique de l'Événement ou Ce Qui N'A Pas Été." *Synergies Pays Riverains de la Baltique*, 13, 22, 123. [PrQ]

RR4932.   Spieser-Landes, David: "Crise Migratoire, Régionalisme Alsacien et Politique Linguistique Française dans *Invitation à Quitter la France* de Martin Graff." *European Journal of Language Policy*, 11, 1, 109-28. [RIT]

KIESLOWSKI, Krzysztof.
See also 4692, 4724.

RR4933.   ● Maréchal, Valérie: *Krzysztof Kieslowski: 'Le Décalogue' ou l'Enfer Éthique*. La-Neuville-aux-Joûtes: Jacques Flament. 309p. [BnF]

RR4934.   Coates, Paul: "'The Way Up Is the Way Down': Curzio Malaparte's 'Il Cristo Proibito' and Krzysztof Kieślowski's 'Three Colours: Red'." *Images*, 24, 33, 47-59. [Cor]

RR4935.   Dabrowski, Radoslaw: "Krzysztof Kieslowski and Ingmar Bergman – Once Again About a Certain Artistic Relationship." *Images*, 24, 33, 87-107. [Cor]

RR4936.   Lubelski, Tadeusz: "Krzysztof Kieślowski's 'Camera Buff': A Revised Version of 'First Love'." *Images*, 24, 33, 129-136. [Cor]

RR4937.   Otto, Wojciech: "Krzysztof Kieślowski's Film Props in the Triptych 'Three Colours'." *Images*, 24, 33, 73-85. [Cor]

RR4938.   Talarczyk, Monika: "Krzysztof Kieślowski's 'Decalogue' as a Quality TV Series." *Images*, 24, 33, 38-46. [Cor]

RR4939.   Viren, Denis: "Non-Accidental Presence. The Reception of Krzysztof Kieślowski in Russia." *Images*, 24, 33, 109-115. [Cor]

RR4940.   Zwierzchowski, Piotr: "The Party in Krzysztof Kieślowski's Films." *Images*, 24, 33, 137-153. [Cor]

LANZMANN, Claude.
See also 370, 474, 4705.

RR4941.   ● Cazenave, Jennifer: *An Archive of the Catastrophe: The Unused Footage of Claude Lanzmann's Shoah*. Albany: SUNY Press. 313p. [Naz]

RR4942.   ● Deguy, Michel: *L'Amitié Avec Claude Lanzmann*. Sainte-Colombe-sur-Gand: La Rumeur Libre. 95p. [Cor]

RR4943.   Andrieu, Louis: "Cultures: Se Souvenir de Claude Lanzmann." *Esprit*, 455. [PrQ]

RR4944.   Amatulli, Margareth: "Claude Lanzmann 'Une Force Qui Va'." *Studi Francesi*, *63*, 2, 394-395. [UaB]

RR4945.   Bellido, Herrero J. C.: "Sucasas, Alberto: Shoah. El Campo Fuera de Campo. Cine y Pensamiento en Claude Lanzmann, Shangrila, Santander, 2018, 460 p." *Agora: Papeles de Filosofía*, *38*, 2. [Cor]

RR4946.   Bhubaneswari, T. S., & Ajeet Singh: "Irony as Trauma & Trauma as Irony in Claude Lanzmann's Shoah." *Contemporary Research*, *3*, 1, 67-71. [WC]

RR4947.   Brooke, Michael: "Shoah: The Four Sisters." *Sight and Sound*, 5, 87. [RIT]

RR4948.   Czesak, Artur: "The Sequence Outside the Church in Claude Lanzmann's Shoah: Some Comments from a Linguist." *Przekładaniec*, 38, Special Issue, 75-107. [Naz]

RR4949.   Kwasna, K., & M. Heydel: "'Why Don't You Tell Them . . .' Unheard Voices in Claude Lanzmann's Shoah." *Przekladaniec*, 38, Special Issue, 27-52. [Naz]

RR4950.   Lanzmann, Claude: "Récit: Le Trésor de Touthankhamon." *Phosphore*, *461*, 3, 24. [WC]

RR4951.   Magilow, Daniel H.: "Obituary: Claude Lanzmann." *Holocaust and Genocide Studies*, *33*, 2, 325-328. [UofR]

RR4952.   Sendyka, R.: "Naturellement: Variant Translations of the Accounts Given by Holocaust Bystanders in Claude Lanzmann's Shoah." *Przekladaniec*, 38, Special Issue, 7-25. [Naz]

RR4953.   Sobesto, J., & M. Heydel: "Bystanders Speaking. The Language Identity of the People of Chełmno in Claude Lanzmann's Shoah." *Przekladaniec*, 38, Special Issue, 54-74. [Naz]

LECONTE, Patrice.

RR4954.   ● Guy, Pierre: *Le Palace Epernay: Un Siècle de Cinéma*. Chaumont: Le Pythagore. 221p. [BnF]

RR4955.   ● Raveleau, Alexandre: *Les Bronzés, la Véritable Histoire*. Paris: Hors Collection. 134p. [WC]

LELOUCH, Claude.

RR4956.   Cristiá, Moira: "Imágenes Robadas a la Represión Chilena. Redes Transnacionales de Denuncia y Cine Contrainformacional Durante la Dictadura de Augusto Pinochet." *Historia y Sociedad*, 37, 173-200. [WC]

LUMIÈRE, Auguste et Louis.
See also 4661.

RR4957.   Albera, François, & L. Le Forestier: "Louis Lumière Metteur en Scène, par Georges Sadoul. Présentation." *1895*, *87*, 1, 112. [Cor]

RR4958.   Martinez, J.: "Pyrenean Indians in Three Dimensions: Discovery and History of 'Euskadi', Film in Relief of Louis Lumière (1936)." *Historia y Comunicacion Social*, *24*, 1, 277-292. [Naz]

RR4959.   Sadoul, Georges: "Louis Lumière, Metteur en Scène." *1895*, *87*, 1, 120. [Cor]

MALLE, Louis.
See also 4720, 4740, 4763.

RR4960.   Baetens, J.: "Ascenseur Pour l'Échafaud en Images Fixes, Louis Malle en Roman-Photo." *Études Françaises*, 55, 2, 57-73. [UofR]

RR4961.   Bazgan, Nicoleta: "Mapping Zazie's Paris in Louis Malle's Zazie dans le Métro (1960)." *Modern & Contemporary France*, 27, 4, 425-40. [PrQ]

RR4962.   Blin-Rolland, Armelle: "Adaplastics: Forming the Zazie dans le Métro Network." *Modern & Contemporary France*, 27, 4, 457-73. [PrQ]

RR4963.   Morrey, Douglas: "'La Nouvelle Vague, Elle t'Emm---!' Louis Malle, Zazie dans le Métro and the French New Wave." *Modern & Contemporary France*, 27, 4, 493-503. [PrQ]

MARKER, Chris.
See also 194, 4671, 4690.

RR4964.   ● *Dossier Zu: Schriftsteller - Chris Marker*. [Köln] [Performance-Archiv "Die Schwarze Lade"]. 1 vol. [WC]

RR4965.   ● Greisenegger, Wolfgang, et al.: *Chris Marker: L'Héritage de la Chouette, das Erbe der Eule*. Wien: Böhlau. 281p. [WC]

RR4966.   Alexander, T.: "A Hint of Industrial Espionage in the Eye: Oriental-ism, Essayism, and the Politics of Memory in Chris Marker's Sans Soleil." *Quarterly Review of Film and Video*, 36, 1, 42-61. [UaB]

RR4967.   Costa, Luiz C.: "História e Memória: A Melancolia de Esquerda em Elegia a Alexandre de Chris Marker." *Porto Arte*, 24, 42. [WC]

RR4968.   Hammoud, Nabil: "Le Monde à Écrire de Chris Marker." *Les Lettres Romanes*, 73, 1-2, 255-275. [Syr]

RR4969.   Poroger, Felipe A.: "A Ilusão do Tempo em La Jetée, de Chris Marker." *Humanidades em Diálogo*, 9, 221-227. [WC]

RR4970.   Wallace, Grace: "'Movies Are Supposed to Move, Stupid': Examin-ing Movement in Chris Marker's La Jetée." *Film Matters*, 10, 1, 86-95. [WC]

MÉLIÈS, Georges.
See also 4727.

RR4971.   ● Fineman, Mia, Beth Saunders, & Tom Hanks: *Apollo's Muse: The Moon in the Age of Photography*. New York: Metropolitan Museum of Art. 192p. [Syr]

RR4972.   ● Méliès, Georges, & Jon Spira: *The Long-Lost Autobiography of Georges Méliès, Father of Sci-Fi and Fantasy Cinema*. [United Kingdom]: Jon Spira. 208p. [WC]

RR4973.   Lexe, Heidi: "Die Reise Zum Mond: Heidi Lexe Über die Kinderlit-erarische Entdeckung des Filmpioniers Georges Méliès." *1000 Und 1 Buch*, 25-27. [WC]

RR4974.   Puig, Peñalosa X.: "Colonialism and Power in Le Voyage dans la Lune (A Trip to the Moon) by Georges Méliès (1902)." *Revista Científica Uisrael*, 4, 2, 28-38. [WC]

MELVILLE, Jean-Pierre.

RR4975.   ● Baratti, Alessandro, & Joséphine Castoro: *"Le Deuxième Souffle" ("Le Deuxième Souffle", 1966) de Jean-Pierre Melville*. [Rome]: Gremese. 142p. [BnF]

RR4976.   Dalenogare, Neto W.: "Escuridão, Resistência e Silêncio em Le Silence de la Mer, de Jean-Pierre Melville." *Significação*, 46, 52. [WC]

RR4977.   Dalenogare, Neto W.: "O Cinema de Resistência de Jean-Pierre Melville." *Artcultura*, *21*, 38, 149-162. [WC]

RR4978.   Gutkin, Len: "The Dandy at Dusk: Taste and Melancholy in the Twentieth Century by Philip Mann (Review)." *Modernism/ Modernity*, *26*, 3, 678-80. [RIT]

MOREAU, Jeanne.
See also 4701, 4733.

RR4979.   ● Rosteck, Jens: *Die Verwegene - Jeanne Moreau: Die Biographie*. Berlin: Aufbau. 396p. [WC]

RR4980.   ● Sauvard, Jocelyne: *Jeanne Moreau l'Impertinente*. Paris: L'Archipel. 285p. [LoC]

OPHULS, Max.
See also 4680, 4688, 4689.

RR4981.   ● Kermabon, Jacques: *Madame de . . . de Max Ophuls: Vertiges de l'Asymptote*. Crisnée (Belgique): Yellow Now. 106p. [LoC]

RR4982.   Cortés, Jesús: "Liebelei (Max Ophuls, 1933)." *Senses of Cinema*, 90. [PrQ]

RR4983.   De-Cárdenas, Federico: "Max Ophüls: Permanencia del Genio." *Ventana Indiscreta*, 21, 70-73. [WC]

RR4984.   Melville, David: "The Gentle Perfume of Despair: Sans Lendemain (Max Ophuls, 1939)." *Senses of Cinema*, 90. [PrQ]

RR4985.   O'Donoghue, Darragh: "The Trouble with Money (Max Ophuls, 1936)." *Senses of Cinema*, 90. [PrQ]

RR4986.   Ophuls, M.: "Max Ophuls et les Producteurs." *Positif*, 701-702, 132-133. [Syr]

OZON, François.
See also 4677, 4711.

RR4987.   ● Ozon, François: *Grâce à Dieu: Trois Actes et un Épilogue*. Besançon: Les Solitaires Intempestifs. 137p. [LoC]

RR4988.   ● Storck, Timo, et al.: *François Ozon: Täuschung und Subjektive Wahrheit*. Gießen: Psychosozial-Verlag. 112p. [WC]

RR4989.   Rouyer, Philippe, & Yann Tobin: "Entretien Avec François Ozon La Parole Était Forte, Il Fallait la Restituer." *Positif*, 696, 15-20. [Syr]

PALCY, Euzhan.
See also 633.

RR4990.   "Cinéma Euzhan Palcy, l'Intransigeante." *Jeune Afrique*, *59*, 3047, 80-81. [Syr]

RR4991.   Maingard, J.: "A Pan-African Perspective on Apartheid, Torture, and Resistance in Euzhan Palcy's A Dry White Season." *Black Camera*, *11*, 1, 201-213. [UaB]

PECK, Raoul.
See also 4663.

RR4992.   Corbet, Alice: "Assistance Mortelle de Raoul Peck: Producteurs:

Arte France, Velvet Film, Figuier Production, Velvet Film Inc., Rtbf, Entre Chien et Loup. 2013." *Les Cahiers d'Outre-Mer*, *279*, 1, 333. [UofR]

RR4993.　Jackson, Robert, Sharon P. Holland, & Shawn Salvant: "James Baldwin: Interventions: A Session at the 2019 Modern Language Association Convention." *James Baldwin Review*, *5*, 1, 197-218. [Cor]

RR4994.　Pastorello, Thierry: "I Am Not Your Negro, Film de Raoul Peck, 2017, 94 min: Un Documentaire Sur la Rage de l'Homme Noir Face au Racisme Blanc aux États-Unis." *Cahiers d'Histoire. Revue d'Histoire Critique*, 144, 203-216. [UofR]

RR4995.　Peck, Raoul, & Avishag Zafrani: "Cinematic Engagement." *Cités*, *77*, 1, 73. [UaB]

RR4996.　Watson, J. B.: "Close-up: Caribbean Cinema as Cross-Border Dialogue: A Voice of Their Own: Narrative Obscurity and African History in the Cinema of Raoul Peck." *Black Camera*, *11*, 1, 180-200. [UaB]

PIALAT, Maurice.
See also 4703.
RR4997.　Thompson, David, & Ginette Vincendeau: "Deep Focus: Maurice Pialat and the New French Realism." *Sight and Sound*, *29*, 11, 42. [Naz]

RAPPENEAU, Jean-Paul.
See also 4845.
RR4998.　● *Le Hussard Sur le Toit: Un Film de Jean-Paul Rappeneau: Scénario Original Intégral et Dialogues, Storyboard Complet du Film, Dossier*. Paris: L'Avant-Scène Cinéma. *L'Avant-Scène. Cinéma*, 668/669. 294p. [WC]

RR4999.　Tobin, Yann: "Entretien Avec Jean-Paul Rappeneau, le Casting d'un Premier Film." *Positif*, 705, 111-113. [Syr]

RENOIR, Jean.
See also 467, 4697.
RR5000.　Bourget, Jean-Loup: "Renoir Père et Fils. Peinture et Cinéma le Bouchon, Essai Sur Pierre-Auguste Renoir et Jean Renoir." *Positif*, 695, 75-77. [Syr]

RR5001.　Davis, Colin: "Cracking Gilles Deleuze's Crystal: Narrative Space-Time in the Films of Jean Renoir, by Barry Nevin." *French Studies*, *73*, 2, 313. [UaB]

RR5002.　Gayme, Évelyne: "La Grande Illusion ou Comment Rendre Populaire la Captivité." *Inflexions*, *42*, 3, 151. [WC]

RR5003.　Schneider, Robert Joseph: "La Marseillaise." *Film Comment*, *55*, 6, 75. [RIT]

RESNAIS, Alain.
See also 4676, 4707, 4730.
RR5004.　● Tourret, Franck: *Alain Resnais, le Pari de la Forme*. Paris: L'Harmattan. 298p. [LoC]

RR5005.　Flood, Maria: "Torture in Word and Image: Inhuman Acts in Resnais and Pontecorvo." *Journal of Cinema and Media Studies*, *58*, 3, 26-48. [RIT]

RR5006.　Koyuncu, Emre: "To Have Done with Representation." *Third Text*, *33*, 2, 247-55. [PrQ]

RIVETTE, Jacques.
See also 443, 4697, 4722.
RR5007. • Tavassoli, Zea Z.: *Balzac Reframed: The Classical and Modern Faces of Eric Rohmer and Jacques Rivette.* Cham: Palgrave Macmillan. 230p. [Syr]

ROHMER, Eric (pseud. of Maurice Schérer).
See also 4707, 5007.
RR5008. • Johae, Antony: *After-Images: Homage to Éric Rohmer.* Salzburg: Poetry Salzburg at the University of Salzburg. 89p. [WC]
RR5009. Cardullo, R. J.: "Seasons Change, or the Tales of Eric Rohmer." *Moderna Sprak, 113,* 1, 266-277. [UaB]
RR5010. Castaldo, Achille: "Ideological Figuration in Rohmer's First Two Moral Tales: 'Voice of Memory', Clinamen of the Image, and Colonial Fantasies." *Studies in French Cinema, 19,* 2, 85-102. [Naz]
RR5011. Handyside, F.: "Words for a Conversation: Speech, Doubt and Faith in the Films of Eric Rohmer and Mia Hansen-Love." *Studies in French Cinema, 19,* 1, 5-21. [UofR]
RR5012. Martín, Sanz A.: "El Cine de Mar Coll: Herencias Catalanas de Eric Rohmer." *Fotocinema. Revista Científica de Cine y Fotografía,* 2, 19, 327. [Cor]
RR5013. Sweeney, Carl: "Éric Rohmer: A Biography." *Studies in European Cinema, 16,* 2, 167-168. [Naz]
RR5014. Szaniawski, Jeremi: "'Mesdames, Mesdemoiselles, Messieurs: Un Classique!': Eric Rohmer's Film Theory (1948-1953) – From 'École Scherer' to 'Politique des Auteurs' by Marco Grosoli." *Senses of Cinema,* 92. [PrQ]

ROUCH, Jean.
See also 216, 4719.
RR5015. Boudreault-Fournier, Alexandrine: "Sherman Rina (dir.), 2018, Dans le Sillage de Jean Rouch. Témoignages et Essais. Paris, Éditions de la FMSH, Coll. Anthropologie, N 54, 356 p., Illustr." *Anthropologie et Sociétés, 43,* 1, 256. [Naz]
RR5016. Gauthier, Nadine W.: "Sherman, Rina (dir.): Dans le Sillage de Jean Rouch. Témoignages et Essais. Préface de Jean-Claude Carrière. Paris: Éditions de la Maison des Sciences de l'Homme, 2018. 351 pp. ISBN 978-2-7351-2391-9. Prix: € 20,00." *Anthropos, 114,* 2, 642-643. [UofR]
RR5017. Scheinfeigel, Maxime: "Colloque International 'Jean Rouch, Passeur d'Images et de Mondes': Quels Cinémas Pour Quelles Anthropologies? (Montpellier – 10-11-12 Octobre 2018)." *Journal des Anthropologues,* 158-159, 301. [Cor]

RUIZ, Raoul.
RR5018. Binétruy, Pascal: "Un Lecteur de Classiques Nommé Raoul Ruiz." *Positif,* 696, 106-108. [UaB]
RR5019. Havenne, Maude: "Raoul Ruiz, Chef d'Orchestre ou Quand la Musique Se Dévoile à l'Écran." *Les Lettres Romanes, 73,* 1-2, 277-289. [Syr]

SAUTET, Claude.
RR5020. • Sautet, Claude, & Joseph Korkmaz: *Entretiens Inédits Avec Claude Sautet.* Paris: Orizons. 312p. [LoC]

SERREAU, Coline.
See also 750, 4728, 4750.
RR5021.   • Serreau, Coline: #*Colineserreau*. Arles: Actes Sud. 206p. [BnF]

TATI, Jacques.
RR5022.   • Ihrig, Wilfried: *Über Paul Celan und: Carl Einstein, David Morley, Jacques Tati und Andere: Aufsätze und Gedichte: Zum 100. Geburtstag von Paul Celan*. Berlin: Epubli. 101p. [WC]
RR5023.   • Tati, Jacques, & Alison Castle: *Tati: The Definitive Jacques Tati: Five Volumes Covering the Complete Life and Work of the Legendary Filmmaker, Screenwriter, and Performer*. Köln: Taschen. 5 vols. [WC]
RR5024.   • Turvey, Malcolm: *Play Time: Jacques Tati and Comedic Modernism*. New York: Columbia UP. 304p. [Syr]
RR5025.   Girard, E.: "The Notion of Space in Monsieur Hulot's Holiday by Jacques Tati (1953)." *Annales de Geographie*, 726, 81-97. [UaB]
RR5026.   Gouttefange, S.: "Subtitling the Profusion of the 'Human Secretions' in Jacques Tati's Playtime: A Major Challenge." *Monografias de Traduccion e Interpretacion (Monti)*, 4, Special Issue, 253-279. [LoC]
RR5027.   Jamard, Jean-Luc, Gaëlle Lacaze, Margarita Xanthakou, & Françoise Michel-Jones: "Corps Sensible, Environnement Urbain Moderniste: À Propos de Playtime de Jacques Tati." *Ateliers d'Anthropologie*, 46. [Cor]
RR5028.   Piazza de Nanno, Antonio: "La Villa Arpel: 'Machine à Habiter', 'Donde Todo Se Comunica' (Mon Oncle, Jacques Tati, 1958)." *Bitácora Arquitectura*, 40, 20-35. [PrQ]

TAVERNIER, Bertrand.
See also 4744.
RR5029.   • Pascal, Michèle, & Bertrand Tavernier: *Christine Pascal: Mémoires Croisées de Deux Sœurs; [Préface de Bertrand Tavernier]*. La Madeleine: Lettmotif. 367p. [WC]
RR5030.   • Tavernier, Bertrand, & Thierry Frémaux: *L'Amour du Cinéma M'A Permis de Trouver Une Place dans l'Existence: Post-Scriptum à Amis Américains; Conversation Avec Thierry Frémaux*. Arles: Actes Sud. 91p. [BnF]
RR5031.   Herpe, Noël, & Michel Kaptur: "Entretien Avec Bertrand Tavernier une Inscription dans l'Histoire." *Positif*, 704, 73-81. [UaB]
RR5032.   Tavernier, B.: "La Trace des Lendemains Entretien Avec Bertrand Tavernier." *Europe*, 97, 1082, 308-311. [Syr]
RR5033.   Torreton, Philippe, & Jean-Luc Cotard: "Capitaine Conan: Un Coup à l'Âme." *Inflexions*, 42, 3, 69. [WC]

TÉCHINÉ, André.
See 4677.

TRUFFAUT, François.
RR5034.   • Gillain, Anne: *Tout Truffaut: 23 Films Pour Comprendre l'Homme et le Cinéaste*. Malakoff: Armand Colin. 287p. [LoC]

RR5035. ● Richter, Verena: *Zwischen Institution und Individuum: Insze-nierung von Adoleszenz in den Filmen von François Truffaut und Louis Malle.* Pader-born: Wilhelm Fink. 330p. [BnF]

RR5036. ● Ross, Lillian: *François Truffaut par Lillian Ross: Textes Issus de the New Yorker, 1960-1976.* [Paris]: Carlotta Films. 39p. [WC]

RR5037. ● Tortolini, Luca, & Victoria Semykina: *François Truffaut: Il Bam-bino Che Amava Il Cinema.* Padova - Italia: Kite. 1 vol. [WC]

RR5038. ● Truffaut, François, & Bernard Bastide: *Chroniques d'Arts-Spectacles (1954-1958).* [Paris]: Gallimard. 524p. [BAnQ]

RR5039. Brodski, Michael: "The Cinematic Representation of the Wild Child: Considering L'Enfant Sauvage (1970)." *Gothic Studies, 21,* 1, 100-113. [UaB]

RR5040. Cohen, Nadja: "Du Récit Épique à la Construction d'un Ethos d'Auteur: Les Journaux de Tournage de Cocteau, Truffaut et Tavernier." *Études Françaises, 55,* 2, 75.[UaB]

RR5041. Raspiengeas, Emmanuel: "Un Beau Mensonge Les Quatre Cents Coups, François Truffaut." *Positif,* 700, 12. [Syr]

VARDA, Agnès.

See 74, 294, 306, 310, 632, 4673, 4684, 4694, 4706, 4717, 4843, 4885.

RR5042. ● Bastide, Bernard: *"Cléo de 5 à 7", Agnès Varda.* Futuroscope: Canopé Éditions. 70p. [BnF]

RR5043. ● Merino, Imma: *Agnès Varda: Espigadora de Realidades y de Ensueños.* Donostia: Donostia Kultura: Euskadiko Filmategia. 206p. [WC]

RR5044. ● Reardon, Kiva, & Mallory Andrews: *The Cléo Reader: 2013-2019.* [Toronto]: [Cléo Journal]. 155p. [WC]

RR5045. "Amy Taubin on Agnès Varda." *Artforum International, 57,* 10, 63-70. [Naz]

RR5046. Antoccia, Luca: "La Strana Coppia a Bordo di un Camion: Agnès Varda e JR: 'Visages, Villages'." *Art e Dossier,* 367, 22-27. [WC]

RR5047. Baez, Luiz: "Apresentação: Agnès Varda, uma Cineasta Heterogê-nea." *Alceu, 20,* 39, 159-160. [Cor]

RR5048. Beceyro, Raúl: "Homenage a Agnés Varda." *Cuadernos de Cine Documental,* 36-39. [LoC]

RR5049. Bluher, Dominique: "Agnès Varda (1928-2019)." *Millennium Film Journal,* 70, 86. [PrQ]

RR5050. Bye, Susan: "Connection and Creativity: Agnes Varda and JR's 'Faces Places'." *Screen Education,* 95, 80-85. [Naz]

RR5051. Byun, Jairan: "Agnes Varda, a History of Women, Cinematic Prac-tice." *The Institute of Humanities at Soonchunhyang University, 38,* 2, 121-142. [WC]

RR5052. Colonna-Cesari, A.: "Au Bonheur d'Agnès Varda." *Connaissance des Arts,* 782. [UaB]

RR5053. Conway, Kelley: "Feeling Seen." *Film Comment, 55,* 3, 14-5. [RIT]

RR5054. Conway, Kelley: "'Visages Villages: Documenting Creative Collab-oration'." *Studies in French Cinema, 19,* 1, 22-39. [UofR]

RR5055. Dumas, Louise, & Agnès Varda: "Varda par Agnès La Dernière Plage d'Agnès." *Positif,* 698, 6. [Syr]

RR5056.   Felleman, Susan: "Agnès Varda between Film, Photography, and Art by Rebecca J. Deroo." *Journal of Cinema and Media Studies*, *58*, 4, 174-178. [UaB]

RR5057.   Flambard-Weisbart, Véronique: "De Sans Toit Ni Loi à Visages Villages d'Agnès Varda: Pavés dans la Mer." *Contemporary French and Francophone Studies*, *23*, 3, 281-289. [Naz]

RR5058.   Furtado, Mendes M. P.: "Exílio, Feminismo e Racismo: Políticas No Cinema de Agnès Varda." *Alceu*, *20*, 39, 171-186. [Cor]

RR5059.   Giraud, François: "Intermediality and Gesture: Idealising the Craft of Filmmaking in Agnès Varda's Lions Love (. . . and Lies)." *Studies in French Cinema*, *19*, 2, 122-134. [UofR]

RR5060.   Heynemann, Liliane R.: "Paisagem e Autobiografia em Agnès Varda: Visages, Villages e as Praias." *Alceu*, *20*, 39, 161-170. [Cor]

RR5061.   Houdart, C.: "La Vie des Formes: Hommage à Agnès Varda." *Nouvelle Revue Française*, 637, 45-52. [UofR]

RR5062.   Jang, Mi-Hwa: "Haptic and Interactivity in Agnès Varda's Digital Essay Film." *The Journal of Literature and Film*, *20*, 2, 321-341. [WC]

RR5063.   Labbé, Mathilde: "La Poésie Déambulée: Agnès Varda et Yannick Bellon Filment Baudelaire." *Captures*, *2*, 1. [WC]

RR5064.   Lemarié, Yannick: "Agnès Varda à V. Agnès, Morituri Te Salutant!" *Positif*, 699, 78. [Syr]

RR5065.   Mauffrey, Nathalie: "Un Imaginaire Collectif au Féminin/ Masculin: Les Veuves de Noirmoutier d'Agnès Varda." *Studies in French Cinema*, *19*, 2, 135-149. [Naz]

RR5066.   Oxen, N.: "Politics of Prehension - Agnès Varda's Essay Films and Alfred N. Whitehead's Process Philosophy." *Allgemeine Zeitschrift fur Philosophie*, *44*, 3, 297-323. [Cor]

RR5067.   Pettengill, Sierra: "Varda by Agnès." *Film Comment*, *55*, 6, 68. [RIT]

RR5068.   Rouyer, Philippe, & Yann Tobin: "Entretien Avec Rosalie Varda et Agnès Varda le Mystère de la Transmission." *Positif*, 698, 9. [Syr]

RR5069.   "Tribute: Agnès Varda Remembered by Mia Hansen-Love and Others." *Sight and Sound*, *29*, 6, 12-13. [UofR]

RR5070.   Varda, Agnès, & Stéphane Delorme: "Le Pont des Arts." *Cahiers du Cinéma*, 755, 92-97. [WC]

RR5071.   Wheatley, Catherine: "Varda by Agnès." *Sight and Sound*, *29*, 8, 58-59. [WC]

RR5072.   Zeric, Arijana: "Return to the Self: Agnès Varda's *Cleo from 5 to 7*." *Film Criticism*, *43*, 3. [UofR]